2142

941
CAM

**The Cambridge
historical
encyclopedia of
Great Britain and
Ireland.**

THE CAMBRIDGE
HISTORICAL
ENCYCLOPEDIA
OF GREAT BRITAIN
AND IRELAND

THE CAMBRIDGE HISTORICAL ENCYCLOPEDIA OF GREAT BRITAIN AND IRELAND

EDITOR

Christopher Haigh

Tutor in Modern History at Christ Church
Lecturer in Modern History at the
University of Oxford

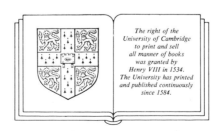

The right of the
University of Cambridge
to print and sell
all manner of books
was granted by
Henry VIII in 1534.
The University has printed
and published continuously
since 1584.

CAMBRIDGE UNIVERSITY PRESS
Cambridge   London   New York   New Rochelle
Melbourne   Sydney

MANAGING EDITOR: Ann Hill
DESIGNER: David Warner

Published by the Press Syndicate of the University of Cambridge
The Pitt Building, Trumpington Street, Cambridge CB2 1RP
32 East 57th Street, New York, NY 10022, USA
10 Stamford Road, Oakleigh, Melbourne 3166, Australia

First published 1985

Printed in Great Britain by W.S. Cowell Ltd,
Ipswich, Suffolk

Library of Congress catalogue card number: 85 – 47568

British Library Cataloguing in Publication Data

The Cambridge historical encyclopedia of Great
    Britain and Ireland.
    1. Great Britain—History—Dictionaries
    I. Haigh, Christopher
    941′.003′21   DA34

ISBN 0 521 25559 7

CONTENTS

1. BRITONS AND ROMANS
c. 100 BC – AD 409
OVERVIEW 10
GOVERNMENT AND POLITICS: *from the late Iron Age to the break with Roman rule* 14
WARFARE AND INTERNATIONAL RELATIONS: *Britain and Rome* 24
ECONOMY: *the arrival of money* 32
SETTLEMENT AND SOCIETY: *from tribe to province* 37
CULTURE AND RELIGION 44

2. SAXONS, DANES AND NORMANS 409 – 1154
OVERVIEW 54
GOVERNMENT AND POLITICS 409-1042: *Saxons and Scandinavians* 59
GOVERNMENT AND POLITICS 1042-1154: *the Norman Conquest and the Anglo-Norman realm* 66
WARFARE AND INTERNATIONAL RELATIONS: *warriors and missionaries* 71
ECONOMY: *farming, trade and manufacture* 78
SOCIETY: *warriors and dependants* 81
CULTURE: *the arts of the heroic age* 88

3. MEDIEVAL EMPIRE: ENGLAND AND HER NEIGHBOURS 1154 – 1450
OVERVIEW 94
GOVERNMENT AND POLITICS: *England 1154-1272* 100
GOVERNMENT AND POLITICS: *England 1272-1450* 105
WALES: *native resilience and English conquest* 110
SCOTLAND: *the land and the kingdom* 112
IRELAND: *the medieval lordship* 115
WARFARE AND INTERNATIONAL RELATIONS 1154-1327: *the Angevin empire* 118
WARFARE AND INTERNATIONAL RELATIONS 1327-1450: *the Hundred Years War* 121
THE ECONOMY OF BRITAIN: *an age of crisis?* 124
ENGLISH SOCIETY 131
CULTURE: *the international style and native variants* 135

4. REFORMATION AND INFLATION 1450 – 1625
OVERVIEW 142
GOVERNMENT AND POLITICS IN ENGLAND 1450-1553: *problems of succession* 147
GOVERNMENT AND POLITICS 1553-1625: *Crown, Church and Parliament* 155
WALES: *integration and conformity* 161
SCOTLAND: *reformation and inflation* 164
IRELAND: *from lordship to kingdom* 167
WARFARE AND INTERNATIONAL RELATIONS 171
A DEVELOPING ECONOMY 175
A DIVIDED SOCIETY 181
CULTURE: *the age of the household* 188

5. DISORDER TO STABILITY: BRITAIN AND IRELAND 1625 – 1783
OVERVIEW 194
GOVERNMENT AND POLITICS: *England and Wales 1625-1701* 199
GOVERNMENT AND POLITICS: *England and Wales 1701-1783* 206
SCOTLAND: *from nation to province* 210
IRELAND: *planters and patriots* 214
WARFARE AND INTERNATIONAL RELATIONS 1625-1689: *wars at home and abroad* 218
WARFARE AND INTERNATIONAL RELATIONS 1689-1783: *a global power* 222
THE ECONOMY: *towards industrialization* 225
SOCIETY: *from crisis to complacency* 230
CULTURE: *the unfolding of native genius* 237

6. POLITICAL REFORM AND ECONOMIC REVOLUTION 1783 – 1901
OVERVIEW 244
GOVERNMENT AND POLITICS 1783-1846: *England, Scotland and Wales* 249
GOVERNMENT AND POLITICS 1846-1901: *free trade, franchise and imperialism* 255
IRELAND: *from ascendancy to democracy* 261
WARFARE AND INTERNATIONAL RELATIONS: *Britain, Europe and the "Pax Britannica"* 265
THE BRITISH ECONOMY: *growth and structural change* 269
SOCIETY: *the emergence of urban Britain* 276
CULTURE: *revolution, romanticism, Victorianism* 282

7. FROM IMPERIAL POWER TO EUROPEAN PARTNER 1901 – 1975
OVERVIEW 288
GOVERNMENT AND POLITICS IN ENGLAND: *realignment and readjustment* 294
TWENTIETH-CENTURY WELSH POLITICS 303
SCOTTISH POLITICS SINCE 1900 305
IRELAND AND BRITISH GOVERNMENT 308
WARFARE AND INTERNATIONAL RELATIONS: *Empire, Commonwealth, Community* 312
THE ECONOMY: *adjustment, affluence, decline* 321
SOCIAL CHANGE: *appearance and reality* 327
CULTURE: *élite and mass* 333

WHO'S WHO 338
FURTHER READING 374
INDEX 377
ACKNOWLEDGEMENTS 392

CONTRIBUTORS

BRITONS AND ROMANS
c. 100 BC – AD 409

A.R. Birley Professor of Ancient History, University of Manchester

Peter Salway Professor of the Archaeology and History of Roman Britain, Open University

David J. Breeze Inspector of Ancient Monuments, Scottish Development Department

J.P. Wild Senior Lecturer in Archaeology, University of Manchester

Martin Millett Lecturer in Roman Archaeology, University of Durham

Thomas Blagg Lecturer in Archaeology, University of Kent at Canterbury

Boris Rankov Junior Research Fellow, St Hugh's College, Oxford (*marginal notes*)

SAXONS, DANES AND NORMANS 409 – 1154

Henry Mayr-Harting Fellow and Tutor in Modern History, St Peter's College, Oxford

James Campbell Fellow and Tutor in Modern History, Worcester College, Oxford

David Bates Lecturer in History, University College, Cardiff

Nicholas Brooks Professor of Medieval History, University of Birmingham

Martin Biddle Director of the Winchester Research Unit

Patrick Wormald Lecturer in Medieval History, University of Glasgow

Trevor Morse Worcester College, Oxford (*marginal notes*)

MEDIEVAL EMPIRE: ENGLAND AND HER NEIGHBOURS 1154 – 1450

J.R. Maddicott Fellow and Tutor in Modern History, Exeter College, Oxford

W.L. Warren Professor of Modern History, The Queen's University of Belfast

Anthony Goodman Reader in History, University of Edinburgh

R.R. Davies Professor of History, University College of Wales, Aberystwyth

Bruce Webster Senior Lecturer in History, University of Kent at Canterbury

James Lydon Lecky Professor of History, Trinity College, Dublin

Michael Prestwich Reader in History, University of Durham

Malcolm Vale Fellow and Tutor in Modern History, St John's College, Oxford

J.L. Bolton Senior Lecturer in History, Queen Mary College, University of London

B.F. Harvey Fellow and Tutor in Modern History, Somerville College, Oxford

Colin Platt Professor of History, University of Southampton

Anthony Smith Pembroke College, Oxford (*marginal notes*)

REFORMATION AND INFLATION 1450 – 1625

Christopher Haigh Student and Tutor in Modern History, Christ Church, Oxford

C.S.L. Davies Fellow and Tutor in Modern History, Wadham College, Oxford

Simon Adams Lecturer in History, University of Strathclyde

Penry Williams Fellow and Tutor in Modern History, New College, Oxford

Jenny Wormald Lecturer in Scottish History, University of Glasgow

Steven G. Ellis Lecturer in History, University College, Galway

D.M. Loades Professor of History, University College of North Wales, Bangor

D.M. Palliser Reader in Economic and Social History, University of Birmingham

Paul Slack Fellow and Tutor in Modern History, Exeter College, Oxford

David Starkey Lecturer in History, London School of Economics and Political Science

Glyn Redworth Research Lecturer, Christ Church, Oxford (*marginal notes*)

DISORDER TO STABILITY: BRITAIN AND IRELAND 1625 – 1783

W.A. Speck G.F. Grant Professor of History, University of Hull

John Morrill Fellow, Tutor and Director of Studies in History, Selwyn College, Cambridge

H.T. Dickinson Professor of British History, University of Edinburgh

Bruce Lenman Senior Lecturer in Modern History, University of St Andrews

David Hayton Research Assistant, The History of Parliament, Institute of Historical Research, London

Ronald Hutton Lecturer in History, University of Bristol

Piers Mackesy Fellow and Tutor in Modern History, Pembroke College, Oxford

J.V. Beckett Lecturer in History, University of Nottingham

Keith Wrightson Fellow and Lecturer in Social History, Jesus College, Cambridge

D.D. Aldridge Lecturer in History, University of Newcastle upon Tyne

Paul Thomas Lincoln College, Oxford (*marginal notes*)

D.R. Woolf St Peter's College, Oxford (*marginal notes*)

POLITICAL REFORM AND ECONOMIC REVOLUTION 1783 – 1901

Lord Briggs Provost of Worcester College, Oxford

Boyd Hilton Fellow, Tutor and Lecturer in History, Trinity College, Cambridge

H.C.G. Matthew Fellow and Tutor in Modern History, St Hugh's College, Oxford

D.G. Boyce Reader in Political Theory and Government, University College, Swansea

D.W. Sweet Senior Lecturer in Modern History, University of Durham

P.L. Payne Professor of Economic History, University of Aberdeen

Michael E. Rose Senior Lecturer in Economic History, University of Manchester

W.E.S. Thomas Student and Tutor in Modern History, Christ Church, Oxford

J.H. Davis Research Lecturer, Christ Church, Oxford (*marginal notes*)

FROM IMPERIAL POWER TO EUROPEAN PARTNER 1901 – 1975

Keith Robbins Professor of Modern History, University of Glasgow

Peter Clarke Fellow and Lecturer in History, St John's College, Cambridge

D.B. Smith Senior Lecturer, History of Wales Department, University College, Cardiff

Christopher Harvie Professor of British Studies, University of Tübingen

Patrick Buckland Reader in Modern History, University of Liverpool

Peter Lowe Senior Lecturer in History, University of Manchester

Barry Supple Professor of Economic History, University of Cambridge; Master of St Catharine's College

Michael Bentley Lecturer in History, University of Sheffield

Gillian Sutherland Fellow, Lecturer and Director of Studies in History, Newnham College, Cambridge

Ann Gross Nuffield College, Oxford (*marginal notes*)

WHO'S WHO

Andrew Hope Christ Church, Oxford

Stephen Thompson Christ Church, Oxford

EDITOR'S PREFACE

The human experience is almost infinite in its detail and its complexity. The history of Britain alone is far beyond the understanding of a single puny mind. So to reduce the past to manageable form, historians sub-divide and simplify; we impose our own selective patterns upon time. We break the continuous flow of events into artificial periods for our own convenience, and we isolate themes which make sense out of the confusion of simultaneous happenings. But the kinds of divisions, simplifications and selections we employ will pre-determine the sort of history we produce. A history of the British Isles which divides its chapters at the "great events" of English tradition, in 1066, 1485, 1688, 1815 and 1914, will be a history which stresses drama and disruption; it will centre upon a version of the *English* past which registers the political milestones in an inexorable progress towards the present. The history of Ireland, Scotland and Wales will be subordinated to English political developments, and the social experiences of the British and Irish are likely to be forgotten in the story of wars and revolutions.

Dictionary definitions of an "encyclopedia" emphasize two features: that it should be a systematic arrangement and a comprehensive presentation of a body of knowledge. The commonest form of encyclopedic arrangement is by short articles in alphabetical order, but this convenient technique is ill-suited to history. Such organization wrenches detail from its context, and provides no panorama within which specific events can be understood. It therefore seems appropriate both to divide an historical encyclopedia into periods, and to present the specific details of the past within an explanatory framework. So this volume offers descriptive entries alongside interpretative essays, and it organizes its material in chronological chapters and thematic sections. It aims to be a work of interpretation and of reference: it is both a history of Britain and an historical dictionary.

The periodization chosen for the book has sought to break free from the conventional "turning points", and to avoid some of the consequences of traditional boundaries. The chapters have been organized around, rather than between, some of the major eruptions in the history of Britain – the Roman invasions, the Saxon incursions, the Norman conquest, the building of the medieval English state, the Reformation, the revolutions of the seventeenth century, industrialization and parliamentary reform, and two world wars. Such events can here be seen in broader contexts, and they have not been permitted to impose their own dramatic domination. On issues such as the impact of immigration in the post-Roman era, or the economic effects of the Black Death, or the speed and results of the Reformation, or the pace of agricultural and technological innovation, or the democratization of politics, the emphases are on continuity and adaptation rather than on crisis and disruption.

A move away from the traditional chronology of English history also makes it possible to offer an account of the British past which is less anglo-centric and less exclusively political. No volume which attempts to treat the history of Britain and Ireland in roughly four hundred pages can be exhaustive, but this book has been structured in an attempt to ensure range of coverage. Where it has seemed appropriate, the political histories of England, Ireland, Scotland and Wales have been treated individually. There are separate sections for political, diplomatic, economic, social and cultural history, though the themes in each period are bound together by an "Overview" of the relationships between them. The main text is therefore divided into sixty-one articles, which together provide as comprehensive a survey as can be packed into a book of this size.

It is a consequence of the complexity of the past and of the specialization of historical study that sixty-one articles need sixty experts. The main contributors are academic historians drawn from twenty-eight universities – fifteen in England, five in Scotland, four in Wales, three in Ireland, and one in Germany. They are not drawn from any interpretative school or generation, and have been chosen to reflect the scholarly variety of the historical profession. These authors have been supported by ten researchers who have written the marginal descriptions and biographies, and supervised by twelve advisers who have vetted text and monitored relationships between entries. This formidable team of eighty-two must be one of the largest and most eminent collections of historians ever assembled between the covers of one book! They have, in all, produced almost three thousand articles, entries, biographies, captions, tables and maps, which have been checked up to ten times in a production process which has stretched over three and a half years. Mistakes will remain, for all are fallible, but few volumes of history can have been combed so meticulously.

An editor who has strained to encourage, cajole, threaten and bribe such a group will have incurred more debts than can properly be acknowledged in a brief preface. He must simply plead that his colleagues should accept a warm but general statement of gratitude for their expertise, their efficiency and their tolerance. He must thank, too, those involved in the technical processes, especially the designer, cartographers, type-setters and indexer, and the mandarins of Cambridge University Press whose faith in the whole scheme *appeared* never to waver. Above all and by name, his thanks must go to Clare Haigh, who endured the personal consequences of the scheme, and to Ann Hill, who made it work.

But this has always been a volume conceived and executed with the readers, rather than the authors, in mind. All contributors have protested at the constraints placed upon them, and all have been subordinated to a conception of the needs of the user. Those who have written on the history of culture deserve particular sympathy, for they were asked to fulfil impossible tasks in short compass, and to relate cultural complexities to unifying themes. The book may be read as continuous history, or used via the index as a reference guide – or the two elements may interact. Readers of the main text will find asterisks directing their attention to marginal elaborations of detail (and cross-references to those which occur later in the volume), while users of marginal entries will find the information they seek placed in context by the adjacent main text. Short biographies of most individuals mentioned in text and marginal entries will be found in the "Who's Who", though, in the interests of economy, artists and scientists are not given their due and those well-described in the text have not received separate biographical notice. The illustrations have been chosen to elucidate and supplement the text, and their captions seek to place them in context. All elements of the book have been designed to fit together, and to form a useful and readable whole.

We have tried to construct a single volume which provides a coherent account of the historical development of the people of the British Isles – from before the first Roman invasion in 55 BC until after the 1975 referendum on entry to the European Economic Community. But two thousand and more years generate a lot of history – especially as few now regard history as just the doings of kings and queens, and the people take their proper place on the stage of the past. We have squeezed in as much as the realities of publishing will permit, though all readers will find their own irritating omissions. But no history is complete, and historians survive by selection: it is the glory of the subject that a different selection is always possible.

Christopher Haigh
Christ Church, Oxford
February 1985

1

BRITONS
AND ROMANS

c. 100 BC-AD 409

BRITONS AND ROMANS
c. 100 BC - AD 409
Overview

A.R. Birley

Contact with Rome took Britain from prehistory into history. Comparison of Caesar's account of his two brief expeditions in 55 and 54 BC, and other comments by Greek and Roman writers, with the evidence of archaeology gives a reasonably full picture of British life in the last century BC. Britain shared the same language and religion as the continental Celtic peoples and the material culture of the island was broadly similar to that found in Gaul. Society was dominated by a warrior aristocracy. Mixed farming was practised, with considerable efficiency, mainly from individual farmsteads, although there were also small settlements that probably housed extended family groups. Whether or not the Britons had towns depends on the definition of an urban settlement. The larger conglomerations were centres for the collection and storage of agricultural produce and it may not be inappropriate to regard them as chieftains' residences. In three important respects the Britons had reached a stage of development that made them suitable candidates for incorporation in the Roman empire. They were producing their own coinage, which indicates a certain degree of trading activity – soon, with increased contacts with Rome, to be exemplified by imports of metal goods, wine and olive oil – and some technological skill; while the use of the Latin alphabet on the coins suggests the beginnings of literacy. They were also capable of building hill-forts, which demonstrates that they had sufficient political organization and engineering skill to shift thousands of tons of soil and prepare and instal thousands of posts. But above all they were efficient farmers, producing a cereal surplus. Of course, there was considerable variation within the island: the use of coinage did not extend north of the Trent, and cereal cultivation was less developed in the highland zone.

It is difficult to be sure about the political divisions of Britain before the mid-first century BC. Caesar refers to the arrival of Belgic peoples a generation before his own invasion, but it is uncertain which of the tribes he mentions were the newcomers. However, it is clear that during the century between the invasions of Caesar and the Claudian conquest, much of southern Britain fell under the control of Cunobelinus (Cymbeline) and his family, based at Camulodunum (Colchester). Meanwhile, a former opponent of Caesar in Gaul, Commius, had established himself as ruler of a smaller kingdom that included much of Hampshire and Sussex. Rome seems to have backed the Commian kingdom as a counterweight to the power of Cunobelinus. It was the expulsion of an heir of Commius, Verica, by a son of Cunobelinus, that was to provide Claudius with his *casus belli* in AD 43.

There is a variety of evidence from which to reconstruct the history of Roman Britain. Rome's greatest historian, Tacitus, was son-in-law of the governor Julius Agricola, and his brief biography includes a summary account – supplemented in places by further detail in his later works – of Agricola's ten predecessors as governor, as well as the story of Agricola's seven years in the post. Thus the first forty years of Roman rule are exceptionally well recorded; and the *Agricola* also contains the most explicit description in Roman literature of the policy of deliberate "Romanization". Thereafter not many episodes are so well recorded. Two sentences in the *Historia Augusta* are the sole literary evidence for Hadrian's building of his Wall and for Antoninus Pius' later Wall in Scotland. Cassius Dio, who wrote in the early third century (and also provides an account of the Claudian conquest), deals with a war in the 180s and with the expedition of Severus in 208-11; a Gallic orator, in a fulsome speech which includes a panegyric of Britain, recounts the recovery of Britain from the usurper Allectus by Constantius Chlorus in 296; while the last great Latin historian, Ammianus Marcellinus, relates the invasions by Picts, Scots, Attacotti and Saxons in the "barbarian conspiracy" of 367, and the restoration of Roman control by Count Theodosius, father of the emperor of that name. Finally, Zosimus and a few other late writers supply some details of the last years of Roman rule, 406-9. Otherwise, the historian would be reduced to reliance on occasional snippets, were it not for the assistance of epigraphy and archaeology. Epigraphic evidence, so important for the history of the Roman empire as a whole, is unfortunately very limited for Britain. Less than three thousand stone inscriptions survive, the great majority from the military districts,

Roman Britain

0	50	100	150 km	
0		50		100 miles
0		50		100 Roman miles

▲ Civitates
⊙ Coloniae
○ Other towns
■ Forts
━━ Main radial roads from London
── Other roads
ICENI Tribes
☐ Extent of Roman Occupation
▨ Land over 200m

N

CALEDONIAN
TRIBES

Inchtuthil
Ardoch Carpow
ANTONINE WALL
DUMNONII Inveresk
Newstead
VOTADINI
Loudoun
Hill
SELGOVAE
NOVANTAE
HADRIAN'S WALL Corbridge
STANE GATE South Shields
Carlisle LOPOCARES
TEXTOVERDI
Moresby Brougham
CARVETII
B R I G A N T E S
Ravenglass
Piercebridge
GABRANTOVICES
Malton
SETANTII
Aldeborough
PARISI
York Brough-on-Humber

HIBERNIA

Manchester
Lincoln
Caernarvon
DECEANGLI Chester
ORDOVICES CORNOVII
CORITANI
ICENI Caister-by-Yarmouth
Wroxeter Wall
Water Newton
Caistor-by-Norwich
Caersws
Leicester
Leintwardine
Godmanchester
CATUVELLAUNI
TRINOVANTES
DEMETAE
Alchester
Colchester
Carmarthen Usk SILURES Gloucester DOBUNNI Verulamium Chelmsford
Caerleon Caerwent Cirencester
London
Richborough
Sea Mills FOSSE ATREBATES Canterbury
Bath Silchester CANTIACI Dover
BELGAE Lympne
DUROTRIGES Winchester
Ilchester Bitterne REGNENSES
Chichester Pevensey
Exeter
Nanstallon Dorchester
DUMNONII

especially Hadrian's Wall and the forts of its hinterland, and the legionary bases at Caerleon, Chester and York. Civilian life in Britain is seriously under-represented in comparison with many other provinces of the empire. Some inscriptions from elsewhere supply important information, but once again this is mainly on the military side. To compensate, in part, archaeological investigation has been exceptionally intensive, although much work remains to be done.

The Claudian invasion rapidly brought the lowland zone of Britain under Roman control, most of it under direct rule, with some areas, notably the Commian kingdom, parts of East Anglia, and the Pennines, left under Roman-protected client-rulers. The conquest of Wales was completed in the 70s, by which time the remaining client-states in England were absorbed and the advance into Scotland had begun. That final stage of the overrunning of the whole island was never to be completed. Julius Agricola, in the late 70s and early 80s, entered the Highlands and defeated the Caledonian peoples, but most of the territory he occupied was soon abandoned. The limit of Roman Britain was marked by Hadrian's Wall in the 120s and effectively Roman control was to be confined to what is now England and Wales, except for a brief period, *c.* 138-62, when southern Scotland was reoccupied, and an even more short-lived attempt, by the Emperor Septimius Severus, to reconquer the whole of Scotland in the years 208-11.

For much of the period of Roman rule the garrison was extremely large, considering that the population can hardly have exceeded five million at the highest estimate. Over ten per cent of the entire Roman army was based in Britain. For the first forty or so years after the invasion, there were four legions. One was withdrawn soon after Agricola's campaigns, but the other three remained for more than three hundred years. They were backed up by a massive force of auxiliary regiments, of which there were at least fifty in the early second century. The total strength of the army of Britain was thus at least fifty thousand men. Virtually all these troops were stationed – after the first few decades and until the last century – in the less developed highland zone. Their presence undoubtedly acted as a powerful stimulant to the economy. They were in the main provisioned from Britain itself and before long from the highland zone, the agricultural efficiency of which must have markedly increased. Furthermore, as soldiers were the only significant body of wage-earners in the ancient world, their spending power was a major factor in the enrichment and development of Britain.

From AD 43 until the early third century, Britain was governed as a single province. The governor, who was also commander-in-chief, was of senatorial rank with the title *legatus Augusti pro praetore.* The Roman senate was composed of about six hundred men, drawn from the landholding élite of the empire, and the legates of Britain were selected from the senior ranks of that body, men who had held the consulship – hence they were often referred to as "consulars". Not surprisingly, Britain's unusually large garrison required an experienced commander and the governor was often the foremost general of his day, as shown by two cases when it was the British governor who was summoned to deal with a military emergency in the East, and by the records of governors' careers. However, they had mostly gained their experience in other parts of the empire: it was exceptional for them to have served in Britain before, as Agricola had. The legionary commanders were also legates of senatorial rank, and from the late 70s a further senatorial official, the *iuridicus,* assisted the governor with his civil responsibilities. In about the year 213 Britain was divided into two provinces. The northern, "Lower Britain", was governed by the legate of the VIth legion at York, who also commanded the bulk of the auxiliary regiments, while the southern, "Upper Britain", was governed from London, with the two western legions, IInd Augusta at Caerleon and the XXth at Chester, under the orders of a legate who was still consular – unlike his junior colleague at York – but lacked the great power of the governors of the undivided province. The reason for the division was political, to prevent rebellion: a governor of Britain, Albinus, had used his army to seek the throne in 195-97. The governors had authority over everything in their province except collection of revenue and payment of the troops. This was the sphere of an official of lower status, an equestrian or "knight" *(eques),* with the title *procurator Augusti.* Since the procurator was directly responsible to the emperor, a means was to hand by which a governor's abuse of power could be watched. One occasion when this was exploited occurred after the rebellion of Boudicca: the procurator Classicianus reported unfavourably to Nero on the conduct of Paullinus, who was replaced.

During the third century, senators were gradually phased out from military command, to be replaced by equestrians. In Britain this process was delayed, since it belonged to the breakaway Gallic empire from 260-74, and implementation of the even more fundamental reforms of Diocletian (reigned 284-305) was also late in Britain, because of the usurpation of Carausius and Allectus, who kept the island independent of the empire from 286-96. After the restoration of central control, Britain was again subdivided, into four provinces; and a fifth was created later in the century. A further reform was the separation of military command from the governorship. Britain, or "the diocese of the Britains", was supervised from London by a "vicar" *(vicarius)* who oversaw the governors *(praesides)* of the individual provinces, and himself reported to the regional praetorian prefect of the West at Trier. The main reason for this elaborate new structure was fiscal, to ensure a more efficient collection of revenue, now the responsibility of the governor. The commanding general of the British garrison, the *dux* or "duke", had his headquarters at York, but his authority extended into several, if not all, the British provinces. Later in the fourth century another general, with a separate command, was installed, the "count" *(comes)* of the Saxon Shore, responsible for the defence of the south and east coasts. Finally, during the last few years of Roman rule, a third general, the "Count of the Britains" is found, with a small mobile force. The garrison seems to have been proportionately and absolutely much smaller in the last period of Roman rule, and most of its units were classified among the least favoured "frontier-force" *(limitanei)* category of troops.

There were few settlers from the rest of the empire in Britain. Three *coloniae* for veteran legionaries were founded in the first century, at Colchester, Lincoln and Gloucester. These doubtless became an important source of recruits for the all citizen legions (although direct evidence is scanty), but the population of these communities will rapidly have become mixed, with a strong British element. A fourth town, York, which had grown up outside the legionary base, was given the honorary status of *colonia* in the third century, probably when it became the capital of Lower Britain. London may have been similarly honoured, at latest in the fourth century, when it was renamed Augusta: it was already a prosperous settlement at the time of the Boudiccan revolt, although not a chartered town, as Tacitus notes. Verulamium (St Albans) received the other type of chartered status, as a *municipium,* soon after the conquest. All these towns must have been assigned an agricultural territory, although there is direct evidence only in the case of Colchester. The remainder of Britain, except for military districts, was organized in *civitates* corresponding, with some modifications, to the pre-Roman tribal structure. Each *civitas* acquired an urban centre – in many cases sited at obsolete military bases, as were the *coloniae.* Chartered towns and *civitates* alike were run by a council, presided over by a pair of annual magistrates, *duoviri,* on the standard pattern of Italy and the western provinces, and were duly equipped with public buildings and *fora.* But it seems only to have been in the second century that elaborate private houses appear, suggesting that the British élite may have shunned urban life

for several generations. Furthermore, there are signs of stagnation in these towns during the fourth century, although at this time a number of smaller centres flourished.

The majority of the population continued to live in the countryside. Substantial stone-built villas began to be built in the mid-60s of the first century and the period of their greatest prosperity is in the fourth, to which most of the best-known mosaics belong. These houses were of course only for an élite minority. Agriculture was the main source of Britain's wealth, but there was also extensive mining – of gold in Wales, lead, from which silver was extracted, in the Mendips, north Wales and the Pennines, copper in Wales, tin in Cornwall, and iron in several areas. There was a widespread pottery industry, notably in the Nene valley, and British textiles were exported.

Religion is a sphere where "Romanization" can be tested. Roman and Celtic existed side by side, or merged – most notably in the great shrine of Sulis Minerva at Bath. As well as their state cult, the Romans brought eastern forms of worship – of Isis, Mithras, and Christianity. The last was already present in the third century, and by the fourth British bishops were attending Church councils. Material evidence is scanty, but includes the remarkable mosaic of Christ from Hinton St Mary and church silver from Water Newton. Further, during the last decades of Roman rule and beyond, a leading figure in the Church was the heretical monk Pelagius, whose writings reveal his high level of education. Although he left Britain in his youth, this confirms the evidence of mosaics that the élite, at least, was imbued with classical culture. Indeed, Tacitus states that Agricola, who fostered the education of the British aristocracy, rated their talents highly. His contemporary, the poet Martial, by his tribute to the charm and culture of a British lady, Claudia Rufina, suggests that Agricola's policy bore fruit. Yet no Briton is known to have risen higher in the imperial service than chief centurion. This may reflect the scanty epigraphic evidence, but it may be that in Britain, not conquered until a century after the other western provinces, education simply did not have enough time to develop. It is noteworthy that in the early fifth century she supplied two emperors of her own, the second of whom, Constantine III, controlled much of the western empire for a few years, while his able army commander, Gerontius, was also a Briton. Paradoxically, it was the rebellion of Constantine and his removal of troops which, having exposed Britain to barbarian attack, led the exasperated inhabitants in 409 to expel their governors and take up arms in their own defence.

13

Government and Politics:
from the late Iron Age to the break with Roman rule

Peter Salway

This period sees both recognizable political groupings and individual political figures emerge into the light of history. From archaeological evidence alone we can observe the appearance of organized societies and make some limited deductions about them, but we cannot put names to tribes or persons in Britain till the island begins to be drawn into the orbit of the Roman empire. From the first century BC, though the Celtic* tongue spoken in Britain was not a written language, references in Roman authors give us important information. Moreover, the coinage* that was developing in Britain, originally under influence from Celtic Gaul, took on Roman features, including the appearance of the names of British rulers in Roman lettering, Latinized titles and occasional mint marks. We cannot automatically assume political affiliations from such manifestations, but they symbolize the fact that the internal politics of late pre-Roman Britain were profoundly affected by being carried on under the shadow of her mighty neighbour.

The details of Celtic political organization are much better known for Gaul than they are for Britain, but there was a strong cultural affinity between Britain and northern Gaul and society and political behaviour also had much in common. That society was highly aristocratic in form and its politics the politics of its warrior élite. Throughout Gaul, tribal identities had clearly emerged. The Celtic peoples were quarrelsome by nature, both between tribes and internally. Though there was in Gaul a tradition of meetings of leading men from groups of tribes, common action was unusual and it is a mistake to think of "national" sentiment. In Gaul, the aristocratic priestly class, the druids*, seems to have had important political influence, but, though Britain was respected by its Celtic neighbours as a repository of druidic lore, British druids themselves play little part in the record of the times.

Comparison of what we know of Britain at the time of the Claudian conquest with a century earlier in Caesar's day conveys the impression that cohesion into clearly identified tribes or states had developed considerably, particularly in the more "advanced" south. The dominant culture was now "Belgic"*, closely allied to that of neighbouring northern France and the Low Countries. But there is still much doubt whether the sharing of tribal names in common with parts of Gaul indicates a more general influx of peoples or, in ways akin to the Norman Conquest, the arrival of an aristocracy that partly conquered, partly absorbed the existing élite. Nevertheless the scope for politics beyond the level of reaction between neighbouring settlements or the family squabble increased. Indeed, the Celtic devotion to the latter combined with the monarchic pattern in these emerging petty states to create tribal, inter-tribal and even international politics.

It is misleading to describe British politics before the conquest in terms of "pro-" or "anti-Roman" parties, since such phrases have nationalistic or ideological overtones that are anachronisms. It was rather a matter of which

Celts in Britain

Celts first mentioned by Greek writers in 6th century BC, around Upper Danube: had already expanded across western Europe, later into Spain and north Italy. Celts or their ancestors in Britain in 2nd millennium BC, but probably not across whole island. Celtic language (linked to Gaulish) extended over southern and central Britain in first millennium BC, by increased contacts with Continent; other forms of Celtic in Scotland and Ireland. Celtic immigration into southern Britain probably not on large scale: leading members of warrior aristocracy and their followings. Celtic society long-lasting in Britain, surviving Roman occupation in north, south-west and Wales.

Gallo-Belgic coinage in Britain

First Gallo-Belgic coins introduced before 100 BC; copies minted locally thereafter in areas of Belgic influence. Coins form almost the only evidence for political history of Britain between 55 BC and AD 43: names of rulers, especially in pairs, can suggest subordination of one king to another or dual magistracy; distribution of coins of individual rulers may indicate expansion of tribes at expense of others.

Druidism

Celtic religion primarily nature cult; druids (priests and prophets) concerned with control of nature by magic and knowledge, in particular keeping of calendar which determined annual festivals around which agriculture organized. Druids unacceptable to Rome through involvement in politics; banned by Claudius. Britain a centre of druid lore; Caesar says druids went to Britain to train.

Belgic peoples

Peoples originating between Seine, Marne and Rhine begin to appear in south-east Britain about 100 BC; influx possibly increased by Caesar's conquest of Gaul 58-51 BC. Material culture, coins, appearance of some tribal names both sides of Channel suggest settlement in south-east by Atrebates, Catuvellauni, Trinovantes, Cantiaci of Kent; beyond these probably only imposition of Belgic aristocracy e.g.

Iceni, Dobunni. South-east thus became most civilized area of Britain with regions unified under single or dual rulers, proto-urbanization and use of coinage; also area most in contact with Roman world.

See **Invasions of Julius Caesar** (page 24)

Catuvellauni

Tribe of Northamptonshire, Bedfordshire, Cambridgeshire, Buckinghamshire and Hertfordshire, possibly that of Cassivellaunus, chief opponent of Caesar 54 BC, with an *oppidum* perhaps at Wheathampstead near St Albans. From 20 BC King Tasciovanus issued coins from Prae Wood (Verulamium), bearing names apparently of subsidiary kings in Catuvellaunian empire. Cunobelinus succeeded at Verulamium; by AD 7 issuing coins at Camulodunum (Colchester), a new capital; succeeded *c.* AD 40 by sons Togodumnus and Caratacus who led resistance to Claudian invasion. Claudius present at fall of Camulodunum which became Colonia Victricensis AD 49, capital of new province until gave way to London.

The tribes of Britain at the start of the Roman period

```
0    50   100  150 km
0    50        100 miles
```

Britons, at any given moment, found it expedient to seek Roman backing. Archaeological discoveries revealing a taste for Roman mass-produced and luxury goods – or the absence of them – should not be taken as evidence for a pro- or anti-Roman stance in any particular locality. It is clear that such goods were status symbols among the Britons, and what the pattern of finds of Roman material in pre-Roman contexts really tells us is who controlled the supply of such items. Such control, particularly of the luxury goods prized by the British upper classes, made the tribes through which they flowed rich and gave their rulers political muscle in relation to other aristocracies that desired them. Similarly, it is now suspected that the British coins in precious metals were less used as a means of exchange in the course of trade than as diplomatic gifts, important symbolic elements in the interchange of politics.

Caesar's invasions* had wrought a temporary alliance of British tribes under a war leader, Cassivellaunus. Historians differ on whether he was, or became, king of the Catuvellauni*, centred in Hertfordshire. But his expulsion of a prince of the Trinovantes* in Essex had been a cause, or pretext, for Caesar's intervention; and the history of Britain from Caesar to Claudius is largely the expansion of Catuvellaunian influence over most of southern Britain. In the same period, the trading pattern between Britain and Gaul shows the bulk of the traffic switching from the routes between Dorset and Armorica* to those between the south and east coasts of England and the Continent from the Seine to the Rhine. The Roman conquest of Gaul and the arrival of large permanent Roman garrisons in Germany transformed the political potential of those who could dominate the British ends of these routes and brought Britain much more closely within the Roman world.

Intense political activity among the British tribes did not bring Rome's intervention till it suited her. Thus neither the flight of Caesar's Gallic friend turned enemy, Commius, to find acceptance as king among his British Atrebatic* kin, nor the taking over by the Catuvellauni of the kingdom of the Trinovantes, expressly forbidden by Caesar, provoked Roman action. The movements are the other way. Internal strife sent several deposed rulers to

Trinovantes

Tribe, probably with Belgic connections, of Essex: surrendered to Caesar 54 BC through fear of Cassivellaunus; protected by treaty with Rome. Coins attest Addedomaros and Dubnovellaunos as rulers, possibly as subjects of Tasciovanus, king of Catuvellauni; coins of Cunobelinus, successor of Tasciovanus, spread over whole territory of Trinovantes. After Claudius' invasion, capital Camulodunum (Colchester) became colonia in AD 49, loss of territory to Roman settlers led tribe to join Boudicca's revolt and destroy city.

Armorica

Region of north-west France involved in trade with southern Britain, early 1st century BC. Armorican coins appear on south coast, especially at Hengistbury Head which acted as entrepôt for hinterland, supplying raw materials for Roman world in return for Roman luxury goods, with Armorican traders as middlemen, in particular tribe of Veneti. Other cultural and commercial contacts with south-west Britain.

Atrebates

Tribe with Belgic name and connections, settled in Britain before Caesar's expedition of 55 BC, when he tried to use Commius, Atrebatic chieftain from Gaul, as intermediary. Commius later broke with Rome, fled to Britain 52 BC, became king of Atrebates centred on Calleva (Silchester). Succeeded by son Tincommius; ruled over broader kingdom, expelled by another son Eppillus, later succeeded by yet another son, Verica; last fled to Rome AD 43 under Catuvellaunian pressure. Eventually kingdom passed to Cogidubnus as client-king, later organized by Romans into three *civitates*: Atrebates centred on Calleva, Belgae on Venta (Winchester), Regini on Noviomagus (Chichester).

15

Rome as exiles. When, however, circumstances at Rome were right, British politics provided reason and opportunity. A struggle in the kingdom centred on the Southampton area drove out its king, followed shortly by a family dispute among the now dominant Catuvellauni that ended in Cunobelinus (Shakespeare's Cymbeline) expelling one son, Amminus, who took refuge with the Emperor Claudius. Claudius needed* a striking military victory to secure his own shaky position; while the transfer of power among the Catuvellauni shortly before the Roman invasion from Cunobelinus to his pugnacious sons Caratacus and Togodumnus meant that both the south and east coasts of Britain were now unfriendly.

Once conquered, the principal objective of Roman governmental arrangements in any new territory was to transfer as much of the burden of administration as possible onto locals. The preferred form was the self-administering and self-financing local authority: *colonia**, *municipium** or *civitas** – a local oligarchy run by loyal men of property in a reflection of the formal structure of Rome herself, which in turn derived from the Mediterranean city-state. Where the native tribes had already developed an oligarchic rather than monarchic form, the transition was much easier. In Britain in the later first century AD and the early second, such a pattern of *civitates* run by an *ordo** developed over most of the province*. The governor*, a Roman senator and former consul, commanded the army and the central administration, supervised the *civitates,* and dispensed justice. Taxation and the control of estates and industrial enterprises, such as mines, that were acquired as Crown property by the emperor (including all the royal estates of defeated tribes) came under a separate officer, the provincial procurator*, who was directly responsible to the emperor. This split administration was a potent source of trouble, but it allowed the emperor both to keep an independent check on the Roman nobles who acted as governors and to retain in his hand the major sources of money.

The disappearance of the Catuvellaunian hegemony almost, but not quite, overnight (Caratacus, till captured, remained a dangerous and active focus for resistance), must have been nearly as dramatic a change in the political scene in Britain as the arrival of Roman rule. New opportunities opened up for other Britons. In the first three decades of Roman rule, indeed, the fact that the province was in an embryo state gave particular opportunities to certain people. The story of those years is the rise and fall of the "client-kingdoms"*. These were often artificial creations: within the original area of conquest, a number of tribes were assembled to make a client-kingdom centred on the south coast. The Iceni* of Norfolk and some peoples towards Wales were also regarded as "allies" of Rome. At least two of these allied political units had kings – Cogidubnus (possibly a Gaul rather than a Briton) in the south, and another over the Iceni. North of the initial province, Queen Cartimandua of the Brigantes* used Roman support to maintain her position within her huge and disunited tribe and her turbulent family. This made her just as surely a client of Rome.

Overall, the Romans' experience of client-kingdoms in first-century Britain was not encouraging. The Iceni revolted twice. In AD 47 they showed their misconception of the Roman notion of "allies" by rising when the governor decided to withdraw their right to bear arms. Under Boudicca they were the point of origin for the cataclysm that nearly destroyed the province in AD 61. Among the Brigantes, Cartimandua's matrimonial exploits ended in her

Drawing of part of an inscription (now lost) dedicating a temple in London: NVM (INI) C (AESARIS) PROV (INCIA) BRITA (NNIA) = The Province of Britain erected this to the Divinity of the Emperor.

See **Motive for invasion of Claudius** (page 24

Colonia
Roman city of highest rank. In full *coloniae*, all citizens were also Roman citizens. Under empire, *coloniae* in provinces often created at former legionary bases, by granting allotments to retired legionaries to provide future recruits for legions, which only accepted Roman citizens. First British *coloniae* were Colchester (Camulodunum) in AD 49, Lincoln (Lindum) end of first century AD and Gloucester (Glevum) AD 96-8. Governed by council (*ordo*), modelled on Roman Senate, with four annual magistrates (*quattuorviri*).

Municipium
Roman city of rank below *colonia*, similarly organized with council (*ordo*) and usually four annual magistrates (two *duoviri*, two *aediles*). Under empire, inhabitants not automatically Roman citizens, but magistrates and families acquired citizenship at end of term of office. Like *coloniae* and *civitas* capitals, had surrounding territory ascribed. Some provinces organized entirely into *coloniae* and *municipia* with their territories. Only one *municipium* in Britain directly attested, Verulamium (St Albans).

Civitas capital
Britain divided into *civitates*, usually based on pre-Roman tribal territories, centred on *civitas* capitals which formed majority of Roman towns, concentrated in south-east and midlands. Capitals often organized on model of *municipia* with *ordo* and magistrates, although latter did not receive Roman citizenship at end of term of office. Created out of pre-existing settlements and settlements which grew up around abandoned forts.

Ordo

Major towns were governed by elected council *(ordo)* normally of 100 councillors *(decuriones)* and created from local pre-Roman aristocracy and other wealthy men, on model of Roman Senate; this process was central to Roman approach to controlling empire: to win over native aristocracy by confirming their position, and allow them to control own people. *Ordo* chose annual magistrates, sent delegates to Provincial Council.

Provincial Council

Council *(Concilium Provinciae)*, formed of delegates from town councils; met annually to pass resolutions praising or criticizing governors and, if necessary, appoint a provincial patron (usually a senior senator) to prosecute governor on its behalf. Main function was to administer annual festival of imperial cult and maintain Temple of Deified Claudius at Colchester.

Province

Under Roman Republic, *provincia* meant magistrate's sphere of responsibility, not necessarily, though frequently, territorial. First emperor, Augustus 27 BC – AD 14, added to those established under Republic several territories which were formed into *provinciae* of two types, those under governors appointed by Senate ("senatorial" provinces) and those under governors appointed by emperor ("imperial" provinces) which included all provinces, like Britain, with legionary troops.

Governors

Under Empire, "senatorial" provinces were governed, as under Republic, by proconsuls appointed by Senate; in "imperial" provinces, emperor acted as proconsul and governed through "viceroys" *(legati Augusti)* or, for smaller provinces, through procurators of equestrian order ("knights"). Only *legati* commanded major armies which included legions; Britain with four (later three) legions was governed by one of most senior. Governors usually served for about three years and had almost absolute powers, including summary direction of trials and sole right of execution.

Provincial procurator

Procurators were senior administrative officers, members of the equestrian order ("knights") ranking below senators, directly employed by emperor. Most senior were provincial procurators who either governed small imperial provinces or, in those governed by *legati* (like Britain), acted as financial officers and watched *legati* (since *legati*, though deputies of emperor, were selected from Senate and so harder for emperor to control). In AD 61 Julius Classicianus, procurator of Britain, appealed to emperor against harsh reprisals of governor, Suetonius Paullinus, following Boudiccan revolt.

Client-kings

Roman empire employed client-kings, especially in 1st century AD, either as buffers on frontiers of empire or in administration of new provinces. Kings were obligated with treaties and in return had Roman backing for their own position, often against rivals for throne e.g. Cartimandua, queen of Brigantes. Within empire, kingdoms usually put under Roman-type administration on death of first client e.g. Iceni on death of Prasutagus.

Iceni

Tribe of Norfolk and north-west Suffolk, possibly Cenimagni who surrendered to Caesar. Produced silver and gold coinage, suggesting Belgic overlordship and dual rulers, but population probably indigenous. Client-kingdom after Claudian invasion; tribe revolted AD 47 when Romans tried to disarm them under *Lex Iulia de vi publica* (see *Pax Romana*). Prasutagus made client-king but Roman depredations on his death led wife Boudicca to revolt. After revolt was harshly suppressed, *civitas* set up with capital at Caistor-by-Norwich.

Brigantes

Pastoralist tribe covering most of northern England, with only precarious unity; aristocracy rich and powerful. Queen Cartimandua acted as client of Rome; returned fugitive Caratacus to Romans AD 51, but later had to be protected against estranged husband and rival Venutius. By AD 73 governor Petillius Cerialis overran Brigantia, defeating Venutius, and in 78 or 79 Agricola conquered whole area. Capital set up at Aldborough (Isurium) but tribe caused trouble again *c.* AD 155.

A formal dedication in honour of Hadrian erected in the forum of Wroxeter (Viroconium Cornoviorum) by the civitas of the Cornovii, dated AD 130.

expulsion in AD 69 by her ex-husband. Her most spectacular service to Rome had been the handing over of the fugitive Caratacus. She had now, however, finally destroyed the credibility of the client-kingdoms in Britain.

Rome was thus committed to the universal extension of the system of Roman-style local authorities. But the Boudiccan revolt* had revealed something far more serious than the personal wrongs done to the queen and her family. That revolt had been joined by the aristocracies of other tribes, including most notably Rome's friends in Britain, the Trinovantes whom the Claudian conquest had freed from the Catuvellauni. A mixture of extreme insensitivity and plain greed on the Roman side had destroyed the confidence of the native aristocracy on whom Rome would have to rely in constructing and running a system of local authorities. The Boudiccan revolt had for the first time shown a real turning against all things Roman.

It was the remarkable achievement of the Roman administrations of the later first century and the second to reverse this tendency. A variety of incentives and pressures gradually transformed the upper classes of Britain into solid provincial Roman gentry. Under sounder imperial administration than had led to the Boudiccan disaster, the British aristocracy could believe they might enjoy those material pleasures of Roman life which they had coveted before the conquest without any serious deprivation other than of the freedom to fight one another. This process of absorbing influential Britons was powerfully assisted by the influx of people from other parts of the empire, creating, at least in the towns, a professional and commercial middle class and a Romanized lower class. It was also strongly affected by the growth of local recruitment* for the Roman army, a system that quite consciously produced Roman citizens* who subsequently took their place in the local community. The attitudes and politics of Britain were henceforth Roman.

If we measure the success of this policy in terms of preventing native revolt against Rome and suppressing the Britons' predilection for fighting one another, it clearly worked – with one possible important exception among the Brigantes in the middle of the second century. But it was not accompanied by an influx of Romano-Britons into the upper reaches of administration and

Causes of Boudiccan revolt
Sparked off by death of Prasutagus, king of Iceni *c.* AD 60; half of kingdom bequeathed to Emperor Nero, but slaves of provincial procurator and centurions of governor's office seized whole kingdom: Boudicca, widow of Prasutagus, flogged, daughters raped, nobles mistreated. Grievances aggravated when Roman money-lenders called in debts and procurator, Catus Decianus, attempted to recoup subsidies paid to chieftains by Claudius. Trinovantes induced to join in revolt by loss of land after colonization of Camulodunum (Colchester).

Boudiccan revolt AD 60
Began AD 60 when Boudicca attacked and burnt Camulodunum, massacred inhabitants; IXth Hispana legion repulsed with heavy losses. Governor, Suetonius Paullinus, dashed to protect London, but commander of IInd Augusta legion refused help, so London evacuated, sacked by Boudicca. Verulamium (St Albans) evacuated and burnt. Total deaths 70,000. Suetonius fell back along Watling Street towards XIVth Gemina and part of XXth Valeria legion: in final battle 10,000 Roman troops destroyed British force, 80,000 British dead; Boudicca committed suicide. Suetonius ravaged territory of rebel tribes into AD 61. New procurator, Julius Classicianus, pressed for milder measures; Suetonius recalled after imperial commission of enquiry.

The development of Roman provincial organization

 o Provincial capitals

 ⊙ Diocesan capital

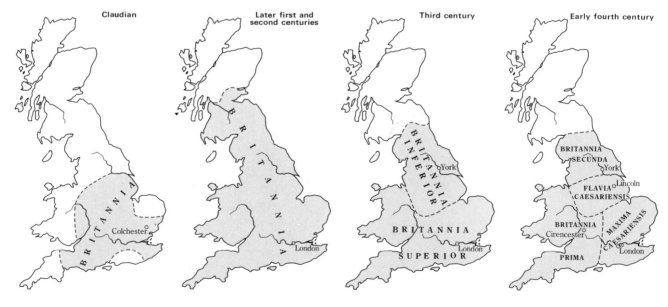

Claudian | Later first and second centuries | Third century | Early fourth century

See **Auxilia** (page 25)

Roman citizenship

Special status universal in Italy under Empire but at first rare in provinces: it gave right to marry and trade under Roman law, protection from summary beating or execution, and right of appeal to emperor; above all, gave hereditary social standing in status-ridden Roman world. Citizenship gradually extended by special patronage, award to magistrates of *municipia,* and to retired auxiliary soldiers and their families. Numbers increased until Emperor Caracalla granted citizenship to all free inhabitants of empire in 212.

Year of Four Emperors AD 68-9

AD 68, C. Iulius Vindex, governor of part of Gaul, and S. Sulpicius Galba, governor of part of Spain, revolted against Emperor Nero. Vindex defeated at Besançon but Nero fled from Galba, committed suicide. Galba arrived in Rome as emperor, but murdered by M. Salvius Otho and imperial guard (January AD 69). Throne disputed by A. Vitellius, governor of Lower Germany; Otho defeated at Cremona. Eastern legions now declarèd T. Flavius Vespasianus emperor; his generals marched on Italy, joined by Danube legions, defeated Vitellius at Cremona. Vitellius killed in Rome (December), Senate declared Vespasian emperor.

Loyalty of Cogidubnus AD 69

AD 69 Britain supported Vitellius until his overthrow; IInd Augusta legion (commanded by Vespasian in Claudian invasion) led way in switching support to Vespasian. Cogidubnus, highly favoured client-king of Atrebates, Belgae and Regini, apparently supported Vespasian and remained loyal to Rome.

politics in the empire at large, as in some other provinces. Instead, Britain's unique position, isolated from the Continent by a sea regarded as formidable and possessing an unusually large garrison that could – except for pay – be wholly supported from local sources, seems to have been responsible for the nature of its involvement in imperial politics.

The army of Britain had taken little part in the Year of the Four Emperors*, AD 68-9. This was partly because the allegiance of the legions was split, partly because of a hostile local environment where the policy of political taming of the locals had not yet been put into effect, and partly due to the loyalty of Cogidubnus*, perhaps the last significant contribution by a client-king on Rome's behalf. But this army's potential was felt at Rome. It developed a reputation over the years for reacting badly to over-strict

A page from a 15th-century copy of the early 5th-century Roman directory, Notitia Dignitatum, *showing the five provinces allocated to the* vicarius Britanniarum.

commanders, and in the course of the second century local recruiting meant a rank-and-file that was largely British. In 185 it showed its strength in an extraordinary incident when a deputation* despatched to Rome was instrumental in the downfall of an unpopular praetorian prefect. In 193 Clodius Albinus*, the governor of Britain and its commander, emerged as one of the eventual three main contenders for the imperial throne after the murder of the Emperor Commodus and the most difficult for the final victor, Septimius Severus, to overcome.

The defeat of Clodius Albinus in battle had less effect on the prosperity of Britain than might be expected. This must indicate limited political support for Albinus among the civilian upper class. Until the end of the third century, the Romano-Britons apparently fell in with their changing political masters without becoming deeply involved. Even the spectacular seizure of Britain in 287 by the rebel general Carausius* does not seem to have had powerful support from the populace. Indeed, there is reason to suspect that even in the garrison – at least among the regular units – there was limited enthusiasm for defending Carausius's successor, Allectus, when the final counter-attack came from the central government. Nevertheless, the political lessons of each occasion in which Britain had become involved in major struggles for power in the empire were that a contender who held Britain was difficult to dislodge militarily and that Britain was a major asset – increasingly so as other parts of the empire were hit by barbarian invasion* and economic decline.

The administrative pattern of Britain remained largely unchanged from the late first century to the end of the third, except that, at some point in the years following the Severan victory, the province was divided* into two as part of a general policy of reducing the size of provinces containing armies that were too large for political comfort. The south, with its capital at London and legionary bases at Caerleon in south Wales and Chester, became Upper Britain; while the north, with York raised to the status of a Roman *colonia*, formed the province of Lower Britain.

The recovery of Britain by the Roman central government in 296 heralded half a century of change. Governmental reform was reflected at the provincial level in a drastic reorganization that separated military command from civil administration. The two provinces in Britain were replaced by four (subsequently five), grouped together in a "diocese"* under a *vicarius*. The *vicarius* reported to a praetorian prefect*, whose headquarters was at Trier, on the Moselle, and who was responsible for the *vicarii* of all the dioceses of the north-western part of the empire. Within Britain, the old provincial procurators disappeared, part of their functions being taken on by the new civil governors*. The principal financial business of the diocese, however, became the sphere of two new financial branches. London* seems to have become the centre for all these civil departments.

Power in the late empire was polarized between the emperor, officials and army on the one hand and the greater landowners on the other. The middle class, and urban communities generally, lost ground. In Britain, this was reflected by a striking increase in the prosperity of the villas* and their estates and a corresponding decline in public spending in the towns. The flowering of villas in this period is in such contrast to the picture in the neighbouring continental provinces that it is probably not just the accident of better survival of historical sources for this age that gives us the impression of greater involvement in politics. And the politics of the fourth century contained a

British deputation to Rome AD 185

In 182, unbalanced Emperor Commodus appointed Perennis as Praetorian Prefect, allowed him to rule empire. Perennis appointed knights instead of senators to command legions; very unpopular. Protests from whole empire included deputation of 1500 men from Britain in 185 (perhaps the governor's bodyguard), who succeeded in having Perennis deposed and executed.

Revolt of Clodius Albinus AD 193

In AD 193, three contenders for throne emerged: Clodius Albinus, governor of Britain backed by Western legions; Septimius Severus, governor of Upper Pannonia backed by Danube legions; Pescennius Niger, governor of Syria backed by Eastern legions. Severus occupied Rome, appointed Albinus Caesar (junior emperor), then attacked Niger, defeating him at Issus 194. Severus broke with Albinus, who invaded Gaul with British troops 196, defeated 197, leaving Severus sole ruler. Britain subsequently divided in 197 (or 213) to avoid concentration of legions under one governor (one in Lower Britain at York, two in Upper Britain at Caerleon and Chester).

Revolt of Carausius AD 287

M. Mausaeus Carausius appointed *c.* 286 by Emperor Maximian to tackle Saxon raids on north-west Gaul; connived with barbarians, condemned to death, but seized Britain 287, declared himself emperor. Maximian attacked Britain 288-89 but forced to make peace; Carausius now functioned as co-emperor, until assassinated by subordinate Allectus 293. In 296 Constantius (junior emperor) and Praetorian Prefect Asclepiodotus led two-pronged invasion of Britain; Allectus defeated, Constantius entered London in triumph.

Barbarian invasions of Roman empire

In 166, tribes of middle Danube region attacked empire and were repulsed; attacks ultimately caused by population pressure from Steppes. Increased in early 3rd century, resulting in continuous warfare on northern frontier and, after fall of Severan "dynasty" in 235, rapid succession of rival soldier-emperors. Continued until Diocletian gained throne 284: established system of four emperors with regional responsibilities (Tetrarchy), which proved impracticable; began army reforms which helped postpone collapse until 5th century in West and much later in East. Britain, as island, escaped worst barbarian pressure, (though not empire's consequent inflation), and was generally peaceful in 3rd and early 4th centuries.

Division of Britain
Britain divided into two provinces to prevent concentration of three legions in hands of one governor like Clodius Albinus; carried out either by Severus in 197 or son Caracalla 213. In Diocletianic reforms Britain divided into four provinces under civilian governors: Prima with capital at Cirencester; Secunda (York?); Maxima Caesariensis (London); Flavia Caesariensis (Lincoln?); at some time after 369, a fifth province was renamed Valentia.

Diocese
When Britain divided into four provinces by Diocletian, each under civilian governor called *praeses* or *rector*, these (perhaps only after 312) formed into diocese (group of provinces), under a vicar *(vicarius Britanniarum)* of the praetorian prefect of the Gauls. This part of Diocletianic reforms was completed by Constantine the Great, dividing civilian and military commands.

Vicar of Britain
Overall civilian governor of diocese of Britain, consisting of four, later five, British provinces. He was a *vicarius* (deputy) of the praetorian prefect of the Gauls; both positions perhaps settled in this form only after 312 when Praetorian Guard disbanded. Vicar was probably based in London.

Praetorian Prefect
Praetorian Prefects originally instituted by Augustus 2 BC as commanders of imperial bodyguard (Praetorian Guard). One, two or three in number, they were most senior knights, and under some emperors the next most powerful men in empire; gradually acquired judicial functions, especially in Italy. Guard disbanded by Constantine 312; prefects became civilian officials, chief regional deputies of emperors with major financial functions. Eventually four territorial prefectures established: The Gauls, Italy, Illyricum (Danube area), the East.

Civilian governors and military commanders
Diocletian's attempt to stabilize and preserve empire involved widespread army reforms, including massive increase in size and creation of professional officer corps. Hence civilian and military command split, new smaller provinces being governed by civilian *praesides* (or *rectores*), who also took over some of financial functions of procurators, under overall control of vicar of diocese; frontier army forces meanwhile placed under *duces* ("dukes" or leaders). Process continued by Constantine, who completed institution of élite mobile field-army, ready to move to aid of besieged frontier forces, led by *comites* ("counts" or companions) of the emperor.

London
Began as trading centre *c.* AD 45; first buildings in timber burnt in Boudiccan revolt AD 60. Provincial procurator possibly already based here. Roman bridge of *c.* AD 80 near London Bridge. Small *forum* built end of 1st century, also governor's palace and Cripplegate fort for his bodyguard. London by now succeeded Colchester as capital. New large *forum* early 2nd century. Major fire *c.* 125, another mid-2nd century, followed by period of decline. Recovery end of 2nd century: wall on landward side, monumental arch, temple of Mithras built. Population declined in 3rd century, but city still prosperous; sharp change from mid-4th century, though riverside wall built. Roman occupation into 5th century, but Saxons later took over.

See **Villas** (page 41)

Carved stone tomb-figure of a military clerk, probably on the governors's staff in London: he carries a case of writing tablets, and wears a sword; the scarf protected his neck from sores when wearing body-armour.

Reconstruction drawing of the Roman governor's palace in London, seen from the south-west.

fundamentally new element, the active interest of the state in ideology and belief*: Christian or pagan, orthodoxy or heresy. Indeed, ancient Britain's most spectacular contribution to world history must be the highly irregular but effective proclamation by the army at York of Constantine the Great* as emperor. On a more local scale, there is reason to think that Constantine did not forget the origins of his power in Britain. And if the age of affluence* in early fourth-century Britain did consolidate power in the hands of the land-owning aristocracy, later events become easier to interpret.

While it is generally recognized that the prosperity of Britain as a whole declined under increasingly severe barbarian incursions for three decades from about 340, the effects of political troubles in the same period were perhaps as acute and may have reached deeper. Twice the army of Britain found itself on the losing side in civil war. The second time, it was followed, in 353, by a political purge of frightening proportions conducted by the infamous imperial agent, Paul, nicknamed "The Chain"*. It is not surprising that the disorders following the great barbarian invasions of 367 were marked by at least one internal conspiracy* – and possibly by the temporary loss to rebels of one of the British provinces. A significant factor was the presence of men of influence, exiled from the imperial Court for crimes against the state, who had been tampering with the loyalty of the troops. So unstable did he judge the political situation in Britain to be that Theodosius the elder* decided to crush the current plot with the least possible fuss and, unlike Paul, forbore to investigate further than was unavoidable. Ironically, an officer who had served under Theodosius in the recovery of Britain, Magnus Maximus*, was able to build up such a strong power base in the restored Britain as to be able to make in 383 an attempt on the throne that came within an ace of complete success.

The vast struggles for supremacy within the empire after the death of Theodosius the Great in 395 probably led to troop withdrawals from Britain in c. 400, and certainly to the cessation of central payment of officials and remaining units shortly after. This isolation was compounded by huge barbarian incursions into Gaul at the end of 406. Of three emperors elevated in quick succession in Britain, the survivor was Constantine III*. The army undoubtedly played an important part in this last attempt from Britain to seize the imperial throne. The retreat of the north-western administration from Trier south to Arles, in the face of the barbarians, however, left Britain out on a limb, even in Constantine's realm. By 409 the Romano-Britons had become disillusioned. What now happened is a curious forerunner of what occurred elsewhere in the West. The great Roman landowners became increasingly dissatisfied with the burden of taxation required to support the superstructure of emperor, Court, bureaucracy and army. They particularly resented and resisted the drain on agricultural manpower represented by military conscription. Moreover there had been a long ideological tension between traditionalist pagan aristocrats and militantly Christian emperors. In 409 the Romano-Britons summarily expelled Constantine's administration. But this time they did not replace him with another candidate for the throne, nor, perhaps observing the arrest and execution of former opponents on the Continent by the central government, did they declare for legitimacy as soon as there was opportunity. Instead they abandoned Roman rule entirely*. There is no evidence to support the notion that this was a proletarian revolution. Rather, we may assume that the successors of that class that had

See **Imperial cult** (page 46); **Christianity in Britain** (page 48)

Elevation of Constantine the Great
After revolt of Carausius, Constantius returned to Britain in 306, now as senior emperor *(Augustus)* in West, to campaign in Scotland against Picts. When he died at York in 306, army declared son Constantine emperor at prompting of barbarian leader Crocus.

4th-century revival of Britain
Period of prosperity in Britain followed 3rd-century stagnation caused by troubles of empire. Revival encouraged by Constantinian reconstruction, general revival of empire after Diocletianic/Constantinian reforms. Prosperity manifested in large villas, schools of mosaicists, hoards of silver etc; peters out in face of political troubles and pressure on northern and seaward frontier from c. 340.

Purges of Paulus Catena ("The Chain")
Constantine II, emperor in West, killed by brother Constans 340. Constans murdered 350, succeeded by Magnentius, who, with troops from Britain, was defeated at Mursa (in modern Yugoslavia) by Constantius II, emperor in East; committed suicide 353. Constantius II, now sole emperor, sent Paul, "imperial notary", to put down disaffection in Britain, seizing supporters of Magnentius. Vicar Martinus, who tried to stop him, committed suicide. Purges ended in 355 when Julian ("the Apostate", later emperor) made *Caesar* (junior emperor) in Gaul and Britain.

Barbarian conspiracy of AD 367
Picts, Attacotti, Scots attacked Britain 367 (in concert with Franks, Saxons who attacked Gaul), helped by treachery of some frontier forces *(areani)*. Fullofaudes, duke *(dux)* of Britain, was besieged; Nectaridus, a count *(comes)*, possibly of the Saxon Shore, killed. Barbarians then broke up, bands raided countryside: some evidence of destruction on Hadrian's Wall, in Pennines. After senior officers Severus and Jovinus failed, Emperor Valentinian sent Count Theodosius to restore order.

Reforms of Count Theodosius
Count Theodosius arrived at Richborough 368, with élite units of field-army, marched on London, destroyed barbarian bands, reorganized army and civil administration, attacked barbarians by land and sea. Order restored by 369; forts rebuilt in north, watch-towers on Yorkshire coast, Saxon Shore forts reorganized; one province, threatened possibly by conspiracy of Roman

exiles, recovered and named Valentia. Reforms ensured final period of prosperity for Roman Britain.

Revolt of Magnus Maximus AD 383
Magnus Maximus, colleague of Count Theodosius, defeated Picts and Scots in 382, possibly as duke of Britain. Used popularity to declare himself emperor 383: invaded Gaul; killed Gratian (legitimate emperor in West); ruled Britain, Gaul, Spain from Trier; recognized by Theodosius the Great, emperor in East. In 387 Maximus crossed Alps, possibly with troops from Britain, occupied Milan, seat of Valentinian II, brother of Gratian. Theodosius attacked; defeated and killed Maximus at Aquileia 388.

Elevation of Constantine III AD 407
In 398-99 Stilicho, senior general of West, repulsed invasions of Picts, Saxons, Irish into Britain, but 401 or 402 withdrew troops to defend Italy against Alaric the Visigoth. In 406 centre of western government moved south from Trier to Arles after barbarians devastated Gaul; Britain becoming isolated. After two British claimants to empire, Marcus and Gratian, were elevated and murdered in turn, Constantine III elevated 407, invaded Gaul and Spain, and by 409 was recognized by Western emperor, Honorius. Constantine invaded Italy 409 but was forced to withdraw by Spanish revolt; surrendered to Honorius 411, was executed.

End of Roman rule
In 409 Britons expelled remaining Roman officials and then Saxons; end of Roman rule (410 letter of Honorius ordering Britons to look to their own defence now thought may refer to Bruttii of south Italy). Provoked by neglect of Britain by Constantine III and empire as a whole. Import of imperial coinage ceased *c.* 402, but Romanized life in towns and villas survived to mid- or late 5th century. Confused period of alliances and wars between groups of Romano-Britons and barbarians. Britons generally successful till 440s; thereafter Saxons took over, though stalled *c.* 490 by major British victory.

been won over in the late first century had now decided that the imperial system, as it now was, took more than it offered. To the landed gentry of Britain, it may well have seemed that their way of life would be better preserved without an emperor than with one.

A section of Roman road crossing Blackstone Edge, Yorkshire.

Warfare and International Relations:
Britain and Rome

David J. Breeze

The invasions of Britain by Julius Caesar* in 55 and 54 BC and by the Emperor Claudius* in AD 43 arose out of Roman domestic politics rather than a serious threat posed to Rome by the British tribes. In fact, although warfare was endemic among these tribes, the superior weapons, armour, training and discipline of the Roman army created an uneven contest. But, while Roman arms were invariably successful in a set-piece battle, the guerrilla tactics occasionally employed by some of the British tribes could delay the inevitable outcome.

The provincial Roman army was divided into two main branches, the legions* and the *auxilia** (literally, support troops). Each legion, recruited from Roman citizens, consisted of about five thousand heavy infantrymen. The soldiers were protected by body armour, helmet and shield and armed with the short stabbing sword (*gladius*) and two javelins. The auxiliary units were, at the time of Caesar, recruited from the allies and friends of Rome and grouped into irregular units usually commanded by their own tribal leaders. By the time of Claudius, these units were organized on a more formal basis, with the commanding officers drawn from the Roman gentry, while the soldiers themselves were mainly recruited from the frontier tribes. There were infantry and cavalry regiments and also mixed units of infantry and cavalry, all about five hundred strong. Towards the end of the first century AD, larger units, roughly double in size, were introduced. The auxiliary soldiers were similarly armed to the legionaries.

The Roman army was so highly trained that, in the words of Josephus, "its battles were bloody exercises and its exercises bloodless battles". It was well drilled and capable of manoeuvring during battle, responding to signals indicated by the movement of the standards or the sound of the trumpet. The Roman army was primarily an infantry force: the main purpose of the auxiliary cavalry was the pursuit and cutting down of the fleeing enemy.

The tribal forces opposed to Rome were very different. Warfare – battle, raid or single combat – was an important part of tribal life, but was based on the individual rather than the regiment. The tribal levy was composed of the warriors (Caesar called them knights) and their retainers. The warriors fought from chariots, long discarded on the Continent, while their retainers appear generally to have fought on foot. Both were armed with a sword (though lighter than the Roman *gladius*), dagger and spear. Body armour does not seem to have been used, but helmets might be worn, and much-needed protection was furnished by a shield.

The Celtic warrior was not particularly concerned with the identity of his enemy and was not organized to conduct a prolonged campaign. Many Roman writers referred to the faction-ridden nature of Celtic society, but it is also clear that the British tribes could combine their forces against the common enemy. In the AD 50s the Ordovices* of north Wales accepted the leadership of

Invasions of Julius Caesar 55, 54 BC
Expeditions to Britain were by-products of conquest of Gaul 58-51 BC, itself a means of maintaining popularity and an army for Caesar. Expedition of 55 a reconnaissance: Britons routed after skirmish, sued for peace. Expedition of 54 with five legions aimed at genuine conquest. Britons united under Cassivellaunus, used chariots and guerrilla tactics. Cassivellaunus' capital (?at Wheathampstead near St Albans) captured after site betrayed by Trinovantes and other tribes. Eventually Cassivellaunus capitulated; Caesar imposed terms including immunity of Trinovantes from Catuvellauni and payment of tribute; recalled to Gaul by rebellion. Terms soon ignored by Britons.

Motive for invasion of Claudius
Invasion of AD 43 prompted almost entirely by political necessity. On assassination of Caligula AD 41, his uncle Claudius made emperor by Praetorian Guard. Supported by army but regarded as crippled idiot by family and Senate; needed successful military expedition to keep army and popular support, withstand hostility of Senate. Invasion of Germany too dangerous; Britain regarded as new world which Caesar and Augustus both failed to conquer. Propaganda value paramount; hence capture of Camulodunum delayed so that Claudius could be present.

Legions
Main fighting units of Roman army, composed of Roman citizens serving 25 years. Between 25 and 30 legions at any time, three (four before AD 86) based in Britain. Each comprised 10 cohorts of 6 centuries (80 men) each, including 120 cavalry, roughly 5000 men in all; led by 60 centurions, usually promoted from ranks, also 6 military tribunes, drawn from nobility, and a prefect of the camp. Commander (*legatus legionis*) was senator of praetorian rank, usually appointed for three years. Legionaries heavily armoured, highly-disciplined infantry. In peacetime, sometimes employed in public building, road construction, mining etc.

Auxilia

Auxiliaries originally recruited from friends and allies of Rome. Organized in *cohortes* (infantry or mixed infantry and cavalry) and *alae* (cavalry), at first of about 500 men each (quingenary), led by centurions (infantry) and decurions (cavalry) and under command of a prefect, usually a knight. From late 1st century AD milliary units (about 800 men) added under command of tribunes. Only 10 milliary *alae* throughout empire, one in Britain at Stanwix near Carlisle. Auxiliaries locally recruited, as legionaries; received Roman citizenship on discharge after 25 years service.

Ordovices

Primitive, pastoralist tribe of north Wales. With Silures of south-east Wales, accepted Caratacus as war-leader when he fled from Claudian invasion; harried Roman advance from AD 47 as Caratacus retreated to Ordovician territory, where he was defeated 51. Ordovician centre of Mona (Anglesey) attacked by Suetonius Paullinus 60 but conquest of tribe delayed by Boudiccan revolt; completed by Julius Frontinus 74-77 or 78 and Agricola's capture of Anglesey 77 or 78. Tribe never sufficiently advanced to have *civitas* capital; remained partly under military control.

Caratacus of the defeated Catuvellauni/Trinovantes, while in the 80s all the Caledonian tribes joined forces under the war leader Calgacus. Their military intelligence could be sound, as evidenced by the night attack on the IXth legion, the weakest division of Agricola's army, and their tactics too. In the early third-century campaigns, the guerrilla tactics of the Caledones and Maeatae were correct, if in the end unsuccessful.

The Roman army was more coherently structured and its campaigns were carefully planned. They followed a set pattern. At the beginning of each season, troops were gathered together from their winter quarters, supplies were collected and intelligence garnered from merchants and travellers. This information included details of the tribes to be attacked, their strength and organization, the geography of the area, together with possible routes. The Romans always liked a just war, even if the pretext had to be manufactured. Thus in 55 BC Caesar stated that he invaded Britain because in almost all the Gallic campaigns support had been received by the Gallic tribes from Britain, and in the AD 80s Agricola invaded Caledonia following threatening movements by the northern tribes. Rarely was the true reason acknowledged, though Suetonius records that in AD 43 Claudius invaded Britain in order to obtain military prestige, and the propaganda value of the successful venture was subsequently fully exploited.

The army, supplies and intelligence collected and the *casus belli* found, the army marched out to find the enemy. Each night it protected itself by throwing up temporary fortifications consisting of a rampart and ditch surrounding the whole force. Through study of the location of such marching

Reconstruction drawing of auxiliary soldiers in the Roman army (left cavalry, *right* infantry*).*

Drawing of a legionary soldier in marching order, carrying his gear and mess-tins on a staff over his shoulder.

camps* it has been possible to trace, in part at least, the route of the armies of Agricola* in the AD 80s and of Septimius Severus in 208-11. Within the defences, the leather tents were pitched in neat rows, small tents for each group of eight soldiers, larger tents for the officers, separated by wide streets for easy movement. It might take several campaign seasons to defeat the enemy. Each winter, the army retired into winter quarters. These were slightly more comfortable, with huts rather than tents.

Few accounts survive of battles in Britain. Most appear to have been straightforward contests, with the Britons, usually because of their superior numbers, frequently underestimating the capability of their opponents. Thus, at two battles in AD 43, the Catuvellauni relied for defence upon a river, only to discover that this was no obstacle to the Roman auxiliaries who swam across in full armour. Caratacus* in Wales and Calgacus at Mons Graupius* chose the site of the battle, utilizing sloping ground in their favour: Caratacus added extra defences in the form of stone ramparts. In the final battle against Boudicca, the Romans were able to choose the ground, fighting in a defile, with a wood behind, so that they could not be outflanked. As a further precaution, the infantry was drawn up in close formation with the cavalry on the wings. Agricola, not so heavily outnumbered at Mons Graupius, chose to fight on a wide front, again with the cavalry on the wings, but with a smaller cavalry detachment and his legions kept in reserve: a wise move as his cavalry reserve was later able to break up a flanking attack. All three battles followed a similar pattern: an initial exchange of missiles, followed by the inexorable advance of the Roman forces, continuing until the Britons broke and fled. In Wales, the steep hill added a further difficulty to be overcome but the legionaries moved up under locked shields: archers dealt with Boudicca's chariots while those at Mons Graupius were routed by the cavalry. At Mons Graupius, for the first time in Britain, the auxiliary regiments formed the battle-line in a set-piece contest.

The aim of the campaign was to force the enemy to sue for peace either by defeating him in battle or by cowing him. Once defeated, hostages would be taken, which would usually have the effect of securing the enemy's acquiescence, and weapons confiscated. Thereafter forts* might be constructed within

Marching camps

Roman army units on campaign constructed temporary camp at end of each daily march, erecting rampart of earth, surmounted by stakes carried with army, to protect leather tents within; could be occupied overnight or for longer period. Area of camp gives good indication of size of force. Many camps discovered in Scotland and Wales, especially by aerial photography; series of regularly-spaced camps of same size allow tracing of some campaigns of Agricola and later of Severus.

Campaigns of Agricola

Cn. Iulius Agricola arrived as governor AD 77 or 78, began final conquest of island, promoted development in south-east. Annual campaigns: (1) subdued revolt in north Wales; (2) completed conquest of Brigantes; (3) and (4) conquest of lowlands of Scotland; during fourth campaign, forts established on Forth-Clyde line; (5) conquest of tribes in Kintyre or Galloway; (6) and (7) campaigns skirting eastern Highlands of Scotland by land and sea. At end of seventh campaign (83 or 84) Caledonian war-leader, Calgacus, defeated at Mons Graupius; Agricola recalled soon after. Trouble on Danube frontier prevented follow-up to Agricola's victory.

Defeat of Caratacus

Caratacus and Togodumnus of Catuvellauni overran neighbouring tribes. Verica, king of Atrebates, fled to Rome, providing pretext for Claudian invasion. Caratacus and Togodumnus resisted invasion in Kent; defeated at Medway, Togodumnus killed. Caratacus fled to south Wales AD 47, and continued Roman pressure forced him north to Ordovices AD 51; accepted as war-leader. Defeated in battle, fled to Cartimandua, queen of Brigantes, but handed over to governor Ostorius; sent to Rome but pardoned because of his dignity.

Reconstruction of a Celtic fighting chariot, based on remains found in chariot-burials and in a votive deposit in Wales.

Battle of Mons Graupius

Agricola finally forced Calgacus, Caledonian war-leader, to battle at Mons Graupius AD 83 or 84. Agricola used 8000 auxiliary infantry in centre, 3000 cavalry on flanks, legions in reserve; Caledonians ranked on hillside behind chariots. After hard struggle Caledonians attempted to take Roman line in rear; reserve cavalry sent in by Agricola, Caledonians routed, lost 10,000 men for 360 Roman dead. Site of battle unknown.

Forts and fortresses

Areas subject to military occupation were held by forts of individual auxiliary units spread one day's march apart, larger fortresses for legions being constructed at key points. In 1st century AD, when army still moved frequently, forts (little more than winter quarters) constructed of timber, with turf ramparts, in characteristic playing-card shape; gates in each of four sides of fort, administrative buildings in centre, timber barrack-blocks elsewhere. From 2nd century, when army dispositions more settled, forts often reconstructed in stone.

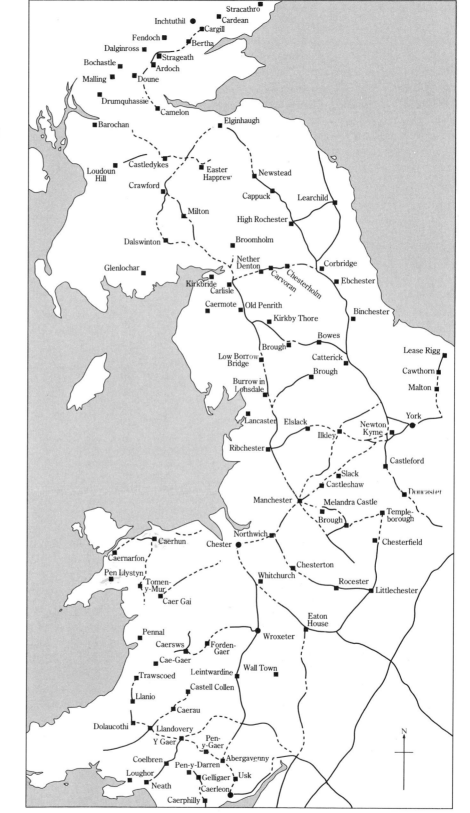

**Roman forts in Britain
in the late first century AD**

| 0 | 25 | 50 | 75 km |

| 0 | 25 | | 50 miles |

| 0 | 25 | | 50 Roman miles |

■ Forts
● Fortresses
— Roman roads
- - - Roman roads (course uncertain)

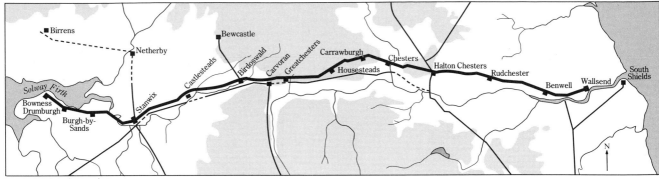

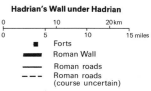

Hadrian's Wall under Hadrian

```
0          10          20km
0        5        10        15 miles
```
■ Forts
▬ Roman Wall
— Roman roads
--- Roman roads (course uncertain)

the territory of the defeated tribe, though this was not always necessary if the tribe could be controlled by the mere threat of force. If a defeated enemy later rebelled, he would be ruthlessly dealt with: in AD 61, harsh treatment was meted out following the suppression of the Boudiccan rebellion, while nearly twenty years later Agricola "exterminated" the Ordovices following a revolt.

It is not easy to distinguish on archaeological grounds between a winter camp and a permanent fort. Indeed it is doubtful if any forts were seen as permanent in the years following AD 43. They would be occupied on a temporary basis as necessary, with the "garrison" possibly changing on several occasions during the years of occupation. Little is known about the pattern of occupation during the first thirty years after AD 43. The army's purpose was to control the newly conquered tribes and to protect them from external aggression. One legion was at first situated at the provincial capital, while the other three were strategically placed for attack and defence in the frontier zone. The position of the auxiliary units is uncertain: they may have been grouped round the legions, dispersed across the province or placed near to the provincial boundary. However, there was certainly no special military frontier at this time: the provincial boundary lay along the borders of the relevant frontier tribes.

The conquest of Wales and the north of Britain in the AD 70s and 80s led to major troop movements, and now the pattern of occupation becomes clear. The legions were moved forward to strategic positions: Caerleon in south Wales, Chester and York. In between lay a network of auxiliary forts, usually ranging in size from three to six acres, placed about a day's march apart – fourteen to twenty miles – and connected by roads. This was not a rigid pattern, for it was varied to suit local requirements. The pattern was maintained in the areas under army occupation into the third century.

The 150 years following the advance initiated by the Emperor Vespasian in AD 70 witnessed several fluctuations in the position of the northern frontier*. Although Agricola pushed northwards, probably to the Moray Firth, and defeated the Caledonians at Mons Graupius, within twenty-five years the northernmost army units had fallen back to the Tyne-Solway isthmus*. Here, Hadrian's Wall* was constructed in the 120s, but less than twenty years after its inception it was abandoned in favour of the reoccupation of southern Scotland and the construction of a new barrier, the Antonine Wall*. This frontier only lasted twenty years before it too was given up: Hadrian's Wall was recommissioned and thereafter remained the frontier until the end of Roman Britain. From 208 to 211, however, the Emperor Septimius Severus campaigned in Scotland* with the intention of completing the conquest of the

Frontiers

At the time of Claudian invasion, increasing emphasis on defence along river frontiers of mainland Europe. Artificial frontiers first emerge in late 1st century. In Britain, first hint that Romans might not conquer whole island comes in Agricola's 4th campaign with establishment of line of garrisons across Forth-Clyde isthmus. Hadrian's contribution to development of frontiers was the linear barrier, first introduced in Germany and Britain in early 120s.

Stanegate frontier

About AD 87 troops withdrew from north Scotland because of trouble on Danube; about AD 105 further withdrawal to Tyne-Solway line, probably because of troop withdrawals for invasion of Dacia (modern Romania). Frontier consisted of forts, fortlets, watch-towers, road (Stanegate). Held until construction of Hadrian's Wall a few miles in front, 122.

Disappearance of IXth legion

IXth Hispana legion last attested in Britain at York in 107/8; replaced by VIth Victrix from Lower Germany, probably *c.* 122 when Hadrian's Wall begun. Once thought that IXth was lost in disaster in north, but tile-stamps show it soon after 107-8 at Nijmegen on Rhine, and four officers of legion are attested later, proving existence into 120s at least. Not attested in list for AD 170, so possibly lost in East under Marcus Aurelius.

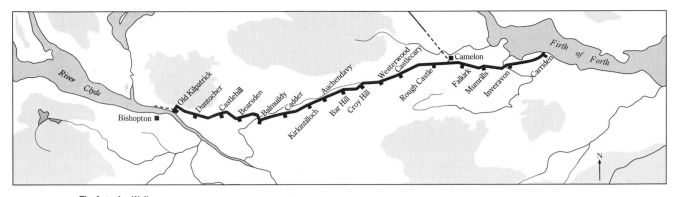

The Antonine Wall

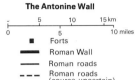

- Forts
- Roman Wall
- Roman roads
- Roman roads (course uncertain)

Hadrian's Wall

Construction probably result of Hadrian's visit, 122. Began with wall 70 miles long, of stone on east, turf on west, ditch in front, milecastle every mile, two turrets between each pair, forts on Stanegate. Plan soon changed to put forts on wall line, detectable by construction over turrets etc; stone wall reduced from 10 to 8 feet wide. Aim of wall was to control movement across frontier and to prevent raids. Troops would fight in open; change of plan to speed up their response to attacks. Garrisoned by auxiliary units, infantry and cavalry. When reoccupied after abandonment of Antonine Wall, system had outpost forts on east along Dere Street, to control Scottish Lowlands, and a military road behind.

Antonine Wall

In 138 Antoninus Pius succeeded Hadrian, built wall north of Hadrian's on Forth-Clyde line; possibly to control Lowlands; also Pius needed military victory for political reasons. Begun c. 142, of turf on stone base, ditch in front, road behind, 37 miles long. Original intention for 6 forts on Wall, fortlets every mile; plan changed, probably to 19 forts, one every two miles; outpost forts added, skirting Highlands. Antonine Wall abandoned c. 163.

whole island and thus presumably solving the problem of continuing irritation on the northern frontier: his aim died with him and his conquests were relinquished by his successor.

The unstable nature of the frontier throughout the late first century and the second century led to the presence of a substantial military force in the north and appointment of some of the best generals of the day to the governorship of the province. However, it had little effect on the disposition of the military forces. The number of forts along the frontier-line was increased by the reduction in the gap between each site from about fourteen to seven miles, while in the 160s the garrisons of the outpost forts of Hadrian's Wall were greatly enlarged. The construction of the frontier complexes was, however, related to an altogether different problem; the desire to prevent (or at least hinder) border raiding and to control the movement of people into and out of the province: access to the province was governed by regulations enforced by the army. At first this was achieved by the construction of watch-towers and fortlets, but the building of Hadrian's Wall recognized that the only effective method of control was through the erection of a linear barrier. The establishment – for convenience – of troops on the Wall blurred the distinction between two very different duties: the local task of frontier control and the wider role of protection. Hadrian's Wall and the Antonine Wall, to be sure, had a defensive role, but they could not stop a major attack and on at least one occasion – about 180 – one of the Walls was crossed and a Roman army defeated.

The campaigns of Septimius Severus were followed, for no clear reason, by a

Campaigns of Severus

Trouble with Caledonians in early 3rd century prompted Emperor Severus to campaign in Britain personally with two sons, Caracalla and Geta. Geta was left as governor, Caracalla and Severus moved north, 208 or 209; tribes forced to surrender territory. More trouble 210; Caracalla sent north with larger force. Death of Severus at York, 211, prevented another campaign; Caracalla and Geta returned to Rome to dispute throne. Conquered territory abandoned; Hadrian's Wall again frontier; peace there for rest of century.

Detail from a commemorative slab on the Antonine Wall showing a Roman cavalryman triumphing over barbarian warriors.

century of peace. This led to a reduction in the size of the army. Many units disappeared from north Britain (though not usually from Hadrian's Wall) at this time, presumably being withdrawn for service elsewhere as their presence in the island was no longer required. When, in the fourth century, a new threat materialized on the northern frontier, in the form of the Picts, new units were sent to Britain to reoccupy these forts.

The fourth century saw not only the reoccupation of the Pennine forts, but the abandonment of those to the north of the Wall. The northern frontier suffered from several attacks during these years, but there were now other pressures elsewhere. In the face of sea-borne raids, new forts* were built – mainly in the late third century – along the coasts of southern Britain from the Wash to the Lune. These forts, unlike their northern counterparts, employed all the latest features of defensive military architecture. However, it is not easy to see how they would have operated. Their known garrisons were military rather than naval, though often the forts were more easily accessible by sea: further, in spite of excavation, barrack-blocks have not yet been recognized in them. They were presumably the shore bases of the fleets* charged with the protection of the province from attacks by pirates and hostile tribes. In the later fourth century, these defensive measures were extended further north by the construction of a chain of watch-towers along the Yorkshire coast, while in the north-west some of the older military establishments were rebuilt.

The fourth century also saw a major reorganization – or rather several reorganizations – of the Roman army. The mobile force of the first and second centuries had fossilized into frontier garrisons in the third century. In the fourth century, mobility was restored by the creation of field armies*. At first, Britain had to rely on the field army based in Gaul, but shortly before the end of the century a small field army was probably established in the island.

The main visible point of contact between Rome and her neighbours so far as Britain is concerned lies in the field of warfare, and here Roman arms were always successful. No barbarians permanently overran the province(s) so long as Britain remained part of the empire. But warfare was not the only relationship. Diplomatic contact was maintained with some of the tribes beyond the frontier. It has been suggested that some of the hoards of coins and silver found beyond the frontier in Scotland and in Ireland, an island never invaded by Rome (though Agricola did consider the possibility), resulted from the payment of subsidies to these tribes. This is not certain, though there was at least one occasion – in 197 – when the governor of Britain paid bribes to one of the northern tribes to prevent it from attacking the province. Plunder, trade, refugees, even the presence of Roman soldiers on campaign, patrol or lost, could help to account for some if not all of these hoards and for the isolated coins and artefacts found throughout Scotland and Ireland, while in later years missionary activity may have played a part. Yet the number of Roman objects found in both Scotland and Ireland is relatively small and suggests that contacts across the frontier, at least in non-perishable goods, were not extensive.

The relationship between Rome and her northern neighbours was always uneven. Though the barbarians might occasionally win, they were never able to secure a footing within the province. Nevertheless the presence of a major power in the southern part of the island had the effect of drawing the northern tribes together, so that by the fourth century the several tribes of Scotland

Saxon Shore forts

In 3rd century, Britain faced new problem of sea-borne pirates; new coastal forts constructed for British fleet from *c.* 225 (Reculver, Brancaster, Caistor-by-Yarmouth) augmenting old bases (Dover, Lympne, Richborough). After pressure increased *c.* 270, Richborough fort built *c.* 280, also Burgh Castle, Dover, Lympne, Portchester, Bradwell, Walton Castle; last fort Pevensey, *c.* 330; other forts across Channel. Had strong walls with external towers to withstand siege; change from earlier defensive architecture. Sometime in 4th century forts placed under Count of Saxon Shore, a high ranking officer. Saxon Shore problematic, unclear how system worked or developed.

Classis Britannica

Our knowledge of *Classis Britannica* (British Fleet) very limited. Fleet existed from invasion, with bases at Richborough, Boulogne; took part in Agricola's campaigns; by 2nd century had bases at Dover, Lympne, Richborough, perhaps Pevensey; last attested mid-3rd century. Saxon Shore forts built from *c.* 225 to act as fleet bases. Fleet recruited from non-Roman citizens, organized into ships and squadrons; commanded by senior Roman knight (Prefect). By end of 3rd century, organized into smaller groups. *Classis Britannica* was involved in Wealden iron industry.

Field army

Gallienus created large cavalry force *c.* 260; Diocletian divorced civilian and military commands and increased number of legions, some only 1000 strong; Constantine completed reforms. Empire now defended by second-grade border troops (*limitanei:* old *auxilia* reorganized), under *duces* ("dukes"), holding forts in frontier zone; supported by élite mobile field army (*comitatenses*) under *magistri militum* (masters of soldiery) and *comites* ("counts").

Picts

Literally "the painted ones". First appear in literary sources 297, thereafter named as principal northern enemies of Roman Britain. Apparently coalesced into kingdom from tribes of central, eastern highlands of Scotland, including Caledones. Constantius campaigned against them 306; involved in Barbarian Conspiracy of 367; Magnus Maximus campaigned against them 382; northern forces strengthened by Stilicho *c.* 398; invaded again 429, defeated by St Germanus. Pictish kingdom survived, producing famous carved stones in Scotland, especially 7th century AD. United with Scots under Kenneth MacAlpin *c.* 843.

Above *aerial view of Hadrian's Wall, looking east over the central section, and showing the defences following the high ground to the north and the ditch and mounds of the* Vallum *running behind it to the south.*

Above right *aerial view of the Roman fort at Housesteads (Vercovicium) on the wall, showing the excavated buildings.*

Right *Hadrian's Wall, looking east towards Cuddy's Crag, showing the standard Roman masonry facing on the inner side.*

Aerial view of the Saxon Shore fort at Portchester, near Portsmouth.

north of the Forth had coalesced into the single kingdom of the Picts*. The Roman army was, on the whole, successful, not only in defending the province but also in maintaining internal order: after the rebellions of the early years there is no record of any civil disorders in Britain, though there were intermittent army mutinies. In one respect of course, the army was not successful: the conquest of the whole island. This was the result of various factors. Agricola's success in the AD 80s was blunted by events on other frontiers, while the death of Septimius Severus at York in 211 brought to a premature end his successful campaign against the northern tribes. In the mid-second century, when peaceful frontiers elsewhere would have allowed Rome to complete the conquest of the island, she was governed by emperors with more limited aims. Thus the Roman frontier was to remain Hadrian's Wall for nearly three hundred years.

Economy:
the arrival of money
J.P. Wild

The inhabitants of Iron-Age and Roman Britain were not unaware of the economic forces that affected their lives; but they rarely sought to manipulate them. Even when a governing authority – an Iron-Age tribal ruler or Roman emperor – interfered in the economy, the objective was usually limited, and selfish. These ancient attitudes, coupled with the real danger of anachronism on our part, make the economy one of the most difficult aspects of the ancient world for us to grasp. The most significant event in the history of Great Britain and Ireland between 100 BC and AD 409 was the imposition of Roman control over lowland and much of upland Britain in the first century AD. In some spheres, the economic impact of Rome was immediate – through taxation and the demands of a hungry garrison, for example – but on other levels, Iron-Age society became Roman provincial society with minimal change.

It has been estimated that four-fifths of the labour force of the Roman empire was primarily engaged in food production. To judge by the density of settlement sites discovered in the past few years, the population of Britain can hardly have been less than five million. If that is so, then only a million made their living outside agriculture. Most Britons before and after the Roman conquest were peasant farmers at subsistence level, as the archaeological record proves. Single farms*, worked by family groups, were the norm, and villages are found only in special circumstances. The nature of the landholding, its productivity and the character of its farm buildings varied with regional geography. At Gussage All Saints on the Wessex Downs, for instance, a three-acre ditched farmyard of Iron-Age date contained two large timber round-houses and numerous grain-storage pits*. Similar farms have been revealed in great numbers on the gravel terraces of major river valleys. In highland Britain, drystone walling took the place of ditches and the emphasis was probably more on stock-raising than on arable: the native farms made use of small square or rectangular "Celtic fields"*, suited to cross-ploughing with a wooden ard*. In the Roman fenland, aerial photography has revealed a landscape of small villages surrounded by "Celtic fields" and separated from one another by open pasture.

By the late second century, the native small-holdings on the more productive soils of southern Britain were replaced by larger agricultural units, at the centre of which were villas. Chedworth in Gloucestershire and Winterton in Lincolnshire are good examples. Here, well-appointed stone-built domestic quarters were flanked by aisled barns and other outbuildings. They were mixed farms and the ideal estate (perhaps 250 acres) would include a range of types of land. Many villas were surrounded by paddocks and larger enclosures, but most of their land shows no sign of man-made divisions within its natural boundaries.

Some indication of the crops available to the British agriculturalist can be gleaned from linguistic and palaeobotanical sources. Wheat and barley were

See **Iron-Age farm settlements** (page 37)

See **Storage pits** (page 37)

"Celtic fields"
Most common type of field-system for arable use in both later pre-Roman and Roman Britain: small rectangular fields, sometimes still traceable from raised boundaries; datable by pottery etc, associated features. Earliest in Britain of Middle Bronze Age (2nd millennium BC) at Plumpton Plain; continued in use into Roman period, villas often retaining earlier fields.

Ard; coulter; mould board
Ard type of primitive, wheel-less, wooden plough without *coulter* (iron blade to cut soil ahead of ploughshare) or *mould board* (board to turn soil over behind asymmetrical ploughshare, facilitated by coulter); most suited to light soils. In use from Neolithic into Roman period, usually requiring repeated cross-ploughing to achieve sufficient depth; patterns sometimes still visible in excavations.

Two sides of gold staters minted for Cunobelinus (CVNO) at his chief settlement Colchester (Camulodunum – CAMV).

See Butser Iron-Age farm experiment
(page 37)

Corn dryers or malt kilns
Stone oven-like features, often with T-shaped flues, frequently found, sometimes in large numbers, on Roman villa estates; some with charred grain. Interpreted as corn-drying ovens to dry grain before storage; or recently, as malting kilns for barley to produce beer.

Mining
Mines, especially of precious metals, usually imperial property. In Britain, initially exploited directly by military with soldiers as work-force; then controlled for emperor by junior procurator, at first via lessees (conductores), usually rich businessmen, sometimes companies, but later directly. Procurators and lessees employed free labour, but perhaps also condemned prisoners.

Dolaucothi
Only known Roman gold mines in Britain at Dolaucothi, Carmarthenshire, employing open-cast workings as well as shafts drained by huge water-wheels. Two aqueduct systems used to supply reservoirs to provide head of water for washing ore. Mines protected by Pumpsaint fort, AD 75-125, to control ill-pacified area and provide escorts for gold shipments.

Cupellation
Method of extracting silver from lead by heating metal in cup-shaped hearth full of bone ash and scooping off silver from top.

Lead pigs
Lead extracted was melted down into ingots or "pigs", weighing 170-190lbs, for transportation; usually inscribed with date, army unit or lessee or district mined. Earliest known pigs AD 49 from Mendips; under Nero, pig shows IInd Augusta legion in charge of production there; by AD 60 private lessee Nipius Ascanius at work; by 91 pig inscribed Brig (anticum) indicates exploitation of Yorkshire field. By time of Hadrian, lessees' names disappear; those of mines, emperor inscribed, perhaps indicating direct imperial control. Last inscribed pigs from Mendips 164-69, so industry perhaps passed into private hands as production declined.

Pewter
Decline in import of fine pottery in 3rd century led to increased demand for domestic pewter tableware, boosting lead and tin mining; popular throughout 3rd and 4th centuries. One centre of industry around Bath near Mendip lead mines.

staple crops. Six-row barley, emmer and oats were cultivated on upland farms, whilst in the lowlands they were supplemented by spelt and the bread wheats. Recent experiments* have indicated that in favourable conditions yields of 26 bushels of wheat per acre were attainable. (Over 60 bushels would be expected now.) Alternative crops included the "Celtic" bean, cabbage, pea, vetch, flax, celery, fennel and cucumber. Herbs such as dill and coriander may have been grown, and probably the grapevine, too. Cultivated strains of pear, plum, apple and cherry were Roman introductions, and there is evidence for the fruit of the walnut, mulberry and sweet chestnut.

Sheep had pride of place on peasant farms in the Iron Age and in the less developed areas of the Roman province: but villa farmers came to prefer cattle and pigs, reflecting the tastes of the more prosperous townsfolk. Improvement in farming technology and a sound level of investment were behind the success of the villa estates. Iron coulters and asymmetrical shares point to the development of a more efficient plough, perhaps with mould-board*, by the fourth century AD. Fixed plant regularly included stone-built corn dryers* or malt kilns. Increased technical knowledge of crop rotation and selective breeding may be presumed. The need to feed the garrison force (about fifty thousand men) gave some impetus to British agriculture. Peasant farmers in the military zone would have been directly affected; but the army, through requisition and purchase, took a significant proportion of the total agricultural product of the province. In return, they taught the provincials new skills in many branches of industry.

Rumours of mineral wealth may have been a factor (albeit minor) behind the invasion of AD 43: certainly the government, acting through the army, set about the exploitation of British precious metal resources* at once. At Dolaucothi*, near Carmarthen, army engineers used the waterpower provided by two aqueducts to locate, extract and crush the local gold ores. Galleries drained by water-wheels were dug to follow the veins underground. Silver was extracted by cupellation* from lead mined open-cast in the Mendips, Clwyd, Derbyshire and north Yorkshire. A series of inscribed lead pigs* (some desilvered) prove military control until at least the late second century. The lead was made into piping and sheet metal, but the total yield of gold and silver must have been small.

Copper and tin deposits in Wales and Cornwall respectively were of less concern to the government, but essential for the impedimenta of everyday life. Copper in alloy with tin as bronze and brass was the standard material of many utilitarian fittings and ornaments for the whole of this period. In later Roman times, tin and lead were combined to make pewter* tableware, a British speciality. Britain was fortunate in having ample iron ore. The Sussex Weald, the Forest of Dean and Northamptonshire were the main centres where ores were mined, roasted and smelted. But finds of smithing hearths on every type of farm and urban settlement prove that the semi-refined blooms were wrought into tools on the spot where they were required. Official involvement in iron working is attested in the eastern Weald, where elements of the classis Britannica were active.

Building activity in Britain, though composed of many disparate elements, was a sensitive indicator of prosperity and confidence. Timber remained the principal building material until the late first century AD, both for military and civil structures. Soon after the conquest, quarries were opened for Purbeck marble and Jurassic limestone, and by the second century most of the regional sources of building stone were being tapped. Tile-making* was probably introduced by the Roman army, not just for roof tiles, but for all sorts of building bricks. Lime kilns supplied the constituent for mortar, concrete, and plaster. The first interior decorators, mosaicists* and wall-painters*, were immigrants, but their trade flourished and the work of several local mosaic workshops can now be recognized. Evidence for the pottery industry abounds. The troops drew supplies from native potters who became increasingly competent; but occasionally they set up works-depots manned by continental potters. Fine tablewares were imported from Gaul for military and civilian customers, but by the third century major production centres in the Nene Valley, Oxfordshire and elsewhere marketed a full range of vessel types and qualities.

Industries with perishable products are less well known than the foregoing, even if they were once more important. By the third century, British woollen* textiles, rugs and capes, were renowned, yet they stemmed from a cottage industry that has left few traces. Surviving remains of shoes and sandals give a glimpse of the craft of the British leatherworker. Specialist food production, for instance of oysters, was obviously lucrative. Salt* for preserving foodstuffs was extracted from brine on many sites in the fens and on the east coast.

The new province attracted investors and entrepreneurs, often with military links. Rights to extract silver and lead, for example, were leased to mining companies and to individuals, usually freedmen* with capital to invest. Name-stamps on mortaria* also show that their first makers were freedmen, but later native Britons or Gauls appear instead. Such craftsmen were prepared, literally, to follow their markets. Slaves were a small part of the province's labour force, mainly appearing as domestic servants. Carriage of

Tiles

Stamps on tiles provide information on production. Tiles for military, official purposes produced by legionary tileries e.g. Holt, Denbighshire, later by auxiliary units also; stamps of *Classis Britannica* on tiles of Folkestone villa imply it may have belonged to fleet commander. Tiles also produced at imperial tileries e.g. at Silchester, municipal tileries e.g. at Gloucester, private tileries e.g. at London.

Mosaics

Mosaics sign of prosperity in towns and villas in Britain. Appear in 1st century AD but rare, probably laid by immigrant craftsmen; flower in late 3rd/early 4th centuries at time of revival of Britain. Some regional schools of mosaics: best at Cirencester 3rd/4th century, characterized by Orpheus in centre of concentric circles of animals; Dorset 4th century, produced Christian mosaics at Hinton St Mary; Petuaria (Brough-on-Humber); Durobrivae (Water Newton) 4th century; distribution generally local. Designs chosen from pattern-books; centre-piece could be pre-fabricated at workshop by masters before laying within borders put down by apprentices.

Wall-painting

Walls of town houses, villas often decorated with frescoes; known in 2nd century from St Albans, Leicester in classical style of Pompeian painting a century before. Like mosaicists, painters apparently organized in groups based on towns. Information on wall-painting in Britain limited since plaster survives less well than mosaics.

Woollen industry

Britain, with large area of pasture, especially in highland territories, famous for wool. British coverlet, *tossia Britannica*, mentioned as gift in 3rd century Gaul; woollen duffle-coat (*birrus Britannicus*), rug (*tapete Britannicum*) listed in price-fixing edict of Diocletian; imperial weaving-mill at Venta (probably Winchester) attested; large wool-combs found at Caistor-by-Norwich, Worlington (Cambridgeshire), cloth-cropping shears at Great Chesterford.

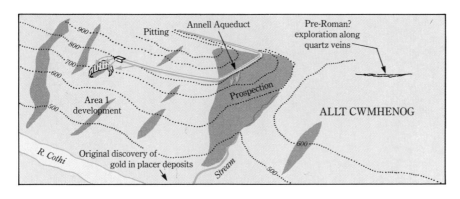

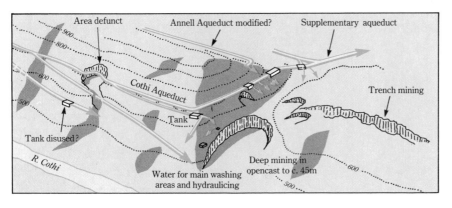

The use of waterpower in the development of the Roman gold mine at Dolaucothi, Carmarthenshire. The diagrams highlight the advanced nature of Roman mining technology, the important role played by the army in mineral extraction and the value to the state of the gold from Dolaucothi.

Salt workings

Salt-extraction practised from 1st century AD, especially in Fenlands, Kent, Sussex, by brine-boiling; salt springs exploited, e.g. at Droitwich, Middlewich (*Salinae*). Salt workings usually imperial property organized under junior procurator; often linked to imperial pastureland.

Freedmen

Freedmen, slaves granted freedom (manumission), received citizenship of master; usually combined master's name with their own. Freedmen still had obligations to master; were debarred from legionary service, town councils, hence formation of *Seviri Augustales* to involve them in public life. Many slaves manumitted as reward for running master's business interests and continued to run business after manumission, a few becoming very wealthy.

Mortaria

Pottery vessels with gritted interior and pouring-spouts for grinding and mixing food in Mediterranean style; army a major market. *Mortaria* produced in Colchester, Kent in late 1st century AD; at Mancetter and Hartshill potteries in midlands from early 2nd to 4th centuries. Oxford potteries produced *mortaria* from late third century.

goods by water was cheaper than by land. Most commodities entering Britain* originated in the western provinces – Chinese silk is one of the exceptions! Italian wine was shipped in *amphorae** to south-west, later to south-east Britain; but from the later first century AD, south Gaul was a leading exporter. Bordeaux and the Rhineland took over the trade later. Spanish *amphorae* brought olive oil and fish-sauce from Baetica – basic ingredients in Roman cuisine. Red-gloss tableware from the potteries of Arezzo in north Italy (Arretine ware), was appreciated by Iron-Age aristocrats,

A piece of 1st-century woollen textile from the Roman fort at Chesterholm (Vindolanda), near Hadrian's Wall; textile production was probably the leading industry in Roman Britain, but few examples survive unless in waterlogged deposits.

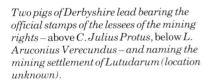

Two pigs of Derbyshire lead bearing the official stamps of the lessees of the mining rights – above C. Julius Protus, below L. Aruconius Verecundus – and naming the mining settlement of Lutudarum (location unknown).

Statuette of Mars from Torksey, Lincolnshire, dedicated to the god and the numina (divinities) of the emperors by two Britons, Bruccius and Caratius, and cast in bronze by the coppersmith Celatus.

and after AD 43 its successor, samian ware*, from workshops in south (and later central and east) Gaul flooded the market for nearly two centuries. In a peak year, over half a million vessels were imported. Some of them crossed the Roman frontier into Scotland. Most shippers handled mixed cargoes and kept ports such as London extremely busy. At the end of the chain were shopkeepers in town *fora* and stall-holders at periodic markets in the countryside. Coinage, currency and taxation were interrelated. Gallic gold coins were circulating in Britain before 55 BC and British issues followed; but they were a means of meeting social obligations rather than of buying and selling. A full market economy may not have functioned until the later second century AD, shortly before the onset of the third-century price inflation*. New coins entered Britain as payments to troops, who used them to buy goods and services from the Britons. The latter returned them to the government in taxation*. Not all taxes were in cash; there was a levy of corn and later of clothing for the army. It is clear indeed, that from the Roman conquest the army was the dominant force in the British economy, at great cost to the government. But by the fourth century, agriculture and local industries were capable of showing a net profit.

Competitive markets for pottery

0   50   100   150 km
0   50   100 miles

— · — Southern limit of the Mancetter market
o Mancetter outliers
· · · · Northern limit of the Oxfordshire market
+ Oxfordshire outliers
▨ Zone of direct competition

Roman trade with Iron-Age Britain
Most frequently recognized import was Mediterranean wine, attested by finds of *amphorae;* many at Hengistbury Head and area of Durotriges on south coast. Wine *amphorae* reached Catuvellauni and Trinovantes, probably via Rhône – Saône – Moselle – Rhine route; often found in aristocratic burials, e.g. Lexden tumulus. Other luxury goods followed wine routes: Arretine pottery, Roman silver goblets etc. In return, several exports recorded early in 1st century AD: corn, cattle, gold, silver, iron, hides, slaves, hounds.

Amphorae and wine trade
Amphorae large pottery vessels of Mediterranean type often buried, presumably full of wine, in pre-Roman aristocratic burials in south-east England: evidence for import of Italian and later Spanish wines. Spanish wine took over from Italian before Claudian invasion, but cut off abruptly after 197, probably when vineyards of Spanish followers of Clodius Albinus confiscated by Severus. Rhenish reliefs suggest German vineyards taking over; silver-fir barrels found at Silchester imply Bordeaux trade. *Amphorae* also used before conquest for import of Spanish olive oil, fruit, fish-sauce (*garum*) for cooking, all indicative of Romanization of taste.

Samian ware
Fine pottery with bright-red glossy slip, often elaborately decorated, used as good-quality tableware. Early 1st century AD southern Gaulish factories captured northern market, gave way to central Gaulish factories at end of 1st century, later

east Gaulish closer to Rhine army market. Army a major market in Britain also, though imported for civilian use as well. Origin and date of individual pieces can be established within fine limits, useful for archaeological dating. Defeat of Clodius Albinus at Lyon in 197 apparently led to end of central Gaulish industry; thereafter little Samian ware imported to Britain.

Inflation in the 3rd and 4th centuries
Heavy inflation of later Roman Empire not fully understood. Attributed to gradual debasement of coinage by emperors to finance wars against barbarian invaders from late 2nd century onwards; accelerated in 3rd century by practice of increasing face values of debased coins for paying troops.

Taxation
Provincial taxation took two main forms, direct (*tributum*), and indirect (*vectigal*). *Tributum* was taxation on land (*soli*) and on individuals (*capitis*), assessed by intermittent censuses, gathered by local councils. *Tributum* sometimes paid in kind, especially corn (*annona*), from 1st century AD; system greatly developed in 3rd century especially to supply larger army of Diocletian. *Vectigal* taxation was e.g. customs (2½%); manumission of slaves (5%); auctions (1%); death duties (5%). Also *aurum coronarium*, tax in gold often levied on province on accession of new emperor. Provincial procurator ultimately responsible for collection of taxes either directly via councils (*tributum*) or junior procurators (*vectigal*), or via lessees (*conductores* or *publicani*).

Settlement and Society:
from tribe to province
Martin Millett

This period demonstrates both continuity and change in settlement patterns. At least in the south, the landscape was densely occupied and intensively exploited, with a well-developed agricultural system by the late Iron Age. Much of the available land was already divided into fields, and individual farmsteads were integral with these field systems. In all areas where good evidence is available, it is clear that mixed agricultural strategies were in use, with both arable and pastoral activities working interdependently. Experimental work on the Iron-Age farm at Butser* (Hampshire) suggests that, contrary to the general assumptions, this type of Iron-Age agriculture could be extremely efficient, and that the technology used was far from primitive. The productive capacity of Iron-Age agriculture is further demonstrated by the abundance of large pits*, apparently corn-storage facilities, which suggest that substantial surpluses were produced, in some seasons at least. This indication lends credence to the occurrence of corn in the geographer Strabo's list of exports from Britain.

The agricultural settlements* producing these surpluses are considerably more varied than had been believed until recently, from settlements with a single round-house (capable of housing an extended family) to those which consisted of clusters of such dwellings with subsidiary structures. The rich material excavated from some of these sites (e.g. Gussage All Saints) shows that they certainly cannot all have been inhabited by peasants. Larger settlement sites (including some of the so-called hill-forts*) occur over significant areas of Britain from the late Bronze Age onwards. They remained in occupation in some areas until c. 100 BC, but changes in the pattern of the larger settlements were beginning to take place. Some of the excavated sites (e.g. Danebury, Hampshire) declined in importance, while others (e.g. Hod Hill, Dorset) continued in occupation. The larger settlements vary in nature, some being densely occupied with an organized disposition of roadways, round-houses, rectangular structures (sometimes interpreted as above-ground granaries), and corn-storage pits. Others may be little more than substantial farmsteads. The large organized settlements cannot, however, be considered urban in any modern sense of the word. Their corn-storage capacity suggests that they acted as centres for the collection, storage and perhaps redistribution of agricultural produce: cereals from Danebury, for example, can be shown to have been brought to the site from the wetlands at least five miles away. Whether this represents tribute collected by a coercive authority or a co-operative venture is beyond the present evidence, although most authorities favour the former interpretation.

Some form of fairly sophisticated social structure is suggested by these centres, based on medium-sized social units which might be seen as tribes in a very general sense, although attempts to link these with historically attested tribes are fraught with difficulties. Variations in their density of distribution,

Butser Iron-Age farm experiment
Reconstructed Iron-Age farm at Butser Hill, Hampshire, to test all aspects of such a settlement. Discovered that ½ - ¾ hectare of land needed to grow grain to fill single storage pit. Large number of pits usually associated with Iron-Age settlements, although not all in use at same time, implies large-scale cereal production and large population.

Storage pits
In Iron-Age settlements, corn for seed and consumption stored in regular clay-covered pits, sometimes lined with wickerwork, alongside dwellings; grain also stored in granaries raised on posts. Very many pits dug over life of settlement; contents regularly went mouldy. Pits allow some estimate of crop production and of population.

Iron-Age farm settlements
Great variety of settlements. Single-house type common in Wessex and north and west; e.g. Little Woodbury: timber round-house 50 feet across, within palisaded farmyard, associated drying racks, raised granaries, corn-storage pits, looms, iron-smelting hearths. Larger settlements, with similar buildings, appear in groups in east midlands, upper Thames region, implying interdependence between settlements. Similar villages in Welsh Marches, Severn Valley, dependent on local hill-fort, implying aristocratic control. Many settlements survive in Roman period alongside villas, though some replaced by them.

Hill-forts
Hills fortified with ramparts and ditches appear in Britain c. 1200 BC; earliest had vertical ramparts, timber fronted and filled with earth; after c. 400 BC replaced by dump ramparts. Some hill-forts refuges or storage sites at first; later timber huts constructed with streets, granaries etc e.g. Danebury. In earlier period, common throughout Britain except east and Pennines, but from c. 400 BC generally fewer though more powerful, implying increased control by local lords; ramparts multiplied, gates elaborated, implying increased warfare. In 1st century BC, hill-forts in south-east replaced by *oppida* as centralized kingdoms emerged.

scale and nature strongly indicate that we cannot envisage a single type of social formation over the whole of the island at this period.

It was societies such as these which inhabited Britain at the time of Caesar's expeditions to Britain in 55 and 54 BC. Although the invasion attempt failed, increased contacts between the British tribes and the Roman empire between 54 BC and AD 43 were the cause of a number of changes in the social organization and settlement of areas in the south and east. In the first instance, there emerges a series of large lowland nucleated sites, often near the locations of subsequent Roman towns. These (for instance at Verulamium* – St Albans and Camulodunum* – Colchester) are often referred to as *oppida**, although there is little evidence about their interiors and nothing which can support their identification with the proto-urban centres which Caesar refers to by this name in Gaul. Some (e.g. Hengistbury Head*, Dorset) began before the Caesarian period, but they were mainly a characteristic of the early decades of the first century AD and were the centres of tribes of increasing size and social complexity. Their emergence coincides with the expanding use of coinage and these developments seem to reflect the growth of early states under the domination of an increasingly powerful social élite. The leaders of the different tribes competed with each other, and these inter-tribal rivalries are hinted at by the classical sources, which demonstrate a continually shifting pattern of alliances between the tribes and the Roman empire.

The location of oppida in southern Britain in the late Iron Age

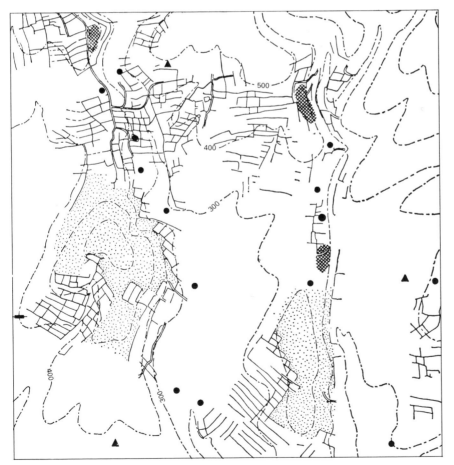

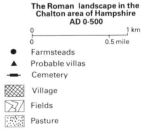

The Roman landscape in the Chalton area of Hampshire AD 0-500

● Farmsteads
▲ Probable villas
⊢ Cemetery
▨ Village
▨ Fields
▨ Pasture

This map shows the intensive occupation and exploitation characteristic of the Romano-British landscape. On Chalton's chalk downland, the high ground was devoted to pasture and the valley slopes to arable fields, farmed from small homesteads, villages and three villas on lower ground. The blank areas are those hidden by modern settlement and cultivation.

In the settlement evidence there are indications of an increased incidence of defended rural settlement sites, and the replacement of hill-forts in the south-east by a smaller number of lowland *oppida*. In addition there is more evidence of continental contact, at least in the lowland zone, through the presence of luxury imports such as wine *amphorae*, tableware and even silver vessels. These objects are not usually found on rural sites, but occur most commonly in graves, and in the *oppida*. Their context and the occurrence of such peculiarities as the Augustan medallion from the Lexden tumulus* at Camulodunum, suggest that some of the objects result from diplomatic gift-exchange rather than trade. This supports the indications of increased social stratification and an increase in the size of tribal groups, perhaps loose

Verulamium

Began as Catuvellaunian settlement at Prae Wood, St Albans, from *c.* 20 BC acting as tribal capital until shift of power to Camulodunum. Roman occupation began with fort in valley below Prae Wood, soon abandoned. Street grid, earth rampart of town established early; by AD 49 timber shops constructed; by 60 possibly a *municipium*; when destroyed by Boudicca took 15 years to recover, but *forum* built by AD 79; theatre, market early 2nd century. Private houses small and of timber until fire of *c.* 155 cleared area; large town houses now built as aristocracy moved in from countryside. Late 3rd-century stone wall, monumental arches built as signs of status. Declined late 4th century; occupation continued to mid or late 5th century.

Camulodunum

Capital of Trinovantes originally at Gosbecks Farm, Colchester, sacred site guarded by dykes. *c.* AD 5-10 fell to Cunobelinus of Catuvellauni; created capital for Catuvellauni and Trinovantes at Sheepen, spread over 12 square miles, enclosed by dykes. Since Catuvellauni regarded as chief tribe of Britain, became site of Roman capital. After XXth Valeria legion moved on *c.* 49, *colonia* founded for legionary veterans: barracks adapted for civilian use, building extended eastward, Temple of Deified Claudius built as centre of imperial cult. Legionary defences levelled, town undefended when burnt in Boudiccan revolt; took 15 years to recover, then expanded north and west, though London now provincial capital. Stone wall built early 2nd century.

Oppida

Contact between Rome and south-east England in 1st century BC brought more developed culture. Single rulers controlled large areas, hill-forts replaced by *oppida* – towns spread over larger areas of low ground, positioned to take advantage of communications; represent stable conditions, proto-urbanization. Remaining hill-fort area less developed; south-east more amenable to Romanization, with major *oppida* developing into prosperous cities.

Hengistbury Head

Headland off Dorset coast occupied *c.* 700 - 400 BC defended by earthworks, ditches; re-occupied 1st century BC becoming trading entrepôt between Armorica and hinterland tribes of Dobunni, Atrebates. Imported Mediterranean wine and oil.

Subsequently became production centre for hinterland raw materials eg. copper, silver, lead, iron, shale. Occupied as peasant settlement into 4th century AD.

Lexden tumulus

One of a number of burial monuments near Camulodunum. Tumulus 80 feet across, contained *amphorae* evidence of burial of Italian, Rhodian wine with body; also Arretine pottery; medallion made of Roman silver coin of 17 BC; all evidence of links with Roman empire. Possibly tomb of Addedomaros, king of Trinovantes.

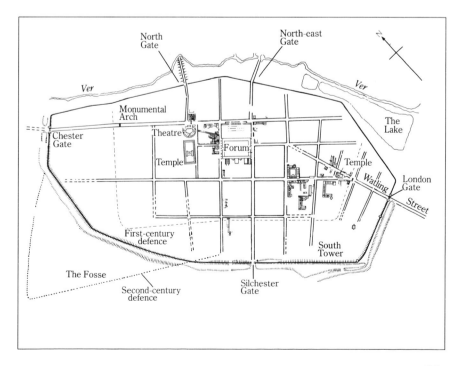

The Roman municipium of Verulamium in the fourth century

0   200 metres

0   500 feet

federations rather than stable units. The rich, late La Tène art* of this period is clearly related to the patronage of the élite in an increasingly competitive and stratified society, and often consists of highly ornamented military objects. This level of organization is suggestive of a well-developed social and political structure, supported by a system of tribute. The areas to the west and north are less well understood from the archaeological evidence, but away from Roman contact, societies seem to have been developing more slowly.

The Roman conquest of Britain, which was never completed, resulted in a large number of changes in the settlement pattern, most particularly in the areas already influenced by Roman contact. These changes, the introduction of rectangular bonded-stone buildings, the development of towns and roads*, and the vast increase in the quantity of archaeological finds, provide rich material for the archaeologist, but at the same time tend to obscure our understanding of broad social trends. In many ways the changes in material culture mask a very large measure of continuity in social organization.

Looking first at the early Roman period, concentrating on the civil aspects, the most obvious changes that take place are the development of villas and the foundation of towns*. The cities were central to the Roman political system, as they represented the centres of government and administration, based ultimately on the Mediterranean city-state. Each territory, centred on a city, was governed by a council made up of the local landed élite; thus Rome ruled its conquered territories indirectly, through limited self-government enshrined in each city's charter. The cities were responsible to the governor, but the essence of the system lay in the co-operation of the élite, who retained and even increased their power and wealth. This system encouraged stability, as it gave the élite a positive interest in Roman control and enabled Rome successfully to rule a huge empire with a small central administration, and without soldiers in each city.

La Tène art
Art of Celtic Iron-Age culture from mid-5th century BC, developing out of earlier Hallstatt culture; named after settlement site of La Tène, Switzerland. Development came about under Classical influences (e.g. depiction of tendrils and palmettes encouraged swirling abstract patterns) as well as oriental and Scythian influences (e.g. frequent use of animal motifs); these translated into abstract patterns, abstracted figures; asymmetrical curves, scrolls; appear in metalwork, pottery in which a high degree of skill attained.

Roman roads
Originally product of army advance; surveyed, constructed by legions to allow rapid movement of troops. Forts linked by roads. Surveyed in straight sections, but curved if necessary; commonly constructed of stones bordered by larger kerb-stones, overlaid with layer of river gravel beaten down to produce firm, smooth surface; often flanked by drainage ditches. Names of Roman roads, e.g. Watling Street, Stanegate, Dere Street usually Anglo-Saxon in origin.

Roman towns
Towns were fundamental to Roman civilization. Organized out of pre-existing settlements, or settlements around early forts, as centres of administration – carried out for Romans by local aristocracy formed into town council; towns thus instruments of Romanization working from native chieftains downwards. *Forum* often first public building, then baths as social centres, temples and theatres, amphitheatres, markets often paid for by local aristocracy with Roman help. Private houses built in stone only later. Town walls generally added 2nd/3rd century.

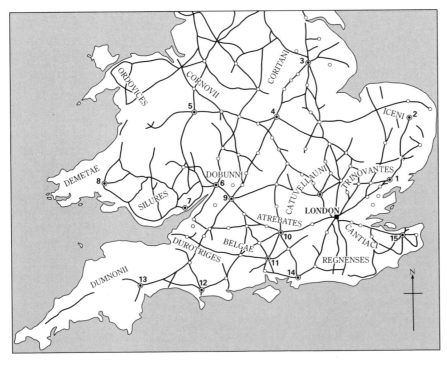

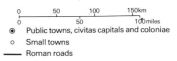

Urban settlements in southern Britain in the later Roman period

⊙ Public towns, civitas capitals and coloniae
○ Small towns
—— Roman roads

Key to civitas capitals:
1 Colchester (Camulodunum)
2 Caistor-by-Norwich (Venta Icenorum)
3 Lincoln (Lindum)
4 Leicester (Ratae Coritanorum)
5 Wroxeter (Viroconium Cornoviorum)
6 Gloucester (Glevum)
7 Caerwent (Venta Silurum)
8 Carmarthen (Moridunum Demetarum)
9 Cirencester (Corinium Dobunnorum)
10 Silchester (Calleva Atrebatum)
11 Winchester (Venta Belgarum)
12 Dorchester (Durnovaria Durotrigum)
13 Exeter (Isca Dumnoniorum)
14 Chichester (Noviomagus Reginorum)
15 Canterbury (Durovernum Cantiacorum)

Fora

Forum a public building erected in Roman town; symbol of organized civic life, housing offices for the *ordo* and for magistrates, as well as shops, market area; often paid for by local aristocrats. In Britain most *fora* built on model of headquarters building of Roman fort: civic offices, including council chamber, at rear, fronted by *basilica* with tribunals for public business, and in front shops around courtyard acting as marketplace; entrance opposite *basilica*.

Villas

Houses in country built in Romanized style, including luxury houses (e.g. Fishbourne), industrial villas (e.g. in Nene Valley, producing pottery), working farms (the vast majority, including most luxury houses). Earliest *c.* AD 60 belonged to Romanized immigrants or officials (e.g. Folkestone) or aristocracy of most advanced tribes (e.g. Park Street near capital of Catuvellauni; often replaced earlier Iron-Age settlements. Constructed and decorated by urban craftsmen, paid for by agricultural surplus produced for towns; most villas cluster round towns; distribution, development dependent on them.

Fishbourne

Early villa of great luxury, at centre of large estate; possibly gift from Roman government to Cogidubnus. Originally site of army supply depot; replaced *c.* AD 60 by "proto-palace" with colonnaded garden, baths-suite, living rooms, servants' quarters. *c.* AD 75 great palace built covering 10-15 acres with four wings and formal garden; living rooms on south overlooking sea; official rooms on west with apsed audience chamber; entrance hall, guest rooms on east, guest rooms on north. Villa destroyed by fire, end 3rd century.

Agricultural innovations

Little evidence that Romans introduced technological advances to Iron-Age agriculture: Celtic fields still used; ploughs with coulter and mould board appeared but date uncertain; corn-drying ovens not widespread until 3rd/4th centuries. Technological advance was late, 3rd/4th century, and empire-wide. Invasion probably did result in greater availability of iron tools, also introduction of new crops, including new fruits (e.g. cherry, vine). Main impact on agriculture was new market of army, towns; encouraged more intensive working of land.

There is little doubt that the sites of many towns were occupied by forts in the conquest period, but many of those forts must themselves have been located at the political centres of the conquered tribal territories. This is most clear at the major centres like St Albans and Colchester. It was the tribal aristocrats who were responsible for the burst of villa building* (e.g. Fishbourne*, Rivenhall, Park Street) and the construction of public buildings in the towns in the period immediately following the conquest. This activity presumably results from the élite investing wealth, to which they already had access, in a new form of display, that is in Romanized building.

Despite the number of villas which did develop in the first century, few were on new sites, and few of the other Iron-Age rural settlements ceased to be occupied. Thus, the Iron-Age settlement pattern continued with an increasing population, and the only major change was the arrival of Roman goods, principally pottery, on the sites. The main changes in the countryside, with many of these sites being rebuilt in stone, took place later in the second and third centuries. In many cases, the initial stone villa was on the same scale as the previous timber structures; thus one sees a Romanization in taste, rather than any improvement in building technique or wealth. Indeed the Iron-Age round-house was primitive neither in the accommodation it offered, nor in the techniques of construction used. Only when small villas developed into larger complexes can any increase in wealth be suggested. Though villas are the characteristic feature of Roman rural settlement, there are only about 650 known examples, a numerically small element in the settlement pattern.

Our knowledge of the non-villa rural settlement is relatively poor, but in some regions (e.g. the Fens, south Yorkshire-Nottinghamshire border) the complexes of rural settlements within field systems are becoming well known. In these areas, land which had been agriculturally marginal was taken into cultivation. This may suggest population pressure, although in other parts (e.g. north Hampshire) there is evidence of desertion of the smaller rural sites in the later Roman period.

These apparent changes, however, are also mirrored in other aspects of the settlement pattern. First, there are a number of nucleated rural sites which seem to be later Roman in date. These may represent a trend away from the traditional isolated farmsteads towards peasant villages, resulting from the growing power of the large landowners and the increasing size of their holdings. Secondly, in the later Roman period the villas represented a major phase of expenditure on rural settlements. This is not only reflected in the buildings, but also in the evidence for innovations in agriculture*, with improved plough types, the introduction of scythes and long balanced sickles.

This increase in expenditure on the countryside may account for the failure of the "public towns" (the administrative centres – the *civitas* capitals, *coloniae* and *municipia*) to continue to develop. Investment in, even replacement of, destroyed public buildings, which had characterized the early period of Roman Britain, petered out in the later Roman period. These towns show only stagnation, with the exception of the construction of city walls*. The élite turned away from civic patronage and towards private display in villas and perhaps patronage of the Church, a pattern seen also in the Mediterranean provinces. In the case of some cities, such as London, stagnation and decline may be more marked than elsewhere.

At the same time as the stagnation of the cities, the so-called small towns* (many of which are actually as large as some of the cities) seem to have had their heyday. Those which are known from excavation show origins early in the Roman period, or even in the late Iron Age, but many only become really substantial in the later period. They have no major public buildings or planned layouts, but instead they tend to contain structures suggestive of craft industry and marketing functions. These sites seem to have resulted from an increase in economic activity and perhaps the development of a market economy. This trend is also suggested by the growth of major industrial centres in rural areas in several parts of the province (e.g. the New Forest and Oxfordshire). The best documented of these industries produced pottery, which was often traded widely within the province.

Although Roman Britain of the fourth century was very different from the island of 100 BC, the structural changes took place gradually in the later Roman period rather than suddenly at the time of the Roman invasion. The development of nucleated centres, both villages and small towns, alongside the farms and public towns may well indicate that major social changes, with increased economic activity and inter-provincial contact, caused a steady breakdown of the tribal structure and a diminution of the power of the controlling élite. These developments are little understood at present. It is nevertheless clear that by 409 many changes in the settlement pattern had at least begun, and may already have taken place.

Small towns
Large variety of small towns in Britain, few excavated. Variety of origins: at pre-existing settlements (e.g. Braughing); from villages around former forts (e.g. Cambridge); outside existing forts, especially on Hadrian's Wall (e.g. Housesteads); as new developments (e.g. Water Newton, Cambridgeshire, a ribbon settlement along Roman road). Variety of functions: farming communities (e.g. Godmanchester); industrial settlements (e.g. Chesterton, centre of Nene Valley pottery industry); spas (e.g. Bath). Differ from major towns in having no administrative function, hence few public buildings.

City walls
Some cities had earthwork defences from 1st century (e.g. Silchester, Verulamium); others built in earth or stone in 2nd century (e.g. Camulodunum), especially towards end (e.g. London). Lack of threat in late 1st/2nd centuries and non-defensive nature of many impressive gateways (e.g. Camulodunum, Verulamium) suggest walls primarily for status. Not until 3rd century are some earthworks replaced in stone (e.g. Verulamium), gates made defensive (e.g. Canterbury), external towers added in 4th century in face of barbarian threat.

Reconstruction model of the palace possibly built for the British client ruler Cogidubnus at Fishbourne, near Chichester.

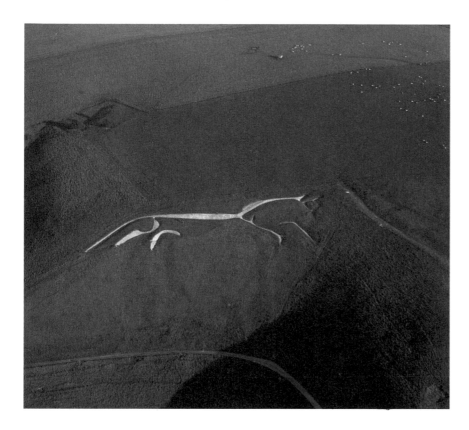

The lifestyle and personal display of the
warrior aristocracy of pre-Roman Britain
was emphasized in some of the finest pieces
of Celtic art. A main characteristic of their
decoration was the masterly use of
curvilinear patterns based originally on
plant motifs, but composed in an essentially
abstract, non-representational manner. On
the bronze helmet and shield (right)
the repoussé and engraving were
combined with glass and enamel inlay. The
design of the Waterloo helmet (1st century
BC) is asymmetrical, but balanced; the
Battersea shield is later (early 1st century
AD), and its symmetry may reveal Roman
influence. Both were found in the River
Thames, and neither may actually have been
intended for use in battle; in particular, the
metal of the helmet is rather too thin.
Instead, they may have been made for
offering to the deity of the river. A similar
combination of warlike and religious
associations may be represented by the White
Horse cut into the chalk hill at Uffington,
Berkshire. Horses pulled the war-chariots of
the aristocracy, but they were also associated
with the goddess Epona. The White Horse
typifies the schematic but often highly
expressive way in which the Celtic artist
viewed the natural world.

Culture and Religion

Thomas Blagg

In their art, language and religion, the native Britons shared in the Celtic culture common to most of western Europe before the Roman conquest. Warfare and personal display were characteristic of their style of life, traditionally emphasized through the splendid decoration of weapons and ornaments with repoussé, enamelled and engraved curvilinear designs and figures. Religious cults* did not generally require the representational images, sacred buildings, texts and inscriptions, which were to be adopted in the Roman period. Votive offerings in rivers and lakes, sacred groves, and the cult of the human head, attest a religion which was manifested more in nature than in art.

In the century or so before the Roman conquest, the Britons were already responding selectively to Roman influence: first, gastronomically, through the import of Mediterranean wine, mainly by the tribes of the south-east. With a taste for wine came one for vessels appropriate to serve and drink it from: the Roman silver cups, bronze flagons and Arretine pottery found in the graves of native nobles. Similarly, *amphorae* for olive oil suggest a Mediterranean cuisine. These luxuries may have enhanced the position of those who adopted them, as embellishments rather than fundamental changes to the life-style of the tribal aristocracy: significant of its attitude to Roman culture, nonetheless.

The political prestige of contacts with Rome is reflected in the British coinage. The earliest, uninscribed, had imitated that of free Gaul. Early in the 1st century AD, some British rulers issued coins which closely copied Roman designs, and were inscribed with the abbreviated names of rulers, mint-towns and, in one case, the Latin "REX" (king). Celtic did not have its own script; literacy and Latin went together.

Native culture was healthy and vigorous; it is no sign of weakness that it was receptive to Roman manners and ideas. One dynamic development in British society was particularly favourable to the eventual assimilation. The establishment of settlements at Camulodunum (Colchester), Verulamium (St Albans), Silchester* and Canterbury* might not have fulfilled a Roman's expectations of a town, but, as administrative, economic and social centres for their tribes, they had already begun to provide the same urban functions as their Roman successors.

So, the soil of Britain was well prepared for the implanting of Roman civilization: but the cultural change was still enormous. The two generations which followed the conquest experienced an astonishing transformation in their physical surroundings, both in town and country, with the laying-out of planned roads and street systems, and the introduction of techniques of construction in mortared stone and tile, and of interior decoration with painted plaster walls and mosaic floors. The purposes of many of the buildings – basilicas, baths, amphitheatres – were as new as the techniques. The *Pax*

Celtic religion
Directed towards placating and controlling forces of nature; priests (druids) performed magical rites, kept calendars to fix four festivals around which agricultural year organized. Local communities had own gods within basic types: great nature gods, e.g. Sucellos, sky god with hammer representing thunder; animal gods, e.g. Epona, horse goddess; fertility goddesses, especially associated with water, e.g. Coventina; mother goddesses e.g. Matres Campestres. All evidence comes through Romanized media e.g. inscriptions, sculpture. When gods were identified with Roman gods (*Interpretatio Romana*) previously weak anthropomorphism confirmed in Celtic mind; thus, building of temples, religious buildings, ban on human sacrifice, etc modified and sanitized religion.

Silchester
Known as Calleva, tribal centre of Atrebates from at least 50 BC, but possibly passing under Catuvellaunian influence until returned to Cogidubnus by Romans. Roman town acquired earthwork defence, street grid, probably in 40s. Became *civitas* capital, perhaps on Cogidubnus' death; acquired *forum* in Flavian period; new earthwork constructed, street alignment changed; inn for travelling officials (*mansio*) and amphitheatre built. Another earthwork built end of 2nd century; masonry wall added in 3rd century; timber houses rebuilt in stone. Several Romano-Celtic temples found, also 4th century Christian church. *Forum* reorganized for metal working in mid-3rd century, suggesting tailing-off of administrative activity. City survived alongside Saxon settlements, perhaps into 6th century.

Canterbury
Belgic settlers replaced Bigbury hill-fort with *oppidum* at River Stour crossing from *c.* AD 10. Timber huts survived into Roman period up to *c.* AD 60. Earliest Romanized buildings in timber; street grid reorganized mid-1st century; city grew under Flavians; theatre built for religious performances *c.* 80-90, rebuilt 3rd century. Public baths,

stone houses built by end of 1st century. No walls until late 3rd century in response to Saxon raids, with defensible gates, external, as well as internal, towers.

Pax Romana

"Roman peace", refers to relatively peaceful conditions prevailing throughout empire from end of 1st century BC to at least late 2nd century AD. Protection from external enemies ensured by frontiers; within empire, native resistance crushed, won over with establishment of towns and spread of Romanization; carrying of arms forbidden by *Lex Iulia de vi publica* ("Julian Law on public violence").

Dress in Roman Britain

Some evidence for dress in literature, relief sculpture. Tacitus's claim that the *toga*, Roman formal dress, became common in Britain under Agricola, an exaggeration; probably worn in Britain only by upper-class Roman citizens on formal occasions. Ordinary dress simpler: tunics for men and women, with cloak (*paenula*), square piece of cloth with hole for head, hood attached. Celts favoured bright colours; brooches, mostly bronze took place of buttons. Shoes either heavy boots with iron studs or sandals laced round leg. By time of Diocletian *birrus Britannicus*, British hooded cloak, popular.

Baths

Public baths essential feature of Roman towns both for hygiene (only wealthiest houses had private baths) and as social centres. Frequently built soon after *forum*; in Britain often modelled on army bath-houses. Bathers progressed from changing room to cold room (*frigidarium*), to warm room (*tepidarium*), to hot room (*caldarium*), to open pores, then back in reverse order to close them again, ending with immersion in cold plunge bath. Warm and hot rooms had underfloor heating (hypocaust) with hot air channelled from furnaces. Men and women usually bathed separately.

Olympian gods and religion.

Olympian deities, each with own sphere of influence, part of official state religion, revived by Augustus as appeal to tradition at institution of new Empire; worship continued, until Christianity superseded it in 4th century AD, as expression of loyalty to state. Appears in worship of Jupiter, Juno, Minerva in shrines (*capitolia*) attached to *fora* of provincial *coloniae* and *municipia*, though no certain evidence in Britain. Altars dedicated by soldiers to Jupiter and rest of triad, Mars etc, official

*Romana** supplanted the cultural ethic of warfare; the result was a new environment. Tacitus describes how in AD 79 the southern Britons were being encouraged to build temples, *fora* and town houses; their leaders' sons were taught Latin eloquence; Roman dress* was frequently worn; the civilized habits of the baths*, strolls in the portico and elegant dinner-parties were, ironically, a sign of the Britons' enslavement by an alien culture. Tacitus's picture may be illuminating, but his view is partial. Religious practices offer a broader canvas for observation and judgement.

Roman administrators, soldiers and merchants brought with them the established gods of the Roman people: Jupiter, Mars, Minerva and other Olympians*; deities associated with nature and fertility, like Silvanus and Ceres; personifications of abstract concepts, like Fortune and Victory. They also brought the Roman manner of worship. Cult images of the gods represented them in human form. They were housed in temples* with columnar façades and tiled roofs. Sacrifices were offered to them on stone altars. Temples, altars, statues and other gifts were vowed in return for the granting of prayers. Inscriptions recorded the dedications, the performance of vows, and the curses which the gods were called to witness.

At an official level, the cult paid to the *genius* (or guardian spirit) of the emperor, and to the deified spirits of dead emperors, gave sanction to the political change which Britain had experienced. An inscription from Chichester records the dedication of a temple to Neptune and Minerva, for the well-being of the imperial family, by the authority of Tiberius Claudius Cogidubnus, native king of the region. Ancient Roman gods, the imperial

gods of Roman army, partly in loyalty to state, partly as thanks to guardian deities. Olympian gods failed to provide spiritual experience; hence growing appeal of eastern mystery religions (like Christianity).

Classical temples

Classical Roman temples based on Greek, themselves based on ancient type of building called *megaron*, large hall with side walls extending forward beyond entrance to form porch with two columns. Roman temple was hall (*cella*) on podium, surrounded by row or rows of columns (peristyle) supporting gabled roof; *cella* housed cult statue. Purely classical temples rare in non-Mediterranean provinces; few examples in Britain include Temples of Deified Claudius (Colchester), Sulis Minerva (Bath).

Both sides of a gold coin of Eppillus, king of the Atrebates (Hampshire-Sussex) just before the Claudian invasion. F COM on the obverse is for Latin filius Commi, "son of Commius", and the Roman model is also followed in the winged victory on the reverse.

dynasty and the local ruler were bound together. The imperial cult* provided a focus for the expression of the province's loyalty to Rome, with the temple of Claudius* at Camulodunum and priestly colleges, the *seviri augustales*, known from other *coloniae* at Lincoln and York. Numerous dedications to the *genius* or *numen** (divine power) of the emperor, found at military sites, show how the cult demonstrated the army's loyalty to its supreme commander. Jupiter and other Roman gods also had their places in the military calendar of festivals. These deities predominate in the religious sculpture and inscriptions of the *coloniae* and legionary fortresses, the communities most representative of Roman institutions. Garrisons of the smaller forts which, as along Hadrian's Wall, were in closer contact with the native rural population, more frequently honoured local gods like Belatucadrus and Cocidius.

In the civilian south, likewise, through assimilation with Roman forms of worship, native gods inconspicuously made their captors captive. The Romans were generally tolerant of other peoples' gods, and tended to identify them with their own. Sometimes this *interpretatio romana** was made explicit, by adding the Roman name of a god to his native name, as with Mars Nodens at Lancaster, Mars Ocelus and Lenus Mars at Caerwent. Sulis*, the deity associated with the thermal spring at Bath, was identified with Minerva. Her temple and the bronze head from her statue, however, are wholly classical in form. Representations of other gods in classical form may conceal Celtic associations. Some Celtic cults are more clearly recognizable as such, when less easily assimilated to Roman religious iconography. There was, for example, widespread worship of the Three Mothers, goddesses associated with fertility and represented seated with loaves, fruit, infants or small animals on their laps. Native ritual and ceremonial practices determined the architecture of so-called Romano-Celtic temples*, the dominant type in the south. The construction techniques are Roman, but the plan (a square central room surrounded on all sides by an ambulatory) is particular to the Celtic provinces of the empire. Examples at Gosbecks (Essex), Worth (Kent) and Hayling Island were built in sanctuaries already established before the Roman period.

Imperial cult

Organized by Provincial Council; delegates appointed priest *(sacerdos)* from their ranks, at annual festival at Colchester, to administer and pay for cult for a year; great honour, but expensive. Centred on Temple of Deified Claudius, presumably built after his death, though perhaps based on earlier altar of Rome and Augustus. Sacrifices were made on behalf of living emperors and dedications set up here and throughout province to *genius* or *numen* of emperor and household; administered in *municipia* and *coloniae* by *Seviri Augustales*. A unifying focus for loyalty to emperor and empire, binding aristocracy and rich, in particular, to Rome in hope of their setting example to populace.

Temple of Deified Claudius

Built at Camulodunum as centre for imperial cult, perhaps replacing earlier altar to Rome and Augustus. Possibly not built until after death of Claudius in AD 54 (unusual to declare living emperor a god). AD 60, site of last stand in city against Boudicca, burnt by her as symbol of Roman domination; rebuilt. Very large, classical in style, housed statue of Claudius. In sacred area *(temenos)* in front of temple stood altar of imperial cult.

Seviri Augustales

In *municipia* and *coloniae* freedmen barred from holding magistracies or serving on council, despite often being wealthy men. To involve them in public life, provide them with status, allowed to serve on board of six *(seviri)* appointed annually by city to organize local celebrations of imperial cult.

Genius and numen

Genius was guardian spirit of anything, anyone, or any place; *numen* was divine power ascribed to anyone, especially to gods or emperors. Inscriptions often dedicated to *genius* or *numen* of emperor or household (*domus divina,* divine house), but others dedicated e.g. to *genius* of fort or army unit, or just of a place (*genius loci,* a phrase to ensure local deity has been addressed).

Interpretatio Romana

Roman practice of identifying any native deity with one of their own, reflecting tolerance of Rome towards other religions. In Celtic regions principal native gods often identified with Mars, Mercury, worshipped as such by Romans. This had profound effect on Celtic religion: local deities received second, Roman, name e.g. Sulis Minerva at Bath; when god depicted in sculpture (a Roman introduction), Roman deity affected conception of Celtic; greatly reinforced previously weak anthropomorphism in Celtic religion.

Sulis Minerva

Sulis, goddess of hot spring at Bath (probably fertility goddess) identified by *interpretatio Romana* with Minerva. When Bath became Roman spa, late 1st century AD, classical-style temple built alongside main basin of hot spring; baths suite added to complex; basin of hot spring covered late 2nd century. Baths frequented especially by convalescent army officers, other affluent visitors; complex dominated town, probably main reason for its existence.

Romano-Celtic temples

Celts had few temples; open-air nature religion involved worship of rude wooden figures within large sacred area *(temenos)*. Romans introduced cult-statues and buildings to house them: temples sited within *temenos,* constructed in Roman manner adapted to needs of Celtic ritual.

Conjectural reconstruction drawings of two temples of British cults assimilated to Roman divinities at Lydney Park, Gloucestershire (Mars Nodens), above, and Nettleton Shrub, Wiltshire (Apollo) top. The temple of Nodens, a healing divinity, had a guest house for worshippers and baths behind.

Bronze figures of Mercury: in classical style, from Bruton, Somerset, above, and, showing Celtic influence, from Southbroom, Wiltshire, left.

Right: relief carving of the Celtic trio of Mother Goddesses (tres matres) from Cirencester (Corinium), holding an infant and fruit on their laps, showing their association with fertility.

47

Cults of eastern origin*, those of Isis, Serapis, Dionysus, Mithras and others, gained adherents in Britain, as elsewhere in the West. Their promises of rebirth to initiates and a more personal communion with the god were part of their appeal. Their extent should not be exaggerated; worship of Mithras, for example, was mainly restricted to military and commercial communities, and none of his known temples suggests a very large following.

There are third-century literary references to Christians* in Britain, but little material evidence for them until the Edict of Milan (313) gave them official toleration. Thereafter, the presence of believers is identified by the Chi-Rho monogram* on wall-plaster or mosaics in villas, notably Lullingstone and Hinton St Mary, and on silverware, among which the Water Newton treasure is probably the earliest collection of church plate yet found in the whole empire. Christianity apparently found its greatest support in towns (e.g. Silchester, Dorchester) and among country landowners. The Britons sent bishops to the Councils of Arles (314) and Rimini (359), and contributed Pelagius to the early Church's list of distinguished heretics. At the same time, despite imperial edicts against paganism, native religion, like the cult of the healing god Nodens at Lydney, survived with resilience.

The rural peasantry, the *pagani,* continued to worship their native gods, and to speak the Celtic language. Some Latin words were adopted, and have been transmitted from British to Welsh. In some cases, there was no British equivalent, e.g. of the Latin for "mule", "wine", "church", but there are also Latin loan-words for more common terms – "arm", "fish", "bridge". The great majority of Romano-British place-names were Celtic, even those of Roman forts. Only forty wholly Latin toponyms are known. In the towns, by contrast, Latin* was widely spoken by the working population, to judge from the potters and tilemakers who scratched graffiti on their wares. This was the Vulgar Latin of common speech, little different from what was spoken by soldiers, traders and craftsmen elsewhere in the western empire. Other graffiti appear to be writing exercises, one from Silchester being a quotation from Vergil's *Aeneid*. Tacitus and Juvenal refer to Britons being trained to be eloquent in what we may presume was the classical Latin of the highly educated minority. Plutarch, at Delphi, met a Greek grammarian who had just come from

Chi-Rho monogram
Monogram representing first two letters of "Christ" in Greek (*see* page 51), first used by soldiers of Constantine the Great at his great victory at Milvian Bridge 312, after he had seen a vision. Appears in Britain in Christian wall-painting (Lullingstone), mosaics (Hinton St Mary), silver plate (Water Newton treasure).

Spread of Latin language
Tacitus speaks of Agricola having sons of British chieftains taught Latin; this prepared them for role in town council (*ordo*). Inscriptions, graffiti suggest spoken Latin common, at least in towns, probably as second language after Celtic; graffito scratched on "Austalis tile" found in London shows even ordinary worker spoke some Latin; most writing probably in Latin. Spread by aristocracy, schools in towns, but most of all army which always used Latin.

Mithraism and eastern cults
Mithraism, like other eastern cults, offered greater spiritual rewards than Olympian religion. Such cults, Isis, Serapis, Dionysus, Cybele, Mithras, involved initiation rites which brought contact with god. Mithraic religion concerned with struggle of Light and Darkness, victory over death, expressed in myth of Mithras slaying bull; promised happiness after death, appealed especially to soldiers and merchants. Temples small, basilican in plan, with raised aisles, cult figures in niche at end of nave, which represented cave in which Mithras was born and was entered down steps. Mithraea at Carrawburgh, London perhaps destroyed in 4th century by Christians who regarded Mithraism as rival religion.

Christianity in Britain
Arrived possibly in 2nd century. First martyr St Alban in 3rd century. Early 4th-century evidence in symbols on silver treasure from Water Newton (Durobrivae), Cambridgeshire, but development obscure until edict of toleration at Council of Arles 314, attended by three British bishops and one deacon. 4th-century churches known at Silchester, possibly Verulamium; 5th-century church at Richborough. Christianity attested in late villas by wall-paintings (Lullingstone), mosaics (Hinton St Mary, etc). Christianity advanced, but Pelagian heresy gained ground: St Germanus sent to Britain in 429 to re-establish Catholicism. Christian missionaries like St Patrick active in 5th century, but widespread paganism survived.

Bath and the cult of Sulis Minerva: the
reconstruction drawing above shows how
the Roman baths might have looked in the
3rd century. The temple that carried the
bearded head of a male Medusa right, and
below on its pediment can be seen in the
enclosure in the foreground. The inscription
DEAE SULI left addresses the goddess
Sulis, identified with the Roman Minerva at
Bath (Aquae Sulis).

The silver dish or lanx (above) *found at Corbridge (Corstopitum) Northumberland, was made in the eastern Mediterranean in the 4th century, when the Empire was* officially Christian. Its decoration in repoussé with pagan gods (Apollo, Diana, Leto and Minerva) probably reflects no more than traditional artistic tastes.

Religious cults of eastern origin became increasingly important in the West from the 2nd century AD onwards. The head of Mithras (above) from the Walbrook Mithraeum, London, is of imported Mediterranean marble, cut to fit into a socket in a body of less expensive material. Not every representation of a god was primarily religious in purpose. Dionysus, shown riding a tiger on a 1st or 2nd century mosaic from London (right) may recall drunken revelry as much as the immortality promised to his initiates.

The chi-rho, *often incorporating* alpha *and* omega, *was the most usual Christian emblem. It is seen* right *in a wall-painting (reconstructed) in the chapel of Lullingstone Roman villa.*

Floor mosaic at Hinton St Mary, Dorset, showing the chi-rho *behind the head of a beardless Christ.*

Above: *the* chi-rho *appears also embossed on thin beaten silver votive plaques from the Water Newton, Cambridgeshire, hoard. The pagan votive plaque from Barkway, Hertfordshire,* top, *represents the type on which the Christian example is based.*

Britain. The view that the Romano-British gentry spoke a rather conservative and stilted "British" Latin has, however, been challenged by recent scholarship.

The extent of literary culture* in Britain is largely unknown. No works by any British writer survive earlier than those of Pelagius, *c.* 400 AD. Vergil's *Aeneid* is the only literary work known to have inspired specific scenes on mosaics and wall-paintings, though a couplet on the Lullingstone mosaic suggests an informed appreciation of Ovid's verse composition. More generally, figured mosaics illustrate numerous themes from classical mythology, notably Jupiter, Bacchus, Neptune and Orpheus. The existence of theatres, however, does not necessarily suggest a great enthusiam in Britain for classical drama; the fact that the few known are associated with temples, as in Gaul, suggests that their purpose was connected with religious festivals.

Culture was no more homogeneous than religion; neither can be judged simply by attempting to balance "Roman" against "native" qualities. For example, the styles of architectural ornament in the major civilian towns of southern Britain were established by different craftsmen, and remained quite distinct from those current in the military north. Both were "provincial"; but one cannot be called more "Roman" than the other. The fact that the purely Roman gods were more frequently worshipped by the army has to be set alongside the totally unclassical proportions of much of the religious sculpture from northern sites, a question of intentions as much as of technical skills. The acculturation of Britain by the Romans produced a rich variety of responses, both passive and creative. Any concept of cultural imperialism is anachronistic and inappropriate to their analysis. The people of Roman Britain included citizen legionaries, native auxiliary soldiers, landowners with British ancestries and Roman names, Greek doctors and teachers, Latin-speaking traders and craftsmen and Celtic-speaking peasants. There were parts for many voices; unison was not required.

Literary knowledge in Britain
Little evidence of much beyond basic education in Britain. Pelagius received good education in Britain, then went to Rome to study law; probably higher education had to be sought abroad. Some knowledge of Vergil's *Aeneid* implied by 4th-century mosaics and frescoes, which depict scenes, and by quotation from the poem in graffiti.

Panel from floor mosaic, depicting scenes from the story of Dido and Aeneas, found in a villa at Low Ham, Somerset.

Mosaic panel in the Roman villa at Lullingstone, Kent, showing the abduction of Europa by Jupiter in the guise of a bull, with a Latin allusion to Virgil's Aeneid *and the jealousy of Juno.*

2

SAXONS,
DANES AND NORMANS

409-1154

SAXONS, DANES AND NORMANS 409-1154
Overview

Henry Mayr-Harting

English history from the Anglo-Saxon settlements to the Norman Conquest represents a development from a "Heroic Age" to a state. This is not to deny an administrative system early on, nor important elements of administrative and urban continuity between Roman Britain and the Anglo-Saxons. But the island became filled with Germanic warrior chieftains and adventurers, who made themselves masters of loose tribal groupings, who were largely untouched by patriotic, ethnic or even family considerations, who fought to display personal bravery and win fame, and who, if their continental opposite numbers like Clovis of the Franks are anything to go by, throve, and indeed lived, on myriads of feuds amongst themselves. We refer to such men as Hengist, Ceawlin and Ida, names known to us rather fortuitously because they were deemed to be founders or early representatives of later ruling dynasties in Kent, Wessex and Northumbria. Of course such warriors fought or treated with the British, and no doubt they thereby strengthened their hold over their fellow Germans. But the British also employed Germanic warriors; certainly they did in the Chiltern region which succumbed only in the late sixth century to Anglo-Saxon pressure. Such warriors could have opposed the Saxons across the Thames, and been opposed by them, with as much zest as Anglo-Saxons ever opposed the Britons. British princes were not different. If Arthur ever existed, his context must have been the feuds and internecine wars of the northern British principalities around 500, before the Anglo-Saxons appeared on the scene there.

The two finest expressions of heroic-age ideals in early Britain are the *Gododdin* and *Beowulf*. The *Gododdin* is a series of poetic laments for the warriors who fell some years before 600, in the great last stand of the men of Edinburgh against the rising power of the Anglo-Saxons in what came to be called Northumbria. These warriors were not only the Gododdin of Edinburgh, but also Britons from Gwynedd, Elmet (around Leeds), Ayrshire etc. One may doubt, however, whether they fought primarily for the British cause rather than for the rewards of fine weapons, gold rings, mead, feasting at a great hall, and the praise of bards. *Beowulf* is an Anglo-Saxon poem

whose eponymous hero is mythical, unlike the warriors of the *Gododdin*, yet his struggles against monsters were occasioned by similar motives. Scholars differ about the date of *Beowulf*, but if it is eighth-century, the commonest opinion, then it probably looks back nostalgically to a kind of society which had really existed but was perhaps passing away in the age of the poet himself.

There are certain social and economic implications in these poems which are of great importance. Their warriors sought their rewards in treasure. The Sutton Hoo ship treasure in the British Museum shows the accumulation of such treasure at the highest level. The excavations of the rich Kentish cemeteries of *c.* 600, with their gold and garnet jewellery, their golden bracteates, their top quality Frankish glass, show how proximity to the Continent and its trade gave the Kentish kings possibilities to distribute luxury goods, or treasure, to the aristocratic warriors who fought for them. It is no accident that King Aethelbert of Kent was one of those early kings who had superiority over others (a *bretwalda*) and that he was considered by Pope Gregory the Great a suitable recipient of the Christian mission of 597.

Not surprisingly, the goldsmith's art was the highest art in such a society: several Gododdin warriors are described as wearing brooches in battle. The Tara brooch in Dublin is an example of the large and splendid penannular brooches with swivel pins for fastening cloaks, which must have been spectacular symbols of achieved status in fighting, like Rolls Royces for modern businessmen. Christianity would bring a whole new world of book art to the Anglo-Saxons, but the art of the smith never lost its importance. Indeed the warriors of Christ also needed it for their chalices, reliquaries and pectoral crosses. At one time it was thought that some of the highest techniques of the smith, enamelling and millefiori inlays, such as are seen in the Sutton Hoo treasure, were known only in Ireland, and that the Sutton Hoo hanging bowl, for instance, must be an Irish export. But excavations at the fortress of Dinas Powys in south Wales have shown that sixth-century British craftsmen also had these skills. Characteristic Irish skills, employed by British smiths in the service of their

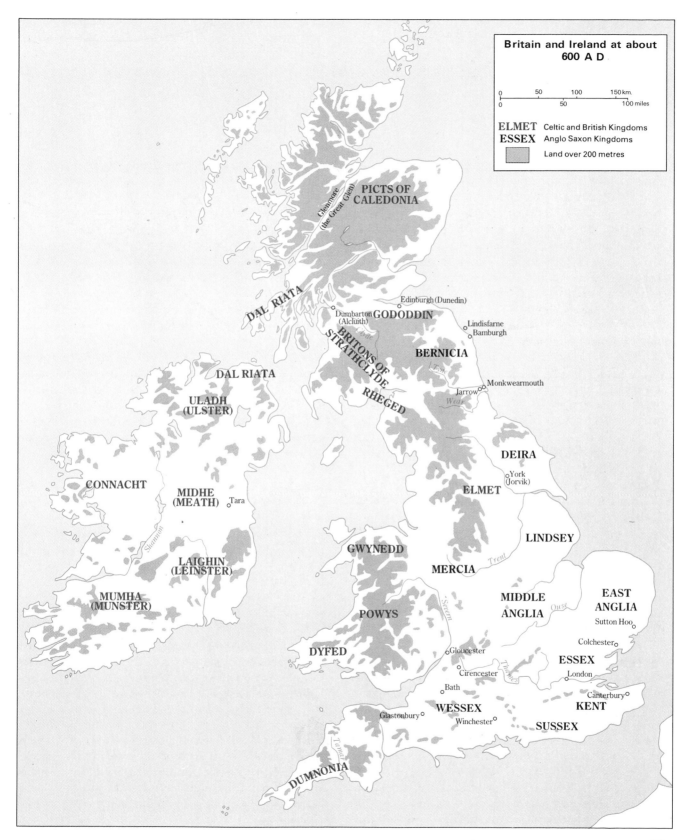

Britain and Ireland at about
600 A D

| 0 | 50 | 100 | 150 km. |
| 0 | | 50 | 100 miles |

ELMET Celtic and British Kingdoms
ESSEX Anglo Saxon Kingdoms
        Land over 200 metres

PICTS OF
CALEDONIA

Glenmore
(the Great Glen)

DAL RIATA

Edinburgh (Dunedin)

Dumbarton
(Alcluith) GODODDIN

BRITONS OF
STRATHCLYDE

Lindisfarne
Bamburgh

BERNICIA

RHEGED

Jarrow Monkwearmouth

Wear

DAL RIATA

ULADH
(ULSTER)

DEIRA

York
(Jorvik)

ELMET

CONNACHT

MIDHE
(MEATH) Tara

LINDSEY

Trent

GWYNEDD

Shannon

MERCIA

LAIGHIN
(LEINSTER)

MIDDLE
ANGLIA

EAST
ANGLIA

MUMHA
(MUNSTER)

POWYS

Severn

Ouse

Sutton Hoo

Colchester

DYFED

Gloucester

ESSEX

Cirencester

Thames

London

Bath

Canterbury

WESSEX

KENT

Glastonbury

Winchester

SUSSEX

DUMNONIA

Tamar

warlords, taken over by an East Anglian *bretwalda* (if Sutton Hoo is to be associated with Raedwald, d. *c.* 625): in what other sphere could one better link the heroic age amongst the Irish, the British and the Anglo-Saxons?

Warriors who sought their rewards in treasure were as mobile as the treasure itself. Mercenary would be a low word to use of Beowulf and his followers, but evidently nothing prevented his appearing wherever the need was great and the price was right. In real life the seventh-century Mercian prince, Guthlac, who also had his followers, was very like Beowulf, a freebooter going wherever there was treasure to be won. We know about him because he happened to become a Christian saint and the subject of an hagiography. Of course one cannot eat treasure. But such men could enjoy, sometimes for months or years at a time, the hospitality of a king's or land-holding nobleman's hall, in a society where hospitality was fundamental to the social ethic. When they obtained lands of their own, it was probably by gift of a king or lord rather than by hereditary right and probably not before they were mature warriors, as Beowulf was when he was granted an estate and as in real life was Benedict Biscop, founder of Bede's monasteries at Wearmouth and Jarrow. Younger noblemen were likely to be landless, mobile and treasure-seeking. The early Anglo-Saxon laws know a class of non-landowning *gesithcundmen*, or noblemen, who disappear from view in the later law-codes. When we seek to explain the rapid shifts of political power amongst the seventh-century English kingdoms, therefore, implicit in the whole story of Bede's *Ecclesiastical History of the English People* (731), the movements of these landless warriors must play a large part.

It would be easy to suppose that the coming of Christianity to the Anglo-Saxons was the vital factor in the transition from heroic-age politics to statehood; but unfortunately, too easy. In the long term, Christianity did indeed play an important part in the forming of an English state, but, in the seventh and eighth centuries, Christianity was itself moulded to the values of the heroic age as it was absorbed. Bede saw Christianity as in many ways frontally colliding with secular society. But one may argue that noble and idealistic as his view was, it was anomalous; *Beowulf* may better reflect the way in which Christianity alone could have succeeded amongst the English aristocracy. "Christianity had been successfully assimilated by a warrior nobility," writes Patrick Wormald, thinking of the deeply embedded Christianity in the poem, "a nobility which had no intention of abandoning its culture or seriously changing its way of life, but which was willing to throw its traditions,

customs, tastes and loyalties into the articulation of the new faith." St Wilfrid is often regarded as the archetypal heroic-age, aristocratic bishop, with his noble birth, his high-minded control of many churches, his warrior companions and his showy generosity.

Charlemagne was the genius who put together the characteristic ensemble of medieval government and statecraft, and the late Old English state was to be powerfully influenced by the Carolingians. But the crucial English developments in this direction occurred under the eighth-century Mercian rulers, more likely parallel with than through the influence of the Continent. First of all, the seventh-century *bretwaldas* exercised power over peoples other than their own by roving and thrusting in particular military expeditions. The Mercians appear the first to try and impose a continuous lordship over areas outside Mercia. This begins with the efforts of Wulfhere of Mercia (658-74) in the region of London. They were also the first to have a territorial strategy. Offa's Dyke was not an agreed or negotiated frontier between Offa (757-96) and the Welsh; it was clearly intended to keep the Welsh and their cattle-rustlers out. But it does show that Offa was thinking territorially about his kingdom. This is a great difference from chieftains who thought of themselves as war-leaders of mobile tribal confederations. Territorial thinking is reflected between the eighth and tenth centuries in the emergence of shires and hundreds with precisely defined boundaries, essential for an effective system of local-government officials, and in the emergence of precise estate-boundary clauses in charters, essential for royal control of land tenure.

It is not surprising that territorial strategy should be a Mercian development. The powerful rulers of the seventh century in Kent, East Anglia or Northumbria all sat on the east coast with direct access to the Continent and to continental trade. But the Mercians were land-locked. They had wealth to export, and part of the secret of their success was that they kept a grip on their natural resources: lead from the Peak District, salt from Worcestershire, and above all, perhaps, wool, cloth and hides. But just when the rewards of access to continental trade were being greatly enhanced, as the proliferation of coins would suggest, they had to struggle against other peoples to gain this access. Whether they gained it through Southampton or the Kentish ports, the vital strategy was control of the Thames Valley. When the Kentish mints finally came into Offa's hands, he had his own name placed on the coins; coins were a form of political propaganda, as well as a means of commercial exchange and a source of profit to the king.

The eighth-century Mercian rulers seem to have been able to harness their resources of land to the raising of labour and fighting forces in a way never achieved by the Anglo-Saxons before. There is debate about this, but if it is true, it was undoubtedly their most important achievement and a big step away from heroic-age politics and economics. Offa's Dyke required large, co-ordinated work forces, and strategic conquest and overlordship required the regular availability of a good army. The Mercians appear to have brought clarity into the uncertainties about whether or not Church lands were subject to the so-called common burdens of bridge-building, fortress work and military service – by insisting that they were. Furthermore, once Church lands were clearly subject to these burdens, rulers no longer stood to lose these all-important services if secular men sought the perpetual right which had hitherto attached only to Church lands by turning their lands into church land or (bogus) monasteries to retain them for the family. Hence grants of bookland (which could remain in the family and be inherited) came to be made to laymen. Such grants were carefully controlled by royal charter – and the lands owed military and labour services. Thus was an important basis laid for the territorialization of the aristocracy.

The biographer of Alfred (871-99), the greatest of all Anglo-Saxon kings, tells us that Alfred divided his Court nobility into three groups, each group by rota to spend a month at Court followed by two months on their estates. Thus by Alfred's time every member of the Court aristocracy was presumed to have his own landed base. Since the arrangement was lifted straight from King Solomon (III Kings, V, 13-14), it is also a nice example of how the Bible and Christianity provided an ideological framework for the development of the English state. The Alfred Jewel is an enamelled figure representing Solomonic Wisdom in a finely wrought gold setting; and Alfred drew a close parallel between himself and Moses in issuing his Laws. Less than a century later, Edgar would be seen as a king in the image not only of an Old Testament ruler but also of Christ. Christianity enormously expanded the perspectives in which rulers could think of themselves, and these perspectives in turn became an engine of expanded royal government. As to the territorialization of the aristocracy, this could affect the ruler in two opposite ways. On the one hand, the working of royal courts in the localities, of tax collection and military summonses, depended on the aristocracy of the region. On the other hand, particularly where the kings had few lands by which support could be attracted, aristocratic families could become powerfully independent forces. It is not so clear as historians have maintained in the past that the great earls who confronted Edward the Confessor (1042-66) were simply the creations of Cnut (1016-35) rather than the culmination of generations of family build-up.

The Church is often seen as the ideal instrument by which the kings could counter the power of the aristocracy in the late Old English state. The tenth century (especially under Edgar 957-75) witnessed a monastic reform and efflorescence, strongly influenced by continental movements. The monastic reformers (especially Dunstan, Aethelwold and Oswald) had a Benedictine religious and liturgical ideal: community life and prayer. To fulfil this ideal they needed the king's patronage, to endow monasteries with lands and recover alienated property from the hands of local aristocratic families. The kings no doubt derived great benefit from this, because the reconstituted monastic estates were almost certainly organized by their abbots to raise contingents of fighting men for the king's armies to combat local disorder and the Danes. These military quotas may have lasted, to remain an important element in the quotas which the Norman kings raised from the churches. But the reformed monasteries of the tenth century were largely aristocratic in composition, and had they been thought to have no function in aristocratic society, they could hardly have been as successful as they were. Therefore the monastic reform should be regarded at least as much in the light of co-operation as of combat between king and aristocracy. At the same time, some of the most important monasteries of the reforming connection of Aethelwold of Winchester were on the borders of Mercia and East Anglia (e.g. Thorney, Ely, Peterborough), which suggests their importance for West Saxon royal control of a politically unstable region.

Management of relations with both aristocracy and Church was fundamental for the success or failure of the West Saxon kingship, *de facto* the only English kingship remaining after the Danish wars of the ninth century, to exercise power in the localities. Aethelred II has been regarded as a weak king, but now we know that he was able to issue effective orders, raising the standard of military equipment with which his warriors fought the Danes. He had considerable support in Mercia, where the West Saxon kings had been able to make extensive land grants to the aristocracy from the former Mercian royal fisc after the collapse of the Mercian kingship in face of the Danes. But the West Saxons had obtained no royal fisc in Northumbria. First, therefore, Aethelred appointed a loyal Mercian supporter, Aethelm, to be earl of Northumbria, but he lacked the landed base to sustain his position. In 1006 he appointed Uhtred of Bamburgh as earl, who had strong local power but only tenuous connections with the West Saxon monarchy. Aethelred's one real foothold of power in Northumbria was the archbishopric of York, to which he appointed the loyal Wulfstan. Wulfstan's activities in drafting royal laws, in local government matters like deciding on true weights and measures, in his determination to bring state power to bear in order to achieve peace and Christian morality, show the importance to the king of the idea that he was "protector of the Church".

It will be obvious that the Danes were of the first importance in later Anglo-Saxon history. The attractions of England to them were a slave trade in captives, a wealth of coinage controlled and collected by a sophisticated government, and prospects of settlement. Their influence on English institutions or even culture is no longer thought to have been great; what matters are the responses which they evoked. The political unification of England was achieved in no small measure thanks to their elimination of all royal houses except the West

Saxon in the ninth century, to the defensive measures taken against them by Alfred, and to the ninth- and tenth-century English wars against them as a settled political power in northern and eastern England. This unification had, it is true, been foreshadowed earlier by the aims of the Mercians and by ecclesiastical unity under the archbishopric of Canterbury. But it would be a mistake to see too conscious a working towards it before the Danish attacks. Furthermore, the continued Danish threat was the factor which induced Edward the Confessor, lacking direct heirs, to espouse the policy of Norman succession to himself. With Normandy and England united, the Danes would be denied their cross-Channel bases for attacking England.

If there was a political and social weakness in the late Old English state, it was not military, nor moral as later Anglo-Norman writers were fond of saying, but partible inheritance amongst the aristocracy, and the search for opportunities to remedy its weakening effects. This was a sphere in which the new Norman aristocracy made a decisive advance.

Government and Politics 409-1042:
Saxons and Scandinavians

James Campbell

The state which Edward, later called the Confessor, came to rule in 1042 was powerful. The Domesday Survey (1086) demonstrates the orderliness of its administration. England was divided into shires, subdivided into hundreds or wapentakes*. Each unit had its court in which local men declared justice under the superintendence of royal agents. With this went a formidable fiscal system. Land was assessed for tax in hides (or *carucates*). Heavy taxes at a fixed sum per hide were raised from *c.* 1012 at the latest. In 1018 Cnut is said to have levied £82,500, more in real terms than most English rulers could raise in a year until the seventeenth century. Some of the weightiest evidence for the power of the state is provided by the coinage system, which was under elaborate central control; each issue, amounting to many millions of silver pennies, being demonetized and replaced by another, from *c.* 980 at intervals of about seven years, by the 1040s every two or three years.

The unification of England had been long in coming about. In the sixth century not only was the island of Britain much divided, so too was the area which later became England. The far north of Britain was in the hands of the Picts*, except that the Western Isles and adjacent mainland were ruled by Irish (*Scotti*, later to give their name to Scotland). Most of the west, including Wales, the south-western peninsula, Cumbria and the west midlands was still British and divided among several kingdoms. The remainder was held by Germanic rulers and peoples. From about the time of the Roman withdrawal, Germans* (mainly Angles and Saxons from what is now north-west Germany) had begun to come to Britain, originally as mercenaries. By about the middle of the fifth century they had created a kingdom in Kent*. By 600 the

descent. Strong under Aidan Mac Gabran late 6th century: Picts forced into alliance. But Aidan defeated by 603 by Aethelfrith of Northumbria (end of Scottish threat to Britain, according to Bede). Medieval Scotland developed from uniting of Dál Riáta with Pictish kingdom by Kenneth MacAlpin, who claimed Pictish throne according to custom of matrilinear succession.

Germanic migrations
Complex process, taking three centuries and involving several peoples from coastal regions of north-west Europe. From 3rd century climatic changes, especially rising sea level, caused their settlements to be abandoned. Germanic warriors employed as mercenaries throughout empire, including Britain. As Roman administration withered in late 4th-early 5th centuries, Germanic peoples filled vacuum. Some military activity, settlements often exploited existing agricultural and institutional resources.

Kent
Most precocious of early kingdoms. Later sources attribute origins to landing of Hengist and Horsa in mid-5th century: Hengist's son Oisc, king at end of 5th century, founder of later dynasty and ancestor of Aethelbert. Bede describes settlement by Jutes, who also colonized Isle of Wight; confirmed by archaeology. Rich culture: some continuity from late Roman period, lavish aristocratic burials, considerable Frankish influence, wide trading contacts. Canterbury continuously occupied. Consolidation and expansion from Isle of Thanet base in 5th century; by 500 frontier established along Medway.

Hundreds and wapentakes
Basic administrative units of late Anglo-Saxon England, subdivisions of the shire. First references to hundred in 10th century, though probably evolved from earlier administrative and fiscal areas. Royal ordinance 959-61 and later law codes prescribe hundred's responsibility for restricting crime and enforcing justice; hundred court to meet every 4 weeks. Wapentake equivalent unit in Scandinavian areas (from *vápnatak,* brandishing weapons aloft to signify approval). Variation in size: in midland shires, hundreds of exactly 100 hides reflect 10th-century administrative reorganization.

Picts
Probably not a homogeneous ethnic group: incorporated all pre-Celtic inhabitants of

Scotland; later Pictish kingdom included some Celtic peoples. Separate northern and southern kingdoms in 6th century, united in 7th century. Increasingly under pressure from Scots, British Celts and Northumbrians, though Pictish victory over last at Nechtanesmere 685 stabilized southern border. Converted to Christianity by 7th century. Mid-9th century kingdom united with Dál Riáta by Kenneth MacAlpin.

Scots *(Scotti)*
Began to raid western Scottish coast 3rd century, frequently in association with Picts. From 5th century infiltrated from northern Ireland into Argyll (Old Irish *Airer Goidel,* "shore of Gaels"). Established kingdom of Dál Riáta (or Dalriada) 6th century, offshoot of Dál Riáta of north Antrim, from whose kings Scots claimed

Bede's Ecclesiastical History
Written at Bede's monastery of Wearmouth-Jarrow, completed 731. The first reliable source for post-migration era: early chronology uncertain but historical structure sound. Settlement of England attributed to Angles, Saxons and Jutes. Poorly informed on areas still under British control; less interested in own period: attempted to list informants.

whole of the eastern seaboard of modern England and much of the interior were under German rule and substantial German settlement had taken place.

In the seventh century Anglo-Saxon kings extended their rule over all, or rather more than all, of modern England, Cornwall apart. Some of these rulers had superiority over most of the others, including those in the non-Anglo-Saxon parts of the island. There was a tendency for small Anglo-Saxon kingdoms (of which there seem to have been many) to be absorbed or merged into larger: for example, during the seventh century the two northern kingdoms of Bernicia and Deira* became Northumbria. In the eighth century the dominant kings were those of the midland kingdom of Mercia; Aethelbald (716-57) and Offa (757-96). In 800 the only kingdoms remaining effectively powerful were Mercia itself, Northumbria, Wessex* and perhaps East Anglia.

By 900 the only English kingdom left was Wessex. Under Egbert (802-39), Wessex absorbed Kent and Essex. Viking invasions*, which had begun in the late eighth century, became very severe by the middle of the ninth, and in the 870s the kingdoms of Mercia, East Anglia and Northumbria collapsed. Under Alfred (871-99), Wessex survived heavy pressure and gained control of much of Mercia. His son Edward conquered East Anglia and most of the midlands from the Danes. From 954 Northumbria was under the permanent control of the West Saxon kings.

During the reign of Edgar (959-975) the power of the West Saxon house was at its height. His son, Aethelred II (979-1016), had to face new Viking assaults. Although the invaders met with repeated military success and were bought off with increasingly large sums, the power of the central authority held surprisingly firm for many years; the state which the Danish king Cnut took over in 1016 was very much a going concern. Neither this change of dynasty nor the reversion to that of Wessex, when Aethelred's son Edward succeeded in 1042, broke administrative continuity.

Many of the elements in the system of government which made Edward's England so formidable a state had long histories. Crucial among these was the system of assessment for taxation and military service in hides*. As soon as we have documents relating to the transfer of land (from the late seventh century), we see that almost all estates were already described in terms of hides. The "Tribal Hidage" (a document of uncertain, but probably eighth-century date) shows a system of assessment in hides from kingdoms and from sub-divisions of kingdoms.

If one key to the nature of the late Anglo-Saxon state is the system of assessment, another is that of shires* and hundreds. Its development had been complex. In seventh-century England the basic unit of local government was the area centred on a royal vill, to which other settlements owed dues and services. Such an area was an economic unit (having, for example, common grazing) as well as an administrative one; and it was probably assessed at a round number of hides. In such a kingdom as Kent it is not clear that there was any unit intermediate between the area dependent on a royal vill (there called a lathe) and the kingdom as a whole. In larger kingdoms, most plainly in Wessex, there were by the eighth century intermediate units, there called shires, each of which had an official called an *ealdorman** at its head. (He was usually of royal or noble birth.) By the early eleventh century England was entirely divided up into shires. Some (like Kent) were former kingdoms; some, such as those in Wessex, were relatively old creations, some, like many of

Bretwaldas ("Britain rulers" or "wide rulers")
Term used in 9th-century *Anglo-Saxon Chronicle* for Bede's list of great kings of early kingdoms, who exercised authority "over all the English south of the Humber". These were: Aelle of Sussex, Ceawlin of Wessex, Aethelbert of Kent, Raedwald of East Anglia and three Northumbrians – Edwin, Oswald and Oswy. No indication that any such authority was formally bestowed, or that it represented enforceable or lasting overlordship. *Chronicle* added to Bede's list Egbert of Wessex, ignoring 8th-century Mercian kings Aethelbert and Offa, whose hegemony was probably more substantial than Egbert's.

Bernicia and Deira
Two kingdoms which were united to form Northumbria. Bernicia established by mid-6th century, centred on coastal fortress of Bamburgh; separate kingdom until late 6th century, and for periods in 7th. Otherwise, unified with Deira, concentrated in Yorks. Dynastic struggle early in 7th century between Aethelfrith of Bernicia and Edwin of Deira: Aethelfrith initially exiled Edwin, but Edwin regained throne with help of Raedwald of East Anglia 616. Edwin killed 632 by Penda of Mercia and Cadwallon of Gwynedd; throne soon passed to Aethelfrith's son Oswald.

Expansion of Wessex
Later tradition ascribes foundation to Cerdic, who landed early in 6th century near Southampton. Archaeology suggests infiltration north from south coast, and west from East Anglia via Thames Valley. Southern group became dominant in 7th century, and expanded westwards, subsequently incorporating British kingdom of Dumnonia (Devon) and consolidating along Tamar after *c*.710. Egbert fought against Cornish in 815, 825 and 838, by which time Cornwall incorporated into Wessex. Egbert took control of Kent, Sussex, Surrey and Essex 825 following victory over Mercians at Wroughton; Berkshire absorbed from Mercia by mid-9th century.

First Viking attacks on England
Began late 8th century, isolated monasteries were favourite targets: Lindisfarne attacked 793, Jarrow 794, Iona 795. First recorded appearance in south 789-802, landed at Portland and killed a royal official; began raiding Kent coast. Joined forces with Cornish 838, but defeated by Egbert at Hingston Down. Continued attacks on south coast: "great slaughter" at London and Rochester 842, Canterbury and London stormed 851,

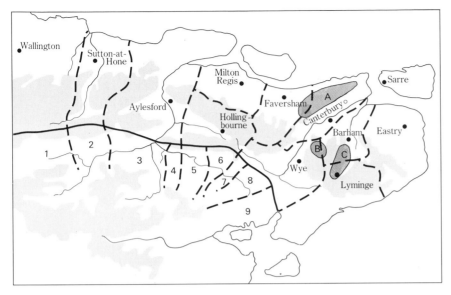

The Lathes of Kent and their wealden commons
in about 675, showing the contemporary coastline

0   15   30km.
0   10   20 miles

● Royal Vills
○ (if abandoned)
▢ Land over 100 m

1 Wallington Common
2 Sutton-at-Hone Common
3 Aylesford Common
4 Milton Regis Common
5 Hollingbourne Common
6 Faversham Common
7 Canterbury Common
8 Wye Common
9 Lyminge Common

Upland forests:
A Blean
B Buckholt
C Haradun

though Aethelwulf of Wessex inflicted crushing defeat at Aclea. Northern raiders were predominantly Norwegian, southern chiefly Danish, though some intermingling and Swedish elements.

Anglo-Saxon Chronicle

Initial compilation in Alfred's reign, probably at Winchester: based on earlier annals, Bede, oral traditions etc. Earliest manuscript written in vernacular by one scribe c. 892: important source for Alfred's Viking wars. Manuscripts circulated to other monasteries, kept up to date locally and largely independently. Four principal manuscripts survive, two of which record events to 1070s; the "Peterborough Chronicle" continues to 1154.

Hides and hidage

Hide a primitive economic unit: the amount of land necessary to support one peasant family. No uniform acreage in early period: varied from area to area. In late period, hide set artificially in some areas, e.g. 120 acres in Cambs. and Isle of Ely, compared with perhaps 40 acres in Wessex. (Areas settled by Scandinavians in 9th and 10th centuries divided into ploughlands.) Hide also the normal unit for assessing royal taxation, though assessment did not necessarily correspond with agrarian reality. Groups of hides maintained walled sections of *burhs*, and in parts of late kingdom 5 hide units provided one man for the *fyrd*.

Shire

West Saxon shires in existence by early 9th century. Names refer to town on which surrounding shire dependent – *Dornsaete*, Dorchester; *Wiltunscir*, Wilton; *Somersaete*, Somerton; *Hamtunscir*, Southampton.

Early administrative boundaries in Mercia disappeared during Viking age, and 10th-century kings created new shires in areas reconquered, centred on a major town. Of five boroughs of Lincoln, Derby, Nottingham, Leicester, Stamford, originally regions of Scandinavian military settlement, four became later shires. Shire court presided over by bishop and sheriff.

Ealdorman

Holder of royal office (frequently inherited) in shire. Responsible for raising and leading military forces of the shire, and implementing royal justice; could have authority confiscated for incompetence or corruption. West Saxon *ealdormen* led armies against Vikings in 9th century. In 10th century came to exercise increased authority, often over groups of shires; some military functions remained. From late 10th century, term replaced by *earl*, under influence of Scandinavian *iarl*.

The stone raised at Castell Dwyran, inscribed MEMORIA VOTEPORIGIS PROTICTORIS ("in memory of Vo(r)tepor the protector"). Vortepor was ruler of the Deisi, a southern Irish tribe which settled in Pembroke and Carmarthen.

61

those of the midlands, were new. No longer did each shire have an *ealdorman*. During the tenth century the sphere of authority of the *ealdorman* (later to be called the earl) was extended to much wider areas. By *c.* 1000 each shire had a sheriff*, responsible to the king for important elements in its administration.

Each shire had its court and in these courts much of the judicial business of the country was done. Their areas of jurisdiction may often have been fairly new. Not only were a considerable number of shires tenth-century creations, but most hundreds were probably created in the same period, though they were often related to older units centring on royal vills. Crucial elements in the judicial system were, however, very old.

The oldest surviving laws* are from seventh-century Kent and Wessex. None survive between those of Ine of Wessex (*c.* 690) and those of Alfred (*c.* 890). Thereafter there is a long series up to but not beyond Cnut. It is chiefly on the laws that the "Germanist" theory of the Anglo-Saxon polity has depended. This emphasizes continuity with German institutions as described by Tacitus in the first century, above all in the extent to which free warriors participated in decision and judgement*. Disputatious issues are involved. It is, however, clear that throughout the Anglo-Saxon period there were important relationships between kings and fairly extensive free classes; and that in

Sheriff ("shire-reeve")
Reeve a minor royal or lay official, mentioned in early sources, with delegated authority in a town or estate; royal *reeves* responsible for enforcing dues, obligations and order. Sheriffs, recorded from early 11th century, assumed some administrative functions of *ealdorman;* directed procedure of shire court and collected royal revenues and taxes; supervised representatives of the hundred in levying geld, received royal writ. Became more important post-Conquest, accounted annually at Exchequer for royal revenues.

Anglo-Saxon law codes
Earliest that of Aethelbert of Kent, early 7th century, after Christian conversion: role of Church recognized and protected. Subsequent 7th century Kentish codes and laws of Ine of Wessex principally concerned with payments for injury, infringement of property rights and breaches of public order. Ine's laws deal with Welsh living under West Saxon control. Alfred's code synthesized elements from earlier Kentish, Mercian and West Saxon codes. 10th- and 11th-century legislation was increasingly complex, dealing more with local administration, implementation of royal justice and economic regulation. Influence of Anglo-Saxon law apparent in legal measures of William I and Henry I. *Leges Henrici Primi* a clumsy compilation of earlier codes.

Witan ("counsellors")
Term applied to king's council in late period; developed from circle of followers who accompanied kings on their travels. No formal existence or constitutional role; an amorphous collection of nobles and ecclesiastics whose advice was sought on particular occasions. Laws of Wihtred and Ine promulgated in association with their greatest subjects. Alfred asked *witan* to declare the law and pronounce on the validity of Aethelwulf's will. In 10th and 11th centuries, came to assume role in royal succession, whenever an elective element was important.

See **Early coins** (page 78)

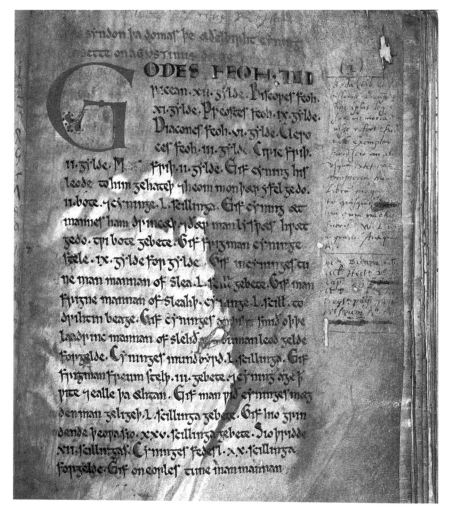

Opening page of the Textus Roffensis, showing part of the law code of King Aethelbert of Kent issued between 597 and 616. This 12th-century manuscript is the only surviving copy of early Kentish legislation.

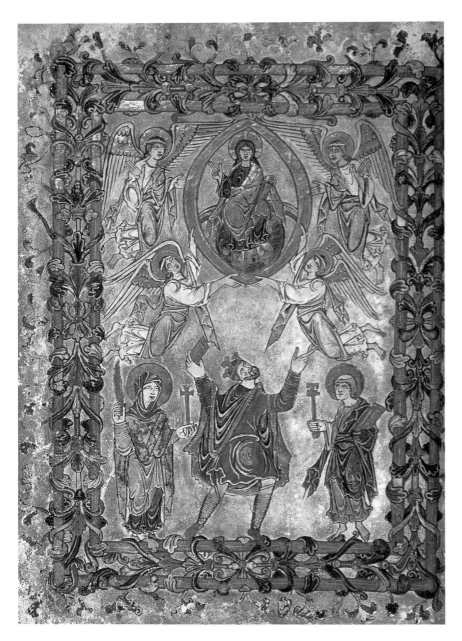

Above: *frontispiece of a mid-10th-century manuscript showing King Edgar offering to Christ his charter to refound the Minster of Winchester.*

Above right: *detail from a page in the 11th-century Stowe manuscript, in which King Cnut presents an altar cross to the new Minster at Winchester.*

these relationships the public courts were important, not merely as the agencies of the ruler, but rather as involving the participation of some of the ruled. Although lordship was always important in Anglo-Saxon England and there were resemblances between its exercise there and on the Continent, England did not become a feudal state in the sense of being one where jurisdiction over the free classes was largely in the hands of feudal lords.

Another sign of the power of the later Anglo-Saxon kings was the extent of their control over the coinage*. Until the eighth century the relationship between kings and coins is obscure. The penny coinage of the later eighth century bears kings' names and was under royal control. Such control reached its apogee in the tenth and eleventh centuries with the development, from *c.* 973, of the elaborate system of replacement.

63

The system of royal succession* was crucial to the development of dynastic authority. In the early period, royal successions seem to have been very open, in the sense that any male from the royal family might succeed. This was a major source of discord and instability in all the kingdoms. But from Egbert's succession by his son Aethelwulf in 839, kings of the West Sussex dynasty, later the rulers of all England, were invariably succeeded by either a son, or a brother, with the exceptions of the succession in 1016 of Cnut, and in 1066 of Harold II. A further reinforcement of royal authority came with the introduction of unction for kings; it first appeared, probably, in 787 when Offa had his son Ecgfrith anointed. By the tenth century an elaborate coronation service had developed. This is the most conspicuous, but by no means the only, example of the relationship between the Church and the growth in power of the state. In short, by the eleventh century, England was a state of a formidable kind. In it, old and new elements were combined in ways which linked the prehistoric, the Carolingian and the feudal worlds.

The English polity had so developed as to diverge from those of the remainder of the archipelago. An observer in, say, c. 600 could have recognized common features throughout. For example, abundance of kings. The Anglo-Saxons then had many, as did the Britons and probably the Picts too. With the Irish one can be sure. Their laws survive, in late manuscripts, but demonstrably in archaic texts unchanged since the eighth century, or earlier, and taking us back into an otherwise prehistoric world. Ireland contained some 150 *tuatha**, each with its *ri*. There was a hierarchy of kings. Rather greater kings had a kind of tribute-taking and present-giving authority over lesser kings, and in turn had greater kings above them.

To an extent one can discern a pattern linking the development of all four areas. It was not in England alone that the ninth century saw a tendency towards unification connected with the impact of, and resistance to, Viking invasion*. Rhodri Mawr of Gwynedd (d. 878) established extensive authority in Wales. Kenneth MacAlpin (d. c. 858) united the Picts and the Scots. Mael Secnail (d. 862) was not the first Uí Néill dynast to claim a kind of authority over all or most of Ireland, but he did more than perhaps any of his predecessors to make good the claim. Except in Scotland, unity did not last. Wales remained disunited, though other rulers of Gwynedd e.g. Hywel Dda (d. 949 or 950) and Gruffudd ap Llywelyn (d. 1063)) had extensive power for a time. In Ireland, though the authority of "high kings" such as Brian Boru (d. 1014) was widely recognized, power was divided among the rulers of several kingdoms.

The Celtic lands were not without institutions which helped the power of the rulers. Kingship was not a static phenomenon in Dark-Age Ireland; and the consolidation of power in the hands of a limited number of rulers must have had institutional bases. The survival from the Irish kingdom of Dál Riáta (in Scotland) of an arguably seventh-century text, the *Senchus fer nAlban*, recording ship-service dues, suggests dimensions to royal authority otherwise hard to trace. In Wales there are indications of elaborate mechanisms for gathering dues* and services, based on *commotes**, the principal subdivisions of kingdoms.

Nevertheless English development stands in strong contrast to that of its Celtic neighbours. It is beyond the Channel that one must look to find most of the parallels to, and at least some of the origins of, the structure and power of the late Old English state.

Royal succession

In early kingdoms, determined by membership of wider royal family and power to make claim effective. Many feuds, murders and changes of dynasty; powerful kings often attempted to eliminate rival dynasties. Royal genealogies frequently glossed over usurpations, and traced ancestry to the gods. Egbert's dynasty united English monarchy in 9th and 10th centuries. Later dynastic disputes of an international nature: Norman victories in 1066 did not extinguish claims of Anglo-Scandinavian royal family.

Tuatha, ri

Pre-Viking Ireland divided into perhaps 100 small kingdoms, of varying size and importance, each occupied by tribe, *tuath*, ruled by king, *ri*. Three grades of kingship: king of 1 *tuath*; king of 3 or 4 *tuatha*; over-king, or *ri ruirech*. Ties of dependence between inferior and superior kings, superior holding hostages from subordinate and offering stipend in return. By 8th century, some kings achieved authority over considerable areas. Royal succession determined in lifetime of reigning king, from amongst eligible members of kindred.

See **Vikings in Ireland** (page 73)

Royal dues in Wales

Annual render of food-rent (*gwestfa*) to king from free kindreds. Bondmen paid *dawnbwyd* twice annually, levied according to territorial divisions. Early evidence scanty, but by 11th century territorial system of levying dues in existence, though perhaps such a system had emerged much earlier in the south-east. Dues chiefly paid in kind: either as hospitality for the king on his travels or produce collected at a royal administrative centre. Service in king's army obligatory by 11th century at the latest. In addition, military conquest rendered subject peoples liable to payment of arbitrary tribute for as long as victorious king could extort it.

Cantref, commote

Administrative, fiscal and judicial units, probably originating in earlier tribal territories. From 10th century, administrative developments gave them more regular identity. In late 11th century Norman invasion also a stimulus, particularly in south. By 12th century *cantref* comprised 100 *trefi* (townships), and divided into two *commotes*, each under the authority of a hereditary chieftain. Officials supervised exploitation of labour of bondmen and collection of royal dues.

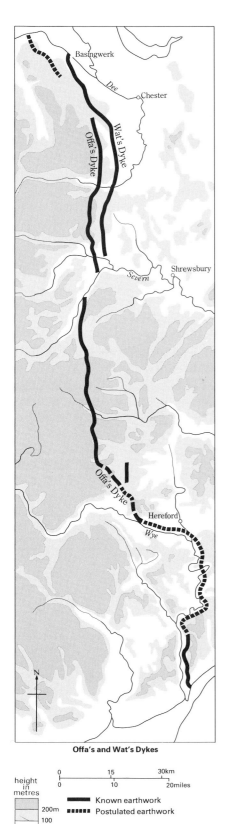

Offa's and Wat's Dykes

height in metres

200m
100
0

0 15 30km
0 10 20miles

Known earthwork
Postulated earthwork

Above: *Tara, a commanding hill-fort in Co. Meath, by tradition the seat from which the Uí Néills ruled as high kings of Ireland between the 4th and 7th centuries.*

Below: *An aerial view of Offa's Dyke, near the village of Newcastle in south-west Shropshire.*

Government and Politics 1042-1154:
the Norman Conquest and the Anglo-Norman realm
David Bates

The most influential single event of the period from 1042 to 1154 was undoubtedly the Norman victory at Hastings on 14 October 1066. In the English kingdom, the Norman Conquest not only initiated the rule of a line of Norman kings, but also entailed the replacement of most of the previous English aristocracy by men whose origins were in Normandy* and other parts of northern France. Henceforth the course of English politics and the development of government were linked to the efforts of king and aristocracy* to preserve a united cross-Channel realm and to the need to fight wars against continental enemies. For Wales and Scotland the results of the Norman Conquest of England were mostly indirect, although the establishment of new castles and aggressively-minded Norman lords in frontier zones put on a much stronger military pressure than had existed before 1066. The Norman kings acquired an overlordship over the king of the Scots from the time of the peace of Abernethy (1072) and maintained the overlordships of their Anglo-Saxon predecessors over the Welsh princes. The evolution towards a more centralized monarchy in England is paralleled to a lesser degree in Scotland.

Throughout this period, English politics were dominated by the uncertainties of the royal succession. In 1041-42 Edward the Confessor was recalled as the son of King Aethelred the Unready (978-1016), to follow Scandinavian descendants of Cnut (1016-35) who had failed to produce male heirs. In 1066 Edward's childlessness caused another crisis, with Harold and Duke William of Normandy only two among a number of potential successors who pressed their claims. In 1087 William the Conqueror's decision to bequeath Normandy to one son, Robert Curthose, and England to another, William Rufus, and in 1135 Henry I's lack of legitimate male heirs, caused long wars of succession. The first of these wars ended in 1106 with Henry I, who had seized the English kingdom in 1100, defeating his brother Robert Curthose at the battle of Tinchebrai and thereby acquiring Normandy; in the second, the succession of Henry II in 1154 ended the conflict* which had started when Henry I's nephew Stephen grabbed the throne against the claims of his daughter and designated heir Matilda (Henry II's mother). With so many feuds, it would be unwise to over-emphasize the political stability of the Anglo-Norman realm. Normandy was always vulnerable to invasion by neighbours such as the king of France or the count of Anjou, and even the desire to keep England and Normandy under one ruler, which motivated all members of the ruling family, would probably not have guaranteed survival against really strong external opposition such as emerged in the later twelfth century. In this context, it was fortunate that the conquest of Normandy in 1141-44 by Matilda's husband, Count Geoffrey of Anjou, kept the duchy in the family when it was transferred to their son Henry II in 1150.

The role of the great magnates in the politics of the Anglo-Norman realm has been the subject of considerable research and reinterpretation in recent

Norman influence before 1066
Hastings represented in contemporary Norman literature as personal triumph for William and proof of innate Norman superiority. But Normans had been influential in England during Confessor's reign: he had been under Norman protection 1013-42; Normans promoted in lay and ecclesiastical aristocracy after his accession. English property granted to Norman monasteries; Rouen traders granted special privileges in London. Earl Godwine's rebellion 1051 precipitated by increasing Norman influence; his rehabilitation 1052 led to outlawing of many Normans.

Duchy of Normandy
Established 911 by decree of Charles the Simple, centred on Rouen. Expanded westwards towards Cherbourg. Immigrant Northmen were rapidly assimilated by native Franks, Gauls and Bretons, and converted to Christianity. Feudal institutions introduced. Rollo, first count of Rouen, baptized 912. Son William Longsword killed 942 by count of Flanders. His adolescent son Richard I rebuffed Frankish attempts at reconquest with help of a Danish fleet. Use of Norman ports by Viking raiders caused quarrel with Aethelred II, settled by treaty 991. Aethelred married Emma, sister of Richard II in 1002. Aethelred took refuge in Normandy 1013, returning to England 1014 with new army.

Extension of Norman control
Many of William's army came for booty and adventure: soon returned. Lands of Anglo-Scandinavian aristocracy gradually incorporated. William acquired lands of Confessor and Godwine family 1066. 1069-72 rebellion of Earls Edwin and Morcar crushed. Earl Waltheof executed 1076, their lands absorbed, together with those of all who resisted. William suppressed revolts in west, midlands and north 1068-75, but Norman advance opposed by e.g. Hereward the Wake 1070-72 in Isle of Ely: Peterborough Abbey burned. Last resistance on Welsh border crushed 1070.

The death of Edward the Confessor, in a detail (right) *from the Bayeux tapestry. In the top scene, the dying king is talking to Harold, with Queen Edith and Archbishop Stigand.*

Scotland invaded 1072: treaty with Malcolm III.

Norman aristocracy

Stable dynastic aristocracy developed in Normandy from early 11th century: toponymic family names, property not to be alienated outside immediate family (previously frequently bequeathed to wide group of relatives and followers); illegitimate children increasingly excluded from inheritance. Several great nobles accompanied William to England and received lands as these came into royal hands; large tracts concentrated in hands of small group of families. Frequent rebellions from *c*.1075, part of wider dynastic disputes within royal family. Dispossessed aristocracy took sides in quarrel between William Rufus and Robert Curthose, and later in civil war between Matilda and Stephen.

Civil War under Stephen

Death of William, Henry I's son 1120 (White Ship), left no clear successor; Stephen could not claim hereditary right in either male or female line – claimed elective status. Unable to secure Normandy, conquered 1144 by Geoffrey of Anjou. Stephen gradually lost support amongst English barons, especially those with Norman lands who drifted towards Matilda. Stephen defeated 1141 and imprisoned by Matilda and Geoffrey de Mandeville. Church, which originally supported Stephen's claim, also increasingly hostile; by 1148 refused to accept Stephen's sons as heirs to throne. 1153 eldest son died; Treaty of Winchester recognized Henry of Anjou as heir, Stephen remaining king for his lifetime. Henry II's accession undisputed, first since 1066.

William the Conqueror's campaigns in England

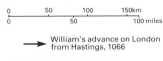

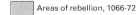

William's advance on London from Hastings, 1066

DURHAM Marcher earldoms

Areas of rebellion, 1066-72

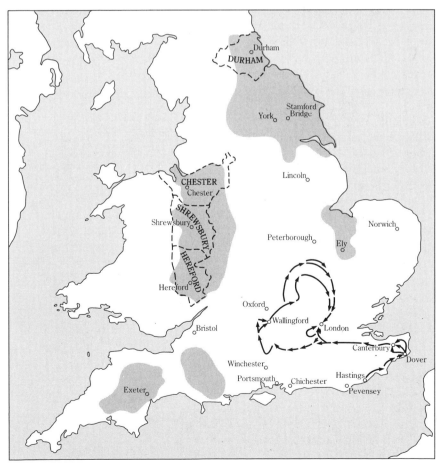

View of the Norman castle and cathedral at Durham which, despite obvious later additions, shows how the Norman buildings dominated the English landscape.

Henry I's Coronation Charter

Previously viewed as constitutional advance, now recognized as limited and pragmatic concession: means of gathering support for confrontation with brother Robert Curthose; some provisions not kept after Tinchebrai. Certain privileges and liberties granted to Henry's free tenants, correcting abuses in feudal arrangments previously a source of antagonism. Removal of "evil customs", e.g. excessive payments (reliefs) demanded for succession to feudal tenancy, exploitation of feudal incidents (transferring property through manipulation of heiresses) and exploitation of right of wardship over heirs until they reached age of majority. Remission of *Danegeld* on knights' demesne lands.

Writ

Sealed vernacular instruction, introduced in Cnut's reign: increasing royal authority over local administration reinforced by spread of royal writ, addressed to sheriff in shire court. Communicated royal directives and proclamations, also notification or confirmation of grants of lands or privileges (in addition to, or instead of, formal diploma). Regular form of words, no witnesses. William I continued use, in vernacular until 1070 thereafter chiefly in Latin. Increasingly employed as substitute for diploma; functions extended in 12th century. Seal attached *sur simple queue*, strip cut along bottom of parchment and wrapped around folded document.

Danegeld

Mid-9th century sources mention tribute paid to Vikings in return for peace. Danegeld first levied nationally by Aethelred II 991-1012. 1012-51, used to maintain navy and king's personal armed retinue, *housecarls*. Normans turned Danegeld into regular tax, not paid on royal demesne and subject of increasing grants of exemption under Henry I. Abandoned after 1162, though revived as *carucage* 1194. Northampton Geld Roll of William I's reign shows that county assessed at 3,200 hides for tax, divided amongst constituent hundreds, then amongst individual villages. *Inquisitiones Geldi,* for south-western counties, similarly.

Domesday Book

William I intended to discover number of hides in each shire, how much land and livestock he possessed, and amount of

years. They are rightly still seen as the aggressive edge of Norman expansion; men were still arriving from Normandy well into Henry I's reign to settle and prosecute war on the Scottish and Welsh frontiers. But the magnates in general possessed a firm grasp of wider political issues and played a crucial part in sustaining the unity of England and Normandy; on several occasions – as in 1091, 1101, and most notably in 1153 – their refusal to support rival claimants in a fight to the finish was decisive in preserving political stability. In the Treaty of Winchester (1153) their influence determined that King Stephen's heirs should be disinherited and the Crown granted to Henry II. The magnates were at the centre of the political stage with, as always in the medieval period, their involvement usually directed into competition for royal favour and for local power. Before 1066, Earl Godwine and his sons became so strong territorially as to enable them to dominate the king; they fought the Confessor's wars for him, his attempt to exile them in 1051-52 was a disastrous failure, and in 1066 one of them, Harold, was able to make himself king. In the Norman period, Bishop Odo of Bayeux often governed England during the absences of his half-brother, the Conqueror, in Normandy, while during the early years of Stephen's reign Count Waleran of Meulan exercised considerable power over the king. It is clear that even under a strong ruler, as Henry I* undoubtedly was, and when the Court was the pre-eminent centre of patronage, the magnates in favour were permitted to acquire lands at the expense of neighbouring families. The messy politics of Stephen's reign, with numerous local acts of violence and treaties between rival lords, reveals the narrower range of magnate political action.

The Norman Conquest of England was, up to a point, simply the transfer of an already powerful monarchy into the hands of a man who announced consistently that he ruled as the Confessor's nominated heir. English institutions such as the writ*, the *Danegeld*, and the system whereby the coinage was regularly reminted, all unknown in pre-1066 Normandy, were therefore employed much as before. Domesday Book*, that great monument to Norman

annual dues owed. Also, who held land of him, how much land and livestock, and total value. Questions to be answered for day Confessor died, day William granted manor to new holder, and day of inquest. Investigators sent out on circuits, collecting information on oath from juries of shire and hundred representatives. Information then rearranged to reflect feudal structure of landholding. Two volumes: Great Domesday covering most of England (north and north-west excluded), Little Domesday covering Essex, Suffolk and Norfolk; latter more detailed, probably reflecting intermediate stage of presentation. Satellite surveys relating to particular areas or lands of particular ecclesiastical tenants.

Land Pleas
1071-75 and 1080 onwards inquiry concerning losses of land and jurisdiction suffered by Ely abbey since 1066. Heard before great assemblies of barons, abbots, bishops and sheriffs. Anglo-Saxon charters produced as evidence of encroachment. Issue not resolved by 1086. Similar enquiry 1072 concerning accusation by Lanfranc that Bishop Odo of Bayeux had encroached on estates of archiepiscopal see. Shire court examined earlier Anglo-Saxon practice. Clumsiness of such procedures encouraged introduction of juries.

See **Feudalism** (page 87)

Military quotas
Norman system independent of earlier Anglo-Saxon obligations, where groups of hides provided one man for *fyrd*. Norman quotas unrelated to hidage, largely arbitrary imposition. Military quotas imposed on Church lands by 1070s. Increasing burden: by end of Henry I's reign tenants-in-chief obliged to perform military service on demand, as condition of tenure. Increasingly, service commuted to money payment for hiring of mercenaries, though duty to guard lord's castle performed in person. Feudal levy called out to defend realm (e.g. against Scots).

Norman Church
Few English abbots or bishops by 1086. William in no hurry to reform. 1070 Council at Winchester presided over by papal legate, deposed Archbishop Stigand, appointed Lanfranc. A realist, Lanfranc accepted papal supremacy in theory, its limitations in practice. Found Church healthy, although Stigand notorious for pluralism and simony. Bishoprics reorganized, relations between Canterbury and York clarified; parish priests secured

thoroughness, compiled in 1086-87 so that William might know better the resources of his new kingdom, is now known to have relied greatly for the collection of information on pre-1066 taxation assessment lists and on the long-established courts of shire and hundred. The over-statement of the *Anglo-Saxon Chronicle* is, however, a potent reminder that the Normans were conquerors: "there was no single hide nor a yard of land nor indeed (shame it is to relate it but it seemed no shame to him to do) was one ox or cow or pig left out". The obvious indications of Norman power are fortifications of a new type, ranging from the king's own White Tower of London to the many mottes and enclosures which can still be traced on the English countryside, and churches of vast dimensions, of which Durham, Norwich and Peterborough provide splendid surviving examples. The division of lands among the new aristocracy must have been supported by a complex organization, aspects of which can be seen in the great land pleas* conducted in William's reign. The Norman lords' acquisition of their lands was followed by the granting of fiefs* to vassals and by agreements between the lords and the king to provide quotas of knights* to serve him. Even if quotas did previously exist, those specifically negotiated between the new king and his magnates can have had little basis in pre-1066 England. The Norman Conquest established a new kind of tenurial relationship between king and magnates, as well as a structure of land-holding within the dominant military class which differed significantly from that of Anglo-Saxon England by placing greater emphasis on the territorial integrity of the fief. The Church* too was taken over by Normans; the frequent meetings of councils under the presidency of Archbishop Lanfranc of Canterbury (1070-89) gave a central direction unknown since the tenth-century reform of Dunstan, Aethelwold, and Oswald.

Under William Rufus and Henry I government became increasingly specialized and centralized. These two kings, both forceful characters, operated in a similar way, although it is only in Henry's much longer reign that the administrative developments can be fully perceived. From *c.* 1109, when it is first mentioned, the Exchequer* and its accounting methods are solidly

from interference by lay patrons; celibacy enforced; monasteries received new inmates and endowments. Anselm quarrelled with William Rufus over Church reform, and took hard line with Henry over lay investiture.

Exchequer
Treasury (*thesaurum regis*) at Winchester mentioned in Confessor's reign. First reference to *scaccarium* in royal writ of Henry I. *Scaccarium* (literally chequered cloth used for accounting) probably developed at Laon under Adelard of Bath. Earliest surviving Pipe Roll, 31 Henry I (1130), shows annual account of payments of farm from the shire, together with annual or extraordinary disbursements from royal revenues, for which sheriff was responsible. Also developed judicial function: Barons of the Exchequer presided over by Justiciar. At first an occasion rather than a place; became established at Westminster under Henry II.

The opening folio of Great Domesday *(1086).*

established in Winchester at the centre of financial administration. Its control was in the hands of a small group of officials, already termed "barons of the exchequer", whose prime *raison d'être* was the conduct of government. Under William Rufus, Ranulf Flambard stands out as the chief organizer; under Henry, it is Bishop Roger of Salisbury*. In general, this is not a period of innovation, but of intensification – the Exchequer, for example, despite its apparent newness, evolved from the Treasury and oversaw the collection of the same kinds of revenue. Henry's reign does appear to have been a period of great expansion in the scope of royal justice*, with a proliferation of itinerant and local justices under the supervision of the Exchequer staff. To judge by the evidence of the surviving royal writs, much larger in total than for previous reigns, much judicial business concerned tenurial disputes between lords and vassals. This, in essence the grafting on to the public courts of shire and hundred of a supervision of the jurisdiction of feudal lords over their vassals, anticipates the systematic procedures which emerged under the Angevins.

Scotland also developed a more centralized monarchy during this period. The reign of King David I (1124-53) is important not only as a time when a Scottish king was able effectively to advance his power southwards, but for the introduction of institutions such as a household, a coinage, castles, feudal tenures, and sheriffs on the Anglo-Norman pattern. Wales remained much more fragmented. The domination over all Wales established by Gruffudd ap Llywelyn (1039-63) crumbled after his death, and Wales remained a land of small principalities despite the achievements of princes such as Rhys ap Tewdwr at the end of the eleventh century and Gruffudd ap Cynan in the early twelfth. As for England, the great earldoms of late Anglo-Saxon England and the dismantling of the Exchequer and devolution of local authority to territorial earls in Stephen's reign suggest that the English kingdom still possessed the potential for alternative, and much less centralized, political solutions. But the Norman period was one in which the predominant trend was towards an ever closer connection between central and local institutions which was to have long-enduring consequences. Political circumstances, the need to maintain a large cross-Channel realm, pushed the kings towards a more efficient exploitation of available resources and towards firmer overall control; the same conditions by and large influenced the magnates to accept this pattern. The whole development drew deeply on the institutions which had evolved in England during the tenth and eleventh centuries. Wales and Scotland retained both individuality and independence, despite some Norman settlement and sporadic military interventions. Both felt the shock waves generated by the Norman victory in 1066 and its aftermath.

Justiciar

In reigns of William II and Henry I "justiciar" simply meant one who dispensed justice. Not recorded by name until Henry II's reign, when position formalized as chief judicial authority in the Exchequer. Position of Bishop Roger of Salisbury more stable under Henry I than had been Odo's or Flambard's: described in contemporary sources as *procurator* or *provisor;* surrogate for king in his absences abroad, a problem inherent in governing joint realm. Long association with Exchequer basis of Roger's control over government: writs issued in his name and by his authority. Dismissed 1139 by Stephen, not replaced.

Royal justice

Scope expanded 11th and 12th centuries. Shire and hundred courts remained, lords' feudal courts added. William I reorganized ecclesiastical courts, bishop hearing cases according to canon law. In William II's and Henry I's reigns local justices appointed in shires to hear cases referred to them by king. Itinerant justices (justices in eyre) also appointed, with supra-regional authority. 1130 Pipe Roll shows accounts rendered for pleas heard by itinerant justices. Penalties collected by sheriffs, whose judicial functions declined. Itinerant justices functioned beside local justices, who frequently came to be appointed from lay and ecclesiastical aristocracy in Stephen's reign.

Writ issued by William I to the citizens of London in 1067: in English, soon to fall out of official use, it begins: "Willm kyng gret Willm bisceop & Gosfregth portirefan [portreeve] & ealle the burhwaru [burghers] binnan Londone frencisce & englisce freondlice".

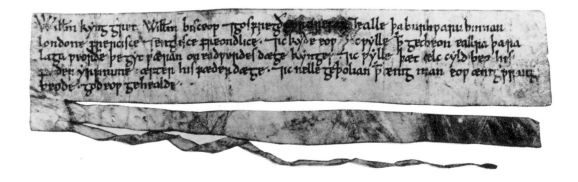

Warfare and International Relations:
warriors and missionaries

Nicholas Brooks

Gildas

De Excidio Britonum, "Ruin of Britain", written *c.* 540. Denunciation of moral and religious standards in post-Roman Britain, especially amongst kings of Wales and the south-west. Germanic invaders the tools of divine wrath. Describes long military struggle between British and Germanic invaders, originally invited to counter Picts and Scots. Much devastation, priests slaughtered. Britons reorganized under Ambrosius Aurelianus, and later won victory at *mons Badonicus* which led to some restoration of stability. Little or no chronology; place of writing not identified; many borrowings from Scripture.

Gododdin

Old Welsh poem attributed to Aneirin. Describes crushing defeat by Aethelfrith of Northumbria at Catraeth of British force from Edinburgh. 300 selected warriors from amongst Gododdin tribe and other British kingdoms including north Wales; led by Mynyddog the Wealthy, who had trained and feasted them for a year at his Court. Military equipment described vividly. Evocation of warrior ethic, particularly loyalty to leader and willingness to fight to the last man (only one returned).

Swords

Placed in aristocratic burials until 7th century. Viking swords found in rivers: objects in ceremonial or sacrificial rites. Literary sources emphasize value, important items of moveable wealth. In Ine's laws, mailcoat and sword worth 40 shillings. Son of Aethelred II bequeathed sword previously belonging to Offa to his brother. In 10th and 11th century, swords formed part of payment of *heriot* for aristocracy (payment to lord, often the king, to secure support for terms of a will).

In the Dark Ages, warfare made sweeping changes to the political map of Britain and Ireland and to the distribution of the various Germanic and Celtic peoples. Yet the military resources available to kings and princes appear to have been very slight. Thus it remains very uncertain whether the Anglo-Saxon settlement of lowland Britain was achieved by mass migrations and land takings, by warrior-peasant settlers or by the largely peaceful infiltration of family groups under the protection either of British rulers or of relatively small Anglo-Saxon war-bands. The British monk, Gildas*, paints a gory picture of the destructiveness of the warfare between Britons and Saxons, and later Irish, Welsh and English annalists and poets write of the great victories achieved by the ancestors of the rulers at whose Courts they served. But the earliest Anglo-Saxon leaders in southern Britain had war-bands that were carried in only two, three or five ships; and a British army of only three hundred warriors was so decisively defeated by the Northumbrian Angles under Aethelfrith at Catraeth (? Catterick) in about the year 600 that the powerful British kingdom of the Gododdin* thereafter disappears from recorded history. Moreover, pagan Anglo-Saxon graves show the spear and the shield to have been the only common implements of war; swords* were the valued possessions of a tiny aristocratic minority, whilst body-armour and helmets seem to be restricted to the graves of kings and princes.

Dark-Age warfare in Britain and Ireland was the regular, often annual, activity of kings and their small aristocratic retinues; it was the means by which they enriched themselves, either from booty and tribute – a powerful king needed to be a generous "ring-giver" to his followers – or from newly conquered lands. Success in battle enabled a king to attract an even larger following of ambitious warriors and this in turn made further victories possible. Hence the snowballing military careers of war-leaders of genius who founded kingdoms or became great overlords: such as Ceawlin of Wessex (565-92); Aethelfrith (593-616), Edwin (616-32) and Oswald (633-42) of Northumbria; Penda (d. 655), Aethelbald (716-56) and Offa of Mercia (757-96); Aidan mac Gabran (574-608) of the Scots of Dál Riáta, Oengus mac Fergus (729-61) of the Picts, or Donnchad mac Domnall (766-97) of the Uí Néill. But it is probably true that wars of conquest were more readily undertaken against peoples of different race who could either be driven out or enslaved, with clerical and lay approval, than against fellow Britons, Irishmen or Anglo-Saxons. It was for this reason that the petty kingdoms of Wales or the *tuatha* of Ireland survived intact, and that the English kingdoms which achieved dominance in the seventh and eighth centuries – Northumbria, Mercia, and Wessex – were those whose subjects had to remain on a permanent war footing to resist border raids and which could expand their frontiers at the expense of the Britons. It was probably for the same reason too that the tiny "Scottish" kingdom of Dál Riáta seems to have been able in the seventh century to call upon land or naval forces of more than a thousand men from all the households of the three *cenela* (clans) of the kingdom. The military organization of the Scottish kingdom* may help to explain how it came to take over the far larger and wealthier Pictish kingdom in the ninth century.

From the ninth to the mid-eleventh century the nature of warfare in both Britain and Ireland was transformed by the advent of Viking raiders* and settlers from Norway and Denmark. There was nothing novel about their

Military organization in early Scotland

Senchus fer nAlban provides two assessments of military strength of Scottish Dál Riáta, first probably mid-7th century, second *c.* 700. Within districts occupied by each clan, number of houses given and total number of men each clan could provide. Ratio different for each district: 1½-2½ men per house. Levy also for ship service: 20 houses provided crews of 14 oarsmen and 1 steersman for 2 boats, i.e. 1½ men per house. Second assessment, based on increased number of houses, reflects expansion of settlement.

Size of Viking armies

Subject of recent controversy. Previously considered to number hundreds, now thought more likely to be thousands. *Anglo-Saxon Chronicle* describes raiding parties in terms of ships, sometimes small precise figures, sometimes large round numbers. Latter probably represent "very many" and should not be interpreted literally. *Micel here,* "great army", which arrived in England 865, much larger, especially when augmented by "great summer army" 871. 9th-century ships probably carried about 30 men, reduced when they carried families or horses (as in 892). Late-10th-century armies larger and more organized; ships carried possibly 60 men.

Contemporary sources for raids

Inevitably contain some degree of bias, as Churchmen only literate class and Church property immediate and obvious target. Threat of aggressive paganism, including bloody sacrificial rituals. Traumatic shock of attack on Lindisfarne 793. Frankish sources especially graphic in describing devastation and slaughter. English sources, notably *Anglo-Saxon Chronicle,* omit such descriptions. Attacks on monasteries (Abingdon, Peterborough, Ely, etc) only recorded in later accounts, though charters mention disruption of agrarian life and difficulties caused by raising tribute.

Wallingford, Oxfordshire, seen from the air, showing the layout of a typical burh. *The line of the ramparts and the high street can be made out. In 1086, the north-east sector of the town was razed by the Normans for a "motte and bailey" castle.*

Vikings in Ireland

First Norwegian raids late 8th century. Coastal stronghold established at Dublin 836; others later at Limerick, Wexford, Waterford, Cork. Turgeis aspired to sovereignty of all Ireland, but captured and drowned 845. From 860s Irish Norse intervened in England, especially in the north: 920-50 attempts to create joint kingdom of Dublin and York, ending with return of Olaf Sihtricson to Ireland 952. From late 9th century Vikings increasingly restricted to coastal strongholds. Expelled from Dublin 902, returned 914. Late 10th century intermittent disputes between Olaf's sons and Brian Boru, who took Dublin 999 and was subsequently recognized as overlord of all Ireland. Brian killed at Battle of Clontarf 1014, but Vikings also lost heavily, effectively ending their supremacy in Dublin, though some Norwegian influence persisted.

Alfred's resistance

Some early successes bought time for military reforms and political manoeuvres. Victory at Edington 878 paved way for treaty, from which Danelaw emerged. Alliance with Mercia: Alfred's daughter married to *ealdorman* Aethelred. Construction of fortified *burhs* begun. Reorganization of army: nucleus of *thegns* and followers, less dependent on shire levies. Army divided in 893: garrisons in *burhs,* and of rest half on campaign, half at home, to ease pressure on economy. New tactics: Viking armies divided and besieged in strongholds until forced to negotiate; scorched earth policy to deprive them of sustenance. New ships built. Some problems: *burhs* not completed on time, ships ran aground.

Burhs ("boroughs")

Ring of defensive forts begun by Alfred, completed by Edward the Elder. Southern England broken into defensive units, everyone being within reach of refuge. Where older towns had Roman walls (Winchester, Exeter, Chichester etc), they were restored. Where not, earth and timber ramparts constructed (Wareham, Cricklade, Wallingford, Tamworth etc). London restored; new *burh* at Southwark. Some *burhs* purely fortresses, others quickly assumed economic significance and became important towns in 10th century. Winchester and other *burhs* laid out in rectilinear street-grids. Later Anglo-Saxon *burhs* characterized by market, mint and court. According to early-10th-century "Burghal Hidage", men from surrounding villages maintained and garrisoned walls, one from each hide.

weapons or their motives. The Vikings were organized in war-bands to enrich themselves by seizing treasure, cattle and slaves; and in time they also sought land to settle with the wealth that they had acquired. The Viking ships were the first truly ocean-worthy vessels in northern waters, and this gave to the Vikings the enormous tactical advantage of surprise. Since their ships could be rowed up any river with three feet or more of water, their mobility made it difficult for the native rulers to organize effective defence, and the victims of such sudden attacks soon became demoralized. From 840 in Ireland and from 851 in England, moreover, Viking activities became more ambitious; larger armies remained longer in the field, used Irish loughs as winter anchorages and fortified winter or permanent camps. But these developments made the Vikings more vulnerable to counter-attack both in Ireland* (where the camps at Dublin, Waterford, Wexford and Cork soon became trading centres) and in England.

The Danish "great armies" which came to England in 865 and 892 were probably the largest forces that western European rulers had had to face for several centuries; but once these armies had settled in East Anglia, eastern Mercia and southern Northumbria and had their own vested interests to protect, they lost their prime advantage of mobility. Thus Alfred of Wessex* and his descendants were able to make telling use of their inherent advantage of numbers. Fortified towns (*burhs**) were laid out and garrisoned, the army

This Viking "long ship", excavated at Gokstad in 1880, had oars for a crew of 32: its shallow draught enabled it to be rowed up rivers, while its sturdy clinker construction, sails and steering rudder made it sea-worthy in almost all weathers.

was reformed to be more mobile and to serve longer in the field, and an attempt was made to provide a fleet for coastal defence. By such methods Wessex survived the Viking storm, and Alfred's successors were able to conquer the kingdoms of the *Danelaw**, making themselves kings of all the English.

A second period of Viking raids, beginning in the last decade of the tenth century, continued until the Danish king, Cnut, assumed the English throne in 1016. These raids were a purely Danish phenomenon, directed by members of the Danish royal house with the aim of extracting·the wealth of England systematically. Their armies were better armed and trained, and they also had larger ships than their ninth-century predecessors. The costs of war for the English therefore increased, in part because of the massive payments of tribute *Danegeld* required to buy off the Danish armies and in part because of the military reforms which Aethelred II "the Unready" (979-1016) had to adopt: English *burhs* were re-fortified in stone, and English armies* were equipped for the first time with body-armour. These expensive developments made warfare even more the preserve of the landed nobility and widened the gulf between the noble and free classes in society.

The advent of the Normans deepened this gulf and revolutionized warfare in Britain. The battle of Hastings was a victory of heavily-armed cavalry over a dismounted force which fought on foot. Though the Bayeux Tapestry* shows that the English and Norman troops were very similarly armed and equipped, the Normans were the pre-eminent warriors of late-eleventh-century Europe because they experimented with couched lances, and adapted their stirrups and saddles to make the mounted knight an effective instrument of war. But we should not exaggerate the social effects of the introduction of knightly warfare to Britain by linking it with the introduction of "feudalism", for the land needed to support a knight was not significantly different from that required to support the similarly armed Anglo-Saxon *thegn**. More important was the Norman importation of the castle. Though there is now a little archaeological evidence that some English *thegns* protected their halls by fortification before the Conquest, contemporaries were in no doubt that the few castles erected by the Norman favourites of Edward the Confessor and the many built by Norman lords after 1066 were a much-resented innovation. Castles enabled the small Norman/French aristocracy to maintain its rule over the English majority; royal power depended upon the king's ability to restrict castle-building to his trusted barons. Already in the reign of William the Conqueror the most important castles were built of stone, but the vast majority of the 2,500 castles known to have been built in England, Wales and Scotland before 1200 were earthwork* and timber constructions, either of "motte and bailey" or of "ringwork" form. The castle therefore became the focus of warfare and the symbol of noble authority, both over the local peasantry and potentially against the Crown.

We do not know enough of the overseas contacts of early medieval rulers in Britain and Ireland to ascribe to any of them a "foreign policy". But this is not to deny the importance of international contacts and influences. The western Church was, of course, pre-eminently an international body. Tradition allows a small but significant papal and Gaulish contribution, besides that of Britons, to the conversion of the Irish to Christianity; more certainly the Anglo-Saxon Church based its organization upon the directions which Pope Gregory I sent to his missionary, Augustine*; subsequent English archbishops had

Danelaw
Term not used until Cnut's reign, but extensive Scandinavian settlement began 9th century. Northumbria divided amongst Viking army 876, parts of Mercia settled 877. Alfred's victory at Edington 878 was followed by treaty effectively partitioning England. East Anglia settled 880. Boundary from Chester, along Watling Street to River Lea and London. Extensive settlement north and east of this line by mixed Scandinavian groups well into 10th century. Military reconquest by Edward the Elder and Athelstan, but place-names, personal names, culture and legal institutions testify to considerable Scandinavian impact, surviving into 13th century.

Battle of Brunanburh 937
Site unidentified. Checked attempts by Scandinavian kings of Dublin to control York. Athelstan had captured York in 927 and expelled Irish Norse under Olaf Sihtricson. Kings of Scotland and Strathclyde and ruler of Bamburgh recognized his authority in Northumbria. Athelstan ravaged Scotland 934 with combined land and sea forces. In 937 kings of Scotland and Strathclyde and Olaf, now king of Dublin, formed coalition and invaded. Penetrated deep into England, met at Brunanburh by Athelstan with combined armies of Mercia and Wessex. Great victory for Athelstan, celebrated in contemporary vernacular poem. Olaf fled to Ireland, but returned 939 on Athelstan's death.

Battle of Maldon 991

Celebrated in epic verse. Scandinavian raids had resumed 980, intermittent attacks until 988. More determined onslaught 991, led by Olaf Tryggvasson, later king of Norway. Kent coast ravaged, parts of Suffolk and Essex overrun. Met by Brihtnoth, *ealdorman* of Essex since 956, and his forces at Maldon. An over-confident white-haired warrior, Brihtnoth conceded tactical advantage of superior ground and refused offer of truce in return for gold. Brihtnoth killed, his personal retinue fought valiantly to avenge him. Poem gives many details on equipment and structure of *fyrd*. Defeat followed by treaty between Aethelred II and Olaf, and first payment of *Danegeld*.

Late Anglo-Saxon army (fyrd)

Alfred's reforms made army more effective, but *ealdorman* still led shire levies, (e.g. Brihtnoth at Maldon). Nevertheless, nucleus was nobles and their personal retainers. Military obligations developed from land tenure. Charters had granted lands on condition military service was performed since 8th century, but obligations became more formal: 5 hides or 6 carucates provided one man. *Thegns* to perform military service in respect of tenure rather than personal loyalty to lord, possibly also from 5 hide units. From Aethelred II's reign, service increasingly commuted to money payment, for hiring of mercenaries. *Housecarls,* introduced by Scandinavian kings, fought to the last at Hastings.

See **Bayeux Tapestry** (page 87)

See **Gesith, thegn** (page 85)

Christian conversion

Mission, led by Augustine, arrived in Kent 597, representing evangelical zeal of Pope Gregory the Great. Conversion of Aethelbert and his aristocracy *c.* 600 paved way for expansion of missionary activity in south. Episcopal sees established at Canterbury, London, Rochester; first West Saxon see at Dorchester-on-Thames 635. Raedwald of East Anglia converted, though later lapsed. Paulinus travelled north *c.*625, allowed to preach in Northumbria: Edwin converted, some success but paganism difficult to eradicate and some areas not visited by time of Bede's death (735). Wilfrid's conversion of Sussex 681.

Detail of the Bayeux tapestry showing Norman cavalry attacking the English army, which fights on foot. It can be observed that the Norman knights adopt various methods of using their lances, that Norman and English equipment is very similar, and that the archer has no body-armour.

each to make contact with Rome, because they needed to wear a papal *pallium** if they were to exercise metropolitan authority legitimately. From the late-sixth century also, Irish monks* (above all, St Columbanus) travelled widely over Europe, and in the eighth century notable English churchmen like Boniface and Alcuin played a crucial role in reorganizing and instructing the Frankish Church. There were secular cross-Channel contacts too. English exiles, such as those escaping from the power of Offa of Mercia, found refuge at continental courts, and a few English rulers, like Aethelbert of Kent between *c.* 580 and 589 and Aethelwulf of Wessex in 856, took Frankish princesses as wives. Trade also brought international contacts: Mediterranean pottery of the fifth to the seventh centuries is found very widely on both secular and religious sites throughout the Celtic kingdoms.

The Viking incursions necessitated contacts with continental rulers who had to cope with the same threat. Alfred married his daughter to the count of Flanders, and a century later Aethelred the Unready married Emma of Normandy to close the Channel ports to Viking fleets. The fame of the English royal dynasty as war-leaders caused leading continental rulers and nobles in the early tenth century to seek the hands of English princesses in marriage. After the death of Cnut (1035), the English throne itself became the subject of an international struggle: the overseas claimants included the successors of Cnut in Denmark and Norway, the English descendants of Aethelred the Unready who had taken refuge in Hungary, and the dukes of Normandy, whose remote claim only became conceivable when it was clear that Emma's last surviving child, Edward the Confessor, was unlikely to produce an heir. William of Normandy's success in 1066 also owed something to his diplomatic preparations* – with the papacy, and with the counts of the Vexin, of Boulogne and of Flanders, who also had marriage and diplomatic ties with the English royal house. For much of William's reign, so long as Edgar the Aetheling could find support in Scotland and so long as Svein Estrithson (1047-76) and Cnut IV (1080-86) of Denmark remained alive, foreign invasion remained an imminent threat.

The Norman Conquest brought, or coincided with, other new forms of international contacts. In the century from 1050 to 1150 the papacy showed an entirely new determination to intervene in the affairs of the Church throughout Britain to promote reform and, above, all to end the practice (which the Norman kings had introduced) of "lay investiture"* of bishops. The rule of the Norman kings also embroiled England in the interminable complexities of Norman frontier disputes in France. Moreover, when Henry I's only legitimate heir was drowned in 1120, the succession to the English throne once more became the subject of struggle between foreign princes. The accession of Stephen, whose brother, Theobald, was count of Blois-Champagne, promised to make the house of Blois the dominant dynasty in northern Europe. In the event, Stephen's inability to consolidate his position in England or in Normandy opened the way for Geoffrey of Anjou, husband of Henry I's daughter Matilda, to overrun Normandy in 1144, and for their son Henry to establish the Angevin claim to the English throne a decade later.

Pallium

Symbol of metropolitan authority, conferred by pope. Circular band of white wool with two hanging strips and 6 purple crosses, worn on shoulders. Delegated papal authority, without which archbishop could not perform duties. Gregory the Great inaugurated practice, *pallium* previously mark of imperial favour. 7th to 9th centuries *pallia* generally sent from Rome. 925-1066, 9 of 14 archbishops of Canterbury received them in person. In Cnut's reign custom developed that archbishops of York should also travel to Rome. Missions assumed political significance; closer papal control over English Church.

Celtic Christianity

Established in Ireland by St Patrick in 5th century, spread to northern Britain 6th century. St Columba founded monastery on Iona 563. Picts converted (?). Monastic communities, with remote cells where hermits lived ascetic life; importance of learning. Inspired by desert hermits of Egypt and Syria. Welsh saints converted much of country 5th and 6th centuries. Synod of Whitby 664 triumph of Roman over Irish Christianity. Major issue the method of calculating date of Easter, though behind this were fundamental questions of Church organization, especially roles of bishops and abbots. Personal achievement for Wilfrid and King Oswy. Some reactionaries returned to Ireland. Welsh Church submitted to authority of Rome 768.

Paganism

Remarkably resilient: backlash in Kent after Aethelbert's death. Pope Gregory had ordered Augustine to destroy idols and temples, but more pragmatic approach adopted: pagan ceremonies and sacred places adapted for Christian worship. Place-names sometimes reflect pagan worship. Folk medicine and superstition preserved many beliefs. Late laws repeatedly forbid pagan practices.

English missionaries

Wilfrid preached in Frisia 678-9. More organized missions followed. Willibrord arrived Frisia 690, consecrated archbishop of Frisians 695. Willibrord a monk, like 8th-century missionaries Wynfrith (Boniface), Lull and others. Boniface, from Wessex, visited Frisia 716, returned there 718 and remained on Continent until death 754; archbishop of German Church 732. Saxon peoples conquered by Franks converted, churches and monasteries founded, at first with English monks and nuns. Close contacts with papacy and

English Church. Requests for religious books to be sent from England. Boniface assisted in reforming Frankish Church. Late 10th - early 11th-century English missions in Norway, Denmark and Sweden.

Pilgrimage

Fundamental in Irish Christianity. Bede's interest in Holy Places. Early royal pilgrims: West Saxon kings Caedwalla 689 and Ine 726 went to Rome, and died there having renounced earthly life. 709 Cenred of Mercia and Offa of East Saxons also, founded *schola Saxonum:* hostel for English pilgrims. Large numbers of English pilgrims 8th century, of all ranks according to Bede. Boniface complained northern Italy full of English women forced into prostitution through lack of money. Pilgrimages continued into 9th century, despite Vikings. Aethelwulf's pilgrimage to Rome 855-56. Burgred of Mercia retired there 874. Cnut's visit to Rome 1027 partly as pilgrim. Large numbers of English in Rome in late Anglo-Saxon period.

William's diplomacy

Norman sources defend his legitimate claim to throne through Confessor's designation, confirmed by Harold 1064 or 5. But expulsion of many Normans from England 1052 and support for House of Godwine necessitated military conquest. Right climate for calculated risk 1066: William's alliance with Baldwin of Flanders, reinforced by marriage to Baldwin's daughter; 1060-67 William guardian of young French king Philip I; death of Geoffrey of Anjou 1060 removed another opponent. Papal approval gained. Support of feudal vassals acquired in great assemblies. Lands and booty inducements, especially to younger sons denied prospects of inheritance by new family customs. Mercenaries recruited from France, Flanders, Maine, Brittany, etc.

Lay investiture

Attempt by secular rulers to control ecclesiastical appointments by investing bishops or abbots with symbols of their authority (ring and crozier in case of bishop), and to receive homage prior to consecration. Condemned by papacy from mid-11th century; principal antagonist German emperor. Practice introduced into England by Normans. St Anselm refused to pay homage to Henry I in 1100. Council of London confirmed compromise 1107: Henry could receive homage and invest bishops with their temporal possessions before consecration, but could not interfere in elections. Wider issue settled by Concordat of Worms 1122, reiterated at Second Lateran Council 1123.

Aerial view (top) *of Pleshey, Essex, showing the Norman motte and bailey with adjacent settlement. The reconstruction drawing* (above) *suggests the appearance of a motte and bailey.*

Economy:
farming, trade and manufacture
Martin Biddle

By the eleventh century, Anglo-Saxon England was a rich country and her people were better fed and taller on average than for many centuries to come. In this England provided a sharp contrast with the rest of Britain, which remained essentially unaffected by the growth of North Sea and Channel trade until the twelfth century.

Coins* provide the clearest evidence for the absolute and relative wealth of Anglo-Saxon England. They had ceased to be used in Britain early in the fifth century, but re-appeared in the mid-seventh, first as gold *thrymsas* and later as silver *sceattas*, the output of which may have reached two to three million coins. True pennies were first issued in quantity by Offa (757-96), and by the reign of Aethelred II (979-1016) as many as forty million coins might be issued in a single type. The quantity and sophisticated management of the coinage reveals the wealth of England by comparison with the rest of Britain and the nearer parts of the contemporary Continent, and shows why England was so attractive a target for the renewed Viking raids of the later tenth century. During the period 991 to 1018 at least £240,500 was paid in tribute to the Vikings, but the amount of silver in circulation was not seriously decreased by the removal of many of these fifty-eight million pennies.

Where did this silver come from and what was the source of England's wealth? Since there is no evidence that silver was mined in Anglo-Saxon England, it could have come only from accumulated stocks or from abroad. The latter seems more likely, because there is clear evidence from the seventh century for the association of coins and coining with the coastal and riverine trading places. At least one such trading place appears in each of the major kingdoms* from the seventh century onwards: Southampton in Wessex; Fordwich, Sarre, Dover and perhaps Sandwich in Kent; London for Kent, Essex and later for Mercia; Ipswich in East Anglia; and York in Northumbria. But there was no comparable development in western Britain and Scotland until the twelfth century, apart from the Viking trading places in Ireland.

A place like Anglo-Saxon Southampton was large (72 acres), densely occupied and laid out from the start with a regular arrangement of streets which were maintained throughout the life of the settlement (*c*.720-*c*.860). Metals, wood, bone and antler were worked, coins were minted, pottery was made and textiles were woven. Imported finds show contacts inland with Mercia and far across the Channel: glassware, pottery and lava millstones from Germany and pottery from many parts of France, with the implication that perishable luxury consumables were imported alongside them. The intensity of the commercial activity is expressed in the extraordinary concentration of coins found: 185 *sceattas* and 113 pennies up to 1984.

Anglo-Saxon Southampton was a *mercimonia*, a "mercantile place". Bede described London as an *emporium* of many peoples coming by land and sea, and Alcuin echoed his words in writing of York. After 880 there was a rapid

Early coins
Late Roman coins and imitative local copies disappearing by 430s. Gold hoarded. Coins now found in rich burials had been minted on Continent. Gold *thrymsas* minted in England from *c*. 640. Several mints in south-east, including London; York also. Some copied from Roman, others from Merovingian models; no identifiable royal styles. By 670s replaced by silver *sceattas*: minting and circulation limited to south and south-east, and Northumbria, where quality deteriorated rapidly, replaced 9th century by copper *stycas* and ringed pellets. Elsewhere, *sceattas* continued until mid-8th century, when replaced by pennies struck from flans stamped out from sheets. Generally obverse bore name of king, reverse location of mint or name of moneyer (later both).

Royal control of trade
Attempts to restrict trade to towns, where king's *reeves* witnessed transactions. 7th-century laws required Kentish men in London to conduct trade before witnesses. Certain grants of privileges to foreign traders or favoured recipients, e.g. Aethelbald of Mercia exempted some ships belonging to favoured bishops or monasteries from dues levied by tax-gatherers at London and Sarre. Control of minting an important prerogative. Edward the Elder and Athelstan tried increasingly to restrict trade to burhs. 10th-century husting in London to regulate trade; continued to meet post-Conquest.

Winchester
Increasingly important from mid-9th century. An Alfredian *burh*. Royal and episcopal complex in south-east corner from 7th century. Alfred's queen, Ealhswith, initiated plans for Nunnaminster, completed in Edward the Elder's reign. Edward also founded New Minster. New street-grid, probably from Alfred's reign: ignored Roman plan which had been obliterated (several pre-Conquest streets discovered in recent excavations); apportioned land for development and settlement. Provision for use as refuge – walls restored. First coins with Winchester

name struck late Alfred's reign, though perhaps coins struck there intermittently earlier. Complex land market and tenurial system developed by late 10th century, reflecting royal encouragement for urban economic growth.

Feorm (food rent)

Earliest form of royal dues, arising from itinerant nature of early kingship; kings travelled kingdom with their retinues, maintained by hospitality of subjects. Domesday *firma unius noctis*, "one night's farm", measure of later tax equivalent – provisions necessary to support king and his retinue for 24 hours. As form of taxation initially paid in kind by free peasantry at royal estate, collected by king's *reeve*. Later increasingly commuted into annual money payment, sheriff responsible for collection. Could be granted away with lands by charter. Remained important form of royal taxation post-Conquest, sheriffs accounting for the "farm of the shire" at Exchequer.

Church dues

Soul-scot was payment to parish priest from property of deceased for welfare of soul: in effect, payment for burial. Possibly originated in pagan custom. Soul-scot of nobility greatly desired. *Church-scot* food-rent for supporting parish priests; early income for clergy, paid by free men according to their holdings, rendered in grain and hens. Later less important as tithe became universal. Tithe of uncertain origin. Initially voluntary grant of tenth of goods or produce for benefit of church, poor or pilgrims. Collection made compulsory in Edgar's reign, paid to minster churches, though churches under lay patronage could receive one third. Receipt restricted to churches on *bookland*. Post-Conquest, lords could use tithe from demesne lands to endow or support monasteries. Collectively, church dues heavy burden on peasantry.

Silver pennies of Aethelred: the "Hand of Providence" c. 979-85 (left, below) and the "Long Cross" c. 997-1003 (right, below).

expansion in the number of towns, from perhaps ten to about fifty by 930, to perhaps seventy by 1000, and by the time of the Conquest more than a hundred places had some claim to be regarded as urban. The amount of coin in circulation may have increased by about the same ten-fold ratio over the same period, yet the fuel which created and sustained this growth is nowhere explicitly identified.

The towns were, however, very small by modern standards. The largest covered 100 to 150 acres and their population can rarely have exceeded 5000. London may have had as many as 20,000 inhabitants by the eleventh century, Winchester perhaps 10,000, but most urban places will have had only 2000 to 3000 inhabitants. Moreover, growth in the urban population does not necessarily imply an increase in the population as a whole: it could be accounted for by a small move from the country to the town. As for the overall size of the population, the latest appreciations of the density of rural settlement patterns suggest that the population of middle to later Anglo-Saxon England has been seriously underestimated and is likely to have been much higher than previous estimates of about two million at the time of Domesday.

Winchester*, for example, had been refounded in the late ninth century and by the mid-twelfth had well over 5000 and perhaps nearer 10,000 inhabitants. It was probably no smaller a century earlier. Its market in urban land was complex and long-established. The trades and industries of the city were highly diversified and conducted in clearly defined areas reflected in such names as Shieldmaker Street and Fleshmonger Street. Local needs were catered for by merchants, metal workers, cloth workers, leather workers, building workers, butchers, brewers and a wide range of other victualling and service trades. Overseas contacts reached throughout western Europe to the Mediterranean and the Byzantine empire, even if not so far as those of Lincoln, which stretched on through the Levant to China. The wealth of Winchester is seen most clearly in its rank as the fourth most-productive mint of late Saxon and Norman England, after London, York and Lincoln, but the source of this wealth is no more clearly identifiable than it is for the country as a whole.

Like the rest of Britain, Anglo-Saxon England was essentially an agrarian society: by the eleventh century only one-tenth of the population seem to have lived in towns. Even if this is an underestimate, English production was overwhelmingly agricultural. Both documentary and archaeological evidence suggest, moreover, that the landscape of late Saxon England was well populated and systematically exploited* and had been since at least the seventh or eighth century. Pollen analysis suggests that there had been no major ecological changes in the post-Roman centuries and no significant increase in the amount of arable land. This picture fits the evidence of the "new topography",

which indicates that Anglo-Saxon exploitation of the land was based on a framework of estates and fields taken over in functioning order from Roman Britain* and gradually modified, rather than on a re-organization and re-colonization of an abandoned wasteland.

The introduction of the heavy wheeled plough allowed fields* to be ploughed in one direction only and thus encouraged the adoption of strip fields. Although long fields and heavy ploughs can be found in the Roman period, the normal tool was the beam ard, which involved cross-ploughing and implied square fields. Until the ninth century the normal Anglo-Saxon plough seems to have been the ard; the heavy wheeled plough and the strip field appear to be developments of the late Saxon period.

The principal crops were six-row barley and bread wheat, the former especially for brewing. Oats were grown for fodder rather than human consumption but rye was not a significant crop. Orchard and garden husbandry and the collection of edible wild foods played a small but significant role. There were considerable regional and chronological variations: for example, hulled wheat *(Triticum spelta)* seems to have given way to naked bread wheat *(Triticum aestivum),* which was more adaptable and produced better flour. Such a change may suggest the use of heavier soils and intensified crop management, and may correlate with the use of the heavy plough. These developments may reflect the need to provision the increasing (and agriculturally non-productive) urban population.

Study of animal bones recovered from urban settlements shows that beef cattle made the principal meat contribution to the diet, with pig providing perhaps only one sixth the amount of meat by weight. At both urban and rural sites, sheep constitute between one-quarter and half of the bone fragments of the three main domestic species. There is much variation between sites and regions, but at Anglo-Saxon Southampton the sheep were relatively large and were usually killed between 2½ and 3½ years old: domestic birds and wild fauna made only a small contribution to the diet.

This pattern allows two main conclusions. First, Anglo-Saxon husbandry was successful in meeting the challenge of victualling the new towns which emerged from the seventh century onwards, and was able to do so with continuing success as the number of towns increased ten-fold. The degree of this achievement can be measured in the bones of the human urban populations. At Winchester the Anglo-Saxon population was both healthier and on average taller than the population of the later medieval city. At Southampton the human remains suggest a remarkably well-fed population, the beef, bread and beer of whose diet has been revealed by study of animal bones and seeds.

Second, sheep were kept for wool production* on a scale (both in town and perhaps even more in the country) which far exceeded contemporary continental practice. This is the first hard evidence for what has long been suspected: that Anglo-Saxon England, like Roman Britain and later medieval England, was a substantial producer of wool and that it was upon the export of wool that the wealth of England was based. On this view the silver whose quantity is reflected in the surviving coins was obtained from foreign merchants. The extent to which this trade was yet in English hands and carried in English hulls, and the degree to which before the twelfth century woven cloth rather than wool formed a significant item of export, are still unknown, but we can see that this economy was firmly based on rural resources which had been fully exploited without significant interruption since the Roman period.

Settlement continuity

Slow process of infiltration and settlement, with continuity in many areas. Settlements established in and around Roman towns and villas, sometimes respecting earlier landholding units. Roman roads and trackways survived. London avoided by Saxon settlements, may have survived behind its defences. Continuous occupation in Canterbury. Apparent choice of "secondary" sites suggests density of existing population. Well-excavated sites of this nature West Stow (Suffolk), Chalton Down (Hants.) Mucking (Essex). Some documentary evidence of continuity of early land boundaries in Wessex.

Field systems

"Celtic" field system characterized by small settlements with rectangular fields laid out in parallel groups. Some continuity after Anglo-Saxon settlement: where, e.g., villas ceased to be economic units, associated fields possibly cultivated in old manner. Now recognized that "open" fields, with communal strip holdings concentrated on nucleated settlement including manor house and church, were a later pre-Conquest development. Complex process of settlement expansion and tenurial reorganization in Anglo-Saxon period: climatic change, land reclamation, fragmentation of lordship, Scandinavian settlement, new techniques and other factors produced diverse agrarian picture.

Wool and textiles

English woollen cloaks a source of dispute between Offa and Charlemagne. 8th-century sources mention export of textiles, including multi-coloured fabrics. Arab sources 9th-11th century allude to fame of English cloth. Trade largely in hands of Frisian merchants. By 1000 toll-records show German merchants buying raw wool in London. Domesday records flocks of over 500 sheep in East Anglia. Increasing demand for English wool in Flanders. By mid-12th century German and Flemish merchants had formed London association (*Hanse*) and toured countryside for supplies of raw wool.

Society:
warriors and dependants

Patrick Wormald

Modern perceptions of society in the early historic British Isles have, like those of prehistoric society, moved away from the "invasion hypothesis". We no longer assume that Anglo-Saxon, Danish and Norman invaders imposed their own ready-made and contrasting social structure on previous inhabitants. Much more is made of patterns of continuity from pre-Roman through to post-Norman Britain; the changes that unquestionably came are ascribed to social and economic forces rather than intervening "racial" cultures. A corollary is that we are increasingly aware of the similarities and parallels between the various societies involved, all of whom ultimately shared in the more or less traumatic experience of "Normanization". This makes it both possible and profitable to consider the social history of Britain and Ireland, "Germans" and "Celts", in the early Middle Ages, as a whole.

But it must first be said that the traditional impression of contrast is soundly based in so far as English, Welsh, Scottish and Irish society has left us with evidence that differs markedly, both in quantity and quality: almost all that the material has in common is its inadequacy, when it comes to reconstructing a realistic social pattern. The only source that reflects British society as anything like it was in the whole period is Domesday Book* (1086), King William the Conqueror's great survey of England south of the Tees and the Ribble; even Domesday was a government-sponsored enquiry which limited itself to social arrangements that were somehow relevant financially to the king and the great lords. Otherwise, early English society must largely be viewed through the law-codes of Anglo-Saxon kings, from that of King Aethelbert of Kent (597-616) to that of King Cnut (1018-23). Any legal source may be suspected of describing society as it should have been rather than as it was, and the Anglo-Saxon codes are far from comprehensive in the topics they cover. For Celtic societies the evidence is almost exclusively legal, and it poses

British survival
Romano-British population and institutions more durable than previously assumed. Gildas evidence for long period of warfare 5th and 6th centuries. Some British successes: *mons Badonicus* perhaps Badbury Rings, Dorset. Archaeology suggests some interruption in Germanic settlement. Wansdyke possibly built by British in 5th century to halt expansion, suggesting considerable resources. Dumnonia survived into 8th century, Cornwall not subdued until 9th. In north, British kingdoms survived for some time: Elmet into 7th century, Strathclyde until 11th. Considerable cultural continuity in Northumbria.

Late Anglo-Saxon settlement
Few excavated sites. Of these several unrepresentative, since they were abandoned in Middle Ages. Some shift in settlement in late Anglo-Saxon period, often from marginal hill-top to valley sites (e.g. Chalton, Hants.); climatic change chief reason. Expansion in Lincolnshire as fens reclaimed; increasing numbers of parishes an indicator. Many settlements not recorded in Domesday Book, especially if appurtenances of larger settlements or constituents of multiple estates. No Domesday or charter evidence for parts of the north. Unlikely that nucleated villages, characteristic of late Middle Ages, had evolved by 11th century. Loose groups of individual settlements.

Domesday Book as evidence for settlement
Survey stressed fiscal potential rather than social and economic structure. Great and Little Domesday not equally useful: latter implies greater population in East Anglia, but probably more edited Great Domesday underestimates elsewhere. Detailed records of boroughs in Little Domesday, elsewhere haphazardly described. London and Winchester omitted. Cumbria, Durham and Northumberland not covered. Variations in methods adopted in each circuit by inquisitors. Inadequacies and inconsistencies in rearranging information collected from system of shires, hundreds and vills according to Norman manorial stereotypes.

Manor
Usual term, as defined in Domesday, for post-Conquest units of landholding, though its essential elements existed previously. Archetypal manor divided between lord's demesne, exploited directly and worked by villeins, and land worked by tenants who owed rent and labour services depending on status of tenure and degree of personal freedom. Lords possessed jurisdiction over tenants, exercised in manorial courts, and wide powers over villeins. Manorial officials exploited lord's demesne with increasing efficiency from 12th century. Considerable variation in size, structure and extent of manorial concentration persisted.

a bewildering variety of problems. The Picts left no laws at all. There is a short, possibly tenth-century, statement of Scottish* custom, which has been succinctly described as "little more than a valuation roll of society". The laws of early medieval Wales* purport to have been issued by King Hywel Dda in the mid-tenth century, but they survive only in later medieval texts which can bear little relation to whatever Hywel originally decreed. Finally, the massive corpus of early Irish* law was certainly written down by the early-eighth century, the probable date of the codification of much of it in the *Senchas Mar* ("Great Tradition"). But this is the work of professional jurists rather than royal politicians and administrators, and lawyers' law is especially inclined to construct elaborate and artificial social schemes; moreover the *raison d'être* of the early Irish learned classes was the preservation of the past, and their law-tracts are so conservative that they say more about the prehistoric roots than the historical development of Irish society. It is necessary to emphasize the limitations of the evidence available because it warns us that common sense and imagination may be as valuable as mere scholarship in its interpretation, and that we may be wise to dwell on general patterns rather than specific details.

For this reason, it may be best to begin with a different, if equally problematic, class of evidence, the secular literature in the vernacular of both Anglo-Saxon and Celtic societies. The Anglo-Saxon heroic epic, *Beowulf**, probably though not certainly composed 675-875, is about a class of young warrior noblemen, who are normally described as *eorlas* ("earls"). They are feasted by their lord the king in his hall, and endowed by him with spectacular treasures, especially sophisticated and expensive weapons; ultimately, they are given land of their own. In return, they are pledged to follow their lord in battle to the point of death, and if necessary to avenge his slaying; they owe the same duty to their kinsmen. The possibility that this was the world of the poem's audience as well as of its heroes is confirmed, in part, by historical sources, beginning with the famous account of the lord's *comitatus* in the *Germania* of Tacitus (c. 100 AD); but still more by the evidence of archaeology. Elaborate weaponry is found in Anglo-Saxon graves, but with a rarity which suggests that only a rich and privileged class possessed it; and the great ship burial at Sutton Hoo* in Suffolk, deposited c. 625, has many echoes of *Beowulf*, from the fact that the Sutton Hoo helmet almost seems to be described in the poem to the common atmosphere which they share: the potentate buried at Sutton Hoo was certainly the master of great treasures. Similarly, Caesar's account of Celtic society in Gaul before the Roman conquest closely parallels that of Tacitus on the Germans; the arguably sixth-century Welsh poems of Aneirin* and Taliesin express a warrior ethic very like that of *Beowulf*; though the special relationship of lord and man is not so much stressed by Irish sagas, their accounts of lavish Court life and of conflict both tragic and sanguinary are even more fevered; and though the Picts left as little literature as laws, the stone at Aberlemno depicts their heavily-armed mounted warriors and the carnage which they wrought. There are reasons, then, for thinking that society was dominated by a military aristocracy throughout the British Isles in the early Middle Ages, and the legal evidence should probably be read in this light.

One thing that emerges from Celtic and Anglo-Saxon law alike is a carefully graded hierarchy of social status, defined by the different sums payable as compensation for killing a man of each class (in Anglo-Saxon,

Scots law

Late 10th-early 11th-century treatise on status "among the Bretts [i.e. Britons] and Scots". Relative *cro* and *galnes* (equivalent to *wergeld*) established for each rank in society – king, king's son, earl, earl's son, thane, thane's son, thane's grandson, freeman, carl. *Cro* of thane 100 cows: payments for other ranks fractions or multiples of this value; each rank had *cro* equivalent to that of son of next rank (earl's equal to that to king's son, for example). Differing grades of freeman, determined by area of land on which he grazed cattle. Importance of kin group in paying and collecting *cro* and *galnes*, though laws tell nothing of machinery by which this was done. Local customary law handed down orally by *brehon*, wise man.

Welsh law

More "advanced" than Irish law, some influence from English codes. Hywel's admiration for Alfred and Athelstan. Oriented towards king and Court, with adaptations for local circumstances. Important role of *cenedl* (kindred) in determining inheritance and regulating *galanas* (blood-feud). System of compensation used, similar to *wergeld*, with payment in cows. Compensation for lesser injuries. Role and status of bards defined.

Irish law

Many ancient treatises devoted to particular subjects, probably composed initially in verse, transmitted orally by *filid* (secular learned men). Unaffected by Roman juristic concepts. Reflected fragmented agrarian society: free society divided into warrior/landed aristocracy, bards, jurists etc, and freemen. Each had defined rights and obligations according to customary law. Very little about slaves. *Fine*, kindred group, responsible for activities of individual. Parties to disputes bound by verdict of *brithemain*, jurists. Compensation for murder and other injury by payment of "honour price", assessed in cows.

See **Beowulf** (page 88)

Sutton Hoo

Probably most important archaeological discovery from Anglo-Saxon period. Royal ship burial, possibly with Swedish connections. Found amongst group of 16 burial mounds near Woodbridge, Suffolk. Ship burials implied in *Beowulf*. Vessel itself 80 feet long, 40 oars. Grave goods included military equipment, rich jewellery and fine possessions, many from Continent or East. Byzantine silver spoons and dishes, east European silver bowls, Merovingian gold coins. No personal effects or remains of body: either not buried there or decomposed without trace. Uncertain whether pagan or Christian burial. Usually associated with Raedwald of East Anglia (d. 625), though coin evidence problematic. Other important aristocratic burials (e.g. Taplow) and boat burials (e.g. Snape) less lavish.

Aneirin, Taliesin

Taliesin Court poet of Urien, king of Rheged. His verse suggests little difference between warrior-aristocracies of British kingdoms and Northumbria. Depicts ferocious battles between rival British leaders. Urien praised as warrior and also as protector of wider community for which he was responsible. British military leaders generous benefactors, poet himself rewarded with spoils from his patrons' campaigns. Rivalry amongst kings to be heralded by bards as greatest warrior. In *Gododdin* Aneirin repeatedly emphasized reciprocal nature of relationship between chieftain and warrior, symbolized by earning of mead which warriors received at lord's hall.

This sumptuously decorated sword-pommel, discovered in Fetter Lane in London, illustrates the quality, and value, of the weapons deployed by the 8th-century Anglo-Saxon aristocracy.

Two of only three known Anglo-Saxon helmets: reconstructed fragments of the 7th-century iron helmet from Sutton Hoo (left), corresponding closely with the description of a helmet in Beowulf; *the 8th-century helmet (top), bearing the name "Oshere", was found intact in the recent excavation in York. A reconstruction of the Sutton Hoo helmet as it may originally have looked is shown* above.

wergeld*, "man-money"). Notionally at least, the central figure in society was the freeman (Anglo-Saxon *ceorl**, Irish *bo-aire*); his *wergeld* in Wessex was 200 shillings, in Ireland, five milch-cows. But below the freeman (and normally owned by him) was the slave, who had no *wergeld* in his own right; and above him was the nobleman, who could have rights over freemen, and who certainly had a higher *wergeld*: 600 or 1200 shillings in Wessex, where he was known as a *gesith**, or later *thegn*. Status was normally inherited both in Celtic and Anglo-Saxon society, but it was not immutable. Manumission was possible, as in any slave* society, and freemen who failed to pay the compensation incurred by their crimes could be enslaved. In Ireland, and perhaps originally in England, free status entailed possession of what the English called a hide, land sufficient to support a freeman's close family, and loss of the requisite property meant loss of full freedom. In Ireland, too, possession of five clients (see below) qualified one for nobility, and there may be a trace of the same principle in the fact that an English law-tract of the eleventh century defines the *thegn* as one who holds five hides; but significantly the same source envisaged that the status of *thegn* could be acquired through "a seat and special office in the king's hall": *gesith* ("companion") and *thegn* ("servant") are both words that seem to express a relationship with the king. Thus, before accepting the social gradations of legal sources at face-value, one should remember that obsession with status* is often prompted by the fact of social mobility. English, Irish and Welsh literature of the period all know the cliché that slaves are now masters of their lords, and Archbishop Wulfstan II of York, who bemoaned the fact in his "Sermon of the Wolf to the English"* (1014), probably wrote the above-quoted tract on status in distinctly nostalgic vein.

It was to the kin that the sums which defined a man's status were paid in the event of his violent death, and the kin who were obliged to seek vengeance if they were not paid. In societies without police, only the prospect of kin-vengeance and the possibility of buying it off with compensation preserved social peace. Kinship* also determined the distribution of property: throughout the British Isles, property was normally partitioned between male (whom failing, female) direct heirs, with distribution to a wider kindred if there were no direct heirs at all. Unfortunately, it is far from clear what the determining principles of kinship were. There is evidence of extended "agnatic" kindreds in Celtic and Anglo-Saxon society alike, which would mean that descendants in the male line of an ancestor up to six generations previously (i.e. fourth cousins) could be involved in the processes of feud and property distribution. But at least in England and Wales, descendants in the female line* and relatives of wives were taken into account. What all pre-Norman societies in the British Isles eventually had in common was a concentration on the "close" or "nuclear" kindred, the three-generation group descended from a grandparent; in later Anglo-Saxon laws, the only obvious function of the "extended" kin-group lay in defining whom the Church would not permit one to marry. In any case, the key determinant of kin solidarity must always have been geography. Distant kinsmen in neighbouring villages might well play a greater role in feud than even archaic law allowed; first cousins at opposite ends of a kingdom would not have been able or willing to intervene.

Obligations to one's kindred are not much stressed in the heroic literature of early medieval Britain and Ireland; poets preferred to dwell on the overriding claims of loyalty to one's lord. The lordship that must have underlain and

Wergeld

Price to be paid to kindred of person killed by kin of slayer in order to avert the bloodfeud. No evidence for midlands or north in early period, but Kent *ceorl's wergeld* 100 shillings, *eorl's* 300. Wessex *ceorl's* 200, *gesith's* 1200 (relative values of shilling probably made these equivalent). Bloodshed unpopular with Church, and late laws increasingly prohibit or restrict it. Complex arrangements for payment by paternal and maternal kindreds, or substitute guarantors. *Wergelds* also marks of personal status. Value of *wergeld* came to be penalty imposed for committing offences such as adultery.

Ceorl

Traditionally considered free landed peasantry, owing no obligations except *feorm*, church dues and military service; supported family on 1 hide of land. This view now recognized as anachronistic and simplistic. *Ceorl's* status defined by *wergeld*, but in fact variety of degrees of status. Tenurial dependency, and ties between man and lord inherent in Germanic society. From 10th century, obligations more closely defined. Smaller landholdings, depression into partial unfreedom, as shown in *Rectitudines* and Domesday. Less decisive role in army.

Gesith, thegn

Early period *gesith* was king's companion, with role in his military retinue. Defined in early laws by size of *wergeld*. Came increasingly to describe nobles settled on estates rather than supported in king's household. Term passed out of descriptive use, replaced from 9th century by *thegn* to describe noble with obligations to king and dependants: lands held in return for services; responsible for ensuring dependants performed military service; rights of jurisdiction over tenurial dependants evolved; role in shire and hundred courts. Hereditary nobility, status defined by *wergeld*, but not closed to *ceorl* who could acquire 5 hides and other trappings of status. Heirs of king's *thegns* paid *heriot* to receive inheritance.

Slavery

Common to Celtic and Anglo-Saxon society: in England slaves valuable chattels. Ecclesiastical opposition to selling slaves abroad (prohibited in Ine's laws), but practice continued and still being condemned by Anselm early in 12th century. Trade routes from Marseilles to Italy, north Africa and Spain. Constant supplies from warfare, vanquished liable to enslavement. Slaves an important object of

Viking raids. A legal penalty, for not fulfilling freeman's obligations, not paying *geld* or performing military service. Hereditary condition, though manumissions began in late period. Domesday records 25,000 *servi*, fewer than in 1066. Manumissions continued as lords found dependent peasantry more attractive than slaves in manorial economy.

Rectitudines Singularum Personarum

11th-century tract on status and obligations in agrarian society: shows variety within peasant class, based on size of holding and nature of tenancy. *Thegns* had responsibilities towards estate dependants, and owed honourable services to king: army, bridge and fort maintenance. *Geneat*, substantial peasant, paid money rent to lord and owed services: carrying reaping, mowing, etc. *Cotsela* (Domesday *cottarius*) paid no rent, but owed periodic days' work on lord's demesne. *Gebur*, similar to later *villein*, owed heavy labour services and payments in produce. Variations in tenurial status, but all freemen. Slaves liable to work at lord's will, but received stipulated amounts of food.

Sermo Lupi

Lupus, "wolf", Wulfstan's literary pseudonym. Bitter diatribe against collapse of moral standards at end of Aethelred's reign; apocalyptic vision of imminent disaster. Claimed no respect for integrity of Church property nor safety of ecclesiastics; Church dues not paid; English no better than heathens; no respect for law – rights of freemen and slaves alike ignored. Breakdown of bonds of kinship and lordship. Adultery, incest and other immoral acts universal. Oaths and pledges (crucial in operation of justice) broken. Echoes *Gildas:* implies Viking attacks in Aethelred's reign were divine retribution.

Kindred

Primary unit of social organization in Celtic and Germanic society. Initial settlement in England by kin groups likely, each occupying territorial areas under military leader from which later political and administrative regions coalesced. Rights and responsibilities of kindred enshrined in customary law, little of which appears in later royal codes, which tended to respond to specific areas of dispute. Role in pursuing blood-feud, or paying and collecting *wergeld*. Kindred possessed tenurial rights, which later could be alienated by grants of bookland. 10th-century developments in royal authority partly operated through kindred, though support for ties of lordship and increasing role of collective oaths and guarantees in legal processes eroded some of its functions.

Bookland

Land granted by charter, which developed from 6th-century private Roman land deeds. Introduced 670s or before. Grants in perpetuity, at first by kings to endow religious houses, later for and by laymen. Royal rights and dues (including *feorm*) alienated with lands, though in 8th-century Mercia, and other kingdoms shortly after, military service and work on bridges and fortifications excluded. Beneficiary could bequeath lands and associated rights at will: to heirs, followers or, frequently, Church. Lands could be leased out, in whole or part, for term of (e.g.) 3 lives. Charters became essential as proof of title, often produced in legal disputes.

Women and property

Evidence only for nobility. Late 7th century - early 8th century, noblewomen granted bookland to found religious houses. By 9th century, women holding bookland in their own right. Later sources show important women inheriting, holding and bequeathing lands, occasionally in defiance of sons or other male relatives. Special provision for widows: from early period customarily a third of husband's lands; but if widow re-married within a year, lands reverted to husband's kindred. "Morning gift", from husband to wife, initially in jewellery, later in land. Remained wife's, reverted to her kindred, and distinct from common property of the marriage.

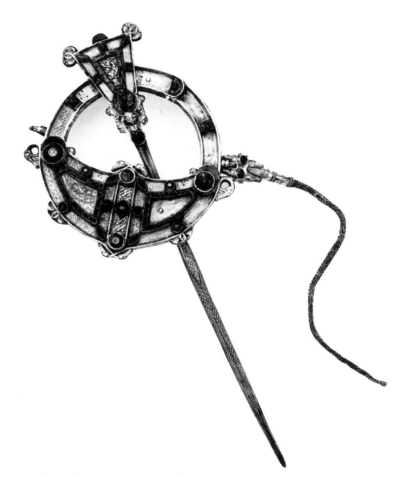

Discovered in unknown circumstances, the "Tara Brooch" illustrates the wealth of the Irish aristocracy in the pre-Viking period.

sustained the life-style of the military aristocracy may also be glimpsed in legal sources. The code of King Ine of Wessex (c. 690) prescribes *manbot*, a sum payable to a lord if his free dependent is killed; the same word and custom resurfaces in fifteenth-century Scotland. Almost from the outset of our evidence, therefore, the lord is *in loco parentis*. Ine's code also shows that men still classed as "free" were allotted land in exchange for labour services which, in the later Middle Ages, would mark them as unfree. English rural serfdom* may have deep roots: it is most evident in the Domesday surveys of areas where Roman villas clustered most thickly. The Welsh laws also bespeak a dependent peasantry, though its labour services are not attested in evidence from the early period itself: they may have been slower to develop than in England, perhaps because there seems to have been an unusually high incidence of outright rural slavery in Wales. In Irish law*, the nobleman has two types of client, both indebted to him for a grant of stock or land and for protection in feud and at law: the "free" client owed military service among other things, and the more securely tied "base" client owed labour service. It is more than likely that these are the same social institutions, dressed up in typically Irish legal language, as military/aristocratic and rural/servile dependence elsewhere in Britain. At all events, by late in the period there was only one type of clientage, with the originally free *bo-aire* increasingly dependent and exploited. In Ireland as in England, social development was all in favour of the lord. Historians, like early medieval poets, tend to dwell on the potential incompatibility of ties of lordship and kindred, suggesting that the former were gaining ground at the latter's expense. The Penitential of Archbishop Theodore of Canterbury*, roughly contemporary with Ine's code, orders seven years penance for avenging a kinsman (the same as for theft) and only forty days for avenging a lord (the same as for looting enemy country). But the distinction between kindred and lordship must to some extent be artificial. In most localities, a freeman's lord is likely to have been the head of his kindred, real or fictional, just as clan chiefs in Scotland today receive nominal acknowledgement from those who share their surname, regardless of actual blood-ties; and in any society, one's best chance of legal redress or vengeance lies with the most powerful person in the locality, whether he is lord or kinsman or both.

The nature of the available evidence may be such as to suggest contrasts between the society of peoples inhabiting different parts of the British Isles in the early Middle Ages, but there are grounds for supposing that social structure and social development were fundamentally similar in all areas. Similarly, the nature and impact of Norman intervention is, on the surface, startlingly different. England was literally conquered: Domesday Book shows a wholesale displacement of its ruling class in favour of the newcomers, and only two Englishmen ranked among the principal landowners holding directly from the king by 1086. The south and east of Wales had much the same experience, but the rest preserved its Celtic polity for another two hundred years. The colonization of Scotland, on the other hand, was by royal invitation, and the new aristocracy mingled with the old. Yet, so far as social structure was concerned, the effects of Normanization were somewhat similar everywhere, and can indeed be exaggerated. Norman "feudalism"* meant differing emphases in the conditions of upper-class landholding, but there was nothing new in the principle that lords were beholden to the patronage of the king and responsible for the rights and obligations of their subordinates. Norman

Villeins

Legally unfree peasants: manorial dependants, owing services to lord by virtue of personal rather than tenurial obligations. Burdensome labour services, few legal rights beyond those enjoyed under customary law. Could be bought and sold as chattels, individually or with families. Much variation, however, within class. Varying land holdings and degrees of economic prosperity. 40 per cent recorded Domesday population were *villani*. In Wales, bondmen provided labour services for lord of *commote*, though of less economic importance than English villeins.

Clientship in Ireland

Lord's social status measured by number of clients – lowest grade had 5, highest 40. Two forms of clientship, both means of economic exploitation for lord's benefit. "Free" clients formed part of lord's following, performed personal service and rented livestock from lord on unfavourable terms for 7 years, when it became client's property. "Base" clients given livestock, or occasionally land, in return for labour services; not wholly unfree. Both free and base clients usually already owned land. Lower down social scale *fuidir* legally and economically dependent on lords, retaining some vestigial legal freedom. Hereditary serfs chattels.

Theodore's Penitential

Probably revised some decades after Theodore's death 690. Influence of Irish Christianity on notions of penance. Penitential prescribes periods of penance for various offences, some against canon law, others of secular nature. Drunkenness amongst monks and clergy said to be prevalent. Fornication and perverted sexual practices strongly condemned, also murder, theft, apostasy and pagan worship. Humanitarian regulations allowing remarriage if existing marriage forcibly dissolved (e.g. one partner taken into slavery). Laymen shown doing penance for range of crimes and sins under direction of priests.

Evolution of the parish

7th-century minster churches built in royal vills, served by monastic communities and entitled to dues from areas appurtenant to vills. Many survived into 11th century. Churches also built under lay patronage, perhaps recalling relationship between lord and pagan priest in Germanic past. Parish and settlement unit usually coterminous. Expansion of parochial system as settlement expanded, though smaller churches had fewer rights to receive dues.

Edgar's laws graded churches, from field church (without graveyard) to head minster. Parishes unequal and irregular by early 11th century. Much lay patronage, bishops often distant figures. Norman reforms attempted to reassert episcopal authority.

Feudalism
Traditionally seen as imposed by Normans, but major elements existed pre-Conquest. A military and political order based on mutual dependence, expressed through formal duties and obligations between king and barons, and between lords and freemen. All land held directly or indirectly of the king. Originated in relationship between lord and follower in Germanic past. Two principal elements: (1) act of homage committed lord to protect vassal, who promised service (chiefly military) in return; (2) lands (fiefs) granted to vassal, who owed obligations commensurate with status of tenure. Formalized chain of obligations, particularly payments to lord to receive inheritance etc. Developed gradually after Conquest, as lands fell into king's hands. Fiefs generally agglomerations of Anglo-Saxon land units.

Bayeux tapestry
Embroidered depiction in pictorial series of events preceding and including Battle of Hastings. Linen cloth 230 feet long, 20 inches wide. Commissioned by Bishop Odo of Bayeux for new cathedral there, consecrated 1077. Undoubtedly made at Canterbury. Depicts Harold's visit to Continent on Confessor's behalf, during which he pledged loyalty to William of Normandy, taking oath on sacred relics. Especially valuable as evidence for contemporary warfare, naval architecture and social scene, including dress. Differences in dress between classes well defined, though little apparent difference between Normans and Saxons.

kin-groups were more narrowly defined than those of pre-Norman societies in the British isles, and laid a new stress on the succession of the eldest male heir to the main family seat, but the pre-Conquest trend everywhere in the British Isles was towards the narrowing of the effective kindred, and the earliest Anglo-Saxon evidence suggests that the eldest son had a prior claim on the main family home. Normans notoriously fought on horseback (when it was tactically appropriate), but the Bayeux Tapestry* shows that English and Norman armies were very similarly equipped, and we know that Englishmen at least rode to and from a battlefield: their military needs would therefore have been just as much of a drain on the resources of society and government.

In the century after the Conquest, the labour services of the tenant peasantry were regulated and intensified, while slaves were correspondingly converted into a tenured labour force; but similar trends had been apparent in pre-Norman England, and also elsewhere in north-western Europe throughout the early Middle Ages. Everywhere in the British Isles, the essence of Norman Conquest was neither more nor less than that one military aristocracy in whole or in part replaced another.

The Picts left no written records of their warriors, but the battle scene carved on a stone slab at Aberlemno, Forfarshire, establishes the existence of a heavily-armed aristocracy comparable with others in the British Isles.

Pictish wealth is demonstrated by the collection of decorated objects in debased silver deposited (probably as a precaution against Viking attack) in a chapel on St Ninian's Isle, Shetland.

Culture:
the arts of the heroic age

Henry Mayr-Harting

In the sixth and seventh centuries the most highly prized arts amongst all the peoples in the British Isles were those of the bards and the goldsmiths, or skilled workers in precious metals. The oral poetry of the former is now largely lost to us, unless there are echoes of it in poems like the *Gododdin* and *Beowulf**, preserved in later forms and manuscripts. The sword pommels, brooches, jewelled pendants of the latter survive largely as they were buried among grave goods during the pagan or early Christian period, for example in the Sutton Hoo ship burial. Written sources tell us that the art of the goldsmith was highly prized, but because of the value of the artefacts, very little has survived. Finely decorated manuscripts, on the other hand, could not be melted down, and the balance of survival has favoured them. Moreover, parchment survives better than textiles, so that although English textile work in the tenth and eleventh centuries was famous, very little remains, besides the English-embroidered Bayeux Tapestry. The material remains of the period might therefore suggest that book art was relatively much more important than it in fact was. Nonetheless some of the highest achievements of the culture were its books*, and they reflect the culture admirably.

Books came to the British Isles in the context of Christianity, and finely illustrated books were mainly for Christian worship. The monastic culture of early Northumbria which produced saints* like Cuthbert (d. 687), ecclesiastical statesmen like Wilfrid (d. 709) and scholars like Bede (d. 735) produced great books, pre-eminent among them the Lindisfarne Gospels (*c.* 698). This book is a synthesis of Mediterranean influences, especially in the figural art of the evangelist portraits, and Celtic influences, notably in the interlace and the curvilinear ornament of the great initials. Another example of the synthesis between Mediterranean Christianity and the northern Heroic Age in early Anglo-Saxon culture is the *Dream of the Rood**, a poem in which the Cross is represented as a loyal warrior companion of Christ suffering the same fate as his Lord, with an awareness and avoidance of Mediterranean christological heresies. This Mediterranean orientation need occasion no surprise. Anglo-Saxon Christians had received their Christianity from Rome and acknowledged the primacy of the Roman see, while the Irish, too, were Rome-orientated, their art showing manifold influences of the Mediterranean. Churchmen like Wilfrid and Benedict Biscop, founder of Wearmouth and Jarrow, travelled to Gaul and Italy to collect books and art, and it was on Biscop's library that Bede's patristic scholarship was based. Canterbury art developed in the eighth century under the influence of Northumbria and its own Italian manuscripts from the age of the Gregorian mission (597). The Canterbury Psalter gave to European culture the historiated initial letters with figural art in them. Also important among the original contributions of the early Anglo-Saxons was the development of insular minuscule, a fluent and legible handwriting which could be more quickly written than the formal

Beowulf
Controversy over date of composition: commonly attributed to 8th century, but some scholars date it earlier, some as late as 10th century. Single manuscript dated *c.*1000, contains many archaic linguistic forms. Similarly, place of composition disputed. If 8th century, perhaps Northumbrian or Mercian Court. Beowulf nephew of king of Geats, people of southern Sweden. Historical setting for fictional events. Major theme Beowulf's struggles with monster Grendel and his mother, who had terrorized Court of king of the Danes. Beowulf subsequently became king of Geats. After 50-year reign, mortally wounded in fight with dragon. Frequent digressions from main narrative, illustrating further heroic traditions which would have been instantly familiar to listeners.

Early books and learning
Importance of Irish influence, both on learning and on script. Both developed 5th and 6th centuries in Ireland through contacts with late classical world. Developments in punctuation, enthusiasm for grammatical texts. Importance of expositional texts in Christian teaching. Iona, Irish monastery founded 563, route of entry into Northumbria. Lindisfarne Gospels show Irish influence on script and ornamentation. Irish influence reinforced by direct English, especially Northumbrian contacts with Mediterranean. Abbot Ceolfrith and Benedict Biscop brought books from Rome late 7th century. Copying, mostly of Gospels, began in England by 670s. Development of characteristic calligraphic script at Wearmouth-Jarrow. Important library there also, used extensively by Bede. Libraries also at Hexham, Malmesbury and Canterbury. Importance of teaching of Archbishop Theodore and companion Hadrian. During 8th century, York became intellectual centre of northern England, its greatest scholar Alcuin.

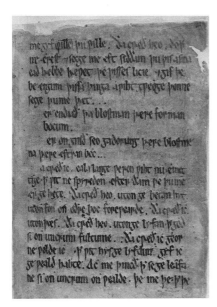

The sole manuscript of Beowulf, *dating from about 1000 – the only example of vernacular heroic verse to survive in full from the Anglo-Saxon or early Germanic worlds.*

The Harrowing of Hell. Mid-11th-century stone relief in Bristol Cathedral.

The early 10th-century church of St Lawrence at Bradford-on-Avon.

Saints' lives

Began to appear in England end 7th century, under influence of: Irish hagiography (e.g. life of Fursey, Adamnan's life of Columba – both used by Bede); late antique texts (e.g. lives of St Martin and St Anthony); and Gregory the Great's *Dialogues*. Earliest English life that of Pope Gregory the Great by monk of Whitby; also of St Cuthbert by anonymous Lindisfarne monk, Bede's two lives of same saint. Life of St Guthlac by Felix, probably East Anglian monk, first half of 8th century. Stereotyped pattern: saint as spiritual warrior, fighting temptation and demoniacal manifestations; performance of miracles, both during life and after death, associated with saint's relics or shrine. Many borrowings from classical saints' lives; others with more historical content. Eddius's life of Wilfrid, written 710-20. Anonymous life of Abbot Ceolfrith 717-25. Bede's lives of abbots of Wearmouth-Jarrow, completed before 731. Less dependent on textual borrowings, some with no miraculous element. Later saints' lives frequently written by continental monks.

Ruthwell Cross

Free-standing stone cross, 18 feet high, at Ruthwell, Dumfriesshire. Best example of Northumbrian sculpture. Carved panels, with unique iconography, show Irish and Mediterranean influence. 5 panels on each broad face of shaft depict New Testament scenes (plus one apparently taken from Jerome's life of Paul the Hermit). Narrow faces contain vinescroll ornamentation. Original carving mid-8th century. Later, passages from poem *Dream of the Rood* added in runic letters. Cross originally stood inside a church, and possibly performed a liturgical function. Similar, though less ornate, crosses elsewhere.

Inscribed round its frame Aelfred mec heht gewyrcan *("Alfred had me wrought"), this jewel consists of a cloisonné enamel figure on a gold plate covered by a "glass" of rock crystal, and framed in gold-work; it probably tipped a ceremonial wand.*

capital and majuscule letters of late Antiquity; a characteristically practical contribution.

A late gospel-book (*c*. 810) in the first great period of Christian culture is the Book of Kells. Like the Lindisfarne Gospels, it has fine Celtic interlace and curvilinear ornament, while its New Testament scenes certainly owe something to east Mediterranean models. But it also has many lively and naturalistic animals playing on its pages, like the otter with a fish on the opening page of St Matthew's Gospel, which has been one of several features recently disposing scholars to see it as a manuscript from Pictish Scotland, the animals being paralleled on Pictish carved stones.

Not until the second half of the tenth century was there another efflorescence of fine book art in Britain. The impression of a hiatus is reinforced by the relatively little evidence for the building of stone churches to compare with Hexham, Jarrow, Brixworth and Bradford-on-Avon from the seventh or early eighth centuries. There is of course the likelihood of flourishing textile and metalwork arts in the period 750-950, the certainty that York had a fine library (on which Alcuin, the adviser of Charlemagne was reared) until its destruction by the Danes, and the knowledge that Offa and Alfred* both cultivated learning in Court schools. The finest manuscripts in the early Middle Ages, however, were produced to meet the requirements either of Court ceremonial or of a vigorous monastic life* and liturgy. It was the English

Continent; Asser, Alfred's biographer, from Wales. Proportion of royal income distributed to monasteries. New houses founded, e.g. Athelney, inhabited by foreign monks. Alfred's daughter Aethelgifu first abbess of Shaftesbury nunnery. School established for education of sons of nobility, who would learn to read English writings; those destined for ecclesiastical orders to go on to learn Latin. Royal officials also to educate themselves. Limited success of reforms: new monasteries did not flourish, uncertain how far standards of learning benefited.

Monastic revival
Partly stemmed from renewed enthusiasm at home, partly from continental influence. By Athelstan's reign, monastic life largely extinguished: remaining houses inhabited by communities of clerks not living according to Benedictine rule. Revival particularly associated with Dunstan (abbot of Glastonbury 943, archbishop of Canterbury 960-88), Aethelwold (bishop of Winchester 963-84) and Oswald (bishop of Worcester 961-92). Continental revival, especially at Cluny (founded 910), Fleury and Ghent, a stimulus. Royal patronage crucial, especially Edgar's. Older monasteries refounded: Glastonbury, Abingdon, Winchester, Ely, Peterborough, Thorney, etc. New foundations (e.g. Westbury-on-Trym and Ramsey) by Oswald. Monastic chapters introduced at cathedral churches. Aethelwold composed common monastic rule, *Regularis Concordia,* derived from continental Benedictine practice and designed to be observed by all communities.

Alfredian renaissance: problems
In Preface to vernacular translation of Pope Gregory the Great's *Pastoral Care,* Alfred complains at decline of learning, especially amongst clergy. Decline of monastic culture, especially ignorance of Latin offices – previously many foreigners had come to England for education and instruction. Before "everything was ravaged and burnt" (by Vikings), churches had been filled with books, but now these could not be understood by churchmen. By beginning of Alfred's reign (871) there were few south of the Humber, and not one south of the Thames, who could comprehend meaning of Latin services or translate one letter from Latin into English. But Alfred exaggerated extent of decline: scholarship remained alive in Mercia. Monastic culture probably in eclipse before Viking attacks.

Alfredian renaissance: remedies
Important didactic works "which may be most necessary for all men to know", translated into vernacular. Copies of *Pastoral Care* circulated to bishops to assist in performing pastoral duties. Late classical works, of value in spiritual and social revival, translated by Alfred and his helpers, drawn from Mercia and the

A late 10th-century English drawing to illustrate the Latin poet Prudentius: "Luxuria" (symbolic of self-indulgence) is shown dancing, watched by a group of knights.

Above: *the opening page of St Matthew's Gospel from the late 8th- or early 9th-century Book of Kells.*

Left: *a detail from the Lindisfarne Gospel illuminated in Northumbria between 689 and 721: the "carpet" page precedes the opening of St Mark's Gospel.*

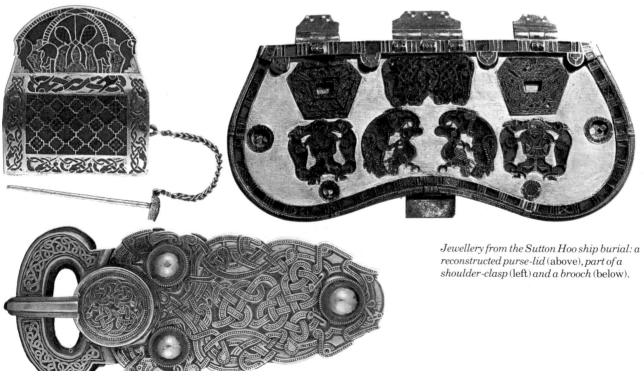

Jewellery from the Sutton Hoo ship burial: a reconstructed purse-lid (above), part of a shoulder-clasp (left) and a brooch (below).

revival of monasticism, strongly influenced by the continental movements of Cluny, Gorze, and Brogne, which provided the context for the great book art (as well as for fine saints' shrines made by goldsmiths) of the later Anglo-Saxon period.

Perhaps the most sumptuous manuscript of this period is the Benedictional made for Bishop Aethelwold of Winchester, whose connection of reformed monasteries in Wessex and Mercia was the most important in tenth-century England. A benedictional contains the blessings pronounced by a bishop at mass, and this book, with its richly coloured full-page illustrations set in acanthus frames, whose immediate origin is Carolingian but whose ebullience is peculiarly English, served the purposes not only of monastic ritual at Winchester, but also of episcopal majesty, in a society where royal and episcopal image-making were closely intertwined. The acanthus frame shows the influence of Rheims and, as Alfred already had close connections with Rheims, some of the cultural foundations of tenth-century Winchester art must be attributed to him. Advances in music accompanied those of visual art, for Aethelwold obtained a music master from Corbie to teach at Winchester, and much tenth-century Winchester music survives, including the score for a liturgical drama of the Resurrection.

The late Anglo-Saxons' mastery of drawing is seen, for instance, in a poignant Crucifixion, probably from Ramsey, which leads us into the spiritual side of the monastic movement. The artistic conceptions in this culture were predominantly linear. Even sculptures like the moving Harrowing of Hell are essentially two-dimensional, and here it is perhaps significant that architecture is not the most noteworthy element of late Anglo-Saxon culture. An important stimulus to English draughtsmanship was the ninth-century Utrecht Psalter, copied at Canterbury about 1000. But there are animated English drawings from before 1000, which show that this vivid, excited and illusionistic psalter was being received into a culture already very open to it. Moreover, whatever the importance of Carolingian models, the drawings of the eleventh-century Bury St Edmunds Psalter or the illustrations of an eleventh-century Canterbury Hexateuch, show that English artists gave rein to their own creative and distinctive inspiration. Several of the Hexateuch illustrations are to Aelfric's* English translation or commentary on these biblical books; and Aelfric himself contributed significantly to give the English the richest vernacular literature of anywhere in its period, not least with his *Catholic Homilies* (991-92), model sermons for English priests.

The Norman Conquest did not mark a cultural break in 1066, since drawings, English textile weaving, the influences of German metalwork, and the use of the vernacular all persisted, but it nonetheless inaugurated a new cultural era in some important ways. Norman abbots and bishops had much precious Anglo-Saxon metalwork melted down, but they imported whole collections of Norman manuscripts which gave a new importance to the ornamentation of initial letters. Above all, in their castles and great churches they brought to England Romanesque* architecture in its full scale and grandeur, and with it a notion of architectural sculpture for which one looks in vain before 1066. It has been well said that the interest of the Normans was in spaciousness, that of the Anglo-Saxons in fine and costly objects. Lastly, the Norman Conquest introduced French, the language of the upper classes for more than two centuries to come, and paved the way for the reception of French learning and culture.

Aelfric's works

Monastic revival gave birth to literary and cultural flowering. Aelfric educated under Bishop Aethelwold at Winchester. Went to new monastery at Cerne Abbas *c.* 987 to supervise monastic school there. 1005 became abbot of another new monastery at Eynsham. His two sets of *Catholic Homilies,* issued early 990s, on lives and passions of the saints, designed to be delivered by priests on important saints' days and festivals. Didactic in tenor, derived largely from Augustine, Jerome, Gregory the Great and Bede. Aelfric interested in Latin grammar and syntax, whose principles were applied to vernacular writings. *Lives of the Saints,* similar content to *Homilies,* written at request of laymen, as was his translation of the *Pentateuch.* Latin *Colloquy* an imaginary conversation between a teacher and members of various trades and callings. *Pastoral letters* instructed parish priests on their duties and reaffirmed the values of pastoral responsibility.

Romanesque

Early features developed in Carolingian Frankia, refined late-10th to early-11th centuries. Reiteration of certain characteristics of Roman public buildings, particularly the basilica. These affected church architecture, especially in ground-plan, structure and decoration. Ground-plan: importance of long nave, proliferation of apses at east end, duplicated transepts etc. Structure: vaulted nave with two or three tiers, semi-circular arches, high towers. Decoration: ornamented capitals especially. Norman Romanesque characterized by simplicity and strength. Thick walls, massive columns and arches, undecorated capitals, Winchester Cathedral rebuilt later 11th century. Groin-vaults in crypt at Canterbury and naves of Ely and Peterborough. Durham Cathedral, begun 1093, shows rib-vaulted nave, begun *c.* 1130, probably earliest in Europe.

3

MEDIEVAL EMPIRE: ENGLAND AND HER NEIGHBOURS

1154 - 1450

MEDIEVAL EMPIRE: ENGLAND AND HER NEIGHBOURS 1154-1450
Overview

J.R. Maddicott

In the second half of the twelfth century, only the facts of geography made Britain an island. By culture, religion and the territorial authority of its rulers, England was joined to Europe, and to France in particular. The kings of England ruled a large part of western France, from the Channel to the Pyrenees. Their nobles held lands in Normandy, spoke French as their first language, liked to read or to listen to the same romances and saints' lives as their French counterparts, and went to France for their favourite sport, the tournament. Both kings and nobles drew the bulk of their wealth from England, but their outlook and interests were in no sense insular. Nor were those of the higher clergy, men who had often been trained in the schools and monasteries of northern France which provided the mainspring for religious reform. They and their subordinates acknowledged the authority of the pope and of the canon law which he promulgated, appealed to his court and accepted the decisions of the judges delegate whom he appointed to act for him in England. The monasteries of the new orders, the most important of which had originated in France, were still more markedly supranational in their organization and allegiances. Such Cistercian houses as Fountains and Rievaulx, their ruins now a part of a timelessly English landscape, were members of one among several orders which belonged not to England but to Christendom.

Only in its government was England truly distinctive. Though its kings ruled over a feudal society of lords and vassals, the development of feudalism had not fragmented their authority. The kings of the twelfth century inherited a centralized monarchy which owed much of its considerable strength to its continuity from a very distant past (barely disrupted by the Conquest of 1066) and to the good fortune which had made England both rich in resources and manageable in size. Their ability to levy general taxes, raise armies, dispense justice and utilize written records gave them a precocious degree of both power and authority unrivalled in any other European kingdom.

By 1450, much had changed. England had become a nation, with a self-awareness, a sense of separate identity and an indigenous culture almost unknown in the twelfth century; and in ways which were subtly connected with this evolution, its kings had paradoxically grown both weaker and more powerful than their Angevin forbears. The "retreat from Europe" was first and foremost a political process. The loss of Normandy to the French in 1204 severed the Anglo-Norman nobility from their ancestral homeland, so that when their descendants returned during the Hundred Years War of the fourteenth and fifteenth centuries they did so as foreign invaders, not as claimants to a usurped inheritance. The subsequent opposition of the nobility to Henry III's foreign expeditions, to the aliens whom he patronized at Court and to the papal clerks whose intrusion into English benefices he permitted, marked the novel development of baronial nationalism in reaction to the policies of the monarch. "Now England breathes again, hoping for liberty", says the *Song of Lewes,* written after Simon de Montfort's victory over Henry in 1264. The sentiment would have been inconceivable a century earlier. During the reigns of the three Edwards, similar sentiments became more widely diffused in English society as they were harnessed to the needs of the Crown, whose foreign wars now made nationalism a force to be encouraged rather than denied. The conquest of Wales in the 1280s could be presented as the civilizing mission of a superior nation towards barbarians; while the much more demanding wars which followed, against Scotland and France, were rapidly transformed from feudal conflicts between lord and vassal into national struggles. During their course, the Crown's success in extracting from its subjects the men and money it needed to wage war came to depend upon the patriotism and sense of common purpose which it could generate among them, and upon its ability to justify its territorial demands. So we find Edward I invoking the legend of Brutus's superiority over the whole of Britain to vindicate his rights to Scotland in 1301, and Edward III branding his French opponent Philip VI in 1346 as a man determined "to root out the English tongue". The king's claims and the national interest were coming to be identified.

The emergence of a distinctive national polity was

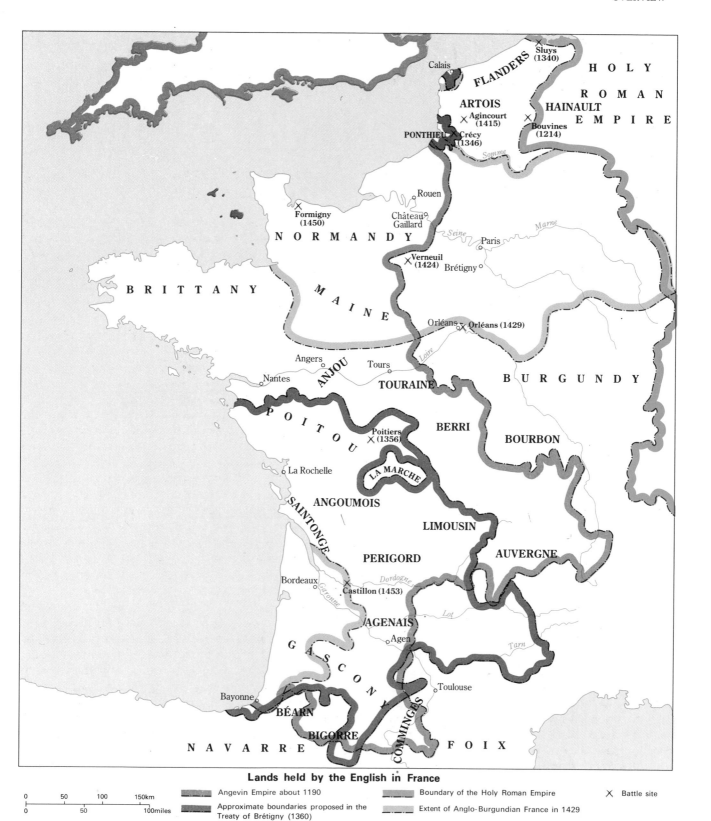

Lands held by the English in France

HOLY ROMAN EMPIRE

HAINAULT

FLANDERS

Sluys (1340)

Calais

ARTOIS

Agincourt (1415)

PONTHIEU

Crécy (1346)

Bouvines (1214)

Somme

Rouen

Formigny (1450)

Château Gaillard

NORMANDY

Seine

Marne

Paris

Verneuil (1424)

Brétigny

BRITTANY

MAINE

Orléans

Orléans (1429)

BURGUNDY

Loire

Angers

Tours

ANJOU

TOURAINE

BERRI

BOURBON

Nantes

POITOU

Poitiers (1356)

La Rochelle

LA MARCHE

SAINTONGE

ANGOUMOIS

LIMOUSIN

AUVERGNE

PERIGORD

Bordeaux

Dordogne

Castillon (1453)

Garonne

Lot

AGENAIS

Agen

Tarn

GASCONY

Toulouse

Bayonne

BÉARN

COMMINGES

BIGORRE

NAVARRE

FOIX

| 0 | 50 | 100 | 150km |

| 0 | 50 | 100miles |

Angevin Empire about 1190

Approximate boundaries proposed in the Treaty of Brétigny (1360)

Boundary of the Holy Roman Empire

Extent of Anglo-Burgundian France in 1429

X Battle site

accelerated by the growth of a more self-sufficient culture, visible in a multitude of ways. The rise of Oxford from the early thirteenth century meant that ambitious young clerks no longer had to go abroad for a university education. The rise of the tournament in England about the same time meant that adventurous young nobles no longer had to seek their sport in France. The evolution of a more definably English law can be traced in the differences between the late twelfth-century legal writer Glanvill, influenced by the customs of northern France, and the legal treatise known as "Bracton", compiled half a century later, which expounds a common law largely purged of French accretions. If we take culture in its narrower sense we shall notice a parallel trend, though in a rather later period. From the second half of the fourteenth century, the growth of English as the language of an elevated literature, seen most notably in the works of Langland and Chaucer, was matched in architecture by the development of the distinctively English Perpendicular style. A common west-European culture still existed: witness the international conventions of chivalry or the plausible case to be made for the origins of the Wilton Diptych, painted for Richard II, on either side of the Channel. But that culture was becoming increasingly fissile. English and French nobles might still read the same romances and saints' lives, but by the fifteenth century they were likely to do so in different languages. In this insular climate it was small wonder that the more cosmopolitan and classicizing air which was beginning to blow from Renaissance Italy had by 1450 been felt by only a handful of English patrons and bibliophiles.

By the end of this period, the rise of English both as a literary language and as the vernacular of the gentry and nobility had contributed to religious changes which jeopardized the traditional links between England and the universal Church. One of the distant origins of those changes lay in the increasingly anti-papal temper of English religion from the thirteenth century onwards. Hostility had been initially provoked by the attempts of the popes, especially Pope Innocent IV (1243-54), both to control more English benefices in order to meet the costs of an expanding papal administration and also to raise taxes on an unprecedented scale for what were essentially military and secular ends. But successful papal exploitation of the English Church was dependent on the compliance of the king, and after Henry III's death that compliance was not to be had. From Edward I's reign the Crown was able to tax the clergy without papal permission and to share in the proceeds of levies imposed on them by the pope. From Edward III's reign it used the

enforced co-operation of the papacy in order to secure *de facto* power to appoint bishops. Its claims were reinforced by a popular anti-papalism which could be given voice in Parliament and which identified a line of French popes, resident at Avignon from 1309 to 1378, with the French cause in the war. Without provoking any great crisis in Church-state relations or martyring an archbishop, Edward III was thus able to transmit to his successors a far tighter control over the Church than Henry II had achieved. The Anglican and Erastian character of the post-Reformation Church was already faintly foreshadowed.

By the end of the fourteenth century, the lay hostility to papal authority which Edward had been able to exploit had contributed to the birth of Lollardy, England's first heresy. The ideas of the movement's founder, John Wycliff, set down in writing in the 1370s and 1380s, subverted the whole ecclesiastical order. Wycliff's emphasis on the authority of Scripture, his denial of the papacy's temporal claims, of the need for priestly mediation between God and man, and of transubstantiation, and his view of the king as the initiator of reform, would have effectively separated England from Rome 150 years before the Reformation. The vernacular Bible which Wycliff's followers made available, and the vernacular tracts in which his views were popularized, emphasized the new role of English as an instrument of religious reform. Despite Lollardy's growth from a widespread lay piety in combination with anti-papalism and anticlericalism, it never became a mass movement nor an effective one. But by 1450 its very existence, as well as the amenability of the clergy to royal influence, demonstrated the increasing localism of English religion. The English Church remained a part of Christendom, but more tenuously and more grudgingly so than in the twelfth century.

The rule of the Anglo-Saxon kings had perpetuated the Roman concept of Britain as "another world", *alius orbis Britanniae*. Its otherness, submerged after the Conquest by the political and cultural dominance of France and by the pan-European religious revival of the twelfth century, had by 1450 reappeared in the new forms which we have described. In the process, the country had acquired a set of political conventions which again served to distinguish England from other European states. Between 1154 and 1215 the Angevin monarchy was very strong by comparison with that of France and immensely strong by comparison with that of any other continental power. Its strengths derived partly from the Anglo-Saxon past, from the tightly regulated political environment of sheriffs, shire and hundred courts, the *geld* and the *fyrd,* which was mainly the achievement of the tenth-century kings. Partly too they derived from the king's ability to exploit for his own fiscal and political profit the undefined feudal customs which governed his relations with his chief vassals – for example, high charges upon heirs for inheritance of their fathers' lands. And partly they were the result of Henry II's development of royal justice, which made the king's courts the usual venue for litigation, carried the king's government into the shires through the itinerant court of the eyre, and created a new source of royal authority by making justice an instrument of patronage, to be granted or withheld. Under Henry II and his sons, this system was exploited almost to breaking point in order to finance and defend the king's possessions in France. The result was the baronial reaction which gave birth to Magna Carta in 1215. In the short term the Charter was little more than a treaty between king and barons, which served to define some of the Crown's feudal powers and some of the subject's judicial rights. In the long term its enforcement during Henry III's minority and its repeated confirmation then and thereafter gave it a status akin to fundamental law. The early development of a powerful monarchy in England had led to its early limitation, in a form which provided England's nearest approximation to a written constitution.

The relations between king and barons which had been at issue before 1215 remained the chief determinant of political stability throughout this period. Despite Magna Carta, the exercise of kingship continued to be governed by unspoken assumptions – or rather by assumptions which were defined only in times of crisis – as much as by written rules. Kings were at all times expected to distribute patronage to the deserving, to take advice from those qualified by blood or service to give it, and to provide effective military leadership in wars, which offered the chance of gain through plunder or promotion. Adherence to these conventions made Edward III and Henry V the two most successful of the late medieval kings; their disregard produced the political conflicts which marked the reigns of Henry III, Edward II, Richard II and Henry VI. The tradition of Magna Carta was perpetuated in the further written limitations on the Crown's authority which sometimes punctuated such conflicts: the Provisions of Oxford of 1258, for example, or the Ordinances of 1311. Yet these restrictions lacked the permanence which the circumstances of Henry III's minority had given to the Charter. A strong king, such as Henry III or Richard II, able to present his prerogative as law and to win noble support through the judicious distribution of patronage, could often defy aristocratic critics who stood outside the Court circle. Even such weak and unintelligent men as Edward II and Henry VI, supinely indifferent to the expectations of their subjects, had favours available which were wide open to exploitation by the unscrupulous and which protected them from complete political isolation. In such circumstances, opponents of king and Court could find a remedy only in active resistance; and the deposition and murder of Edward II, Richard II and Henry VI showed how hard it was to impose peaceful constitutional restraints on kings unwilling to accept them.

They showed, too, the increasing viciousness of politics from the fourteenth century onwards. In the early Middle Ages, kings had been accustomed to treat leniently the baronial rebellions which were a commonplace in all feudal societies. Rebellion was the accepted and quasi-legal resort of the mistreated tenant, the ultimate sanction behind the contract for mutual benefit which lay at the heart of relations between lord and vassal. Edward I's brutal executions of captured Scottish rebels marked a sharp move away from these milder conventions, and one soon carried into domestic politics. Once the military and tenurial realities of feudalism had withered, as they largely had by the fourteenth century, and the king's position was closer to that of a sovereign than of a party to a contract, rebellion was taken more seriously and punished more savagely, as Edward II's opponents found in 1322 and Richard II's in 1397. The deposition of kings was not only a measure of constitutional desperation, but a response to a less inhibited and more violent exercise of royal power.

The nobility's expectations of royal government were thus more consistent than their reactions to its abuse. If in 1450 their likely responses still remained the chief constraint upon the king's freedom of action, they were no longer the only one, for by then the growth of Parliament had given other social groups some access to power. Here again, Magna Carta had done much to determine the future, providing the impetus for institutional growth by linking taxation to consent. Initially, under Henry III, that consent was required only intermittently and from the greater baronage alone. The paucity of expensive foreign campaigns meant that the Crown's financial needs, pressing though these often were, could usually be met from its traditional resources. But under the three Edwards, and especially from 1294, large-scale warfare necessitated regular levies of direct taxation, bringing into being a Parliament which comprehended not only barons but also the knights and burgesses who represented the taxpayers of the localities and whose consent was now equally essential for the support of the king's ambitions. Taxation for war gave sharper point to traditional aristocratic protests against royal favourites, whose enrichment under an Edward II or a Henry VI could be shown as depleting the national resources needed for victory. More important still, it limited the king by forcing him to attend to his subjects' complaints before he could secure a grant. The process had begun under Henry III, when on three occasions the barons had granted a tax only in return for the king's confirmation of Magna Carta. But it was not until Edward III's reign that the regular redress of the Commons' grievances began to be set against supply, in a form of political bargaining which was to last into the seventeenth century.

War thus promoted institutional limitations on kingship more effective than the reforming codes enacted from time to time by the Crown's baronial opponents. Yet it also made the Crown vastly more powerful. Through Parliament, and the royal requests for men, money and supplies which might be sanctioned there, the king could tap the resources of all his subjects. Through those who attended from town and country, he could publicize both his policies and the reforming statutes which were often the price paid for their financing. Backed by Parliament, the king was now potentially stronger than he had been in the days of the feudal autocracy of the Angevins: to a far greater degree he was able to exploit the wealth of the nation and not merely that of his great men.

The expansion of Parliament was a response not only to military exigencies but also to social change. In the years around 1200, legal protection for the right to inherit and to alienate land had been extended to all free men, thus limiting the powers of feudal lords and giving to their knightly tenants a new and judicially enforceable independence. From about the same time, the top ranks of this group grew in prominence as jurors and sheriffs, tax collectors and arrayers of troops, constables of castles and keepers of forests; they became an administrative élite upon whose support in the counties royal government was ultimately dependent. The lack of a professional salaried civil service in the localities (in strong contrast with France) had made the English Crown reliant upon "amateurs", often men with powerful local interests and connections, whose control of offices was both an effective barrier against royal absolutism and also a main cause of the disorderly feuding which often divided provincial society in the later Middle Ages. It was the support of such men that Edward I and his successors sought in Parliament. From these changes there had evolved by the fifteenth century a

political society far more complex than that governed by Henry II. Kingship had become a matter of management, and no longer just the management of the great. The growth of the Commons, the local weight of the gentry, the ties of bastard feudalism which bound together lords and retainers, all meant that the Crown had to take into account and to conciliate a public opinion which had hardly existed in the twelfth century.

These practical limitations on royal government were reinforced by the nature of the society which the king ruled. By the fifteenth century the upper classes were becoming more stratified. The peerage, now arranged in ranks, was separating from the gentry, who were themselves more hierarchically ordered. Yet stratification implied little in the way of privilege. Unlike the French *noblesse,* neither the English nobility nor the gentry were exempt from taxation, and the resilience of the English Parliament owed much to their shared subjection to this burden. It created a common political interest which would not allow Henry VI to divide and rule, as his French contemporary Charles VII was able to do. The real division in English society had lain elsewhere: at its bottom rather than its top, and between free and unfree rather than between noble and non-noble. From Henry II's reign the villein had been denied that access to the royal courts which was the right of all free men. Yet this line too had now been eroded. The decline in population brought by the Black Death had accelerated the decline of villeinage which was already underway before the plague's arrival. It withered from the late fourteenth century as landlords, now faced with a surplus of land and a shortage of tenants, found it increasingly difficult to lease holdings on the old service terms. As stratification became more apparent at the top of society, so it became less apparent at its base. Yet, for almost all its members, that society remained a very open one, in which rank conferred social precedence rather than legal privilege, great differences of wealth were not reflected in class antagonisms, and social mobility went hand in hand with social deference.

The cohesion of English society was sustained by a prosperity greater and more widespread than that of the twelfth century. In terms of the European economy, and by comparison with the great commercial centres of Italy and the Low Countries, England might indeed be backward; yet the standard of living of her people was remarkably high. Their diet of meat, the richness of their clothing, the wealth of their parish churches, the silver plate to be found in taverns and private houses, were all commented on by contemporaries in the late fifteenth century. It is customary and proper to point out that these comforts were ensured largely by a stagnant level of population, itself the result of recurrent visitations of the plague. The survivors, able to profit from high wages, high demand for manufactured goods, low rents and the general availability of land, were the lucky ones. But one perceptive observer writing in the 1470s, Sir John Fortescue, made a less obvious connection between national prosperity and the national polity. In a country where the king could not levy direct taxation as he pleased (as he could in France), where there was no indirect taxation of consumables (as there was in France), where the weight of taxation was distributed with reasonable equity (as it was not in France), and where the powers of both king and nobles were subject to legal and political constraints, neither the state nor the aristocracy inhibited economic growth as they did in other European countries. It was in part the evolution of the English constitution that was reflected in the social and economic differences between England and the continental neighbours with whom she had once been so closely associated.

Government and Politics:
England 1154-1272

W.L. Warren

When he became king of England, Henry II (1154-89) was already duke of Normandy, count of Anjou, and (in right of his wife) duke of Aquitaine. The mastery and integrity of his French dominions* remained his overriding political concern. Though he inherited claims to the overlordship of Wales and Scotland he was content to secure stable relations with the native rulers. Even his intervention in Ireland was designed to contain the Anglo-Norman adventurers already there, and his intention was to consign it to his youngest son John as a separate realm. Only the unforseen succession of John to all his father's dominions permanently linked England and Ireland. The French connection was to remain a preoccupation of royal policy for over a century. In consequence a determined attempt to fashion a united kingdom of the British Isles was postponed until the end of the thirteenth century – too late for it to be achieved without prohibitive cost.

On the other hand, Henry II, with impetuous and largely triumphant self-confidence, consolidated the monarchy of England and transformed its government*. The king's frequent and prolonged absences on the Continent highlighted the age-old problem of how to delegate royal authority without either handing it over to feudal lords or endowing local officials with too wide a discretionary power. The solution that was devised (resting on self-regulating administrative mechanisms, cross-referenced record keeping, a division of functions which obliged officials to work in unison, specific instead of generalized commissions, and routine procedures authorized in precisely formulated writs) had the effect of transforming the old methods for managing royal rights into effective means for carrying royal authority directly and systematically into the shires. One immediate consequence was to make royal justice routinely accessible to all freemen by standardized procedures (the "common law"*) which rapidly expanded in response to popular demand. In the shires the exercise of royal authority rested on the co-operation of the lesser landholders and ordinary freemen, setting a trend for "self-government at the king's command", and forging a community of interest between Crown and country. The resilience of the new administrative machine* was demonstrated in the reign of the dashing but improvident Richard I (1189-99) who spent no more than six months in England, and who for long periods while on crusade or in captivity in Germany was beyond the reach of his ministers.

The translation of royal authority into executive action challenged the scope and competence of the authority of feudal lords and of the Church, which was at the same time developing the jurisdiction of ecclesiastical courts and claiming exclusive control over all clergy. In steadfastly resisting Henry II's attempt to define the limits of clerical independence and jurisdiction*, Archbishop Thomas Becket became a hero to all who resented the king's overbearing assertiveness, but his dramatic martyrdom (1170) obscured his failure to promote a struggle for supremacy between Church and state. Henry

Angevin inheritance
"Angevin" is the adjective derived from the name Anjou. Henry II had an hereditary right to Anjou, Maine and Touraine through his father Geoffrey of Anjou, and to England and Normandy through his mother Matilda. In 1152 he married Eleanor, daughter and heiress of William, duke of Aquitaine and count of Poitou. By 1154 Henry controlled England and more than half of present-day France.

Henry II's government
Effectiveness of justice increased through royal justices hearing civil and capital criminal cases prepared by sheriffs ("General Eyre"). Corruption of sheriffs and officials checked and efficiency increased by administrative purge (Inquest of Sheriffs, 1170). Severer criminal code and improved enforcement through Assizes (precursors of statutes) of Clarendon 1166, and Northampton 1176. Royal revenues accounted, and officials supervised, by sophisticated administrative processes of Exchequer. Communication between government and officials founded on use of adaptable, precisely formulated writs. No conscious anti-baronial policy, but baronial resentment of increasing royal power over freemen in shires evident in 1173-74 revolt.

Common law
Evolved under Henry II; covered whole country; derived from customary law but capable of expansion and improvement in response to cases encountered by justices. New procedures were devised for civil property cases (Petty Assizes): complainants bought returnable writs ("returned" by sheriff to justices certifying action taken) requiring sheriff to summon defendants and twelve jurors, knowing facts of case, before itinerant justices; extended to proprietary right (Grand Assize) cases 1179.

Court of Common Pleas
Justices appointed to hear cases in which the king was not a party, sitting in the *Curia Regis;* permanently at Westminster after 1215; distinct from courts held by

Justices in Eyre; the judges in Common
Pleas (and its criminal equivalent, King's
Bench) evolved into professional class of
justices.

Angevin administration
Formally consisted of the king's household
and the provincial aspects. The former
(Chancery and Chamber supplemented by
the offices of the marshal and constable)
travelled with the king; the latter contained
the central court *(Curia Regis),* Exchequer,
Treasury, Court of Common Pleas and
itinerant justices, all presided over by vice-
regal justiciar. But administration was not
a bureaucracy of officials, rather a network
of adaptable men.

Constitutions of Clarendon 1164
Henry II's attempt to define customary
rules governing Church-state relations in
England: clergymen should have no
communication with Rome without royal
permission; appeals to papal court should
not take place until cases had been heard in
appropriate English courts; king's
permission needed before spiritual
penalties could be imposed on barons and
royal officials; some cases heard by
ecclesiastical courts (for instance debt)
should now be heard by lay courts; trial of
clergymen accused of crimes should be
subject to royal supervision, and
punishment of guilty clergy should be
similar to that of laymen.

*Records of the royal chancery (charters,
letters patent and letters close) were kept on
skins of parchment sewn together and rolled
up. Systematic record-keeping was essential
to the 12th-century development of more
effective royal government.*

*Aerial view of Dover Castle, showing Henry
II's keep (1180-90) and the outer works, with
Constable's gate, built in the reign of Henry III.*

II's concern lay in pragmatic solutions to pressing problems, not ideological conflict. Crown and papacy reached an understanding to protect their own over-riding interests (which coincided in promoting centralized control against local autonomy); and the bishops, like the barons (defeated in the insurrection of 1173-74), had to accommodate themselves to royal government. Thereafter opposition shifted from open resistance to criticism of the ill-effects of royal monopoly, particularly its enhanced scope for discrimination against the disfavoured, the arbitrary enforcement of royal rights, and the distortions which royal convenience imposed on the transition from custom to settled law. But criticism was frustrated by the lack of constitutional devices for the redress of grievances, for the development of a largely self-sufficient royal government had undermined the old sanction which obliged kings to win the co-operation of their barons by making concessions. Only a crisis of confidence in royal control could induce acts of self-limitation by the Crown. It came in the reign of John (1199-1216). King John was not lacking in enterprise or intelligence, but he had a facility for alienating everyone who mattered (including the papacy*) and a fatal hesitation in the face of conspiracy. The humiliation of the loss of Normandy, and the collapse of his continental strategy for recovering it with the defeat of his allies at the battle of Bouvines (1214), emboldened many of his barons to disavow their allegiance*. The price of renewing it was Magna Carta* (1215).

The Charter reflects a hotchpotch of specific grievances rather than any coherent constitutional theory. Nevertheless it carried constitutional implications, limiting the arbitrary exercise of royal will by defining Crown rights precisely, and prescribing the proper exercise of government by the Crown and its officers. In granting the Charter, the Crown conceded that it ought to be constrained by agreed law. But as a formula for peace it failed. King John died in the midst of a civil war against opponents who preferred the option of reuniting England and Normandy by putting themselves under the French Crown. The throne was rescued for John's infant son, Henry III (1216-72), by those of his supporters whose interests lay chiefly in Wales, Ireland, and southern France. Magna Carta was reissued as a royalist manifesto, an earnest of good intentions but shorn of its most hampering restrictions. Its confirmation by Henry III himself in 1225, "of his own spontaneous goodwill", established it as a bill of rights; but in its revised form it lacked sanctions and so rested on the good faith of the king. In consequence it required repeated confirmation (which prevented it becoming merely a piece of past history), and the good faith of the ruler became the test of political rectitude.

Magna Carta tacitly recognized that government was the king's business, both as his duty and his right. But while Henry III was a minor the king's government had in effect to be put into commission. It functioned by co-operation between the bureaucracy and the barons, but significantly many judicial decisions were postponed until the king should be of age. When Henry III assumed control of the authority which was rightfully his, consensus politics gave way to personal monarchy, buttressed by a newly formulated ideology of kingship. Unlike his predecessors, Henry III had no experience of the world before he was crowned and grew up in tutelage. He took advice on how to be a king from those who had everything to gain from his patronage, and most notably from Frenchmen from south of the Loire – who had formerly resisted Henry II as an outsider, but clung to Henry III against the encroachments of the Crown of France. The king's patronage of "aliens"* was the most

The Interdict 1208-13
A general suspension of all religious services in England ordered by Pope Innocent III 1208 to force John to accept Stephen Langton as archbishop of Canterbury. Innocent was obeyed, but John turned Interdict to advantage by placing ecclesiastical property under royal control and exacting payments from clergy, which solved his financial problems. The Interdict (and John's subsequent excommunication) were lifted when John, fearing French invasion and seeking allies, agreed to become Innocent's vassal 1213.

Rebellion of 1215
Led by Robert Fitz Walter and Eustace de Vesci, the rebels, numbering about one-third of English baronage (many having personal grievances against John's harsh methods of government), took advantage of the collapse of John's strategy at Bouvines 1214. They renounced homage and fealty and captured London; military stalemate enabled moderates led by Archbishop Langton to negotiate a settlement. Terms of Magna Carta were agreed at Runnymede, a meadow between Windsor and Staines.

Magna Carta
Charter of liberties sealed by John, containing sixty-one clauses: guaranteed privileges of the Church; defined feudal obligations between king and barons; limited royal rights, particularly in forests, and outlawed abuses of administrative power; prevented king from manipulating the law to his advantage; made law courts generally open to free men; provided for a standing committee of twenty-five men, elected by the barons, to act as guardians of the law and receivers of complaints against the king.

Aliens
Royal employment of dependable Poitevins (Peter des Roches by John; Peter des Riveaux and his own Lusignan half-brothers by Henry III) as administrators was connected with royal attempts to exclude the English baronage from royal government, and also with need for Poitevin allies if continental possessions were to be recovered by England. Their preferment could sometimes be justified by their kinship with king, but they were targets for political attack: in 1258 the barons expelled the Lusignans.

Franchise

A jurisdictional privilege giving a lord royal rights over an area or community: for example, "the franchise of return of writs" meant that lord's bailiff undertook legal administrative tasks usually performed by king's sheriff. Henry III investigated the right to, and use of, franchises in 1254; in Edward I's reign *Quo Warranto* inquisitions were held to examine the rights of franchise holders to their privileges. Statute of Gloucester 1278 sought to define and regulate franchises, as did *Quo Warranto* statute 1290.

persistent criticism of the barons, who saw themselves as his "native born counsellors". It also highlighted a rift between royal and baronial interests, for while the king strove to restore the Angevin "empire", the barons found compensation for the loss of Normandy in the more direct and efficient management of their English estates and identified with an incipient "nationalism".

An efficient bureaucracy converted personal monarchy into personal government. Under Henry III the mechanisms of central government were refined to a form which sufficed until the sixteenth century. His predecessors' framework was filled out, its parts better articulated, its methods rationalized. It also thrust more deeply into the shires, challenging the grip of franchise* holders even on policing and petty crime. But although the structure implied a centralized state, the realm was still thought of as the king's personal "estate", and to baronial demands that the chief officers be publicly

Above: *the popular view, from an early 14th century manuscript, of Archbishop Becket disputing with Henry II over Church-state relations and clerical autonomy.*

Henry III fashioned an elaborate imagery for an exalted monarchy. Matthew Paris's drawing (top) *shows the king carrying his new relic of the Precious Blood in procession to Westminster Abbey in 1247. In promoting* the cult of Edward the Confessor, Henry III *also expressed his conception of kingship:* (above), *the coronation ceremony from* The Life of St Edward *commissioned by Henry III.*

accountable, the king replied that he would be as free in the management of his estate as the barons were in theirs. The baronial opposition should not be equated with the rebels of 1215, but rather with those who reissued Magna Carta as a royalist manifesto; and for long it resembled a dispute among shareholders about the management of a family business. Ideological arguments, however, converted divergent interests into constitutional attitudes. To the king's paternalist conviction (expressed in art and architecture as well as frequent harangues) that as God's vicar he bore responsibility for the welfare of his people, the barons opposed the view of themselves as spokesmen for the "community of the realm".

It is characteristic of Henry III's policy that he welcomed the friars but banned the Inquisition. In practice however, his government signally failed to justify the aspirations of his kingship. It was unresponsive to developing needs, omitted to control corruption and oppression at the lower levels, and hence forfeited popular support; his grandiose continental policy collapsed in financial disaster and put him at the mercy of his barons. They resolved in the Provisions of Oxford* (1258) to take control both of policy-making and the machinery of government, through a formalized Council and a structure of committees to provide for baronial participation and consultation. But they could not agree on how to reform "the state of the realm", especially when challenged from below to apply to the management of their own fiefs and franchises the reforming scrutiny which they required of royal government. The only escape from anarchy seemed a restoration of the king's authority*. The leader of the irreconcilables, Simon de Montfort, imposed his own solution after capturing the king at the battle of Lewes (1264); but though sustained by idealism and populist enthusiasm, his régime threatened to be ruthlessly authoritarian. He was brought down a year later at the battle of Evesham by a decisive combination of royalists and ex-reformers. Henry III's reign had identified the problems of reconciling Crown and community, but acceptable solutions had yet to be found.

Provisions of Oxford 1258

Henry III surrendered power to baronial critics to gain support for taxation needed to pay for "Sicilian Business". Provisions forced him to share royal power, imposing a permanent baronial council on him, requiring him to meet baronial representatives three times a year, and placing appointments of justiciar, treasurer and chancellor in their hands.

Provisions of Westminster 1259

The barons nominated Hugh Bigod to hear complaints in every county against sheriffs and other royal officials, which formed basis of Provisions of Westminster: these contained detailed technical reforms of English common law, beneficial to the ordinary free man.

Barons' War

From 1259 Henry III gradually restored royal authority. Pope Alexander IV absolved him from obeying both Provisions, which he renounced 1262. Royal power collapsed under pressure, directed by Simon de Montfort, for implementation of Provisions 1263, but new régime under Simon was insecure. Both sides begged St Louis to resolve crisis. Louis' Judgement of Amiens 1264 ruled uncompromisingly in Henry III's favour. This caused civil war with early success for Simon (Lewes 1264) but final victory to Henry (Evesham 1265). Dictum of Kenilworth 1265 defined process whereby rebels might recover confiscated lands. Statute of Marlborough 1267 reaffirmed Provisions of Westminster and the version of Magna Carta issued in 1225. Peace quickly imposed.

The opening page of Magna Carta, 1215.

Government and Politics:
England 1272-1450

Anthony Goodman

Henry III was buried in 1272 in his beloved Westminster Abbey, but his heart was to be taken to Anjou, to lie near the remains of his grandparents, Henry II and Eleanor of Aquitaine. He was the last king of England to be commemorated as an Angevin, and the first post-Conquest ruler to be buried near London – an example followed in the case of four of the seven kings who ruled between 1272 and 1450. Their posthumous association with Westminster and the resplendent shrine of their English predecessor Edward the Confessor was fitting, for Westminster had become the centre of English government.

The Chancery, Exchequer and Privy Seal offices, and the courts of King's Bench and Common Pleas, were customarily housed in Westminster Palace. The king's household, though still itinerant, was often to be found there – a small army, precisely ranked, of guests and servants, including key royal officers (e.g. the keeper of the Great Wardrobe, and the keeper of the Signet Seal). Such officers were sensitively responsive to the royal will, and might be in charge of the management of the king's disposable income or the drafting of his correspondence.

The real power of kings and their government varied dramatically in the period. Edward I dominated Wales and Scotland, but the world of his son Edward II shrank to a cell in Berkeley Castle. Whereas Edward III died honoured by his subjects after a reign of fifty years, his successor Richard II suffered the tragic fate of Edward II. The health of Henry IV, the first Lancastrian king, broke after repeated rebellions. But his son Henry V was perhaps the most popular of English medieval kings, and Henry VI's kingship went unchallenged from babyhood to mature manhood. The effectiveness of rule depended on the strength of subjects' belief in the naturalness of royal exercises of sovereignty, as well as on the *esprit de corps* of small bodies of Westminster and household clerks. Except in a few exempt regions (such as the bishopric of Durham), the king's writs were everywhere executed as a matter of course, whether by his sheriffs' officers or by lords' stewards in their franchises. Magnates did not elaborate dynastic claims to regional sovereignty, like the lords of the Isles in Scotland or the dukes of Brittany in France: they increasingly stressed their kinship with the kings of England. There was no plurality of dukes, counts or cities claiming a customary exercise of devolved royal powers, as in the Holy Roman Empire. Indeed, royal sovereignty was defended against the claims of foreign jurisdictions. In 1366, Parliament rejected the feudal overlordship of the realm claimed by the papacy in virtue of King John's homage. The Statute of Praemunire* (1393), which confirmed limits placed on the papal court's exercise of spiritual jurisdiction, insisted that the Crown had "no earthly master". In 1416 Henry V's brother Gloucester, sword ceremonially drawn, rode his horse into the sea at Dover to prohibit Sigismund, king of the Romans, from exercising imperial power in England.

The Jewel Tower, built at Westminster in 1365-66 to house the personal valuables of Edward III.

Statutes of Provisors 1390 and Praemunire 1393
Former stopped any clerk accepting a favour (e.g. an ecclesiastical office) from pope; latter prohibited introduction to England of citations, excommunications and bulls of provision from Rome, and forbade papal court to hear lawsuits respecting English churches. Not strictly enforced but gave kings bargaining power with pope. Reflected Commons' hostility towards papal use of Church in England as source of wealth, to neglect of English interests.

England was itself an expanding imperial power. The mythical history of Great Britain, particularly the stories of King Arthur's rule and conquests, strengthened convictions of the rightfulness of Edward I's assertions of sovereignty over Wales and Scotland, and of Edward III's and Henry V's incursions in France. The pickings to be gained from the Crown's claims abroad were widely appreciated. But there were domestic risks inherent in expansionist royal policies: they aroused expectations difficult to fulfil, which might coincide only fleetingly with dynastic aims. Disappointments produced discontent, such as that expressed by Cheshire soldiers in 1393, angry because peace threatened their livelihoods. The risks of discontent were magnified by the enormous costs of wars which, from the 1290s onwards, tended to be increasingly ambitious, prolonged and inconclusive. But the Crown's income from customary revenues was insufficient even for non-military demands: available cash was swallowed up by the royal household's huge running costs. Much revenue continued to be used for patronage, with Crown lands let out on often generous terms by Exchequer leases. The most significant achievement of kings in this period was their success in raising vast sums from their subjects to finance war, a process which stimulated political and institutional change.

A foreign visitor in 1466 remarked on how English sailors fell on their knees before the king's letters and kissed them. But Englishmen's zeal for sovereignty owed more to their anti-alien sentiments than to a love of kings. Indeed foreigners suspected that such expressions of loyalty masked an ancient inclination to rebellion and regicide, such as had burst forth to destroy Edward II in 1327 and Richard II in 1399. In fact these orderly depositions afford testimony to the sense of national unity in the period. In no other kingdom were there such flourishing cults to victims of royal tyranny, such as those at the tombs of Edward II's arch-opponent Thomas, earl of Lancaster (executed 1322), and Henry IV's opponent Archbishop Scrope (executed 1405). Above all, there was the cult of St Thomas of Canterbury, who had resisted Henry II: tyranny was still a lively issue. Edward I and his successors were as determined as their ancestors to exercise their wills unfettered, but the thrust of their arbitrariness, though often enraging their subjects, was narrowed by the direction of their ambitions, and by the institutional and political conventions these were helping to evolve. They were not interested in undermining Magna Carta, and showed no consistent zeal to exploit the full range of feudal incidents. Only Edward I's *Quo Warranto* enquiries (1278-94) threatened an expansion of royal, at the expense of baronial, jurisdiction. By the mid-fourteenth century, kings entrusted the normal business of royal government in the localities* to resident gentry and burgesses, who acted under commission as sheriffs, escheators, keepers of the peace* with judicial powers, arrayers mustering military levies, and collectors of subsidies.

One means of monitoring how the king's will was being discharged locally lay in the device of summoning leading subjects to give the king advice and judgement in Parliaments*, in conjunction with his leading officials. Edward I developed parliamentary precedents in his frequent summons of representatives of shires, boroughs and clergy: the order that he sometimes made for them to come with full powers to give counsel and consent on behalf of their communities was to become standard. By 1322 the summons of Parliaments including representatives was so habitual that, according to the Statute of York, it was customary to discuss and establish national concerns in Parlia-

Edward I's statutes
Extended common-law statutes promulgated on royal authority in Parliament (which did not yet make law). Statute of Westminster 1275 codified existing law; Mortmain 1279 prevented grants to religious corporations whereby king and lords lost rights over land; Acton Burnell 1283 improved procedure in debt cases; Rhuddlan 1284 modified Exchequer procedures; Winchester 1285 attempted to revive ancient police institutions, particularly local public courts; *De Donis* 1285 enabled men to place conditions on descent of land which heirs might not lawfully break; *Quia Emptores* 1290 protected rights of feudal lords by outlawing sub-tenancies.

Local officials
Powers and duties of sheriff were increasingly restricted; more business was placed in hand of officials recruited, as the sheriff increasingly was, by the king from substantial county gentry. Escheators dealt with king's rights as feudal landlord (wardships, marriages, reliefs); coroners kept record of pleas of Crown and held inquests into matters in which king had legal interest (murders, shipwrecks). Other officials appointed to supervise estates in royal hands, collect customs in ports and keep the royal forests.

Justices of Peace
Evolved in 14th century from Crown's practice of appointing unpaid local commissioners to carry out administrative duties in their counties. In 1368 judicial powers were entrusted to such commissions by statute: justices were to maintain peace and the Statutes of Winchester 1285 and Northampton 1328; enquire into labour law offences, weights and measures, forestalling and regrating; and determine felonies and trespasses. Act of 1390 stipulated eight justices for each county. System entrusted local government to men who, through ownership of land, possessed local power and authority.

Parliament
Writ summoning elected representatives to 1295 Parliament was model for future: representatives were to have full power to do what was ordained by "common counsel" (negotiation between king and lords); counties and boroughs were obliged to do what representatives had accepted; representatives had no authority to refuse assent or determine what should be done. Their appearance with these powers (and, thereby, the emergence of recognizably modern Parliament) owing to king's

The stained glass memorial in the parish church of West Horseley, Surrey, to Sir James Berners, a household knight of Richard II, who was impeached and beheaded in 1388.

ment, with the assent of the prelates, earls, barons and "community of the realm". Indeed in its form and functions, Parliament had settled by the mid-fifteenth century into what was to be its traditional mould, with a House of Lords and, in the House of Commons, members debating subsidy demands and promoting bills under the eye of the Speaker.

Parliaments were summoned by the king often annually, which expedited consideration of petitions; the attendance of representatives publicized judgements made there by king and council, and bound the "community of the realm" more firmly to obey new statutes, support decisions about national affairs and contribute to aids. But, for many, the benefits of the Edwardian elaboration of links between Crown and community may have been outweighed by its drawbacks – insistent and often arbitrary royal demands for money, supplies and services, especially for war abroad. In the last decade of his reign, Edward I faced demands for new constitutional safeguards. Baronial frustration probably contributed to the harsh opposition which his less competent son Edward II soon encountered: he was forced to accept the reforming Ordinances of 1311*. Edward III's reckless and oppressive financing of grandiose campaigns precipitated a series of parliamentary crises* (1339-41). Having provoked opposition at home and exhausted his credit abroad, Edward came to rely for defence subsidies on bargains struck with the knights of the shire and burgesses in Parliament: they gained a near-monopoly of the right to grant taxes, a situation which kings were on the whole prepared to accept since it guaranteed a good return.

Under Edward III, shire knights and burgesses acquired the habits of meeting as a single assembly*, and of consulting frequently with delegations of peers. Representatives learned traditional, unifying aims – to maintain the defences of the realm and its interests abroad with their taxes, but to ensure that these were kept low and spent appropriately and, wisely. The political courage which they were capable of whipping up was strikingly demonstrated in one of the last parliaments of Edward's reign, the "Good Parliament"* of 1376. They communally impeached nobles and merchants whom they

desperate need for war taxation. 13th-century precedents moulded Parliament's form: to restore harmony after Barons' War, Edward I regularly took advice, promulgated legislation and made judicial decisions in greatly enlarged Council meetings to which rich and influential knights, burgesses and merchants were sometimes summoned.

Ordinances 1311
In 1310 Edward II consented to appointment of certain bishops and earls to reform government. Ordinances published in Parliament 1311: contained attack on Piers Gaveston, regarded as an evil counsellor and monopolizer of patronage; required financial retrenchment, better use of royal revenues and patronage; stipulated baronial consent to royal grants and appointments of state and household officials and sheriffs; reformed abuses of legal procedures by Crown officials; demanded annual Parliaments for

complaints against royal administration. Sought greater accountability of royal government to Lords, not fundamental constitutional change.

Consequences of Bannockburn
Scots' defeat of English at Bannockburn 1314 led to humiliation of Edward II, evident in unhindered Scottish raids on England, and acquisition of power by Thomas of Lancaster (Edward's enemy since his involvement in Gaveston's execution 1312). In spite of an agreement with the earls (Treaty of Leake, 1318) Lancaster, though rich and powerful, could not dominate England. Edward II rebuilt a Court party around the Despenser family.

Boroughbridge 1322
Edward II attacked and defeated Lancaster (executed 22 March) at Boroughbridge, Yorkshire (16 March). York Parliament (May) repealed Ordinances and proscribed king's enemies. Power of régime led by

Despensers buttressed by Scottish truce 1323: Despensers' acquisitiveness made them unpopular. Opposition centred on Queen Isabella, who removed to France with exiles and lover Roger Mortimer; she invaded England 1326, toppled the Despensers and, by parliamentary process, deposed her husband 1327. In 1330 Edward III seized power, executed Mortimer and restored political stability.

Crisis of 1339-41
Edward III had to find subsidies for allies and fruitless Low Countries campaign 1338-40; there was armed resistance to tax collectors in Essex 1340. Commons required redress of grievances before taxation 1339; no tax should be levied without parliamentary assent; confirmation of Magna Carta and Forest Charter; and, for first time, appointment of named councillors 1340; in 1341 statutes passed (later annulled) requiring ministers and justices to swear to observe charters.

believed had defrauded the enfeebled king, and successfully petitioned for new councillors. When, during the early years of Richard II's and Henry IV's reigns, the realm's defences and the royal finances appeared to be crumbling, the Commons again showed determination – and presumption – in trying to influence the conduct of government.

Richard II believed that parliamentary criticism and interference infringed his prerogative: his usurping successor Henry IV was perforce more tolerant. Richard had cause for alarm, since Commons' discontent in 1386* and 1388* was violently exploited by an alliance of magnates, led by his implacable uncle Thomas, duke of Gloucester: Henry's enemies, the Percies, could muster only extra-parliamentary support. Rebellious nobles, such as Gloucester in 1387, Henry of Bolingbroke in 1399, and the Percies in 1403 and 1405, were reviving the tradition that they had a right to take up arms as the natural defenders of the liberties of subjects. In fact, most of the higher nobility never rebelled, but burnished their personal loyalty to the king, cherishing their access to him in the household and basking in their developing privileges as hereditary peers of parliament. Nevertheless, the growing links between the Crown and the wider political community helped to undermine the traditional role of the higher nobility, providing some with incentives for rebellion.

For the gentry's need to rely on a Simon de Montfort or a Thomas of Lancaster to defend them against royal arbitrariness was lessening in the fourteenth century. But magnates needed the goodwill of a more powerful "magisterial gentry" to protect their scattered property interests, often vulnerable to trespass and suits over title. To get goodwill, and a variety of technical services, magnates needed to grant fees, rewards and annuities to their officers and neighbours, binding some by indentures. Feudal ties, often now much attenuated, no longer sufficed to gain faithful service. The systematization, particularly under Edward III, of grants to nobles of royal lieutenancies abroad, captaincies of military retinues on land and sea, and wardenships of the northern Marches, provided them with welcome additional sources of patronage. The widespread tendency for income from land to fall in the later fourteenth and early fifteenth centuries and then stagnate probably increased

The interior of the Chapter House of Westminster Abbey where the Commons met for the 1376 Parliament.

Commons as a body prosecuted offenders before the Lords. Royal government regained initiative in subsequent Great Council 1376 and Parliament 1377, securing taxation which Good Parliament had refused.

Wonderful Parliament 1386
Parliament of 1385 had demanded annual review of royal household expenditure. Wonderful Parliament voiced Commons' disillusionment with Richard II's ineffective foreign policy, mistrust of courtiers and suspicion of royal financial policies; impeached chancellor and appointed a continual Great Council composed of lords and bishops, with powers to control all royal revenues and supervise household expenditure. In 1387 Richard left Westminster with his advisers and friends, who formed a council rivalling that appointed by Parliament.

Questions to judges 1387
Richard II questioned a group of judges regarding king's rights in law; answers were uncompromising defence of royal prerogatives, which challenged authority of Parliament: reforms of 1386 unlawful, their upholders traitors; Parliament had no right to redress of grievances before taxation; impeachment without royal assent was unlawful; king alone could choose royal

Statute of Treasons 1352
Of great legal significance because it clearly enumerated six kinds of treasonable offence: plotting death of king, queen or their eldest son; violating queen, king's eldest unmarried daughter or wife of his eldest son; levying war against king; assisting or encouraging his enemies; counterfeiting royal seals or money, importing counterfeit money; killing chancellor, treasurer or any judge of the realm.

Parliament and constitution
Edward III's war expenditure meant that he had to govern with Commons' assent, for negotiated direct taxation was the least politically divisive means of obtaining finance. 1362 statute established that Parliament must assent to all lay taxation (clergy continued to negotiate directly with king over taxation in Convocation). This

established the role of Parliament, and Commons in particular, in the constitution. Commons' sense of corporate identity and procedures developed under Edward: Parliament became a crucial aspect of political life; kings could only ignore it if they were financially independent (by avoiding war).

Good Parliament 1376
Was highly critical of royal government, accusing officials of corruption and peculation, and financiers of profiting at king's expenses: a product of weak government during Edward III's dotage, political incapacity of John of Gaunt, and dismal military failures in war. Good Parliament important for election of first Speaker (Peter de la Mare) to represent Commons throughout Parliament in discussions with king and Lords, and for use of impeachments procedure whereby

councillors, who were not responsible to Parliament; Parliament could do nothing without king's assent. Judges' answers provoked major political crisis.

Merciless Parliament 1388
In November 1387 five of greatest lords of realm "appealed" (accused) five of Richard's closest adherents of treason, on grounds that they had exerted undue influence over king and used royal power to benefit themselves. Appeal was heard by Lords in Parliament, found proved, several executed. The Appellants appointed ministers and council to rule, but in 1389 Richard dismissed them, installed a council of moderate, experienced administrators, and pursued conciliatory policies during early 1390s.

Richard II's "Tyranny"
Peace with Scotland and France gave Richard II his opportunity for recovery; three Appellants were convicted of treason; one exiled, one executed, Thomas, duke of Gloucester, murdered. Parliament of 1397-98 annulled acts of Merciless Parliament, forcing those involved to sue for pardons. Richard demanded oaths of loyalty from Lords and Commons; exacted blank charters which placed subjects' lands and property at his mercy; extracted forced loans; denied men access to common-law courts; and terrorized population with private army.

Deposition of Richard II 1399
Richard II's gravest error was the exile of Henry of Bolingbroke and seizure of his estates. Bolingbroke landed at Ravenspur (Yorks) 1399, gained northern lords' support and captured Richard II. The aftermaths of the Good and Merciless Parliaments had shown that no workable constitutional settlement could be imposed on a king: accordingly Lords and Commons in Parliament renounced fealty to Richard II and accepted Bolingbroke's claim that the Crown was his by right.

The Lancastrian dynasty
Established by usurpation; uncertainty of Henry IV's title provided justification for many rebellions. He claimed throne by successful conquest, recognition by Parliament and hereditary right. Hereditary title seemed most significant to noblemen because it determined descent of lands and titles. (Unfortunately for Henry IV, a better hereditary claim existed, that of young Edmund Mortimer, earl of March, descended from Edward III's second son; Henry IV was son of Edward III's third son). Despite this obstacle Henry V, by his

the dependence of magnates on Court favour; they sought offices and rewards for themselves, supplementary means of rewarding their clients, and other ways of enhancing their incomes, such as the grant of licences to set up property trusts, and of the wardships and marriages of heirs.

The Crown found it hard to satisfy all these appetites. The parliamentary subsidy, the main device by which it had expanded its revenue, could not be blatantly used to reward the higher nobility; moreover, a high degree of reliance on taxes exposed the whole field of royal patronage to the suspicious scrutiny of the Commons. The conquests which Edward III and Henry V made abroad, fruitful prospects for nobles, turned sour. Competition for royal favour consequently intensified. The hunt for offices and good lordship came to permeate much of noble society: caucuses headed by magnates sought favour at Court and dominance in their localities. Such "affinities" tended to manipulate the law and to intimidate through violence. The king who channelled his favours too narrowly through coteries of friends and household officers, as Richard II and Henry VI were inclined to do, risked rebellion by disgruntled magnates and the alienation of gentlefolk nauseated by the oppressive greed of courtiers.

Sir John Fortescue, after a long and distinguished career in the service of the Lancastrian kings, described England as a realm in which the king might not rule the people by other laws than those they assented to, and might not set impositions on them without their consent. His confidence reflects the stability of the institutional bases of relations between Crown and community of the realm which had evolved in the fourteenth century. But he also noted elements of political instability. There was the propensity of the common folk to rebel. Their rebellions, as the Great Revolt* of 1381 and Cade's Revolt* of 1450 above all demonstrated, were no longer just against the authority of a borough or manor court: artisans and peasants were combining politically (sometimes, indeed, with gentlefolk) to reform the government of the realm. But Fortescue was more concerned about the threats posed to kings by those whom he termed "overmighty subjects". It was the instability at the top rather than at the bottom of society which threatened peaceful rule.

achievements, established Lancastrian legitimacy: his son Henry VI's minority 1422-37 was free from plot and rebellion.

Hotspur's Rebellion
Percy family had been well rewarded for aiding Henry's usurpation, but had grievances: manifesto claimed that they had not known of Henry's desire for throne; Hotspur (Sir Henry Percy) accused Henry of packing Parliament and breaking promises made at his accession. Percies resented Henry's favour towards Neville enemies, his refusal to ransom their Scottish captives, and his slow repayment of their debts incurred in royal service.

Battle of Shrewsbury 1403
Henry IV defeated rebel Percy forces led by Hotspur, before they could join forces with Glyndŵr; victory established secure hold on

throne, and enabled Henry to increase power of Neville allies in north.

Cambridge Plot 1415
Aristocratic plot to assassinate Henry V at Southampton: Henry was to be replaced by Edmund, earl of March (who informed Henry of plot) and Percy influence restored in north. Richard, earl of Cambridge, and main plotters were executed; Henry V wisely ignored other conspirators, and faced no further noble plot.

See **Peasants' Revolt** (page 134)

See **Cade's Rebellion** (page 147)

Wales:
native resilience and English conquest

R.R. Davies

Medieval Wales proved to be a very difficult country to conquer. The Normans made their first incursions into the country within a year of the battle of Hastings but the process of the conquest of Wales took more than two centuries to complete. The reasons for this delay are manifold: the mountainous terrain, the fragmented character of the native Welsh polity*, the piecemeal and uncoordinated nature of Norman penetration into Wales, the spasmodic nature of royal interest and intervention (for the campaigns of 1114, 1121, 1157 and 1165 were little more than punitive forays), the diversions of political turmoil in England (notably during Stephen's reign) and the undoubted fact that Wales was peripheral to the interests and ambitions of most of the Anglo-Norman and Angevin kings and barons.

By the later half of the twelfth century, a stalemate – or an equilibrium – had been reached in the Norman attempt to subjugate Wales. By then the Normans had established themselves firmly in the lowlands of southern Wales*. In these areas their military control was underpinned by rural settlement and the establishment of boroughs and priories. Elsewhere, however, Norman control was fitful and uncertain, amounting to little more than a loose military superiority and the collection of tributes from the native population. Henry II formally accepted this *status quo* by acknowledging fully the position of the native Welsh princes.

By the later twelfth century three major principalities had emerged in native, unconquered Wales (*pura Wallia* as it was called): Deheubarth, Powys and Gwynedd*. Political hegemony passed from the one to the other; but during the thirteenth century it came to be lodged firmly in Gwynedd under two remarkable princes, Llywelyn the Great (d.1240) and his grandson, Llywelyn ap Gruffudd, "the Last" (d. 1282). Their achievements were many: they secured firm control within Gwynedd itself at the expense of rival claimants within their own dynasty; then, through persuasion and force, they gradually brought all other native Welsh princelings under their authority; finally, they took full advantage of the political dissensions within England (notably during the later years of John's reign and during the turmoil of 1258-67) to push back the tide of Anglo-Norman advance in Wales and to forge native Wales into a single political unit. Their remarkable achievements were recognized in the Treaty of Montgomery (1267), when Henry III was forced to concede both Llywelyn ap Gruffudd's territorial gains and his newly-claimed title of Prince of Wales.

But the success of Gwynedd and the survival of native Wales were largely built on the incompetence of English kings; it only required the single-mindedness and masterfulness of one king to reveal that painful truth. In two devastating campaigns of 1276-77 and 1282-83 Edward I demolished the new-born principality of Wales. Llywelyn ap Gruffudd himself was killed near Builth in December 1282*, and his lands and principality were eventual-

Welsh Polity
Three major principalities defined by geography and kinship, with loose federation of lesser princes exercising some independence; lordship was exercised over *commotes,* local social units in which ties of kinship provided some unity.

Welsh March
Region created by military enterprise and seignorial activity of Anglo-Norman lords between 1067 and 1284; stabilized by conquest of Wales, which made Marcher lords' defensive role nearly irrelevant, but not abolished until 1536. Lords exercised practically regal authority; lordships gave great concentrations of military and territorial power to their owners.

Deheubarth, Powys, Gwynedd
Welsh princes were restricted to the mountainous and isolated parts of Wales by Anglo-Saxon kings. Gwynedd in the north, Powys in the east and Deheubarth in the south were the chief principalities, each a distinct group dominated by a powerful family. The inaccessible terrain greatly limited the extent of each prince's territorial power. Despite political disunity, Welshmen regarded themselves as a community *(Cymry),* united by common language, customs, culture and laws.

Treaty of Conwy 1277
Its terms suggested that outright conquest of Wales was not Edward's first aim: Llywelyn was required to do homage and fealty to Edward, surrender all lands conquered by Edward and undertake to pay all his debts to English Crown; in exchange Edward confirmed Llywelyn's title of prince of Wales and allowed him to retain his remaining possessions under Welsh laws and customs.

Rebellion of 1282
Begun not by Llywelyn but by his brother David, though Llywelyn joined it, as did many Welshmen who resented growing aggressiveness of English rule in Wales.

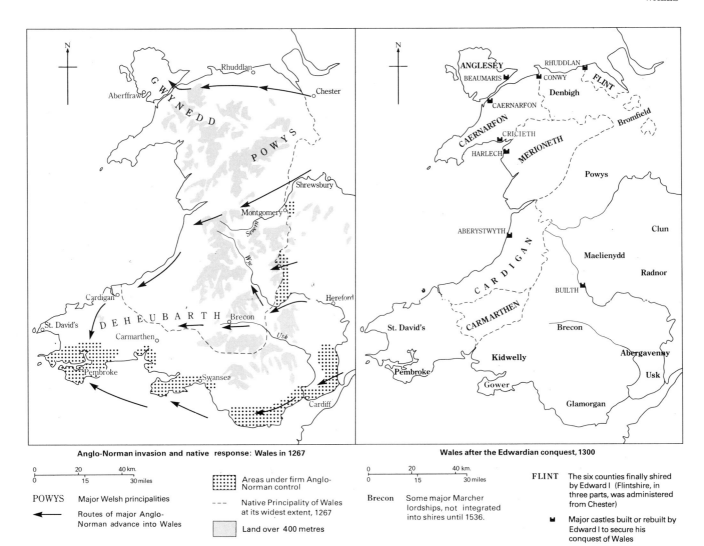

Anglo-Norman invasion and native response: Wales in 1267

0 20 40 km.	
0 15 30 miles	

POWYS   Major Welsh principalities

⟵   Routes of major Anglo-Norman advance into Wales

Areas under firm Anglo-Norman control

- - -   Native Principality of Wales at its widest extent, 1267

Land over 400 metres

Wales after the Edwardian conquest, 1300

0 20 40 km.	
0 15 30 miles	

Brecon   Some major Marcher lordships, not integrated into shires until 1536.

FLINT   The six counties finally shired by Edward I (Flintshire, in three parts, was administered from Chester)

◼   Major castles built or rebuilt by Edward I to secure his conquest of Wales

Edward I's castles

Victory in 1277 and 1282 inaugurated heavy investment in Wales by Edward I in castle building, castle repair and foundation or improvement of towns (usually settled by Englishmen). Large expenditure on the five castles of Snowdonia (Conwy, Caernarfon, Cricieth, Harlech and Beaumaris) and on Builth and the castles and towns of Flint, Rhuddlan and Aberystwyth.

Statute of Rhuddlan 1284

(or "of Wales") extended shire system to much of Wales: Welsh law and customs to some extent preserved – criminal law anglicized, civil law remained Welsh; commote retained as centre of justice and administration with Welsh local officials; new administrative centres established at Caernarfon and Carmarthen.

ly bestowed on Edward's son. The military and governmental settlement which followed the crushing victory was comprehensive. A series of magnificent castles* (such as Harlech, Caernarfon and Conwy) was built to ensure the permanence of the military victory; shires on the English pattern were created in the conquered lands of north and west Wales; governmental headquarters were established at Caernarfon and Carmarthen to administer the newly-conquered lands; in the Statute of Rhuddlan* in 1284 English common law was introduced, without, however, altogether extinguishing native Welsh law and custom; and the Welsh Church, which had been brought more closely into alignment with English and European practice and organization in the twelfth century, was now even more firmly fettered under English control. In only one respect was the settlement incomplete: Edward made no attempt to absorb the great Marcher lordships of eastern and southern Wales into his territorial and governmental settlement.

In spite of serious revolts in 1287 and 1294-95, the Edwardian conquest proved final. Many Welshmen learnt to live easily enough with it and indeed to benefit from it. Others, however, harboured resentment at the way in which they were ruthlessly exploited and at the privileges bestowed on

English settlers, especially in the boroughs. Yet others dreamed of an united Wales under its own native dynasty. Out of these resentments and dreams was forged the revolt of Owain Glyndŵr* which swept Wales in the years 1400-08. Its success was based largely on the political turmoil of Henry IV's reign; its ultimate failure persuaded Welshmen that in future their political aspirations had to operate within the framework of English conquest and control.

Owain Glyndŵr's rebellion

His feud with Lord Grey of Ruthin sparked Welsh revolt; proclaimed Prince of Wales 1400; proposed joint Welsh, Irish and Scottish rebellion 1402; captured Edmund Mortimer, who joined rebellion, opening links with Percy rebellion 1403; captured Harlech and Aberystwyth 1404; summoned Welsh Parliament; arranged Tripartite Indenture 1405, ravaged western midlands; lost Harlech and Aberystwyth 1408 in English recovery; revolt subsided, Wales reconquered.

Tripartite Indenture 1405

An agreement between Glyndŵr, Edmund Mortimer (earl of March's uncle) and Henry Percy, earl of Northumberland, to depose Henry IV and divide England between them into three regions. Archbishop Scrope of York, complaining of bad government, heavy taxation and raids on coast, rebelled in Yorkshire; captured by Ralph Neville, earl of Westmorland, tried and executed 1405. Northumberland and allies fled; later defeat of their forces at Bramham Moor (Yorks) 1408.

Scotland:
the land and the kingdom

Bruce Webster

Scotland's history has been made by the land, much of it harsh hill country, impressive to the tourist but yielding little to the farmer. The lower parts can be rich, especially around the Moray Firth and in the fertile plains of Angus, the central Lowlands and the Tweed valley; and these regions, each cut off from the other by mountains or moorlands, were to dominate the country's development. Over Highlands and Islands, life depended on subsistence farming, hunting and fishing, with cattle the only product for export. In the more fertile lands of the east, arable farming was dominant; and over the southern hills the Border abbeys pastured flocks of sheep whose wool, exported mainly through Berwick, made Scotland one of the important suppliers in western Europe. Towns were small, mainly local markets; but a few, Berwick, Perth, Dundee and Aberdeen, had a significant foreign trade.

Lacking any obvious centre of power, Scotland was slow to move from a tribal kingship towards the kind of territorial monarchy that had been developing in other countries since the tenth century. For long the various "peoples", Picts, Scots, the several British kingdoms of Strathclyde and Lothian, and the Scandinavian overlords of the north and west, lived in temporary and fluctuating alliances and rivalries. By 1153, the Canmore dynasty had for almost a century been uneasily accepted, with occasional English support, as rulers of a single kingdom; but power remained with those who controlled the localities.

By 1153, however, a basis was already emerging for a more effective royal authority. The Canmore dynasty's English contacts made it possible to introduce into Scotland nobles from the north of England, Bruce and Balliol for instance, from the Welsh March Walter son of Alan, or even directly from

Scotland in the Middle Ages

0	50	100	150 km
0	30	60	90 miles

Land over 200 metres

"Cum Universi" 1192
Papal bull granted to William the Lion: declared Scottish Church, comprising nine named dioceses, to be immediately subject to Holy See; no one except pope or his legate (representative) could pronounce interdict (papal prohibition restraining clergy from performing divine service); only a Scot or a man specially deputed by pope might act as legate in Scotland.

France. There was never a Norman "conquest" of Scotland but there was the establishment of an alien aristocracy who came to dominate the better lands. At first, at least, they were a natural support to the dynasty that had introduced them.

The Church was also a source of strength. For centuries the Scottish Church had been remote from the rest of Christendom, developing in its own way and without the organization that had long been normal in more settled countries. By the twelfth century, however, a diocesan system was emerging, and in 1192 the papacy recognized the identity of the Scottish Church and its independence of all authority save that of Rome itself*. This immeasurably strengthened the authority of the monarchy; and the kings themselves helped by founding in Scotland many new monasteries, giving much land into the control of institutions which looked directly to the kings for support.

Scotland's first university, St Andrews, was founded in 1411. The mace of the Faculty of Arts was completed by 1419. It is of silver, partly gilt, and may be of Scottish workmanship.

The Douglas fortress of Hermitage Castle in Liddesdale, Roxburghshire, symbolizes the power of the family in a remote area.

113

Silver-gilt boss of the Bute mazer, a maple-wood drinking bowl; the lion probably represents Robert Bruce and the arms are those of his leading followers.

At the same time, elements of a territorial administration appeared: sheriffs based on royal castles, acting at once as a local judiciary and as agents for the collection of revenue and the administration of royal lands. Yet in medieval Scotland the local administration was never controlled by a centralized bureaucracy. Scottish "central" government was simply the king and his household: the chamberlain handled his revenues, the clerks of his chapel wrote his documents and kept his records. All could and did move with him as required. It was not till the fourteenth century that a more permanent base seemed to be emerging in Edinburgh.

In 1153 Malcolm IV inherited an authority which was effective over the Lowlands, the central and eastern Borders, and the lands on the southern coast of the Moray Firth. He had little if any power elsewhere. William the Lion tried, not very successfully, to increase his authority both in Galloway and to the north of the Moray Firth; Alexander III was able in 1266 to secure the nominal cession of the Scandinavian territories in the west*. Yet the Highlands remained hard to control and the Western Isles were a distinct region throughout the Middle Ages: their trading and personal links were with Ireland, Man and the west of England, and politically their nobles were as ready to ally themselves with England as with their own king.

The Canmore dynasty ended with the tragic death of Margaret, grand-daughter of Alexander III, in 1290*, which led Edward I of England to press his claims to overlordship and ultimately, in 1296, to attempt the conquest of Scotland. The resulting resistance* (the Wars of Independence, 1296-1357) had, by the mid-fourteenth century, secured the independence of Scotland; but it had also dramatically altered the political structure of the country. The leaders in the wars, especially the family of Douglas, gained so much land in the Borders that the kings from David II onwards found it difficult to exercise any authority in the area. During the captivity of James I (1406-24), the Douglas family enjoyed unchallenged power in the south; a power that was only curtailed in the 1450s, when James II dispossessed the main branch of the family of its lands. Like his father James I, James II could exploit the personal authority of the monarchy with a high-handedness that revealed his

Treaty of Perth 1266
Followed unsuccessful campaign in Western Isles by Hakon IV of Norway, who suffered a reverse at battle of Largs 1263 and died on campaign; apparent that Lords of Isles preferred lordship of Alexander III of Scotland rather than kings of Norway, whose naval power was waning. Treaty restored peace between Alexander and Magnus, son of Hakon: Man and Western Isles sold by Norway to Scots.

Scottish succession
Alexander III's only surviving heir at his death 1286 was young grand-daughter, Margaret of Norway, for whom a regency government was established; she died 1290. Claimants to throne were descendants of William the Lion's brother: (1) John Balliol, grandson of his eldest daughter; (2) Robert Bruce, son of a younger daughter. The dispute was submitted to Edward I, who took this opportunity to have his overlordship recognized by claimants; 1292 Edward ruled in Balliol's favour and Balliol was enthroned at Scone.

Scottish revolt
Scottish barons were aggrieved by Edward I's encouragement of appeals from Scottish law courts to England; seized power from Balliol, allied with France. English expedition defeated Scots (Dunbar 1296), Balliol surrendered kingdom to Edward I. William Wallace rebelled 1297, defeated at Falkirk 1298; English expeditions 1302-4 temporarily subdued Scotland; Robert Bruce (grandson of claimant) revolted 1306.

Bannockburn 1314
In 1309 the Scottish clergy formally recognized Bruce as King of Scots: after a series of successful campaigns the Scots besieged Stirling castle, a vital English stronghold. Edward II mustered an army to relieve it, which was heavily defeated at Bannockburn (24 June 1314), where Scottish archers and infantry successfully overcame English cavalry. Victory led to consolidation of Bruce's power.

"The Bruce"
John Barbour (archdeacon of Aberdeen) composed *The Bruce* by 1375: a vernacular work of over 13,000 lines in couplets; glorifies Robert Bruce and his captains, celebrates "freedom" of Scotland; an invaluable source for historians.

personal power, though it did less to establish an even-handed system of justice, something which even in the fifteenth century still depended on the intermittent activities of the king's council, as and when urged by the king himself.

In 1455 James II ruled a country that was fiercely and self-consciously nationalist. Its nobles and churchmen were familiar travellers in Europe; foreign *objets d'art,* manuscripts and literature were imported and imitated by native craftsmen and writers. But the wars against England had not only encouraged continental contacts; they had given rise to a distinctively anti-English national culture, evinced in the development of a nationalist school of historical writing, and in the exaltation in literature of the heroes of the Wars of Independence, Wallace, Bruce* and Douglas. James II still lacked much that was elsewhere regarded as the natural administrative apparatus of effective kingship, but there was now no question that he ruled over a single nation.

The second Great Seal of Robert I, 1317, showing Robert, armed and mounted.

Ireland:
the medieval lordship

James Lydon

In 1155 Pope Adrian IV authorized King Henry II to invade Ireland*. Eleven years later Henry received the homage of the Irish king of Leinster. Finally, in October 1171, he led a major expedition to Ireland to establish his rights over the island and its people, including those Anglo-Normans who had been winning extensive and independent lordships for themselves there. King Henry bound them and most of the Irish kings in a dependent relationship to himself. He reserved a large royal demesne, which included the Scandinavian ports*, issued charters to Dublin and to many religious corporations, and left behind a chief governor and the embryo of an administration which would

Laudabiliter 1155
Papal bull (or letter) granting Henry II permission to invade Ireland to promote ecclesiastical reform: the Irish Church retained many Celtic characteristics. Pope Adrian IV (an Englishman) knew success demanded the appointment of reforming bishops, supported by a powerful and sympathetic king; Henry II was the obvious candidate. Henry finally invaded 1171 to prevent his vassal Richard de Clare ("Strongbow") forming an independent kingdom of Ireland, after Strongbow had inherited the kingdom of Leinster and defeated Rory O'Connor, high king of Ireland, in battle.

The Scandinavian ports
Dublin, Limerick, Cork, Wexford and Waterford; each was from the 10th century the centre of Viking settlements, from which Norse rulers threatened to topple native dynasties. Norse power waxed, unchecked by the Irish, until the High King Malachy defeated Dublin (Battle of Tara, 980), and the Munster hero Brian Boru overcame Limerick at Sulcoit (968) and ended the Scandinavian menace by defeating Norse forces at Clontarf (1014).

An illustration from a 14th-century French manuscript showing Thomas Despenser earl of Gloucester, coming face to face with Art MacMurrough, king of Leinster, in 1399.

Trim Castle, County Meath, built on the River Boyne in about 1230 to protect the Pale of Settlement from marauders. With its extensive perimeter, it was designed for a large garrison.

protect his rights in future. The new lordship of Ireland developed rapidly. Dublin became its capital, home of an Exchequer, Chancery and civil service which was to provide a central administration controlling a system of local government based on shires and liberties. The common law of the England was introduced, with justices, courts and a legal system through which it could be administered. A network of manors, boroughs and new parishes spread a new social order. The Church was feudalized and many new religious foundations helped to strengthen the increasingly English character of the settlement. Most of Gaelic Ireland was affected. Many local lords were dispossessed or left in possession of greatly reduced lordships. Intermarriage between the leading settler families and the ruling dynasties of Ireland softened for the Irish nobility the inexorable spread of the feudal settlement. The new order soon produced prosperity, manifested in the cathedrals, parish churches and stone castles which, in the thirteenth century, became a feature of the Irish countryside. Exports increased rapidly, founded on an agriculture which had been transformed by the settlers. The new wealth created a demand for imported luxuries. The government, too, benefited and was able to produce a surplus revenue for the king. By the late thirteenth century Ireland seemed well on the way to becoming a thoroughly Anglicized, reasonably stable and prosperous lordship attached to the English Crown, with its own Parliament* and institutions of government.

But a century later King Richard II had to lead two great expeditions to Ireland in rapid succession in an attempt to salvage a tottering lordship. Ireland had been invaded by the Scots* in 1315 and for nearly four years had been torn by war, famine and death. Even earlier, Irish chieftains in the localities had successfully resisted the completion of the feudal settlement and even forced a withdrawal in certain places. Many settlers had accommodated themselves to the new circumstances by dealing on their own terms with the

Irish Parliament

First recorded meeting was 1264: began as enlarged meeting of royal council, became judicial, consultative and legislative assembly. There were three houses: the spiritual and secular peers, the commons and the lower clergy. The commons were summoned in 14th century to discuss taxation, but did not become an integral part until end of that century. The area represented in Parliament was small and always shrinking: the members were few and easily controlled by government and lords who dominated the Council.

Scottish invasion

Victory at Bannockburn enabled Edward Bruce, brother of Robert, to invade Ireland 1315. With support from Gaelic Irish he overcame all resistance: crowned king of Ireland 1316. But he failed to take Dublin; driven northwards by army led by Roger Mortimer of Wigmore, killed at Dundalk 1318. Edward II failed to make use of victory to restore centralized rule; Bruce invasion a major cause of collapse of English lordship in Ireland.

Statutes of Kilkenny 1366
Important codification of laws for Ireland, designed to impose social, political and economic stability; promulgated by Irish Parliament summoned by Lionel of Clarence (Edward III's son), governor of Ireland. Attempted to prevent, by statutory provision, "degeneracy" (process of Gaelicization, whereby Anglo-Irish descendants of Anglo-Norman settlers were adopting laws, language, customs and culture of native Irish): neither the statutes nor Edward III's enormous military expenditure in Ireland under Clarence (1361-64) and William Windsor (1369-71) greatly increased royal control.

Richard II and Ireland
Peace with French and Scots enabled Richard II to challenge rebellious Gaelic chieftains: in 1394-95 Richard and a well-equipped army quickly overcame the men of Leinster and many other regions. Richard recruited Leinster men to attack and occupy Gaelic lands further west, leaving the Leinster lands to English lords: the plan failed. Richard's second expedition 1399 was cut short by Bolingbroke's English rising: Anglo-Irish lords and Gaelic chieftains became practically independent in 15th century.

The Pale
Area ruled from Dublin during 15th century (counties of Dublin, Meath, Kildare and Louth). Governments realized that centralized rule of all Ireland was impossible and power was divided between Gaelic chiefs, Anglo-Irish lords and Dublin. Official policy concentrated on defence of Pale through castles, forts, watchmen, beacons and ditches.

Irish. Control from Dublin began to break down. Revenues declined sharply in the early fourteenth century, and before long the English taxpayer was increasingly forced to subsidize Ireland. War became more frequent as the settlement (now known as the "land of peace") continued to contract and the "land of war" gained ground. The great Anglo-Irish families, Butlers, Geraldines, Berminghams and Powers being the most prominent, had mostly to fend for themselves. The Church became more sharply divided into that "among the English" and that "among the Irish". Instability followed and inevitably contributed to the economic decline which Ireland experienced in common with western Europe. The Black Death made plague endemic, with catastrophic results for the manors and towns of feudal Ireland, further weakening the settlement. Desperate attempts by successive Dublin governments at recovery by military means produced no solution. Major expeditions from England in the 1360s, 1370s and 1390s* achieved little at huge expense. A poverty-stricken Lancastrian government in the fifteenth century could not afford to maintain this level of expenditure on Ireland. In an attempt to cut losses, the Irish government increasingly restricted itself to a small area in the east, including the Pale*, which was defended with fortifications. Elsewhere it relied on the local Anglo-Irish nobility to preserve the lordship intact. These lords used a system of maintenance, partly based on Irish customary exactions, to retain armed retinues. They became self-reliant, semi-autonomous, and to some extent Gaelicized. The greatest of them, Butlers and Geraldines, sought to control the Dublin government and to use it in their own interest. By 1449, when Richard of York came to Ireland as chief governor and heir to the great de Burgh lordships in Connacht and Ulster, Ireland was ready to be exploited by him and he seized the opportunity to bind the leading Anglo-Irish nobility to his house.

Aspects of Irish life reported to Giraldus Cambrensis during his tours in the late 12th century: (left) coracle paddlers from Connacht, wearing only rawhide girdles;

(above) the inauguration rite of the kings of Tyrconnell, with the new king standing in a tub of broth and sharing broth and meat with his people.

Warfare and International Relations 1154-1327:
the Angevin empire

Michael Prestwich

The fact that the kings of England held lands in France as vassals of the French monarchs dominated foreign policy from the reign of Henry II to that of Edward II. While the rulers of England were prepared to perform homage to those of France, they resisted French attempts to exercise effective jurisdiction over their continental possessions. In the resulting conflicts, the extent of the English lands in France was steadily reduced.

In 1154, through a mixture of conquest, inheritance and marriage, Henry II came to rule an immense dominion stretching from the Scottish borders to the Pyrenees. There was no real unity to this conglomeration of territories, often termed the Angevin Empire, though Henry's plans to divide his lands in France between his sons eventually failed. Henry II did not challenge French overlordship directly: he withdrew from an attempted conquest of Toulouse in 1159 rather than oppose Louis VII in person, and he performed homage both to Louis and his son Philip II. The rebellions of his sons in 1173, 1183 and 1189 were more of a problem to Henry than the hostility of the French: though the latter took advantage of the rebellions, it was only after Henry II's death that they offered a major challenge to the English.

Richard I's participation in the Third Crusade* added to his chivalric renown, but also to his debts. The defence of Normandy against Philip II was increasingly costly, particularly with the construction of the great castle of Château Gaillard*. Yet it seems that England's financial resources were adequate: disaster only came when, in John, a king who lacked powers of leadership succeeded to the throne. John's refusal to attend Philip's court led to judgement being given against him, and so to the French conquest of Normandy in 1204. John's attempts to regain his losses, with the aid of a great coalition of princes from the Low Countries and Germany, came to nothing when the Emperor Otto IV was defeated by the French at Bouvines* in 1214. In the course of the civil war at the end of John's reign the French even invaded England*, though with little success.

Although Normandy had been lost, the English still retained lands further south. Ineffective expeditions in 1230 and 1242 failed to reverse the loss of Poitou, but Gascony and some other lands in the south-west remained English. In 1259, in the Treaty of Paris*, Henry III formally gave up his claims to Normandy, Maine, Anjou and Poitou, and agreed that he held Gascony as a fief of the French king. Conflict was not renewed until 1294, when Edward I refused a summons to the *parlement* of Paris. Like King John, Edward built up a grand alliance* against the French, but when he landed in Flanders in 1297 he received little support, and had to agree to a truce. In the peace negotiations a marriage was agreed between Edward and Philip IV's sister, and this new link was reinforced in 1308 when Edward II married Philip's daughter Isabella. Yet lengthy diplomatic proceedings failed to resolve the outstanding issues, and in 1324 English possession of Gascony was

Third Crusade 1187-92
Response to Christian defeat at Hattin (1187) by Saladin, Moslem overlord of Syria and Egypt, who seemed about to destroy the Crusader states. After Philip II and Richard I had settled their political differences, Anglo-French armies left France (1190): they besieged Moslem-held Acre (captured 1191); Richard defeated Saladin at Arsuf and relieved Jaffa; made truce with Saladin 1192.

Château Gaillard
Castle on River Seine built by Richard I 1196-98 at enormous cost: a crucial strongpoint for defending Seine routes to Norman capital (Rouen) and for launching attacks. A masterpiece of military architecture, but it was lost to Philip II by John 1204.

Bouvines 1214
Major battle in Flanders, signifying emergence of Capetian France as a great power and the end of Angevin pretensions in northern France. John had planned to attack Philip II's territory and regain possessions lost in 1204; organized a coalition in Low Countries hostile to Philip, including Emperor Otto; sent expedition to Flanders under William, earl of Salisbury, and campaigned himself in Poitou. Philip negotiated truce with John immediately after his decisive victory.

French invasion 1216-17
John's repudiation of Magna Carta renewed civil war: Prince Louis of France invaded England, claiming the throne through his wife Blanche (grand-daughter of Henry II), and supported the rebels. At John's death 1216 Louis held London, eastern England and the Channel ports; royalists protecting young Henry III held western England. Royalists attracted support for the Crown by reissuing Magna Carta 1216: during 1217 William Marshal, earl of Pembroke, defeated rebels and French at Lincoln and at sea off Sandwich and arranged settlement by Treaty of Kingston. Louis left England and William Marshal's government revived royal authority thereafter.

Treaty of Paris 1259

Henry III surrendered to Louis IX of France all claims to Normandy, Maine, Anjou and Poitou. Louis acknowledged Henry's lordship over Gascony, on condition that Henry became his vassal. The treaty gave England peace and friendship with France for 35 years but left Gascony open to French kings' intervention (as overlords).

Edward I's Grand Alliance

Created 1294-95 to counter Philip IV's intervention in Gascony and deter him from further expansion; included counts of Flanders, Bar and Holland, the duke of Brabant, and Adolf of Nassau, king of Germany. In 1297 Edward made defensive alliance with Flanders; his Flemish expedition followed invasion of Flanders by Philip. Edward I weakened by cost of foreign subsidies and war on four fronts (Flanders, Gascony, Scotland, Welsh rebellion of 1294-95), and mounting domestic opposition to his governmental methods: truce covering Flanders and Gascony agreed 1297; Gascony formally restored to Edward 1303 (Treaty of Paris).

Early 14th-century drawings in the Holkham Bible Picture Book which show (top) mounted knights in combat with lance, sword and battleaxe, and (below) common soldiers engaged with longbows, swords and other weapons.

The ruins of Château Gaillard, overlooking the River Seine south-east of Rouen.

119

again threatened in the War of Saint-Sardos*. By 1327 there was little left of the once vast Angevin empire.

English interests and ambitions were not confined to France. Henry II formed marriage alliances with Sicily*, Castile and Saxony, and there are hints that he hoped to intervene in northern Italy. It was under Henry III that foreign policy became most far-reaching, with a plan to make his second son, Edmund, king of Sicily. Nothing came of this, however, save acute financial embarrassment. Nor were the ambitions of Henry's brother Richard to the German throne crowned with any real success, despite his election in 1257.

The crusade was not only important under Richard I, but also under Edward I*. When he came to the throne in 1272 he was on his way home from a crusade, and he always hoped to lead another expedition. He tried hard in the 1280s to create the peace in Europe* which was a prerequisite for a successful crusade, and took the cross himself in 1287, but because of his problems nearer home was never able to achieve his ambition.

The conventional view is that in this period the feudal host, composed of men serving in return for land, was transformed into a paid army. In fact the central element of English armies, the cavalry of the royal household, changed little throughout these years, and there was always some reliance on paid men, often foreign mercenaries. Feudal service continued to be demanded, but the size of the quotas asked for was radically reduced in the first half of the thirteenth century. Yet even under Edward I many magnates disliked serving for pay, and brought contingents far in excess of their formal obligations to fight in Wales and Scotland. Continental warfare was not so popular, however. As armies became larger under Edward I, up to 30,000 strong, recruiting, transport and victualling became far better organized.

The aim of warfare was more often to put opponents under economic pressure by ravaging lands and burning villages, or by taking castles, rather than to engage in set-piece battles. English troops fought no really major battles on the Continent in this period, although at home there were the civil-war battles of Lewes (1264) and Evesham (1265), while in Scotland both Falkirk (1298) and Bannockburn (1314) were major encounters. It was the fall of Château Gaillard in 1204, however, not a field battle, which sealed the fate of Normandy, and it was in military architecture and siege techniques that the major advances in military technology took place. There was probably little difference between the tactics employed by English and French armies in the twelfth and thirteenth centuries: both depended extensively on heavily armed cavalry. A greater reliance on archers began with Edward I's Welsh wars, and with the Scottish wars of the early fourteenth century new tactics were developed. By 1327 the English knights were instructed to be ready to fight on foot, and the way was prepared for the techniques of using archers and men-at-arms in combination which were to prove so devastating in the Hundred Years War.

War of Saint-Sardos 1323-25
Charles IV of France sought Edward II's homage for Gascony; Edward failed to comply. Charles started building a fortified town at Saint-Sardos, under English jurisdiction: Sir Ralph Basset, English governor of Gascony, attacked Saint-Sardos, hanging a French official 1323. War broke out when Charles invaded Gascony to compel Edward to acknowledge his authority; Edward agreed to truce 1325; his son did homage to Charles IV who returned Gascony.

The Sicilian Business
In exchange for recognition of Edmund as king of Sicily in 1255, Henry III agreed to send Pope Alexander IV troops and to pay papal debts (on pain of excommunication and interdict in default, which occurred 1258, precipitating English barons' opposition movement). Sicily was attractive for its wealth and strategic location but, controlled by Alexander IV's enemy Manfred, difficult to conquer. Henry III possibly sought to accumulate the Hohenstaufen possessions in his own family and become Europe's greatest power.

Edward I's Crusade
Took cross in 1268; departed in 1270 for Tunis, then went on to Acre, to fight Moslem leader Sultan Baibars, who, preoccupied by Mongol attacks in northern Syria, was reluctant to engage him; led two raids into Palestine, survived Moslem assassination attempt. Left Acre 1272, reached England 1274, having achieved little.

Edward I as peacemaker
Edward spent years 1286-89 in Gascony, composing struggle between king of Aragon and Charles of Salerno for the kingdom of Sicily. His efforts contributed to a general settlement, but Scottish succession problems 1290 demanded his attention, preventing him from organizing another crusade.

Warfare and International Relations 1327-1450:
the Hundred Years War

Malcolm Vale

Battle of Crécy 1346
Edward III's Norman expedition exploited earl of Derby's victories in Gascony: Philip VI intercepted Edward at Crécy, heading for Calais; English archers inflicted heavy French casualties; Edward subsequently captured Calais 1347. Rout of Scottish invasion by archbishop of York, Nevilles and Percies (Neville's Cross, 1346) and Thomas Dagworth's (lieutenant in Brittany) victory at la Roche Derrien 1347 added to English triumph.

Battle of Poitiers 1356
Papal mediators at Guines 1354 suggested Edward should renounce French throne for sovereignty over Aquitaine, Poitou, Anjou, Maine, Touraine and Calais. Breakdown of negotiations renewed war; at Poitiers, Black Prince (Edward III's son) defeated and captured King John of France.

Treaty of Brétigny 1360
Edward III gained full sovereignty over Gascony, Poitou, various counties and lordships, and town and environs of Calais; fixed King John's ransom at £500,000, offered to renounce claim to French Crown under certain conditions (not fulfilled). After 1369, English war effort was poor: two unsuccessful *chevauchées,* defeat for Pembroke's fleet off La Rochelle 1373, devastation of English coast by Franco-Castilian fleet 1377. By 1375 (Truce of Bruges) English held only Calais and coastal strip from Bordeaux to Bayonne. Political instability in England and France after 1380 prevented major war until Henry V's reign.

Armagnacs and Burgundians
Feuding and civil war amongst French nobility gave great advantage to Henry V. Incapacity of Charles VI stimulated struggles for control of royal government and patronage; escalated into civil war in 1407. In 1414 and 1416 Henry V had secret agreements with Duke John of Burgundy; in 1417, when Henry invaded Normandy, Burgundy was at war with opponents amongst French nobility (including Dauphin Charles), thus reducing opposition to invasion. Murder of Duke John by

The great war between England and France which began in 1337 and effectively ended in 1453 was merely the last phase of a much more protracted conflict. Since the union of England with Normandy, Anjou and Aquitaine in the twelfth century, her kings had been vassals of the French Crown for these continental fiefs. The breaking of this feudal connection by Edward III (1340) ushered in the final stage of a gradual but inexorable movement of alienation. Edward's claim to the throne of France (through his mother Isabella, daughter of Philip the Fair) transformed a feudal dispute into a dynastic war. This was in turn to become a conflict between two "nations" in the fifteenth century. The so-called "Hundred Years War" can therefore be divided into two major phases: from 1337 to 1417, and from 1417 to 1453. The second invasion of Normandy by Henry V (1417) was an important turning point in the conflict.

During the fourteenth and early fifteenth centuries, the English war effort tended to concentrate upon raiding expeditions into France, designed to harass and terrorize the enemy. It was in the course of two such raids, or *chevauchées,* that the English victories at Crécy* (1346) and Poitiers* (1356) took place. These enriched many English captains, especially as a result of ransoms and booty taken from the French Crown and nobility. In 1360, at the Treaty of Brétigny*, Edward III was prepared to exchange his title to the throne of France for a greatly enlarged Aquitaine, which the Black Prince was to rule. French refusal to restore these south-western lands, and appeals to France against the Prince's government by certain Gascon lords in 1368-69, led to a renewal of the war. By 1415, internal divisions* among the French nobility persuaded Henry V to pursue his claims with greater expectation of success, and his strategic and moral victory at Agincourt* heralded an English war of conquest. The character of the war changed: a permanent English occupation of northern France (which was unknown under Edward III) was now envisaged, so that a new reality might be given to otherwise purely theoretical claims. Lancastrian France and the duchy of Normandy became viable units of government and administration under Henry V and

Dauphin's men 1419 precipitated alliance between Henry V and Duke Philip of Burgundy.

Agincourt 1415
Henry V found his path to Calais blocked by large French force: English fought on foot defending position against French cavalry; English bowmen wreaked havoc. French force heavily defeated with losses including three dukes and Constable of France. Agincourt fuelled English enthusiasm for war (Parliament immediately granted

generous financial assistance); it encouraged Henry V to undertake systematic conquest of demoralized French enemy, and it seemed to legitimize the Lancastrian dynasty.

during the subsequent regency of his brother John, duke of Bedford. However, the financial sub-structure of the Lancastrian dual monarchy of England and France was not secure. The war of conquest was increasingly unable to pay for itself and a spiral of debt, over-assigned revenues* and consequent bankruptcy plagued the last twenty years of the English presence in France.

The political basis of the English war effort throughout the period had been a system of alliances with both greater and lesser nobles within France and the old Angevin dominions. By 1435, grave weaknesses had become apparent in this political structure. The defection of Philip the Good, duke of Burgundy (1419-67) to the side of Charles VII of France (1422-61) undermined the English régime's stability in the north; while the worsening position of English finances, and a decreasing supply of land and rewards for loyal Gascons, produced a crisis of allegiance in the south after 1442. By 1450 the French were able to reduce Normandy with relative ease, although some entrenched English captains proved both difficult and costly to dislodge. In the south-west, the final débâcle of 1453 was preceded by a campaign in 1451 which effectively brought the greater part of English Gascony (except for Bordeaux and Bayonne) permanently into French hands*. Despite Henry VI's marriage to Margaret of Anjou in 1445 and the truce* which preceded it, the traditional methods of promoting Anglo-French harmony – royal marriage alliances and intensive diplomatic activity – had ultimately failed. Hostilities were brought to an end only by military force: the Anglo-French deadlock was broken, and nothing remained of the English presence in France except the town and March of Calais, intangible claims to sovereignty (which were never formally renounced), disappointed supporters (some of

Overassignment
Assignment was the practice of discharging royal debts by delivering to creditors a tally (notched stick depicting sum due) to present to local revenue collector for payment. Overassignment occurred when sums issued by tally exceeded the revenue available, thus disappointing royal creditors.

An assault on a fortified place, illustrated in Jean de Wavrin's Chronique d'Angleterre *(illuminated in Flanders c. 1470): the outer defences are attacked while a siege-gun is brought to bear on the inner walls and towers.*

Treaty of Troyes 1420

Agreement on future relations between Charles VI of France, Duke Philip of Burgundy and Henry V. Henry married daughter of Charles, and was accepted as heir to France (thus establishing double monarchy of France and England which Henry VI inherited). Effectiveness of treaty depended on support of Philip and speedy elimination of Dauphin.

Congress of Arras 1435

Diplomatic meeting between French, Burgundian and English representatives as result of which Philip the Good, duke of Burgundy, renounced Treaty of Troyes and recognized Charles VII of France. Loss of Burgundian alliance undermined English position in France, already serious owing to death of John, duke of Bedford, an able soldier and statesman. Although Paris was lost, England held on to Normandy for a further 14 years.

Truce of Tours 1444

Henry VI and his chief minister William, earl of Suffolk, hoped the king's marriage to Margaret of Anjou would be basis of lasting peace; but they only gained a two-year truce with Charles VII, extended until 1449.

Loss of Normandy and Gascony

When war resumed, English garrisons in Normandy fell quickly to Charles VII's troops; defeat of relief force from England at Formigny in 1450 ensured collapse of English Normandy. In 1451 French overran Gascony: Lord Talbot's relief force was defeated at Castillon 1453, amidst carnage caused by French artillery; ended English rule over Gascony.

whom sought exile in England), and regional memories of greater autonomy under the English régime than under the French administration which replaced it.

The major military developments of the war were two-fold: the perfection by the English of battlefield tactics which relied upon a combination of dismounted men-at-arms and archers armed with the longbow; and, from the 1370s onwards, an increasing use by both sides of firearms and artillery. Although guns had appeared in western Europe by 1327, they remained small and generally ineffective for some time. It was only in the last quarter of the fourteenth century that large siege guns, or bombards, began to make some impact upon warfare. The final campaigns of the Hundred Years War (1449-53) owed much to the superiority of French siege artillery, although field artillery was still in its infancy. Charles VII's French standing army (1445), however, gave pride of place to heavy cavalry, and fighting in the field underwent something of a revival in the subsequent decades. But there were relatively few pitched battles between Verneuil (1424) and Castillon (1453), and it was the steady reduction of fortified places by the French which, in military terms, won the war for them.

The collapse of English rule in France demonstrated that Henry V's war aims had proved impossible to achieve. Although it was essentially an Anglo-French conflict, the Hundred Years War was also a French civil war, in which the great nobles fought both the Crown and each other in a struggle for independence and autonomy. The measures taken by Charles VII's government to mitigate and heal divisions within France between 1435 and 1461 deserve a prominent place in an explanation of why the English lost their continental possessions. As a result of the war, Englishmen and Frenchmen became more conscious of their separate identities, but this was a relatively late development. The war made many Englishmen rich, but Crown finances were severely strained. A permanent occupation of extensive territories abroad was now shown to be beyond the resources of the English kingdom: whereas Edward III had kept his war aims firmly within the bounds of political feasibility, Henry V did not reckon with the changing political circumstances of the fifteenth century.

A sea-battle, probably in 1416, from a drawing in the Beauchamp Pageant *manuscript of about 1485-90.*

The Economy of Britain:
an age of crisis?

J.L. Bolton

In 1150 the economy of Britain was on the eve of an age of expansion. Between 1100 and 1300 the population probably increased from about two million to about five million in England, by far the most heavily populated of the home countries. There were perhaps 400,000 people in Scotland by 1300, but it is very difficult to make even an informed guess at the populations of Wales and Ireland. These totals seem low by modern comparison, yet it must be remembered that the majority of the people lived on and off the land. In England there was only one major town by European standards, London, with a population of perhaps 30-40,000 in 1300. York had some 10,000 people at that time, but most English county towns had populations of only 2-3,000. In Scotland there were only four major "burghs" and, whilst in Ireland and Wales the Norman settlement had stimulated urban growth, the towns were for the most part small. What mattered was the land and what it could produce, for there lay the major problem of the medieval economy. The levels of technical ability and productivity were low. The only ways of maintaining the fertility of the soil were by leaving a portion of the cultivated area fallow every year and by the use of as much animal manure, the most generally available fertilizer, as possible. A delicate balance had to be struck between arable and pasture. If too much land was turned over to cereal production, (wheat, barley, oats and some rye were the main crops grown), then the number of livestock which could be kept would fall, with serious consequences for arable agriculture. Crop yields were poor. On the manor* of Alciston (Sussex) in the late fourteenth century the average yield per acre was about 17 bushels of wheat, 26 of barley, 22 of oats. Alciston was one of the best managed and most fertile of medieval manors, but by comparison a modern farmer would expect at least four times as much from the same amount of land, using far less labour. So the crucial question, before the advent of the plague, was: could enough food be produced to supply the small urban and industrial sector of the economy, and feed all the people? If production was to be raised, it could only be by taking more and more land into cultivation.

That explains a major phenomenon of the twelfth and thirteenth centuries all over the British Isles, the enormous expansion of the cultivated area. At first, this happened within the boundaries of existing settlement, but eventually an all-out attack was made on forests, fen and marsh land and on the hills. In England, more land was cultivated than at any other time in its history, except during the World Wars of the twentieth century. In Scotland, a statute of 1214 compelled landholders to cultivate more land, either by plough or spade; in the lordship of Brecon, a hilly area in the Marches of Wales, arable was more extensive than at any other time; whilst in the Anglo-Norman area of Ireland peasant colonization proceeded apace. But it is doubtful whether food production kept pace with demand. Between 1180 and 1220 there was rapid price inflation in England. It seems likely that the population had begun

Manor
Agricultural estate over which lordship was exercised: usually divided into demesne land (in lord's direct control) and customary land (worked by lord's tenants in return for rents and services). Demesne was either farmed to produce food for consumption and market, or leased out for cash income; demesne work was done by paid estate labourers (*famuli*), skilled hired labour and tenants owing labour services to lord.

High-farming
Agricultural organization in 13th and 14th centuries when lords worked their demesne lands directly, using hired labour and customary labour services (intensified whenever possible). Rising prices for agricultural produce stimulated growth of skilled estate management; emergence of sophisticated written records; and the writing of treatises on agricultural organization and methods (e.g. Walter of Henley's book on husbandry).

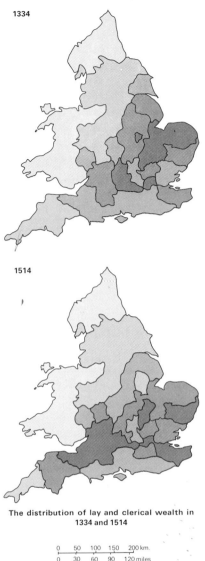

1334

1514

The distribution of lay and clerical wealth in 1334 and 1514

```
0    50   100  150  200 km.
0    30   60   90   120 miles
```

Ranking of counties

- 1 - 9
- 10-19
- 20-29
- 30-38
- Not taxed

Bury St Edmunds was a flourishing cloth town in the Middle Ages. Its prosperity is reflected in the church of St Mary, the product of generous benefactions in the first half of the 15th century.

to outrun the food supply, and during the course of the thirteenth century prices more than trebled, whilst wages remained static and in real terms fell, pointing to surplus manpower in the economy.

To many historians, the thirteenth century has seemed the high point of the Middle Ages. Certainly it saw major changes in farming, the growth of towns and of trade, local, regional and international. Great landlords, lay and ecclesiastical, who before 1180 drew most of their income from leasing out their lands, soon realized that there were rich profits to be made from farming for the market*. As the leases fell in, they reorganized their estates to produce both grain for the home market and wool for the export trade to Flanders and Italy. As their incomes rose, they spent lavishly on building, on luxury goods, on hospitality and ostentatious living, although their burden of taxation grew increasingly heavier. Towns of all sizes expanded, partly because the population itself was growing, but mainly because they both served and supplied the needs of the countryside. Whilst there were markets in villages (and between 1198 and 1453 some 2,800 grants of market were made, over half of them in the first three quarters of the thirteenth century), urban markets were held more frequently and could provide a wider range of goods, either made in the town itself or imported. The surest sign of urban expansion was the creation of new towns by charters from the Crown or a lay or ecclesiastical lord. New Salisbury was founded in this way, and the ports of Hull, Lynn and Boston were developed as wool exports to Flanders expanded. By the first quarter of the fourteenth century the number of towns in England had doubled, and there were some 300 places with urban characteristics. Edward I's conquest of Wales led to the foundation of new towns around his northern castles and the Anglo-Norman settlement of Ireland seems to have stimulated urban growth. All this must be seen in perspective. Throughout Europe, new lands were being brought into cultivation, older towns were expanding, new towns being founded, and compared with north Italy, Flanders or Germany urban growth in the British Isles was limited.

Economic expansion was not to everyone's benefit. Great landlords and wealthy townsmen may have prospered, but for many the prospects were not

Labourers reap and bind the corn into sheaves (above). A laden corn-wain is pushed uphill (above, right). Corn is brought by pack-horse to the miller at his windmill (right), where a woman shoulders a sack of flour. All from the Luttrell Psalter (c. 1340).

so bright. By the end of the thirteenth century, there are signs that in some parts of Britain there were too many people for the land to support. It is no longer possible to talk of general rural overpopulation. There is as yet no evidence of acute land pressure in Scotland by 1300, and there was no lack of pasture, either, for stock rearing or for converting to arable in north Wales. But in certain areas of England there was an agrarian crisis. It has been estimated that nearly sixty per cent of the English peasants were unfree, and most of them lived in the manorialized counties of central and southern England. Some forty per cent of these manorial tenants had to live off ten or fifteen acres of land, or less, and, given the low productivity of the soil and their compulsory payments to their lord, they teetered on the edge of subsistence. In a good year, all was well, but a run of bad harvests might bring disaster. Equally, the incomes of some lesser landlords, knights, esquires, the middling ranks in the countryside, clearly failed to meet their social pretensions. They borrowed heavily*, and when they could no longer meet their debts, they were bought out by the greater landholders, anxious to increase their demesnes*. But for every failure one can find a success, a man who had risen by financial acumen, or service to the Crown or to a great lord. Some families failed, others prospered, and there was no general crisis of the knightly class.

Expulsion of the Jews 1290
After 1066 Jews were indispensable moneylenders for kings and noblemen, and the king afforded them special protection. However, growing intolerance of religious heterodoxy, generated by Fourth Lateran Council 1215, and hostility of indebted landowners towards Jews, made close royal association with them politically unwise; the emergence of Italian bankers as great lenders and Jewish impoverishment by punitive taxation made close association financially unnecessary. Consequently it seemed expedient for Edward I to expel Jews in 1290.

Demesne
Land or other property (like ponds, mills and weirs) held by a landlord himself (and not his tenants): it was worked for his profit, with his tenants' labour services or labourers employed for the purpose. Before the Black Death great landlords used their demesnes to produce agricultural goods for the market and to supply their own

se: quomam ipfe cognoutt figmen

(Above left) *woodmen clearing a coppice, from a "Labours of the Months" manuscript calendar;* (above) *a water-mill, with eel traps in the stream (Luttrell Psalter);* (left) *builders and masons at work, from the mid-13th century Book of St Alban by Matthew Paris.*

household needs; after it, as agricultural profits fell, demesnes were more often leased out to peasant farmers, merchants and neighbouring gentlemen.

Wool trade

Wool sold predominantly in Flanders was England's main export until 14th century, reaching over 36,000 sacks annually, but falling drastically to 8,000 sacks 1450. This collapse was due to: falling population; socio-economic crisis in Flanders; Edward III's taxation on wool exports; growth of cloth exports; and a monopoly of wool exports to Flanders achieved by a company of English merchants. To meet tax bills the monopolists charged consumers high prices and paid producers low ones, thus stimulating English cloth production.

That still left about a third of the tenants in the manorialized areas of England living on the brink of subsistence, along with substantial numbers of the urban poor, particularly since the major industry, the production of cloth, had been badly hit by Flemish competition in the course of the thirteenth century. Nor was there any compensation in the expansion of wool exports*, since in 1300 most of the trade was in alien hands. The Italians, with their large reserves of liquid capital, were more than a match for their English rivals. The economy had expanded in the period 1150-1300, but there had been no growth, no *per capita* increase in wealth, no major industrial development to absorb the manpower surplus to agriculture. Tin and lead mining, and building in stone flourished, but they brought prosperity to a few areas only. For peasant smallholders in manorial England, life was grim.

It was to become even grimmer in the second decade of the fourteenth century. The English population faced heavy taxation for war with Scotland, seizure of crops and stock to supply the armies and then, between 1315 and 1325, natural disasters struck the whole of the British Isles. Due to appalling weather, the harvests failed in 1315 and 1316 and again in 1322, and there were widespread cattle and sheep murrains which affected the agrarian economy through loss of the wool clip and shortage of draught animals. In the north of England the economy was wracked by Scottish raids, and Ireland suffered from the Bruce invasion of 1315-16, which brought devastation to a land already wasted by famine and murrain. It has been argued that this "general crisis" of the early fourteenth century led to economic change, to population decline, to falling prices and rising wages in the 1330s and 40s, to retreat of settlement and to great landlords in England abandoning farming for the market and returning to leasing their lands, for a fixed income from rent. Yet the evidence to support such an argument is hard to find. Some land, in the north of England, in Shropshire, Sussex and the counties to the north and west of London did fall out of use, but the older established villages were still full of people. Holdings often had to be subdivided to cope with a population which seems to have replaced itself rapidly after the disastrous famine years. If prices fell in the 1330s and 40s, then so did wages, due to monetary deflation caused by the outflow of silver* in the opening stages of the Hundred Years War. Some landlords did abandon direct farming and switch to rents, but they were very much the exception rather than the rule. It was thus on a high-farming economy that the plague fell in 1348.

The "Black Death"* is usually regarded as a disaster, a turning-point in the economy which brought the end to expansion and a return to subsistence farming, decline in trade and industry, impoverishment and contraction for the towns. The first attack of plague, lasting from 1348 to 1351, was devastat-

Bullion outflow

Occurred because Edward III spent heavily on subsidizing continental allies and paying his own army serving abroad, after having acquired his subjects' bullion through taxation. In theory, a country which loses bullion quickly experiences price and wage falls because there is less money available for acquiring the same amount of goods and services.

Black Death

An epidemic of bubonic plague which reached Melcombe Regis in Dorset June 1348, spreading through England 1349 and arriving in Scotland 1350. Black rats, fond of human habitations, carried fleas with plague bacterium, so mortality was highest in crowded towns. Principal symptoms were fever and boils (buboes) in armpit and groin, death usually following in five or six days: pneumonic (when someone with a respiratory infection contracted the plague) and septicaemic variations were more deadly still.

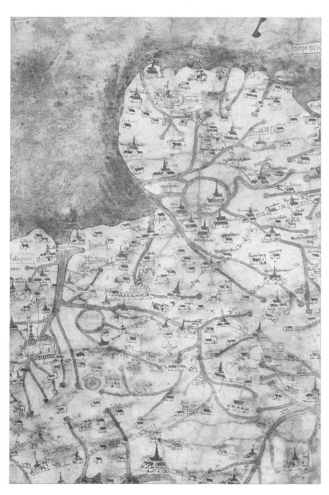

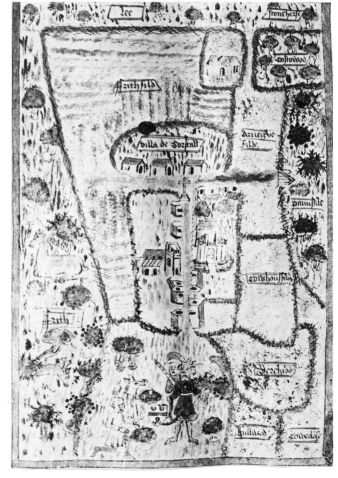

15th-century Flemish manuscript illustration showing dyers at work.

Far left: *the mid-14th century Gough map shows an elaborate network of roads, and suggests that communications may not have been as bad as is often suggested.*

Left: *a 1444 survey of the village of Boarstall in Buckinghamshire, showing the open fields with their strips of land for separate cultivation.*

ing, striking at all parts of the British Isles. In England, perhaps a third of the population died, and yet recovery seems to have been rapid, the economy having suffered little more than a hiccup. Vacant holdings were soon filled, demesne farming continued and the labour legislation* (Statute of Labourers, 1351) was scarcely needed, again pointing to a surplus of manpower in the countryside before the plague came. It was to take the cumulative effects of a series of outbreaks, in 1361-62, 1369 and 1375, before the English population declined by between one third and a half. Recurrent outbreaks of plague and other diseases kept it at that level until the end of the fifteenth century. But in Scotland only two major outbreaks of plague are recorded, in 1349-50 and 1362, and, although the possibility of further outbreaks cannot be ruled out, the population decline was not as severe as in England. The fifteenth century may have been a period of slow growth in Scotland, not stagnation at all. On the other hand, there can be little doubt that the Bruce invasion and the plague brought economic decline to Ireland, with lands lying vacant and untilled, and a similar combination, the plague and the effects of the Glyndŵr rebellion in the early fifteenth century, brought economic hardship to Wales.

But, was the decline in population necessarily such a disaster for England? There are good grounds for believing that the general standard of living rose. The same amount of wealth was shared by fewer people, villages on marginal land could be abandoned, leaving more than enough good arable and pasture to support the population. Great landlords found, by the 1370s, that with low prices and high wages, demesne farming was no longer profitable. They managed to sustain it for twenty or so years after the Black Death, largely by using their coercive powers to force the peasants to work for them and by exploiting the financial obligations of villeinage*, but in the mid-1370s economic circumstances changed. By 1450 manorialism had collapsed, and villeinage in England was dying. Lords had to accept that peasants were no longer prepared to perform labour services or live under the constraints of villeinage. For the English peasantry the fifteenth century was one of quiet prosperity.

Some would argue that that meant hard times for the lords. They were forced to become rentiers and, since supply of land now exceeded demand, their incomes ought to have fallen. There was no salvation either in turning to sheep farming, since wool prices were low and demesne pastures as well as demesne arable were leased. Yet for every example of a landlord facing hard times, one can find another of a great lord prospering. Much the same is true of towns and trade. Whilst Lincoln and Leicester suffered from both declining population and a flight of industry to the cheaper and unregulated* countryside, Salisbury and Bury St Edmunds, serving the Wiltshire and East Anglian cloth industries respectively, flourished. In the cloth manufacturing

Labour legislation
1349 Ordinance and 1351 Statute of Labourers were responses to Black Death: attempted to provide supply of cheap labour by fixing wages at pre-plague rates and requiring landless men to accept employment at these rates, their own lords having first claim on their services. Enforcement (placed in hands of country gentlemen named as Justices of Labourers) was vigorous immediately after 1351, and

perhaps also shortly before Peasants' Revolt. As population fell, land went out of cultivation and landlords competed for labour, the legislation became difficult to enforce and caused hardship for labouring poor.

See **Villeins** (page 133)

Urban regulation
In towns, guilds and corporations imposed restrictions on trade and industry by regulating working hours, wages and prices, and imposing long apprenticeships, as well as controlling entry into crafts and trades in the towns. Advantageous for those already in a trade or craft; regulation also benefited consumers when guilds endeavoured to keep the quality of goods high.

areas of the south-west and East Anglia, new towns developed from existing villages, like Castle Combe or Lavenham, which by 1524 was the thirteenth richest town in England. By 1450, cloth had replaced wool as England's chief export. Heavy customs duties on wool to pay for the campaigns in the Hundred Years War meant increased costs for England's main competitors, the Flemish cloth towns which themselves were suffering from civil war and social unrest. Gradually, in the second half of the fourteenth century, the English industry regained the home market and then, by the 1430s and 40s, became the leading European supplier of fine and medium quality broad-cloths. By 1440, cloth exports* were worth only ten per cent less than wool exports had been at their height in the early fourteenth century, when the population was almost twice the size. Exporting finished goods rather than a raw material brought more profit, more employment and more spending power, especially in the south-west, East Anglia and the North Riding of Yorkshire, where the industry was based.

And there lies the key to understanding the apparent contradictions in the late medieval English economy, the high degree of regional variation. Wealth and people were shifting from the midland grain belt, stretching from Gloucestershire to Cambridgeshire, to the south-east around London and to the cloth manufacturing and tin mining areas of the south-west, where the continued demand for land meant steady rent income for lords and a prosper-ous squirearchy and peasantry producing for the market. In the midlands, although some profited from raising cattle, since pasture was abundant and the demand for meat increasing as the general standard of living rose, lords found it difficult to collect rents and towns declined. There was no one economy but a series of regional economies, and for some of them the fifteenth century brought prosperity to all classes of society.

It would be wrong to end on a note of euphoria. Compared with continental rivals, north Italy, south Germany and the Netherlands, England was some-thing of an economic backwater. There was only one city of any size, London, the economy was still predominantly agrarian and forty per cent of the valu-able export trade was in Italian and German hands. They took the cloth to lucrative distant markets in the Baltic and Mediterranean, whilst English merchants concentrated on the short routes to Flanders and the Nether-lands. Little capital was being invested in mining or metallurgy, the founda-tions of European capitalism or, cloth apart, any other industries. The British Isles were still on the fringe of Europe, geographically and economically.

Cloth exports

By 15th century cloth (particularly cheaper, coarser types such as kerseys) was England's greatest export, bringing considerable wealth to merchants. Usually well over 40,000 broadcloths (24 yards by 1½ or 2 yards) were exported each year. English cloth reached markets in Scandinavia, north Germany, the Netherlands, France and Spain. German merchants of the Hanseatic League competed with Englishmen for the profitable export of cloths, and Hanse privileges were confirmed by 1474 Treaty of Utrecht.

A 14th-century sketch of the punishment awaiting a baker who gives short weight: he will be dragged through the streets on a hurdle and then made to stand in the pillory.

English Society

B.F. Harvey

Throughout the Middle Ages, the main stream of social theory accepted that society was a hierarchy in which inferior owed respect to superior. But at the beginning of this period status, although essential to the system, was not elaborately ordered or sharply emphasized. English society in 1150 is most aptly described as "feudal". England was never highly feudalized, and the development of lordship and vassalage* was not accompanied by the fragmentation of public authority. Here "feudal" signifies that, as well as the family and the local community, dependent tenure was essential to social arrangements. At the higher levels of society, which we shall consider first, land was normally held of a lord in return for homage* and fealty*, and for services which often included some form of military service or payment in lieu. Except at the highest levels of all, payments in cash or kind were also very common.

Because our view is coloured by modern notions of property and ownership, we find dependent tenure hard to understand: in feudal England neither lord nor tenant "owned" the land. By the early thirteenth century, however, the tenant was much nearer to being an "owner" than his predecessor of 1100 or even 1150. The decay of the classic feudal relationship over these years is exemplified in three developments which derived much of their effect from the rapid rise in population from about two millions in c.1100 to between four and five millions in 1300. This rise brought about an increase in rents and prices. But most of the services that a lord could ask of the tenant whom he had enfeoffed were fixed in amount or in value. Nearly all the economic advantage of the rise in land values went to the tenant and scarcely any to the lord. In the same period, feudal tenants won two important rights: they could now transmit their lands to an heir; and they could alienate land if they wished. In practice, feudal fiefs* had long been heritable and to some extent alienable, but it was not until the late twelfth century – and in the case of alienability a little later still – that the law securely underpinned these customary rights, dispelling the idea that they were favours to be purchased. Family sentiment provided the impetus for the attainment of heritability. Many feudal tenants who coveted the right of alienation did so in order to enfeoff* younger sons and daughters with a portion before the heir took all at death: they were seeking to ameliorate the harsh consequences of the feudal rule of primogeniture.

These changes denote a large-scale shift of wealth and importance to the small landowners of Angevin England – to the men of knightly rank who held a manor or two of a lord but who rarely enfeoffed others with manors. These gained at the expense of great landowners, the earls and barons, and those of the middling sort. The friction so occasioned was a conspicuous feature of English society in the first half of the thirteenth century, and engaged the attention of the reform movement of 1258-65.

The effective bonds between lord and man that dependent tenure no longer

Vassalage
The term for dependent status of members of the nobility, who were knights professing arms, after they had done homage to a lord.

Homage
A ceremony establishing the relationship between a lord and man: the lord, standing, took in his hands the clasped hands of the kneeling man, who acknowledged his dependent status: kisses were exchanged revealing their accord and friendship. Homage symbolized a man's obedience to, and dependence on, his lord, who undertook to protect and aid his man.

Fealty
Ceremony whereby vassal, laying hands on Gospels (or sacred relics) swore to be faithful to a lord. Fealty was a unilinear act by vassal; lords rarely swore oaths to vassals.

Fief
An estate in land held on condition of homage and service (usually military) to a superior lord; service was agreed between lord and tenant but soon became customary. Early 12th-century kings treated fiefs held of them as life estates; the Angevins bowed to noble pressure for heritability, enshrined in Magna Carta. Alienation means conveying land to another party by sale or gift: if this occurred a lord was concerned not to lose the service or dues owed for the fief.

Feoffees
Persons to whom lands were granted (enfeoffed) by owner; they became owners in common law. "Enfeoffment to Use" was important legal device (from 14th century) whereby landowner granted part of estates to feoffees (normally family or close associates) but retained use and revenues until death. At grantor's death feoffees disposed of estates according to instructions left by him (usually in "last will"); he could direct lands' descent and make provisions as desired. Added advantage for those, especially lords, holding land directly from Crown was that, feoffees being common-law owners, the Crown could not extract feudal rights from lands on grantor's death.

provided were supplied by retaining. The central feature of this complex institution was a contract between lord and man, whereby the latter promised services in return for an annual fee and livery of clothing. Although many contracts were for life, retainers received their rewards in instalments that could be withheld, and this saved these bonds from the atrophy that overtook those of classic feudalism. There was no sharp transition from dependent tenure to retaining; and the roots of retaining lie deep in the feudal period. But fees and livery were used much more frequently from the late thirteenth century than previously. Retaining was admirably suited to the stratified society now taking shape.

In this society, the horizontal divisions separating social ranks became clearer than formerly, and the bonds uniting those who shared the same rank were in consequence strengthened. Here, too, the chronology of change was very untidy. A typical product of the period and mentality was the sumptuary law of 1363, which prescribed the appropriate quality of clothing for every grade in society. Evidently the more extravagant fashions of the period were threatening some sartorial conventions believed by Parliament to be essential for the maintenance of the traditional hierarchy. Social distinctions were not those of a class system. Birth, the practice of arms and the possession of heraldic arms, royal creation, the ties of retaining, occupation, wealth – especially landed wealth – all counted in deciding status, but in proportions that may have been as hard to define then as they are now. Nevertheless, it is clear that some profound changes occurred at the higher levels of society. In about 1300, when the idea of an aristocratic élite was not far developed, all landowners whose income enabled them to support the status of knighthood shared in the nobility of the earls and barons. Among this large company, numbering perhaps between 2,000 and 3,000, some were of course wealthier and more powerful than others, but socially the criterion that mattered was knighthood or the capacity to assume that rank. By the mid-fifteenth century, however, only the peers of parliament*, themselves ordered in distinct grades, were universally regarded as noble. Knights were now well on the way to becoming mere gentry; but in that fallen state they were conscious of their superiority to the squires and gentlemen, who formed the lower ranks of gentle society, for this too, like the nobility, was now graded.

At these levels of late medieval society, the possession of landed wealth was a *sine qua non* of entry and of survival, and, since it was accepted that standards of living must mirror status, it was important to possess an estate of the right size. Here, as often in the history of the period, demographic developments impinged on social arrangements. In the second half of the fourteenth century, as a result of the Black Death and later epidemics of plague, the population of England fell dramatically. In consequence, though not as swiftly as we might expect, the rental values on which landowners depended for their incomes declined too. It became necessary, therefore, not only to possess an estate, but also to augment it, and how some landowners succeeded in doing this – whether by purchase, by royal favour, or, as most often, by marriage – and how others failed to do so is inextricably interwoven with the political history of England under Richard II and his successors. The fall in the rental value of land, occurring as it did in a period when standards of living rose, is one reason why so few families managed to sustain the burden of noble status in the fifteenth century. Around 1450 there were fewer than eighty peers of parliament.

Court of Chancery

Developed in first half of 15th century to hear cases and give judgements in Equity: probably received great impetus from development of enfeoffment to use; if feoffees ignored or disputed their instructions, there was no remedy in law for aggrieved because feoffees were common-law owners – but chancellor could instruct feoffees to comply. Cases concerning contracts, particularly commercial, were also important.

Parliamentary peerage

Developed in 14th century: originally noblemen whom king summoned by writ directly to Parliament. By about 1350 men who had been summoned once were attending parliaments regularly, as were their heirs after them. Development of tail male (strict legal settlement providing that a nobleman's lands and title would descend to his lineal male heir, postponing or altogether eliminating inheritance by female heirs) essential for evolution of peerage. In 15th century it was accepted that dignity of peerage was tied to lands. Peerage could be widened through creation by royal patent, a method first adopted by Richard II. By 1450 parliamentary peerage was hierarchically stratified through invention of new titles: dukedoms 1337, marquessates 1385 and viscountcies 1440.

Franciscan friars

Greatest spiritual impression in 13th century England made by Franciscans (Friars Minor or Grey friars): arrived 1224; spread rapidly in following twenty years, establishing friaries (usually in towns) and gaining patronage from wealthy urban classes; especially influential in Oxford. Followed ideals of St Francis of Assisi: itinerant, evangelical preachers; humility; worldly poverty; and regular life free from constraints imposed by monastic rules. Ideals compromised during 13th century as friars gained wealth and office.

Dominican friars

Dominicans (Friars Preacher or Black friars) followed teaching of Saint Dominic: reached England 1221; influential but less spiritually significant than Franciscans; scholarly order, self-consciously devoted to rational defence of Christian faith, therefore attracted to universities, being very powerful force in their organization.

Secular clergy

Those clergy who did not live a regular (i.e., by a monastic or similar "rule") life; they were parish and chantry priests, chaplains, clerks in administrative jobs (as in the royal administration) and university teachers. Higher clergy were the abbots, bishops and archbishops.

Anticlericalism

Lay hostility to: influence of clergy, especially bishops, in politics; legal privileges of clergymen and jurisdiction of church courts; papal taxation and intervention in English ecclesiastical affairs. Anticlericalism only serious during political crises, particularly when governments were short of money and wanted to tap ecclesiastical wealth (as in 1370s); connected with rise of lay literacy and professions, which suggested that clerks were simply professional men not deserving special privileges, and growing voice of gentry (envious of episcopal wealth) in Commons.

Manorial courts

The manorial lord's court supervised the life of the manor: it punished certain minor crimes, such as assault, regulated relations between tenants, and was a useful source of income for lord.

Villeins

13th-century judges defined them as those forbidden access to royal law courts and wholly subject to their lords' private courts. A villein sometimes owed onerous labour services to his lord; needed licence to buy, sell or sub-let lands; was taxable at will by his lord; was tied to the manor and unable to leave without permission; and could be compelled to use his lord's ovens and mills. But inheritances, rents, fines and labour services were defined by customs which had practically the force of law.

Causes of Peasants' Revolt

Immediate cause was heavy, inequitable burden of three poll taxes 1377-81 and oppressive conduct of tax collectors. Longer term causes were: resentment of government's failure to defend coast; inefficiency and corruption of government; rejection of legal disabilities of villeinage and economic burdens of servile tenure; hatred of restrictive labour laws which reduced peasant mobility and kept wages low. Also influence of egalitarian moral teaching of poor clergymen and utopian ideals of agitators, possibly influenced by Wycliffite teaching and radical interpretation of Gospels.

How did the clergy fit into this stratified society? The question would have surprised contemporaries, to whom the difference between a monk and a friar* or between these and a secular clerk* was as great as any distinguishing the whole clerical order from the laity. Among the secular clergy, inequalities of wealth were too great for a single view of that body to be realistic. Thomas Arundel, when bishop of Ely (1374-88), spent more than £1,000 per annum on his household of about eighty persons: many parish priests and stipendiary chaplains in his diocese were probably making ends meet on £5 per annum or less. Most of the higher clergy gave fees and livery with gusto, and monasteries did so to the limit of their means. If friars did not often give livery, they received it on occasion. In all its arrangements, as for example seating at table, society habitually took note of distinctions of clerical status. In their several ways, it may appear, the clergy fitted harmoniously into late medieval society. The appearance is perhaps deceptive. A sense of the incongruity of this degree of conformity to the world is often expressed in the religious and secular literature of the period. Many critics of the monks questioned the legitimacy of the endowments that enabled them to live so easily. The way of life of prelates like Arundel did much to ensure that anticlericalism* was stronger now than ever before. But anticlericalism embraced many more than the Caesarian prelates: this in fact was the one standpoint from which all the clergy looked alike to the laity.

The vast majority of the common people lived in the countryside, and we shall consider only those who were, in this general sense, "peasants". Over their way of life the strong regional differences characteristic of medieval England had paramount influence, and generalization is correspondingly difficult. Moreover, social structure is imperfectly reflected in the manorial documents on which we must chiefly rely. Our attention will be focused on the clarification of legal status in the late twelfth century, and on the consequences of the fall in population in the fourteenth.

Until the reign of Henry II, the status of common people was a matter of degree. Some men and women were freer than their neighbours; others, less free. But except for the fundamental divide separating slaves from all others, there were no clearly marked divisions; and slavery was obsolete before 1150. Henry II, however, opened the royal courts, hitherto the preserve of the great, to all free men and thus created a new division in society – between those who were free at common law and those who were not. It took a long time for actual social arrangements in manor and village to be affected. But the law now conferred on the humblest free tenant the same kinds of benefits as were enjoyed higher up the social scale by the tenant in fee, and the long-term effect of this development was to ensure that seignorial authority over peasant lands held in free tenure would be of the lightest kind. Even in the highly manorialized parts of the country, perhaps as much as a third of the land was affected. Moreover, the condition of the more dependent peasants who were denied the benefits of the common law – the so-called villeins* – now acquired a significance lacking when only the great were indubitably free. In a sense, therefore, the status of the peasantry both improved and deteriorated in the second half of the twelfth century: freedom was articulated with a new clarity, but so was dependence.

In doubtful cases, status was often tested by the degree of the peasant's involvement in the cultivation of the manorial demesne: regular agricultural services, particularly services such as digging and threshing, signified villein status. But villeins owed money rents as well as labour services, and by the thirteenth century the rents were in most cases the larger part of the burden. Villeinage dues were always much heavier than the often nominal rents owed by free peasants; but, since they did not rise proportionately to land values in the late twelfth century and the thirteenth, these dues were, by 1300, lighter than leasehold* rents. In general, however, villeinage did much to keep peasant society poor and to ensure that the scale of most enterprises down to the fourteenth century was small.

The fall in population in and after 1348, and the surplus of land that resulted, brought about no sudden change. Slowly, however, peasant society became more sharply differentiated, as the winners – who had always existed – took advantage of the new opportunities and augmented their holdings. By now villeinage was shorn of some of the features which had made it a disabling handicap earlier. But many lords now used their seignorial authority to keep the dues owed by villeins uneconomically high and to maintain the anachronistic limitations on their freedom of action. The Peasants' Revolt* of 1381, which made the abolition of villeinage one of its principal aims, voiced the frustration of the victims of this exploitation. Villeinage was not in fact abolished in 1381, but the sting went out of it on most estates in the course of the next two decades.

The scarcity of labour after 1348 also exacerbated relations between lord and villein, but its main social effects were probably felt within the peasant community itself. In medieval England, labourers were not a separate class. Some held land or belonged to land-holding families. Many, however, were landless or nearly so. The status of such people had always been uncertain: the labour laws enacted on the morrow of the Black Death were probably making explicit some long established conventions. In the end, the main beneficiaries of this legislation were the substantial peasant farmers who were now becoming the pre-eminent producers for the agricultural market, where, indeed, they had long been important. Their precarious foothold in commercial husbandry would be lost if the wages that they had to pay were to rise too fast and too far. It is at this level of society that we glimpse some of the most acute tensions occasioned by the economic changes of the later Middle Ages.

Leasehold
Arrangement by which a peasant held land for such time and such rent as he had negotiated with the lord of the land: lord could alter terms of lease when it ended; thus he could adapt to economic change more easily than with customary tenures. Leasehold not subject to labour services, tallages (lord's tax), death duties and (in some cases) entry fines.

Peasants' Revolt 1381
Erupted at Brentwood (Essex), spread to Kent and East Anglia. Led by Wat Tyler and John Ball (a priest), rebels reached London; with help of urban rebels, ransacked city and murdered Archbishop Sudbury (Chancellor) and Robert Hales (Treasurer). Richard II and Mayor William Walworth negotiated with rebels, granting their demands. Walworth, defending Richard, killed Tyler; Richard calmed rebels, who dispersed peacefully. In East Anglia, rebels killed Chief Justice and Prior of Bury St Edmunds; subdued by Bishop Despenser of Norwich.

Carthusian monks in choir, with mementi mori *above their stalls, in a miniature from Henry VI's Psalter, c.1430.*

Late 13th-century stone effigy in Dorchester Abbey, Oxfordshire, of an unknown crusader knight.

Culture:
the international style and native variants

Colin Platt

Between the earthworks of a Norman castle immediately to the west and the fragmentary remains of a Benedictine priory-cell to the south-east, the diminutive parish church of Kilpeck in Herefordshire preserves its full apparel of stone carvings as fresh today as when cut in the mid-twelfth century. They are triumphant masterpieces of the Herefordshire School, as much Scandinavian as local in inspiration, yet, if it had not been for Kilpeck's remote situation on the edge of the Welsh March, such work must even then have seemed bizarrely old-fashioned. Just a few miles to the east, in a church which is as small and every bit as isolated as Kilpeck, the Kempley frescoes are Byzantine-inspired. They are of equally high quality and are only a little later in date. And they tell us of a society which had lately turned its back on the immediate past, finding fresh inspiration in a Mediterranean world to which Angevin political ambitions had introduced it. Contemporaneously, there were Sicilian-trained artists at work in late-twelfth-century Winchester. There is little insularity in an art of this kind, and its achievements, as one might expect, were considerable.

Appropriately classical echoes, the fruit of such exchanges with the South, are present in the work of William of Sens, rebuilder of the choir of Canterbury Cathedral in the 1170s. They are there again in the arcades of Castle Hedingham church, or in the capitals of the new hall at Oakham Castle. However, this so-called "proto-Renaissance" was short-lived in the North, and what absorbed it was something undoubtedly more stimulatingly original, the full flowering of first-period Gothic. While the great cathedrals of northern France were rising at record speed, similarly ambitious building programmes were launched in contemporary England, with St Hugh's reconstruction of Lincoln Cathedral beginning in the 1190s, and with an entire new cathedral at Salisbury finished (all but its spire) in less than forty years. No builder in mid-thirteenth-century England would rival the king in an overweening ambition to do better. Even Henry III's drive could not bring to completion his most-favoured project at Westminster. Yet the marks of Henry's refined taste are still everywhere apparent, whether in the development of tomb sculpture or the sophistication of the tilers of Clarendon and Chertsey, in the emergence of a delicate "Court style" in painting or in the encouragement of the embroiderers of the native *opus anglicanum,* among them Henry's own Mabel of Bury St Edmunds.

Henry's influence on the arts long outlasted his own reign, and its flavour remained distinctly international. Westminister Abbey had itself been a building in the French taste, rather than in the English. In painting, the Court style of Henry III and his successors was modelled on the current fashion in France. In military architecture, and most particularly in the north Welsh castles of Edward I, the primary inspiration was continental. Nevertheless, this is not to say that native traditions had entirely disappeared. At St

Church reform
In 13th century was inspired by Fourth Lateran Council 1215, which aimed to provide a body of disciplined, educated clergy armed with an orthodox creed and qualified by character and training to instruct parishioners. Episcopal authority was enhanced by enforcement of constitutions (episcopal commands to parish clergy) and regular diocesan synods. Ecclesiastical solidarity was developed in the emerging Convocation (ecclesiastical parliament) which often resisted papal and royal taxation of the Church and defended ecclesiastical privileges against secular encroachment.

Universities
Oxford grew from schools established by late 12th century, having three important 13th-century foundations (Balliol, University, Merton). Cambridge had origins in group of scholars who settled there at Henry III's invitation in 1229. Both developed quickly in 13th century; were responsible for training great majority of clerical intelligentsia. New colleges founded regularly in 14th and 15th centuries. Most students took six-year Master of Arts course in seven liberal arts (grammar, rhetoric, logic, astronomy, music, geometry and arithmetic). Eight-year higher degrees were available in theology, medicine and law.

13th-century tiles from Chertsey Abbey, Surrey, showing Richard I as crusader.

Albans Abbey, for example, both the line-drawing of pre-Angevin England and its practice of historical enquiry were kept alive in the works of Matthew Paris and his school. Only a little later, there was the development of a lively and distinctive regional art, no longer necessarily monastic, in a fine group of East Anglian psalters, while the contemporary knight effigies at Dorchester, Hanbury, Ingham and elsewhere – naturalistic, restless, and unsleeping – are as English as the bones that lie below them.

It was just that restless military energy that contributed to the outbreak in 1337 of a prolonged dynastic squabble with France, now known as the Hundred Years War. The growing alienation between the English and the French, promoted by the long cycle of victory and defeat overseas, manifested itself increasingly in all sorts of ways, not least in the separation of their arts. Of course, much of English castle architecture in the later Middle Ages remained largely French in its inspiration, for its patrons had learnt most of what they knew about war on French soil. But an English castle, for all that, rarely looks (except in details) like a French one, and the differences were to be even more marked in church building. After the perverse extravagance of the Decorated* style, one of Henry III's imports *via* Westminster Abbey, English masons turned increasingly from the developing *style flamboyant* of fifteenth-century France to favour the austere geometry of Perpendicular*. The greater monuments of this native style – the nave of Canterbury Cathedral, the hammerbeam roof of Westminster Hall, the west front of Beverley Minster – attracted expert attention on the Continent. In due course, elements of English Perpendicular reappeared as far afield as Bohemia, Portugal and

Decorated style

English modifications of French-inspired Early Gothic, with greater attention to detail in decoration, to graceful and flowing lines, and much use of figure sculpture. It evolved from *c.* 1250 and had reached a perhaps extravagant peak by *c.* 1330: e.g. Exeter Cathedral. Characteristics are elaborate façades (Lichfield Cathedral), ribbed vaulting (choir of Ely Cathedral, *c.* 1324-28), fine tracery (York Minster's west window, *c.* 1330), complicated arcades with clustered piers, and extensive use of the structurally weak but graceful ogee arch.

Perpendicular style

Developed in 14th century; first great example is Gloucester Cathedral choir begun in 1330s by master-mason William of Ramsey. Features of style include: tracery with vertical lines, rectilinear wall panelling, four centred arches, broad "casement" moulding, fan vaulting (first used for wide span at Sherborne Abbey 1430-40). Naves of Winchester and Canterbury Cathedrals (1360-1410; 1380-1410) are typical in increased height of nave and clerestory. One of finest architects and master-masons was Henry Yevele, who built Westminster Hall.

Exterior and nave of Salisbury Cathedral: begun on a new site in 1220, completed, except for the spire, before 1260.

The carved stone porch of Kilpeck Church, Herefordshire (far left), *and the painted chancel walls and vault of Kempley, Gloucestershire* (left).

Spain. They formed part of a trading and artistic exchange which had reversed direction for a while, as English broadcloths penetrated new markets overseas and as Nottingham carved alabasters, coming into their own from the fourteenth century, found purchasers among church patrons throughout the West.

One of the areas in which the English alabaster workers found favour was in the fashioning of monuments, especially in the carving of sepulchral effigies. Most famous of the earliest alabaster effigies is that of Edward II at Gloucester Abbey (now the cathedral), which shows the development of a realism in sculpture which anticipates some of the elements of a portrait art more usually associated with the Renaissance. English memorial sculpture never reached the peaks of excellence of the Burgundian tombs. But Burgundian realism is anticipated already in the mid-fourteenth-century: Blanche Mortimer's effigy at Much Marcle (Herefordshire) has its draperies spilling, as they would have done in life, over the edge of the tomb-chest. Death, in a period of endemic plague, provided rich fuel for inspiration.

If death and its mysteries were one source for the artist, chivalry was undoubtedly another. Frequently, the two came together. Prominent on Blanche Mortimer's tomb are the heraldic escutcheons of her husband's noble line and of her own. Similarly, the great collegiate chantry at Fotheringhay (Northamptonshire), now the merest fragment, was at least as much a celebration of the living Yorkist clan as of the dead magnates who had contributed to its endowment. Chivalric motifs took many forms in art, rarely absent from any major project of the period. However, they are most obvious, as one might expect, in late-medieval castle and palace architecture – in the great towers (Caesar's Tower and Guy's Tower) of the Beauchamp show-front at Warwick Castle, or in the overwhelming mass of Edward III's splendidly re-fashioned castle-palace at Windsor. Edward's Windsor was to be the home of his innovatory Order of the Garter*, and Garter symbolism would have been prominent in its buildings at that time. For his grandson, Richard II, the White Hart meant more. In the Wilton Diptych, Richard wears his own White Hart livery-badge as he kneels before the Virgin and Child, and so do the angels of the company he confronts.

Richard's individual profession of faith before the Christ Child was entirely characteristic of his period. Earlier in the same century, a more personal religion had begun to find favour, under the influence of English mystics like Richard Rolle (d. 1349) and under the pressure of a common disillusion with the Church. Men were turning inwards towards their parish churches, financing a general rebuilding in the localities*, especially active in the fifteenth century and unparalleled since the transformations of the twelfth. Many

In this miniature of about 1400, Geoffrey Chaucer reads his work aloud to a company of courtiers and their ladies.

Order of Garter
Epitomized the military ideals of Edward III's reign when jousting, pageantry, lavish entertainment and courtly, chivalric behaviour preoccupied the aristocracy, though within the context of Christian piety. Stories of King Arthur influenced Edward, who undertook to create a Round Table for his knights. The Order was established 1348 with the symbol of a blue garter: its membership was twenty-six knights, presided over by the king; membership soon regarded as great honour. Order symbolized the mutual commitment of king and knights to search for justice and fame through valorous deeds, ever faithful to one another.

Ecclesiastical endowments
In late medieval England, traditional monastic houses were less frequently founded by pious patrons, although Henry V did establish two. Benefactors were more attracted by collegiate churches, served by secular clergy, and chantry endowments (which supported a chaplain to sing masses at an altar in a church or in a separate chapel). Guilds of townsmen and individual founders from landed classes made such endowments. Collegiate churches often had attached grammar schools or alms houses; provision was often made for chantry priests to teach children. Education and lay piety were closely linked.

Wycliff's doctrines
John Wycliff was a radical Oxford philosopher and theologian, protected by John of Gaunt (who needed academic propaganda to support his attack on Church), despite condemnation of his teachings by pope and a synod of English Church 1382. Produced many treatises: *De Dominio Divino* and *De Dominio Civile* attacked governmental structure of contemporary Church, rejecting clergy's possession of worldly wealth; *De Eucharistia* denied orthodox doctrine of transubstantiation. Wycliff's lectures at Oxford influenced students, who disseminated his opinions.

The Wilton Diptych, c. 1399, and a detail showing angels wearing the White Hart livery-badge.

The Risen Christ with Mary Magdalen: detail from the Syon cope of about 1300, one of the finest examples of English embroidery, opus anglicanum.

Guy's Tower, Warwick Castle, completed in 1394.

The monument to Blanche Mortimer (d. 1347) in St Bartholomew's church, Much Marcle.

parishioners sought to secure their souls by private deals with God in the purchase or endowment of memorial masses. A few, more adventurous, dabbled with heresy, making common cause with the Lollards*.

Here, then, was one kind of intimation of the future. Another was the nascent humanism of the vernacular poet* Geoffrey Chaucer, influenced by (among other things) Giovanni Boccaccio's *Decameron*. After Chaucer, many doors opened in fifteenth-century England to at least a whiff of the Renaissance from the South. There was John Lydgate, for example, the monk-poet of Bury St Edmunds, who had known Chaucer well. And there was John Whethamstede in the next generation, twice abbot of St Albans and last of that long line of St Albans scholars which had included Roger of Wendover, Matthew Paris and Thomas Walsingham, who preferred classical authorities to those of his own times, and who wrote in what he believed to be the authentic language of Antiquity. A growing regularity in domestic and military planning; the first efforts to accommodate and to make proper defensive use of the gun; the pursuit of a deliberate architectural symmetry where nothing of the kind had been considered necessary before: in 1450, these were suggestions only – the merest gleam in the eyes of the abbot of St Albans and his circle. But they were present.

Lollardy

Most important heresy in late medieval England, with views drawn indirectly from Wycliff. Lollards usually artisans (especially textile workers); some knights had Lollard sympathies in Richard II's reign, but Lollardy's association with sedition (in Peasants' Revolt and Oldcastle's Rebellion) later made heresy unpopular with landed classes. Lollards produced vernacular Bible and devotional literature, studied at private meetings; they were critical of value of sacraments, clerical celibacy and property, and veneration of saints; rejected pope as Anti-Christ.

De Heretico Comburendo 1401

Parliament's response to Lollardy was this statute "concerning the burning of a heretic": unlicensed preaching was forbidden, and determined heretics were to be burned at stake by secular authorities after conviction in Church courts. There was sporadic persecution of heretics in 15th and early 16th centuries: statute finally repealed 1559.

Oldcastle's Revolt 1414

Sir John Oldcastle (old friend of Henry V) was found to possess heretical books; but king would not protect him; tried 1413, refused to recant, denounced ecclesiastical hierarchy. He escaped from Tower, raised futile revolt near London 1414, enjoying little support from landowners, some from artisans and clergy; captured and executed (1417). Revolt associated Lollardy with sedition, rendering conservative landed classes hostile towards it and pushing government into supporting repression.

Vernacular poetry

Chaucer (c. 1340-1400) was the genius of medieval vernacular poetry: his *Troilus and Criseyde* and *Canterbury Tales* (1387-1400) are masterpieces of form, characterization and description. Though influenced by Italian and French works, he wrote distinctively *English* literature. Near contemporary, alliterative, masterpieces were Langland's *Piers Plowman*, *Gawain and the Green Knight* and *Pearl* (both anonymous), written in vigorous regional dialects of west and north-west England. Apart from Thomas Malory's (c. 1408-71) *Morte d'Arthur* (1469) work of other poets, John Gower (c. 1330-1408), John Lydgate (c. 1370-1450) and Thomas Hoccleve (c. 1368-1426), was less accomplished, although popular carols (religious and secular) and ballads contained many beautiful verses.

Mystery (Miracle) plays

Cycles of vernacular plays (as many as 48 in the Wakefield cycle) performed by members of urban guilds at Whitsuntide or Corpus Christi festivals; cycles would last from dawn to dusk, and involve many townsmen. The best surviving are from Chester, Coventry (both from the 1370s), York and Wakefield (c.1425). Although they illustrated liturgical themes and were based on Bible stories, some were comical, others satirical. Also popular were Morality plays (such as "Castell of Perseverance", c. 1405) descended from religious homilies, in which virtues and vices were illustrated by allegory, and morals drawn.

4

REFORMATION
AND INFLATION

1450 - 1625

REFORMATION AND INFLATION 1450-1625
Overview

Christopher Haigh

History is change, and the historian's job is the explanation of change. But since the evidence which the past has left us is voluminous and complex, we tend to simplify our task by dividing history into periods, reducing each period to a unifying movement, and labelling such movements as the major forces of change. Thus the history of the period 1450-1625 has often been presented as a succession of "rises", "the rise of the monarchy", "the Reformation" (or "the rise of Protestantism"), "the rise of the gentry", "the rise of Puritanism" and "the rise of Parliament". But some recent historians have been rather less impressed by the pace of change in these years, and now believe that dividing the past into progressive movements exaggerates change, elongates causal sequences and makes history seem more crisis-ridden than it really was. The process of revising the history of this period by stressing continuity and doubting the strength of "modernizing" forces has come to be called "revisionism", and it has led to much debate. While historians do not argue very much about whether particular events took place, we do dispute the significance of these events. This is a highly controversial period, and what is presented in this "overview" is very much a "revisionist" interpretation, not an anodyne compromise.

The English disorders of the late-fifteenth century, known somewhat misleadingly as "the Wars of the Roses", resulted from the nature of political and social relationships. The king had various offices, fees and lands which he could use to attract men to obey him. A nobleman in the king's favour could influence the distribution of royal largesse and supplement it by patronage from his own estates and household, so he could attract lesser men to serve him in the hope of reward. The "affinity" thus created could constitute a formidable political and, indeed, military force, and so gave the king good reason to favour its leader. This system, "bastard feudalism", was potentially unstable, since patrons and affinities were in constant contention, but a wise and vigorous king could preserve order by balancing his grants. But Henry VI was neither wise nor vigorous, and with conflicting titles to the throne there was competition not just for office but for the highest office of all, the monarchy:

great families and their followers fought out claims to national supremacy, and lesser figures with their own local disputes took sides according to their calculations of interest. But although most noble families were involved in the wars in their earliest stages, there was increasing reluctance to risk life and fortune in the turbulence of civil war. This left the succession to be decided by small forces: Bosworth, which gave the Tudors the throne for 118 years, was fought by perhaps 10,000 men, commanded by a dozen nobles. Thus, though men were killed in battle and some of the defeated were executed or exiled, the importance of the wars should not be overestimated: the realities of political life (and, even more, the lives of those who played no part in politics) did not change, whoever sat on the throne.

Henry VI, Edward IV, Richard III, Henry VII and, indeed, Henry VIII ruled their subjects in much the same way, by alliance with the regional magnates whose support was essential to orderly government. Kings rewarded their friends and punished a few enemies, but they also needed to buy the support of some who had stood against them and others who had stood by. Deviation from these norms led only to trouble: Richard III's creation of a powerful Howard interest and his use of northerners in southern county government lost him the support he was to need when Henry Tudor invaded in 1485. The nobles who had caused such trouble in the late-fifteenth century were remarkably quiescent in the early-sixteenth, perhaps as inflationary pressures made them more dependent on royal favour: they were content to rule their counties for the king or jockey for position at Court, though that jockeying could itself be troublesome. It led to disaster for the duke of Buckingham in 1521, after a group of nobles challenged the chancellor, Cardinal Wolsey, and more serious difficulties began in 1527 when a noble faction weaned the king from reliance on the cardinal, using Anne Boleyn as a bait. The king's "great matter" of his marriage raised a whole swarm of political bees, some of which will be considered later.

As there were few real differences between the governmental systems of these kings, it would be wrong to think, as historians once did, of the dawn of a new

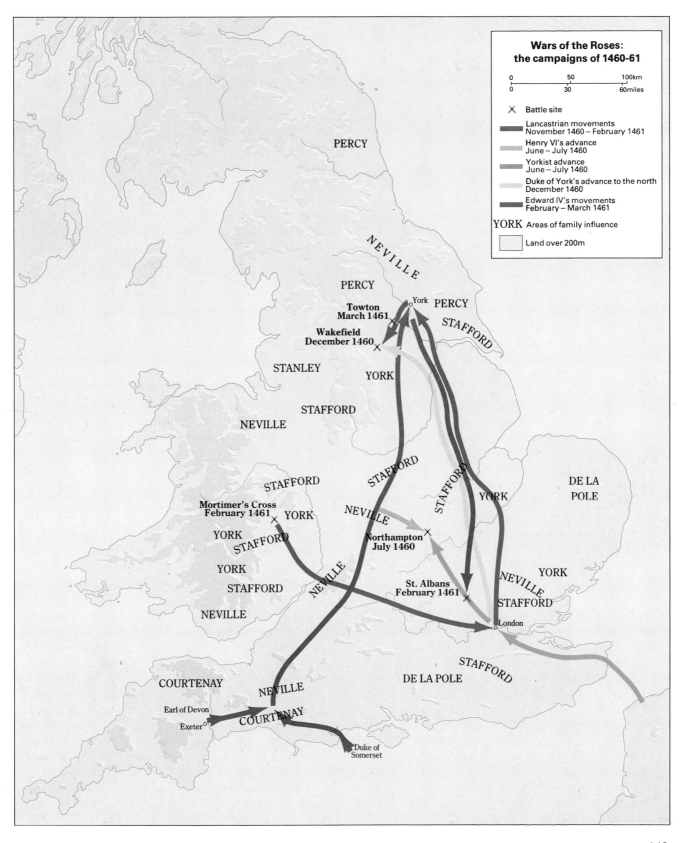

PERCY

NEVILLE

PERCY

NEVILLE

York PERCY

STAFFORD

Towton
March 1461 ×

Wakefield
December 1460 ×

STANLEY

YORK

STAFFORD

NEVILLE

STAFFORD

STAFFORD

STAFFORD

YORK

DE LA
POLE

Mortimer's Cross
February 1461 × YORK

NEVILLE

YORK
STAFFORD

Northampton
July 1460 ×

YORK
STAFFORD

NEVILLE

NEVILLE

St. Albans
February 1461 ×

YORK

NEVILLE

STAFFORD

London

COURTENAY

NEVILLE

STAFFORD

DE LA POLE

Earl of Devon

COURTENAY

Exeter ○

Duke of
Somerset

Wars of the Roses:
the campaigns of 1460–61

| 0 | 50 | 100km |
| 0 | 30 | 60 miles |

× Battle site

Lancastrian movements
November 1460 – February 1461

Henry VI's advance
June – July 1460

Yorkist advance
June – July 1460

Duke of York's advance to the north
December 1460

Edward IV's movements
February – March 1461

YORK Areas of family influence

Land over 200m

political age in 1460 or 1485. A better case has been made for a major shift in the 1530s, when Parliament legislated on new issues, central government was reformed and the administrations of Wales and Ireland and the English provinces were reorganized. These changes have been termed "the Tudor revolution in government", and interpreted (together with the Reformation) as the deliberate creation of a modern, centralized, sovereign state. But the novelty and rapidity of change have been exaggerated: development took place through gradual adjustment rather than radical innovation, and was the result of political manoeuvre rather than planned reform. Above all, we should not confuse the formal system of administration with the realities of political power. Offices, new and old, were part of the patronage system and, with other favours, were used to buy the co-operation of men with influence: the king continued to rule in alliance with local notables. The balance of power in the alliance had moved decisively in the king's favour, especially as the creation of new offices and the increased wealth of the Crown (from confiscated Church property and rising customs revenue as trade expanded) made it a more attractive patron. But this means only that a system which had worked imperfectly in the mid-fifteenth century because the king was too weak was much more effective in the mid-sixteenth when the Crown was much stronger.

There were dramatic alterations in the policy and personnel of government in 1529-32, 1536, 1539-40, 1546-47 and 1549, but such adjustments took place within the ruling order and the overall framework of government and politics remained stable. Even the crisis of 1553, when Mary Tudor raised a regional rebellion against the central government at Westminster and forced the duke of Northumberland to hand over power, led to remarkably little disruption; despite the division within the political nation public order was maintained, and there was a good deal of continuity between the régimes. Above all, the central feature of politics – that government was only possible by co-operation between the Crown and the leaders of local society – remained. There were therefore limits to the power of the monarchy, and the king ruled by consent, in three senses: first, consent to legislation had to be secured from the nobles and gentry in Parliament; second, a law had to be approved by magnates and justices if it was to be implemented by them in the counties; and third, even ordinary people had to give some limited consent by their co-operation in local government as constables and jurors, and by their obedience.

It was this administrative weakness, rather than any

strong support for Protestantism, which explains why the Reformation was comparatively peaceful: in England, Wales and Ireland, the Reformation was imposed by the state, but in a hesitant and piecemeal fashion which made each individual stage more or less acceptable. While it is true that some men, especially lawyers, wanted the power of the Church reduced, and others, especially merchants and artisans, had been converted to Lollard or Lutheran heresies, it seems that few wanted alteration in religion. "The Reformation" was neither a mass national movement nor a preconceived plan implemented step by step by Henry VIII, Thomas Cromwell and Thomas Cranmer: it is a historians' label for a sequence of often accidental events, which resulted from short-term political expedients and could have turned out differently. When Henry VIII failed to persuade the pope to divorce him from Catherine of Aragon, he forced the English Church to annul the marriage and he married Anne Boleyn; in consequence, to prevent papal reversal of the decision, he caused Parliament to recognize himself as supreme head of the Church. To raise money for defence against the expected foreign invasion, Henry suppressed the religious houses from 1536, and to secure allies among German Lutherans reformist measures were introduced into the Church – and when, in 1539-40, Franco-Imperial disputes encouraged Henry to court Charles V, ecclesiastical policy was reversed and Cromwell was executed. Religious change was contingent partly upon foreign policy and partly upon Henry's affections: politicians sought to influence the king by working through his wives and his cronies in the Privy Chamber.

The forward thrust of the Reformation was resumed in 1547, again for accidental reasons. The date of Henry VIII's death, January 1547, was crucial, for if it had come six months earlier, when the conservatives were in the ascendant, the young Edward VI's government would have been dominated by them. But in Henry's last months a reformist alliance led by the earl of Hertford (uncle of the prince of Wales) used its control of key offices to ensure that power passed into their hands at the accession of the boy king, and they resumed a cautious policy of religious reform. In 1549 control was seized by John Dudley, earl of Warwick, and a group of conservatives, but when Warwick's own future was threatened he cut his erstwhile allies out of government by a series of Protestant innovations. At the popular level, Protestantism advanced in towns such as Bristol, Canterbury, Colchester, Coventry, Ipswich and London, and among weavers and other artisans in the rural textile areas; English Bibles and Protestant books began to circulate widely. But after the succession crisis of 1553, the new Queen Mary reached London on a wave of conservative sentiment: the Reformation had apparently failed and the old religion seemed safe. For in seeking to undo the Reformation Mary was not, as has sometimes been thought, attempting the impossible, since Protestantism had as yet gained only very localized support. The statutory restoration of Catholic worship was achieved and enforced without much difficulty, and papal authority was reinstated after guarantees had been given to the owners of former Church lands. The Marian persecution, in which some 280 Protestants were burned at the stake, seems to have caused surprisingly little trouble at the time: there were murmurs at the executions of well-liked individuals, but revulsion from the persecution in general was a product of anti-Catholic propaganda in later reigns. If Mary had produced a child, or if she had lived long enough to make it too dangerous for her successor to alter religion once again, it seems that England and Wales (as well as Ireland) would have remained substantially Catholic – and without the alliance of a Protestant England, it is difficult to see how the Reformation could have succeeded in Scotland.

Thus there was nothing inevitable about the Reformation. The new religion proved attractive to some social groups and some areas, but the pace of conversion was slow and it would not have got far without the backing of the state. The accession of Mary's half-sister, Elizabeth, in 1558 finally threw the support of the state behind Reformation: her government of former Edwardians immediately began to impose Protestantism. In Scotland, Catholicism was driven out along with the French interest, and Mary, Queen of Scots, was deprived of her throne by a clique of nobles, who then ruled through the boy James VI. In both kingdoms, state support gave the expanding corps of Protestant preachers an opportunity to evangelize, which they did with considerable, but not uniform, success. The process was a long one, for it took time to train preachers, and the hierarchical Church of England was not organized for missionary activity. But the development of new evangelistic structures, with town lectureships and various forms of team ministry, led to success in the towns. In the countryside, however, where three-quarters of the men and nine-tenths of the women could not read, a Protestant religion which stressed the importance of Bible-reading and sermon-going, and which sought to enforce strict morality and observance of the sabbath, was less attractive. Though the forms of worship moved gradually in a Protestant direction, it is likely that the fundamental beliefs of ordinary people changed very little: even in the early seventeenth century, the committed "godly" were conscious that they were an isolated minority in a world of sinners, papists and witches.

The instability at the centre of English politics which set in after 1527, when factions were polarized over dynastic and religious issues, ended about 1570. The first decade of Elizabeth's reign saw political competition between groups led by the secretary, Sir William Cecil, the earl of Leicester and the duke of Norfolk. But a major crisis in 1569-70 (when a rebellion in the north sought to advance the claims of Mary, Queen of Scots, to the throne and perhaps to restore Catholicism) discredited Norfolk and his allies and forced Cecil and Leicester into the uneasy alliance which ensured stability for the next twenty years. Though there were several minor Catholic plots against Elizabeth's life, regular invasion scares and the Armada challenge of 1588, the middle decades of the reign were remarkably orderly. The expansion and streamlining of local government brought more of the growing gentry class into co-operation with the régime, while the attractions of metropolitan culture, a colourful Court and profits from wardships kept nobles and gentry quiescent.

Though historians have seen "the rise of the gentry", "the rise of Puritanism", and "the rise of Parliament" in the reign of Elizabeth and after as the long-term causes of the Civil War, such a view is now often thought misleading. We should not assume the inevitability of revolution, and to seek lengthy social or religious or constitutional causes may be to misinterpret the reigns of Elizabeth and James I. The gentry did not really "rise", since they had been a leading element in local society for centuries: rather they expanded in numbers (as richer peasants increased their lands at the expense of the less successful and so improved their status), but in so far as they could be incorporated into the ruling order by offices and patronage this strengthened government by broadening its base. "Puritanism" was, until it was driven into opposition to the bishops from 1625, little more than committed Protestantism, which represented the mainstream of reformed opinion in the Church rather than some later deviation: it was not a challenge to Church or state, though it did cause friction in some parishes. Again, Parliament was not seeking to expand its powers at the expense of the monarchy: though Elizabeth and James caused some concern by seeking to reserve some matters, especially dynastic, foreign and religious policies, to themselves, there were few clashes and they were speedily resolved – for the interests of both ministers and MPs were best served by fruitful co-operation.

There were difficulties in the 1590s, as a result of pressures of war against Spain and in Ireland and high food prices caused by harvest failures. At Court, financial problems led to fiercer struggles over patronage, perhaps exacerbated as larger numbers of gentlemen chased the restricted favours of a parsimonious queen. In the counties, official demands for taxation and army recruits at a time of economic depression brought sullen resistance and occasional disorder, and the passing of Elizabeth in 1603 was greeted with just the mixture of relief and nervousness there had been at her sister's death. The arrival of a new king from Scotland solved some problems and caused others. Since James had a wife and children, the succession was clear, and since he was pacifically inclined he ended the Spanish war in 1604. But he had some difficulty in reconciling the conflicting promises he had made to secure unchallenged accession, and pursuit of a grandiose scheme to unite his separate kingdoms into a new "Great Britain" caused resentment and had to be abandoned. The main political problems related to finance: at least since the 1530s, the Crown's own revenue from its lands and customs had been insufficient for its ordinary expenditure, and parliamentary taxes granted for special purposes had been regularly raided for current expenses. Inflation had worsened the position, Elizabeth had sold lands to pay for war, and the yield of the subsidy shrank as commissioners deliberately under-taxed their friends. From these depleted resources James had to buy the loyalty of his new subjects, keep his Scots content and project an image of monarchy which ensured obedience.

Though he cut a poor figure at its end, James's reign was a success: he had united the crowns, if not the realms, of England and Scotland, and brought Britain and Ireland under one rule; he had avoided expensive foreign wars and defused the threat of religious dissidents. The extravagance of his Court prompted criticism and his lectures to Parliament caused irritation, but political conflict was more concerned with the distribution of favours than great divisive issues. The squabbles over foreign affairs, monopolies and taxation in the Parliaments of 1621 and 1624-25 were in part the results of factional competition, and there was no sustained bid to extend the role of Parliament. The roots of 1642 should not be sought in the reign of James I.

There had been no major deterioration in government, and the political framework had seen few alterations. From the 1530s onwards, the Privy Council came to be composed almost entirely of administrators and courtiers; there were few magnate members, and sometimes no bishops at all. The great lords went to Court for celebrations and entertained the monarch on progress, but their involvement in government, central and local, seems to have declined: some served as lords-lieutenant, but the real work of ruling the counties was done by the growing numbers of justices of the peace. The crisis of 1570 broke the power of the Dacres, Nevilles and Percies in the north, and the Howard dominance of East Anglia ended in 1572. Financial problems eroded the regional influence of some families, such as the Cliffords, and the divisions of estates among heirs-general weakened the position of others, such as Stanleys and Talbots. But despite the "inflation of honours", when James and the duke of Buckingham sold peerages, the nobility retained great social, and some political, prestige: the House of Lords was a major political force, nobles were important channels for patronage, and new families of political aristocrats, Cecils, Herberts and Russells, built up local authority. Though the Church, with its preachers and its network of courts, was still an important weapon in the maintenance of order, it had lost its independent power: bishops needed the support of the royal Council, and country rectors needed the support of the squire. But these were not fundamental changes in the system of government. A monarchy with a small bureaucracy and no standing army or police force was still dependent for its coercive authority upon the co-operation of local notables, and their assistance was bought by the distribution of patronage. Though Britain grew more populous and more prosperous, though the gap between rich and poor widened, though towns grew and new industries emerged, and though the official religion of the state was altered, there was a remarkable political continuity. James I ruled much as Edward IV had done.

Government and Politics in England 1450-1553:
problems of succession

C.S.L. Davies

In 1450 the duke of Suffolk, leader of the faction which dominated Henry VI's government, was impeached and murdered. The people of Kent, gentry as well as commoners, rose in a rebellion* against corruption and ineffectiveness in local and national government. The next decade saw a rapid worsening as factions contended to control government. For a while (1453-55) Henry was clinically insane and Richard, duke of York, governed as Protector, with some success. When Henry recovered he was a pawn in the hands of his queen, Margaret of Anjou, determined to safeguard the rights of her son, Prince Edward (born 1453) and to avenge herself on Richard. The first of the spasmodic battles of the so-called Wars of the Roses* broke out in 1455 at St Albans*, to be followed by more in 1459 and 1460. In 1460, for the first time, York advanced a claim to the throne. The lords in Parliament, under military threat, accepted his argument*, saving their oaths to Henry by allowing him to hold the throne for life, but disinheriting his son; York meanwhile was to have charge of government. This compromise collapsed when Queen Margaret gathered her forces. York was killed at Wakefield* (December 1460). His son, in a desperate throw, had himself proclaimed king as Edward IV* by a handful of peers and the citizens of London (March 1461). Against the odds he crushed Margaret's forces at Towton. Lancastrian resistance was effectively ended.

The great landed magnates dominated these events. Land meant power; armies could be raised from tenants and dependants. Ambitious men sought "good lordship" from those who could help them to office in Church or state or browbeat officials or juries. The prevalence of "retaining"* gave the system an additional twist at this time; the payment of an annuity in return for (not necessarily military) service. Retainers (themselves often gentlemen, sometimes even peers) could swell their lord's army with their own men, and provide a professional officer cadre. The system was fluid (some retainers

Cade's Rebellion 1450
Major uprising in Kent May - July 1450, led by Jack Cade and several future MPs. Complaining of local and national corruption and against backcloth of high taxation and English failure in Normandy, rebels defeated royal army at Sevenoaks, entered London and executed Lord Treasurer Saye, before being forced to flee. Also complained of low birth of royal councillors, wanting inclusion of dukes of Norfolk, Exeter and especially York, who returned from Ireland and tried to establish his pre-eminence in government of the realm. Rebels were forced to flee, and Cade killed.

Wars of the Roses
Label invented by Sir Walter Scott (and unknown to contemporaries), for the sporadic political and dynastic troubles between Battle of St Albans 1455, and Henry VII's reign. Depicted as struggle between house of Lancaster (claiming descent from Edward III's 4th son) and house of York (claiming descent from his 3rd son), but conflicts more complex. Misleading term, since neither "Lancastrian red" rose nor "Yorkist white" ever uniquely identified houses; and in 30 years from 1455 about 60 weeks of active campaigning took place. 16th-century propagandists depicted Tudor dynasty as restoring peace and prosperity after Yorkist usurpation.

Battle of St Albans 1455
Traditional start of 15th-century civil wars. During King Henry's madness, York was made regent instead of Queen Margaret; with king's recovery, animosity of queen's friends to York and Nevilles redoubled. York and Nevilles attacked their enemies in king's retinue at St Albans, killing Somerset and Northumberland and capturing Henry.

Act of Accord 1460
In aftermath of defeat of king and queen's forces at Northampton, the duke of York was acknowledged by October Parliament as heir to the throne and Protector of the realm, and given yearly grant of 10,000 marks.

Battle of Wakefield 1460
Leaving Sandal Castle to face superior royal forces, Richard of York was killed and his severed head, wearing a paper crown, displayed at York. Royal forces then marched south to London.

Accession of Edward IV 1461
Proclaimed king because his father York's death and Margaret's implacable opposition to disheritance of her son rendered compromise impossible. Margaret, failing to seize London (where some citizens possibly alarmed at prospect of billeting queen's northern armies), retired northwards, leaving Edward to enter capital. His *coup* was only endorsed by handful of peers in London and popular acclamation arranged by soldiers.

Livery and maintenance
Traditional aspects of retaining, being the wearing of a lord's uniform or "livery", and a lord's interference with law courts to "maintain" a follower or his cause. Sometimes thought to have weakened national unity by focusing loyalty on lords; eventual limitation by statute seen as success for Tudor monarchs.

served more than one lord), and the Wars of the Roses therefore involved a series of short, if bloody, battles, not sustained campaigns; clients were all too ready to abandon a losing cause and to seek better lordship elsewhere.

A skilful king could use this system of "bastard feudalism"* for his own advantage, by careful control and balancing. There was a potential for disorder, but violence was not in the interests of the nobility as a whole. Their own lives and possessions were heavily at risk in civil war. Once blood was spilled, however, events took on a momentum which it was difficult to check. The 1450s did see on a local level the escalation of several inter-noble feuds to dangerous proportions. Towton* showed that peace could be better guaranteed by King Edward than by Henry VI (or Margaret). The majority of peers hastened to make their peace with the new régime.

Edward's first ten years were disturbed by the ambitions of his cousin, Richard Neville, earl of Warwick. York's strength had been based on alliance with the Nevilles, but Edward worked to emancipate himself from their control. His marriage (1464) to Elizabeth Wydeville was taken, even if not so intended, as a gesture of independence; it certainly frustrated Warwick's negotiations for a French marriage for the king. Fighting broke out again in 1469. Edward fled to exile (1470), Warwick restored Henry VI* and began negotiations for the return of Queen Margaret. Before these unnatural allies could combine, Edward returned, crushed Warwick's troops at Barnet*, and Margaret's at Tewkesbury (1471). Warwick and the Lancastrian prince of Wales, Edward, were killed; Henry VI, on hearing the news, died in suspicious circumstances. With its rivals dead, the Yorkist dynasty was secure. The remainder of Edward's reign (1471-83) passed with little incident except for the execution of his brother George, duke of Clarence, in 1478. (Clarence had successively betrayed both Edward and Warwick in 1470-71 and now presumed too much on his brother's charity.) In spite of a reputation for self-indulgence, Edward worked hard at the details of government, reducing disorder and building up a healthy financial balance, while advancing the interests of his children, his other brother Richard, duke of Gloucester, and his wife Elizabeth's relations, often at the expense of the nobility.

Edward died at forty, in 1483. His son, now Edward V, was twelve. A festering enmity between Gloucester and Elizabeth Wydeville explains at least Richard's initial moves in the familiar sequence of his seizure of the young king, his having himself proclaimed king as Richard III, and the disappearance of Edward and his brother into the Tower*. The duke of Buckingham, who had helped Richard to the throne, rebelled, for reasons still obscure. These divisions in the Yorkist party gave hope to the exiled Henry Tudor, whose "Lancastrian" claim (through his mother Margaret Beaufort) had won little support hitherto. The wariness of many peers to commit themselves meant that Richard's advantage, though substantial, was not overwhelming at Bosworth* (1485). An uncovenanted bonus was Richard's death; the first English king to die in battle since Harold in 1066.

Four-fifths of the nobility took part in the battles of 1460-1; only one-fifth in that of 1485. None of the Yorkist kings excited much positive loyalty; neither did Henry VII who had to exercise constant vigilance against real or pretended claimants*. Like Edward, he extracted bonds* for good behaviour from nobles and others, and also tried to heal political wounds by gradually restoring lands and titles to former opponents, although his approach was far more methodical and circumspect than Edward's had been. He resumed Edward's policy of

Bastard feudalism
Term sometimes used to describe society in late medieval England where ties of loyalty no longer depended on lords granting land to vassals in return for service in war and peace, but on paying cash annuities to retainers, who contracted (by indenture) to serve for life or a fixed period under stipulated conditions. Alleged to have been unstable system, forcing lords to compete fiercely for power and wealth and support their retainers in violent disputes.

Battle of Towton 1461
Largest battle of the civil wars, with up to 50,000 combatants, Towton witnessed heavy losses and destruction of Lancastrian might by Edward IV. Margaret and Henry VI escaped.

Henry VI's readeption 1470-71
With his brother dismissed, Francophile policy ignored, and daughter's marriage to duke of Clarence hindered, Warwick's support for Edward IV lapsed. Warwick, Clarence and Archbishop Neville denounced Edward's high taxation, subversion of justice, and Wydeville partiality. Edward surrendered to enemies after forces defeated by northern rebels (Edgecote 1469) but soon released. Warwick and Clarence left for France, forming alliance with Margaret of Anjou. With French help, Warwick and Clarence landed in Devon 1470, and forced Edward IV into exile: Henry VI restored as king 6 October 1470 - 11 April 1471.

Battles of Barnet and Tewkesbury 1471
Edward IV landed near mouth of Humber 1471, marched south attracting support in midlands. Clarence rejoined him near Warwick and Edward entered London. At Barnet, 14 April 1471, Warwick and John Neville killed. Margaret landed at Weymouth, heading for Lancastrian north Wales; intercepted by Edward in Gloucestershire, she was captured and her son killed at Tewkesbury, 4 May 1471.

Princes in the Tower
Edward V reigned 9 April - 25 June 1483, but he and brother Richard were declared bastards owing to father's prior betrothal which invalidated Wydeville marriage; their uncle became Richard III. Princes sent to Tower, and soon disappeared, possibly murdered.

Battle of Bosworth 1485
After landing at Milford Haven in Wales, Henry Tudor faced the king at Bosworth Field, Leicestershire, 22 August 1485: a small-scale battle, the king being supported

THE HOUSES OF YORK AND LANCASTER

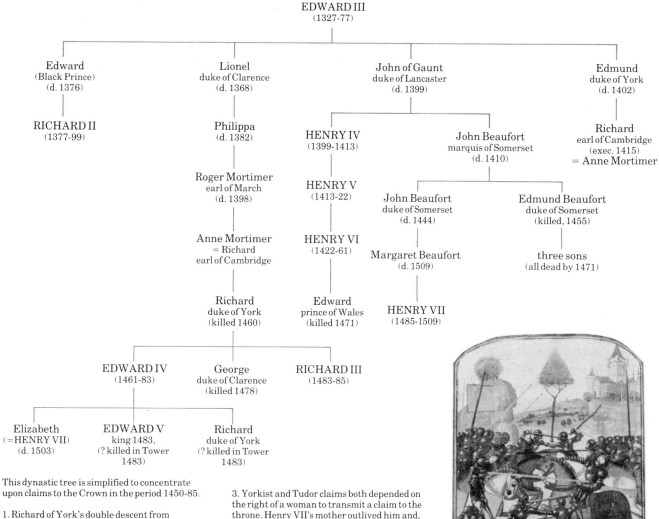

This dynastic tree is simplified to concentrate upon claims to the Crown in the period 1450-85.

1. Richard of York's double descent from Edward III gave him both a claim, *via* Lionel of Clarence, which could "trump" that of the House of Lancaster, and a claim to succeed if the Lancaster line were to die out (and the Beauforts were held to be debarred).

2. The Beaufort claim to succeed the main Lancaster line was vitiated by John Beaufort's having been born a bastard. The family was later legitimated, but specifically barred from the royal succession in 1407.

3. Yorkist and Tudor claims both depended on the right of a woman to transmit a claim to the throne. Henry VII's mother outlived him and, by modern doctrine, should have been queen in her own right.

4. Henry VII carefully avoided basing his claim on his marriage to Edward IV's daughter. He dated his reign from the battle of Bosworth (22 August 1485), had himself crowned on 27 October and married Elizabeth on 18 January 1486. Nevertheless, Henry VIII, a son of Elizabeth of York, might claim to be king on legitimist Yorkist principles.

The Battle of Barnet, 1471, in a contemporary Flemish miniature. Edward IV is shown personally killing Warwick – a symbolic not literal representation of events.

by only seven peers and the usurper by two or three, it was desertion of Stanleys that led to Richard's death and Tudor accession. Though Bosworth seen as end of civil wars, Henry VII had still to face several conspiracies and minor invasions.

Battle of Stoke 1487
Imposter Lambert Simnel was crowned "Edward VI" in Dublin, supported against

new Tudor dynasty by both English and Irish nobles, and 2000 German mercenaries supplied by his "aunt" Margaret of Burgundy. The rebels suffered heavy casualties at Battle of Stoke (near Newark), 16 June 1487, and Simnel was captured.

Perkin Warbeck's claim
From Tournai, he was put forward as the younger of the princes in the Tower from

1491. Henry chose to isolate "Richard IV" from European support by series of diplomatic agreements. Warbeck tried to invade England 1497 but was captured.

Bonds
Sums of money forfeited on failure to perform a duty or maintain allegiance to king, becoming more frequent under Henry VII after 1500.

increasing revenue and combatting disorder without fundamentally altering the machinery of government. He needed luck as well as ability; above all, in surviving just long enough to avoid yet another royal minority.

Henry VIII's self-confidence resulted from his peaceful accession, the first since 1422. Cardinal Wolsey's government (1513-29) pursued an active foreign policy, introduced a more efficient tax*, prosecuted breakers of the enclosure laws and generally maintained order and political stability while improving the administration of justice. Queen Catherine's failure to produce a male heir involved Henry in a frantic search for nullification of his marriage*. Papal intransigence led to the downfall of Wolsey, and eventually (1532-34) to a series of measures abrogating papal jurisdiction over the English Church and subjecting it to the king as its "Supreme Head". With Thomas Cromwell as minister, Henry proceeded to dissolve the monasteries*, while pushing the Church in an increasingly Protestant direction; the provision of an official English Bible* (1537) was the most important step in this direction. From 1539 reaction set in, with the Act of Six Articles*, followed (1540) by the fall of Cromwell*. Henry's last years were devoted largely to war, with France and Scotland; though the Chantries Act* (1545) heralded a renewed attack on Church endowments and by implication on doctrine. Henry's second marriage, to Anne Boleyn, had produced a daughter, Elizabeth, before Anne was executed* and the marriage retrospectively annulled (1536). The birth of Prince Edward (1537) to Henry's third wife retrieved the situation. But none of Henry's three subsequent wives produced children. An Act of Parliament (1543) inserted Henry's (technically illegitimate) daughters Mary and Elizabeth into the line of succession after Edward, while allowing Henry to determine the further succession by will*. Edward succeeded (1547) as a

Subsidy
Parliamentary tax based on (variable) assessment of an individual's wealth in landed income or goods. Created 1512 to finance Henry's early wars. (Yielded £170,000 between 1513 and 1516). Overshadowed old "fifteenth and tenth", a fixed parliamentary levy imposed on localities and worth £30,000.

Amicable Grant 1525
Extra-parliamentary levy by Wolsey of up to ⅙ lay goods and ⅓ clerical possessions, to pay for renewed attacks on France. After some years of forced loans and heavy subsidies, the Grant provoked open resistance among cloth-workers of East Anglia and Kent; Londoners objected, claiming all benevolences (money-gifts) to Crown outlawed by 1484 statute. Henry VIII halted collection, alleging it had been levied without his authorization.

The king's divorce
(Sometimes known as the king's "great matter".) In 1527 Henry revealed qualms about marriage with Catherine of Aragon, said to contravene Old Testament ruling against marrying brother's widow. Problem of Catherine's brief marriage to Henry's

late brother Arthur had been raised before 1509 marriage to Henry; papal dispensation then granted, but Henry later argued pope incapable of dispensing with scriptural law. Causes of breakdown of once-successful marriage included king's conviction that lack of male heir was punishment from God; as aunt to emperor, Catherine impeded better Anglo-French relations sought since 1525; and Henry's infatuation for Anne Boleyn.

Valor Ecclesiasticus 1535
Royal commissions surveyed all Church property in England and Wales in 1535; their evaluation, the *Valor*, revealed monastic revenues of £160,000, and as much again for rest of clergy; became basis of clerical taxation.

Dissolution of monasteries 1536-40
Allegations of monastic laxity produced by royal investigation were used to justify 1536 Act dissolving smaller monasteries and granting their property to the king. A campaign ensued to force remaining houses to offer their dissolution, confirmed by Parliament 1539. By 1540, 800 houses had been taken over, bringing Crown new revenues. But laity, not Crown or Church,

were beneficiaries of massive transfer of wealth and patronage: by 1547 two-thirds of ex-monastic land sold by Henry to finance his wars. Destruction of English (and Irish) monasticism carried out primarily to meet royal financial needs.

English Bibles
In 1520s Bibles in English were burnt by Church, fearing availability of Scripture would undermine its authority, but circulation increased during Reformation. In 1537 Cromwell licensed Coverdale's translation; in 1538 he ordered every parish church to have an English Bible; official "Great Bible", mainly Coverdale's work, appeared in 1539. Conservative disquiet over translations led in 1543 to restriction of Bible reading according to social status.

Act of Six Articles 1539
Repressive conservative statute which sought to enforce Catholic doctrine on six controversial issues: transubstantiation, communion in one kind, clerical celibacy, vows of chastity, private masses and auricular confession. Fearing diplomatic isolation, Henry VIII sought to stamp out heresies in England and Calais: several enquiries or "quests" launched under Act, especially in London, before repeal in 1547. Called by critics "whip with six strings", "bloody statute".

Fall of Cromwell 1540
Arrested for treason less than 2 months after creation as earl of Essex: declared guilty, by act of attainder, of having plotted to fight Henry and marry Princess Mary, usurping royal power, and of heresy. Kept alive in Tower long enough to provide evidence for annulment of Cleves marriage, then beheaded. Probably fell because his association with Cleves marriage and the alliance with German princes became an embarrassment to Henry.

Chantries Acts 1545 and 1547
1545 Act empowered confiscation by king of all charities, whether chantries, hospitals, guilds, or colleges, claiming Henry would make better use of their wealth. Dissolution hardly begun on Henry's death; new Act 1547 differed by stating theological objections to chantries – their main purpose was to fund priests to say masses for dead, thereby implying existence of purgatory, an intermediate stage to heaven with little scriptural justification. Crown received over £600,000 from dissolution of chantries as land passed into lay hands.

Succession Act 1534

Stated children of Boleyn marriage (i.e. so far, Elizabeth) heirs to throne and bastardized Mary (daughter of Catherine). Ordered nationwide oaths to this effect, which, being refused by More and Fisher, led to their imprisonment. Henry's chequered marital history necessitated further acts in 1536, 1543.

Fall of Anne Boleyn 1536

Anne executed with accomplices on implausible charges of treasonable adultery and incest; her marriage to Henry was declared void, making Elizabeth Tudor illegitimate. Fall due to alliance of religious conservatives (who believed marriage to Protestant Anne hindered understanding with Rome and inheritance of Mary Tudor) and Cromwell, who feared political power of Boleyn faction. Henry then married Jane Seymour.

Henry VIII's will

1543 Succession Act acknowledged rights of Mary and Elizabeth, though maintaining their "illegitimacy", and empowered Henry to determine further succession by will. December 1546 will gave precedence (after Edward, Mary and Elizabeth) to descendants of his younger sister, Mary, ahead of descendants of Margaret of Scotland. Henry's death 27 January 1547 kept secret for 3 days while councillors Hertford and Paget took steps to alter the will. Instead of collective government by a named council of equals, Paget claimed Henry's real intention was to make Edward Seymour Protector or virtual regent, and that the councillors should receive new lands and titles.

Henry VIII in state, presenting a charter to the Company of Barber-Surgeons, 1540. The painting is attributed to Holbein.

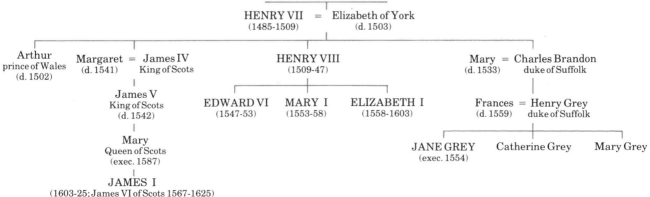

THE TUDOR FAMILY

minor. Henry had intended the minority government to be conciliar, but a *coup* carried on round his deathbed led to Edward's maternal uncle Edward Seymour being installed as Protector and duke of Somerset.

Overweening self-confidence characterized Somerset's government. Inept handling of the 1549 rebellions* led the Privy Council to overthrow him. His successor, John Dudley, duke of Northumberland, more tactfully manipulated the Council and avoided the title of Protector. Through the new Prayer Books* of 1549 and 1552 Edward's governments prescribed an unequivocally Protestant mode of worship. Concern for his religion probably explains Edward's nomination of his cousin Jane Grey (Northumberland's daughter-in-law) to succeed him. His will lacked parliamentary sanction. Mary proclaimed herself queen and successfully roused the country in defence of her interests. Respect for Henry VIII's line played its part in her success; so too did the knowledge that she stood for a return to the traditional religion.

Political stability remained precarious. The Tudors had acquired the legitimacy of long continuance. Retaining was less blatant after some exemplary prosecutions* under Henry VII and Wolsey. Great nobles were still a focus of loyalties, however, their influence decisive in suppressing or surreptitiously encouraging rebellion. But good management and good fortune had produced a long period of internal peace, allowing both a broadening of the political base away from the nobility who had been dominant in the crisis conditions of 1450-71; and allowing, too, the strengthening of the state.

The subjection of the Church* regularized to some extent the existing situation; the king had long appointed bishops, and the grant of legatine powers to Wolsey by the pope consolidated, in effect, supreme power over Church and state in the hands of the king's minister. But the "supreme

See **Peasants' revolts** (page 186)

Books of Common Prayer 1549 and 1552
First Edwardian Prayer Book drafted mainly by Cranmer, its exclusive use for church services ordered by Parliament in 1549 Uniformity Act. Emphasized evangelical ideas of communal or congregational worship: services in English not Latin, and eucharist changed from a re-enactment by the priest of Christ's sacrifice into a commemoration of his death and triumph. With Christ's real presence in the bread and wine not denied, and Church ceremonial retained, most religious conservatives accepted first Prayer Book. Second Uniformity Act 1552 enjoined a more radical religious settlement: Prayer Book was heavily modified, and in "black rubric" (a last-minute addition by the Privy Council) bodily presence of Christ in eucharist explicitly denied.

Eucharist
Central act of Christian worship, where bread and wine offered after fashion of New Testament Last Supper. Catholics believed in a "real presence" of Christ's body; the priest's words changed the substance of bread and wine into the body and blood of Christ (transubstantiation). Lutherans also believed in a "real presence", in which Christ's body coexisted with the bread and wine (consubstantiation). Radical Protestants denied a "real presence", seeing the communion as a commemorative act. The 1552 religious settlement was the only one in England to include an explicit denial of real presence.

Acts of Attainder
Parliamentary declarations that named individuals were guilty of treason, resulting in their execution and forfeiture of all land to Crown. Their avoidance of public trials made them useful in destroying politically embarrassing figures. Many attainders were later reversed in order to reinstate heirs.

Edward VI's own "Devise for the Succession". The first version ignored the claims of Mary, Elizabeth and the Stuart line, and left the throne to the "heirs male" of the women of the Grey family. When it became clear (probably in May 1553) that Edward would not live long enough for any of the women to bear a son, the "devise" was amended to make Jane Grey herself the only living heir.

Submission of the clergy 1532

English Convocations (the Church assemblies for York and, more significant, Canterbury provinces) forced by king and Commons to accept that all existing and future canon (Church) law be subject to royal approval. Sir Thomas More resigned the chancellorship as result of this major assault on Church independence.

Supremacy Act 1534

Did not create king's title of "supreme head of the Church of England", merely accepted this rightfully so, then defined and sanctioned the legal powers which the title entailed. Act repealed by Mary 1554, but royal supremacy revived by Elizabeth under title of "supreme governor" 1559.

Treason Act 1534

To protect Reformation régime, Act extended definition of treason to cover words (not just deeds) encompassing king's death, and also the denial of royal supremacy. Treason by words repealed by Somerset 1547.

Royal Injunctions of 1536 and 1538

Instructions issued under royal supremacy by Cromwell as vicegerent-in-spirituals, designed to give practical effect to changes in doctrinal emphasis. August 1536 Injunctions pronounced against superstitious beliefs on pilgrimages, relics and images; required clergy to expound 1536 Ten Articles, and to teach Lord's Prayer, Creed, and 10 Commandments in English. Injunctions of September 1538 ordered removal of images, keeping of registers of baptisms, marriages and burials, and placing in churches of a large Bible in English.

Council of the North

Like Welsh council, originated under Yorkists, as personal council for future Richard III, lieutenant in north. Lapsed under Henry VII, but restored 1525 as council under duke of Richmond, Henry VIII's illegitimate son. Reformed and given wider jurisdiction in 1537, with permanent base at York: a convenient regional court and supervisory body, but abolished 1641.

The title-page of the 1539 Great Bible from a 1540 edition: watched approvingly by God, the king hands out the scriptures to Archbishop Cranmer and Thomas Cromwell, who pass them on to a grateful people.

headship"* had symbolic importance; it had practical implications, in the supervision of episcopal jurisdiction, the determination of doctrine*, and the take-over of monastic lands, and of chantry endowments, and eventually (1552) church plate by the Crown. The monastic lands (possibly some fifteen per cent of the entire landed wealth of the country) would have permanently transformed the Crown's financial position, but for the unprecedented military expenditure of the 1540s. Cromwell's régime saw too the abolition of surviving noble franchisal jurisdiction, the reinvigoration of the councils of Wales and the North*, and the Welsh Act of Union (1536). The 1530s and 1540s saw a whole range of social and economic regulation, including attempts to establish a national system of poor relief and to control prices. The incidence of violence had been reduced to more acceptable levels; government vigilance, and

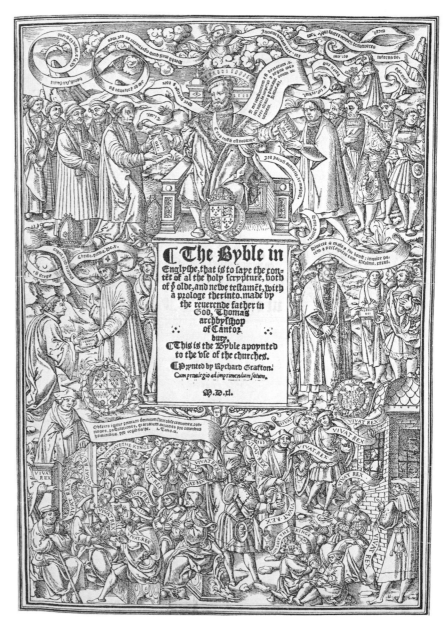

speedier remedies through the extended jurisdiction of Chancery* and Star Chamber*, stimulating in turn some modernization of the archaic proceedings of the common-law courts, played their part.

Many of these changes involved parliamentary legislation. The scope and volume of legislation, the challenge to traditional concepts involved in the Reformation legislation, increased the standing of Parliament. This was not at the expense of the Crown; rather king and Parliament worked together to increase the importance of statute law against the vaguer, more diffused, concept of authority in which natural law, the international law of the Church, statute and prescription had jostled together.

These changes were not accepted without protest; notably the 1536 Pilgrimage of Grace*, and the 1549 rebellion in the West Country against Edwardian religious innovation. Given the extent of changes which attempted to overthrow customs as emotionally charged as the provision of masses for the dead, and to work a revolution in man's concept of fundamental truth, it is surprising how little overt opposition there was. But while the government could carry through institutional changes such as the abolition of the monasteries, beliefs and attitudes were a different story. Many of the church ornaments which should have been confiscated in 1552 were hidden away to re-appear in Mary's reign. The Prayer Books may have been quietly ignored in many villages. The state under Henry VIII and Edward VI had arrogated to itself the power to determine, in theory, a range of issues, from the nature of salvation to the price of beef, on a scale so far unprecedented. (What, wondered Thomas More, would happen if Parliament were to declare that God were not God?) It had inevitably overreached itself. The second half of the sixteenth century was to be a period of consolidation.

Chancery
Lord Chancellor's court sitting at Westminster, which by application of "equity" (the chancellor's sense of fair play) could try cases less rigidly than the common law. Until 1536, particularly important in guaranteeing the inheritability of land.

Court of Star Chamber
Name given to King's councillors when sitting as judicial body, usually in Star Chamber at Westminster: used by Wolsey especially to deal with interference with local courts by great men and property disputes involving breaches of the peace. Could not inflict loss of life or property.

Pilgrimage of Grace 1536
Series of rebellions engulfing Lincolnshire and six northern shires. First came Lincolnshire revolt of October: largely spontaneous local reaction to central interference in the county and to rumours of further religious change; suppressed in just over a fortnight by small force under duke of Suffolk. More dangerous was Yorkshire rising: York occupied by 16 October and a rebel force of over 30,000 gathered. Led by Robert Aske and some nobles and clergy, Pilgrimage of Grace (as Aske called it) proposed national conservative political and religious programme: repeal of recent interference in bequeathing of property; removal of Cromwell; end to monastic dissolutions (reversed by rebels); restoration of pope, and of Mary Tudor to the succession. Revolt petered out when king promised concessions (never implemented); rebel leaders and many commons executed.

Remigius van Leemput's mid-17th-century version of the wall-painting by Holbein in the Privy Chamber at Whitehall. Edward VI stands before the mural, which shows Henry VII with Elizabeth of York and a dominating Henry VIII with Jane Seymour.

Government and Politics 1553-1625:
Crown, Church and Parliament

Simon Adams

Mary I proclaimed herself queen on 10 July 1553 at Kenninghall House in Norfolk; a steady stream of defections from her rival assured a near-bloodless accession* within a fortnight. Loyalty to the principles of inheritance had overcome fears of a religious reaction, but over 800 persons went into exile in well-organized communities during the course of the reign. After January 1555 at least 280 persons (mainly commoners) were executed for heresy – a vivid demonstration of the consequences of a Catholic restoration*. Parliament obediently repealed the earlier Reformation statutes in 1553 and 1554, but it could not be relied upon to go further; in 1555 a Crown bill to penalize the exiles was thrown out. In order to pacify opposition, lay possession of the former monastic estates was accepted, while the structural weaknesses of the Church – together with the absence of a missionary clergy – inhibited the revival of Catholicism.

The queen herself – kind-hearted, utterly conventional and grimly devout – provoked further discontent by her marriage to Philip*, son of the Emperor Charles V. Following a major, if bungled, rising* in early 1554, she was plagued by a series of conspiracies. Moreover, her failure to produce an heir forced her to accept the half-sister she disliked as successor. Entry into war against France for the Habsburg cause in June 1557 resulted in financial disaster and the loss of Calais (7 January 1558).The reaction to persecution and foreign rule was skilfully exploited by the propaganda of the exiles, and a powerful myth of popular and patriotic Protestantism was created thereafter which shaped political consciousness for over a century after Mary's death in 1558.

The forty-four year reign of Elizabeth I (1558-1603) provided time for the slow consolidation of the Protestant Reformation. Her first Parliament* (1559) returned the Church to a marginally more conservative version of 1553; the adoption in 1563 of a doctrinal statement acceptable to predestinarian

Accession of Mary 1553
Lady Jane Grey, granddaughter of Henry VIII's sister, Mary, and Northumberland's daughter-in-law, "reigned" 6 - 19 July 1553, in accordance with Edward's will, which sought to override statutory succession. Throne was claimed by Henry's daughter Mary, who began raising East Anglian followers; Northumberland set out to fight her. As support for Mary grew, Privy Council abandoned Jane, leaving Northumberland to capitulate in Cambridge (later executed). Mary's *coup* claimed as only successful Tudor rebellion.

Restoration of Catholicism
In October 1553, all Edwardian religious legislation repealed by Parliament (restoring Henrician position of Catholicism under a royal supremacy), with exception of 1547 Chantries Act; April 1554, rivalries in Council caused Lord Paget to defeat in Lords heresy bill of his rival, Bishop Gardiner; November 1554 pope's authority acknowledged, but only after papal dispensation allowing retention of ex-Church lands. The 3 parliaments of 1553-54 suggest property at least as important as religion to MPs and peers.

Spanish marriage 1554
Treaty for marriage between Mary and Philip of Spain concluded January 1554: any child of marriage to inherit England and Netherlands, and whole Spanish empire if Philip's son, Don Carlos died. Married July 1554, Philip was accorded title of king though his political influence was controlled. Critics of marriage feared Spanish domination.

Wyatt's Rebellion 1554
January-February 1554, after announcement of Spanish marriage, Sir Thomas Wyatt raised 3,000 Kentishmen to march on London, (planned risings in Devon, midlands, and Wales collapsed owing to government's foreknowledge). Queen Mary rallied supporters in London, and rebels were repulsed. Aims of conspiracy unclear: Wyatt may have intended to go beyond blocking Spanish marriage and make Elizabeth queen. In the purge following Wyatt's execution, Jane Grey beheaded; also calls for Elizabeth's death.

Elizabethan "settlement" 1559
Parliament restored royal supremacy, but under title of "supreme governor" of the Church. Uniformity Act restored second Edwardian Prayer Book, but compromised on question of real presence: the 1552 phraseology which implied communion was only a symbolic act was supplemented by 1549 words which suggested Christ's body really present in eucharist. Elizabeth's Council had difficulty getting legislation accepted, especially through resistance by Catholic bishops and nobles who forced concessions.

Royal Injunctions 1559
Orders to Church, published to Protestantize churches and enforce re-introduction of Book of Common Prayer, and implemented after a visitation. Based on 1547 Injunctions, stipulating use of Edwardian vestments, including square caps; contained less provocative version of statutory oath of supremacy. 1559 visitation deprived c.300 clergy.

Calvinists* (the Thirty-Nine Articles*) completed a structure that remained largely intact until 1640. From the universities came a growing stream of graduate Protestant clergy: in 1560 nineteen per cent of the clergy of the diocese of Worcester were graduates, in 1640 eighty-four per cent. Less successful were efforts to remedy the wide disparities in clerical status and income, while the desire of the more evangelical clergy to impose a rigorous discipline on the laity met with little support. An open confrontation provoked by the queen's conservative views on clerical dress* saw the emergence of a Puritan* party within the Church, which after 1570 took on an openly presbyterian hue. By the 1580s an underground semi-presbyterian system ("classes"*) existed in several counties. But after 1581 the presbyterians were themselves outflanked by the separatists, miniscule in number but potent in their challenge to the royal supremacy. A particularly outspoken radical propaganda campaign (the Marprelate Tracts*) caused a strong reaction between 1589 and 1593, in which at least four separatists or radicals were executed and others banished. These struggles in turn produced a more self-consciously episcopal bench of bishops and inspired the publication in 1594-97 of Richard Hooker's *Of the Laws of Ecclesiastical Polity**, a definition of the Church of England as an independent Protestant episcopal Church.

The fissiparous tendencies in Protestantism were counterbalanced by equally strong pressures to maintain a common front against an internal and external Catholic threat. Until the 1590s, sympathetic privy councillors (notably Lord Burghley, the earl of Leicester and Sir Francis Walsingham) were generally able to protect the Puritans. During the 1590s the Court became more hostile, but the war with Spain rallied most Protestants behind the queen. By contrast the same pressures served to paralyse Catholicism. Some five hundred clergy refused to accept the régime in 1559, of whom a number went into exile on the Continent. There they organized a seminarian and missionary movement* – 803 priests were trained between 1568 and 1603, of whom 649 were sent into England – largely dominated by the Jesuits. But the seminarian concentration on the gentry and Jesuit involvement in schemes for military reconquest (following the publication of the Papal Bull of excommunication* in February 1570) limited their success. The existing treason laws were extended, 125 priests were executed, and the Catholic nobility and gentry found themselves trapped in a conflict of loyalties. A confused and demoralized rebellion broke out in the north* in 1569, but in 1588 the Catholic gentry hastened to demonstrate their loyalty.

Catholic loyalism was in part inspired by respect for the rights of inheritance, but it was also due to the position in the succession occupied by Mary, Queen of Scots*, until her execution in 1587. Elizabeth's refusal to marry (obvious by the later 1560s) made the succession clearly a Stuart one, though after 1567 Protestants could look to the godly James VI. Nevertheless, the tensions arising from the succession question – combined with Puritan dissatisfaction over the religious settlement – created a new climate in Parliament. Both the House of Commons (389 MPs in 1553, 489 in 1624) and the electorate were expanding; MPs were more self-conscious and self-confident. Concerted efforts to force the queen to commit herself to marriage* and the establishment of a Protestant succession in 1563 and 1566 were followed by increasingly well-organized co-operation between Puritan divines and some MPs, culminating in the attempt to introduce presbyterianism by statute in 1587*. On the other hand, Elizabeth's financial prudence kept parliamentary

Calvinists
Followers of the teachings of French-born John Calvin and his disciples. Calvin's *Institutes* (1536-59) was a monumental, systematic account of Christian doctrine (which also described strict system of Church government without bishops). Most characteristic Calvinist belief was predestination: Catholic stress on good works was challenged by view that man is so irredeemably sinful that only act of God at beginning of time predestined some to heaven and consigned others to hell. Predestination accepted by most Elizabethan and Jacobean churchmen.

Thirty-Nine Articles
A revision of Cranmer's 42 Articles of 1553, the 39 Articles were passed by Convocation of 1563 and imposed Protestant doctrine on Church of England. Articles avoided too direct an attack on certain Catholic beliefs, leaving room for real presence by attacking a purely symbolic eucharistic doctrine as well as transubstantiation. But Article 17 sanctioned belief in predestination, and the Church's right to regulate rites and ceremonies was affirmed.

Vestiarian controversy
Since Edward VI's reign, clerical vestments formed contentious issue as they emphasized separation of priesthood, contrary to Protestant sentiment, and power of Crown and bishops to supplement scriptural provisions. Pressed by Elizabeth, in 1566 Archbishop Parker issued "Advertisements" enforcing distinct clerical dress and other ceremonial matters, but was resisted by "Puritan" ministers.

"Puritans"
Vague and variously-defined term, originally of abuse for "hotter" Protestants with overriding attachment to scriptural authority; also implications of sobriety of dress and morals and willingness to impose these on others. United more by evangelical attitudes than by coherent doctrinal beliefs. Might usefully be confined to those who, while accepting royal supremacy and concept of national Church, hoped for further Protestant reform of English Church from within, agitating for changes in structure of Church organization and in ceremonies and practices. Elizabeth's refusal to alter settlement drove some Puritans towards secession, and meant Puritans mainly influential on local level, in imposing "puritanical" sanctions against Sunday games or gambling in villages or towns under Puritan magistrates.

"Classes"
Series of unofficial evangelical cells or meetings within established Church, involving mutual instruction and correction within fellowship of ministers. Established with support from sympathetic local gentry or municipal councils, it remained a disparate movement, despite national conferences in Cambridge and London in late 1580s, and was broken by pressure from Whitgift.

Marprelate Tracts
Series of 7 scurrilously funny attacks on established Church and individual bishops, appearing from October 1588. Search for the underground presses led to exposure of Puritan network. Welshman John Penry executed 1593 for involvement in publication; author(s) unknown but probably Job Throckmorton.

Hooker's "Ecclesiastical Polity"
Series of 8 books published from 1594, some posthumously: part of Whitgift's propaganda campaign against presbyterianism, became main Anglican apology, justifying Elizabethan settlement and especially the episcopal system. Argued Scripture not sole basis for Church's teaching by emphasizing importance of reason, ecclesiastical tradition, and authority of state.

Catholic missionaries
In 1568 William Allen founded seminary at Douai in Netherlands, which trained English priests for the Catholic community in England; first priests sent to England 1574, and other colleges founded later; first English Jesuit missioners landed 1580. Captured missionaries were first executed under 1352 Treason Act, but from 1585 it was treason simply to be Jesuit or seminary priest. Though some plotted against government, work of most priests was pastoral, migrating around system of "safe houses".

Papal Bull of excommunication 1570
Regnans in Excelsis decreed Elizabeth's excommunication and deposition, releasing subjects from their allegiance. Issued in aftermath of Northern Rebellion, it confirmed official fear of Catholics, provided propaganda opportunity for Protestants, and was largely ignored by Catholic community in England.

Recusancy laws
1559 Uniformity Act imposed one shilling fine for each absence from prescribed services of established Church, but with growing fear of Catholics fine increased 1581 to huge sum of £20 per month. The fines were not widely exacted, but the

threat was used to intimidate Catholics into conformity; laws tightened 1587, 1597, 1606. Persecution of Catholics varied with political circumstances, but Elizabeth temporized in face of Parliament's preference for stronger action.

Northern Rebellion 1569
Flight to England of Mary, Queen of Scots, 1568 galvanized discontent both in north and at Court. Duke of Norfolk planned to oust Cecil from power, marry Mary and have her acknowledged as heir to throne; earls of Northumberland and Westmorland believed championing of Mary and Catholicism would restore them to former prestige; others wanted Elizabeth replaced by her Scottish cousin. When plotters were summoned to answer, northern earls raised retainers, tenants and wider support, taking control of Durham and restoring mass. Despite widespread sympathy for rebel cause, decisive action by royal commanders crushed rising; earls fled, fierce repression followed, involving *c.* 400 executions.

Plots for Mary, Queen of Scots
Elizabeth's illegitimacy in Catholic eyes made Mary rightful queen: Mary's presence in England from 1568 incited numerous conspiracies, starting with Norfolk's marriage plan. In 1586 interception of her letters revealed Mary's assent to Elizabeth's murder in Babington plot: Mary condemned for treason; beheaded 1587 at Fotheringay Castle.

Elizabeth's marriage schemes
Marriage to an Englishman would involve Elizabeth in factionalism, but she considered Robert Dudley, earl of Leicester. After rejecting Philip II and Habsburg and Scandinavian princelings, move to French alliance caused Elizabeth to flirt with duke of Alençon when diplomacy demanded, especially 1578-79. 1563 Parliament petitioned queen to marry and name

Detail from the title-page of the 1563 edition of Foxe's Acts and Monuments, *depicting an idealized Protestant congregation listening to the preaching of the Word.*

successor; 1566 Parliament tried to use taxation to force action: both were campaigns by Privy Councillors to put pressure on queen. Civil war over disputed succession was likely result if Elizabeth had died before Mary, Queen of Scots.

Admonitions to Parliament 1572
Widely circulated first *Admonition* (June) written by London clerics, John Field and Thomas Wilcox, and part of attempt to reform Church through Parliament, rather than through queen or bishops. Called for return to simple hierarchy of pastors, elders and deacons; administration of the eucharist to a sitting, not kneeling, congregation, from which papists and unworthy were excluded; and for the revival of excommunication. Field and Wilcox imprisoned in Newgate and future archbishop Whitgift composed a reply. This prompted *Second Admonition* (possibly by Thomas Cartwright) which also called for a presbyterian system, with each parish supervised by its own consistory. Cartwright escaped abroad (1573-85); Field and Wilcox harassed by Church authorities.

Cope's bill and book 1587
Anthony Cope, MP for Banbury, committed to Tower after presenting to House of Commons a bill repealing the Book of Common Prayer, and proposing a more radical book containing new rites and ceremonies acceptable in a presbyterian Church. Opposition from MPs prevented the bill from being read. Queen demanded from Speaker both bill and book. Peter Wentworth argued against Elizabeth's limitation of free speech in Parliament; committed to Tower, with 3 other MPs.

Elizabeth as patriot-goddess: one of the "Armada" portraits painted by an unknown artist, between 1588 and 1592, to stress the glory of the Queen and the power of her state. Through the windows, the arrival and defeat of the Spanish Armada are depicted.

taxation to a minimum until 1589. The price was paid, however, in the expansion of fiscal feudalism* and various forms of indirect taxation: the prerogative rights of wardship and purveyance, extensive use of monopolies* and customs privileges as political rewards, and the increased burden on county rates of rearmament of the militia* with firearms and gradual introduction of the Poor Law. During the war years of the 1590s the system began to crack: although Parliament voted multiple subsidies (four in 1601), major attacks on purveyance and monopolies were mounted in 1597 and 1601.

Elizabeth's success owed much to luck – and her peculiar combination of arrogance and charm, prudence and obstinacy, intelligence and prejudice. While absolutist to a degree when pressed, she also knew how to strike a patriotic note and enjoyed playing to the crowd. Moreover, the general competence of her ministers and servants and their shared ideology gave the régime an internal coherence. On religious, social and economic issues, councillors were generally in agreement; major disputes were usually caused by foreign policy. The only real breakdown in this relative unanimity occurred in the 1590s, when the earl of Essex, believing his military plans to be sabotaged, attempted to take over the Court. His failure, in turn, led to his attempted *coup d'état** against his rival, Sir Robert Cecil (8 January 1601).

The repercussions of this bitter faction struggle underlay the endemic factionalism of the next reign. As king of Scotland, James VI had attempted to secure his position in the English succession by being all things to all men; he was equally enigmatic as king of England. James I completely transformed the structure of the Court by a massive inflation of honours* (the peerage alone expanded from 55 in 1603 to 126 in 1628) and by the displacement of many of the leading Elizabethan families (despite his retention of Robert Cecil

Fiscal feudalism, wardship, purveyance

Crown income came from 4 main sources: Crown lands, customs dues, parliamentary taxation, and various charges exacted from holders of land by military (feudal) tenure – "fiscal feudalism". Wardship allowed Crown to administer property of under-age landowners and to arrange suitable marriages – at profit to Crown or grantees. Purveyance, originally feudal duty to supply royal household with cheap produce, became under Elizabeth direct levy on counties, worth *c.* £35,000 in 1590s.

Monopolies

Crown licences granting exclusive rights of manufacture or retail of certain goods. Some monopolies were means of promoting industrial growth, as in 1560s revival of glass-making industry; others, such as Raleigh's monopoly on playing-cards, seen as irritating perks for courtiers. Commons criticized abuses of monopolies, which became more extreme as cost of Spanish war mounted. Elizabeth revoked monopolies on essentials like starch, bottles and salt in 1601, but abuse became even worse under James.

Militia

Comprehensive county militia system organized from 1558, but in 1580s training (of all able-bodied men between 16 and 65) could cost each shire up to £400 per annum, and more in 1590s. By 1588, 26,000 men (out of total militia of less than 200,000) were specially trained for use of guns, armour, and horse. Development of militia (and trained bands within them) under counties' lords-lieutenant decreased Crown reliance on bastard feudalism in raising armies.

Essex's Rebellion 1601

After decade of rivalry between Essex and Robert Cecil over office and influence in Elizabeth's government, by 1600 Essex was in disgrace after disastrous Irish campaign 1599 and heavily in debt after loss of royal favours. With about 300 personal followers who also felt alienated from Court, Essex attempted to seize ageing queen and destroy Cecil. Wild plot carefully monitored by Cecil; Essex executed.

Sale of honours

In contrast to Elizabeth's parsimonious creation of peerages and anger at Essex's liberal creation of military knights, James increased number of English peers from 55 at his accession to 81 in 1615, and reaching c.120 by 1625. Inflation of honours due to king's generosity, but also need to reward Scottish adherents and win support among English as well as to raise revenue by sales. Rank of baronet – hereditary knighthood below peerage – introduced 1611 for sale to help foster Ulster Plantation.

Hampton Court conference 1604

Followed Millenary Petition of 1603, calling for abolition of certain ceremonies and vestments. 1604 conference between James, English bishops, and Protestant divines seeking further reformation of Church: agreed to new biblical translation (resulting in Authorized Version 1611), and to minor Prayer Book amendments. Commitment made to improve educational standards of clergy, reduce pluralism (the holding of more than one church benefice by an individual) and to establish preachers in Wales, Ireland, and north of England.

Gunpowder Plot 1605

Celebrated attempt to murder James, his queen, and elder son Henry by placing gunpowder in cellars of Parliament on 5 November, by handful of Catholic gentlemen led by Robert Catesby, with help of Guy Fawkes. James I's failure to ease conditions of Catholics persuaded Catesby to try desperate means to stir up Catholic rising. Plan leaked out, conspirators arrested, tried, executed. Plot led to renewed penal legislation against Catholics 1606, and increased Protestant fears of popish conspiracies.

See **Spanish match** (page 174)

Detail from the portrait by Daniel Mytens of James I in about 1621, when he was aged about fifty-five, showing the king looking mentally and physically worn out.

as his chief minister until the latter's death in 1612). At the Hampton Court conference* in 1604 he proclaimed his satisfaction with the overall state of the Church; his appointment of a generally Calvinist episcopate caused open Puritan nonconformity to decline. Yet his tolerance of individual Catholics (who included his queen, Anne of Denmark) led to a new Catholic presence at Court, and factionalism took on a distinctly religious colouration. After an initial panic caused by the Gunpowder Conspiracy* of 1605, enforcement of the penal laws against Catholics was only sporadic, partly because of James's *rapprochement* with Spain. The projected "Spanish match"* for Prince Charles created such political tension that in the latter years of the reign James ruled through what were in effect two separate administrations.

More immediate, however, was the impact of James's prodigality and financial imprudence. He inherited a debt of some £350,000 from Elizabeth; by 1608 it had reached £1 million; after a brief reduction it reached £900,000 again by 1618. Attempts to persuade Parliament to fund the Crown's ordinary expenditure provoked – after an initial grant in 1606-7 to cover the inherited debt – demands for curtailed expenditure and reform of existing fiscal grievances. A compromise proposed by Cecil in 1610 (the Great Contract*) was accepted by neither side, forcing the Crown to rely more heavily on fiscal feudalism, increased and new customs duties, monopolies, and open sale of titles and offices. These devices, legitimated by the royal prerogative, created new constitutional clashes with the House of Commons and led to the premature dissolution of the Parliament of 1614*.

The latter years of the reign were dominated by the strains produced by the Thirty Years War. A resort to Parliament in 1621 for military finance provoked a debate over the prerogative* and a dissolution, when the king ruled discussion of the Spanish marriage out of order*. Moreover, while some compromises were made over monopolies and other grievances a new source of controversy had arisen over the influence of the king's most notorious favourite, George Villiers, duke (in 1623) of Buckingham. The Spanish negotiations were brought to a climax by the journey of Buckingham and Charles to Madrid in 1623, but the duke's attempt to lead James into war with Spain was stalemated in 1624 by the king's refusal and Parliament's suspicions. It would be inaccurate to state that James's death in March 1625 precluded a major crisis, yet the Protestant consensus that had so marked Elizabeth's reign was clearly no longer evident at Court. While Parliament had neither taken the initiative nor produced a coherent "opposition", the running battles between Crown and Parliament since 1604 demonstrated that the Tudor system of government could no longer function effectively.

Great Contract 1610

Lord Treasurer Salisbury (Robert Cecil) came to provisional agreement with Commons that Crown be granted fixed annual sum of £200,000 in place of profits of fiscal feudalism (including systems of wardship and purveyance). Against background of disagreement over sums and James's reluctance to sanction financial reforms, Great Contract failed.

Addled Parliament 1614

Parliament summoned 1614 to vote supply and confirm Elizabeth of the Palatinate's son as heir after Prince Charles: dissolved after 2 months without legislating or granting money. Some historians see this parliament as reflecting the tensions which led to Civil War, emphasizing Commons' indignation at Crown interference with elections, and continuing attacks on royal prerogative; others see conflicts arising from policy disagreements and rivalries among James's councillors.

Prerogative

The inherent powers of the Crown, not deriving from statute but still exercised within framework of law. Included the declaring of war and peace, the pardoning of criminals, the creation of peerages, and summoning and dissolution of parliaments. Monarchs emphasized different aspects of prerogative: Henry VII stressed his feudal overlordship in financial dealings with aristocracy; the Henrician supremacy was the extension of prerogative to deal with ecclesiastical matters; Elizabeth claimed her marriage and other affairs of state appertained to her prerogative, which she took to mean that Parliament could not discuss these matters without invitation. Although James implied prerogative granted by God and therefore not subject to common law, in practice there were few disputes with judges.

Protestation 1621

Commons were asked to provide funds to support opposition to Spain in the Palatinate; in defiance of king's wishes, Commons debated wider aspects of foreign affairs and treatment of Catholics at home. In ensuing messages, James objected to rights claimed by Commons, and announced his intention to punish any member who discussed affairs of state or the proposed Spanish marriage for Charles. Commons made a Protestation, or assertion, of the "ancient and undoubted birthright" of Englishmen to debate any subject in Parliament, without fear of arrest or punishment. James tore out the Protestation from Commons' journal, and dissolved Parliament.

Impeachment

In effort to resolve continuing crises over monopolies, 1621 Commons resorted to direct action by impeaching two leading monopolists (both connected with Buckingham), so reviving practice obsolete since 1459: Lower House acts as accuser of an individual, Upper House as judge. Revisionist historians now stress importance of Court vendettas rather than institutional maturity of Parliament as reason for impeachments: political rivalry behind attack on Chancellor Bacon by Edward Coke 1621 and Buckingham's use of impeachment against Cranfield 1624. Attempted impeachment of Buckingham 1626 was to remove him from Charles's administration, forcing redistribution of office and royal patronage.

An engraving of the House of Commons in 1624, showing the cramped conditions in St Stephen's chapel, Westminster, where the Commons held their sessions between 1550 and 1834.

Wales:
integration and conformity

Penry Williams

In the middle of the fifteenth century, Wales was divided into two distinct regions. In the west and north-west was the Principality, the lands conquered by Edward I, apportioned by him into shires and ruled on the English pattern. Eastern and southern Wales, conquered earlier in piecemeal fashion by Anglo-Norman nobles, was morcellated into Marcher lordships, substantially independent of the Crown in administration, jurisdiction and military power.

The great magnates of Lancastrian and Yorkist England derived much of their might from these lordships. From his base in the earldom of March, Edward IV launched his successful bid for the throne in 1461; Henry Tudor landed in Wales in 1485. But with the accession of Henry VII the political weight of the Marcher lords had almost gone, for most major lordships had passed to the Crown, and with the execution in 1521 of the duke of Buckingham, lord of Brecknock, the king was political master of Wales. Yet the government of the region was still confused, thanks to the proliferation of separate lordships, held by the Crown but independent of the normal system of administration; and disorder abounded. Tentative proposals for reform were made in the first half of the reign of Henry VIII, but only the urgent need for greater control generated by the Reformation, allied to the practical energy of Thomas Cromwell, put them into effect. In 1536 and 1543, two Acts of Union* were carried, transforming the administrative structure of Wales. The powers of the Marcher lords were greatly diminished, though not abolished; seven new shires (Denbigh, Montgomery, Radnor, Brecknock, Pembroke, Glamorgan and Monmouth) were created and added to the existing shires of the Principality (Anglesey, Caernarfon, Merioneth, Flint, Cardigan and Carmarthen). The apparatus of English county government was introduced into all shires: sheriffs, justices of the peace*, members of Parliament, and, later in the century, lords-lieutenant and deputy-lieutenants. Welsh laws, including those of inheritance, were replaced by English; and English was to be the language of government. But in two respects the administration of Wales differed from that of England. Common-law jurisdiction was exercised by itinerant courts known as the Great Sessions*; and supervision of the entire region was entrusted to the Council in the Marches of Wales*, founded under Edward IV and now more firmly established. The changes did not at once produce a well-governed society: violence and feuding remained endemic until the end of the period. But there was gradual improvement in the imposition of order. Government by justices of the peace was preferable for most men to the "pleasure of peculiar lords".

The success of this policy was largely due to the welcome given it by the gentry of Tudor Wales. From the end of the fourteenth century, a class of gentleman-landowners had been emerging: although poorer than their English counterparts, they resembled them in living mainly off the rents of their tenants and in passing on their lands by primogeniture*. Tudor rule gave

Acts of Union
In 1534 Cromwell began policy of incorporating Wales into England, by removing trial of felons from Marcher courts to sessions in neighbouring English counties. 1536 Act of Union destroyed Marcher independence and created new counties on the English model, ruled by justices of the peace. 1543 Act of Union consolidated existing legislation and established Great Sessions.

Justices of the Peace
In 1536 JPs were introduced by Cromwell into shires of Principality, along with Glamorgan and Pembroke. JPs chosen from local gentry to enforce the law, so allowing measure of local Welsh self-government.

Great Sessions
1543 Act created 4 Courts of Great Sessions, each with own circuit and permanent judiciary, to administer common law in 12 Welsh shires (border counties came under Westminster courts). Council in Marches of Wales retained wide discretionary powers.

Council in the Marches of Wales
One of the most successful elements of Yorkist and Tudor policy to impose royal control on outlying districts through vice-regal provincial councils. Grew in significance from early 1470s when Prince of Wales's council received supervisory powers for Wales and Marches; reconstituted by Wolsey for Mary Tudor in 1520s. In 1534 Bishop Lee appointed President, delving into all judicial matters and supervising Cromwell's statute-enshrined policies for Wales. Some conflict with Westminster courts later.

Primogeniture
System of inheritance whereby property descends to eldest male heir, as opposed to partible inheritance (or *gavelkind*) where possession divided between heirs. Primogeniture only partly adopted in Wales by early 17th century.

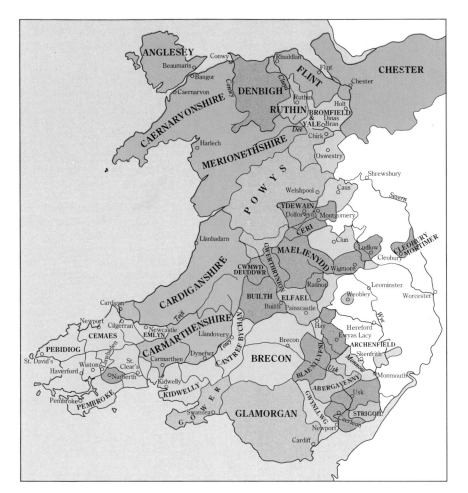

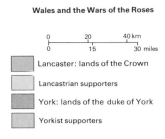

Wales and the Wars of the Roses

	Lancaster: lands of the Crown
	Lancastrian supporters
	York: lands of the duke of York
	Yorkist supporters

them independence from the Marcher lords, social and political dominance in their counties, and legal backing for the undivided inheritance of their estates. The Reformation also assisted the process of integration. The gentry for the most part conformed, though without enthusiasm, to the Protestant settlement; the dissolution of monasteries and chantries enlarged their estates; religious conformity brought political rewards. The translation of the Prayer Book and New Testament into Welsh in 1567, and of the whole Bible* in 1588, aided acceptance of the Church of England. There were pockets of Catholicism in the north, in Montgomeryshire and in Monmouthshire, but most of Wales conformed, although the peasants, while not Catholic, were a long way from being truly Protestant. Wales presented a marked contrast to Ireland, whose population was becoming fervently Catholic, and to Scotland, where the presbyterian creed was dominant. It has often been asserted that Tudor rule and the sixteenth-century gentry between them virtually destroyed upper-class Welsh culture and language. This is false. The "language" clauses of the Acts of Union permitted the continued existence of Welsh and there was no attempt to suppress the native tongue as there was in Ireland. The translation of Prayer Book and Bible positively encouraged Welsh prose. Landowners patronized Welsh poets and historians. Not until after 1660 did most of the gentry become anglicized, separating themselves from the peasantry and accelerating the erosion of Welsh culture.

Welsh Bible

1563 statute ordered translation of Bible and Book of Common Prayer into Welsh. Prayer Book and New Testament produced by William Salesbury and Bishop Richard Davies, published 1567. Salesbury's work, especially New Testament, criticized for over-use of Latinized words and phrases. William Morgan published whole Bible 1588. Major influences on development of Modern Welsh as literary language.

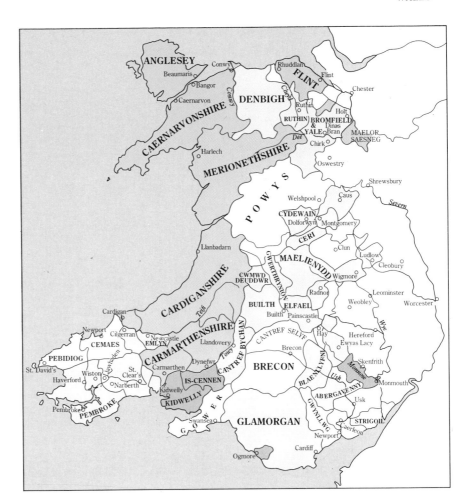

Lands of the Crown in Wales in the reign of Henry VII

0 — 20 — 40 km.	
0 — 15 — 30 miles	

Principality of Wales

Lordships of the Duchy of Lancaster

Crown lordships

Wales after the Act of Union, 1536

0 — 35 — 70 km	
0 — 25 — 50 miles	

Borders of the new counties

Counties of England and the Principality

Lordships
1 Denbigh
2 Ruthin
3 Bromfield & Yale
4 Chirk
5 Powys
6 Cydewain
7 Gorddwr
8 Ceri
9 Maelienydd
10 Gwerthrynion
11 Cwmwd Deuddwr
12 Elfael
13 Builth
14 Brecon
15 Blaenllyfni
16 Pebidiog
17 Cemaes
18 Pembroke
19 Emlyn
20 Cantref Bychan
21 Is-Cennen
22 Kidwelly
23 Gower
24 Glamorgan
25 Abergavenny
26 Gwynllwg
27 Strigoil

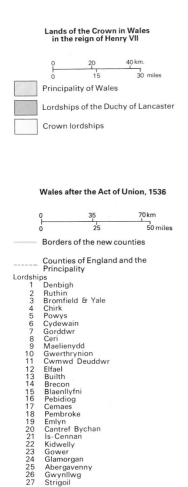

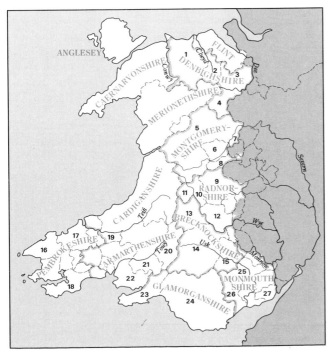

An artist's impression of Raglan Castle in Gwent, seat of the Herberts, earls of Pembroke, during the Wars of the Roses: it was clearly a stronghold, but the oriel windows made it vulnerable to attack; magnificence was more important than impregnability. The castle passed to the earls of Worcester in the 16th century.

163

Scotland:
reformation and inflation

Jenny Wormald

1455 saw the final destruction of the second of two families, Stuarts and Black Douglases, who qualify as Scotland's "overmighty magnates"; it was a dramatic event but in no sense a turning-point. For the ease of the destruction, with no support from other nobles for a family under attack by the Crown, only underlined the unquestionable strength of the Stuart monarchy. 1625 was the year when the last of that royal house who had personally ruled over Scotland died. That was a very great turning-point indeed.

The intervening period was one of astonishing self-confidence. Scotland was a society under virtually no pressure. Thought of normally as lawless and backward because of its relatively undeveloped administrative and legislative institutions, it was in fact unusually stable, precisely because the government made so few demands on the governed, for their bodies or their money; Scotland was rarely at war, that most massive strain on a country's resources and equilibrium. Her kings could combine displays of individual ruthlessness with a light rein on the kingdom in general, and the undisturbed localism of society made the repeated royal minorities which bedevilled the monarchy much more tolerable than in more highly governed states. The Scots never appreciated the point so obvious to the world outside, that their kingdom was small, insignificant and impoverished; for apart from Flodden* and Solway Moss*, senseless battles both, they never had to back their diplomatic confidence with military proofs. James IV's miserable death in the Flodden mud, at the only major battle of his life, was a dismal end for a man who had throughout his reign made his presence felt in Europe, mainly by nagging the papacy and secular powers to sink their differences and unite under the Scottish banner in crusade against the Turks; his vision may have clashed with their more immediate interests, but it ensured that he was heard abroad, and it chimed remarkably with the aspirations of his subjects. For they too were Europeans, no longer distracted, as the defensive Scots of earlier centuries had been, by English aggression. Merchants and scholars continued to find their way into the markets and universities of Europe. The first group hardly ranked as major traders, but they were successful enough; Scotland was not absolutely, as opposed to comparatively, poor. The second entered into the intellectual and religious ferment of Reformation Europe; they persuaded surprised continental scholars that the Scots were civilized and cultured beings, and they had a profound effect at home.

The Reformation, according to the traditional story, "happened" in Scotland in 1560, primarily through the efforts of a Calvinist God and his servant John Knox. The reality is much more complex. Scotland did not trail belatedly into line with other reformed countries; the acts of the Reformation Parliament of 1560 merely set the seal on a process whose origins go back to the 1520s, when merchants brought into the east-coast ports goods and Lutheran tracts. The king's resistance to Protestant reform was a major theme of the personal rule

Hugo van der Goes's Trinity altarpiece, showing James III attended by St Andrew. The third figure is probably James III's eldest son, the future James IV.

Battle of Flodden 1513
James IV agreed to support Louis XII against Holy League, and mounted major campaign against England. Disastrous battle at Flodden Hill (eastern Cheviots): English army under earl of Surrey killed James, 3 bishops, 11 earls, 15 lords and up to 10,000 others, at cost of 1,500 English soldiers. Accession of 18-month-old James V followed.

Battle of Solway Moss 1542
English attacks on Scotland in preparation for Anglo-Imperial invasion of France were undertaken by duke of Norfolk, nominally pursuing Henry's claims to sovereignty over Scotland. Large Scots army entered Cumberland, but disintegrated when faced by English force at Solway Moss. Few casualties, but James V died three weeks later, after this humiliation; succeeded by week-old daughter, Mary, Queen of Scots.

Parliament of 1541
In face of diplomatic uncertainties and some religious dissension at home, James V used Parliament to enforce obedience to Church: Acts passed protecting church images and papal authority, and requiring reverence to Virgin, saints, and all sacraments.

Devotio moderna
The 15th-and 16th-century revival of emphasis (especially in Netherlands) on internal spiritual life (through meditation and reading of devotional works), as opposed to importance of externals such as ceremonies and sacraments. Erasmus, leading humanist and Biblical scholar, tutored James IV's illegitimate son, Alexander, in Italy, and corresponded with principal of Aberdeen university.

Aberdeen university
Founded in 1495 under Bishop Elphinstone's patronage, and last of country's three 15th-century universities (others being St Andrews and Glasgow). Became notable centre of humanist learning, as only university to teach any Greek and medicine, and close academic links established with Kinloss Abbey under reforming abbots.

"Rough Wooing"
English policy towards Scotland 1543-49 which involved persistent ravaging of the Borders and south-east, culminating in Somerset's policy of garrisons. So called as attempt to enforce Greenwich Treaty 1543, betrothing Prince Edward to infant Mary, Queen of Scots.

Reformation Parliament 1560
Protestant Parliament dominated by east-coast lairds altered the religion but not structure of Scottish Kirk: accepted "Confession of Faith", acknowledging justification by faith and a form of predestination, condemning transubstantiation but affirming real presence. Papal authority was abolished and mass made illegal. Queen Mary (still in France) did not consent to these measures, and problems of episcopacy and Church endowments remained.

The Italianate façade of Crichton Castle, Midlothian, added to the medieval structure c. 1585 by the 5th earl of Bothwell. The classical arcade and Florentine Renaissance detailing show the sophistication of some Scottish domestic architecture at this time.

The Devil preaching to the witches at North Berwick, from News from Scotland, *printed in London 1591.*

of James V (1528-42); we do not know his private religious beliefs, and it may be unfair to ascribe his strenuous defence of the old Church only to the quantity of money he was able to wring out of the papacy, and its political advantages in his foreign dealings with Rome, the Emperor, France and England. But the king's will held the reformers at bay in Scotland, and leading Protestant scholars fled south to Cromwell's patronage and English benefices. Though James V, like Henry VIII, had his Reformation Parliament* (1541), it was a Parliament used to impose reform within the Catholic Church. Leading Catholic scholars, influenced by Erasmus, Ximenes and others, inspired by the *devotio moderna**, reinforced the political lead, notably in the north-east where there was spiritual and cultural flowering associated with the abbey of Kinloss, the university of Aberdeen* and later the diocese of Orkney; and the drive for reform was continued in the great series of reforming councils of the Church, presided over by Archbishop John Hamilton, in the decade before 1560.

James V died in 1542, leaving a baby daughter, Mary, Queen of Scots, to succeed him, and it was this absence of a monarch capable of rule which gave the Reformation its extraordinary character. The initial reaction was an outburst of Protestant hope and enthusiasm, as the vernacular Bible was legalized in 1543, alliance with Protestant England appeared imminent, and the regent, James earl of Arran, enjoyed a brief reputation as "the most fervent Protestant that was in Europe". Only the first had any permanence; friendship with England gave way to the "Rough Wooing"*, and, as it turned out, the regent was incapable of deciding what his religion was. For two decades, Scotland was in limbo, her foreign relations veering uncertainly between England and France, her religious state indefinable; while mid-Tudor England swung from extreme Protestantism back to Catholicism because of the religious proclivities of its rulers, Scotland – without a ruler – dithered. In the 1550s Mary of Guise, regent for her daughter from 1554 and one of the most attractive and able personalities of the period, held the ring. But her success in marrying that daughter to the dauphin Francis, and the English shift away from Rome after 1558, brought the regent and the Protestants into collision; her death in 1560 and the expulsion of her French troops made possible that dramatic moment in August when Parliament defied the Crown*, and abolished the Mass and the authority of the pope.

1560 was no more the end of the story than the beginning. Protestants at the time knew very well that their victory was extremely shaky; the strength of Catholicism in Scotland and the support of foreign Catholic powers could undoubtedly have been mobilized at least to challenge if not overthrow their gain, had Queen Mary* been a ruler of any purpose or political skill. Her lack of both ensured that the old Church would not revive; it was also crucial in determining the nature of the new, for yet again the reformed Church was establishing itself without any lead from the secular arm. Decades of self-help produced a radical Church which consistently resisted any form of state control, while demanding the state's support for its work. The battle fought out between the great reformer Andrew Melville and his followers, and King James VI, focused upon the issue of the powers of Kirk and state*; was the king merely a member of Christ's congregation, or was he its head on earth? Neither side won. James died in 1625 leaving that extraordinary anomaly, a presbyterian church with bishops.

If the Reformation was not belated, inflation, it seems, was. Such incomplete information as exists suggests that both population and price rises did not significantly affect Scotland until the late sixteenth century. When they came, they combined with the trauma of religious reform to produce an uncertain and unsettled society. The Calvinist response to the threat of vagrants – the sixteenth-century unemployed – was to measure them indiscriminately against the virtues of hard work and thrift, and find them wanting; there is no leavening in the harsh poor law* of awareness that work might be created. The Crown's response, in the person of the hopelessly spendthrift James VI, was equally simple and equally disturbing; taxation, raised not for emergency needs but for the expenses of the king, became regular after 1581. Not all suffered. There were still wealthy merchants and wealthy landowners; there was a reformed ministry which, though not in every case well-off, was certainly better-off than its pre-Reformation counterpart. But government became more intrusive. Taxation alone would have ensured that, and it was grafted on to the new aspirations of a literate laity; for the gradual process by which, in the previous two centuries, laymen had begun to push their way into the clerical enclaves of law and administration had now reached the point where the laity reigned supreme and the reformed Church firmly withdrew the services of its ministers from the state. Late-sixteenth century Scotland presents a series of apparently conflicting pictures, with its brilliant and cultured Court, its utterly assured churchmen, its self-confident gentry and merchants – and its localism disrupted; its natural leaders, the magnates,

Portrait of Mary Queen of Scots by François Clouet. It probably shows her in 1559 at the age of seventeen, in mourning for her father-in-law, Henri II of France.

present, and make arrangements for following year. Bishops ignored, and rights of local Kirk assemblies guaranteed. James increasingly evaded provisions of Act.

Restoration of episcopacy
Heeding Kirk's petition for representation, James began restoration of bishops: 1597 Parliament authorized king to appoint "prelates" to membership; in 1598 James denied any desire to appoint English-style bishops, and Assembly narrowly agreed that Crown and Kirk choose 51 prelates. Move towards "diocesan" bishops when James's only 3 prelates were given reduced revenues of vacant sees. 1606 Act restored the rank of bishop; and by 1610 introduction of archiepiscopal high commissions. Apostolic succession passed on by English bishops.

Synod of Perth 1618
James VI persuaded Kirk assembly at Perth to accept Five Articles: kneeling at communion; observance of Christmas and Easter; confirmation; communion at home for the sick; and private baptism. In 1621, partly through help of the 11 parliamentary bishops created since 1600, Articles were accepted in Parliament, lessening gulf between Kirk and Church of England.

Poor law
Late 16th century saw increase in vagrancy, partly due to population pressures, and heightened awareness of problem, resulting in poor law legislation of 1570s and 1590s. Relief seen as duty of Kirk, so parishes had to maintain registers of genuinely sick and impotent; need assessed by church elders.

Abdication of Mary 1567
Second marriage to Henry, Lord Darnley, culminated in his complicity in 1566 murder of musician and secretary, David Riccio. Mary then allegedly plotted with earl of Bothwell Darnley's brutal murder. Marriage to Bothwell weakened Mary's position, and his activities alienated queen from other Protestant lords. She was imprisoned July 1567 in Loch Leven Castle; forced to abdicate 24 July, nominating 4 regents for James VI. She escaped May 1568; soon fled to England.

"Black Acts" 1584
Assertion of royal supremacy over the Church by régime led by James Stewart, earl of Arran. Parliament asserted king head of the Kirk; ministers should not preach politics; Assembly to sit with royal permission; Crown to nominate bishops.

"Golden Act" 1592
Reassertion of Kirk's independence at a time when James VI needed Protestant support. Affirmed second *Book of Discipline*, and right of General Assembly to meet once a year, if king or commissioner

Witch-hunts 1590s
Result partly of James VI's own encouragement and of the 1590s economic depression which created tensions within communities, the witch-hunt was carried out by standing commissions till James lost interest and revoked them in 1597. Denunciation, often by local minister, led to torture to reveal names of accomplices; execution was by strangulation then burning.

uncertain of their role; its poor feeling the chill wind of state and Kirk intervention as opposed to the kindlier dealings of kinsmen and neighbours; and that dark side of religious belief, its first great witch-hunt*, in the 1590s. Furthermore, Scotland had, from 1603, an absentee king, that focal point and personalization of society now removed. Yet its overall self-confidence was not severely dented; the king was still a Scotsman, and Scotsmen could enjoy the irony of having given England a king. Only with Charles I, and visible royal indifference to the country which claimed the Stuarts as its own, did the long-established structure of Scottish society collapse.

Ireland:
from lordship to kingdom
Steven G. Ellis

Lordship of Ireland
Divided into 2 parts: the "Englishry" where Anglo-Irish lords, such as Butler earls of Ormond, held land in fief from Crown but were largely independent of it, plus the Pale, a concentrated area of English rule around Dublin; and the "Irishry" where Gaelic chiefs ruled according to Irish custom.

Poynings' expedition 1494-96
After earl of Kildare supported Perkin Warbeck, he was deprived of lord deputyship 1492 and Sir Edward Poynings was sent as lord deputy in 1494. He failed to extend military influence in north, but sent Kildare to London on treason charge. In 1494-95 Drogheda Parliament acknowledged its dependence on Henry VII and Council in England, and accepted validity in Ireland of English laws. Expense caused abandonment of mission and return to Kildare's deputyship.

Ireland in 1450 was a land divided between the English and Gaelic worlds. The north, west and midlands shared their Gaelic customs and language with parts of Scotland, but politically were highly fragmented into over sixty independent lordships. The more fertile south and east comprised the effective area of English lordship*, a region of some strategic importance within England's medieval empire, its population fairly anglicized. Superficially, English rule there seemed little more stable than in France, with a weak administration unable to counteract Gaelic raids, or prevent emigration to England and the spread of Gaelic customs among the colonists. In reality, however, it enjoyed widespread support and the lordship's problems stemmed largely from the accentuated impact of Henry VI's regal shortcomings on government in a borderland: the so-called Gaelic Revival (1300-1450) was opportunist, based on no significant politico-military developments, and with the resurgence of royal authority in England came a gradual strengthening of the English interest in Ireland.

No doubt the prominent role of the colonial community in the Wars of the Roses first alerted successive kings to the inadequacies of royal control there: the Fitzgerald earls of Desmond and Kildare generally supported the Yorkists, while the Butler earl of Ormond was attainted in 1461. Yet the traditional response, government through an outsider with an enlarged retinue for offensive action, required heavy subsidies from England. Except during political crises, therefore, the Yorkists and Henry VII preferred to rely on a local magnate and govern the lordship much as other borderlands. Kildare, with his following in the English Pale and the minor Gaelic lordships beyond, was the normal choice as governor. Given the now limited objectives of royal policy – self-sufficient administration of the traditional English districts – he ruled effectively. The English revival stemmed partly from the economic upturn throughout Europe, which benefited the lordship's towns and manorial economy more than the backward Gaelic districts and helped swell Crown revenues. Yet central control over outlying counties was gradually strengthened, magnate feuds curtailed, piecemeal administrative reforms were made and the Pale's defences developed.

Under Henry VIII, however, new problems were encountered. The king planned the piecemeal assimilation of Gaelic Ireland into the Tudor state, but refused additional resources for this task. Kildare, made scapegoat for the failure of an unrealistic policy, rebelled* and was destroyed. An English governor and small garrison were intruded and the Irish Reformation Parliament* (1536-37) enacted the major ecclesiastical and administrative measures recently passed in England. The changes extended the king's claims on his Irish subjects and his control over the Dublin executive, but overall government remained weak and costs escalated. From 1534 Tudor policy dithered between proposals for conquest and schemes for financial retrenchment.

In 1541 Henry was proclaimed king of Ireland* and the Gaelic nobles were offered English law and charters for their lands in an attempt at their peaceful (and economical) assimilation. The experiment died with the king, to be followed by the garrisoning and plantation* of key border districts to insulate

Kildare Rebellion 1534

"Silken Thomas", son of earl of Kildare, rebelled, hoping to secure Kildare's reappointment despite Cromwell's attempt to undermine Geraldine influence. Offered Irish overlordship to pope or emperor in place of schismatic Henry. Revolt took over a year to quell at cost of £40,000; Kildare ascendancy destroyed.

Reformation Parliament 1536-37

Acknowledged Henry as "the only supreme head in earth of the whole church of Ireland", declared succession to be in heirs of Boleyn marriage, and made it treason to call Henry heretic, schismatic, or usurper; later agreed to monastic suppression. Parliamentary opposition came only from proctors of lower clergy, an element unknown in English Parliament.

Kingdom of Ireland

In 1541 Irish Parliament accepted Henry VIII as king, not just lord, of Ireland: signified end to limited royal involvement based on traditional division of country, and replacement by unified realm governed from Dublin. Deputy St Leger attempted peaceful linking of Crown with Gaelic lords by "surrender and regrant" 1541-43, whereby Irish possessions were guaranteed in return for acceptance of English law. Policy interrupted by Henry's later wars.

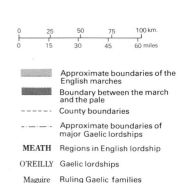

The lordships of Ireland, at about 1534

| 0 | 25 | 50 | 75 | 100 km. |
| 0 | 15 | 30 | 45 | 60 miles |

Approximate boundaries of the English marches

Boundary between the march and the pale

----- County boundaries

-·-·-·- Approximate boundaries of major Gaelic lordships

MEATH Regions in English lordship

O'REILLY Gaelic lordships

Maguire Ruling Gaelic families

Leix-Offaly Plantation
Failure of Henrician policy to create united Ireland led mid-Tudor governments to concentrate again on Pale: to protect it from cattle raids and foreign intervention, "plantation" of neighbouring lordships with English settlers began in Edward's reign, increased under Mary and later confirmed by Irish Parliament. Gaelic landowners were expropriated and confined to one-third of their collective holdings.

Connacht and Munster Councils
Sidney's 1565 appointment made with view to extending to Connacht and Munster a bureaucratic layer of royal government imposed by force. Connacht presidency erected 1569 under Sir Edward Fitton; that for Munster 1571. There Sir John Perrot and his provincial council tried to impose rule over nobles through common law, but with support from troops and martial-law powers.

Nine Years War 1594-1603
Perhaps against policy of conquest rather than English overlordship. Tyrone raised rebellion in Ulster with semi-trained army of c. 6,000 men, five times greater than Deputy's forces; cost Crown ultimately nearly £2 million to put down. Destruction of 1,500 English soldiers at Yellow Ford, north of Armagh, 1598, was significant Tudor setback in Ireland and caused Munster to rebel. In 1599 earl of Essex sent with largest army yet, but soon deserted his post and returned to Court. His replacement, Lord Mountjoy, despite Spanish intervention at Kinsale 1601, starved out native Irish and defeated Tyrone, who surrendered 1603.

the Englishry from the Irishry. Under Lord Deputies Sussex (1556-64) and Sidney (1565-71, 1575-78), however, the government groped towards a more radical strategy for military conquest which combined earlier initiatives with the establishment of regional councils for Connacht and Munster*. Yet the enforcement of religious reform was neglected and Elizabeth (though spending heavily) rarely allowed her governors sufficient men or money: the Old English, neglected and distrusted, protested against arbitrary government, while Gaelic chiefs were provoked rather than crushed. The result was a series of revolts, becoming successively more serious throughout Elizabeth's reign. The government alienated potential supporters and afforded ample opportunity to dissidents of all shades to organize rebellion. The conquest was finally completed against fierce Gaelic resistance* led by Hugh O'Neill, earl of Tyrone, who sought Catholic Old-English support and was assisted in 1601 by 3,500 Spanish regular troops.

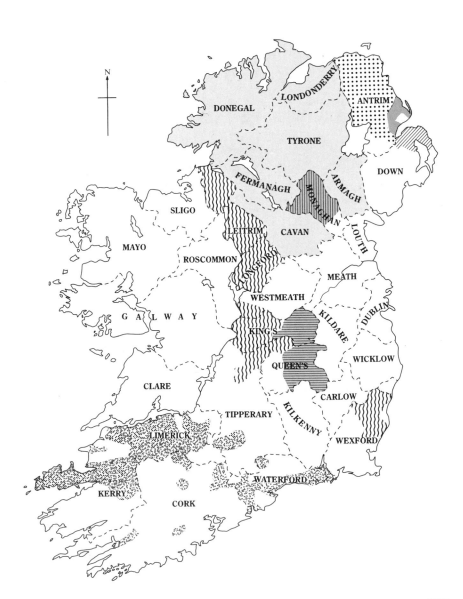

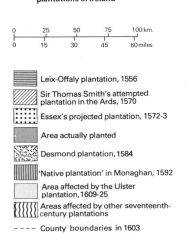

Tudor and early Stuart plantations in Ireland

| 0 | 25 | 50 | 75 | 100 km. |
| 0 | 15 | 30 | 45 | 60 miles |

- Leix-Offaly plantation, 1556
- Sir Thomas Smith's attempted plantation in the Ards, 1570
- Essex's projected plantation, 1572-3
- Area actually planted
- Desmond plantation, 1584
- 'Native plantation' in Monaghan, 1592
- Area affected by the Ulster plantation, 1609-25
- Areas affected by other seventeenth-century plantations
- - - - County boundaries in 1603

James I inherited a country much wasted but tractable at last. But if English law and customs now spread rapidly, so too did post-Tridentine Catholicism*; plantation recommenced, notably in Ulster* and parts of Munster, but the Old English were displaced from office. In general, strong government was again sacrificed for short-term economy. The basis of the Crown's indigenous support thus remained narrow: by 1625 a group of New English adventurers was manipulating government against Catholic Old English and Gaelic nobles and gentry. Thus, far from solving their Irish problem, successive monarchs had, by their reluctance to pursue a consistent and realistic policy, merely promoted a gradual but costly transformation in its basic characteristics.

Post-Tridentine Catholicism
Name given to reformed Catholicism after Council of Trent 1545-63 which was intellectually and morally reinvigorated, and less susceptible to pressures of Protestantism or of the State.

Plantation of Ulster 1608-12
Flight of several Ulster lords 1607 allowed Crown annexe almost all of Armagh, Cavan, Coleraine, Donegal, Fermanagh, and Tyrone. Land was assigned to English and Scottish immigrants, Crown servants in Ireland and (around Coleraine) City of London. Catholic Gaelic landowners replaced by ruling Protestant élite.

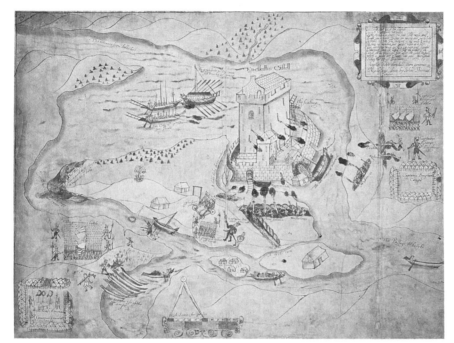

Watercolour sketch, annotated, dated and signed by "John Thomas, Solder", of the English siege of Enniskellin Castle, Co. Fermanagh, in February 1593/4.

Watercolour of the defeat near Wicklow of a royal force under Sir Henry Harrington by Irish rebels, 1599.

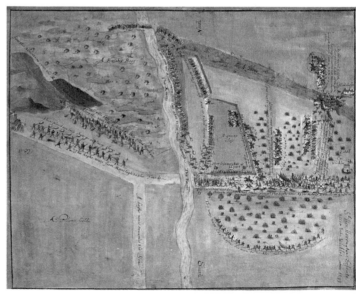

Warfare and International Relations:

D.M. Loades

At no time during this period was England more than a second-rate power, and for much of it her influence upon European affairs was negligible. Her importance lay mainly in her strategic position, and as the chief source of high quality woollen cloth.

In the grand strategy of European politics, England was first and foremost a counter to be moved against France, with the automatic corollary that Scotland was primarily a counter to be moved by France against England. Consequently, in the late-fifteenth century Edward IV and Henry VII either participated or threatened to participate in a succession of shifting anti-French alliances. The interests of the French were focused on Italy for much of this time, and English engagement or disengagement therefore tended to follow the fortunes of the Italian wars. In 1519 this situation was substantially altered by the election of the Habsburg Charles of Spain as the Holy Roman Emperor Charles V. For the next forty years European diplomacy was dominated by the political (and personal) struggle of Valois against Habsburg. English policy was generally pro-Habsburg, but the situation was complicated by Henry VIII's break with the papacy in 1533, and by the growing influence of Protestantism after his death in 1547. Between 1559 and 1572 a new pattern emerged, as France sank into the turmoil of civil war, and Scotland was permanently detached from the French interest by the triumph of Protestantism. In this pattern, an opportunist assortment of French Protestants and *politiques,* rebellious Netherlanders and Ottoman Turks sought to curb (or escape from) the overwhelming power of Spain. With this assortment

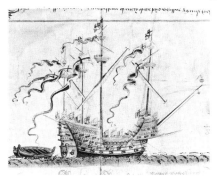

The rebuilt Henry Grace à Dieu (Great Harry) depicted in the 1546 Navy roll, by which time she had been lightened to 1000 tons and 133 guns, compared with her 1514 specification of 1500 tons and 186 guns.

Engraving of the French assault on Brighton in 1514: shallow-draught galleys landed troops, and the bigger carracks gave cover.

171

England became increasingly associated; to the extent of open war from 1585 to 1604. The re-emergence of France after 1598, and the increasing militancy of the Counter Reformation, created a third pattern, but after 1604 England was only marginally involved as James I tried to bridge the increasing ideological gulf through intricate dynastic diplomacy more appropriate to the High Renaissance.

In 1450 England was at the end of a period of military power. In that year the French recovered Normandy, and in 1453 Gascony, leaving only Calais in English hands. For the next forty years England was mainly on the receiving end of her neighbours' attentions. The French, prompted by Margaret of Anjou, Henry VI's queen, supported the Lancastrians; the Burgundians, particularly after the marriage of Edward IV's sister Margaret to Duke Charles in 1468, supported York. The re-adoption of Henry VI in 1470, the return of Edward in 1471, and the successful invasion by Henry of Richmond in 1485, were all powerfully influenced by these preferences. Despite the disappearance of autonomous Burgundy after 1477, the implacable hostility of the Dowager Duchess Margaret towards Henry VII could be seen in the support which she and her son-in-law the Emperor Maximilian lent to the pretensions of Simnel and Warbeck. Apart from fending off these undesirable attentions, the main efforts of Henry VII were directed towards securing recognition by neighbouring dynasties*, maintaining peace, and using the preoccupations of others to increase his own security. The marriages of his son Arthur to Catherine of Aragon in 1501, and of his daughter Margaret to James IV of Scotland in 1502, were his most positive and lasting achievements in this field. He was also sympathetic to the lobbying of merchants (who were good taxpayers), as the *Magnus Intercursus* of 1496 (with the Netherlands) and his support of the Merchant Adventurers against the Hanse bear witness.

With the advent of the young king Henry VIII in 1509, the defensive and manipulative tactics of the previous reign were abandoned. War with France and Scotland* (1512-14) gratified the aggressive instincts of the king, worked off some of the dangerous frustrations of the nobility, and brought the appearance of victory. The appearance was deceptive; neither the victory of Flodden, nor the capture of Tournai, nor even the marriage of Henry's younger sister Mary to Louis XII, was of any lasting significance. The most important consequence was financial exhaustion. Having failed to bring off a *coup de guerre,* Henry's chief adviser Cardinal Wolsey next attempted a *coup de paix,* but the elaborately-worked Treaty of London* (1518), which was designed to make England the arbiter of Europe, was struck dead in a year by the Imperial election. An attempt to wage war on the Emperor's behalf in 1522-23 was humiliatingly frustrated by poverty, and for the next decade the increasingly urgent priority of the king's "great matter" dictated a rapprochement with France, the only power which could conceivably give him any effective support in jettisoning his unwanted wife, Catherine – who was the Emperor's aunt. In the event that support was not forthcoming, and Henry was left to solve his problem in his own way. Charles V was nothing if not a pragmatist, and the death of Catherine in 1536 brought an end to his half-hearted encouragement of the English opposition. However, the hostility of the papacy was implacable and Henry's very survival depended upon keeping Francis I and Charles V at loggerheads. After a brief alarm of peace between them in 1539, a reassuring animosity quickly reappeared. Henry had no need

Treaty of Medina del Campo 1489
Gave Henry VII recognition by Spain and provided for marriage of Arthur, prince of Wales, to Catherine of Aragon 1501. Ferdinand agreed not to aid English rebels. Alliance with Spain then became pivot of English diplomacy: after Arthur's death, Henry VIII maintained alliance by himself marrying Catherine 1509.

Magnus Intercursus 1496
Treaty with Burgundy which allowed English merchants to trade freely in the Netherlands, thereby ending trade embargo ordered by Henry in 1493 to oust Warbeck from Low Countries. Merchant Adventurers (incorporated 1407) controlled export of white (unfinished) cloth from London to Antwerp; though dependent on Royal support and privileges, they were a highly important "pressure group" in mercantile and foreign affairs.

Henry's early wars 1512-14
To relieve French pressure on Italy, pope and Spain conceived Holy League for joint attack on France with Henry and Emperor. Henry sent 10,000 troops to Gascony 1512; led 30,000 men into northern France 1513, occupying Tournai. Louis XII resorted to "auld alliance" with Scots, who attacked northern England: Scottish army routed and James IV killed at Flodden 1513. Wolsey rose to power through organizing armies and concluding peace with France, 1514.

Treaty of London 1518
"Universal Peace" negotiated by Wolsey, which bound most of powers in Europe to avoid aggression or risk united opposition of the others. Seen as manifestation of humanist ideal of peace throughout Christendom: soon failed.

Field of Cloth of Gold 1520
Spectacular "summit meeting" near Calais between Henry and Francis I, ostensibly to help maintain peace between France and Habsburgs but also intended to emphasize England's potential as a continental power.

Henry and the Lutherans
1530s formed a unique period in English diplomacy 1489-1572, because of collapse of Spanish alliance after Aragon divorce. Hostility of Catholic powers to England's schism forced Henry to flirt with Protestant princes of Germany. Though nothing was achieved (except brief marriage to Anne of Cleves 1540), Henry considered heading league of Lutheran princes and permitted discussions of theological differences with Lutherans 1536, 1538.

Cleves marriage 1540

Haunted by fears of Franco-Habsburg *détente*, Henry agreed to matrimonial alliance with Cleves, north-western German duchy which had renounced papal authority. Henry married Anne of Cleves January 1540, but annulled in June on grounds of non-consummation. Marriage a factor in downfall of Cromwell.

Henry's last wars

In 1542, Henry attacked Scotland in preparation for Anglo-Imperial war against France 1543. With 40,000 troops, Henry invaded France 1544 and captured Boulogne. Charles V deserted English ally 1544, leaving Henry to defend his conquest alone. Peace with France 1546.

Military developments

Important changes late 15th century, making wars more costly and defensive. Dominance of artillery led to expensive fortifications: lower fortress walls to reduce target area; sophisticated outworks, including, ditches, inclines, to hinder artillery's approach; creation of bastions from straight walls to avoid blind spots where besiegers could attack. Fortifications of south coast and Boulogne among Henry's main expenditures in 1540s, prompting sales of ex-monastic lands.

Garrisoning of Scotland

Somerset aimed at subjugation of Scotland by nurturing Protestantism to counteract French influence and through erection of permanent English fortresses in Scotland. Garrison policy hugely expensive, and French troops forced abandonment 1549.

Calais

England's last continental foothold: captured by Edward III after Crécy 1346, remained in English possession until lost in 1558, during Mary's disastrous war on behalf of her Habsburg relatives. Calais had prospered as outlet for English wool, and served as base for military action.

Peace of Cateau-Cambrésis 1559

Ended Italian wars by French renunciation of claims pursued since 1494, in return for Habsburg surrender of territory on Franco-German border. Treaty concluded England's 1557-59 war against France and in reality English accepted loss of Calais.

Detail from an anonymous painting showing Henry VIII and his Court embarking, probably for the meeting with Francis I at Boulogne in 1532.

to become involved in order to promote his own security, but in the last five years of his life his natural aggressiveness again asserted itself*. He attacked Scotland in 1542 and France in 1543, winning vastly expensive victories on both fronts (Solway Moss and Boulogne) but failing to secure any substantial advantage, and died in 1547 enormously in debt after spending most of the confiscated assets of the Church.

The wars which Henry left were assiduously and shortsightedly pursued by the first mentor of Edward VI's minority, Edward Seymour, duke of Somerset and Lord Protector. Despite a victory in the field (Pinkie Cleugh) and the aid of the embryonic Scottish Reformation, Somerset overreached himself at home and abroad and it was left to his supplanter, John Dudley, duke of Northumberland, to extricate a virtually bankrupt country by humiliating treaties which abandoned Scotland and Boulogne. As the young king's health deteriorated, Northumberland sought to frustrate the accession of Catherine of Aragon's daughter, Mary, by drawing closer to the French, but the association was extremely unpopular in England and contributed to his downfall. Ironically, it was left to Mary to begin the transformation of attitudes which was soon to constitute Spain into the chief and hated enemy. Mary's adherence to the Habsburg alliance was predictable and instinctive. She married Philip of Spain primarily because his father Charles V (for whom she had a profound respect) wished her to. Charles wanted this marriage, not for any advantage which it might bring to Mary, but to help Philip to secure the Netherlands inheritance and to complete the encirclement of France. These priorities soon became apparent when Philip forced England into war with France in 1557, and disrupted the recent and painfully negotiated reconciliation of England with the papacy by attacking the Papal States in 1556. As a result of this war, Calais* was lost and the Habsburg alliance discredited.

For Elizabeth, as for her grandfather, the first priority was, and remained national security. Having embraced a Protestant settlement, she was committed to the prolonged hostility of the papacy, but judicious intervention in Scotland in 1560 brought the reformers to power in that kingdom and laid the foundations for union. For a quarter of a century thereafter, England enjoyed much needed peace while Elizabeth, driven partly by the logic of her country's Protestantism, and partly by the collapse of the European balance of power,

came to terms with her new and exposed position. In 1570 Pope Pius V declared her excommunicate and deposed, and in 1572 she found what diplomatic shelter was available in a defensive alliance with France (Treaty of Blois*). The weakness of France, and the increasing power of the Catholic League, reduced the value of this alliance, but Elizabeth did her best to retain some advantage through a prolonged and indecisive flirtation with the duke of Anjou. It was, however, the near collapse of the Netherlands revolt in 1584 which finally forced the queen back into continental commitments. The Treaty of Nonsuch* (1585) gave minimum help to the Dutch, but tempted Philip into the disastrous gamble of the Armada*. The English rightly gave God the credit for this victory, and Elizabeth found herself confronted with an increasing Protestant chauvinism which she did her best to curb, but which protracted the war for twenty expensive years and gave an important emphasis to English commercial and maritime enterprise*.

The accession of James VI and I finally removed Scotland from the realm of foreign affairs, and the new king wisely brought the long Spanish war to an end*. James's vision of himself as an arbiter, however, tempted him into folly. In 1615 he married his daughter Elizabeth to the (Protestant) Elector Palatine – a reasonable and comprehensible move; but when he tried to follow this up by marrying his heir, Charles, to the (Catholic) Infanta of Spain*, he lost his subjects' support completely. The failure of this ambitious policy, his own declining faculties, and the short-sighted importunities of Charles and Buckingham then drove him back at the end of his life into the continental war which he so much (and so rightly) disliked.

Treaty of Blois 1572

A mutual defence alliance between England and France, designed to prevent Spanish interference by guaranteeing help if either was attacked by a third party. Alliance with France a major shift in English foreign policy.

Treaty of Nonsuch 1585

Though refusing Dutch rebels' offer of sovereignty, Elizabeth agreed to limited involvement against Spain: to provide and support 5000 foot and 1000 horse for duration of war, in return for control of two Channel ports. Signified failure of her policy to avoid open conflict with Philip.

Spanish Armada 1588

Invasion project designed to re-impose Catholicism on England and put an end to Elizabeth's support of the Dutch. Fleet of *c.* 130 ships with 19,000 infantry left Lisbon but failed to link up with Spanish army in Netherlands for joint invasion. Lack of safe anchorage exposed Spanish ships to fireboat attacks by English, whose fleet was successful at Battle of Gravelines. Further Spanish losses in bad weather as they tried to escape round Scotland.

Maritime enterprises

Growing hostility to Philip II led to increasing infringements of Spanish trade monopolies. John Hawkins led slavetrading expedition to West Indies 1562, kinsman Drake sailed to Africa by 1565. At San Juan de Ulua 1568, Spanish fleet attacked Hawkins's ships, outraging English opinion. Close connection of politics and piracy illustrated by queen's licence to privateer granted 1572 to Drake, and 1578 appointment Hawkins as Treasurer of Navy. Drake first Englishman to circumnavigate globe 1577-80. Martin Frobisher 1576-78 and John Davies 1585-87 attempted to find Arctic north-west passage to Pacific, which would avoid Spanish routes.

Peace with Spain 1604

Ignoring those wishing continue expensive Spanish War, James signed Treaty of London: promised no direct aid to Dutch, but James refused to concede Spanish monopoly of trade in New World.

Spanish match

From 1610 James actively tried to spread peace in Europe by daughter's marriage to Protestant Elector Palatine and finding Spanish wife for his heir. In 1623 Charles and Buckingham bullied James into allowing them to travel in disguise to Madrid to find Habsburg bride, despite king's misgivings and parliamentary preference for sea-war against Spain. The resulting fiasco led them to cajole James into reversing his foreign policy, by aggressive alliance with Louis XIII and future marriage to Henrietta Maria.

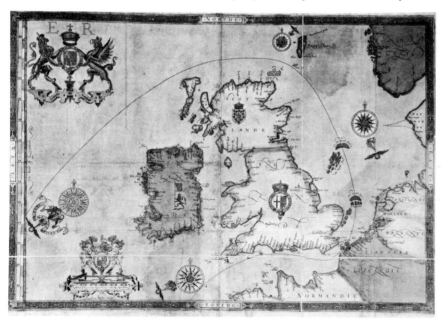

The course of the Armada and its English pursuers, in a map published in 1590.

A Developing Economy

D.M. Palliser

Economic history cannot meaningfully be parcelled up by exact dates, but in Britain 1450-1625 stands conveniently for the first phase of the "pre-industrial" period, that crucial transition from an underdeveloped, primary producing economy to an industrializing one. It was not, of course, a steady transition: the period 1450-1520 saw only gentle change, with population, prices and most production stable, while thereafter population, prices and output increased more rapidly. Some sectors of agriculture and industry were more dynamic than others; and in an age when there was no "British economy", but an overlapping series of regional economics, some areas moved rapidly towards a commercial economy while others remained largely at subsistence level.

Nearly everyone still lived in the countryside. Perhaps only five per cent of the English population in the 1520s lived in towns of over 5,000 people (half of them in London), while in the rest of Britain and Ireland probably only Edinburgh came into this category. There were many smaller "towns" as well – some 650 market towns in England and Wales in 1588, and 200 burghs of barony in Scotland – but many were mere villages in size. Yet it would be wrong to picture Britain as filled with subsistence farmers scratching an inefficient living from arable open fields* set in a sea of forest and waste, as some textbooks still do. The pattern and prosperity of settlements, agriculture and marketing varied greatly over quite short distances. Since most wealth was still agricultural, it is scarcely surprising that the richest areas were the southern and eastern parts of Britain, and that almost all large towns lay in the same region.

In England and Wales the uplands consisted of hill pasture and scattered hamlets and farms. Even in the lowlands, in "wood pasture"* regions like Arden and the Weald*, scattered settlements and pasture farming predominated, often combined with small-scale rural industries. Only the third type of region, the remaining lowland valleys and plains, approximated to the stereotype of manorial villages* with unfenced arable fields, though many of these were being gradually enclosed. Scotland was similary divided between the mixed farming Lowlands and the pastoral Borders and Highlands, Ireland between a largely pastoral Ulster and Connacht, and a manorial, village-based arable farming in much of Leinster and Munster.

Population remained low for nearly two centuries after the Black Death, but it was increasing again by 1520 and still more rapidly by the mid-century*; it rose by over seventy per cent between 1540 and 1625. Whereas in the fifteenth century landlords' incomes and tenants' rents had been low, and labourers' wages high, with population increase the sixteenth century saw those conditions reversed. At the same time there was growing concern about beggars and paupers, marked by the series of Tudor poor laws* enacted between 1531 and 1601. Some historians view these changes as evidence for relative

Open fields
Mixed farming system of village land where, classically, "open" or unhedged arable fields were divided into narrow strips and given to tenants to ensure balance of good and bad land. One field lay fallow each year, in rotation, to regain fertility and provide communal grazing land; common rights over meadow pasture and waste. System unsuited to large-scale production for market and required high degree of democratic supervision through village-meetings; most common in (lowland) midlands; rare by 1500 in Kent, Suffolk, Essex and Devon; unknown in Fens and of little use in highland areas.

Wood pasture
Pattern of lowland cultivation, found in Royal Forests, and much of Essex, Sussex, Kent, Dorset and Wiltshire: some arable farming, but emphasis on dairying and livestock, with woodland crafts and rudimentary industry. Homesteads tended to be isolated, necessitating less sophisticated social structure and less local co-operation.

Weald
Originally term used for any wooded area; but especially area between north and south Downs covering much of Kent and Sussex (and parts of Surrey and Hampshire). Weald one of largest wood-pasture areas in England; also developed industry through iron deposits and availability of timber: in 1570s three-quarters of England's 70 blast-furnaces found there.

Manorial villages
In open-field villages, dwellings were usually concentrated centrally around church and manor house; influence of landlord and local co-operation through institutions of medieval manor often survived.

See **Population trends** (page 182)

See **Tudor poor laws** (page 185)

overpopulation, with output failing to keep pace with demand, and a widening gap between landholders and landless as food prices rose rapidly. Yet population growth was modest by the standards of Third World countries today (0.56 per cent per year in England 1541-1656), and even by 1625 the total had probably not recovered to pre-Black-Death levels. There was therefore no good reason why the country should have been unable to feed itself, except in years of harvest failure. Nor is it certain that beggars and paupers were multiplying faster than the population as a whole.

What *is* certain is that the stable prices and wages of the fifteenth century gave way to price inflation between the 1520s and 1650s (severe in Scotland only from the 1560s) in which food prices and land rents outstripped wages. The causes remain in dispute: there is much to be said for the common-sense correlation with population growth and rising demand, but monetary factors were also important. The silver value of Scottish coins fell steadily from 1513 to 1600, whereas in England a severe debasement* by Henry VIII and Somerset (1544-51) was followed by fifty years of stability, but by a doubling of the volume of coin in circulation. The English debasement was also imposed on Ireland, where its effects were longer lasting: debased coin was barred from circulation in England in 1561, but in Ireland not until the 1650s.

Great debasement

Employed in 1540s (after Wolsey in 1526 showed its usefulness) as means of financing continental and Scottish wars; reduction of (mainly) silver content in coins profited Crown by over £1¼ million. Much popular complaint, especially of 1546 silver shilling which was rapidly disfigured in circulation and somewhat reluctantly accepted. Contributed to inflation. Major source of Crown revenue in Scotland throughout 1580s and 1590s.

Cottage industries

Predominant early modern system of production, whereby goods were manufactured at home, e.g. shoes, pots, leather goods. Often combined with system whereby capitalist merchant hired or loaned expensive equipment or raw materials to domestic workers: "putting out" of cloth mainly in West Country, Home Counties, East Anglia and north-west England, often where poor land or partible inheritance created large, under-employed labour force. Whole families would be involved: e.g. children carding wool, women spinning it into yarn, and men weaving fabric.

Farming regions in England, 1500-1640

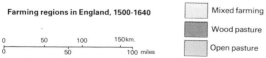

- Mixed farming
- Wood pasture
- Open pasture

Top: *silver groat of Henry VII, 1485-90.* Above: *testoon, or shilling, of Henry VIII, 1544-47. In the debasement, the silver content of the testoon fell successively from 75 per cent, to 50 per cent and finally 33 per cent, and the copper colour of the alloy soon showed through. There were stylistic changes, too, from the formalized representation of the monarch to a naturalistic rendering of the familiar features of Henry VIII.*

Fen drainage

Little attempt to drain East Anglian marshes till late 16th century, then locally unpopular but complicated system of ditches and small canals (sometimes with wind-pumps) removed water to rivers. Little overall alteration, though, to region's pastoral nature for another century.

Enclosure

Creation of consolidated land-holdings by various methods, including amalgamation of properties; extinction of communal rights; actual "enclosing" with hedges or ditches. Normally achieved by consent and in 15th century, but friction caused when arbitrary enclosure led to tenants' eviction, or unemployment ("depopulation") through creation of one large farm. Numerous statutes against certain types of enclosure, especially conversion of arable land to pasture, as latter required fewer workers: 1517-19 and 1548-49 nationwide enclosure commissions to investigate complaints. Most problems incurred in open-field midlands; serious revolt 1607 in eastern midlands over conversions to pasture.

Sheep-folding

Since animal dung was most important fertilizer, arable and pastoral farming often combined, especially in East Anglia, with sheep grazing and dunging on fields later used for growing corn.

It has been suggested that the Tudor price rise was the most markedly inflationary period between 1250 and 1900. It is estimated that by the 1610s foodstuffs cost on average five times as much as they had in the 1510s and industrial products nearly three times, while another calculation suggests that the "cost of living" (combining agricultural and industrial prices) rose by 350 per cent over the same period. The rise in food prices, more rapid than in wages or industrial prices, had a markedly differential effect. Shrewd land-owners and merchants could make large profits which they spent lavishly on land, housing, furnishings or plate; smallholders could hold their own if their plots made them self-sufficient in food; but the landless found expenses rising and income falling. However, this harsh stimulus encouraged many cottagers and labourers to take up secondary employments* such as nailmaking and stocking knitting; and such diversification laid the foundation for a more widely-diffused prosperity when the pressures of population and prices eased after 1650.

Some historians have gloomy views of agricultural productivity during this period, seeing a recession in 1450-1520, with falling profits, declining cultivation and the continued desertion of whole villages, and the 1520-1625 period as one of crisis in which primitive farming methods prevented output from keeping pace with increasing population. Both views are probably too pessimistic. Recorded farming innovations multiplied after the 1560s, including fen drainage*, carrot and rape cultivation, manuring, stock-breeding, and water-meadows (the artificial enriching of valleys by silt). Most widespread of all were increases in yields by enclosing land*, by alternating its use as arable and pasture, and by folding sheep* on the arable to dung it. They are so widely recorded that some historians have detected an "agricultural revolution" between c.1560 and 1675. More soberly, others have drawn attention to a considerable growth in regional specialization and commercial farming for the market after c.1570. (In Ireland, commercial farming spread rather later: after 1600.) All these developments are undeniable, though an increase in the quantity of records surviving after the mid-sixteenth century has exaggerated their novelty. Many can be traced back into the period 1350-1520, and it now looks as if the preparation for the agricultural revolution began then rather than later.

In particular, two legacies of the fifteenth-century population minimum

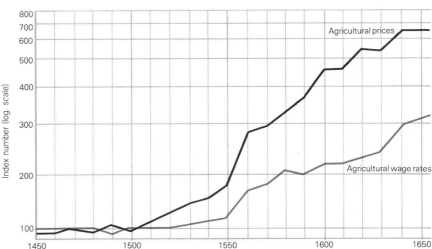

Agricultural prices and wage-rates in southern England

1450-99 = 100

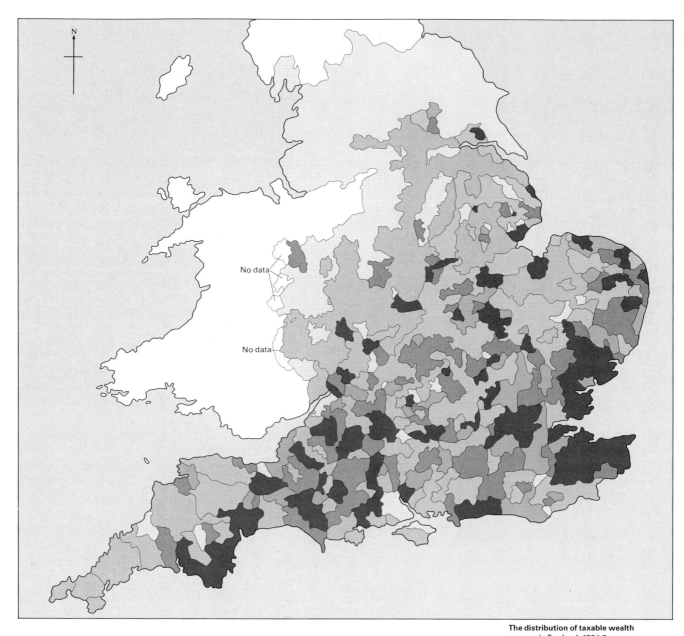

No data

No data

The distribution of taxable wealth in England, 1524-5

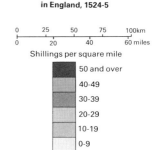

| 0 | 25 | 50 | 75 | 100km |
| 0 | 20 | 40 | | 60 miles |

Shillings per square mile

50 and over

40-49

30-39

20-29

10-19

0-9

were crucial, for England and Wales at least. A better balance was struck between arable and pasture, and middling tenant farmers enlarged their holdings at the expense of both manorial lords and smallholders. During the population rise of 1520-1650 those tenants, with some legal security, generally held on to or enlarged their holdings, creating a capitalist agriculture which squeezed out many smallholders and turned them into landless labourers, but which also increased productivity. That was one reason why England ceased to suffer nationwide famines after 1596-98 (or possibly 1622-23), and why restrictions on corn exports were eased after 1624. Francis Bacon could boast that whereas England had formerly been "fed by other countries", in his day "she fed other countries". It made for a stark contrast with Scotland and France, where severe famines continued throughout the seventeenth century.

New industries in England: (below) an engraved soda-glass goblet, made in 1584 by Giacomo Verzelini, a Venetian glass-maker who arrived in London in 1571 and was granted a monopoly for making Italian-style table glass; (right) a polychrome tin-glazed earthenware dish of 1600, the earliest known surviving example of London delftware, thought to have been made in the Dutch pottery at Aldgate.

"New draperies"

Made from inferior wool, these cloths were suitable for warmer climates as lighter (and cheaper) than traditional materials: exported especially to Mediterranean. In home market, purchased by the poor, and by the fashionable who valued their adaptability. Technology imported with exiled Flemish Protestants from 1560s; East Anglia, Kent and Essex specialized in manufacture.

Another major development was the expansion of the cloth industry, boosted by the swing to pasture. Cloth was already England's largest export by 1450, and the home and overseas markets continued to expand, despite slumps in the 1550s, 1614-16 and 1620-24. Between about 1470 and 1554, the growing exports were of traditional woollen cloths shipped mainly to Antwerp for north European markets. After mid-century, this outlet was disrupted by war in the Netherlands, and furthermore the expanding market for cloth was the Mediterranean, where lighter and cheaper fabrics were in demand. Fortunately one problem threw up an answer for the other: many Flemish weavers, religious refugees from the wars, were welcomed into England after 1565, where they helped establish the "new draperies"*, lighter textiles suitable for some southern European markets. The English cloth trade with the Mediterranean flourished, especially after the collapse of the Italian and Spanish cloth industries from the 1620s.

Cloth was probably the largest industry in Britain, but its role in exports has overshadowed others geared mainly to the home market, such as leather crafts and pottery. The Weald of Kent and Sussex was a major rural industrial area for ironworking and glassmaking; coalmining developed rapidly in Tyneside, Nottinghamshire, south Wales and Fife after about 1540. Skilled continental immigrants, encouraged by the English Crown, introduced the manufacture of cannon, gunpowder, paper, sailcloth, drinking glasses and other products which reduced dependence on imports. There were similar attempts to introduce new industries to Scotland and Ireland, but with less success.

It was an age of commercial, as well as industrial, growth. The concentration of overseas trade on the Netherlands was followed after 1554 by an expansion of geographical horizons, with cloth exporters seeking markets in Russia* and the Baltic, southern Europe, Turkey*, and for the first time beyond Europe, in return for naval supplies, wine, Asian silks and spices, and American tobacco and sugar. The African slave trade began in the 1560s, largely to serve the lucrative markets of Spanish America which were invaded at the same time; and the East India Company*, founded in 1600, signalled the start of direct trade with the Far East. Yet such luxury and long-distance commerce can distract attention from the steady growth of internal trade. London's rapid growth encouraged the beginnings of a national market: Newcastle coal and Welsh cattle were brought to the capital in large quantities as early as Elizabeth's reign, and Scottish cattle joined them after 1603. Ireland exported wool, timber, fish, hides and live cattle to mainland Britain in return for manufactures. Even heavy cargoes could be sent long-distance cheaply by water: by the 1580s Newcastle coal was being shipped, albeit in small quantities, to the Mediterranean, and England was Europe's largest exporter of lead.

Industry and commerce did not, however, necessarily entail urban growth. The late medieval textile boom occurred in small towns or industrial villages like Lavenham and Long Melford, leaving marvellous "cloth churches" as legacies of their industrial greatness, while old cloth towns like Lincoln, Beverley and Winchester decayed. Indeed many of the greater medieval towns – York, Canterbury, Salisbury and Coventry among others – decayed so much between about 1450 and 1550 that it is now fashionable to call the period one of general "urban crisis", and with some justice. Industries (not only cloth) moved into the countryside; there were too few rich merchants to pay the cities' tax assessments; and the Reformation often added the *coup de grâce* by ending religious plays, processions and pilgrimages. However, rural industries at the same time turned villages into new towns – Birmingham, Manchester, Sheffield – while after about 1570 the older, larger towns began to grow again.

The capital was in a class of its own, and growing rapidly larger. In Henry VIII's reign it housed 2.5 per cent of the English population, but by 1650 its population numbered 400,000, some 7 per cent of the national total; and it was second only to Paris among west European cities. The Italian Botero considered in 1588 that London was the only English city that "deserves to be called great", and when an Englishman reached Persia in 1568 he found that the Shah's courtiers had heard of London but not of England. The growth of London was, on balance, beneficial to the British economy, stimulating trade and industry by its voracious demands; but it frightened Elizabeth, James I and Charles I, who all tried vainly to limit new building and new immigrants. They expressed fears of overcrowding, riot and disease, and with reason: the capital continued to suffer severe epidemics of plague while it was diminishing as a national killer. Yet an unhealthy environment did little to deter floods of immigrants to London from all over England and even from Wales and Ireland. Ireland was also able to spare people to boost the growth of Dublin, which numbered perhaps 5,000 in 1600 but 50-60,000 in 1685, when it was the second largest city in the British dominions.

Muscovy Company
Founded 1555 to promote trade with Russia after collapse of Antwerp market: forerunner of other joint-stock companies. First voyage 1555 financed initially by 240 shares, at £25 each, with profits distributed according to shares held. Sponsored 1580 voyage searching for Arctic route to China. Lost monopoly 1587, and occasionally found it hard to find the heavier cloth needed for northern markets, possibly owing to competition for wool from new draperies.

Levant Company
Granted monopoly of trade with eastern Mediterranean in 1581, after a secret mission to Sultan had secured privileges in Ottoman Empire for English merchants. Traded cloth for raw silk; Turkish carpets also highly prized.

East India Company
Granted royal charter 1600 with 218 original members, allowing exclusive trade in and around Indian Ocean. Joint-stock company as common capital financed voyages, since long-range trading extremely expensive. Last of great Elizabethan trading companies; example of beneficial use of monopolies.

Model of the Royal Exchange, which was built in 1566-70 by Sir Thomas Gresham as a meeting-place for London financiers and merchants.

A Divided Society

Paul Slack

Although there is much that is controversial and uncertain about social change between 1450 and 1625, there is one feature on which most historians would agree: that over that time-span a period of relative stability was replaced by one of obvious instability. Society in 1520 was still very like what it had been in 1450. By 1625, on the other hand, it had changed, if not fundamentally then at least visibly and tangibly. As late Elizabethan and Jacobean literature shows, people at the end of the period saw themselves in a society beset with uncertainties and in continuous flux, and they spent a good deal of time proclaiming the virtues of "order" and "degree" against dangers which seemed to lurk all around.

One reason for this transition was the rapid inflation, whose economic effects have already been described. The cost of living, which was stable until about 1510, rose five-fold between 1510 and 1625: an unprecedented rise after a century of price stability. The majority of people who were dependent on the market for their food and clothing were hit hard because wages did not keep pace with prices. It has been estimated that between about 1500 and about 1620, the purchasing power of wages was cut by sixty per cent. That was probably not as severe a drop in living standards as it looks. Many consumers were protected to an extent against inflation, because their meals and sometimes their lodgings were provided by their employers. But it was a fall, nevertheless, and it seriously affected wage-earners in towns and wage-labourers in the countryside – perhaps a third of the population by 1625. The days of plenty for ordinary Englishmen in the fifteenth century, when the price of food was low, land plentiful and wages high, were over. There were many other people, however, who profited from inflation: especially those who owned land and had surplus produce to sell in the market. The wealth of the gentry and yeomen farmers rose rapidly; and although the greatest landowners were unable at first to raise their income from rents in line with inflation, they were beginning to catch up by the end of the period. By 1625, too, the wealth of landowners was stimulating consumer demand for foreign imports of luxuries and for home-produced textiles, and thus benefiting many merchants and retail tradesmen. In short, inflation redistributed wealth from the lower classes to the upper and upper-middle classes in the century after 1520.

A second, and related, determinant of social change was a rise in population. We do not know precisely when or why population at last began to grow after the long stagnation of the later Middle Ages. The main reason was probably a decline in mortality. The great killing diseases like plague continued to affect Britain throughout the period. A quarter of the population of London may have died of plague in 1563; the population of England as a whole fell by about six per cent because of an epidemic of influenza between 1557 and 1559. But major mortalities of this kind seem to have declined in frequency after a great plague in 1479. As a result, expectation of life at birth was exceptionally high

"The Rich Man and the Poor Man". An engraving from Stephen Bateman's Crystal Glass of Christian Reformation, *1569.*

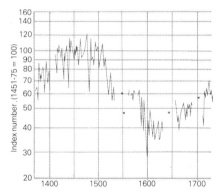

The changing value of wages 1400-1700 (equivalents of wages of building craftsmen expressed in a composite unit of consumables)

181

(38 years) in the late-sixteenth and early-seventeenth centuries, the first period for which we have any reliable evidence*. It is possible also that fertility was increasing in the early-sixteenth century, because of a fall in the age at marriage. The age at first marriage was always high in pre-industrial England: it was 28 for men and 26 for women in the early-seventeenth century. But it had probably been a year or two lower than that in the early and mid-sixteenth century, thus providing a temporary boost to fertility.

Consequently the population of England (we have no accurate information about other parts of Britain) rose rapidly for a century from 1520 to 1620. It had been about 2 million in 1450. In 1520 it is estimated to have been still less than 2.5 million. But by 1620 it had probably reached 4.5 million. The consequences were profound. One was an increase in the proportion of children in the population, and hence in the number of mouths to be fed by each bread-winner. That put a strain on the family economy of the poor. At the same time competition for land increased, and, since primogeniture was the commonest form of inheritance, younger children had to move to find a living. Demographic growth produced extensive migration by the landless poor. Many of them moved to previously underpopulated areas of forest and upland pasture, others headed towards towns, and above all to London, whose population increased remarkably in the second half of the period.

Like the redistribution of wealth, this redistribution of population had implications for the social structure. It produced a marked contrast in social relationships between two distinct types of settlement. In the "fielden" areas of lowland England, which were primarily corn-producing, villages had a clear social hierarchy, headed by a group of wealthy yeomen and often a lord of the manor, and with a growing class of permanent agricultural labourers beneath it. But in forest and pastoral areas, found especially in western and northern England and in Wales and Scotland, there was a much more egalitarian society of cottagers, using common pasture to augment their own smallholdings, and often engaged in rural industries as well. The first sort of society formed the archetypal approved model of the orderly village. The second was regarded as a novel source of disorder, an "open" society of dispersed settlements where industry and agriculture intermingled anarchically, and where vagrants, beggars and rioters were bred. Finally, a third kind of society, an urban one, was emerging in London. Other towns were too small to be wholly

Population trends

Parish registers from 1538 record baptisms, marriages and burials, and Cambridge Group for History of Population has collated data from 404 registers. By process known as "family reconstitution", it has been possible to discover average sizes of families, age when children set up own homes, etc., and to estimate population totals.

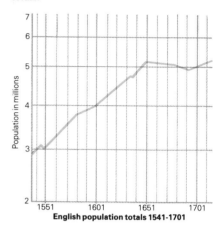

Population in millions

English population totals 1541-1701

Peerage

Highest estate under monarch, who alone could promote to its ranks, consisting of dukes, marquesses, earls, viscounts and barons; and by extension archbishops and bishops. Enjoyed great wealth and influence, but no special judicial or territorial powers. Recognized as Crown's advisers and used in local government, its main formal privilege was right to vote in Upper House of Parliament. About 40 peers in late 15th century, rising to 55 in 1603, to 126 in 1628. Titles normally passed to eldest male descendant; extinction occurred only through failure of male issue or act of attainder.

divorced from the countryside, but in the capital there was a social environment where upward mobility was rapid and relatively easy, provided one had inherited or acquired capital; and where social distinctions were not obvious. At the end of the period, contemporaries were already complaining that it was difficult to tell from dress and behaviour who were masters and who were servants in the metropolis. London's growth, like that of forest settlements, was another social threat which governments tried, in vain, to prevent.

There were other changes which seemed to undermine the integrity of those horizontal status categories which contemporaries used to define gradations in their social structure. At the top were the nobility* and the gentry. The distinction between the two was never as clear-cut as some historians have suggested, but it narrowed appreciably in the second half of the period. The great magnates and large landowners of the later Middle Ages just about held their own in economic terms. Though suffering severely in the years around 1600 they were beginning to increase their incomes again by 1625, and they held as much of the land of England in 1690 as they had in 1436 (roughly 15 per cent). But they lost their military power for ever and with it their unquestioned political predominance. The gentry*, on the other hand, expanded both their wealth and their power. They had owned 25 per cent of the land in 1436, but they had more than 45 per cent by 1690, largely thanks to the dissolution of the monasteries, which benefited them more than any other class. This has led some historians to talk of a "rise of the gentry" in the century after 1540, although it should be pointed out that they did not have very far to rise.

A more distinctive feature of the period was the "expansion" of the gentry. For while the wealth of this status group increased, the number of people enjoying it increased still more. There were probably roughly 5,000 knights, esquires and gentlemen in the mid-fifteenth century: by 1625 there were more than twice as many. Some of the newcomers were merchants who had made substantial profits from foreign trade. More of them were yeomen, profiting from price inflation, who were able by the end of the period to live in the style of a gentleman and obtain a grant of arms*. Four thousand grants of arms were made between 1560 and 1640. The demand for honours, including the new title of baronet*, was enormous in the early seventeenth century, and several books were published defining "gentility" for the instruction of those who had

Gentry
Contemporary yet imprecise social rank for class below peerage, ranging from knights and esquires to simple gentlemen: a man was a gentleman because others accepted him as such. "Gentility" consisted in living without physical labour off landed income, acceptance of duty to govern localities, shared social values, (such as largesse, valour), and similar educational backgrounds (increasingly at universities for a little culture and Inns of Court for smattering of legal knowledge). Though esquires might approach wealth of some peers, many gentlemen were hardly more prosperous than yeomen.

College of Arms
Following 15th-century reorganization, college was official guardian of gentle status; could register men worth £10 a year in land or £300 in moveables as gentlemen. Every 20 or 30 years heralds visited each county, acknowledging family pedigrees and coats-of-arms of gentry, disowning others. In 1603, 641 "official" gentry in Yorkshire; but c. 1000 assumed that rank. College's purpose was to recognize (not hinder) attainment of gentry status.

Baronetcies
Hereditary knighthood created in 1611 in England and 1618 in Ireland. Originally associated with Irish colonization, after 1617 openly sold; prices fell from £700 1619 to £220 in 1622. Also sold late 1620s and early 1640s by Charles I.

Visscher's Long View of London, *1618, showing nobles' houses to the west, old St Paul's cathedral, houses and shops on London Bridge, and ships moored between the bridge and the Tower.*

just acquired it. The result was a very much larger social and political élite in 1620 than had existed in 1450, and a very much more competitive and less easily managed one. Despite the wish of Queen Elizabeth and her ministers to keep the social structure unchanged, they were unable to prevent the number of justices of the peace in most counties from rising rapidly after 1558.

If the number of people in the upper ranks of society was rising, and probably rising faster than the population after 1540, so too was the number at the other end of the social scale. In the years around 1520 the extent of poverty began to impress itself on contemporaries, whether in the form of beggars in towns or of vagrants on country roads, and for the next century the problem increased in size until it came to be regarded as the major social issue of the day. There was also an increase in the number of those who, while not destitute, might find themselves in abject poverty if they were ill or suddenly unemployed: artisans in towns and, above all, labourers in the countryside. The growth of wage labour in agriculture was particularly important because it meant the beginning of the end of the traditional English peasant: the moderately prosperous farmer who had occupied the vital middle ground between the labourer and the prosperous yeoman. Recent studies suggest that he began to disappear in the later sixteenth century, largely because of the impact of inflation. He either moved up to yeoman* status and a share in the attitudes and authority of the élite, or he joined the ranks of the labourers. This change was gradual and was only just beginning by 1625, but it represented a polarization in rural society which mirrored that larger polarization between the fortunes of rich and poor which marked the whole century after 1520.

We have so far looked at the social structure in terms of horizontal classes or status groups. But in England (and even more so in Wales, Scotland and Ireland) there were also vertical loyalties cutting across these distinctions. The most important were the ties of neighbourhood and local community, which gave villages and counties a sense of identity of their own. There were also ties of clientage and patronage between lords and gentlemen, between landlords and their tenants and servants, and between employers and employees. None of these was unaffected by social and economic change in the period, although they were stretched or redefined, never destroyed. The most obvious casualties were the old "bastard feudal" links of dependence between lord and retainer. They were gradually replaced by more flexible ties of patronage. Local identities may also have been weakened by greater geographical mobility, the growing dominance of London, and government centralization. This can be exaggerated: Englishmen still referred to their county as their "country" in 1625, for example, and provincial loyalties were even stronger on the Celtic fringe. But there is much evidence in the second half of the period, and at the level of the propertied classes, that local accents and customs were coming to be regarded as quaint and backward, and that a national élite culture, in terms of manners and styles of language and dress, was emerging.

These changes may help to explain the stress which was laid in publications of the sixteenth and early seventeenth centuries on the importance of the family and the household. These were regarded as vital instruments for the imposition of social discipline when other social bonds seemed to be dissolving. It has also been argued, though this is more controversial, that in reality people in the sixteenth century came to depend much more on the nuclear family, and less on an extended kin system, on their lineage or clan. Whether this was so or not, by the later sixteenth century, when we first have good

Yeomen
Technically those with freehold land worth £2 p.a., guaranteeing right to vote for Parliament, yeomen were small-scale owners of land or prosperous tenant farmers. Seen as lowest stratum of society capable of governing, yeomen served as jurors, constables and churchwardens; in villages without resident squires, two or three yeomen families might exercise leadership. 1543 Act restricted Bible-reading to males of rank of yeoman and above.

Husbandmen
Rarely owned land but farmed holdings of c. 10-30 acres. Tenancies differed enormously from 99-year leases in west of England (often freely renewed) to temporary grants where rents rose at each renewal. Rare for husbandman to leave estate exceeding £20 value. Probably suffered as result of Tudor inflation, as landholdings were too small to profit from higher food prices, and many became wage-labourers.

Patriarchalism
System of social regulation based on superiority of oldest males, according to rank. Deference to age related to reliance on experience and memory. Women socially and legally inferior: unable to vote; severely limited ability to trade; only widows could control their property. Reformation perhaps depressed status of women: closure of nunneries and destruction of guilds and charities, often charitable organizations with women playing significant roles; decline in emphasis on Virgin Mary and (female) saints; stressed husband's role as exponent of God's Word to household. Omnicompetence of Parliament – in religion, wages, property etc – partly stemmed from patriarchal ideas: social superiors had duty to regulate all aspects of life of inferiors.

Sumptuary laws
Laws restricted luxury clothes (or weapons) according to wealth or status, for both economic and social reasons. 1463 statute of Edward IV restricted velvet, satin or counterfeit silk to men above rank of knight and wives, on grounds that excess was repugnant to God and enriched other countries at England's expense. Pressures on social structure from growing population and redistribution of wealth led to concern about "confusion of degrees", as witnessed by 19 proclamations dealing with clothing between 1516-97 alone.

Statute of Artificers 1563

Ordered imposition of maximum local wages annually assessed by local JPs: partly reaction to higher wage demands resulting from temporary labour shortage following influenza and hunger of 1550s. All men under 30 to practice craft originally trained in; unemployed men to take farm work and women to take domestic service; obligation to remain in locality of birth.

Witches

English witches, unlike those of Scotland or Continent, not associated with Devil or broomsticks, but rather with causing injury or death to man or beast through misuse of "natural" magic. Alleged "witches" usually poor, elderly women living on fringes of community. After population pressures increased poverty and tensions in villages, if old women were refused charity by neighbours, any following misfortunes were blamed on revenge by the "witch". Fear heightened by Reformation, with destruction of saints, processions, which previously offered antidote to witches, leaving prosecution as only form of protection. Witchcraft a capital offence in England 1542-47 and 1563-1736; about 1,000 "witches" executed.

Sabbath regulation

Loss of 43 holy days (other than Sundays) after Reformation led to emphasis on sanctity and uniqueness of Sabbath: Sunday work forbidden by law, some calling for harsh punishment of Sabbath-breakers. Particularly strong moves early 17th century to ban Sunday sports and drinking.

Tudor poor laws

Saw gradual sophistication in understanding causes of poverty. 1531 Act distinguished between those unemployed (or in need) due to sickness or old-age and those wilfully vagrant; only the former were given right to beg in own parish. 1536 Act made parishes or towns responsible for genuine poor, through voluntary alms-giving. 1572 legislation introduced compulsory poor-rates (following examples of London and Norwich) and accepted that some vagrants were unable to find employment; physical punishment still prescribed for genuinely "idle". 1598 and 1601 summaries of existing legislation created "overseers of poor" to levy contributions and create jobs; in force till 1834.

Group portrait of William Brooke, Lord Cobham, and his family attributed to Hans Eworth, and dated 1567.

evidence for it, the English household was a small and close-knit social unit with a familiar "modern" look to it. The average size of household was 4.75, and most households were made up of parents and children alone. Only ten per cent of them had other resident kin, and only twenty-eight per cent contained servants.

There were great social variations, however. The households of the poor were generally smaller (often three members or fewer), and those of the rich larger, because they had more servants. Service was in fact a central social institution, and one which separates the early modern household from our own. The children of the poor got employment in the houses of their betters as domestic servants or servants in husbandry (that is, young farm workers who lived in). As a result, a majority of the population lived in the minority of households which contained more than six people. Whether as a master or as a father, however, the head of the household was in the crucial social position as the first source of authority*; and it is not surprising that contemporary commentators such as William Perkins emphasized his importance when social and economic change seemed to be undermining hierarchy and deference outside the family.

There are many other signs of contemporary concern about the problems of authority and order in the second half of the period. From the 1530s onwards there was a gradual increase in the number of laws trying to control popular behaviour: punishing vagrants, witches*, bastard-bearers and those who did not attend church*, and tightening up the machinery for detecting crime of all kinds. At the same time, local authorities started to pass by-laws which were socially regulatory: against drunkenness, alehouses and disorderly popular recreations. There were carrots as well as sticks to prevent popular disorder, notably the poor laws*, beginning in 1531 and finally codified in 1601, which gave some relief to the destitute. Private benefactors were similarly establishing almshouses, loan funds for poor tradesmen, and charities for the poor in increasing numbers in the century after 1540. The formal and informal mechanisms for social control were much more elaborate in 1625 than in 1450.

There is some evidence that the social fears which lay behind these measures were justified. Vagrancy, petty theft and bastardy, for example, were increasing, and probably increasing faster than population in the hard economic times (for the poor, that is) between 1580 and 1610. On the other hand, some sorts of disorder declined in incidence over the period. The amount of naked violence fell, as property-owners fought out their disputes in the courts and took the law less often into their own hands. The business of every court in the land expanded enormously between 1500 and 1625. Rebellion also ceased, partly because of the military decline of the magnates, partly because of the disappearance of the peasantry who once led it. The last major peasant revolt was that in Norfolk in 1549*; the last serious provincial rebellion was the Rising in the North twenty years later. Despite the poverty, popular dissidence and crime to which contemporaries were so sensitive, the country was in some obvious respects more orderly in 1625 than it had been in 1450.

It was also in obvious ways much richer. Patterns of public consumption grew vastly more extravagant and more varied in the course of the sixteenth century. Any collection of Tudor portraits shows that the dress* of the nobility was much more elaborate and theatrical at the end of the sixteenth century than at the beginning. Gone were the sober gowns of men in the late fifteenth century, and the loose flowing dresses of women; in came padded doublets for men, farthingales for women, and starched ruffs, jewellery, lace and embroidery for both sexes. No one who worked with his or her hands could dress like that, of course. But the social élite set the fashion, and the dominance of "fashion", largely determined and catered for in London, was one mark of the new wealth of the élite in Elizabethan England.

Conspicious consumption and rapid changes of taste were demonstrated in other areas too: in the new "prodigy" houses of the nobility and gentry, for example, and in their diet. The meals of the upper classes were always gargantuan, but by 1600 they were much more varied in quality and probably better nutritionally. Some of these changes percolated down the social scale to the middle ranks of urban and rural society. Yeomen as well as gentlemen rebuilt their houses in the later sixteenth and early seventeenth centuries in what has been described as the "great rebuilding of rural England". Inventories of yeomen, merchants, and craftsmen show that glass windows, chimneys,

Peasants' revolts 1549
Against background of inflation and unsettling religious changes, much of southern England saw spontaneous anti-enclosure riots spring 1549; quelled by local gentry. More dangerous rising in Devon and Cornwall in June: Catholic clergy (but few gentlemen) and peasants revolted against new religion, Prayer Book in English and probably sheep tax; rebels besieged Exeter, but suppressed by hastily-assembled royal army. In East Anglia, friction between sheep-farming landlords and arable-farming commons produced some rioting and mass demonstrations in rebel camps. Mousehold Heath (outside Norwich) was main camp, led by Robert Ket. Grievances mainly economic: no exploitation by landlords, protection of common land from enclosers, lower rents. Savagely suppressed by army under Warwick, August 1549.

Dress
Doublets were close-fitting jackets with or without sleeves, traditionally worn with hose (stockings). Though simple in shape, could be richly worked to display wealth; earl of Leicester in 1588 left 7 doublets and 2 cloaks worth £545. Ruffs, starched, elaborate collars, and farthingales, framed hoops worn under skirts to enlarge them, both examples of impractical fashions adopted to heighten grandeur and emphasize distance of wearers from manual labour.

A scene of popular merry-making in Bermondsey, with a distant view of the Tower of London across the Thames to the north. Citizens of various degrees, from peddlars to merchants and their families are seen in this painting by a Flemish visitor, Joris van Hoefnagel, of about 1590.

Portrait of Robert Dudley, earl of Leicester, by an unknown artist c. 1575. Leicester's embroidered silk doublet is tightly waisted and pointed below, being padded and stiffened with buckram to resemble armour.

A Procession of Queen Elizabeth I, c. 1601, attributed to Robert Peake the Elder. There have been many interpretations of this picture – that it may celebrate a wedding or a victory or a visit. It is probably an idealized representation of a triumphant Queen, surrounded by the nobles and ladies of her Court.

changes of clothes and linen, spare beds and domestic utensils were common in the last fifty years of the period. They had been rarities in 1450. Books were another new item in middle- and upper-class inventories in the later sixteenth century, reflecting the phenomenal educational expansion which transformed intellectual life in the two centuries after the invention of printing. Over 300 new schools were founded between 1500 and 1620, and the book trade expanded even more rapidly: 259 new works were published in 1600 alone and by 1640 the annual number had doubled. By the 1620s all gentlemen, five out of ten craftsmen and tradesmen and more than half of all yeomen could sign their names and therefore, probably, read.

There can be little doubt, therefore, that the quality of life for everyone except the poor improved immeasurably over the period. The exception is, however, an important one. We have seen that the poor were a growing class, and there is no sign that their standard of living improved before 1625, though it began to do so very soon afterwards. But we should not paint too black a picture of their lot. They were not as undernourished, as precariously close to subsistence level, as their French counterparts, and some Englishmen knew it and were proud of the fact. But in the bad harvest years of 1595-97 people did die of starvation in some of the poorer parts of England, in the highlands of the north and the south-west, and in Wales, Scotland and Ireland too; and by 1600 there were new slum areas in towns, overcrowded alleys with single-room dwellings in which malnutrition, plague and other diseases levied a dreadful toll.

We have no means of knowing what the total number of the poor (however defined) was in 1625. We cannot count them as easily as we can the gentry, partly because they existed on the margins, off the centre of the historical stage – in highland areas, forests and the suburbs of towns. But they were numerous, and they point the social contrasts which have been the theme of this essay. The prosperous peasant society of the later Middle Ages had given place to one with a much more evident economic and social divide between the labouring "commons" on the one hand and the leisured gentlemen and comfortable "middling sort" on the other.

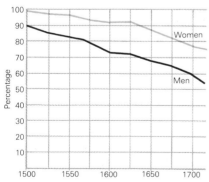

Estimated illiteracy of men and women in England 1500-1700

Culture:
the age of the household

David Starkey

The years 1450-1625 are the first age of the Renaissance in England. Here we are concerned with the social setting of the "re-birth" as much as with the artistic achievement itself. In the native lands of the Renaissance – Italy, the Rhineland, and the Low Countries – its cradle was the city; in England, it was the great household, and the greatest household of all, the royal Court.

The great household dominated later medieval England. Its obvious rivals – the towns and the Church – were relatively weak and in any case were interpenetrated by its own forms: a guild, monastery or college was a communal household; while the households of the bishops looked very like those of the secular nobility. For the arts, this dominance meant that the household was the prime supplier of patronage and posts (although the poet John Lydgate, for example, was a monk of Bury St Edmund's, he received a royal pension, taught the sons of the nobility, and largely wrote for their parents); it also determined the status of the artist and much of the content of the arts as well.

To understand this we need to know more about the household itself. Its core, of course, was the family; but around the family was a much larger penumbra of servants. And the more important the head of the household, the greater the number of servants: a knight had a dozen; an earl a hundred or two; the king five hundred or more. To accommodate these numbers, vast sprawling houses like Knole* were built and they were the largest centres of conspicuous consumption in the country.

The result was to put both the artist and the arts in a decidedly dependent role (so much so that such terms are manifest anachronisms). Whereas in the urban cultures of Italy and the Netherlands the artist was a professional among professionals and regarded accordingly; in England he was a servant, while the arts themselves were frankly utilitarian. The master-builder (the word "architect" was scornfully rejected by Ben Jonson as a pretentious foreign import even at the very end of our period) built and maintained accommodation for the great household; the writer, painter and musician amused its members in peace and prepared propaganda for them in war: the king's Serjeant Painter was an heraldic artist, who painted banners and badges; the royal minstrels made the ceremonial noises that marked each stage of the Court day, and even a privileged musician of Henry VIII's Privy Chamber*, like the great lutenist Philip Van Wilder, was also a royal musical odd-job man, repairing the king's broken lute strings and tutoring the royal children. The same goes for literature. Not only did its dominant themes of courtly love and the knightly romance reflect the values and interests of the nobility and gentlefolk, they also answered to the social reality of life in the great household, where the day was spent in hunting and jousting* (for which the romances provided the ethos and the decorative themes) and the evening in "dalliance in the ladies' chamber" (when love poems would be recited or

Knole
Huge mansion near Sevenoaks, Kent, virtually appropriated from Archbishop Cranmer by Henry VIII. Enlarged in 1540s by Henry, liking its refreshing air; granted by Elizabeth to Sir Thomas Sackville (earl of Dorset under James I). Built around 3 large courtyards, Knole retains massive Tudor gateways but also more delicate Jacobean skyline.

Privy Chamber
Innermost suite of apartments in royal palace where monarch led "private" life; its members also attended informally (and secretly) to political matters. Under Henry VIII, sovereign's attendants in most intimate bodily functions were great gentlemen who were able to influence policy-making: also controlled access to king at crucial moments. Privy Chamber later declined politically with succession of child and two women; situation complicated under James I with growth of Bedchamber and influx of Scots.

Jousting
Martial and dangerous pastime favoured by aristocracy and youthful Henry VIII, where 2 horsemen charged each other, hoping to unhorse opponent with levelled lance. Also tilting, trying to spear small metal rings with lance. Tournaments (or "tilts") enacted before Court ladies, especially Catherine of Aragon. Many of Henry's later councillors or personal attendants, e.g. Lord Russell, his original boon-companions. From *c.* 1580, elaborate Court tilts to celebrate anniversary of Elizabeth's accession.

Madrigals

Musical settings of poetry for 4 - 6 voices: first significant English exponents were William Byrd *c.* 1542-1623 and Thomas Morley 1557-*c.* 1603, who made full musical use of word-play and variety of sounds in English language. Madrigals highly emotional, ranging from melancholic to zestful. Especially popular under Elizabeth and James I as private household entertainments, with each vocal line printed in separate part-books.

sung* and their rituals played out). Again, the dominant relationship of the household – that of master and servant – acted as the model for most other relationships (whether in literature or life): between God and man (whence a religious "service"); between man and woman (whence the lover-servant's vows of fealty to his "mistress"); and between king and subject (whence Sir Thomas More's description of himself as "the king's good servant"). Finally, taste or aesthetic was shaped by the great household. The household's ideal was "magnificence": a relentless worship of lavishness, elaboration and expense. In the visual arts the counterpart of this was the overloading of ornament; in literature, the turgid prolixity most notable in Lydgate, for whom length was a virtue in itself.

In principle, the Renaissance was opposed to all of this. Artistically, it substituted decorum and the observance of rules for idiosyncrasy and

The Queen's Gallery (above right) for the Westminster tournament of 1511 is covered in straightforward heraldic badges and livery colours, but some thirty years later (right) on a similar structure of the 1540s, with similar badges (Henry VIII's portcullis and Katherine Parr's queen emerging from a rose), the decorations are set in delicate classical fantasies. The decorations of these temporary structures for Court entertainments clearly shows the shift from Gothic to Renaissance forms.

indulgence; politically, it emphasized peace rather than war (the *raison d'être* of the nobility) and the common good instead of a selfish and individualistic honour; religiously, it aimed to sweep away empty ritual, sterile philosophy and a presumptuous bargaining with God (as in indulgences*) and to replace them by a lively faith kindled by the pure Word of God*. This conflict of "old" and "new" is explicit in Erasmus (who is rude about the nobility's ignorance of letters and their fondness for hunting, fighting and the keeping of multitudes of idle servants), and it provides the emotional and intellectual steam of Book I of More's *Utopia*.

But as these names – both darlings of the Court – suggest, the "new", for all its hostility to the existing culture, entered England not by revolution from below but politically from the top. In the later fifteenth century the Crown had been "refounded" by a strengthening of the informal machinery of the royal household*. This had become larger and its servants were now masters of their own households. The result was to make it different in kind from the other great households, in short, a Court. The king was again rich enough to resume large-scale patronage; while the vicious competitiveness of the Court itself mirrored the fruitful strife of the Italian city and provided the perfect seedbed for the "new".

At first the "new" was taken up by the Court as an unthinking matter of fashion and enjoyed wide-based support: so that Holbein's patrons on his first English visit (1526-28) included not only the increasingly conservative More but also a random group of courtiers involved in the Greenwich pageant* of 1527 for which Holbein was a principal designer. But with the divorce crisis, politics became dominated by ideologically committed factions, and one of these, the "reformers", led successively by Anne Boleyn, Thomas Cromwell and Edward Seymour, duke of Somerset, increasingly monopolized the patronage of the *avant garde:* Holbein, permanently based in England from 1532, became their protégé and their houses – Lacock, Dudley Castle, Longleat – carried the new architectural forms deep into the countryside. At the same time and again associated with the "reformed" religion, which demanded a sophisticated literacy from its adherents, the gentry, who had hitherto been apprenticed (as it were) in other great households, began to undergo a more

Indulgences
Grants of remission of penalties for sins committed: Catholic Church argued that Christ's sacrifice (and merits of Virgin and saints) so superabundantly meritorious that Church could pass on credit to others (even in purgatory) for their sins. Indulgences earned by pious acts or purchased: Luther attacked Rome over indulgences from 1517, arguing each man saved through own faith in Christ.

"Word of God"
From late 15th century, humanist revival of Greek and Hebrew and psychological authority of printed word brought about new reverence for scriptural authority. Most Protestants believed Bible revealed all necessary for salvation; some thought to go beyond Scripture was sinful. Catholics affirmed that pope and Church – heirs to Peter and Apostles – received continuing revelation from God to supplement Scripture.

Utopia
Latin book by humanist Sir Thomas More, published in Louvain 1516. Part I is wide-ranging commentary on state of England: condemns Christian princes for waging war; and enclosure of arable land for pasture, creating unemployment. Part 2 describes drab, authoritarian, non-Christian but communal and egalitarian society. First English translation 1551.

Nicholas Hilliard's painting of Queen Elizabeth of about 1575 shows the royal portrait transformed into icon.

Drawing of c. 1558 by Antonius van den Wynegaerde of Hampton Court Palace, begun by Cardinal Wolsey and extended by Henry VIII.

A feast in the house of Sir Henry Unton, c. 1596. A masque is in progress, accompanied by a "broken consort": treble violin, cittern, pandore, base viol and lute. This detail is taken from a memorial portrait telling the story of Unton's life, which was commissioned by his widow.

Household administration
Replacement of ancient Exchequer's financial control by King's Chamber, especially under Edward IV and Henry VII; permitted king's personal supervision of resources. Sometimes contrasted with Cromwell's bureaucratic innovations of 1530s, when autonomous new departments of government were created.

Greenwich pageant 1527
From 1527, Henry allied with French because imperial capture of pope impeded projected divorce. Change of policy announced through 1527 pageant to greet French representatives: Latin play depicted Wolsey and Henry (with French help) releasing pope and combatting Lutheran heresies; setting included perfumed water from fountain behind olive tree, representing benefits of Universal Peace. In an under-literate age, such symbolism was a major means of communication.

Universities
Period saw great expansion within two existing English universities. Numerous colleges founded in humanist desire for better educated clergy, e.g. Christ's and St John's, Cambridge, (both founded by Henry VII's mother, Margaret) and Wolsey's Cardinal College (now Christ Church), Oxford; later, colleges founded to strengthen Protestantism, especially Emmanuel, Cambridge 1584 and Wadham and Jesus, Oxford. More gentry (not intending Church career) spent time at universities after *c.* 1550: one-third of 1563 MPs were university men, but by 1593, over half. 15th century saw foundation of three Scottish universities.

Inns of Court
Four London law "colleges": Lincoln's Inn, Gray's Inn, Middle and Inner Temple. Provided smattering of legal education required by sons of landowners, future JPs. Increasingly a "finishing school" for gentlemen – often after a year at university – as opportunities to study history, scripture, music, fencing, and other signs of gentility. Larger numbers of students than universities combined; lack of scholarships meant few poorer students. Popular from 1550 and throughout 17th century.

formalized education in schools and universities*. The first fruits of this were gentlemen-authors, like the poets Sir Thomas Wyatt and the earl of Surrey, who wrote of the great game of politics with the urgency and insight of participants (quite unlike the merely ringside view of earlier servant-writers, who, like even More in his *Richard III,* had seen politics as "king's games, as it were stage plays, and for the more part played upon scaffolds, in which poor men be but the lookers-on").

But the Henrician Renaissance quickly petered out. On the one hand its political leadership was destroyed, partly by its own internecine strife and partly by the Marian reaction. And, on the other, the restoration of the "reformed" political establishment under Elizabeth – ironically – cut England off from the Continent, where the Counter-Reformation was largely triumphant. The result of this incompletion and isolation was the wonderfully strange hybrid culture of Elizabethan England. This was both innovatory and revivalist. In painting, the Renaissance form of the portrait was retained, but Renaissance "realism" was abandoned in favour of a neo-Gothic stiffness in which the sitter became an image, encased in clothes and hung with jewels. The most extreme form of such secular icons was the portraits – regulated by proclamation – of the Queen herself*. In architecture, as at Wollaton, classical detail was blended with fairy-tale gothic forms; in literature, as in Spenser, chivalric romance was treated in Italianate verse, and the ideal of knighthood itself reinterpreted for an age of religious wars. These violent juxtapositions penetrated the very language: a murdered man's blood would "The multitudinous seas incarnadine, Making the green one red". And, as this example from Shakespeare's *Macbeth* suggests, it is this multiplicity of forms, values and vocabulary (in contrast with the earlier monopoly of "the age of the household") that gives the age its vitality.

With the Stuarts there are signs of a contrary movement. Contacts with the Continent were resumed and royal patronage, frozen by Elizabeth's meanness, revived (if haphazardly). The effects showed soonest in the visual arts. The first of the new-style connoisseur-collectors, Thomas Howard, earl of Arundel*, wanted nothing of England's past but Holbeins, for which he admitted he had a "foolish curiosity". Otherwise he collected the ancient Roman or modern Italian or Flemish. His taste in paintings and sculpture was followed by Henry, prince of Wales, and the duke of Buckingham; while in architecture his protégé Inigo Jones, who had travelled with him to Italy, began single-handed a second and technically much more accomplished Renaissance, whose triumph (still incomplete in 1625) was the Queen's House, Greenwich. These innovations, incomprehensible to most and offensive to some, were wholly identified with the Court (Buckingham was royal favourite; Jones Surveyor of the King's Works). And this identification of the Court with an alien culture came when the Court's domination of politics, established a century previously, was in manifest decline. The ensuing double isolation of the Court, both politically and culturally, opened the way for developments it had originally sponsored to turn against it: literary self-consciousness contributed to a heightened political consciousness; the republican tendencies of classical literature began to come into the open. The Renaissance, long domesticated at Court, was recovering its original bite.

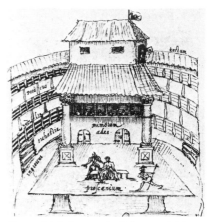

Pen and ink drawing by Johannes de Witte of the interior of the Swan theatre in 1596.

Portraits of Elizabeth

An important form of political propaganda: 1563 proclamation forbade further likenesses of queen (not having perfectly captured queen's "person, favour, or grace") till one master likeness made and distributed for copying. From *c.* 1580, portraits became more allegorical and propagandist: celebrated "Armada Portrait" shows divine intervention in battle through the storms that blew up, so connecting Elizabeth with God's destiny for England. All portraits showed Elizabeth as young woman: depiction of old age would raise anxieties about succession.

Theatres

Second half of Elizabeth's reign saw arrival of commercial theatre; previously only religious plays and private bands of actors. First commercial, purpose-built building, "The Theatre" erected in Shoreditch 1576; later south bank of Thames preferred, e.g. for Shakespeare's "Globe". Popular audiences (provoking fears of immorality and irreligion) watched from galleries round central yard. Shakespeare's greatest dramas written under James I: strong political overtones, stressed need for authority and restitution of peace by Tudors.

Arundel collection

Thomas Howard, earl of Arundel, from 1615 started first large private art collection in England. Collected statuary from Europe and Levant, even undertaking archaeological work in Italy with Inigo Jones. Collector of Holbeins and Dürers, patronized Van Dyck and Rubens.

Wollaton Hall, Northamptonshire, built by Robert Smythson between 1580 and 1588.

5

DISORDER TO STABILITY: BRITAIN AND IRELAND

1625-1783

DISORDER TO STABILITY: BRITAIN AND IRELAND 1625-1783
Overview

W.A. Speck

At first sight the period has no coherence whatsoever. On the contrary, the civil wars under Charles I are generally regarded as one of the greatest watersheds in the history of the British Isles, while the Revolution of 1688 was another major turning-point in their development. The contrast between the "Century of Revolution", as the Stuart era has been called, and the political stability now widely held to be the salient characteristic of the early Hanoverian period, appears complete. Nor do the terminal dates offer obvious chronological breaks. Although 1625 saw the accession of a monarch, this did not necessarily punctuate the long-term social, economic and cultural trends which have been seen as culminating in conflict.

And yet these 158 years do have a certain unity. Charles I inherited not a pre-revolutionary situation but a political consensus. This broke down when he promoted Arminianism and thus precipitated ideological divisions in his kingdoms. The peaceful solutions sought before the final appeal to arms involved curbing the royal prerogative and making the king's ministers accountable to Parliament. They thus posed a constitutional problem which remained central to British politics for over a century and a half. Charles I's reply to the Nineteen Propositions sent to him at York in 1642, prescribed the terms of a debate over the relationship between the executive and the legislature which was to preoccupy political theorists, at least until the French Revolution drastically changed the agenda. When under pressure, Charles I argued that the constitution was not that of absolute but of limited monarchy. The Crown's powers were restricted by those of the Lords and of the Commons. When these were in exact equilibrium the system was superior to any other polity in the world.

During the ensuing years the constitution collapsed, until there was neither Crown nor Lords, while radical solutions to the *impasse* were sought, some Levellers even advocating a democracy based on manhood suffrage. Yet the traditional triad reasserted itself even before the Restoration, in the form of Protector, second chamber and lower house. The year 1660 saw the restoration of Lords and Commons as well as of the Crown.

They worked together, if not always in equilibrium, for the best part of twenty years. During the Exclusion crisis, however, they fell apart, as the majority of the peers rallied to the king, while the bulk of the Lower House supported measures to exclude the heir to the throne, James, duke of York, from the succession. For most of the 1680s Parliament was in abeyance, as it had been in the 1630s, so that the Lords and Commons were again unable to act as a check upon the Crown. And once again revolution followed, though this time bloodlessly. The Revolution of 1688 restored the three constitutional powers, this time on a permanent basis. By the reign of George III it had become axiomatic that, in theory at least, they formed the finest constitution under the sun.

Although men used the same language, however, they did not necessarily share the same assumptions. In 1641, for instance, it was widely accepted that the powers of the Crown, Lords and Commons had been in equilibrium in the reign of Queen Elizabeth, and that subsequently the balance had become disturbed. There was nevertheless serious disagreement about how this had come about. Where the earl of Strafford and his supporters insisted that it had happened because the Commons had over-reached themselves, Pym and his associates blamed the Crown for exceeding its bounds. Their diagnoses, and consequently their proposed remedies, were diametrically opposed. An analogous situation obtained under George III. Again it was generally agreed that the constitution had become unbalanced in recent years. The king, however, was apt to blame the Commons for encroaching upon his prerogative, while his critics were inclined to the view "that the influence of the Crown has increased, is increasing, and ought to be diminished". Indeed the period ends with a clash between Crown and Commons over this very issue. George III cashiered the Fox-North coalition in 1783, complaining that they were bent on depriving him of his remaining prerogatives, while they insisted that he was subverting the constitution by dismissing them when they controlled a majority in the Lower House.

Contemporaries established connections between the

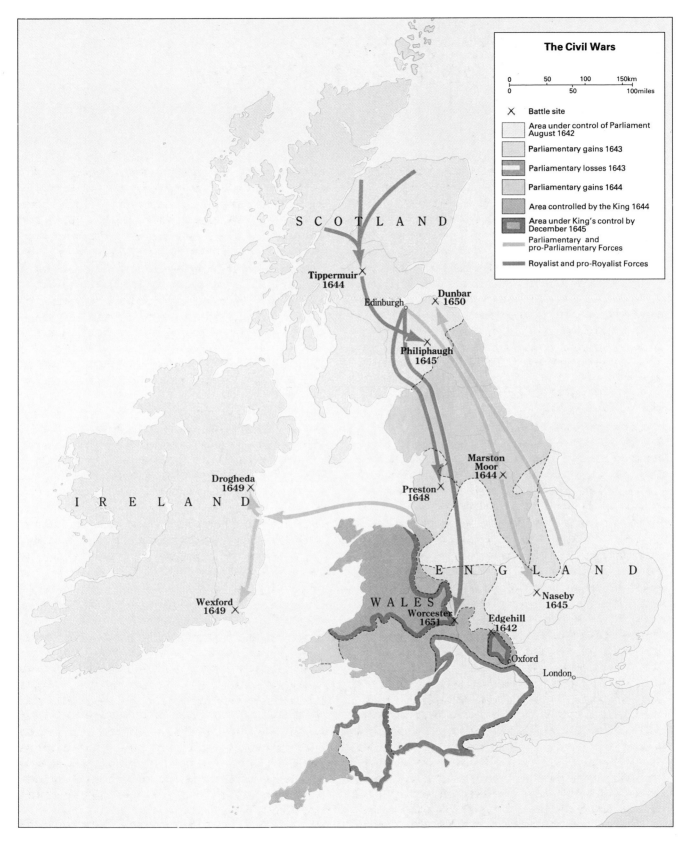

The Civil Wars

0   50   100   150km
0   50   100miles

✕   Battle site

Area under control of Parliament
August 1642

Parliamentary gains 1643

Parliamentary losses 1643

Parliamentary gains 1644

Area controlled by the King 1644

Area under King's control by
December 1645

Parliamentary and
pro-Parliamentary Forces

Royalist and pro-Royalist Forces

S C O T L A N D

Tippermuir
1644 ✕

Edinburgh ○

Dunbar
✕ **1650**

Philiphaugh
1645 ✕

I R E L A N D

Drogheda
1649 ✕

Marston
Moor
1644 ✕

Preston
1648 ✕

E   N   G   L   A   N   D

Wexford
1649 ✕

W A L E S

Worcester
1651 ✕

✕ **Naseby**
1645

Edgehill
✕ **1642**

Oxford ○

London ○

balanced constitution and social trends. James Harrington argued in *Oceana* (1656) that the Civil War had come about through a shift in the ownership of land from the Crown and the Lords to the Commons, resulting in a corresponding transfer of power, thus dissolving the traditional constitution in which none of them preponderated. In *Cato's Letters* (1720-22), Thomas Gordon and John Trenchard asserted that it had been restored again in the Glorious Revolution, but that since 1688 the development of a financial-military complex had increased the power of the Crown at the expense of the other two elements.

Modern investigations of Harrington's proposition did not substantiate his claims. Although the majority of the Lords sided with the Crown in the Civil War, while most MPs opposed Charles, no great economic differences have been established between landowners who led the rival armies into conflict. The main positive conclusions to emerge were that the majority of the landed élite wished to be left out of the hostilities, but were drawn in by an active minority, ideologically divided by constitutional and religious issues generated mainly since the accession of Charles I. Most magnates hoped to preserve the peace of the counties over which they presided. County communities were resistant to the demands of central government throughout the seventeenth century. Charles I's levying of ship money, Cromwell's impositions of major-generals, and the interference of both Charles II and James II in local government by the process of *quo warranto,* all provoked reactions from the localities. Tension between centre and provinces only relaxed with a tacit understanding at the Revolution that the government would respect a large measure of local autonomy.

Divisions within the ruling class were more significant in generating political conflict than any struggles between it and other classes, at least until the late eighteenth century. When they resolved their differences and closed ranks, they could suppress agitation from below. Thus when they regrouped in reaction to the threat of social revolution during the Interregnum, they ensured the restoration of the king and their own ascendancy. They divided over the constitutional and religious issues posed by the prospect of a Catholic ruler. When the reality fulfilled the prophecies of those who had warned that the accession of James II would be a disaster, they again rallied together to oppose his challenge to their hegemony. After his flight and replacement by William and Mary they once more became polarized into rival parties, in an ideological cleavage which was to survive well into the eighteenth century.

Division was exacerbated by the rise of professional and business interests which were viewed as a threat by landowners. The emergence of a professional standing army, which predates the Revolution but became a fixture thereafter, and of a bureaucracy to sustain it, placed a permanent financial burden on society. To cope with this unprecedented situation, taxation had to be increased and revenue anticipated by public borrowing, the main direct tax falling on landed incomes, while investors in the national debt received attractive returns on their investments. There resulted a transfer of income from taxpayers to state creditors during the wars against Louis XIV. This provoked protests from the former, especially those who paid land tax, against the latter. Their complaints were skilfully and unscrupulously exploited by propagandists, chief amongst whom was Jonathan Swift. These argued that there was a conspiracy to bleed the mainly Tory landed interest to death, in order to line the pockets of Whiggish military and moneyed men.

Society absorbed these strains largely because the nineteen years of warfare between 1689 and 1713 were followed by twenty-six years of virtually undisturbed peace. Even when wars were resumed after 1739 they did not impose as heavy a burden on the country, because meanwhile Britain's resources had expanded, enabling her to sustain her recently acquired great-power status. Throughout the seventeenth century, with the exception of the 1650s when Cromwell presided over a military state, Britain was largely ineffectual in Europe. This was due less to a lack of resources than to a reluctance to make them available to the Crown for a dynamic foreign policy. By contrast, after the Revolution not only did resources expand considerably, but the political will to use them aggressively was much more positive and determined.

The buoyancy of the economy in the mid-eighteenth century may be attributed to long-term demographic and productive trends which can be traced back to the reign of Charles I. The period is demographically as well as politically distinct. It marks a breathing space between the pressure of a growing population upon resources which characterized the sixteenth century, and was to overtake the country again during the 1790s. The upwards trend in overall numbers was checked and even reversed in the second half of the seventeenth century. While the figures begin to rise again quite rapidly in the early eighteenth century, they did not outstrip food supplies until immediately after this period. Agricultural productivity continued to provide surpluses for export almost every year before 1783, though soon after that date Britain became a net importer of foodstuffs. The abundance of relatively cheap food during the reign of George II might even have produced a rise in real incomes, generating spending power which stimulated the manufacture of consumer goods. Meanwhile the commercial revolution, occasioned by demand from a rapidly growing affluent society in the American colonies and at home, also encouraged industrial growth. The industrialization which occurred from increasing home and overseas markets was nevertheless modest in comparison with the changes which transformed British society after 1780. At the same time, the performance of the agricultural, commercial and manufacturing sectors of the economy from the 1680s onwards was strong enough to sustain the development of political stability.

It has also been held responsible for the apparent disappearance of political agitation from the lower orders. Between the Levellers in the 1640s and the Corresponding Societies of the 1790s, there is hardly a whisper of the demands for democratic participation which they articulated so forcibly. Of course, the political aspirations of those below the privileged classes are notoriously difficult to fathom. It could be that the rift in the ruling class during the Civil Wars allowed humble men to enunciate attitudes which they held all the time, but whose expression was normally suppressed. If this is the case, then popular radicalism was not eliminated in the 1650s, but went underground, to re-emerge in the 1790s. Yet it is strange that it never came to the surface at all, even when the ruling class was again divided, between the late 1670s and the 1720s. The rival Tory and Whig parties appealed for wide public support in their frequent clashes on the hustings, but the crowds who followed their banners, or the mobs they used to intimidate their rivals, shouted their superiors' slogans and not their own. The participation of the electorate was an extension of the rivalries within the ruling class, and rarely generated any demands outside the dialogue between the élites of the two parties. This could account for the otherwise puzzling acquiescence of the voters in the curtailment of their rights by the Septennial Act of 1716, which reduced their opportunities to participate from one every three years in theory, and two in practice, to seven in theory and over six in practice until the General Election of 1784.

The ascendant Whigs not only evaded the electorate but passed such repressive legislation as the Riot Act of 1715 and Waltham Black Act of 1723. Yet though these measures provoked dissatisfaction with the Hanoverian dynasty, which even expressed itself in popular Jacobitism shortly after the accession of George I, this too took out an option held up by a disaffected section of the élite,

and not one which was spontaneously produced from below. Moreover by 1745 the lower orders, in England at least, demonstrated their acceptance of the régime and their rejection of the Pretender in no uncertain manner during the Jacobite rebellion. It seems that by then they had no quarrels of their own with a system which had not only eliminated subsistence crises, but was sustaining a modest improvement in their standard of living.

By 1745, too, the divisions within the ruling class had been largely healed. The fierce religious animosities which marked the Stuart period, and had brought politics to boiling point on more than one occasion, became lukewarm under the Hanoverians. The zeal which pitted Arminian against Puritan, or high churchman against low churchman and dissenter, cooled into widespread indifference during the eighteenth century. Although nonconformists were prevented by the Corporation and Test Acts from holding municipal or national offices, in practice the state acquiesced in their breach of these statutes, and indemnified them from prosecution for violating them. Despite an abortive attempt to repeal the acts in 1736, the dissenters remained among the most loyal subjects of the first two Georges. Their loyalty was strained during the War of American Independence, when many sympathized with the colonists. But it was not until the late 1780s that they began to agitate in earnest for the repeal of the restrictive legislation. Meanwhile the rise of Methodism had rekindled religious zeal, albeit mainly below the ruling class. And although Methodists were at first thought to be subversive, they remained staunchly loyal to the constitution in Church and state.

The dynastic disputes which had been an issue in politics since the Exclusion crisis were also finally resolved with the defeat of the Jacobite rebellion. To some extent the issue was artificially kept alive by Sir Robert Walpole, who accused the Tories of Jacobitism in order to justify their proscription from office. His successors either considered his accusations to be exaggerated, or that they were self-fulfilling prophecies, forcing the proscribed Tories to seek salvation from the Pretender, for they partially lifted the ban on the very eve of the Forty-Five. During the rebellion, the mass of Tories showed their preference for the Hanoverians rather than for the Stuarts. Although the Young Pretender conquered Scotland, the rebellion also indicated that the majority of Scots were at last reconciled to the Union passed against their wills in 1707. In the Fifteen, a significant proportion of all classes in Scottish society had supported the earl of Mar's stance against the Hanoverian régime. Thirty years later the Stuart cause found few supporters outside the Highland zone and the north-east coastal strip.

By the late 1750s the nation was entirely united behind the Pitt-Newcastle ministry. Opposition within Parliament was virtually non-existent, and the government could count on the support of all sections of society. Pitt even raised regiments in the Highlands for service in North America. In the succeeding decades, however, George III presided over the collapse of a consensus which he had inherited, rather as his predecessor Charles I had done. One of the causes of this was that sections of the increasingly influential middle strata of society felt shut out of decision-making circles.

During the seventeenth century, the professional and business communities had expanded enormously along with urbanization. Even the older professions grew. While the numbers of Anglican clergymen probably remained constant, their dissenting colleagues increased as nonconformity became accepted. The medical and legal professions proliferated after 1680. An enlarged military and naval establishment and bureaucratic apparatus also emerged. At the same time there developed a whole new world of finance in the City of London and in country banks, while economic growth added to the legions of merchants and tradesmen who were to earn for Britain the reputation of being a nation of shopkeepers.

These changes in the middle range of the social spectrum were to some extent reflected in cultural life. Under Charles I the Court was the centre of culture. The king was the greatest connoisseur of art ever to sit on the throne, and his taste was emulated by his courtiers. In their country houses they reproduced the Court in miniature. Even drama became associated with the Court, by contrast with the Elizabethan and Jacobean eras. Indeed so much were the king and his adherents identified with the arts that baroque architecture, Italian (and therefore Catholic) paintings, and plays were all condemned by Puritans not only for being sinful, but also for being associated with the Caroline Court.

Under George III the Court still provided patrons with a lead. The king himself patronized Zoffany and gave a pension to Dr Johnson. The aristocracy, too, dominated cultural life, with their Palladian mansions crammed with *objets d'art* brought back from the Grand Tour. Many professional and business men, who were in a dependent client relationship with the aristocracy and gentry, aped the landed élite, setting themselves up in houses in the country, or building town houses which emulated those in the new squares and terraces of Bath and the West End of London. In provincial Assemblies they pooled their resources to avail themselves publicly of the concerts and balls which the owners of great country houses could afford for their private entertainment.

At the same time the growth of the market economy freed many businessmen from their client status and facilitated distinctly bourgeois cultural activities. Clubs of all kinds sprang up in London and the provinces, catering primarily for the middle ranks of society. A mass readership for newspapers and pamphlets developed, particularly amongst the urban bourgeoisie, which made writers less dependent upon patrons and more reliant upon sales. Daniel Defoe pioneered the exploitation of this new literary audience, discovering and catering for its insatiable appetite for fiction as well as for news. Where the élite imported foreign works of art or commissioned their own portraits, the urban middle classes bought Hogarth's prints, which were specifically engraved to adorn their walls. Even the London theatres became more the haunt of the professional and business community than of the Court aristocracy and gentry, who preferred the more fashionable opera.

The political aspirations of this emergent middle class were articulated by John Wilkes. Although he couched his demands for the liberty of the subject in traditional language, their implications were truly radical. Wilkite rhetoric spoke of the balanced constitution as theoretically perfect, and merely wished to purge it of abuses. But middle-class demands for parliamentary reform were really challenging the system itself. They thus prepared the ground for the far more fundamental constitutional changes which were to occur after 1783.

Government and Politics:
England and Wales 1625-1701

John Morrill

Between 1625 and 1701 England and Wales experienced one bloody and one bloodless revolution. None of this seemed possible when Charles I was crowned. The position he inherited was a strong one: there were no rival claimants to his thrones; no organized religious parties to cross him; no recent tradition of lawlessness either amongst the political élite or amongst vaga-bonds on the margins of society. These were the problems which brought civil wars to much of Europe in the sixteenth and early seventeenth century, and which had threatened England in the past. Charles's reign did, however, begin with a reminder of the main structural problem faced by his predecessors: an inability to raise the money and resources to wage successful war. He fought

Charles I and his Court in Greenwich Park, painted by Jan van Belcamp and Adriaan van Staelbent in or very soon after 1632: in the middle distance, Inigo Jones's Queen's House is nearing completion and behind is old Greenwich Palace.

Spain (1624-30) and France (1626-29) but gained nothing. Worse, he tried to finance the wars by compelling his subjects to lend him the money Parliament had failed to provide, and by imprisoning without charge that minority who refused to pay. Parliament's response – the Petition of Right* – further embittered relations. Nonetheless the return of peace in the 1630s, the royal and national prosperity that flowed from England's neutrality in continental affairs, and the streamlining of royal government seemed to vindicate Charles's decision in 1629 to rule without Parliament*. He gave power to many critics of the duke of Buckingham (assassinated in 1628) and seemed set fair for a long and comfortable reign. Under the surface, however, there was much resentment. Charles's attempts to impose a uniformity of practice on local governors offended provincialist sensibilities; royal finances were cushioned only by the use of emergency powers, such as ship money*, in dubious circumstances; those courts* which had grown out of the royal Council (Star Chamber, High Commission) were used to harass and punish a small but vociferous number of protestors. But with the founding of the New England colonies, most of those who could not stomach royal policies preferred to emigrate rather than to contemplate resistance. Constitutional anxieties were, however, relatively minor. Few doubted that a limited reorganization of the powers of the Council and its offshoots, and a change of personnel in office, would restore stability. Religious anxieties mounted far more strongly. Charles sponsored a religious faction, led by William Laud, whom he raised to be archbishop of Canterbury. This "Arminian*" group smacked of popery in its beliefs and practices. Even worse, Charles seemed indifferent to the growth of Catholicism at Court. Those bred on tales of the Marian burnings, of the Armada and of the Gunpowder Plot, bitterly resented and feared the influence of the papal envoys and the news that the queen took her children with her to mass.

Nevertheless, resistance was difficult to contemplate. It took a remarkable series of errors by Charles to persuade even a minority of his subjects that he was deranged and unfit to govern. Charles blundered into a war with Scotland* and tried to use Irish and Highland Catholic armies (together with an English army largely officered by Catholics) to impose his will on rebellious Scottish Protestants. He even contemplated using Spanish and papal grants to pay for those armies. Charles was twice defeated by the Scots and was forced to summon Parliament. The "Long" Parliament* – the first ever which could determine the duration of its own sitting – saw itself as having a unique and unrepeatable chance to get things right. Constitutional grievances were quickly sorted out, though Charles's manifest ill-grace in conceding demands made his critics seek fresh guarantees. Such issues did not, however, provoke the passions which could lead to civil war; rather religious issues turned a crisis of confidence in the king into rebellion and revolution. A militant minority obsessed by fears of a Catholic takeover (fears given substance by the massacre of Protestants in Ireland) determined to replace the Church government and worship discredited by Laud and his allies by a more evangelical, disciplined form of Protestantism. Opposed to this minority was another minority of men deeply committed to the teachings and practices of the Church of England, or at least to the notion of a hierarchical Church order that paralleled and supported the political and social hierarchy. With the great majority dithering and petitioning for peace, these minorities took up arms and cajoled and bullied others into war*.

Petition of Right 1628
In 1626 Parliament failed to vote taxes needed for war; Charles I continued to collect customs dues (tonnage and poundage) and raised a "forced loan". Refusals to pay precipitated "Five Knights' Case" in which judges confirmed king's right to imprison men without showing cause. Parliament of 1628 responded with Petition of Right, asking king to declare arbitrary imprisonment and tax collection without parliamentary consent illegal. Petition also prohibited use of martial law and billeting of Buckingham's troops for French war. King assented 7 June, 1628, insisting that Petition merely confirmed old, not created new liberties.

"Eleven Years' Tyranny" 1629-40
(Or "personal rule" of Charles I.) King resolved to rule without Parliament and was nearly successful; only advent of Scottish rebellions (1638-40) forced him to call new Parliament. "Tyranny" of period has been greatly overstated; on the whole, decade was one of peace, cultural achievement, economic stability and expansion of trade. Principal grievance was probably not Parliament's rights but increasing encroachments of Laudians on traditional Protestant forms of worship. Critics of Laud such as Prynne, Bastwick and Burton were silenced by imprisonment (and punished by having ears cut off). Other grievances included raising money by fining those worth £40 a year in land for not taking up knighthood, and fines for those found to have encroached on royal forests. Grant of monopolies to companies for production of soap and other goods continued to be unpopular.

Ship money
Tax levied by Charles I 1634-40, traditionally paid by coastal areas for support of ships in navy; Charles levied it from these areas in 1634 but extended it to inland areas in 1635. Wealthy gentleman John Hampden refused payment but court case (1637-38) ended narrowly in favour of king. Resistance to ship money was uncommon, most paying without protest until additional burdens of Bishops' Wars. Parliament declared it illegal in 1641.

Prerogative courts
Courts directly under royal (rather than common law) control, these developed great powers under Tudors. Included Star Chamber, Council of North and Council in Marches of Wales, and High Commission (the last for ecclesiastical cases). These became increasingly unpopular in early 17th century, both because many MPs were

common lawyers and because these courts could be used to carry out unpopular Crown policies. Long Parliament disposed of Star Chamber and High Commission (June-August 1641).

Arminianism

Technically a term applied to teachings of Dutch theologian Jacob Arminius (1560-1609), who rejected strict Calvinist emphasis on double predestination. In England, term "Arminian" was often applied in looser sense to Laud, archbishop of Canterbury (1633-45) and his followers. Arminianism was associated with arguments for "divine right" of episcopal government, belief in limited free will of Christian communicant and liturgical reforms designed to improve "beauty of holiness". Seen as crypto-Catholicism by John Pym in 1620s, and became major grievance of 1630s. Ultimately it drove many Anglican supporters of episcopacy to support Puritan minority in Long Parliament and Civil War, leading to abolition of episcopacy (1646-60).

See **Bishops' Wars** (page 210)

Short Parliament 1640

Forced by need to raise money after first Bishops' War, in April 1640 Charles summoned Parliament for first time since 1629. When House of Commons refused to vote supply before Crown had redressed grievances, Charles dissolved Parliament after only three weeks. Sudden dissolution angered majority of MPs and led to great intractability of both Houses in Long Parliament, six months later.

Canons of 1640

Controversial Church laws passed by Laudian-controlled Convocation of clergy after dissolution of Short Parliament in May 1640. Canons declared legitimacy of many Laudian liturgical and doctrinal "innovations", reconfirmed divine right of monarchy and illegality of resistance to royal authority, instructing parish clergy to pronounce this from pulpit four times a year. Offers by Laud to repudiate canons early in Long Parliament failed to silence opposition, which encouraged petitioning for complete abolition of episcopacy "Root and Branch" (December 1640).

Long Parliament 1640-60

Summoned November 1640 on advice of Council of Peers when Scottish invasion forced Crown to brink of bankruptcy. After attainting Strafford, prolonging its own life against involuntary dissolution, enacting bill for triennial parliaments and

abolishing prerogative courts, Parliament set about religious and constitutional reformation, embodied in Grand Remonstrance November 1641, gradually driving moderates to support king. Led by John Pym and others, Commons gradually developed into an executive body. It soon lost faith in king who, after initial assent to reforms, attempted on 4 January 1642 to arrest Commons ringleaders. Failure of king and Parliament to agree on control of troops for repression of Irish rebellion (November 1641) led to final breach in relations and outbreak of Civil War August 1642. Purged of moderates in 1648 and expelled by Cromwell in 1653, "Rump" of Long Parliament was twice recalled after Oliver's death. When members "secluded" in 1648 were readmitted, February 1660, Long Parliament finally dissolved itself and prepared way for Convention Parliament to restore Charles II.

Nineteen Propositions 1642

Parliament's last major manifesto before outbreak of war two months later: severely curtailed royal powers, asserting parliamentary rights to approve royal ministers and education and marriage of king's children; also demanded parliamentary control of army, stricter execution of anti-Catholic laws, reformation of Church by synod, and closer alliance with Dutch and other Protestant states. Parliament undertook in return to grant king revenue. Propositions drove many moderates to king's side.

King's Answer 1642

Charles's reply to the Propositions was a moderate document. It argued that England was not an absolute monarchy nor a democracy but had a government mixed of monarchy, aristocracy and democracy, represented in Parliament by King, Lords and Commons. The survival of social order said to require preservation of this "mixed" constitution.

After four years of fighting (August 1642 to April 1646) the king was defeated. But his enemies were hopelessly divided. To beat him, they had had to use ruthless methods* that dwarfed the petty tyrannies of Tudor and Stuart monarchs. Since there were 50,000 troops in arms with pay months in arrears, no relief from high taxation or other arbitrary measures was in sight. The king tried to take advantage of the consequent disillusionment* by appealing for a return to "the old King and a new Parliament". The army leadership, backed by a handful of supporters in Parliament and in the radical churches* in London and the provinces, claiming that the sufferings of the people had to have a deeper, divinely ordained purpose, purged* Parliament to prevent a

See **Militia Ordinance and Commission of Array** (page 218)

Independents and Presbyterians

In strict sense, these names refer to religious parties in 1640s; Independents advocated church government by autonomous congregations, while presbyterians demanded a more rigorous, centralized government through local and national synods of lay elders and ministers. However, terms soon acquired political meanings. By 1645, "Independents" were parliamentary faction committed to victory in Civil War, "Presbyterians" committed to reaching terms with royalists as soon as possible. These groups not identical with religious groups of same names; many political "Independents" were presbyterian elders. Parliament set up a presbyterian scheme in 1646, but never fully implemented and from 1647 there was effective religious toleration.

See **County Committees** (page 219)

See **The Levellers** (page 232)

See **Milleniarism and the Sects** (page 232)

Pride's Purge 1648

Coup d'état conducted by Colonel Thomas Pride December 1648, on orders of army council, expelling MPs who wished to re-open negotiations with king after second Civil War. "Secluded" members included many former parliamentary stalwarts such as William Prynne. Purge allowed radical minority, in league with army leaders, to bring king to trial and execute him.

sell-out and put the king on trial for treason. Charles I was executed* on 30 January 1649. England was declared a republic, the House of Lords abolished, and religious toleration declared (the Church of England having been abolished in 1646). But after this initial revolution the radical cause atrophied. A series of constitutional experiments was tried: a sovereign, single-chamber Parliament* (1649-53); an assembly of "saints", men "fearing God and of approved integrity", handpicked by the army leadership (1653); a paper constitution imposed by the army (the Instrument of Government 1653-57) and a second one imposed by an elected Parliament (the Humble Petition and Advice 1657-59). The radicals believed in popular sovereignty but were painfully aware that free elections would sweep them from power and restore the monarchy. They wanted to broaden the basis of their support, but could not do so while their position rested on brute military force and on the high taxation needed to maintain the army. Oliver Cromwell as head of state* believed that the people of England were like the people of Israel in the time of the Exodus. They were now in the desert being led by God towards the promised land and it was his job to keep them on the path. Cromwell was willing to do anything – impose military governors* on the regions, imprison without trial, impose arbitrary taxes or stage *coups d'état* – which would have that effect. Government was "for the people's good, not what pleases them". This further alienated the majority of the political nation, who even offered Cromwell the crown in an attempt to make him more subject to the ancient rule of law.

Convention Parliament 1660
Following final dissolution of Long Parliament, elections were held for a new Parliament. The Convention Parliament (so-called because it met without royal summons) restored Charles II; granted him an annual fixed income in lieu of feudal dues; settled disputes over land confiscated in wars and Interregnum; and passed Act of Indemnity and Oblivion which ratified royal pardon to all persons not specifically excluded, for offences committed in previous twenty years. Its acts were subsequently confirmed by later Parliaments. Term "Convention" also applied to Parliament of 1689, which offered crown to William of Orange.

Execution of Charles I 1649
Following Pride's Purge, army grandees convened special High Court to try Charles I. King refused to answer charges of treason against people of England, because subjects had no power to judge king. King was found guilty 27 January 1649, and executed 30 January. On scaffold, Charles conducted himself nobly, reiterating principles of "Answer to Nineteen Propositions" and his devotion to liberties of the people. Regicide made him martyr of royalists and confirmed majority of England in monarchical sentiments. Several regicides were executed at restoration of Charles II.

The Commonwealth 1649-53
On execution of king, power lay with a sovereign Parliament of those MPs (less than a third) who survived Pride's Purge; its failure to agree on electoral reform before dissolving itself led Cromwell to expel Rumpers April 1653. Attempt by officers to govern through "Nominated Assembly" (known as "Barebone's Parliament" after one of its members) failed when radical members (especially Fifth Monarchists wishing to establish rule of Christ and his saints) abolished Chancery and attacked tithes and ecclesiastical patronage, regarded by gentry as property rights. Moderates dissolved Assembly December 1653, surrendering power to Cromwell and Council of Officers.

The Protectorate 1653-59
After collapse of Barebone's Parliament, Cromwell ruled England as Protector under hastily-written Instrument of Government. He had considerable difficulty with Parliament and his attempt to govern through major-generals caused widespread resentment among local gentry. Though he refused crown, Cromwell accepted greater powers under Parliament's Humble Petition and Advice 1657, which established a second house of Parliament and a quasi-monarchical court. Richard Cromwell succeeded Oliver as Protector September 1658; after brief, unsuccessful Parliament, Richard was deposed by coalition of army leaders and republican MPs, leading to recall of Rump and restoration of Commonwealth April 1659.

See **Rule of Major-Generals** (page 219)

Declaration of Breda 1660
Manifesto issued by Charles II prior to his Restoration: assured earlier opponents of him and his father of a general pardon, from which only regicides (and a few other parliamentarian ringleaders) were exempted; left problem of lands of Crown, Church and 700 royalists confiscated and sold by Long Parliament to be decided by a Parliament. Declaration also promised payment of arrears to army and measure of religious toleration to "tender consciences", which his first Parliament refused to grant.

Detail from the painting by the visiting Flemish artist, Weesop, of the execution of Charles I outside Banqueting House in Whitehall, 1649.

The second Great Seal of England, 1651, showing the Commonwealth Parliament assembled in the House of Commons.

See **Dissenters** (page 234)

Clarendon Code

Series of statutes of Charles II's "Cavalier Parliament" (1661-79), named after Lord Chancellor Clarendon (though he disapproved of large parts of it). Code re-established Anglican Church and ended Cromwellian toleration of sects and independent congregations. Corporation Act 1661 obliged town officials to swear oaths of allegiance, supremacy and non-resistance, to reject Solemn League and Covenant of 1643 and to take Anglican communion. Act of Uniformity 1662 installed revised Book of Common Prayer and Thirty-Nine Articles; about a tenth of all parish clergy resigned their livings, unable to comply with its requirements. Conventicle Acts of 1664 and 1670 suppressed dissenting congregations. Five Mile Act (1665) barred nonconformist ministers from going within five miles of their former parishes and of corporate towns, unless they took oath of non-resistance.

Test Acts

First of these 1673 excluded Catholics from military and civil office: early victims were Lord Treasurer Clifford and Lord Admiral James, duke of York (afterwards James II). Repealed in 1829. Second Test Act 1678 excluded all Catholics except York from Parliament. Acts were called "tests" because they required office-holders to receive Anglican communion, swear allegiance to monarch and his supremacy over Church of England, and repudiate Catholic doctrine.

The Cabal

Acronym for group of ministers (Clifford, Arlington, Buckingham, Ashley and Lauderdale) who controlled Charles II's Council 1667-74; less cohesive than name implies. Buckingham enjoyed support of Ashley and ascendancy till 1669, but thereafter lost influence to Clifford (a Catholic) and Arlington, eventually joining Ashley in supporting Country party in Parliament. Lauderdale ruled Scotland as High Commissioner, playing little part in English government. Due to pro-French leanings which produced third Dutch War, Cabal fell in 1673-74.

Despite his high-handedness, it was only his blend of social conservatism and religious zeal which kept country squire and russet-coated captain in balance, and, after his death in 1658, both the acquiescence of the gentry and the unity of the army collapsed. In May 1660 Charles II found himself called back as the only alternative to anarchy.

The Restoration settlement was a magnanimous one. There was a full indemnity for all but those who signed Charles I's death warrant. Former royalists and parliamentarians, cavaliers and Cromwellians were asked to share power in the Privy Council, in the civil service and in local government. The king was declared to reign by divine right, he was reinvested with all the powers his father had not freely surrendered, he was given a substantial income and a free hand to control the army. In practice the reforms of 1640-41 had removed most of his ability to bully local governors, and he had also lost the ability to raise emergency taxation so that he was even more dependent upon Parliament whenever he wished to pursue an active foreign policy. In fact, Charles II had more ability than ambition. His early manhood had been so consumed with passion to secure his rightful throne that once he sat on it all ambition was spent. Charles was forced by a vindictive Parliament, and by the response of the Puritan leaders, to abandon his plans for a broad Church* embracing a variety of traditions; he also failed to secure religious toleration* for those who did not want to be members of any national Church. Though he returned unsuccessfully to these endeavours several times during his reign, he always abandoned unpopular policies if the political temperature began to rise. He was clever but ruthless, allowing loyal ministers to be impeached by Parliament or driven from office, and allowing innocent men to be executed on evidence he knew to be perjured during the scares of the Popish Plot* in the late 1670s. Despite his flexibility, Charles would never surrender powers he believed he had inherited by divine right. When the earl of Shaftesbury tried to have the king's Catholic brother James excluded* from the succession, a constitutional manoeuvre that would have established that kings derived their power from a contract with their people, Charles resolutely resisted him. Intense political lobbying at the hustings and at Westminster led to a crystallization of two political philosophies and two parties*. The Tories were devoted to divine right monarchy, non-resistance to that monarchy, and the exclusive claims of the Church; the Whigs were committed to the Protestant succession, a monarchy circumscribed by Parliament and to a wider measure of religious freedom. Charles had an iron nerve, a solid majority in the Lords, and enough money to hold out against the Commons. He weathered the storm and lived to take revenge, proscribing his opponents from public life.

James II quickly squandered the strong position he inherited. He was a staunch Catholic with an unimaginative mind and a self-righteous manner. Until June 1688, he expected to be succeeded by his Protestant daughter, Mary, married to the Dutch ruler William of Orange. James certainly did not set out to establish a military despotism for their benefit. Rather, he determined to establish full religious and civil equality for his Catholic subjects in the expectation that there would be massive conversions to the Roman faith which in turn would make it impossible for his successors to reintroduce religious persecution. Equality meant far more than lifting of sanctions against Catholics, however. It meant setting up Catholic dioceses, taking over Oxford colleges as seminaries, and ultimately exempting Catholics from the Anglican Church courts and from paying Anglican tithes. It meant positive discrimination for Catholics in the appointment of army officers, civil servants, local governors. Initially, all this had to be done by prerogative action supported by the judiciary, which in turn had to be purged and purged again to ensure compliance. But to make the achievement permanent, James had to secure election of a Parliament which would endorse his actions; his efforts to obtain one led him to much more drastic measures including the sacking of three-quarters of all JPs and the remodelling of two-thirds of all borough charters. This constituted a revolution in office-holding far more extensive than anything attempted in the 1640s and 1650s. The birth of a male Catholic heir in June 1688 (though many persuaded themselves that the baby was a fraud smuggled into the royal palace), and the trial of seven bishops* led major figures from across the political spectrum to invite William of Orange to England to protect the Protestant religion and ancient liberties. William took a risk in responding, and invaded with an army less than half the size of the one James kept in readiness. Some Whigs supported William in arms; most Tories sat still, hoping William would succeed but bound by their belief in passive obedience and non-resistance to do nothing actively to oppose James. In the event, the king had a form of nervous breakdown and fled the country without a fight. William then demanded that he and his wife be made joint rulers. In a series of fudged compromises, this was achieved. The throne was declared vacant and William and Mary were invited to occupy it; they agreed to a Bill of Rights* which bound them not to repeat James's misdeeds; they granted religious toleration to all Protestants. The Tories looked forward to the restoration of the proper and divine order of succession after the deaths of James and William in the person of James's other daughter, Anne.

Popish Plot 1678
Equivalent of modern "red scare": normal fears of Catholicism, high in period, were exacerbated again in 1678 by allegations of adventurer Titus Oates of Jesuit plot to murder Charles II and establish absolutist, Catholic government under James, duke of York. Murder of Godfrey, the JP who took Oates's evidence, seemed to confirm Oates's tale; several Catholics executed for participation in conspiracy which later turned out to be false alarm. Plot was complicated by revelations that Lord Treasurer Danby had secretly negotiated with French king to provide pension for Charles.

Exclusion crisis 1678-81
Political crisis triggered by Popish Plot, involving attempt of elements of "Country" party, led by Shaftesbury, to exclude Catholic James, duke of York, from succession in favour of Charles II's bastard son, James, duke of Monmouth. Other issues included corruption of royal ministers and "management" of proceedings in Parliament by Court party, and fear of French-controlled arbitrary government. Elections for Parliament in March 1679 returned anti-Court majority

Titus Oates was presented as the Englishman who single-handedly exposed conspiracies aimed at the re-introduction of Catholicism. This print of 1679 shows the pope jumping with shock at Oates's revelations.

to Commons, as did quick dissolution and new elections. Exclusionists (called "whigs") failed to pass Exclusion Bill and turned instead to attack on royal ministers. In third Exclusion Parliament held at Oxford March 1681, Whigs openly campaigned for Monmouth's succession. Charles, having acquired a pension from Louis XIV, was able to dissolve this Parliament after a week and ruled without Parliament till his death. Whig leaders were disgraced, Shaftesbury fleeing into exile.

Whigs and Tories

Immediate consequence of Exclusion crisis was emergence of organized political parties. Under leadership of Shaftesbury the Country party organized nationwide petitions 1679 in favour of excluding James from throne. Opponents of these Petitioners were called "Abhorrers", but each party gave the other more lasting names: Petitioners called Abhorrers "Tories" (name refers to Irish bandits) while they themselves became known as "Whigs" (after Scottish presbyterian rebels of Civil War). Both parties survived crisis. Though Whigs were crushed in 1681, they later collaborated with Tories to depose James II.

"Seven Bishops' Case" 1688

From early in his reign, James II silenced Anglican ministers, set up a Commission for Ecclesiastical Causes (reminiscent of High Commission), and purged Anglicans from every level of central and local government. This culminated in the Declaration of Indulgence, giving full equality of religious practice to all Christians. Protests of Archbishop Sancroft and six bishops against royal order that Declaration of Indulgence be read from pulpits caused "Seven Bishops" to be tried for sedition; all were acquitted (29 June 1688).

Bill of Rights 1689

Act ratifying Revolution of 1688-89, declaring William and Mary joint monarchs, condemning James II for attempting to subvert laws of England, and excluding all Catholics from throne. Bill incorporated earlier "Declaration of Rights" offered to William, and established supremacy of Parliament.

Triennial Act 1694

Designed to ensure regular meetings of Parliament, at least once every three years, and to limit lifespan of Parliaments to three years. Earlier Act of 1641 demanded Parliament meet at least once in three years but set no limit to its length; this was repealed in 1664 under new Act which

By 1701, the desperately muddled and incoherent settlement of 1689 had been overtaken by events. In order to protect England from Louis XIV, who sought to restore James by force of arms, William had to maintain a standing army and a large bureaucracy, and he built up a body of "place men" (civil servants) in the Commons to ease government measures through the House. When the death of Princess Anne's last child in 1701 made the long-term succession uncertain, the king's critics took the opportunity of the Act of Settlement* to introduce measures to prevent the continuation of William's innovations. But two developments of the reign were of lasting significance. One was cabinet government*, a small group of ministers drawn from within Parliament, who enjoyed the support of the Houses and could guarantee parliamentary support for government business. The other was the creation of a National Debt*, that vast capital sum raised to wage war with Louis XIV. This debt was never to be repaid. Already by 1701, annual sessions of Parliament were required to raise the necessary taxation to meet interest payments. At long last, faced by the threat of a foreign invasion to impose popery and arbitrary government, Englishmen submitted themselves to universal, rational and substantial taxation. The bureaucracies of war and finance which had eluded the Stuarts were created to keep them out, and they gave the Hanoverians the means to conquer and to defend a world empire.

stipulated triennial meetings but made no provision for enforcing them (allowing Charles II to ignore it 1681-85). Problem was solved in 1694 Act, which was superseded in 1716 by Septennial Act.

Act of Settlement 1701

Statute providing for Protestant succession if William III or Anne died heirless: required sovereign to be member of Anglican Church, restricted him from leaving England without parliamentary permission. Act first named Sophie, electress of Hanover (grand-daughter of James VI and I) whose death in 1714, a few months before Anne's, left Britain to her son George I. Act also gave Parliament traditionally royal power to dismiss judges, and sought to inhibit cabinet government, "placemen" in Parliament, and other aspects of growth of the executive.

Whig Junto

Group of ministers within Whig party, the Junto held power under William III and later Anne. Giving support to Marlborough's war effort from 1696, Junto included Lords Somers and Wharton, Charles Montagu, earl of Halifax, and Charles Spencer, earl of Sunderland. Economic policies of Montagu during Nine Years War (1688-97) resulted in creation of National Debt and of "sinking fund" for its gradual repayment (never completed). From 1697 Junto governed weakly, at odds with William, until resignation of Montagu and dismissal of Somers (1699-1700). Junto

Whigs returned to power in 1708 during War of Spanish Succession, but increasing unpopularity of war and the Sacheverell case led to fall in 1710.

See **Bank of England** (page 225)

William of Orange landing at Torbay, 5 November, 1688. This engraving of the event was published in Amsterdam in 1689.

Government and Politics:
England and Wales 1701-1783

H.T. Dickinson

The Act of Settlement of 1701 confirmed the rejection of divine right monarchy in favour of parliamentary monarchy, imposed further limitations on the Crown, and guaranteed the Hanoverian succession. Supported by both Whigs and Tories, it was ultimately to pave the way for the balanced constitution and the political stability of the eighteenth century, though some of its terms were soon amended and the intense rivalry between Whigs and Tories continued for at least another two decades. The Tories were no longer so firmly attached to divine right, indefeasible hereditary succession and the prerogatives of the Crown, and the Whigs had retreated from any firm commitment to the original contract, natural rights and the sovereignty of the people. Nevertheless, there were still serious disputes between Whigs and Tories on a whole range of issues. The Whigs supported the Revolution settlement and were committed to the Hanoverian succession. They supported religious toleration for Dissenters and, though most parliamentary Whigs were landowners, they sought an alliance with the financial and commercial interests. Prepared to wage a land war against France, they were ready to face the inevitable financial and administrative consequences. The Tories, on the other hand, were divided about both the Revolution settlement and the Hanoverian succession, though most of them eventually came to terms with both. They were staunch defenders of the Church of England and regarded themselves as the representatives of the landed interest. Having little sympathy with the war against France (1702-13) they criticized its enormous expense and resented the way it benefited courtiers, financiers and military men.

Party rivalry was intense in the early eighteenth century, but developments which would ultimately assist the growth of political stability were already far advanced. The rapid expansion of overseas trade and the requirements of a state engaged in major wars abroad had led to a steady growth in the administrative machinery of government and a revolution in the system of public credit. The increased number of government officials expanded the patronage at the disposal of the Crown, and hence improved its ability to manipulate opinion and to manage Parliament. The creation of the National Debt, which meant that Parliament had to approve the large sums needed by the government and vote the taxes necessary to meet the interest on these loans, eventually improved relations between executive and legislature.

But the opportunities for political stability could not be fully exploited while the political nation remained sharply divided. Party rivalry did decline after the accession of George I in 1714, however, because the Hanoverians trusted the Whigs but regarded the Tories as tainted with Jacobitism. Abortive Jacobite rebellions* in 1715 and 1745 confirmed these prejudices. The long years of Whig supremacy under Walpole and the Pelhams did not

Sacheverell Case 1710
Dr Sacheverell was a High Anglican preacher of exuberant verbosity. His widely publicized sermon of 1709 advocated the doctrine of non-resistance and criticized members of the Whig government: the Whigs impeached him, provoking a barrage of Tory pamphleteering and riot from the London mob. Impeachment procured a slender Lords' majority against Sacheverell and a mild sentence: a moral victory for the Tories, contributing to their rise to ministerial domination 1710-14.

Fall of the Whigs 1710
The Whigs were damaged by cumulative war weariness: the apparent unattainability of the "no peace without Spain" demand combined with misjudgement over the Sacheverell case to weaken a government already undermined by manoeuvres of Tory, Robert Harley. He replaced Queen Anne's confidante, Sarah Churchill, with his kinswoman Abigail Masham, manipulated the pamphlet press and introduced disruptive duke of Shrewsbury to the government, persuading key Whigs to acquiesce in the dismissal of their leaders, Sunderland and Godolphin. With Harley supreme and a peace policy pursued, the remaining Whigs soon left.

Schism Act 1714
High Church Tories, mirroring the sentiments of the devout Anne, had repeatedly sought to curb Occasional Conformity (by which Dissenters could qualify for public office by taking occasional Anglican communion). Once in power, Tories were able to legislate against Occasional Conformity in 1711, and added Schism Act in 1714, by which nonconformists were forbidden to keep schools. This would destroy their existing system, and present educational monopoly to the Anglicans. With the Queen's death and the Hanoverian succession, it became a dead letter and was repealed in 1719.

Political journalism 1701-56
Savage exchanges on religious and war policy in Anne's reign stimulated sales and development of newspaper and pamphlet

satires, notably from Defoe and Swift. Peaks included Sacheverell Case and peace negotiations, 1711-14. Walpole (prime minister 1721-42) suffered e.g. from *The Craftsman* and from theatrical satire, responding in kind. Under the Pelhams, war was again a stimulant.

South Sea Bubble 1720
Dramatic rise in the value of South Sea Company stocks followed its link with National Debt 1719. Ignorance of a nascent City financial system, royal and government involvement and example of "Mississippi Scheme" in France inspired wild speculation and profiteering. "Bubble" burst but scandal at Court and government crisis resolved by Walpole's intervention (he was untainted), and by fortuitous deaths of Stanhope and Craggs.

George I and Prince of Wales quarrel 1717
Mutual detestation characterized relations between Hanoverian kings and heirs. A quarrel at the christening of the prince's first child signalled beginning of this cycle, promoting foundation of prince's separate establishment at Leicester House, thereafter focus for factious opposition to king's government.

See **The Fifteen; The Forty-Five** (pages 212-213)

Excise Crisis 1733
Walpole utilized control of Commons through ability, patronage and personal regard of the Crown (notably through Queen Caroline) to retain position. Land tax reduction appealed to landowning Lower House, but plans for a higher and inland excise to make up revenue shortfalls seized upon by opposition – who played upon fears of Excise authorities' powers of search and entry and of high prices, to incite mob pressure and Commons dislike – forcing Walpole's retreat.

Walpole's resignation 1742
Cabinet disloyalty (manifested in the Excise Crisis 1733 and defection of episcopal support in the Lords 1736 and 1737) combined with ill health to weaken Walpole's political domination. Although death of ally, Queen Caroline, may have strengthened his direct links with George II, royal confidence was insufficient against opposition focused around Prince Frederick. The opposition raised patriotic pressure over Spanish atrocities, forcing Walpole into war 1739. Wartime inefficiency and electoral defeats drove Walpole from office, though he continued to advise George informally.

immediately destroy the Tory party, but did lead to one-party government in Britain. Divided and proscribed, the Tories ceased to be a viable, alternative government and could no longer find enough emotive issues to create a sustained opposition to the Whigs. Twenty-five years of peace, lower interest rates and land taxes, and the government's refusal to countenance a serious onslaught on the Church of England, enabled the Whigs to cut much of the ground from beneath the feet of the Tories. Since they were largely confined to the negative criticisms and obstructive tactics of the natural backbenchers, the Tories were reduced to being a permanent, but largely ineffective, opposition to successive Whig administrations led by Sir Robert Walpole (1721-42) and then the Pelham* brothers (1744-57).

Although the Whig and Tory parties survived into the reign of George II (1727-60), a measure of ideological consensus was clearly apparent in the middle decades of the eighteenth century. Both Jacobite Tories and radical Whigs ceased to have much of a following within the political nation. The majority of both parties defended the rights of private property and sustained an hierarchical social order in which precedence was given to the great landowners. They supported a political system in which the few governed the many and they stressed the inestimable virtues of mixed government and a balanced constitution. The constitution was admired as a mixture of monarchy, aristocracy and democracy, in the shape of King, Lords and Commons. Each of these institutions had a special function: the King was the head of the executive, the Lords was the highest court of appeal, while the Commons controlled the raising of taxes. All three institutions also combined to form

Broad Bottom Ministry 1744-46
The Old Corps, Walpole's followers, survived him, led by Newcastle and Henry Pelham. Complaints over conduct and expense of War of Austrian Succession and accusations of pro-Hanoverian bias were directed against king's minister, Carteret, and the Pelhams demanded his removal. George II resentfully complied, the resulting "Broad Bottomed" administration being so called due to the admission of country Tories to ministerial and local office. Attempted recruitment of Pitt and Chesterfield and royal obstruction provoked mass resignation in 1746.

Supremacy of the Pelhams 1744-57
After eclipse of Walpole and Pulteney, a mass resignation in 1746 confirmed dominance of Pelham brothers (Henry, and Thomas Pelham-Holles, duke of Newcastle). Pelhams combined strict government budgeting with responsiveness to popular national belligerence.

Satirical prints were effective weapons for critics of government. In this detail from Ready Money: the prevailing Candidate *of 1727 the bribery and corruption of 18th-century politics are indicted.*

the sovereign legislature. Because no one part of the legislature could control the other two, and because all three parts had to act in concert, the balance of the constitution was preserved. This complicated system of checks and balances was praised for establishing harmonious relations between King, Lords and Commons, and for creating an equilibrium between government and Parliament. The constitution appeared to achieve the greatest number of advantages and the fewest evils of any political system. It maximized the constraints upon power and prevented its abuse, while also ensuring that the people enjoyed as much liberty as was consonant with political stability. It was praised above all for establishing the rule of law and for protecting men of property from the twin dangers of arbitrary tyranny and mob rule.

While the political nation was almost unanimous in its support for these constitutional principles, there were many who were far from happy with existing political practices. To maintain the constitutional checks and balances, Whig politicians employed methods which alienated political rivals and smacked of political corruption. Political stability depended upon the skill with which the leading Whig politicians managed to control the two main components of the political system: the Court and the House of Commons. The king had to be won over and political rivals dominated or outmanoeuvred. Although admiration for the constitution, loyalty to the king, and a lingering attachment to Whig principles could be found among many MPs, these attitudes were not enough to guarantee any government a majority in the House of Commons. Ministers also had to appeal to ambition and self-interest. It was their influence at Court that enabled the chief ministers to exploit the extensive patronage available to the Crown. This patronage could be used to build up a body of supporters (the Court and Treasury party) in the House of Commons. Other means had to be employed, however, to win over the independent back-benchers who made up a majority of the Commons. Subtle man-management and expert knowledge of parliamentary procedure were essential. Able ministers also made shrewd assessment of what was politically feasible and careful calculations of how to manipulate and influence opinion in Parliament and across the nation at large. Sufficient taxes had to be raised without creating widespread resistance. Order had to be maintained at home, while Britain's vital interests abroad had to be promoted. Powerful vested interests had to be allowed to secure the legislation which they desired from Parliament, while remaining free from too much government interference in their own affairs.

Septennial Act 1716
By extending length of Parliaments to up to seven years, Act gave stability to 18th-century political system. Lengthy tenure of MPs increased value of parliamentary seats while lessening accountability to electorate. This stimulated the use of patronage and corruption in elections.

The Idea of a Patriot King 1749
Political treatise by Bolingbroke, written 1738, published 1749. Against picture of corrupt government leading to ruin of England, set ideal of revived and disinterested royal government under a "patriot king", who would maintain constitution and serve all. Said to have influenced earl of Bute and his pupil, George III.

Political journalism 1756-83
War in 1756-63 encouraged journalism. Government propaganda in the *Briton* inspired Wilkes and promoted debate on press freedom. Letters dominated a proliferating newspaper press, notably from "Junius". This fluent critic of Grafton's and North's ministries (1769-72) is usually assumed to have been Philip Francis. In 1771 a city- and Wilkes-inspired campaign secured *de facto* reportage of parliamentary debates which, with literary and theatrical affairs, came to replace the political letter. The scandal sheet predominated.

Ministerial instability 1760-70
George III, influenced by Leicester House hatreds fanned by his tutor Bute, repudiated his grandfather's ministers, Pitt and Newcastle, and their war policy. Whigs resorted to nuisance tactics and press warfare. Their suspicions bedevilled George's search for an acceptable prime minister: Pitt's maverick behaviour in and out of office, Grenville's insensitivity, the Rockinghams' naivety, and Grafton's incompetence combined with genuine clashes of principle and mob activity (arising from post-war depression) to produce political chaos. Ultimately resolved under amiable Lord North, acceptable to both Parliament and king.

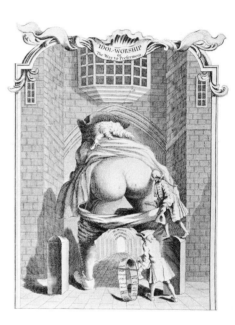

Idol Worship or the Way to Preferment, *1740, shows candidates for high office kissing the bare backside of Sir Robert Walpole before entering the Palace of Westminster.*

The Vision or Ministerial Monster *in 1762 depicts Prime Minister Bute as a hideous monster destroying English rights, while breast-feeding ragged fellow Scotsmen.*

The North Briton case 1763
Disgruntled office-seeker and journalist, John Wilkes, used the *North Briton* as a mouthpiece for his whiggish patrons: scurrilously critical of the Peace of Paris, he provoked arrest for seditious libel. Use of archaic General Warrants procedure misfired, resulting in Wilkes' acquittal and successful action for wrongful arrest.

Middlesex elections 1768 and 1769
John Wilkes elected to Parliament at Middlesex 1768, but, imprisoned on old charges, was repeatedly expelled from a privilege-conscious Commons. Violence at Brentford and St George's Fields. Wilkite movement gained momentum, linked with American grievances and backed by city politicians and radicals. It comprehended many petitions, culminating in that of Middlesex 1770, middle-class support and working-class violence and riot. Wilkes remained excluded from Parliament till 1774. Demands for parliamentary reform ignored.

The Yorkshire Movement 1779-80
Demands for parliamentary reform and radicalism were muted by Wilkite split of 1771 and patriotic majorities of North's government. Christopher Wyvill led Yorkshire or Petitioning Movement which soon spread, enshrining landowning discontent at high taxes, government failures in war and county under-representation. Preceded by a Wilkite revival in the Middlesex election of 1779, it was taken up by parliamentary oppositionists. But Rockinghamites mainly concentrated on economical reform, culminating in Dunning's motion on Crown influence 1780 and Burke's 1782 reform.

See **Boston Tea Party; American War of Independence** (page 224)

Fox-North coalition 1783
Defeat in America brought opposition Whigs back to power. When Rockingham died 1782, Shelburne and Fox quarrelled over the peace negotiations; Fox resigned, but combined with North to oust Shelburne and "storm the closet". When the apparently cynical coalition seemed to engross Indian patronage in the 1783 East India Bill, George removed them, appointing the youthful Pitt.

Political methods such as these meant that people with power and influence could prosper, while those without such advantages were ignored or defeated. This encouraged the latter to claim that the balance of the constitution was being seriously, perhaps fatally, disturbed by the power of the Crown. Extensive Crown patronage was seen as creating a new threat of arbitrary power. Ambitious ministers were in a position to corrupt public life and to undermine the independence of Parliament. Electors were being bribed, while places, pensions and sinecures were offered as rewards for those MPs who would support the ministry's policies. If this situation were allowed to go unchecked, Parliament might continue to exist, but its power to influence and restrain the Crown would be destroyed. The spirit of patriotism* and the love of liberty in the nation would be sapped by the corrupting effect of money and ambition. These sentiments formed the basis for the opposition to Walpole, and were expressed by Gay, Pope, Swift and Bolingbroke.

But it was in the reign of George III (1760-1820) that a more vigorous opposition arose, with the aim of reducing Crown patronage and achieving a radical reform of Parliament. The new king failed to achieve harmonious relations with leading politicians, and there was a decade of instability* (1760-70); John Wilkes* voiced the grievances of the middling orders; and the loss of the American colonies* (from 1776) humiliated the government and alarmed the nation. The result was a vocal, organized and widespread opposition. By 1780 there were demands for a reduction in Crown patronage to eliminate political corruption, and a reform of Parliament* to widen the political nation. And yet, by 1783, this reform movement was already in decline and support for the constitution revived. George III's new prime minister, William Pitt the Younger, proved to be one of the most able politicians of the eighteenth century, while the ending of the war without catastrophic consequences removed the issue which had done so much to fuel opposition. Political stability was soon restored on much the same lines, and by the employment of similar methods, as under the first two Hanoverians.

Scotland:
from nation to province

Bruce Lenman

Under James VI and I's rule after 1603, the Scottish Privy Council, which ran the country for its absentee monarch, evolved a pattern of conservative government well suited to the highly decentralized nature of the traditional Scottish polity and acceptable to the aristocracy, whose co-operation was essential. Though born in Dunfermline in 1600, the new monarch Charles I was brought up in England and at once displayed a genius for generating opposition in Scotland. His first move was an Act of Revocation in 1625 which cancelled all grants of Crown property since 1540 (before the Reformation), and rescinded all grants of ecclesiastical property, or the erections of such property into secular lordships. Though meant to secure reasonable provision for the "Kirk by Law Established" through negotiated compromises rather than confiscation, the measure deeply alienated the aristocracy.

From 1630 Charles quarrelled with his capital, Edinburgh, over taxation and his assaults on its burghal autonomy. Eventually, the Arminian religious policy of the Crown united nobles, burghers, and even the lower orders against Charles. James had employed bishops as viceroys only in "the dark corners of the land": Charles showed determination to make them dominant in central government. Already under James they had been used in the Committee of the Articles* to render the Scottish Parliament a mere royal rubber-stamp. When Charles ill-advisedly tried to impose a new code of canons (1636) and a new liturgy (1637) on the Church of Scotland by royal order, he offered his disgruntled nobility a priceless opportunity to check him.

In an age of inflation and inelastic rents, the nobility were economically, as well as politically, insecure. They do not seem to have intended to do more than recall Charles to the ways of his father. The sovereign's Arminian theology was widely distrusted as neo-papistical, but it was the elevation of royal and episcopal authority which lay at the core of a crisis exacerbated by royal stubbornness. The signing of the National Covenant* early in 1638 marked a further escalation of the confrontation, but in it the discontented Scots, ably led by nobles like Rothes and divines like Alexander Henderson, did not openly criticize the episcopal order in the Kirk. Only with the Glasgow General Assembly later in 1638 did they move to a presbyterian stance.

Since a purely presbyterian order challenged a central pillar of monarchical policy, war was inevitable. The two short 'Bishops' Wars*", finally concluded by the Treaty of Ripon* in 1640, marked the total collapse of royal policy. The Covenanting cause was supported by a wide spectrum of Scottish opinion from the Campbell chief, the earl of Argyll, to the future arch-royalist earl of Montrose. The Covenanting victory was to be sealed by a working alliance with the English ruling classes assembled in the Long Parliament, which was the single most important consequence of the wars. Under the leadership of Argyll, the Covenanters pushed through a constitutional revolution in 1640-41 in which the Scots Parliament was not only unshackled from royal fetters,

Lords of the Articles
Committee of Scottish Parliament, dating from 15th century but particularly important in this period. It organized and presented legislation to full Parliament, which could not debate or amend bills, only accept or reject them. From 1621 the Crown gained control of Committee through electoral system whereby bishops (all royal nominees) elected 8 pro-Crown nobles to committee, who in turn elected 8 bishops; these 16 then chose pro-government shire and burgh representatives. Abolished by Covenanters, the Lords were re-established at Restoration under system of 1621, but with less complete success. In 1686, Parliament actually defied a narrow vote of committee in favour of religious toleration. Committee was abolished in 1690.

National Covenant 1638
1636 Book of Canons demanded individual ministers' acceptance of forthcoming Book of Common Prayer and endorsement of episcopal system. In 1637 Charles imposed new Prayer Book, modelled on English book; it met instant objections by clergy, nobles and lairds, and riots in Edinburgh ensued. Opponents of Book organized into committee of the "Tables" to protest, issuing National Covenant in 1638; this bound all Scottish subjects who signed to resist ecclesiastical innovations unless approved by General Assembly. When Assembly met November 1638, it was controlled by presbyterians and abolished episcopacy, excommunicated several bishops and abandoned both Canons and Prayer Book.

Bishops' Wars 1639-40
So-named because blamed on English bishops, especially Laudians, who with king sought to reimpose the episcopal Church abolished by Covenanters and crush rebellion against royal authority. First war ended without conflict when Charles's lack of funds compelled Treaty of Berwick June 1639 satisfying neither side. After Charles failed to raise money from Short Parliament, he resumed war with Irish money. Scottish army invaded England, defeating English at Newburn and seizing Newcastle. Treaty of Ripon

followed; Charles was forced to summon Long Parliament.

Treaty of Ripon 1640

After occupying Newcastle (August 1640), Scots negotiated Treaty of Ripon (October 1640): Scots occupied six northern counties and were paid £850 per day by the king pending final settlement, which was concluded in London by Long Parliament (June 1641). Under this the king removed garrisons of Berwick and Carlisle, agreed to ratify recent legislation of Scottish Parliament, to instigate reform of English Church and pay Scots an indemnity of £300,000 before they left England.

Solemn League and Covenant 1643

Agreement between Scots and English Parliament whereby Scots aided Parliament in Civil War and Parliament undertook reformation of Church on presbyterian lines. Westminster Assembly of Divines included eight Scots but failed to agree on imposition of presbyterianism. Scots played active role in war and their cavalry helped defeat Prince Rupert's royalists at Marston Moor 1644.

Engagement and Scottish royalism

Engagement was 1647 treaty between Charles I and Scottish faction of royalists and moderate Covenanters, who agreed to restore king to power if he would establish presbyterian Church in England for three-year trial period. After disastrous defeat of Scottish army by Cromwell at Preston August 1648, power in Scotland passed to Kirk party led by Argyll, less sympathetic to king. But Charles's execution turned most of Scotland against English Commonwealth, leading to proclamation of Charles II. Defeats at Dunbar 1650 and Worcester 1651 crushed Scottish resistance; country was ruled by England and militarily occupied until 1660.

but was also effectively given power to elect the executive and judicial officers of the state. Charles acquiesced in these developments during a visit to Scotland in 1641, but only because he could see civil war coming in England and was desperate for Scottish assistance or at least neutrality. With the Irish rebellion and the subsequent seismic split in the English ruling class which was the prelude to the outbreak of civil war in August 1642, the Scots were placed in an impossible position.

Regional opposition to the Covenanters had always existed in the north-east (around Aberdeen) and in parts of the Highlands. The insistence of Argyll and other hard-liners that it was not safe to let Charles I defeat the English Parliament led to the Anglo-Scottish Solemn League and Covenant* of 1643, whereby a Covenanting army entered England to turn the tide of war. In exchange, the English Parliament gave what proved to be an unrealistic undertaking to move towards a new Church order for both England and Scotland, on a presbyterian basis. Royalism in Scotland found a political leader in Montrose who, with support from Highland clans and MacDonalds from Ulster, waged a series of brilliant campaigns in 1644-45 which ultimately collapsed in débâcle. Their terrible violence alienated Scottish opinion, but fatally damaged the Covenanting cause.

Further division followed when Charles I surrendered to the Scots in 1646. Argyll and the hard-liners sensibly handed him to the English Parliament, and withdrew into Scotland. The duke of Hamilton persuaded the bulk of the Scots nobility, despite bitter opposition from the Kirk and Argyll, to join together in "The Engagement"* (1647), whereby they invaded England in 1648 to try to restore Charles to power. This dangerous scheme, supported by all "moderates" met total defeat by Cromwell in battle near Preston. Argyll set up the last possible independent Scottish régime on a narrow basis, for the English naturally insisted on the exclusion of Engagers from political life. With the execution of King Charles in January 1649, any possibility of co-existence with an increasingly radical England vanished. Charles II was proclaimed in Edinburgh. He returned to Scotland first on the Covenanters' terms, but after the defeat of their army at Dunbar by Cromwell he benefited from a royalist

The Arch-Prelate of St Andrewes in Scotland reading the new Service-booke in his pontificalibus assaulted by men & women, with Cricketts stooles Stickes and Stones.

An engraving by Wenceslas Hollar of the riot that broke out in St Giles's Kirk, Edinburgh, in 1637 when the new Laudian Prayer Book was used.

resurgence north of the Forth, the new military frontier. An independent Scotland vanished when its last army, headed by Charles, was crushed at Worcester on 3 September 1651 by Cromwell.

Scotland was placed under commissioners despatched from England; heavily garrisoned by an occupation army disposed in several formidable citadels; and eventually totally incorporated in one Commonwealth with England and Ireland. Its economy was by 1652 prostrated by war, taxation, famine and plague. Its nobles were deprived of their extensive hereditary jurisdictions. Glencairn's rising in 1654 was confined to the Highlands and defeated, but it did frighten the Cromwellian authorities into more conciliatory attitudes to the Scottish upper classes. Some economic recovery came in the later 1650s, but the restoration of the Stuarts and of Scottish independence in 1660 was greeted with relief.

The Restoration in Scotland was as much a restoration of the nobles as of the monarch. King and nobility had reunited at the Engagement, and many ex-Covenanters like the earl of Lauderdale were prominent in Restoration politics. Religious dissent was a major and often a violent theme of the period. The Restoration Kirk combined episcopal and presbyterian features, but from the start about a third of the parish ministers refused to accept the restoration of bishops and had to be extruded from their charges. Despite several rebellions*, the régime of Charles II was more firmly in the saddle than ever at his death in 1685. Royal autocracy administered at local level by a nobility restored to its jurisdictions was helped by reviving prosperity and a run of good harvests. Many features associated with post-1707 Scotland – political reaction, cultural revival, and an emphasis on improvement – really date from 1660.

It required the inept heavy-handedness and strongly Roman Catholic policies of James VII and II to destroy Scotland's Restoration settlement. At the outset of his reign he easily crushed a rising by Argyll and his Campbells, but by 1688 his assaults on local self-government, in pursuit of his catholicizing policies, had so alienated the élites that they stood sullenly by while a minority

Rebellions of 1679 and 1685
After 1660 Charles II ignored his committment to presbyterianism and re-established episcopacy in Scotland, though without surplices or Prayer Book. Attempt to suppress nonconformist conventicles led to minor rebellion in 1666; despite Letters of Indulgence 1669, allowing banished ministers to return to their churches, many conventicles continued. In 1678 Lauderdale, High Commissioner, fearing rebellion, billeted Highland troops on south west. Following murder of archbishop of St Andrews 1679, major rebellion, in which Glasgow fell to rebels or "Covenanters". Rising was crushed by Monmouth, and its leaders executed or transported. Minor rising led by preacher Richard Cameron in 1680 was more easily suppressed. 1681 Test Act required all ministers and office-holders to repudiate covenants. Rebellion led by Argyll in 1685 in support of Monmouth against James VII and II failed to gain support.

Killiecrankie, July 1689
Battle between Highland followers of Viscount Dundee, in support of deposed James VII, and royal troops under General Mackay. Though Jacobites were successful on this narrow pass near Pitlochry, Dundee was killed, and his leaderless army disintegrated after failing to take Dunkeld.

Massacre of Glencoe 1692
Chief of MacDonalds of Glencoe had failed to take oath of allegiance to William III before deadline of 1 January, 1692, though he did so on 6 January. Lord Advocate Dalrymple ordered Captain Robert Campbell to make example of MacDonalds and kill all under seventy. Campbell's troops, billeted in MacDonald houses in Glencoe, massacred nearly thirty on 13 February 1692. Dalrymple was forced out of office; Jacobites (supporters of exiled James VII) suspected William III of having ordered slaughter.

Union of 1707
Failure of Scottish colonial venture in Darien on Isthmus of Panama 1695-99 blamed on jealousy of English merchants and Westminster Parliament; 1703 Scottish Parliament declared intention of choosing its own successor to Queen Anne unless Scots received equal trading privileges. Negotiations for complete union began 1706: Scots agreed to send 16 peers and 45 MPs to English Parliament in return for full trading privileges (and equal customs duties); they were recompensed for losses of Darien. Common coinage, but Scotland retained its law courts and laws. Union Treaty approved by commissioners January 1707. Scottish Parliament met for last time March 1707.

The Fifteen 1715
Scotland was centre of Jacobitism. In 1715, following Hanoverian succession, earl of Mar led episcopalian and Catholic Highlanders into rebellion, arousing

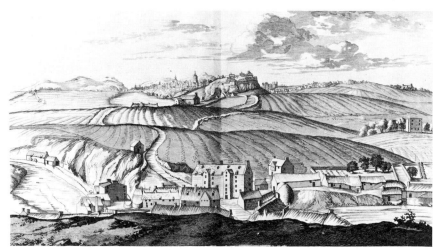

significant Lowland support. Rebels occupied Perth and Jacobites on both sides of border joined them. Pro-Hanoverian duke of Argyll saved Edinburgh from capture by Jacobites. At Sheriffmuir both sides fought a draw, but Mar retreated to Perth. Arrival of Pretender in December failed to stop desertions; James and Mar fled to France. Disarming Act removed further threat from armed clans, and estates of Jacobite landlords were forfeit to Crown. Further rebellions followed.

The Forty-Five 1745

Charles Edward Stuart, "Bonnie Prince Charlie", landed in western Highlands in August 1745 and raised clans, mainly from episcopalian and Catholic Highlands. Rebellion received little support in presbyterian Lowlands, unlike the Fifteen. Nevertheless, Pretender's army, led by Lord George Murray, captured Perth and Edinburgh. Charles invaded England as far as Derby, but soon retreated back into Scotland, followed by duke of Cumberland and an army of loyalist Scots. Charles's attempt to take Stirling failed and desertions began: by April 1746, 5000 Highlanders faced Cumberland's 9000 at Culloden; Highlanders routed. Charles fled to Skye and eventually to France. This was end of Jacobite hopes forever.

Scottish industrialization

By middle of 18th century, Scotland shared England's colonial trade; Glasgow became Britain's biggest importer of tobacco, and also imported large quantities of sugar and rum. Biggest industry was linen, production of which increased twelve-fold from 1728 to 1800. Tobacco trade declined with loss of American colonies and cotton industry grew, especially in Renfrewshire and Lanarkshire. Scottish iron industry developed from about 1760, though never as well as linen and cotton. Better transportation in form of wagonways and canals aided mining industry (particularly coal), while Glaswegian James Watt's steam engine helped industrialize all Britain; invention of threshing-machine by Andrew Meikle (1787) improved Scottish agriculture.

Left: *a view of Edinburgh from Thomas Slezer's* Theatrum Scotiae, *1689.*

Right: *detail from David Morier's vivid impression of the Highlanders' charge on the left wing of the duke of Cumberland's army at Culloden on 16 April 1746.*

of activists took advantage of the Glorious Revolution in England to overthrow Stuart government in Scotland. The first Jacobite rising under Claverhouse on behalf of James was poorly supported and collapsed after its leader's death at Killiecrankie* in 1689. As the Scottish bishops proved incorrigibly Jacobite, presbyterianism had to be established in 1690, at the cost of dissent by half the clergy. Freed from the tyranny of the Lords of the Articles, the Scottish Parliament proved difficult to manage. William III regarded Scotland merely as a source of troops and taxes. Scandals like the massacre of Glencoe* in 1692 and the Darien fiasco (when the Scots tried to establish a colony in Central America) led to pressure for incorporation with England, first from William and later from Queen Anne.

The need to secure the Protestant succession precipitated the Act of Union of 1707*. By buying Hamilton, the leader of the Scottish opposition, English ministers could push through a pre-arranged package, abolishing the kingdom of Scotland, but offering nobles, burghs, and the Kirk guarantees for their special interests. Unpopular in the country at large, the Union rapidly lost support among those aristocratic groups who had rammed it through the last Scots Parliament, partly due to economic discontent, and partly because Westminster promptly violated both its spirit and its letter. After an abortive Jacobite invasion in 1708, there was a very serious rebellion in 1715* supported widely in both the Highlands and the Lowlands and probably capable in co-operation with English risings, of shaking the Hanoverian succession, had it not been led so badly by the earl of Mar. A tiny Jacobite rising in the Highlands in 1719 was a fiasco, but with considerable economic growth by the 1740s, especially in mining, and the cattle and linen trades, the Union settlement grew secure, and the Forty-Five*, though it reached Derby, was an unsuccessful *coup* by a minority of Highlanders led by Prince Charles Edward Stuart, and not a national rising. Prosperity did not come because of the Union, but it did come in time to save it. The growth of Glasgow, by the Atlantic trades and the linen industry, is a good indicator: it had 13,000 inhabitants in 1708, but 43,000 by 1780.

The ancient heritable jurisdictions of Scotland were abolished by statute in 1747. The forty-five North British MPs and sixteen "Representative" peers at Westminster were a venal pro-government block elected on an increasingly corrupt franchise and intermittently organized by a political manager such as the earl of Ilay (later 3rd duke of Argyll, who died in 1761). Scotland's unusually large university establishment provided the basis for the intellectual efflorescence known as the "Scottish Enlightenment"*, while her economically resurgent nobles, including the ex-Jacobites, integrated themselves into the Westminster system by political subservience and by raising regiments to fight in the Seven Years War and the War of American Independence. By 1784 the forfeited estates were restored to the ex-Jacobite families. In North Britain the upper classes had become and have remained a junior branch of the British ruling élite.

Scottish enlightenment

Continuing dominance of Latin and, after Reformation, English, as languages of education and polite letters restricted native cultural development in Scotland, though her five universities (against England's two) allowed wider higher education. "Enlightenment" was signalled by opening of Advocates Library in Edinburgh 1682. Latin declined rapidly and interest in vernacular was revived, as in verse of James Macpherson (who "translated" Gaelic sagas of "Ossian", soon shown to be Macpherson's own invention) and later, in work of Robert Burns. David Hume's sceptical philosophy and his controversial *History of England* were important. A greater historian was William Robertson, whose *History of Scotland* 1759 and *History of Charles V* 1769 are classics. The Adams dynasty of classical architects produced notable work, and Adam Smith's economic writings were influential.

Decline of clans

The clans were an ongoing threat to peace which government resolved to eliminate. Disarming Act 1746 prohibited arms-bearing, similar Act prohibited wearing of kilt or clan tartan. 1747 Act abolished heritable jurisdictions, removing rights of chiefs to act as judges, and replacing hereditary sheriffs with Crown-appointed ones. Tenure by military service was abolished. Introduction of Lowland methods to Highland agriculture and rise of industry also contributed to death of clan power. By the time Jacobite estates were restored to owners in 1784, many clan chiefs had become absentee landlords. Lesser tenants farmed and fished on small, self-sufficient crofts, which stimulated individualistic economy in place of old clan collective spirit.

Ireland:
planters and patriots

David Hayton

The pressure of the early Stuart régime upon Irish Catholics eventually produced an eruption in 1641 when the Gaelic Irish rebelled and were joined by their co-religionists among the "Old English", the establishment of this united front, institutionalized as the "Catholic Confederacy", marking an important stage in the process whereby racial divisions in Ireland became subsumed into a simple religious conflict. It had been in an effort to make the kingdom more profitable, and to feather his own nest, that Lord Deputy Wentworth* had threatened the property of the Old English*. Fearing even worse from the Puritans in the English Parliament, these Old English took up arms, protesting loyalty to the king but determined to preserve their own rights, including that of participating in government through an Irish Parliament, in which they aimed to see their own position entrenched.

Their Catholicism prevented the Old English from making common cause with King Charles's army when the Civil War broke out in 1642, and by the time the Confederacy collapsed in 1649, permitting the royalists and some of the Catholic forces at last to coalesce, it was too late. In 1649-50 Cromwell

The Graces

Charles I's need for revenue for French and Spanish wars and his pro-Catholic sympathies led to attempts to conciliate Irish opinion: in 1626, 26 "graces" or concessions were offered, and in 1628, 51. These stimulated Protestant hostility and a reversal of policy in 1629 with a proclamation against Catholic religious houses.

Wentworth and "Thorough" 1633-41

Sworn Lord Deputy 1633, Thomas Wentworth pursued ruthless methods. Extorting parliamentary subsidies, yet reneging on promised concessions, he hounded "Old English" officials. In 1634 he forced the Church of Ireland to adopt the 39 Articles. Commercial policy, e.g. his tobacco monopoly and revival of plantation policy, offended most of the community.

A glittering occasion for the Anglo-Irish Protestant élite: the duke of Dorset's state ball at Dublin Castle probably in November 1731. The painting is attributed to William van der Hagen.

Catholic rebellion 1641

Discontent at Wentworth's régime, his removal, and crisis in London provided opportunity for revolt, beginning in Ulster. Bloody massacres of Protestants by Catholics, later exaggerated, reinforced traditional English anti-Catholicism and provoked ferocious reaction (e.g. "No Quarter" Ordinance, 1644).
Parliament and Charles disputed control of any army of repression while the Adventurers' Act 1641 encouraged Protestant private enterprise to seize Irish Catholic land.

The "Old English"

The population of Ireland can be divided into: (1) the disloyal "native Irish" inhabitants; (2) long-resident "Old English", subject to varying degrees of Gaelicization or Catholicization; (3) newer loyal English – Protestant, privileged and usually land- or office-holding; (4) recent Scots settlers in Ulster.

Drogheda and Wexford 1649

In 1649 Cromwell was appointed Commissioner for three years to mop up royalists and Confederates. In September he destroyed the Drogheda garrison and populace, part a deliberate policy of terror, part a response to the governor's refusal to surrender. Wexford suffered a similar fate, massacres and author passing into resentful Irish folk memory.

suppressed resistance with excessive ferocity, notably at Drogheda*. Ireland was temporarily united with England, Irish Protestants sitting in the Protectorate Parliaments, and attempts were made, through large-scale confiscation and plantation, to strengthen the English presence. However, while the "New English" element in the landowning class was substantially reinforced, the Cromwellian settlement failed to introduce the requisite substructure of English yeomanry. Only in Ulster was Protestant immigration to take place on such a scale, but the Scottish presbyterians there remained a separate entity, distrusted by the "English".

The restored monarchy left intact much of what the Cromwellians had done, a compromise on the land question confirming in possession many of the

Francis Wheatley's painting of 1779, showing the Volunteers, a radical Protestant para-military force, firing a salvo in College Green, Dublin.

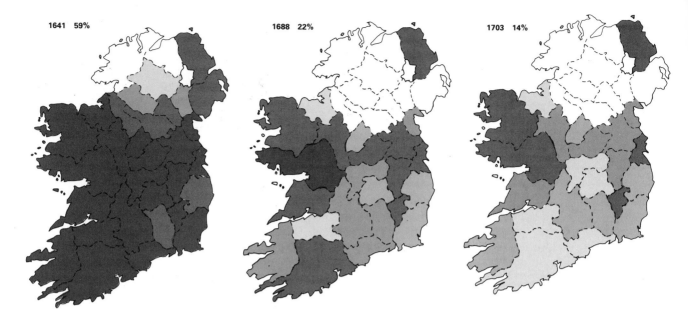

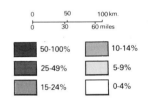

The proportion of land held by Catholics in Ireland

0	50	100 km.
0	30	60 miles

▓ 50-100%		▓ 10-14%	
▓ 25-49%		▓ 5-9%	
▓ 15-24%		□ 0-4%	

new planters*. High Anglican bishops regained control of the established Church after the Puritan interlude, though without being able to coerce the vast majority of Irishmen who remained outside it, until, in the late 1670s, the Popish Plot and the disturbances in Scotland obliged the government to take tougher measures against Catholics and presbyterians. Otherwise Restoration viceroys contented themselves with quietly developing the resources of the Crown. The accession of James II, however, brought a sudden and fundamental change of policy in favour of the Catholics, with the result that when ejected from England James found refuge in an Ireland controlled for the most part by his own supporters. His Irish Parliament in 1689, dominated by the Old English, reversed the land settlements and attainted Protestant "rebels" in turn.

James's counter-revolution perished in 1690 at the Battle of the Boyne, Catholic defeat bringing a further reinforcement of the Protestant landowning class*. The relationship of this class to England was now one of mutual dependence: a small minority of the total population, they relied on English military backing, yet were themselves the only allies the English had in Ireland. Thanks to the financial lever which the demands of imperial military strategy afforded them, they were able to retain their Parliament, from which Catholics were excluded, and develop it into a regular institution of government. The Poynings' law procedure ensured that bills were monitored at Whitehall, and the Westminster Parliament retained the right to legislate for Ireland, so that when Irish and English interests conflicted the latter prevailed. But Irish MPs could nevertheless do much for themselves, and might on occasion override the wishes of the English government in Ireland – as in their sabotage of William III's treaty with the Catholics and substitution in its place of a savage penal code designed to eradicate the Catholic religion and deprive "papists" of their civil rights.

In 1690 the planters still regarded themselves as "the English in Ireland". Gradually a sense of Irishness began to take over, and a brand of political patriotism similar to that of the American colonists emerged. All along, some Protestants had claimed a share in the libertarian fruits of the Whig revolu-

Act of Explanation 1660
Fleetwood replaced Cromwell, pursuing a "transplantation" policy by which thousands of Catholics were physically displaced 1654-55 in favour of Protestant migrants and demobilized soldiers who drew lots for Adventurers' land. The 1660 Act confirmed Interregnum land policy on Charles II's Restoration, excepting only royalists and "innocent Papists".

Navigation Acts 1662, 63, 67
Irish trade was formally subordinated to the Imperial interest: 1622 Act, restricting wool exports from Ireland; 1663 Act, directing and limiting trade with the colonies; 1667 Act, halting English importation of Irish cattle. Further embargoes, e.g. wool again, 1699, followed.

The 1688 Revolution
After James II's flight to France, he crossed to Ireland to rally support. Exhaustive *quo warranto* methods produced a Catholic Irish Parliament 1689, but the victories of William III and Baron von Ginkel at the Boyne 1690 and Aughrim 1691 resulted in the Treaty of Limerick. The Jacobite army

was allowed to cross to foreign service; religious privileges reverted to the Restoration settlement, soon to be overturned in Ireland by vengeful Protestants.

The Protestant ascendancy
Displacement of Catholic officials and landowners and subordination of the Catholic peasant majority to a Protestant caste of landowners and office-holders followed defeat of James II. Fear of Ireland as a back-door for foreign invasion, reinforced by French support of Jacobitism, led to tighter subjection. To Poynings' laws were added new oaths of office 1691, educational, military and penal disabilities 1695, an Oath of Abjuration 1703, and the savage 1704 "Act to prevent the further growth of Popery".

The Scots and Ulster
Wet years and bad harvests led to massive further migration of Scots presbyterians to Ulster from 1695. Although benefiting from 1719 Toleration Act, these and other nonconformists remained subordinate to established Church. First great Irish emigrations were those of Scots from Ulster in 1718, 1729 and the bad years 1739-41.

Wood's halfpence 1722-24
The acquisition by William Wood of exclusive right to mint copper halfpence for Irish circulation aroused intense Irish opposition, including the "Drapier's Letters" by Jonathan Swift 1724. These criticisms were grudgingly accepted by Walpole's government, which withdrew the monopoly and pensioned off Wood.

Protestant ascendancy and resistance
Despite Jacobitism's decline, the Protestant ascendancy was reinforced by a Declaratory Act 1720, explicit disfranchisement of Catholics 1728, and further measures on arms and education 1734, 1740. Agrarian agitators, the Whiteboys, rose in Munster 1761, followed by the Oakboys ("Hearts of Oak") in Ulster 1763, provoking Tumultuous Risings Act of 1766 and greater viceregal intervention under Townshend.

The Money Bill
Irish surpluses in 1749 and 1751 had been commandeered by Westminster government, but appropriation in the bill of 1753 was rejected by Dublin Parliament, led by Speaker Henry Boyle and supporters seeking partisan advantage. They were dismissed, but restored by 1755. The agitation aroused patriotic enthusiasm and alarmed the English.

tion, setting out the former Old English case for the autonomy of the Irish Parliament, though at first only a few would go this far. In 1697-1704 and 1717-24, there were protests in the Dublin Parliament and the country at large against the "oppressions" of England, mainly in economic matters*, without any real political support for the idea of "independency". Such effusions were usually provoked by transient economic crises: timely concessions, or the diversion of Irish energies into different channels (as when Irishmen became absorbed in the party struggles of Whigs and Tories in Anne's reign) would staunch them. In the first half of the eighteenth century, the Irish political classes were content to work within a constitutional framework which gave them security, a say in legislation, and, via the "undertaker system" (by which viceroys contracted out parliamentary management to local politicians), a reasonable share in patronage, in quantity if not always in quality.

This consensus began to break down in the 1750s, which witnessed another patriotic convulsion, the so-called "Money Bill"* dispute. Here the patriotism was more strident, the constitutional issue clearer, and the agitation accompanied by a failure in parliamentary management stark enough to prompt English ministers to reappraise their approach. There was talk of reducing the influence of "undertakers"; more radically, of union as a possible solution. The viceroyalty of Lord Townshend*, 1767-72, saw a successful, though unpremeditated, campaign against the "undertakers". Unfortunately Townshend's recovery of the reins of management only underlined the reality of Ireland's subordination and thus stoked the patriotic fire. The American example, the withering of fears of popery as the Jacobite threat subsided, the politicization of the Ulster presbyterians, so long excluded from the establishment, all had combined to produce an atmosphere increasingly hostile to English constitutional paternalism. The Volunteer movement*, a Protestant pseudo-militia, demanded legislative independence* at bayonet point, and in 1782, through an alliance with the English Whigs, the Irish parliamentary opposition was able to secure this great objective without violence. "Ireland is now a nation", declared the "patriot" orator Grattan. In terms of political power, however, this "nation" was still exclusively Protestant.

Townshend and the Undertakers 1767-72
Townshend, appointed Viceroy in 1767, sought enlargement of the Irish army establishment. Exasperated by demands and obstruction from "undertakers" he by-passed them, using patronage and pensions to build a new "Castle" party, assisted partly by the new MPs of the Irish Octennial Act 1768. His rule was marred by Steelboy ("Hearts of Steel") disturbances in Ulster 1769-70, parliamentary opposition, the rejection of a money bill 1768 and riots in Dublin, 1771.

The Volunteers 1778-83
Irish Protestants had been disgruntled by Townshend's heavy-handedness, and by the rejection of an absentee landlords' tax 1773, while American economic and political agitation and the terms of North's 1775 and 1778 peace overtures were noted. The first

Belfast Volunteers formed in 1778, and other groups followed: ostensibly to combat the threat of French invasion, this armed Protestant militia threatened an English government beset by difficulties.

Legislative independence 1782-83
North's ministry appeased an armed ascendancy and an Irish Commons (led by Henry Flood and Henry Grattan) which by 1779 was threatening to withold financial co-operation. A Catholic relief Act 1778 was followed by trade concessions 1780. Demands for legislative independence and an Irish Declaration of Rights 1782 were met by the Rockinghamite ministry. Further Catholic relief, and dismantling of Poynings' laws and 1720 Declaratory Act in 1782 were followed by British Renunciation Act 1783. Volunteers turned towards parliamentary reform agitation, over which Grattan and Flood quarrelled.

Warfare and International Relations 1625-1689:
wars at home and abroad
Ronald Hutton

For most of the mid-seventeenth century, England's effectiveness as a world power was reduced by three interrelated factors: the lack of obvious enemies and allies, the inadequacy of the governments' financial resources, and domestic instability. The opposite coast of the Channel was divided between three states. Two, France and Spain, were monarchies of dangerous strength and a hostile, Roman Catholic, religion. The former contained a Protestant minority who appealed for English protection, the latter possessed a colonial empire which tempted attack. The third power, the new Dutch republic, had in common with the English a Protestant faith and an interest in keeping Spanish power balanced by the French, but was also England's greatest commercial rival. To fight a war, the Stuart kings normally depended upon parliamentary grants, which required debate and could be denied altogether if relations between monarch and subjects were strained. At the opening of the century this taxation consisted of a percentage of an individual's reputed wealth, based upon assessments long obsolete and providing considerable opportunity for evasion. While the cost of warfare rose, the yield of these grants declined, and most MPs were too ignorant or too afraid of unpopularity for the necessary reforms to be made.

All these problems contributed to the disasters in 1625-28, when Charles I attempted to regain the German lands of his brother-in-law the Count Palatine, which had been occupied by Spain. To this end he attacked first the Spanish and then the French*, whom he hoped to coerce into supporting the effort against Spain. After a succession of petty failures, the king's military operations, and his reputation abroad, collapsed because his parliamentary grants proved inadequate. The resulting confusion and bitterness combined with political and religious tensions to make the partnership of King-in-Parliament unworkable in 1629, and Charles had to make peace abroad. His administration began searching immediately for a solution to its military impotence and found one in ship money, a levy made under the royal prerogative to improve the navy, which required a fixed sum from each county. It did much to solve both the problem of managing a Parliament and that of raising the amount required by the government. Upon its proceeds, an excellent fleet was built up, and Charles was about to renew the war with Spain in 1637 when domestic problems once more intervened.

The rebellion which broke out in Scotland in that year injected an enduring element of violence into internal English affairs, and intensified the problem of military effectiveness, upon which the survival of régimes, and not merely their prestige, now depended. In the Bishops' Wars of 1639-40, Charles's armies were so completely outmatched by the Scottish rebels that they never offered battle. This was partly because the insurgents were fighting to preserve their religion, which most Englishmen were content to permit them. But also, in their desperation, the Scots raised money and equipment by arbitrary

Amboina massacre
Traditionally close relations with Protestant United Provinces declined in 17th century as religious amity gave way to commercial rivalry. Ten English merchants on island of Amboina in Moluccas killed by Dutch 1623. Incident occasioned departure of East India Company from area, and may have been factor in cooling of Anglo-Dutch relations for next three decades, prior to outbreak of series of wars with Dutch. However, most Protestant commentators in England were prepared to overlook Amboina atrocity, regarding Dutch as invaluable allies in any conflict with Spain.

War with Spain and France 1624-30
Failure of Buckingham's Spanish match project left him allied with factions in Court and Parliament pressing James I to enter Thirty Years War on Protestant side. Maritime war with Spain ensued in 1624, and 1625 Cadiz expedition failed. Attempt to fight in Germany through mercenaries under Mansfeld and volunteer forces under Vere proved unsuccessful. English claim to search French shipping led to simultaneous war with France, with England ineffectively supporting Huguenot rebels at La Rochelle. King's ability to fight limited by failure to gain supply from Parliament of 1626. Murder of Buckingham 1628 and fall of La Rochelle allowed Peace of Susa with France 1629. Spanish war ended in 1630, and with it England's involvement in Thirty Years War.

Militia Ordinance and Commissions of Array 1642
Irish Catholic rebellion 1641 triggered crisis in relations between Charles I and Long Parliament, whose leaders dared not trust king with control of army. Issue of control of militia for domestic defence worsened dispute, Parliament passing Militia Ordinance February-March 1642, so called because without royal assent it was not an Act. Charles attempted unsuccessfully to enter Parliament's garrison at Hull and issued proclamation forbidding subjects to obey Ordinance. To raise his own troops, king issued

"commissions of array" to royalist leaders and gentry, reviving method used before establishment of county militias by Mary Tudor. Each side accused its enemy of illegality and both methods of levying forces proved unpopular.

County committees
Created by Parliament in 1642, to administer Parliament-controlled areas of country, subdue royalist resistance, enforce religious reforms and, above all, to raise finances for conduct of war. Controlled at first by important gentry, power gradually shifted to more radical lesser gentry as war progressed; many committees ruled with far greater tyranny than had Charles I, as did central committees of Parliament. Taxes included weekly "Assessment", a direct tax; an excise on most goods (including food); further funds were raised by "sequestering" estates of "delinquents" (royalists and, often, neutrals) who could then "compound" for their property with cash.

New Model Army
Parliament first organized armies into "associations" of several counties, and the main field army under earl of Essex. Early defeats and failure to press for final victory after parliamentary success at Marston Moor 1644, occasioned major military

Woodcut of a pillaging soldier, printed on the cover of a tract of 1642, The English-Irish Soldier.

means and so acquired these things with a speed which eluded Charles as he operated the system of legal levies. Parliament was recalled in 1640, and found itself resorting to an array of novel taxes to pay first the Scottish army occupying north-east England and then a force to put down the Irish rebellion of 1641. In 1642, however, Charles and the leaders of Parliament took up arms against each other, and the great Civil War commenced. Both sides were soon driven to demand fixed sums from counties* in the manner of ship money, and many of the rival leaders, like the Scottish rebels, fought with the fervour of men whose beliefs, lives and property were at stake, and forced the means to maintain their war effort from the rest of the population. The result was perhaps the most unpleasant experience that the English people has ever undergone, when about a quarter of adult males were in arms against each other and trade and the provision of justice ceased in many areas. By 1647 Parliament held England and the king, but faced Charles's undefeated supporters in Ireland, a strong party in Scotland disposed to ally with him, and a grave risk of rebellion by English royalists reinforced by thousands of civilians who wished only to remove the burden of the parliamentarian army. That army, however, had developed into a formidable machine*, led by men selected for merit and paid by unprecedentedly heavy taxation which it could itself compel. Between 1648 and 1651 it overcame all opposition, putting down a set of English risings* and conquering the rest of the British Isles. To ensure its continued survival, and that of its ideals, the army first coerced and then purged the Parliament which had raised it, and forced the abolition of the monarchy. During the following decade its hold upon the central government remained, while its army officers* played an increasing part in local administration.

re-organization, promoted by rising "Independent" faction in Parliament. All parliamentary armies united 1645 into "New Model" under Fairfax; existing leaders were forced to resign by "Self-denying Ordinance" prohibiting MPs and lords from holding commands; Cromwell, second-in-command, was exempted. Decisive victory over royalists at Naseby 1645 all but ended first war. Elite nature and Puritan inclinations of New Model soldiers and officers have been greatly exaggerated; army was successful because better administered (especially in terms of pay) than its predecessors. From 1647 army became politically potent, objecting to Parliament's attempts to disband it or send regiments to Ireland without payment of arrears.

Second Civil War
Charles I surrendered to Scots Covenanters 1646, and began to play off Scots against English, then Parliament against army. Failure of Charles to agree to presbyterian system for Church led Scots to surrender him to Parliament 1647. Following failure of negotiations between king and Parliament, army generals seized king; army then submitted "Heads of Proposals",

calling for electoral reform, biennial parliaments and some religious toleration. King escaped to Isle of Wight and signed "Engagement" with Scots (agreeing to trial period for presbyterianism in England). Scots invaded England in summer 1648 on king's behalf; simultaneous royalist risings occurred in Kent, Essex and Wales. This second Civil War was short-lived: Cromwell routed Scots at Preston in August.

Rule of Major-Generals
After dissolution of first Protectorate Parliament 1654 and brief royalist rising under Penruddock in Wiltshire, Cromwell divided England into eleven districts, each under a "major-general". Local gentry, the "natural rulers" of countryside, objected to this apparent imposition of direct military rule. Though most major-generals attempted to cooperate with JPs and other local officials, some over-zealously interfered in attempt to enforce reformation of morality. Heavy "decimation" tax on estates of royalists was used to pay for system, adding to its unpopularity. Second Protectorate Parliament 1656 forced recall of generals, but episode left lingering distaste for repressive Puritanism and military rule.

The military strength of Interregnum régimes enabled them to quell three revolts at home and to attack the Dutch and the Spanish in succession*, gaining Pula Run, Jamaica and Dunkirk. However, they underestimated the expense of these wars, while Cromwell courted popularity by permitting a reduction in taxation below the requirement of his military establishment. The resulting financial crisis played a great part in the fall of the republic. At the Restoration, the army was disbanded but Charles II inherited a powerful navy and the wartime system of tax assessment. These permitted him to attack the Dutch in 1665-67* and to win battles, only to be defeated by the cost of further efforts which his Parliament proved unwilling to meet. In the ensuing treaty he merely exchanged Pula Run for New York. The real beneficiaries of this war were the French, who, having already bought Dunkirk from Charles, were left free by the Anglo-Dutch conflict to destroy Spanish power in the Netherlands. The growing might of France provoked alarm in England, but Charles chose to ally with it* for a war of vengeance upon the Dutch in 1672-74. Parliament soon forced him to treat, and growing tension in domestic affairs left the English unable to wage foreign war for over a decade.

The weakness of public finance vanished naturally in the 1680s, when a trade boom increased customs revenue sufficiently to support an army without parliamentary supply. This James II deployed against his subjects, to crush Monmouth's rebellion* and to enforce an unpopular religious policy,

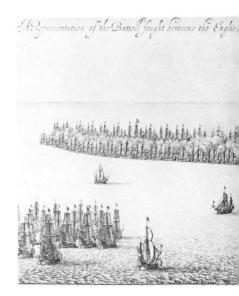

Engraving of the 1645 Battle of Naseby (from Joshua Sprigge's Anglia Rediviva, *1647), when the New Model Army achieved a crucial victory.*

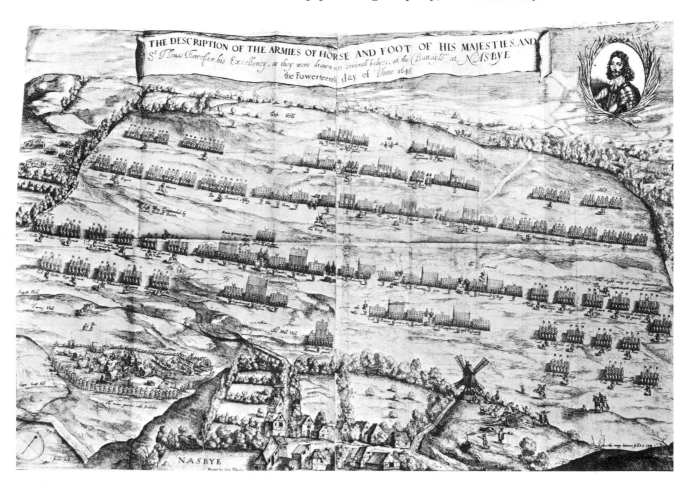

Hollar's engraving of the St James's Day Fight, 25 July 1666, when the English fleet heavily defeated the Dutch off North Foreland: one of the few English successes in an increasingly unpopular war.

First Dutch War and Spanish War

Interregnum foreign policy was more aggressive than that of early Stuarts. 1651 Navigation Ordinance attacked Dutch "middleman" role in colonial and European trade; strict enforcement by strong navy and demands for salute from Dutch in English Channel led to war 1652. Death of Dutch admiral Tromp and abilities of English commanders Blake, Ayscough and Penn forced Dutch to conclude Treaty of Westminster 1654: Dutch paid compensation for Amboina massacre (1623), and agreed to pay for fishing in English waters. Gains were soon squandered in war with Spain 1655-59, although England captured Dunkirk from Spain (sold to France in 1662); in West Indies, navy took Jamaica.

Second Dutch War 1665-67

Like first war, undertaken for commercial reasons. Initiated by English capture of Dutch colony New Amsterdam (now New York). Series of indecisive naval battles fought, the Dutch enjoying French support from January 1666. Poor finances forced English fleet to stay in port, allowing Dutch to sail up Medway and badly damage English ships June 1667. War ended in Treaty of Breda, which resolved very little. Short-lived "Triple Alliance" between England, Dutch and Sweden followed in 1668; Charles sought escape from this almost immediately.

Treaties of Dover 1670 and Third Dutch War 1672-74

Pro-French and Catholic tendencies of Charles II and some Cabal ministers led to alliance with France and agreement to attack United Provinces. By 1670 secret Treaty of Dover (of which only Clifford and Arlington were informed), Charles undertook to declare his conversion to Catholicism and eventually restore Catholicism in England. After Buckingham signed public, official version of treaty, omitting religious sections, third Dutch war ensued 1672. Money was raised for navy by withholding payment to government creditors in "Stop of Exchequer" 1672. Third war, unlike first two, was fought for diplomatic, not commercial reasons; English popular opinion soon objected, believing Catholic French to be true enemies. Fall of Cabal

leaving Louis XIV a free hand in Europe. The Dutch, fearing conquest by the French, invaded England in 1688 to secure its resources, or at least its neutrality. James, unnerved by treachery in his army and opposition in the country, fled to France to prepare a counterstroke.

This "Glorious Revolution" removed most of the checks upon England's effectiveness as a military power. It left the English endangered by an obvious enemy, the French, and allied with an obvious partner, the Dutch. It gave them a Dutch king, William III, who was obliged to surrender to his Parliaments many of the traditional royal powers in order to obtain their co-operation in a war effort. This shift in the constitution left the Commons willing to vote heavy taxation and to guarantee government borrowing, and the regular Parliaments which followed provided a means for the expression and resolution of domestic discord. It is part of a single pattern that the 1680s witnessed the last battle on English soil, at Sedgemoor, the 1690s the foundation of the Bank of England, and the 1700s the victories of Marlborough.

ministers resulted, though Charles continued war to indecisive conclusion of Treaty of Westminster 1674.

Monmouth's Rebellion 1685

Uprising against James II on his accession, with aim of installing on throne its Protestant leader, duke of Monmouth. Adherents, primarily from western counties, joined Monmouth on his landing at Lyme Regis, when he denounced James as an usurper. Trapped by loyalist troops at Bridgewater, Monmouth was forced into battle of Sedgemoor where he was routed. Monmouth was executed; some three hundred supporters were hanged after Chief Justice Jeffreys' "Bloody Assizes"; several hundred more were transported to colonies. Simultaneous invasion of Scotland by earl of Argyll was also put down with ease.

Warfare and International Relations 1689-1783:
a global power

Piers Mackesy

The Revolution of 1688 transformed England into a great power at the centre of the European stage. For generations her political will had been paralysed by domestic strife, and her growing wealth withheld from the Crown by Parliament. Constitutional changes now bridged the gulf between the executive which conducted foreign policy and war, and the legislature which provided the funds; and new financial institutions such as the Bank of England placed government's financial credit on a sound footing. A series of foreign kings strengthened Britain's connections with the European scene. With the accession of William III the country was plunged into a struggle with France which lasted off and on for 125 years, with Spain as a secondary enemy.

For a generation after William's accession Britain was engaged in almost continual warfare, in the War of the League of Augsburg* (1689-97) and the War of the Spanish Succession* (1702-13). England's first concern was to defend the Protestant succession against James II and the Old Pretender, backed by Louis XIV; but her common goal with the allies she financed, chiefly Austria and Holland, was to maintain the balance of power against the ambitions of Louis in the Netherlands and Germany, and then in Spain where the death of Charles II threatened a union of the French and Spanish crowns.

The Spanish succession was settled, after Marlborough's brilliant campaigns*, by the Peace of Utrecht. A Bourbon took the Spanish throne; but the crowns of France and Spain were to remain separated, and the Spanish Netherlands were given to Austria. Britain's power was now seen to be immense; but there followed a long period of what passed for peace, maintained by Sir Robert Walpole's understanding with the French Cardinal Fleury. Walpole had learned from the wars that the one thing likely to unsettle the now stable British political system was war, with its high taxation and contentious aims and strategy. Moreover, the long peace denied to the Jacobite Pretender opportunities to challenge the Hanoverian dynasty, which had succeeded on the death of Anne in 1714. These peaceful years, however, were punctuated by naval interventions in the Baltic on ten occasions up to 1727, either on behalf of George I's claims as Elector of Hanover in territories on the Lower Weser, or to secure Britain's supply of ship-building materials. In the Mediterranean there were two clashes with Spain over Spanish violations of the Peace of Utrecht, both resolved by superior British naval power.

Major war broke out in 1739 against Spain over commercial rights in Spanish America (War of Jenkins' Ear*), predictably bringing down Walpole's ministry; and it soon merged into a general European war (War of Austrian Succession*), in which French successes in the Netherlands were partly balanced by British colonial successes. The Peace of Aix-la-Chapelle (1748) left much unsettled, especially in the colonial world.

War of the League of Augsburg 1689-97
A continuation of William of Orange's feud with Louis XIV, whose aggressive policies forced the European powers into concerted action. 1688 Revolution reversed the Stuart policy of appeasement in return for French subsidies. The Jacobite threat was crushed in Ireland 1690-91, but at sea (La Hogue, 1690, Beachy Head, 1692) and in expensive campaigns on the Continent the English lacked decisive success. Treaty of Ryswick created a breathing space before revival of the Spanish succession question.

The Spanish Succession
A tenuous French claim to all or part of the Spanish empire remained unresolved due to the unexpected longevity of Charles II of Spain. After 1697, exhaustion and defeat inclined Louis XIV to caution: agreement seemed possible between France, Holland and England for the amicable division of the empire by 1698 Partition Treaty. William III feared the French threat would be reinforced by Spain's maritime resources and Mediterranean and colonial power. The death of an heir designate in 1698 brought a Second Partition Treaty, but Charles II's will entrusted all to French Bourbons. Louis accepted the will and antagonized the English by recognizing "James III".

War of the Spanish Succession 1702-1713
William III's ideals survived him. The Whigs, bolstered by Marlborough's victories and his wife's influence upon Anne, directed a continental and belligerent policy. Despite victories at Blenheim 1704, Ramillies 1706 and Oudenarde 1708, Marlborough was unable to counter public disenchantment over an expensive and apparently aimless war by decisive victory. Defeat at Almanza 1707 thwarted the allies in Spain, while heavy losses at Malplaquet 1709 and French revival at Denain threw allied war aims into confusion. The rise of Harley and the Tories to Anne's confidence led to temporary eclipse of the Whigs and a compromise 1713 Treaty of Utrecht.

Stanhope and Sunderland 1715-20
Accession of Hanoverian George I altered British alignments. His Whig sympathies and frequent returns to Hanover strengthened continental link. His ministers played on George's German interests, with Stanhope pursuing a vigorous policy of European alliances: with France and Holland 1717, Spain 1718, and Prussia and Sweden 1719. Naturally, opposition criticized the apparent pre-eminence of German over British interests.

The "Boy Patriots" 1737-38
Group of young, aspiring opposition Whigs, based on the Leicester House circle. They capitalized on Prince Frederick's wrangles with George II and Parliament over his household allowances, were reinforced by return of Bolingbroke 1738, and stirred public opinion against Walpole's pacifism and in favour of a war against Spain. They included the Grenvilles, Bedford and, notably, William Pitt the Elder.

War of Jenkins' Ear 1739
Possession of Gibraltar and of commercial rights since Utrecht soured British relations with Spain. Captain Robert Jenkins was manhandled by Spanish coastguards 1731; his testimony, fanned by "Patriot" opposition in 1738, together with cabinet pressure, forced Walpole to abandon his peace policy. Ill-preparedness of the navy contributed to poor performances and Walpole's resignation.

War of the Austrian Succession 1740-48
When Charles VI of Austria died 1740, Maria Theresa stood to inherit the Habsburg estate through the Pragmatic Sanction of 1713. German states repudiated the Sanction; so did France, entering the conflict in 1744. Britain supported Maria Theresa and Austria against France. At Dettingen 1743 George II became the last English king to lead his army in battle.

The Seven Years War 1756-63
Anglo-French imperial rivalry in India 1751 and North America 1753-55 drifted into war. Newcastle's search for allies linked Britain and Prussia: a diplomatic revolution. Early losses of Minorca 1756 and Hanover 1757 provoked public outcry, with Admiral Byng the scapegoat for Minorca. Brilliant young commanders, Clive in Bengal (Plassey 1757) and Wolfe (Quebec 1759), achieved military success, and there were gains in the West Indies: Pitt successfully combined "blue water" foreign policy, relying on naval and colonial victory, with continental subsidy of allies. But high land taxes, backbench war

Most dissatisfied was England's old ally Austria; and the eight years of peace which followed, disturbed by growing Anglo-French colonial conflict, ended in 1756 with the realignment of Austria with France, which Britain counter-balanced by an alliance with Prussia. The Seven Years War* (1756-63) saw Britain engaged in a truly global war with France and Spain. Overseas she won Canada, islands in the West Indies, and a pre-eminent position in India. In Europe she defended her colonial gains by protecting Hanover and keeping Frederick the Great of Prussia in the field under the assaults of four converging powers. To aid the Prussian ally, William Pitt the Elder attempted to hold French forces in the west by a series of coastal raids. These were inconclusive; and the defeat of the British-subsidized army defending Hanover under the duke of Cumberland (Convention of Kloster-zeven, 1757) gave France possession of Hanover and threw open Frederick's western flank. Even Pitt, who in opposition had railed at Britain's military commitment to the Electorate, was forced to intervene. From 1758 a British army campaigned in Hanover, which was saved from becoming a French

weariness and the partnership of Bute and George III led to Pitt's rejection. Bute's Peace of Paris 1763 was criticized as too generous.

Engraving (of 1735) showing the duke of Marlborough and Prince Eugene of Savoy advancing on French positions at Malplaquet, 1709. Although Marlborough had a nominal victory, the huge losses in a hard-fought battle contributed to growing hostility in Britain to further participation in the War of the Spanish Succession.

Watercolour by Robert Clevely of the occupation of Rhode Island by a mixed British force in 1776, during the American War of Independence.

bargaining counter, and after the battle of Minden (1759) Frederick never had to fight a French soldier.

Britain's strategic problem in these wars became increasingly complex. Priority for money and resources had to be given to the navy, since command of the sea was the essential condition of all other efforts: of security at home, colonial operations and the reinforcement of allied armies in Europe; and indeed of the trade and financial confidence on which credit and subsidies depended. Naval superiority over France had been won in the wars of William and Anne after a shaky start. In the War of the Austrian Succession the usual peacetime run-down of the navy to save taxes exacted its toll; but superiority was gradually re-imposed, and the principle was established that global command of the oceans depended on the home fleet blockading French naval bases, especially Brest. In the Mediterranean the acquisition of Minorca (1707) provided a base (temporarily lost in 1756) for naval and military operations. It came to be recognized that, in order to contend with France and Spain simultaneously, a two-power naval standard had to be maintained.

The priority given to the navy meant a shortage of men and money for the army. The British population was small compared with the French. While the navy could be manned by pressing, there was no compulsory service for the army; and some residual prejudice against standing armies left over from the seventeenth century checked the army's expansion. Its training in peacetime was disrupted by continual changes of quarters and dispersal to keep order and check smuggling; in war rapid expansion delayed its improvement. The need for large garrisons at home and in the colonies left very limited forces available for field operations, and there was bitter public controversy about whether they should be deployed to aid European allies or to conquer colonies. In practice a balance had to be struck between these alternatives. Colonial acquisitions were popular; and unlike most other powers the British government was highly responsive to public opinion, and to commercial pressure groups such as the East India Company* and the West India merchants. But in reality the value of trade with Europe was greater, and the risk of allowing France and her allies to extend their power on the Continent was too grave to ignore. The Netherlands had to be defended against France, and Portugal against Spain; and allies had to be gained and supported to contain the resources of France which could otherwise be diverted into a naval challenge. This meant troops as well as money: in every war British armies fought on the Continent, in spite of the British public's suspicion of its allies.

The necessity of European alliances was illustrated during the American War of Independence* (1775-83). After the Seven Years War Britain had become friendless in Europe, while France took a deliberate decision to avoid European entanglements and concentrate on exploiting her rival's colonial troubles. With a huge army in America, Britain found her Atlantic communications disrupted by the French navy, which entered the war in 1778, followed by Spain (1779) and Holland (1780). This maritime coalition succeeded in shaking British naval superiority. In the Caribbean several islands were lost; and the French navy's intermittent irruptions into American waters won a spectacular success by causing Cornwallis's surrender at Yorktown (1781). Though shortage of money and seamen eroded French naval power towards the end of the war, Britain's will to recover the American colonies had been undermined and the lesson was clear for the future: isolation in Europe could spell disaster.

Stamp Act 1765
After 1763, French menace removed from North America. Desiring political control, governments decreed stop on frontier expansion; retrenchment inspired the Grenville Molasses Act 1764 and Stamp Act 1765, a tax on official paper: all bitterly resented in America. Stamp Act provoked riots and was repealed 1766 by inexperienced Rockingham ministry, encouraged by British merchants and driven by Pitt's oratory.

East India Regulating Act 1773
Clive's military success in India and growing profits increased East India Company's political weight and led to politicking, mismanagement and stockjobbing at home, peculation and irresponsibility abroad. Overestimates of Company's assets brought a "bubble" of speculation and then collapse, with revelations of corruption, war and famine abroad, and banking crisis of 1772. North's 1773 Act included financial aid, some government supervision and attacked the buying of company votes. Burgoyne's accompanying enquiry pilloried Clive, who died shortly thereafter.

Boston Tea Party 1773
Charles Townshend attempted to tax America through duties on luxury goods. As with Stamp Act, non-importation agreements and violence ensued, culminating in Boston Massacre 1770. Dislike of extremism and commercial necessity brought calm 1770-73, with North repealing all but tea duty 1773. Arrangements to sell cheap Indian tea – helping the bankrupt East India Company and sneaking the taxation principle into the colonies – backfired. Dumping of tea into Boston harbour resulted in the "Intolerable Acts" 1774, which rallied American opinion. Crisis and war followed.

American War of Independence 1775-83
After early clashes at Lexington, Concord and Bunker Hill 1775, Britain needed swift success to discourage European intervention. An ambitious campaign marred by poor co-ordination ended with Burgoyne's surrender at Saratoga 1777. France, Spain and Holland entered the war. In 1781 successful combined Franco-American operation won the land war by compelling surrender of Cornwallis, isolated at Yorktown. But Admiral Rodney's victory (The Saints 1782) strengthened Britain's bargaining position at the Peace of Paris 1783.

The Economy:
towards industrialization

J.V. Beckett

Between 1625 and 1783 the British economy underwent a process of consolidation and development which, whilst not dissimilar to other areas of Europe, laid the foundations for industrialization. The positive reaction of the agricultural sector to low prices, coupled with a vibrant internal market, enabled England in particular to avoid the widespread economic problems experienced by most of seventeenth-century Europe. Industrial innovation, which had the effect of raising productivity, included such significant developments as Darby's coke smelting process in the iron industry (1709), Newcomen's and Watt's steam engines (1712,1763), and, in cotton textiles, Hargreaves' jenny* (1768), Arkwright's waterframe* (1769), and Crompton's mule* (1779). A world-wide commercial network was created, into which Ireland and Scotland were integrated. Both became highly commercialized, and exported considerable quantities of agricultural and manufactured goods through England to the rest of the world. All these developments rested on a sound base: favourable population and price trends, improved communications, a commercial infrastructure capable of supporting the trade network, generally supportive state action, and a "financial revolution"* brought about partly by the need to raise large sums of war finance.

Putting quantitative flesh on to the qualitative bones is hampered by the paucity of accurate statistics. For the eighteenth century, however, it has been suggested that agriculture accounted for perhaps 45 per cent of output in 1700, but only 33 per cent in 1800, whereas industry and commerce rose from 30 to 40 per cent over the same period, with the most significant change taking place in the last quarter of the century. The annual rate of growth accelerated markedly, from under half of one per cent in the period 1700-40, to nearly one per cent between 1740 and 1770, but little change occurred in the structure of national product: the major transformation of the economy was still to come after 1783.

The long population rise experienced by sixteenth-century England continued into the early seventeenth century, but from the 1650s gave way to seventy years or so of stagnation. Thereafter, the general pattern was of steady growth accelerating from the mid-eighteenth century, almost certainly as a result of rising fertility, which was partly the result of a fall in the age of women at first marriage. A similar trend occurred in Ireland and Scotland. Within these overall figures the most significant feature was urban growth. The proportion of the total English population living in towns of 5,000 inhabitants or more increased from 16 per cent in 1700 to 27 per cent in 1801. London experienced the most spectacular growth, its population increasing from around 400,000 in 1650 to 948,000 in 1801. In Scotland, the Glasgow and Edinburgh areas were the fastest growing in the second half of the eighteenth century, whilst in Ireland Dublin grew from around 60,000 in 1700 to nearly 200,000 by 1801, at which time Cork had 60,000 inhabitants.

Hargreaves' spinning jenny
Population growth and war boosted demand for cloth in excess of available supply, resulting in bottlenecks which encouraged innovation. Hargreaves' textile spinning machine ("jenny" after his wife) was patented 1768 at 16 spindles; by 1784 it worked 80. Together with effective steam engines, innovation in textiles, England's strongest traditional industry, brought increased productivity and enabled child and female to replace expensive male labour, thus increasing profits and capital available for further progress.

Arkwright's waterframe
A water-powered textile spinning machine, patented by Richard Arkwright in 1769; used from 1771 in his new factory at Cromford, Derbyshire. Frame was widely copied, leading to litigation to protest patent; a key influence in growth of factory production.

Crompton's mule
A machine for spinning yarn for use in manufacture of muslin; invented by Samuel Crompton in 1779, and widely used.

Bank of England
Need for unprecedented sums to finance Nine Years War with France led to formulation of permanent National Debt 1692 and of Bank of England 1694. Bank consisted of shareholders who lent the government money at interest; originally created for twelve years, it lent the government £1,200,000 at 8% per annum and £100,000 p.a. for expenses. Permanent charter granted in 1708. Bank issued its own notes and in 1750 assumed responsibility for National Debt, but its notes were not mandatory legal tender until 1830s.

Prices followed a similar pattern to population, holding steady or even declining from a high point reached in the 1640s at least until the mid-eighteenth century. Relative grain prices moved downwards, except in years of poor harvests, to a point where the 1730s and 1740s were decades of real depression in many of the corn-producing areas. It was only from the 1760s that population increase took up the slack in production, with a consequent increase in prices.

The effect of this stagnation in population and prices on the rest of the economy was considerable. Real wages improved as a result of falling food prices and an increase in money wages as the labour supply slackened. Part of this excess found its way into an improved diet, as a result of which the price of meat and dairy products held up when that of grain fell, and pasture farmers suffered less severe consequences in the 1730s and 1740s. What proportion of this surplus income was channelled into industrial products is less certain, although there was a long-term increase in the output of consumer goods at lower prices. Price evidence suggests a buoyant demand for home manufactured goods during the period 1750-80.

Despite these population and price movements, and in contrast to its European counterpart, the agricultural sector increased productivity*. Farmers sought to increase output to maintain their profit margins. They also responded to rising demand from the Continent for grain, from the domestic market for both meat and dairy products (consequent upon rising real wages), and from the growing proportion of the population resident in towns. Wheat yields increased from around 11 bushels per acre in the first half of the seventeenth century to roughly 20 in 1700 and to 22 by 1800, whilst corn output in England and Wales increased by 43 per cent during the eighteenth century. Even so, domestic consumption exceeded home production by the 1760s. English grain exports to the Continent dwindled, to be replaced by a net import surplus; Scotland resorted to bringing in supplies from north America; and Ireland solved its supply problems through the widespread adoption of the potato.

Productivity and output improvements were achieved in two major ways.

Agriculture improvements
Jethro Tull (author of *Horse Hoeing Husbandry* 1731) publicized more effective seed drilling and hoeing. Progressive farming became fashionable, and, favouring the great magnates, profitable. "Turnip" Townshend (after 1730 resignation from politics) reduced wasteful winter slaughter with root crops for animal feed. Later, Thomas Coke of Holkham; Rotherham, inventor of a modern plough; Arthur Young, author and agronomist; "Farmer" George III, keeper of a model farm; and Robert Bakewell of Dishley, scientific animal breeder, contributed to increased agricultural output.

Enclosure
Integral to the process of agricultural improvement, enclosure helped destroy the old "open field" system, providing for effective drainage, crop rotation, and hedging. Could be achieved by local agreement, but in 1760-93, 1611 Enclosure Acts were passed. These favoured richer, more extensive landowners: resulting suppression of common and grazing rights caused hardship, often riots.

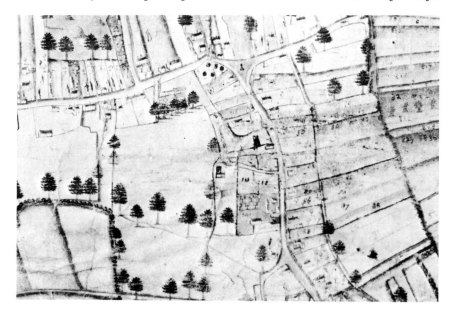

The village of Laxton, Nottinghamshire, as depicted on an illustrated survey map of 1635: the houses of the villagers, on two streets near the parish church, are surrounded by the numbered strips of the open fields and by pasture land.

Engraving from D. Loggan's Cantabridgia Illustrata *of 1690 showing barges delivering coal to Magdalene College, Cambridge, while the canopied "tilt" boats carry passengers for fares.*

One was the spread of "convertible husbandry", whereby land which had been permanent arable or permanent grass now alternated between the two. After seven to twelve years in grass, while the sowing of legumes (such as clover) combined with animal dung and urine to increase soil fertility, it was then ploughed up for two to twelve years. The quantity of crops could be as much as double that obtained on land in permanent tillage. However, this practice was most appropriate for light, easily worked soils of marginal fertility, rather than the old corn territory of the claylands where fewer opportunities were available for farmers to cut costs. The need to respond to this, and the growth of a national market for agricultural produce during the seventeenth century, facilitated the second means of improving productivity, regional specialization. Landowners responded to the prevailing conditions either by promoting the cultivation of labour-intensive crops, and market gardening, or, more widely, by turning down their land permanently to grass, in order to tap the more stable prices of dairy products. When marginal and waste lands had been converted, and the limits of enclosure* by agreement reached, landowners turned to legislation to complete the process. As a result, in the first period of sustained parliamentary enclosure, the 1760s and 1770s, the major concern was with open field arable, particularly in the midlands. In the long term this meant a shift in arable farming away from the wet clay lands towards the lighter, sandy and loam soils, many of which had previously been held as heaths and commons. Improvements of a similar nature reached lowland Scotland by the 1780s. Overall, the productivity improvement through the period was a result of more extensive, intensive and efficient use of resources, which produced a percentage increase in output during the eighteenth century approximately double that of the two preceding centuries.

Industry experienced few spectacular changes, but sufficient investment and innovation to suggest the passing of the pre-industrialized economy by 1783. Measuring output is hazardous, but it seems that England experienced brisk activity in the later decades of the seventeenth century, followed by somewhat slower growth in the early eighteenth. A renewed upward trend can be traced from the mid-1740s as technical developments and the use of power enabled industry to escape its major supply restraints. Significant regional specialization was also taking place, characterized by a long-term shift away from the south towards the north and midlands. This was typified by the decline of the Wealden iron and Devon cloth industries.

Textile production remained the major British manufacturing interest. The output of woollen goods was increasingly geared towards the European "new draperies" market. By the early eighteenth century, worsted stuffs from Norfolk and Yorkshire, flannel from Lancashire and stockings from Nottinghamshire had ousted the old export staple of kerseys, and was increasingly undermining the prosperous serge manufacture of seventeenth-century Devon. Linen was widely produced in Lancashire, as well as being the major manufacture and domestic export of eighteenth-century Scotland and Ireland. In Lancashire the industry was slowly transforming itself into its more famous successor – the cotton industry. Silk production, mainly in the midlands, was boosted by Huguenot immigration, protection against French imports, and the introduction of the silk-throwing mill.

Possibly the most notable industrial progress was made in the extractive industries. Coal mining was stimulated initially by the growing demand from domestic users – hence the benefit accruing to the north-east and west

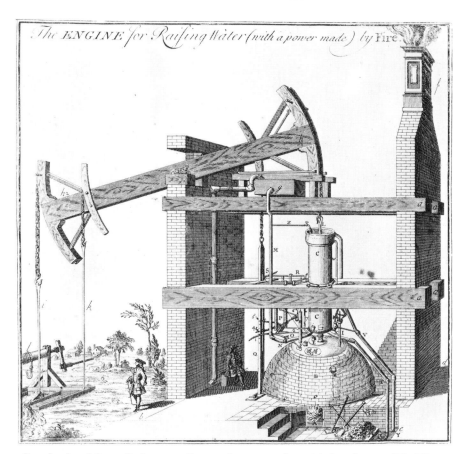

The ENGINE for Raifing Water (with a power made) by Fire

The earliest illustration (1717) of Thomas Newcomen's invention, the "atmospheric" pump, which revolutionized mine drainage.

Cumberland from their respective seaborne trades with London and Dublin – and later from processing glass, salt and metals. Total coal production may have risen from 2.98m tons a year in 1681-90 to perhaps 7.5m tons in the early 1780s. The industry benefited from significant technological advances in drainage (the Newcomen engine), ventilation, and the use of wagonways for transporting coal. Despite increasing productivity, the iron industry was still unable to meet demand. In the 1650s eighty-six blast furnaces were producing around 23,000 tons annually, while by the 1740s forty-nine were turning out 30-33,000 tons. Simultaneously, however, imports of bar iron were rising, at least until the increasing use of coke smelting* after 1750 enabled production to mount more rapidly. Significant industrial developments also took place in, amongst others, sugar refining, tobacco processing, brewing, the making of pottery, and shipbuilding.

British trade underwent a "commercial revolution" between 1625 and 1783, in which the mutual exchange of manufactured goods with Europe expanded into a world-wide trade of finished goods in return for food and raw materials, together with a large transit (or re-export) trade. Imports grew by around 400 per cent and domestic exports by over 300 (rising to nearly 600 with re-exports). Behind these figures lay a significant structural change: imports of manufactured goods grew by 17 per cent between 1699-1701 and 1772-74, but raw materials doubled, and the 400 per cent increase in retained raw cotton between the 1720s and 1770s reflects the significance of such imports for industrial diversification. On the export side, woollen goods fell from 80 per cent of the total in the early seventeenth century to 42 per cent in 1772-74.

Steam engines
Engines were invented by Thomas Savery (steam vacuum pump 1698) and Thomas Newcomen (atmospheric steam engine *c.* 1712), and widely used in mining. James Watt produced improved steam engine with separate condenser 1763, and in partnership with Matthew Boulton (from 1774) gained commercial success. Engines reduced demand for adult male labour, and contributed to industrial take-off of 1780s. Later revolutionized transport with invention of steam locomotive.

See **Coke smelting; Cort's puddling process** (page 272)

Navigation Acts 1651-96
Inspired by 17th-century economic theory of mercantilism. This assessed national wealth by gold stocks, achieved by favourable trade balances secured by a system of quotas and tariffs. Navigation Acts sought to exclude Dutch from English trade, and colonial trade was rigidly subordinated to English interests. The colonies were to provide an exclusive market for the mother country's manufactures and reciprocate with raw materials, eschewing trade with other countries.

East and West Indies trades

English trade with India began *c.* 1591: East India Company chartered 1600, reorganized 1708. Silk, calico, cotton and bullion imports were important but the tea-drinking boom crucial, despite the high duties. Clive's victories (1751-60) brought security and over-optimism. However the West Indies trade took precedence: the Asiento (right to supply slaves to the Spanish empire) granted to England's African Company in 1713, stimulated slave trade profits; the Sugar Islands were considered invaluable and were prizes in the many wars.

"The Wealth of Nations" 1776

Adam Smith's "gospel" of free trade criticized the mercantilist system's costly wars and imperial rivalry. By 1783, North had considered lowering tea duties, Shelburne advocated "reciprocity" with America, and Pitt the Younger was influenced by Smith. Landowners and the manufacturing lobby, led by Lord Sheffield and Josiah Wedgwood, were less enthusiastic.

Canal development

Transport in England benefited from relatively short distances, plentiful inland waterways and an established coastal traffic. Transport of coal was an important catalyst for improvement and the object of the Worsley-Manchester canal, built 1759-61 by John Gilbert and James Brindley, for the duke of Bridgewater. The duke was the most outstanding of a group of entrepreneurial landed magnates who could afford to invest in the expensive transport projects. Carriage by canals and rivers was slow, but competitive compared to roads.

Turnpikes

Turnpike trusts, empowered by Act of Parliament, could maintain and repair specific roads and charge a toll for their use. Nearly 300 such Acts were passed in the 1750s and 1760s, and another 400 before 1836. Trusts provided finance and some regulation, and stimulated the careers of engineers (e.g. Metcalf, Telford and Macadam). Other roads were generally poor and travellers were subject to the depredations of highwaymen and footpads.

A framework knitting machine illustrated in 1751 and based on the original stocking frame invented by William Lee in 1589.

Although linens, silks and cottons brought textiles up to 54 per cent of total exports, the real growth was in metalwares and other manufactured goods, up from 10 per cent in 1699-1701 to 44 per cent in 1772-74.

This import-led advance was made possible by navigation laws* and a protective tariff policy in the later seventeenth century, and by Britain's emergence from the Anglo-Dutch and Anglo-French commercial rivalry of the period 1651-1763 as the dominant power in the extra-European commercial world. The rapid rise of the East India Company's trade in the seventeenth century was complemented by the exploitation – partly through imported slave labour – of the north American and West Indian colonies*. As a result, America became an important "new" market for manufactured goods, the proportion of total exports sent there from England and Wales rising from 12 per cent in 1699-1701 to 42 per cent by 1772-74.

The development of the internal market, partly through the movement of coal, iron and foodstuffs, together with the extension of overseas commerce, was possible only as a result of subsidiary changes. Transport improvements were particularly significant. Between 1660 and 1750 some forty English rivers were subject to legislation designed to improve their navigability, while the 1760s and 1770s were the first decades of canal building*. By 1750 the major trunk roads radiating out from London had all been improved, and energetic turnpiking* activity over the following decades brought better roads to the extremities of England. Other consequences of commercial change included the expansion of the mercantile marine, greater sophistication in the conduct of the financing of trade (London became a centre of international commerce), and the growing importance of the outports, especially Liverpool, Bristol, Hull, Newcastle and Glasgow. Finally, this expansion of activity was helped by and in turn stimulated the development of sophisticated banking.

Society:
from crisis to complacency

Keith Wrightson

The first characteristic of society in Britain in the century and a half before industrialization was its geographical and social diversity. England, Scotland and Wales remained predominantly agrarian countries and their peoples lived for the most part in tiny rural communities, interspersed with small country towns and a handful of major cities. These were, to be sure, subject to the powerful integrating influences of government, the national Churches and legal systems and a steadily developing network of internal trade. Yet they retained much of their national, regional and local distinctiveness.

At the same time, society was highly stratified, encompassing massive differences in living standards and life chances. Contemporary commentators were well aware of all this. Some of them saw the social order as a finely graded hierarchy stretching down from the nobility and landed gentry to cottagers, labourers and vagrants and including a score or more of occupational and status groups. A less formal view of society identified three broad clusterings of social groups; "gentlemen", "the middling sort of people", and the "lower sort" or "poor". Both modes of perception were valid, though they emphasized different aspects of stratification. The former laid stress upon its complexity and upon the intricacy of the criteria by which social status was evaluated. The latter focused attention upon the existence of constellations of social groups which shared broadly defined but distinguishable social and cultural milieux. "Gentlemen" were above all the landowning élite, though gentility was also accorded to the wealthy leaders of commerce and the professions. The "middling sort" encompassed the economically comfortable lower ranks of trade and the professions, master craftsmen and prosperous farmers. The "lower sort" or "labouring people" relied for their living upon cottage holdings and wage labour in agriculture or manufactures. Their lot was to work and to obey.

Whichever method of description was preferred, contemporaries recognized that the social order was neither fixed nor rigid. It was subject to constant modification as the fortunes of particular groups waxed and waned, and it was open to individual social mobility. In broad essentials, however, it endured. As to the proportion of the population falling into any particular category, there was considerable national, regional and local variation. Those claiming gentility were always a tiny minority. For the rest, it can be said that England was distinguished by having both a larger proportion of prosperous "middling" people and a larger wage-labour force than either Scotland or Wales. The well-being of the "middling" section of society was frequently commented upon by foreign visitors: but by the later seventeenth century wage-labourers commonly constituted half or more of the population of particular localities.

The realities of social inequality were well to the fore in contemporary perceptions of society. There were also, however, strong bonds which softened the harshness of social distinctions. Most of these derived their strength from the intimacy occasioned by the small scale of life. Few rural communities

The seating plan of Myddle parish church, Shropshire, drawn by Richard Gough in 1701, reflected the social order of the community. Gentlemen, such as Mr Acherley, sat at the front, near the pulpit (top left); *yeoman farmers, including Gough himself, were placed centrally; cottagers and labourers occupied pews near the south door* (bottom right).

Act of Settlement 1662

Relief of poverty under poor laws was administered at parish level; 1662 statute defined eligibility for parish relief, and empowered overseers to expel paupers not born or employed in a parish back to their native parish. In theory, the poor were only entitled to aid from their native parishes, and officials would often use any means to get rid of wandering poor, evicting unwed mothers in labour to prevent bastard offspring being "settled" on their parish.

Hardwicke's Marriage Act 1753

Designed to prevent clandestine, hurried or fraudulent unions by clarifying confused marital law of England. The publication of banns, explicit residence requirements and notice of parental approval combined with a stricter definition of legitimacy to protect heirs and their property. Runaway suitors thereafter aimed for Gretna Green and the Scottish border.

numbered more than 500 souls. The towns accounted for at most a fifth of the population in 1700 and many were large villages rather than truly urban centres. Provincial cities commonly had fewer than 10,000 inhabitants and only London offered a truly metropolitan experience.

Within local communities the family was the basic unit not only of residence, reproduction and consumption but often also of production. As in other societies of north-west Europe, households were predominantly small in size and "nuclear" in structure, though many of them also included living-in servants or apprentices. Marriage* was to a very large extent conditional upon the achievement of economic independence. In consequence it was generally rather late, usually being contracted in the mid-to-late-twenties, while a substantial minority remained unmarried. In the highest reaches of society marriages were influenced by parental arrangement, but for most young people choice of a spouse was relatively free. Parental consent was desirable and approximate social "parity" between prospective partners was expected, but such expectations were compatible with freedom in courtship. In domestic relations much stress was laid upon the authority of husbands over wives and of parents over children, though in practice there was a strong and socially approved ethos of companionship in marriage and parent/child relationships were much less authoritarian than is sometimes assumed. Given the high mortality rates of the period, many marriages were prematurely broken by death and remarriage was frequent and swift, while the deaths of infants and children were commonplace. Such demographic realities, however, should not lead us to assume that family life was fragile or characterized by low emotional expectations, for there is much evidence of strong emotional bonding within the family.

Beyond the immediate family, ties of extended kinship were of limited practical significance for the bulk of the English people – though they retained

The Saltonstall family, painted by David Des Granges c. 1636-37. Although an intimate domestic scene, the grouping of the figures emphasizes the authority of the father as household head, and the painting is viewed by some historians as a harsh comment on patriarchal dominance. The wife lies in childbed. Births were regular in early years of marriage, a child every two years being usual. At the same time, high infant mortality often meant that the number of surviving children was not large. Death in childbed was a real hazard for women and underlay the higher than average mortality among married women in their twenties and thirties.

more force in Scotland, notably among the Highland clans. Bonds of "neighbourliness" within the local community, however, were strong, underpinning daily co-operation and finding periodic celebration in calendrical festivities, religious observances and recreational life*. For the gentry, their community was the county society of their social equals. For the common people, it was the more circumscribed arena of parish and township. It would be mistaken, however, to imagine either as an idyll of neighbourly harmony. County society was periodically fractured by rivalry and faction: in the 1720s York gentry had separate Whig and Tory assembly rooms. Local communities varied in their structure and their social relations. Ties of neighbourhood were qualified not only by personal conflict, but also by the realities of social differentiation; and though relations between superiors and subordinates were often governed by the conventions of paternalism and deference, they could also break down into sharp group hostilities. If overt class conflict was relatively muted, there were sufficient tensions within the established social order to qualify the contemporary ideal of a stable and harmonious society.

Many of the characteristics sketched above were to endure throughout our period. It was not, however, without change. To many, indeed, the events of the Civil Wars and Interregnum seemed to threaten the stability of the social order. No concerted popular uprising accompanied the breakdown of royal authority, but there were numerous attempts by the common people of particular English localities to seize the time for the rectification of economic grievances. Again, the demand for liberty of conscience, the ferment of radical ideas* in London and the army and the proliferation of sects* all challenged conventional values, while the exigencies of war and republican administration heightened popular political consciousness and broadened participation in government. In all these ways the war years and their aftermath were among the "highest of times". Yet the long-term social consequences should not be exaggerated. After 1660 traditional social relationships and patterns of authority were largely reasserted and the succeeding century was, to all outward appearance, one of remarkable social stability.

Behind the apparent equilibrium of the later seventeenth and eighteenth centuries, however, significant changes were at work throughout Britain, bringing about modifications in the structure of society and the fortunes of particular groups. The aristocracy were able to recover the ascendancy which had been shaken in the earlier and mid-seventeenth century, aided by economic trends which favoured the possessors of great estates. Among the peers and greater gentry the period was marked by a stupendous level of conspicuous consumption, evidenced in their great houses, their splendid attire, their retinues of servants and their participation in the social seasons of London, Edinburgh and such fashionable watering places as Bath. This prosperity was shared at a more modest level by the squires and lairds who remodelled their country seats in fashionable styles and aped in their provincial assemblies the fashions of the capital. And if some of the lesser gentry found their economic position under threat at the turn of the seventeenth and eighteenth centuries, many others did well enough and held their own.

Perhaps more significant change was to be seen in the middling ranks of society, which expanded in numbers, diversified in composition and grew in both wealth and sophistication. Financial, commercial and industrial development resulted in the emergence of a "monied interest" of rentiers and financiers, swelled the ranks of merchants and master manufacturers, created a

Holidays and recreations
Puritan attempts to limit holidays, banning some such as Christmas outright, met with fierce resentment and only half-hearted compliance in local communities. Though denounced as superstitious, such festivals as May Day broke up the year and provided a social "safety-valve" in which hostility between neighbour and neighbour, and inferior and better, could be let off. Recreations like bull- and bear-baiting, Whitsun ales and fairs and sports like bowls and wrestling continued to be popular until middle of 19th century. But there were continued efforts by Church courts to limit Sunday recreations, especially to prevent drinking and dancing in service times.

Alehouse
Equivalent to today's pub, alehouses were licensed by JPs. Books of Orders required suppression of superfluous houses, though many unlicensed ones sprang up. Attendance at alehouses on Sundays and other religious occasions proved troublesome, as did disorderliness and drunkenness. The most concerted attempt at suppression was made in 1655 during rule of Cromwellian major-generals. In later 17th and 18th centuries, more effective regulation by JPs, excisemen and brewers; alehouses acquired greater respectability, while remaining centres of social life in local communities.

Levellers
Radical groups created during Civil War: led by John Lilburne, Richard Overton and others, they wished creation of republican constitution with sovereign one-chamber legislature chosen by nearly-universal manhood suffrage; issued many pamphlets urging popular government against tyranny of king, Parliament or army generals. Proposals issued in "Agreement of the People", 1647, amended 1649, debated by army at Putney 1647 without acceptance. Mutinies by Levellers and allies in army (concerned mainly with threat of disbanding without arrears of pay) were crushed ruthlessly in 1649, and with them the Leveller movement.

Diggers
A small radical group, led by Gerrard Winstanley: after occupying common land on St George's Hill, Surrey, April 1649, Diggers denounced private property. They were believers in non-resistance and were easily subdued, never posing a threat to Parliament or army leaders.

Hollar's engraving of 1656 showing James Nayler, a Quaker accused of blasphemy, having his tongue bored through with a hot iron.

bustling world of small tradesmen and increased demand for professional services. Though the period saw a decline of England's freeholding yeomen, their niche in rural society was filled by large tenant farmers, a group also emerging in greater numbers in lowland Scotland. Urban development was such that by 1750 London had some 675,000 inhabitants and Edinburgh 57,000, while at least seventeen provincial cities had populations over 10,000, this growth being complemented by that of country towns whose tradesmen and professionals served the needs of prosperous rural customers.

The prosperity and self-confidence of the "stout midriff" of British society fuelled change in both living standards and cultural life. Greater purchasing power was employed to acquire the "decencies" of life (a trend towards a novel consumerism encouraged by the astute salesmanship of manufacturers and well-reflected in surviving inventories of household goods). Handsome new houses with classical trimmings transformed the streets of provincial towns, paid for by a "pseudo-gentry" who made up in genteel pretensions for what they lacked in broad acres. Moreover, there was greater spending on leisure and entertainment, a proliferation of coffee houses*, theatres, libraries, pleasure gardens, booksellers and provincial newspapers and an expanded preoccupation with fashion. It was an age of commerce and of commercialization.

Such prosperity was shared in part by labouring people. A stable population and cheaper foodstuffs in the century after 1660 brought modest rises in real

Millenarianism and the sects

Abolition of High Commission 1641 and disruptions of Civil War put an end to local ecclesiastical discipline, encouraging emergence of radical sects in 1640s and 1650s. Many of these held "millenarian" beliefs: they were convinced that rule of Christ and saints on earth for millennium was imminent. Fifth Monarchists (so-called because Christ's fifth monarchy was supposed to follow four ancient ones) were especially influential in Wales. Even more radical were Muggletonians, whose leader claimed semi-divine powers; and Ranters, who aroused horror by their sexual license and blasphemy. Sectaries were usually of poorer social and economic background than presbyterians or even most Independents.

Quakers

Most enduring of sects founded during mid-17th century was Society of Friends, more commonly known as Quakers because they were supposed to respond physically to "inner light" which was their source of godliness – rather than authority of ministers or even the Bible. Friends' refusal to defer to social superiors by removing hat was one of many attributes which gave Quakers reputation as disturbers of social order. Leader James Nayler severely punished for blasphemy by Parliament in 1656, despite sympathy of Cromwell. Under leadership of George Fox, Quakers endured post-Restoration persecution, evolving into industrious and pacifist Friends of today.

Duelling

The private duel, an imported custom from France, revived with the Restoration, reflecting the laxity of morals and predilection for riotous and theatrical entertainment associated with the period. Popular London haunts, like Covent Garden, featured almost nightly bloodshed. Even the king's dwarf, Hudson, fought a duel. A Hanoverian habit, too: George III's reign recorded 172 duels, involving many notables including Wilkes, Germain, Charles James Fox, Garrick and Sheridan.

Coffee houses

Initially erected as substitute for alehouses, first at Oxford in 1650, coffee houses outlived Interregnum becoming popular alternative form of meeting-place, with emphasis on quiet conversation and reading of newsbooks while drinking coffee, not alcohol. Short-lived attempt at suppression by royal proclamation ended after ten days in 1675. Some houses soon offered gambling; others became banking houses for goldsmiths; Edward Lloyd's was important London meeting-place for shipping underwriters and centre of commercial news. The houses spread to provinces by 1690s, Bristol having most after London. They declined towards end of 18th century as tea-drinking became more fashionable and as more exclusive "clubs", which began as early as 1700, sprang up as rivals.

Censorship

Collapse of official censorship in 1641 stimulated unparalleled production of newsbooks and journals, though governments attempted several times to re-impose censorship (1643, 1645, 1649, 1655). All newsbooks except government ones were outlawed in 1655 and 1659. In 1662 new Licensing Act restricted numbers of printers and authorized searches for illegal presses and seditious material; John Twyn was executed for seditious printing in 1664, and by 1666 the *London Gazette* enjoyed near monopoly of news. But lapse of Licensing Act in 1679 produced new spate of political tracts during Exclusion crisis. Licensing revived 1685-94; after this, press was regulated under libel laws.

wages and after 1700 banished the spectre of famine* (though periodic dearth years still brought real hardship). Tobacco, sugar, tea and cottons were modest luxuries widely enjoyed. Cheap print catered for a population in which, by 1750, perhaps two thirds of men and one third of women could read (a significant improvement on the situation of 1640). Yet the benefits of economic growth remained strikingly unequal in their distribution and, if some did well, the contrasts between the haves and the have-nots in society were if anything accentuated. Agrarian change undermined the partially independent domestic economies of many smallholders and cottagers, as farms were engrossed and commons enclosed, and there was an increase in the wholly wage-dependent population. Moreover, the spread of industry was a mixed blessing: many cottage-workers were grindingly poor and their employment uncertain. The worst effects of proletarianization were not to be seen until the 1790s, but by 1760 there was an increase in dependence upon the poor rates which worsened as population began to rise and real wages were depressed. In 1753 Fielding could speak of "whole families in want of every necessity of life" in London's pauper suburbs, while the housing of the rural poor could be described as "mud without and wretchedness within".

The marked contrasts evident in material life can also be discerned in the world of beliefs, attitudes and values. The religious extremism of the Civil War years left a legacy of disillusion, cynicism, or at best emotional exhaustion, after the abject failure of the drive for godly reformation of Church and society. The Church of England was able to reassert its monopoly of power in 1662, but it never regained its spiritual hegemony. Indeed despite periodic persecution of dissenters*, it scarcely tried. By 1700 Latitudinarianism* ruled in the Anglican Church, placing its stress upon reason rather than revelation, accommodating divinity to the world-picture of Newtonian science and valuing moderation above vulgar "enthusiasm". In Scotland, restored episcopacy met fierce resistance in some areas. The presbyterian triumph of 1690, however, was followed not by resurgent Covenanting zeal, but by divisions, secessions from the Kirk and the emergence of the "polite church" of the Moderates. Meanwhile, liberty of conscience was formally, if grudgingly, recognized throughout Britain and freedom of belief could rapidly become freedom to doubt. Among the educated, Deism* and anticlericalism were common enough and if a religious view of the world persisted for most, rational sensibility and private moral judgement had displaced the biblicism and intense self-inquisition of puritan piety.

Famine and dearth

Periodic harvest failures brought soaring prices, and hunger for poor consumers dependent on market for their bread – especially workers in rural industries. Relief measures by local officials and especially rising agricultural output alleviated problem in 18th century. Last major British famines (outside Ireland) affected north England and Scotland in 1623 and Scotland in 1690s, though local shortages still caused suffering and riots through 18th century.

Great Plague and Great Fire 1665-66

England, especially London, suffered outbursts of bubonic plague in 1603, 1625, but last and greatest occurred in 1665-66, killing 70,000 to 100,000. But increasing dominance of brown rat and decline of plague-carrying black rat caused virtual disappearance of plague as epidemic killer after this. 1665 episode immediately followed by second tragedy in London: Great Fire 2-5 September 1666, which broke out in a baker's shop and consumed four-fifths of city of London, destroying 87 churches and over 13,000 houses. Only twenty people died, and destruction allowed Wren to rebuild St Paul's cathedral and

many smaller churches, also permitting great improvements in street design and housing standards.

The Gin Age

Gin was introduced in 1690s from Holland: far cheaper than wine or brandy and easily distilled, its ready availability solaced the squalor and brutality of urban living, especially in the 1720s. John and Henry Fielding as London magistrates attempted restriction and Acts of 1729, 1733, and 1736 attacked the habit, but such efforts often provoked violence. By 1756 the problem was effectively taxed out of existence.

Dissenters

Enforcement of 1662 Act of Uniformity effectively excluded presbyterians, Baptists, Independents and smaller sects from membership of national Church. Dissenters, or nonconformists, found unlikely allies in Charles II and James II, prepared to grant indulgence if it could also be extended to Catholics; but Declarations of Indulgence 1662-63, 1672-73, 1687, 1688 were unacceptable to Anglican majority in Parliament. Despite vigorous persecution of dissenters, especially in early 1670s and early 1680s, numbers grew. Toleration Act 1689 allowed dissenters their own teachers and preachers, but they could not hold public office (though many sat in Parliament); from 1727 annual indemnity acts allowed them local office. In 1715 there were slightly over 300,000 dissenters in England and Wales, by 1800 nearly 400,000. Early dissenters were often of gentry or aristocracy, but by 1750 artisans, tradesmen and some wealthy merchants were in overwhelming majority.

Latitudinarianism

Growth of intellectual scepticism stimulated by religious fanaticism of mid-17th century led many clergy and laymen to tolerant, undogmatic outlook, which held each man responsible to his own conscience in worshipping God. Leading 17th-century exponents included William Chillingworth, John Wilkins and Archbishop John Tillotson. In early 18th century, Latitudinarians continued to press for comprehension of nonconformists within broader Anglican Church, and received some support from George I and George II since they were a counterweight to "High Church" party.

Deism

Quite different from Latitudinarians were "Deists" such as Charles Blount, Matthew Tindal, Viscount Bolingbroke and John Toland, whose *Christianity not Mysterious*

1696 aroused theological controversy. Where Latitudinarians stayed within framework of Christianity (usually Protestant), Deists often departed from it to search for philosophical and ethical principles held in common by all religions of the world, past and present, rejecting dogma and ceremony in favour of simple "natural religion".

In this anonymous painting (above), *persons of fashion and leisure promenade in St James's Park and the Mall (c. 1737), in a conspicuous display of wealth and confident superiority.*

Hogarth's Gin Lane, *1751, illustrates the squalid world of the metropolitan poor at the height of the "Gin Age". The distiller and cellar "dram-shop" thrive, as does the pawnbroker, at the cost of violence, disease and premature death among their demoralized clientele.*

The moral earnestness and providential world-picture of the early seventeenth century, however, did not entirely evaporate. They lived on in the evangelical wings of the established Churches and in the numerous dissenting denominations, and found expression in both the Societies for the Reformation of Manners* and in charitable efforts to counter the materialism and insouciance of the age. Godliness, however, was out of style. The established Churches were often spiritually moribund and pastorally negligent. English Dissent witnessed both a decline in numbers and a narrowing of its social base, and by 1750 had become predominantly urban and middle class in complexion. As for the labouring poor, many still gave their allegiance to the established Churches or to dissenting congregations, but there was also widespread neglect of formal religious observances, a legacy, in part, of their alienation from the cultural aggression of Puritan godliness. They were largely left to themselves until the advent of Methodism*, which achieved some success in both Wales and the industrial communities of northern and western England. Limited in their contacts with formal religion, the labouring poor nevertheless remained deeply aware of the supernatural. Magical beliefs were widespread and deep-rooted in a pre-scientific perception of the natural world. In this, as in its boisterous rituals and customs, plebeian culture was distinctly distanced from the "enlightened" world of polite society.

In the third quarter of the eighteenth century British society, diverse, complex and dynamic as it was, retained many features of a traditional social order. In the face of change it had proved remarkably stable. Highland Scotland maintained its threatened cultural identity even after the smashing of the clan system in the years after 1746. Elsewhere, the existence of sharp social conflict might be inferred from the savagery of the criminal law*, with its myriad capital offences (many of them established after 1690). Yet the terror of the law was tempered by considerable discretion in its enforcement. Again, social instability might be discerned in the frequency of riot* in the provinces. Yet rioters were generally parochial in their concerns, limited in their aims and restrained in their actions. They posed no serious threat to the established order. As for their rulers, they stood four square in defence of their property and their privileges, but they had neither the need nor the desire to be consistently oppressive. Indeed, the traditional leaders of society were supremely confident and complacent; little heeding the anachronisms and inadequacies of their social institutions, scarcely aware that the society which they ruled was about to give birth to a new industrial order.

Societies for the Reformation of Manners

Puritan zeal during the Interregnum was followed by the licence of Restoration society: moral laxity persisted in Court, society, literature and theatre. By Anne's reign prominent non-jurors denounced contemporary lapses while low-church Anglicans and dissenters expressed disapproval through Societies for Reformation of Manners. Their criticisms foreshadowed the revival of standards by later Wesleyan and Evangelical movements, and reflected concern at the moribund nature of the Church.

Somerset Case 1772

Despite enlightenment condemnation of black slavery, notably from Montesquieu, slave-cultivated sugar riches were considered of paramount importance. The philanthropist, Granville Sharp, defended several blacks, obtaining a decision in the case of Somerset which seemed to free slaves in England. Sharp remained active, e.g. the Zong Case 1783, and the anti-slavery cause gained the support of James Ramsay, an experienced and eloquent West Indian parson.

Methodism

Originally a movement within Anglican Church, founded by John Wesley in 1730s, so-named for "methodical" routine of work and prayer adopted by members. With emphasis on salvation for all and on balance between faith and works, Wesley appealed to masses in open-air sermons from 1738. Local societies and annual governing conference organized from 1744; Anglican dislike of "enthusiasm" and fear of grassroots element in Methodism drove Wesleyan preachers and their adherents into separation from the Church of England by 1795. Several splinter groups emerged in 19th century: in Wales, Methodism leaned towards more traditional Calvinist belief in predestination. Number of adherents rose from 24,000 in 1767 to 77,000 in 1796 and flourished especially among labourers and miners, particularly in industrializing north.

Waltham Black Acts 1724

Added 50 capital offences to the ever harsher penal code. Defence of property and the privileges of gentility preoccupied a judiciary and legislature dominated by rural magistrates. The game laws, e.g. of 1671 and 1770, restricted hunting to wealthy landowners; sentences of death, flogging and transportation were prescribed for theft and poaching. In practice, mercy was frequently extended through pardons and petitions.

"The Mob"

The mob was an accepted part of 18th-century life. Politicians cynically employed it to pressurize government, notably in the 1733 Excise crisis, against Byng 1756-57 and later in Wilkite violence 1768-71. In 1766 Spitalfields weavers protested against unemployment and naval mutinies occurred. Demobilization problems and depression followed the frequent wars. Anti-Catholic rioting featured over the Quebec Act 1774 and during the Gordon Riots 1780 (when procession to petition Parliament against "growth of popery" led to days of riot and looting).

Royal Marriages Act 1772

Hanoverian monarchy did not set high moral tone: George I had two German mistresses, his son was a notorious womanizer, Frederick, prince of Wales, a rake. Although George III was religious and uxorious, relatives and offspring were not. Indiscretions of duke of Cumberland provoked 1772 Act, which sought to bring royal marriages under influence of sovereign and Privy Council. Act failed to end scandals or raise reputation of royal family.

Culture:
the unfolding of native genius

D.D. Aldridge

The seventeenth and eighteenth centuries witnessed an unparalleled creativity in the arts, and pertinacious scientific enquiry into the natural world and the universe. Philosophic analysis of society attained new psychological force in the hands of the west countryman John Locke*, the Anglo-Irishman Jonathan Swift, the Scotsman David Hume; and the careers of William Hogarth and Samuel Johnson are testimony to the artist's struggle for the recognition of his social function in an era of material advance and increasing professional exclusiveness.

The relative significance of British and continental antecedents cannot be discussed here, but the prominence of painters and sculptors of foreign extraction is sufficiently obvious, and this was not primarily due to the cosmopolitanism of much royal patronage. In the seventeenth century an Anglo-Dutch cultural and maritime relationship was particularly evident: the science of optics and the skills of lens production were practised by Robert Hooke and Isaac Newton* under Dutch influence when the two nations were equally concerned with navigational and surveying techniques, and the international repute of Robert Boyle's experimental philosophy was secured as much by Leyden as by the British universities or the Royal Society*. Between 1672 and 1707 the Van de Veldes so firmly established marine painting in England that direct homage was still rendered them in the nineteenth century. Samuel Cooper, the greatest English portraitist of the seventeenth century, though born in London, may have been of Low Countries blood; and the greatest wood-carver of the period, Grinling Gibbons, was born in Rotterdam. His contribution to the decoration of Christopher Wren's St Paul's, the greatest single artistic achievement by any Englishman, is plain enough, and Wren himself was beholden to Dutch patterns for the spires of many of his city churches* – as were his contemporaries to the vernacular architecture of Jacob van Campen. John Milton was at one with Vondel of Amsterdam and Junius of Leyden in their championship of humanism against the doctrines of high Calvinism.

Locke's "Essay Concerning Human Understanding" 1690
On fleeing to Holland with discredited patron Shaftesbury 1683, Locke completed this cornerstone of British "empirical" approach to science and philosophy, which broke with earlier philosophical treatments of nature of human knowledge. Locke argued, against thinkers such as Lord Herbert of Cherbury and René Descartes, that human soul or mind was *tabula rasa,* an empty sheet of paper containing no innate ideas, even of God; the mind receives and organizes experiences, through the senses, into ideas of increasing complexity. In 18th century, David Hume made Locke's views the basis of his sceptical philosophy.

Newton's "Principia" 1687
A revolutionary work of mathematical and physical science, *Philosophia naturalis principia mathematica* influenced all further enquiry in mathematics and physics till 20th century. About 1665 Newton had discovered law of gravitational force of large celestial bodies: that intensity varies with inverse square of distance. In 1679-80, building on earlier work by Kepler, he found that the orbit of a planet is an ellipse with centre of gravitational force as one focus. In 1685 came his discovery that every particle of matter in universe attracts every other with force inversely proportional to square of distance between them. Under pressure from friend Edmund Halley (discoverer of Halley's comet), Newton set down his discoveries in *Principia* 1685-86, exhibited it at Royal Society that year and published it 1687. In 18th century it gradually superseded Cartesian teachings in European universities.

Royal Society
Interregnum witnessed sudden flourishing of scientific investigation and movement for educational reform by foreign and English philosophers and *virtuosi* (persons of many interests), who looked to Francis Bacon as their hero without necessarily following his limited, unmathematical methods. Royal Society (established 1660, granted royal charter 1662) drew together best of learned chemists, musicians, architects and men of letters. Early members included Christopher Wren and Isaac Newton. Members were often disorganized and unsystematic in conducting experiments, but Society provided stimulating environment within which Boyle's chemical discoveries and Newton's universal laws could be propagated.

Wren's London churches
87 parish churches were destroyed in whole or part by the Great Fire 1666. Christopher Wren's ambitious plan for complete rebuilding of city was rejected, but he was responsible for reconstructing churches. By 1678, 14 new churches were complete; in 1721 the last of 51 was opened. These churches were designed with Anglican liturgy in mind, and built of Portland stone, with some red brick for walling. Wren did not personally supervise all these churches, and they are of varying quality. 25 survive today: outstanding are St Mary Le Bow, for its steeple, and the interior of St Stephen Walbrook.

The Queen's House, Greenwich, begun 1616, completed by 1635, demonstrates Inigo Jones's mastery of Palladian classicism.

"The Club"
Beginning with Whig "Kit Kat Club" 1700 and Tory "Cocoa-Tree" coffee house, political and intellectual groups began to meet in London regularly. Though many welcomed lower orders and some such as the "Hell-fire Club" specialized in wild celebrations and debauchery, others were more refined and restricted membership jealously. Greatest of these societies was the Literary Club, or simply 'The Club", founded by lexicographer and scholar Dr Samuel Johnson and painter Sir Joshua Reynolds. This group included Burke, Goldsmith, Boswell, Gibbon and Adam Smith; it met regularly from 1763 to 1783. Such clubs suggest emergence of men of letters as social group separate from aristocratic patron, on whom authors had depended until early 18th century.

Court art
The early Stuart Court attracted the finest foreign (especially Dutch and Flemish) painters, including Mytens, Rubens (painter of Whitehall Banqueting House ceiling) and Anthony Van Dyck, whose period in England 1632-40 epitomized cultural achievements of 1630s. A master of portraiture, he captured Charles I's Court on canvas. Works were politically important at time; studies such as *Charles I on Horseback* (1633) sought to create image of king as martial hero in tradition of St George, Constantine and Henry V. After Restoration, Court art was still dominated by foreigners, Godfrey Kneller and Peter Lely being the best known.

The masque
Now a dead literary form, but in 1620s and 1630s a vital, lively art combining visual, dramatic and often musical elements in allegorical entertainments. Essentially a Court activity often featuring members of royal family in leading roles, masque reached its height in partnership of Ben Jonson and Inigo Jones, which produced *The Fortunate Isles* 1625 among others. Jonson's verse combined with Jones's use of elaborate props and light effects turned royal Court into a marvellous fairyland, though perhaps distancing it from outside world.

Mantuan collection
On death of brother, Henry, 1612 and Anne of Denmark 1617, Prince Charles inherited large collections of paintings; he

In Ireland, no native literature evolved amongst an overwhelmingly Catholic populace ruled and penalized by an Anglo-Irish hierarchy. But the country's attachment to Rome gave it its own cultural links with the Continent via the Irish Colleges in France and those native Irishmen who attended French or Italian military academies, or became engaged in business overseas. To seventeenth-century English and Scots, Ireland seemed a sinister threat, and no less sinister because impoverished. It was sometimes a refuge for British Catholics, such as the Scots portraitist John Michael Wright (who painted his "Sir Neil O'Neill" there in 1680), but more often the scene of starved military campaigning: his Londonderry background has relevance to George Farquhar's treatment of military life in his play *The Recruiting Officer* (1706). But in Trinity College, Dublin, and Kilkenny Grammar School the country had two sixteenth-century educational foundations of renown. The Yorkshire-born William Congreve, author of *Love for Love* (1694), attended both, as did Swift and the master-essayist Oliver Goldsmith – before he continued on to Edinburgh, Leyden, Padua and finally, in 1763, to a founder-membership of the "Club*" begun by Joshua Reynolds and Samuel Johnson. Whether on the quays of Leyden, in the taverns of Fleet Street, or the gardens at Vauxhall and Streatham, Goldsmith, as an Anglo-Irishman who only banished poverty towards the end of his life, never forgot his "Irishness" or its cultural connotations. Edmund Burke's "Irishness" was rather different, because of his Protestant-Catholic parentage: another founder-member of the "Club", this sensitive man threw himself into the privileged Westminster of his day only to be spurned as he illuminated it with his oratory and insights. His political tracts remain imperishable literature, but Burke had hardly less influence upon taste through his 1756 essay *On the Sublime and the Beautiful.*

But eighteenth-century Dublin had a cultural life which was more than Anglo-Irish veneer: its theatre was enlivened by the revolutionary Shakespearean acting of David Garrick and Charles Macklin, as well as the vitality of the blind playwright John O'Keefe and the versatile operatic impresario Owen MacSwinny, and it was the Dublin Charities Association which in 1741 assured the first public performance of Handel's *Messiah.* By the century's

established a continental network of agents to purchase works of art. 1623 visit to Spain exposed Charles to state collections of Madrid and he began seriously to create a British rival. From that year, negotiated for collection of Gonzaga dukes of Mantua, eventually spending over £25,000 by 1628 on superb collection of works by Mantegna, Giorgione, Titian etc.

Palladianism

Architectural style of early 17th century, whose greatest exponent was Inigo Jones, based on buildings and teachings of Italian Andrea Palladio, influenced by principles of ancient Roman, Vitruvius. Emphasis in Palladian buildings, such as Jones's Banqueting House at Whitehall, is on straight lines, simple unadorned style and rigid adherence to symmetry. Palladianism was eclipsed in later 17th century by grander classical style of Wren, best seen in his St Paul's Cathedral, and in extreme ornamentation of Baroque style, found in John Vanbrugh's Blenheim Palace and Castle Howard. Palladianism revived in early 18th century in Lord Burlington's Chiswick House; rival styles of period included "rococo" (a French import based on assymmetrical soft curves rather than clear lines) and by rugged, "natural" effect of Gothicism, exemplified in Horace Walpole's home, Strawberry Hill.

end, Dublin was adorned by the civic architecture of James Gandon and Thomas Cooley, comparable to Edinburgh's "New Town" – which was city planning of European significance carried out by the Adam brothers, Sir William Chambers and James Craig. Dublin's Liffey bade fair to be transposed to the Venetian Brenta through Lucan House (1775), the work of Samuel Johnson's favoured architect Agmondisham Vesey, while out in the country Edward Lovett Pearce and others were commissioned by a privileged few to build great Palladian houses like Castleton, Russborough and Kilshannig. Burke's concept of the "Beautiful" was truly visited upon Irish fields, for these were splendid derivations from a potent early seventeenth-century classicism introduced into England by Inigo Jones.

Not until the closing decades of Elizabeth's reign had there been a mature English response to the heritage of the Renaissance. But, however that had been delayed, the fact that Jones found professional fulfilment in courtly* circles betrays their receptiveness to Renaissance culture: the theatrical requirements of James I and Charles I drew on all Jones's resourcefulness as a beguiling designer of masques*. These, though, were "insubstantial pageants", and it was during two Italian journeys that Inigo Jones carefully observed the profound functionalism of Andrea Palladio's architecture. In varying ways Whitehall's Banqueting House, the Queen's Chapel at St James's, above all the Queen's House at Greenwich, reflect this potent influence from Italy, one which significantly contributed to a moment of the highest refinement in England. Here Charles I's munificent art patronage* was unprecedented, and some of the greatest productions of Italian and Flemish art entered England and were destined not only for royal palaces but for houses such as Wilton and Little Hadham (with their Italianate gardens as evidence of further indebtedness). Much later, during the years 1719-27 when Palladianism* was revived in England under the patronage of the extrava-

Arthur Devis's group portrait of 1749 summarizes the life style of the country gentry. The family are shown relaxing in the open air, and the saplings of their newly landscaped estate can be seen in the distance.

239

gantly questing earl of Burlington, Palladio's genius and Jones's eclecticism had become one and the same inspiration: from the inventive minds of Colen Campbell (author of *Vitruvius Britannicus)* and the unlettered William Kent sprang Chiswick, Mereworth and Holkham, all the children of an entranced experience of early eighteenth-century Italy.

British *cognoscenti* continued to embrace the classical heritage throughout the eighteenth century: just as in 1620 Jones could complete a sculpture gallery beside the Thames for the earl of Arundel, so 150 years later Robert Adam was similarly employed by William Weddell at Newby Hall in Yorkshire. In sciences, yet to be divorced from art, Mayerne and Harvey, graduates of Paris and Padua and physicians to James I and Charles I, respectively researched the chemistry of pigments and the circulation of the blood (1628) just as, in the later eighteenth century, George Stubbs consummated for all time the work of sixteenth-century Italians in the anatomization of the horse and, in partnership with Josiah Wedgwood, advanced the enamelling of a pottery production inspired by Graeco-Roman ceramics. Charles I's own preoccupation with the past worlds of Raphael and Titian was savagely terminated in 1640, but Van Dyck had already recorded for future generations the mien of a new aristocracy with a secularism which seems prescient. Spiritually distanced from the devotional grandeur of his master and fellow Catholic, Rubens, Van Dyck has an artistic link with the Protestant non-conformist Gainsborough so demonstrably close that it shrivels the century which separates them and subsumes the accomplishment of a Lely or a Kneller.

Grand Tour
Part of education for sons of nobility and wealthier gentry, who toured capitals of Europe, generally under supervision of a tutor. Practice remained popular through 17th and 18th centuries, providing a supplement, or even an alternative, to university. As aristocracy became artistic and intellectual patrons, tours became less an education for future rulers than an introduction to European culture, concentrating on development of aesthetic and intellectual tastes.

Libraries and scholarship
Increasing literacy led to wider demand for books, and lending libraries sprang up from 1725. Equally important were major libraries collected by scholars and noblemen, many of which were united in British Museum in 1754. Throughout period, English scholars rivalled Europeans: Richard Bentley (1662-1742) being greatest classical scholar of his age. Restoration antiquaries studied past by editing records and texts; interest in English language culminated in Johnson's huge dictionary (1755). History-writing developed strongly, with scholarly tradition of John Selden, William Dugdale and Thomas Madox progressing in parallel with literary historiography from Bacon's *Henry VII* 1622 through Clarendon's *History of the Rebellion* 1701 to Hume's *History of England* 1754-62. But in Edward Gibbon's *The Decline and Fall of the Roman Empire* 1776-88, best elements of both streams were merged, producing a work of great originality and erudition.

Music in England
England attracted many foreign composers in this period but also produced some outstanding native ones, from Lawes brothers in early 17th century through William Davenant, composer of Britain's first opera, *The Siege of Rhodes* 1656, to Henry Purcell's choral music at end of century. George F. Handel arrived from Hanover 1710; his *Messiah* 1741 and *Music for Royal Fireworks* 1749 were great works in Baroque tradition, but had few successors. The next generation saw a shift from grandiose opera of Handel to its satire form in Gay's *Beggars' Opera* 1728. Thomas

An aerial view of Wimpole Hall, Cambridgeshire, showing both the south front and the Capability Brown landscape of 1767 to the north. The west wing, chapel and library wing are by James Gibbs, 1713-30, and the central block was refaced by Henry Flitcroft c. 1740.

The Roman Hall at Kedleston, Derbyshire, by Robert Adam 1760-70, one of the most monumental interiors that he produced.

Arne was of lasting importance, and great foreigners such as J.C. Bach continued to come to England. Arne and others developed the "glee", a typically English unaccompanied voice composition.

Theatres
From 16th to 18th centuries, dramatists and theatre-owners needed government approval for plays performed publicly. But Puritans objected to theatres which promoted lewd morals and violated scriptural rubrics against men masquerading as women (females did not appear on public stage till Restoration). Long Parliament closed theatres by ordinance 1642, but many continued to operate clandestinely, resulting in raids and fines for spectators 1647. After re-opening at Restoration, dramatic satire became popular, resulting in attempted suppression by government during Exclusion crisis of 1679. In 18th century theatres continued to thrive and expanded to provinces: attempt by Walpole to regulate them in Playhouse Licensing Act 1737 failed. Larger theatres such as Garrick's at Drury Lane encouraged bigger audiences and period also saw beginning of serious revival of Shakespeare.

Gin Lane
Restoration and early 18th century produced much social and political satire in art. The great engraver and painter Hogarth specialized in depicting seamy side of London life in works such as *Marriage à la Mode* 1745. His engraving *Gin Lane*, depicting evils of contemporary gin craze, so aroused public anger that Parliament passed Gin Act 1751.

Royal Academy
Attempts by 17th-century *virtuosi* like Edmund Bolton to create an academy for study of fine arts and literature, on French model, were fruitless. Royal Academy was founded 1768 by Crown architect Sir William Chambers and other artists, after power-struggle within Incorporated Society of Artists (1765) led to secession of many members. Sir Joshua Reynolds president until 1790. Academy membership originally restricted to 40: these included Oliver Goldsmith as professor of ancient history and Dr Johnson as professor of ancient literature. From 1771, meetings were held at Somerset Palace.

The effects of Puritanism's brief triumph and defeat cannot be treated here, but they were profound. The dissenting backgrounds of Daniel Defoe (*The Shortest Way with the Dissenters* 1702) and Tom Paine (*Common Sense* 1776) surely induced in them the same lucid irony and the same potent rhetoric. But nuances in the revulsion from Puritan extremism are infinite indeed: it was possible for the unbowed Milton to write *Paradise Lost* in the alien world of the 1660s, but that world was already also John Dryden's, one of polemic certainly but one in which culture was no longer threatened by fanaticism. No one could have more warmly responded to the tradition of English lute playing and the Anglican anthems of Henry Lawes than Milton, but Matthew Locke's bequest of viol fantasia forms to Purcell included also music for the theatre. With Henry Purcell, music for the opera *Dido and Aeneas* (1689) or for occasions such as Queen Mary's funeral in 1695 assured England a status in great music making*, to be honourably sustained by Boyce and Arne. The towering musical and dramatic genius of Handel, himself indebted to Arne, should not conceal the wealth of English balladry and song which helped to bring the Three Choirs Festival into being (1724) and assure unprecedented success for John Gay's *Beggars' Opera* (1728). The managerial skill of the great mimic, John Rich, at Covent Garden, and a public which flocked to Garrick and Woffington and operatic stars from abroad as happily as it made its way to the pleasure gardens, gave a fresh robustness to the English theatre*. And that theatre fertilized the careers of artists: while Hogarth's own sources were mimicry and the motley, it was through landscape or genre painting that Francis Hayman, Paul Sandby (founder members of the Royal Academy* 1768), George Lambert, Philip de Loutherbourg (who taught Gainsborough to experiment with light) became associated with the stage. In Scotland, conversely, it was the stage which promised to forward landscape painting, although the poet Allan Ramsay, author of *The Gentle Shepherd* and probable founder of Britain's first Circulating Library (*c.*1725), encountered the authority of the Kirk in his theatre ventures. His son and namesake, who with Hogarth established the informal portrait in England, found professional fulfilment outside Scotland, but William Adam, the architect father of the

Adam brothers and author of *Vitruvius Scoticus,* had sufficient scope in government contracts at home. By 1760 the Highlands were attracting sight-seers, and Robert Fergusson was about to lead the revival of the Scots vernacular which would herald the coming of Burns.

While wealthier houses might be furnished with fine Dutch or French artefacts, and their gardens formalized after continental fashions, there was a virile confidence in England's artistic resources. A proudly patrician society had defended political liberty and the perquisites of property-ownership in the Revolution of 1688, and a national awareness could only be fostered by the great successes in the French wars. Whether the younger Wren was French-influenced or not, his exceptional mathematical skills and acute sense of spatial values was a special, home-bred genius. This is no less true of the thrilling imagination in stone of Nicholas Hawksmoor; and these two reticent men seem comfortably to inhabit the charted universe of Newton's *Principia* (1687) and to belong to the sanguine society reported by Steele and Addison in the *Tatler* and *Spectator** (1709-14) and later probed in fiction by Richardson and Fielding. There was also in literature a search for a reasonable linguistic precision: from Dryden through Swift to its culmination in Johnson's *Diction-ary* (1755) there was an urge to regularize. Yet there remains a strong element of paradox between the language of Alexander Pope, with its incisive observa-tion and unerring rhythms, and the abandonment of the horticultural disci-plines men had subscribed to in the recent past: in his garden at Twickenham (1720) Pope was the first to adopt a designed irregularity. Within thirty years, however, Lancelot "Capability" Brown's landscape art would sweep away for ever the sixteenth- and seventeenth-century inheritance. Pope would hardly have sympathized with "Capability's" interpretation of "artful wildness" and the breadth of Brown's vision seems far removed from Pope's introspection, induced in the poet by his Catholic faith and physical deformity. And in his river imagery Pope seems closer to the transient world of the seventeenth-century metaphysical poets than to the certainties of a Brown or a Humphrey Repton, or even the landscape paintings of Richard Wilson, for all the nostalgia in their didacticism. Wilson experienced all too keenly the artist's insecurity and, along with Pope, saw that the pellucid Thames at genteel Twickenham was destined to become fetid with writhing humanity at the Fleet Ditch. Yet in its turn Wilson's countryside was more arcadian than Joseph Wright of Derby's (landscape's "Grand Style" fades out in the 1760s), and Wright's treatment of light seems inspired more by the spectroscope and the foundry than the Campagna's sunlight. The eighteenth century's quivering balance must be thrown by the industrial "leap forward", and Burke's concept of the "Sublime", symbolized in mountain pass and plunging waterfall, transmuted by the drift mine and the steam-hammer.

Portrait of the Artist on a Grey Horse, *1782, painted by George Stubbs in enamel on a ceramic tablet.*

Literature: mock epic to novel

Restoration witnessed flourishing of political verse and satire such as Dryden's *Absalom and Achitophel* 1681, written against Whigs in Exclusion crisis. Same period saw Milton's great epics *Paradise Lost* and *Paradise Regained,* but general trend of poetry was toward formalism in construction (dominated by clever "rhyming couplet") and frivolity in subject. Literary patronage declined in 18th century; many authors chose to raise money by having readers subscribe for their works in advance. 18th century also saw a substantial increase in number of women authors (such as the "bluestocking" Elizabeth Carter, Mary Delany and Hannah More), and movement toward "realism" in narrative depiction of life, particularly in work of Henry Fielding. But most important was rise of novel, beginning with Richardson's *Pamela* (written in the form of letters, hence called "epistolary novel") and continuing with Fielding's *Tom Jones* and Jane Austen's books.

"Tatler" and "Spectator"

Journals founded by essayist Richard Steele with Joseph Addison. Steele, Whig publicist and royal gazetteer, published *Tatler* three times per week 1709-11 writing under pseudonym "Isaac Bickerstaff". *Tatler* contained news, essays, and dramatic criticism, often with political satire which cost Steele his gazetteership in 1710. In 1711, Steele and Addison inaugurated *Spectator*, published daily: modelled on *Tatler* but without political content, professed "an exact neutrality between the Whigs and Tories". Though *Spectator* ended in December 1712, these journals stimulated essayists and critical writers; prototypes of modern literary journals.

6

POLITICAL REFORM
AND
ECONOMIC REVOLUTION

1783 - 1901

POLITICAL REFORM AND ECONOMIC REVOLUTION 1783-1901
Overview
Asa Briggs

It used to be conventional to begin a new period of British history in 1815, the year of Waterloo, when the long wars against France were brought to a triumphant end. Thereafter there was peace until 1914, except for the Crimean War of the 1850s and many "little wars" fought on remote frontiers. These were years of liberal reform at Westminster and of administrative reform at Whitehall. As part of such an interpretation, the "Great War" of 1914-18 was seen as the next major break, although it was recognized that the death of Queen Victoria, who reigned from 1837 to 1901, was a break of a different kind, symbolic and social. The feeling of forlornness when she died, the *Annual Register* remarked, had never been paralleled, except, perhaps, on the death of King Alfred.

The long reign of Queen Victoria, who was unique amongst monarchs in giving her name both to an adjective and to a noun, Victorianism, imposed an artificial unity on a period of change and resistance, when there were many sharp contrasts of structure, fortune and experience not only between its different phases but in any single phase. It even influenced, also somewhat artificially, interpretations of the years between 1815 and 1837, which came to be thought of as "pre-Victorian" with strands of "Victorianism before Victoria". Two royal jubilees in 1887 and 1897 became landmark dates, when past experience was assessed and re-ordered.

Yet there was an equal artificiality in generalizing, as contemporaries and subsequent historians did, in terms not of Queen Victoria's reign but of the nineteenth century itself, "the wonderful century", as the scientist A.R. Wallace called it in 1898, when he attempted what he called "an appreciation of the century – of what it has done and what it has left undone". Old England, he felt, had become a new country. Samuel Smiles had said the same thing, bringing in Scotland and Wales as well, decades before. For critics, however, the wonder was misplaced. Another author with scientific and historical interests, H.G. Wells, described "the epoch" as "a hasty trial experiment, a gigantic experiment of the most slovenly and wasteful kind". Victorian Englishmen were "restricted and undisciplined, overtaken by power, by

possessions and great new freedoms, and unable to make any civilized use of them whatever".

A very different historian, who was less impressed by the influence of science and technology, G.M. Trevelyan, was equally uneasy about what had happened. "I must sadly and deliberately confess", he wrote at the end of the century, "that to my mind every important person has done everything either wrongly or at the wrong moment from 1895 onwards", while as far as culture was concerned the rot had set in far earlier. He argued that a common effort was required "to make the good as presentable, as obvious, as cheap, as the bad is today". And when in 1937 he came to produce a second edition of his widely read *British History in the Nineteenth Century and After,* first published in 1922, he added that "the twentieth century had been kept in a perpetual movement and unrest by the headlong progress of inventions, which hurry mankind on, along roads that no one has chosen, a helpless fugitive with no abiding place".

By then, the nineteenth century was beginning to look very different in perspective from what it had seemed in 1898 or 1901, and G.M. Young had produced his brilliant essay on *Victorian England: Portrait of an Age* in 1934. Not surprisingly, the image Trevelyan had used was conjured up again after the Second World War by Basil Willey in his *Nineteenth Century Studies.* "In our own unpleasant century", he wrote, "we are mostly misplaced persons, and many feel tempted to take flight into the nineteenth as into a promised land, and settle there like illegal immigrants for the rest of our lives."

Trevelyan chose 1782, the year before the recognition of American independence by treaty, as the opening date of his *History,* for, as he rightly put it, it would have been absurd to have begun it exactly with the new century "at a moment's pause in the battle with revolutionary France and in the most terrible years of the initial agony of our own industrial revolution". Whether or not the term "initial agony" is appropriate – some historians would prefer "exhilaration" – or whether or not 1782 (one of the last year's of "quiet, old England") is a better starting date than 1783 or 1793 (when Britain was drawn into the military strugglest France) in order to understand both the subsequent sequence of events and what lay behind them, it is certainly necessary to go at least as far back as the 1780s.

This was a decade of unprecedented economic growth, associated with the development of industry, and of equally unprecedented political change, associated above all else with the French Revolution of 1789 and the reactions to it. Industry, which came to be thought of in the nineteenth century not as a laudable human quality but as a dominating sector of the economy, did not stand still at any point in that century. What began with coal, iron and steam was to lead through still more coal to steel and electricity. Nor was it to stop there. The sense of economic revolution might be dimmed as invention came to be taken for granted and new ways of working, living, thinking and feeling became matters of habit and routine. Yet industrialization continued as a process, with many indirect as well as direct consequences, including the making of a new industrial middle class and a new kind of working class. Likewise, ideas and aspirations unleashed by the French Revolution retained their power both to inspire and to alarm and were significantly extended, though to a lesser extent in Britain than in France, during the course of the nineteenth century. There was no revolution, but there was an increasing sense of a "labour movement" with its own logic and its own momentum.

Historians have been in no more agreement than contemporaries were about how best to interpret such long-term processes of change or, for that matter, the late-nineteenth century development of "imperialism" – which it would have been difficult to predict in 1783 with the "collapse of the old colonial system" and the final "loss of America". There was always an argument about empire, as there was about industrialization, urbanization, liberalism and democracy. Facts were multiplied in an age of statistics, but values were divided. There were built-in difficulties of communication, despite the transformation of physical communications, associated in the first instance with canal and railway, particularly the latter (pre-railway days were compared with days before the Flood), and of social communications, associated with the Press, penny postage (1840) and the telegraph. (By the end of the century there was the telephone also, and the beginnings of wireless.) Moreover, during the course of the "wonderful century" many traditional certainties were eroded even when they were not destroyed. It was not so much atheism or agnosticism as indifference which made possible increasing "secularization", although individuals often underwent searing spiritual crises and from time to time there was bitter religious controversy, particularly on science and religion – which reached its most dramatic moment after the publication of Charles Darwin's *The Origin of Species* in 1859.

It was not until later in the century, however, that morality seemed threatened as well as belief, for during the 1870s, often described as a watershed, George Eliot, a confessed agnostic, maintained earnestly that if God was incomprehensible and Immortality inconceivable, Duty, the third key word in the Victorian value system, was peremptory. There was, in fact, no rapid or universal shift from acceptance of Duty to assertion of Will, but by the 1890s many mid-Victorian (and older traditional) values were being questioned. It was not only a small socialist minority that pointed to the inadequacies of self-help: there were liberals and conservatives who shared in the critique. "Character" also was under assault: there was as much talk of feet of clay as of pillars of society. "Respectability" began to look threadbare, and earnestness itself began to seem dull. George Bernard Shaw and Oscar Wilde were in agreement that the virtues of the poor, while they might be readily admitted, were "much to be regretted". "The best of the poor are never grateful. They are ungrateful, discontented and rebellious."

Not surprisingly, it became unfashionable to dwell on a word like "improvement". Indeed, "the age of improvement", a useful label, derived from contemporary language, for the whole period between 1783 and 1867, was certainly over by 1880. The 1880s were difficult years of confusion and conflict, and even when, during the late 1890s, there was a reaction against the so-called "late-Victorian revolt" – and Wilde was in exile – there was no return to the liberal mood of the 1850s and 1860s. The century ended in a burst of strident popular nationalism – not, of course, universally shared – which reached its climax on Mafeking night in May 1900, when, following the news of the end of the siege of a town in South Africa, there was, in Trevelyan's guarded phrases, "an orgy of relieved feelings and relaxed dignity".

When the great French historian Élie Halévy resumed his interrupted *History of the English People in the Nineteenth Century* at the year 1895, leaving a gap in the middle and later decades of the century, he felt that he was no longer dealing with the same themes or even with the same society. "The period between 1895 and 1914 does not belong to the British nineteenth century, as I understand it. It is at most the epilogue of that century." There was more noise but less confidence, more conflict but also more collusion. At the very time when the Empire was being deliberately extended there were more doubts about it: at the very time when trade unions were drawing in new groups of workers, management, increasingly separated from ownership, was losing its dynamism. "The impartial observer", he decided, "would be disposed to conclude that employers and workmen, for all their hostile rhetoric, had formed an unconscious alliance against that appetite for work, that zeal for production by which British industry has conquered the markets of the world."

Similar views have been advanced more recently by American historians, particularly by Martin Wiener, who has pointed to a decline of the "industrial spirit" which had been so evident at the Great Exhibition of 1851, held in the newly-built Crystal Palace. "It is a historic irony", he has claimed, "that the nation that gave birth to the industrial revolution, and exported it throughout the world, should have become embarrassed at the measure of its success." Pre-industrial values had persisted among aristocracy and working classes, had influenced employers, many of whom preferred countryside to town or city, and were dominant among people who, in other countries, might have been called intellectuals. Moreover, an improved educational system did much to perpetuate them. Public schools and universities were more interested in classics than in engineering, while primary schools, provided by local authorities on a systematic basis only after 1870, reinforced class difference. Secondary education, necessary in its own right and as a link within the system, was neglected.

Like all general interpretations of English social history, treating that history as a model to be admired or a warning to be heeded, such theses leave much out of the reckoning and much that is unexplained. Nonetheless, sensitive observers in 1901 itself were in little doubt on two points. Industry had not been unreservedly accepted, and parliamentary democracy had not been fully achieved. Indeed, it was felt to be a matter of pride that English, if not British, social history was distinctive in these respects. Industry had been kept in its place. So had rich men. Democracy had seldom been treated as ideology. Trade unionists were pragmatists, not theoreticians. Although there were eloquent advocates of greater equality and a few of total equality, "deference" was still an acknowledged feature of politics, society and culture.

There was a peculiarly rich infrastructure, and there were many powerful intermediate institutions, some old, some new, between the individual and the state. Moreover, the economic and the administrative role of the state was restricted. This was not only because of suspicion of collectivism, a suspicion some dismayed conservatives thought was a declining force, or distaste for high taxation, but because the scope and scale of local government had been extended during the nineteenth century, as had the initiatives and resources of voluntary organizations, many of them active pressure groups. It should be added, however, that an influential new civil service had been created, based on merit, not on patronage, and with stronger links with the universities than business had. It had also developed an almost instinctive sense of institutional morality. For the Fabian socialist, Graham Wallas, this was the one great political invention of the nineteenth century.

Other observers might have stressed the new role of the political party. In 1783, when the coalition between Charles James Fox and Lord North, considered by many to be a monstrous coalition, broke down and the king turned to William Pitt the Younger, there was little sense of how important party would become in the nineteenth century, which ended with the emergence of a new Labour party. "Connection" did not lose all its importance, but both Liberals and Conservatives, the two main parties, changed their organization considerably from the 1860s. There were still structures of "interests", but the extension of the electorate in 1832, 1867 and 1884 had begun to change the terms as well as the organization of politics. As early as 1846, during the fascinating parliamentary debates on the repeal of the corn laws, Disraeli had argued forcefully that "it is only by maintaining the independence of party that you can maintain the integrity of public men, and the power and influence of Parliament itself", yet his argument was no more convincing at the time than was his opponent Sir Robert Peel's appeal to public service even if it meant splitting party. All that can be said, as Sir Lewis Namier observed in 1952, is that Disraeli's view was "more in harmony with the realities which were then shaping, and which, when once shaped, were soon to be mistaken for primordial elements of the British Constitution". Nor was the role of party completely clear when Walter Bagehot produced his brilliant essay on that constitution in 1867.

The study of the formation of political parties demands examination of grass-roots change at the constituency level as well as of personalities at the centre. (So, too, of course, does the formation of "class".) Yet the political and constitutional history of the nineteenth century cannot be written without paying meticulous attention to the motivation of personalities: of Peel, when he decided to repeal the corn laws; of W.E. Gladstone, who, starting as a Tory, evolved his own long-popular version of liberalism; of Joseph Chamberlain, radical liberal, who formulated first a civic and then an imperial gospel and who, having played a key role in the splitting of the Liberal party in 1886, was to go on in the twentieth century to

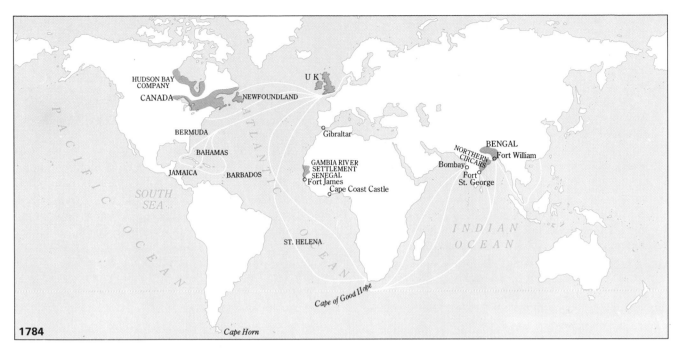

1784

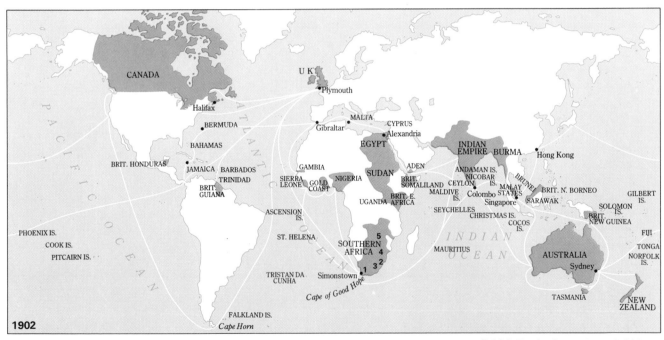

1902

British Territories, 1784 and 1902

| 0 | | 3000 | | 6000 km. |
| 0 | 2000 | | 4000 miles | |

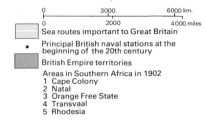

Sea routes important to Great Britain

Principal British naval stations at the beginning of the 20th century

British Empire territories

Areas in Southern Africa in 1902
1 Cape Colony
2 Natal
3 Orange Free State
4 Transvaal
5 Rhodesia

split the Conservative party also. Chamberlain was also one of the first politicians to appreciate the tactics of caucus politics. Finally, the queen herself cannot be left out of the picture, nor her husband Prince Albert who died in 1861. In general, the power of the Crown declined between 1783 and 1901, although there were times when Queen Victoria suggested the opposite, and, according to Disraeli, in ironical mood, had Albert lived, he might have conferred upon the country the blessings of absolute monarchy.

Disraeli was a novelist as well as a politician, and his great rival Gladstone was at least as interested in Homer as he was in free trade, the greatest of all the liberal gospels. There were few experts in the hundred years after 1780 and more people with a broader interest in knowledge than there were to be in the late-nineteenth and twentieth centuries, when the influence and organization of professionals grew. The literature of the years 1783 to 1901 was richly varied, with the novel as a major medium. Jane Austen and Walter Scott, the novelists of the early century, were greatly preferred to George Eliot and George Meredith by A.J. Balfour, who became prime minister in 1902 and wrote eloquently, if critically, about the Victorian heritage. At least two novelists, Charles Dickens and Anthony Trollope, have been read, often uncritically, for the light they throw on the age, an age which has even been described as "the age of Dickens". The poet of these years, Tennyson, has been less widely read than the romantic poets who preceded him.

The drama did not thrive until the end of the century, when Wilde's plays pointed wittily to many of the preoccupations of a generation more aware of disturbance than of order. It is to *The Importance of Being Earnest* (1895), for example, that we must turn to recover the most succinct account of the implications of the agricultural depression of the 1880s and 1890s which affected many (but not all) farmers and landlords. "What between duties expected of one during one's lifetime, and the duties exacted from one after one's death", says Lady Bracknell, "land has ceased to be either a profit or a pleasure. It gives one position, and prevents one from keeping it up. That's all that can be said about land."

Much more *can* be said about land in any year between 1783 and 1901, and much more was, although the proportion of people working on the land diminished during the period and the state of the harvest came to matter less than it ever had done before in history. The rhythms of the trade cycle counted for more. Economists and sociologists have frequently turned to the nineteenth century both to collect basic facts about a complex economic system and to advance theories about its past evolution and future prospects. Their evidence and conclusions, conflicting though they are, are a necessary part of the historian's evidence. So, too, is the evidence of demography. Early in the period there were fears of over-population, affecting among other things attitudes towards poverty and the poor. At the end of the period there were fears of under-population. The peak size of the family, the major institution of the mid-Victorian years, was reached during the 1860s. This was the golden age of *pater familias* and "home, sweet home". Little children, of whom there were many, had to be seen and not heard. There was also a double standard of morality for women and men. These particular balances did not and could not last. Census returns, first collected in 1801, revealed quite different demographic patterns in 1901 from those in 1871. And the "new woman" had already made her appearance. Between 1901 and 1914 much which had been taken for granted even in an age of change was no longer secure, so that when H.G. Wells dreamed of a modern utopia he began by insisting that no stable utopia was ever possible.

Government and Politics 1783-1846:
England, Scotland and Wales

Boyd Hilton

To a rare degree in British history, the period from 1783 to 1846 possesses a thematic unity which distinguishes it markedly from what came before or after. It was a period of economic upheaval, in which Britain shifted from being a predominantly agricultural and commercial society to being the world's first industrial nation. Many of the most contentious political issues of the day, corn and currency laws for example, were really questions of whether government policy should be directed towards encouraging this shift, or trying to reverse it. Accompanying the economic changes was the most sustained and dangerous cycle of revolutionary discontent and working-class protest in British history. This prompted a few political concessions on the part of the governing aristocracy, but more significant was the emergence of governmental machinery designed to maintain law and order, which in turn led unintentionally to the foundation of the modern centralized and bureaucratic state.

The power of the Crown declined significantly. Although George III (until he became incurably mad in 1810), George IV, William IV, Victoria, and her consort Albert, could all influence the course of political intrigue, the monarch's power to control the policies of the state was severely reduced. In the decade before 1783 the king had exercised a virtually personal rule, and so was held responsible by part of the political nation for the loss of the American colonies. But as the scope and scale of government business increased during the long French wars, less and less passed through the monarch's hands.

Massacre at St Peter's or "BRITONS STRIKE HOME"!!!

Cruikshank's cartoon, Massacre at St Peter's, or Britons Strike Home!, *lampooning the Manchester yeomanry who charged the crowd at St Peter's Fields on 16 August 1819.*

Except possibly where foreign policy was concerned, the Crown was being reduced to little more than a figurehead of state.

Effective power remained in the hands of a territorial aristocracy, whose representatives still dominated both Houses of Parliament. They faced an active and vociferous radical movement, particularly strong in the years following the foundation of the London Corresponding Society* in 1792 and in the economically depressed years* after the end of the war in 1815. The "massacre" of Peterloo* at Manchester in 1819 left an enormous psychological scar on a polity which prided itself on its ability to contain discontents. Yet the aristocracy survived, largely because the middling ranks, terrified by the violence of the French Revolution, set their faces against any sort of revolutionary radicalism*. Realizing this, a Whig government in 1832 enfranchised a large mass of merchants and manufacturers, professional and trades people, who were coming to regard themselves as making up a "middle class" between aristocracy and people. This Great Reform Act* also gave political recognition to the Industrial Revolution by removing separate representation from a large number of depopulated boroughs, giving it instead to important new towns like Manchester and Birmingham. In some ways it was only a gesture to middle-class interests. Radical demands for a free and secret ballot* were

London Corresponding Society
Founded 1792 by London artisans, for circulation of radical literature. Treated as insurrectionary threat by government, leaders arrested and investigated by Commons committee 1794; emasculated by restrictions on public meetings in Two Acts 1795; suppressed 1799 under Corresponding Societies Act.

Postwar depression and repression
Postwar adjustment brought depression, with agrarian disturbances, machine-breaking and revival of popular reform agitation. Two meetings at Spa Fields 1816 (second ending in violence) and attack on Prince Regent led to suspension of Habeas Corpus and restrictions on public meetings 1817. Peterloo and other reform meetings 1818-19 led to Six Acts 1819: forbade training in arms and drilling; authorized seizure of arms; simplified prosecutions; forbade seditious assemblies; punished blasphemous libels; restricted the press.

Peterloo 1819
Panic charge by troops upon peaceable crowd of 60,000 at reform meeting at St Peter's Fields, Manchester; eleven killed and at least 400 injured: reflected Lancashire magistrates' fear of uprising during distress of 1819.

Combination Acts
Acts of 1799 and 1800, introduced in Revolutionary War panic, to stifle trade unions by making combinations for higher pay or shorter hours illegal. Ineffective: at least 50 illegal unions in Nottingham alone 1799-1824. Repealed 1824.

First Reform Act 1832
56 English boroughs totally disfranchised, 30 deprived of one Member; 22 new two-Member boroughs and 19 single-Member boroughs created in England. 26 English counties divided into two two-Member seats, seven given additional Member. Five extra seats in Wales, five in Ireland, eight in Scotland. £10 residential franchise supplemented by £10 copyhold and £50 tenant-at-will franchise. Electorate

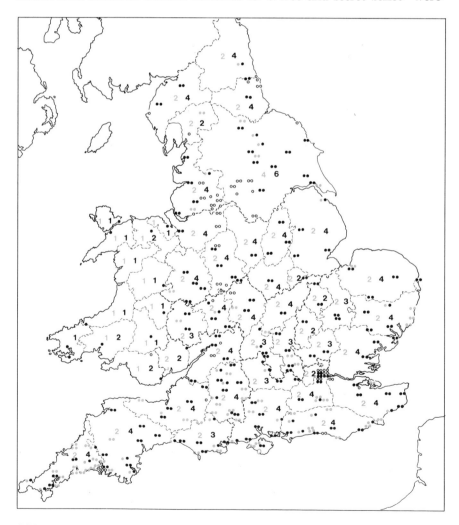

Changes in Parliamentary Representation between 1831 and 1832

County representation

1 1831

1 1832

Borough representation 1832

○ Member lost

● Member retained

O Member created

increased by 50% in England and 57% overall; about 20% of English adult males could now vote.

Secret ballot

Featured in cabinet committee reform proposals of 1831, but omitted from First Reform Act: rallying issue of Philosophic Radicals during 1830s, declared "open question" by cabinet 1839. One of Chartist six points, lost prominence during 1840s; revived with franchise extension 1867, implemented 1872.

Chartism

Working-class movement for extension of franchise. Six-point Charter drafted 1838: universal suffrage, secret ballot, annual elections, payment of Members, no property qualification for MPs, equal electoral districts. Three petitions (1839, 1842, 1848) made no impact on Parliament. Ranged from quasi-revolutionary Chartism to self-improvement. Dominated by Feargus O'Connor through *Northern Star*.

Sir George Hayter's 1833 painting of the first House of Commons to be returned under the Reform Act of 1832.

refused, while the parliamentary power of the country gentlemen was strengthened with more county seats and the abolition of many "nomination" and "rotten" boroughs. More importantly, the Act identified political power with economic achievement. Until 1832 parliamentary representation had been a haphazard jumble of legal and historical rights, without any logical order or precise discrimination. After 1832 the right to vote was identified with certain definite economic categories – ten-pound householders in the boroughs, forty-shilling freeholders in the counties. The working classes, frustrated by the desertion of their middle-class allies, saw that no improvement in their living conditions would be possible until they had opened up the political structure of the state. Hence Chartism* (*c.* 1837-48), an impressive but ultimately unsuccessful conglomeration of protest movements, which focused on the need for annual parliaments, the ballot, and universal suffrage. It collapsed with the return of economic prosperity after 1848, leaving the British upper classes more than ever complacent about their ability to innoculate themselves against that continental epidemic, revolution.

The real threat to aristocratic power was more insidious, and came from the state. As population shifted from countryside to city, so the real power of the landlords to direct the lives of ordinary people – a power which had been exercised on their estates and in the quarter sessions – declined. This point can be illustrated by those two vital problems of keeping the peace and relieving the poor. At the start of the period, responsibility for maintaining law and order was in the hands of local officers such as magistrates and lords lieutenant. But Peterloo finally brought home to politicians the dangers of trying to govern large cities along lines devised for rural areas and small towns.

Gradually police* forces were set up, the important steps being taken in 1829, 1835, and 1839. They were directly responsible to the Home Office and their function was to prevent rather than merely repress disorder. Thus it was that, working directly with the military and local police, governments were able to cope with Chartism without recourse to the kind of "political"repression that Pitt had indulged in, and indeed without involving Parliament at all. On the question of poor relief, landlords made a valiant attempt in 1795 to retain the affection of, and control over, their labourers, when in many parts of England (but mainly in the south) they enacted the "Speenhamland"* system, to cushion the poor against high wartime food prices. It may have helped to stem the depopulation of the countryside, but its financial cost to the landlords proved so great that pressure built up after 1815 for a severe reduction in the provision of relief. The New Poor Law* of 1834 marked the landlords' virtual surrender of charitable functions to the state, for, though the workhouse system then instituted was not always administered as harshly as was intended, and though many landlords retained influence over the new poor-law unions, from 1834 the provision of relief was subjected to national guidelines and was notably less generous than it had previously been. Indeed, the poor law serves as a reminder that *centralization* did not imply greater interference by the powerful in the lives of ordinary people, but rather the reverse, for central authorities were far less paternalistic than local magistrates had been. An increasingly *laissez-faire* attitude was taken to social evils, so that it took valiant efforts on the part of individual philanthropists to secure any alleviation of harsh economic conditions – such as Lord Shaftesbury's campaign to limit the number of hours worked by women and children in textile factories*. In some respects, the richest country in the world remained backward in the matter of welfare policy.

Laissez-faire policies derived partly from the prevailing climate of opinion, dominated philosophically by Bentham and morally by a widespread belief in the need for individual "self-help" and hard work. But there were sound practical reasons for them as well. Throughout the period there was serious concern over Britain's enormous public debt, which first built up during the American war to stand at £232,000,000 in 1783, and then escalated to a massive £843,000,000 by 1818. All peacetime governments were concerned about the prospect of a national bankruptcy, such as had precipitated revolution in France, and to reassure the important fundholder interest they all made a priority of retrenchment, which left little financial scope for social and welfare spending.

Although the language of politics became increasingly dominated by class rhetoric, most of the important political divisions, those which took place within the political nation, were of a vertical rather than a horizontal nature, and had two main foci – religion and economics. Throughout the period, nonconformist dissenters struggled to achieve political rights and liberties. The sudden and unexpected repeal of the Test and Corporation Acts* in 1828 set in motion a chain of reform movements which left the Church of England looking increasingly battered and beleaguered. Before then the struggle of Roman Catholics to be relieved of their civil disabilities had been an intermittent but important polarizing issue, though it was finally settled in 1829* when a Tory government yielded to the threat of violence in Ireland. Then there were constant battles on such issues as corn laws, currency, taxation, and tithes, in which agricultural and manufacturing sectors struggled for control of

Police
Peel's Metropolitan Police Act 1829 created first paid uniformed force in Britain, under direct control of home secretary; Municipal Corporations Act 1835 obliged every borough council to elect Watch Committee responsible for policing borough. Police Act 1839 allowed county justices of England and Wales to establish paid forces, under a chief constable approved by home secretary. Cost fell on county rate, and only 28 counties had adopted Act by 1856, when County and Borough Police Act made maintenance of police force obligatory.

Speenhamland system
System of outdoor relief adopted by Berkshire Justices meeting at Speenhamland 1795, in wake of poor harvest and hungry winter; payments to poor on scale reflecting price of bread and number of dependants; widely imitated in midlands and rural south.

New Poor Law 1834
Wartime inflation saw aggregate poor relief rise; postwar deflation increased unemployment so relief burden continued to rise. Ratepayer resistance and criticism by political economists led to Royal Commission on Poor Laws 1832: reported 1834, arguing that indiscriminate relief demoralized beneficiaries; recommended abolition of outdoor relief and maintenance of workhouse inmates at level below that of lowest paid workers. Poor Law Amendment Act 1834, created central Poor Law Board and regularized election of guardians, but retained discretionary outdoor relief.

Factory movement
First legislative limitation of hours of labour by Apprentices Act 1802; first major Factory Act 1833 prevented employment of under-9s and limited under-11s to 9 hours, under-18s to 12 hours daily, instituted factory inspectorate. Movement for 10-hour limitation gathered force during 1840s; 1844 Factory Act limited employment of under-13s to 6½ hours and that of all women to 12 hours; Acts of 1847 and 1850 finally limited employment of women and persons under 18 to 10 hours. Legislation only applied to textiles.

Pitt's financial reforms
To tackle inherited war debt, Pitt stimulated Customs revenue by reduction of duties on tea, wines and spirits 1784-86; created new Sinking Fund 1786; 1787 Consolidation Act simplified public accounts, abolishing all existing Customs and Excise duties and replacing them with fewer, simpler duties, product of which was

carried into one consolidated fund, from which public expenditure would be met.

Repeal of Test and Corporation Acts 1828
Test Acts 1673 and 1678 (preventing non-Anglicans from holding public office) and Corporation Act 1661 (excluding them from municipal positions) remained on statute book though seldom enforced. Protestant Society planned repeal campaign 1826, and United Committee of Congregationalist, Baptist and Unitarian ministers formed 1827. Russell successfully moved repeal 1828, though slightly qualified by amendment binding Dissenters not to use civic position to attack established Church.

Catholic emancipation 1829
Catholics denied franchise, election to Parliament, and public office, though Irish Catholics granted vote 1793. Reform prompted by success of Burdett's emancipation motion in Commons 1828, and by O'Connell's victory in County Clare by-election 1828. 1829 Act repealed all civil disabilities to which Catholics were subject, with provisos protecting established Church and excluding Jesuits from England. Catholics remained barred from lord chancellorship, lord-lieutenancy of Ireland, and universities. Provoked considerable resentment within Tory party.

Corn laws
Domestic wheat producers protected intermittently since Middle Ages and continuously since 1660s. Need to shield agricultural sector from post-war deflation and continental gluts led to 1815 law prohibiting all foreign corn imports when domestic price fell below 80s per quarter; Act of 1828 introduced sliding scale by which duty fell as home price rose; scale revised to provide less protection by Peel 1842.

Resumption of cash payments 1821
Bank of England's obligation to convert notes to gold on demand suspended during Revolutionary Wars 1797; encouraged belief that wartime inflation reflected over-issue of banknotes. Return to convertibility thus seen as guarantee of stability of prices and foreign trade: Peel's Act of 1819 stipulated resumption of cash payments within four years, achieved by Bank 1821. Speed of resumption exacerbated deflationary effects; notes appreciated by 40% instead of anticipated 5%. Fall in price level benefited exporters but harmed domestic producers and agricultural interest.

economic policy. The main theme here is the gradual erosion of agricultural protection, so that the period closes with the repeal of the corn laws*, when the "field of coal" defeated the "field of barley". Still more important, perhaps, was a division of interest between those who owned and those who owed money. The former category included all those who invested in the public funds (*rentiers*) as well as in canal and railway companies. The latter included many of the people who actually created wealth, farmers and master manufacturers for example, but who often had to borrow money in order to carry on their operations. What made the distinction important was the sharp decrease in the value of money following the suspension of cash payments in 1797, and the subsequent increase in its value following the return to cash payments* (the gold standard) in 1821. Such fluctuations obviously affected the economic position of the two groups, shifting the balance first against and then in favour of the owners of money. After 1819 all governments followed a policy of dear money and deflation, which favoured the *rentiers* and provoked a strange but persistent alliance between ultra Tories (mainly backwoods landowners with heavy mortgages and other debt charges) and working-class radical spokesmen.

Despite these vertical divisions, politically the period was surprisingly stable, a consequence no doubt of the upper classes' need to close ranks in the face of popular disaffection. It is therefore not surprising that the period was dominated by the Tory party, which was in office for nearly fifty-one out of sixty-three years. The party was founded by Pitt, who called himself a Whig but came to be regarded as a Tory because he was opposed by the official Whig party of Rockingham and Fox, and it was subsequently led along very similar lines by Perceval, Liverpool, Canning, Wellington, and Peel. The Whigs were only able to achieve power when the Tories divided among themselves, as they did in 1827-30 and again in 1846. Politics took on the appearance of a two-party conflict; feeling ran high, and was carried out from Parliament into public discourse by such fiercely partisan reviews as the Tory *Quarterly* and Whig *Edinburgh*. After 1832 each party tried to attract and register* those

Monetary legislation 1819-44
Restrictive effects of return to gold 1821 offset by lack of control over credit offered by private banks and over commercial discounting side of Bank of England's business: speculative crash of 1825-26 blamed on inflationary issues of country banks. Two acts of 1826 forbade note issue below £5 and authorized provincial branches of Bank of England and joint-stock banks outside London. Measures of monetary regulation by Bank smoothed passage of Bank Charter renewal 1833, but Bank widely blamed for crises of 1836 and 1839. Peel revised Charter by Bank Charter Act 1844: fiduciary note issue limited to low ceiling, with further issues to be backed by gold; banking and issue departments of Bank strictly separated.

Ministry of all the Talents 1806-7
Coalition formed after Pitt's death, under leadership of Grenville: predominantly Foxite, with Charles James Fox foreign

secretary, but also included conservatives Sidmouth (formerly Addington) as lord privy seal and Ellenborough as lord chief justice. Only major reform achievement was passing of Wilberforce's Bill to abolish slave trade within empire 1807; fell on proposal to allow Catholics to hold army commissions.

Electoral registration
No electoral register in either counties or boroughs before 1832, so that right to vote had to be proved at poll. 1832 Reform Act provided for annual compilation of register: lists compiled by parochial overseers but subject to appeal to revising barristers. Need to ensure registration of all supporters stimulated local party organization during 1830s; Anti-Corn Law League sought to enrol supporters 1844-46 by creation of county freeholds.

sections of the community which had just been given the vote. The election of 1841 was a new kind of contest in which the parties appealed directly to the electorate for support, and in which one party at least, the Whigs, offered it a package of measures (free trade). Though this was not to happen again until 1868, it was a pointer to future trends, and in 1841 far fewer voters than usual acted non-politically by splitting their votes (giving one to the Whig candidate and one to the Tory), and there was a far more uniform national swing than usual. The election saw a landslide victory for Peel's Tory party, which did well in many boroughs besides sweeping the county seats.

However, the appearance of a two-party system was somewhat deceptive, for both Whigs and Tories were deeply divided. The passage of Catholic emancipation in 1829 removed from the political scene the only issue on which the Whigs were *not* divided. Their decade of office 1830-41, with first Grey and then Melbourne in charge, revealed all too clearly the differences of aim and emphasis between old Whigs, liberals, Radicals, and their Irish and nonconformist allies. The Tories meanwhile comprised an uneasy alliance between backbench country squires on the one hand and on the other professional, government-minded administrative politicians (largely Cambridge men under Pitt at the start of the period and Oxford men under Peel at the end). A majority of squires supported the Tories, because they could not forgive Fox for his support of the French Revolution, but their loyalty to a Tory government was conditional on its coming forward with congenial policies, and they frequently voted against such governments on individual issues, as when they voted to repeal the property tax* in 1816. Peel's great victory in 1841* gave him the confidence to insist on pushing his measures through Parliament, threatening to resign if the country gentlemen would not vote obediently. He succeeded, even securing an increase in the parliamentary grant to the Roman Catholic College at Maynooth* in 1845, and also the repeal of the corn laws* in 1846. But the price of success was that he finally shattered the precarious coalition that was the Tory party, condemning it to political weakness for the following thirty years.

The Kennington Common meeting of Chartists, photographed in 1848.

Repeal of property tax 1816
1798 wartime tax was due to lapse on cessation of hostilities. Government proposed renewal 1816 at half rate for two years: opposition from mercantile community and county meetings. Whig parliamentary opposition scored rare success, mobilizing forces to defeat renewal.

General Election 1841
Dominated by issue of protection, returned 368 Conservatives and 290 Whig/Liberals – first Conservative majority under reformed system. Conservative strength in English counties and small boroughs, also older commercial centres and ports. Industrial areas predominantly Liberal, new (1832) London boroughs exclusively so. £10 borough householders strongly Liberal, county electorate stridently Conservative.

Income tax
Lapsed 1816. Reintroduced by Peel 1842 to meet budget deficit: standard rate of 7d in £ on incomes over £150 p.a. Threshold reduced to £100, at lower rate, by Gladstone 1853, with plan for extinction of tax by 1860. Standard rate ranged between 1/4d in £ at height of Crimean War expenditure and 2d in £ in mid-1870s; Gladstone again proposed extinction 1874.

Maynooth
Catholic seminary near Dublin, founded 1795 with annual parliamentary grant: grant became target for anti-Catholics in Parliament, especially after emergence of Tractarianism in 1840s. Grant not increased since 1813, and Peel's Bill of 1845 proposed trebling of grant: resented by both Tory Anglicans and Dissenters and passed only with Whig support, contributing to Tory divisions.

Repeal of corn laws 1846
Failure of Irish potato crop 1845 taken by Peel to justify repeal of corn laws: he proposed suspension of corn laws with a view to repeal, but failed to secure cabinet approval and resigned, only to return when Russell refused office. In 1846 Peel proposed reduction of protection over three years, then virtual abolition; measure passed Commons with Whig support, but bitter opposition from county Tories. Two-thirds of Tories in Commons had opposed repeal; 69 protectionists then voted with Russell to defeat government over Irish Arms Bill, bringing about Peel's resignation.

Government and Politics 1846-1901:
free trade, franchise and imperialism

H.C.G. Matthew

The split in the Tory party in 1846 proved remarkably conclusive. No major figure who followed Peel over corn-law repeal again held office as a Tory, and most – Gladstone, Sidney Herbert, Aberdeen, Graham, Newcastle – found themselves in office in coalition with Whigs, liberals and Radicals. Russell's government (1846-52), with tacit Peelite* support, repealed the Navigation Acts (1849) and the 1851 Great Exhibition* celebrated the triumph of the industrial, free-trading ethos and marked a new tone in affairs: the propertied classes' confidence that the British political system had withstood the storms of the 1830s and the 1840s and now looked forward to an era of relative political calm based on commercial prosperity.

Russell's government fell in 1852 over a militia bill, and the Conservatives (as the Tory remnant now usually called themselves) took office in the first of three minority governments with Derby as prime minister and Disraeli as chancellor of the exchequer (1852, 1858-59, 1866-68). Failing, though not as badly as some had expected, to win the 1852 General Election, the Conservatives were replaced by a Whig-Peelite-liberal coalition under Lord Aberdeen, with Gladstone as chancellor, Palmerston as home secretary and Russell as foreign secretary. This government furthered free trade with Gladstone's "Peelite" budget (1853), and introduced the first stage of a civil service* open to competition (1853), but drifted into war with Russia in the Crimea. The poor performance in the war led to the government's disintegration in February 1855, and its replacement by a government of Whigs and liberals led by Palmerston. After winning the 1857 General Election, Palmerston's government was mainly concerned with foreign and imperial affairs, and fell when it attempted to pass a bill to increase the penalty for conspiring to murder. The second Derby-Disraeli minority was defeated when it introduced a reform bill, and failed to win the general election it called in 1859.

Palmerston was then successful when Aberdeen had failed; a man of all parties himself, he put together a coalition of Whigs, Peelites, liberals and Radicals which he sustained until his death in 1865 following a triumphant general election. In the 1850s the Peelites had vacillated, distrusting Palmerston and Disraeli in equal measure; from 1859 they were committed to the Liberal party, if not to all aspects of the liberal cause. Gladstone consolidated

A contemporary comment on the repeal of the corn laws, 1846. Robert Peel, the baker, stands at the door of his cheap bread shop while the duke of Wellington, who had earlier supported a reduction in tariffs, carries a placard.

Northcote-Trevelyan report 1853
Report on civil service recruitment by Sir Stafford Northcote and Sir Charles Trevelyan, influenced by Gladstone: advocated extension to entire service of examination system already used in eleven departments, with supervision by central board. Loss of patronage and reduction of departmental discretion offended many within system; government accordingly confined itself to creation of Civil Service Commission to scrutinize applicants and nominees. Open competition not introduced until 1870.

Peelites
Tories remaining loyal to Peel after 1846 corn-law split: most of Peel's ministers, together with free-trade backbenchers, mainly representing small and middling boroughs. Reunion with Tories mooted 1851, 1855 and 1858, but never likely; Peelites joined Whigs in Aberdeen coalition 1852, and most moved over to new Liberal party in 1859.

Great Exhibition 1851
International exhibition of industry, science and commerce instigated by Prince Albert: held at Hyde Park in purpose-built Crystal Palace; attracted over six million visitors, up to five million of them carried by railway.

the party in the Commons around a series of free-trade budgets*, especially that of 1860 which was co-ordinated with the treaty negotiated with France by Richard Cobden*.

The Liberal party, as the governing coalition was coming in the 1860s to be called, was broadly based in its support in the country: industrialists, free-traders, nonconformists, Roman Catholics on the mainland and in Ireland, the multiplicity of reforming pressure groups which characterized Victorian politics, all looked to it for parliamentary representation. So also did those who as yet had no vote. Ex-Chartists and Radicals had moderated their aims since the 1840s: the Reform League* called merely for household suffrage (i.e. the male head of each household to have a vote). Whereas Tory support was almost wholly Anglican, Liberals spanned the whole religious spectrum from Roman Catholics through Anglicans and nonconformists to unitarians and to secularists such as J.S. Mill (a Liberal MP 1865-68). The Liberal party successfully combined and co-ordinated the demand for religious pluralism with that for fiscal and economic progress through free trade, the latter term implying a range of moral and political attitudes in addition to its strict, fiscal meaning of no protective tariffs.

In the 1850s several attempts were made to introduce a reform bill, some by those such as Russell who felt the 1832 Act needed carrying further, one in 1859 by the Conservatives who wanted to change an electoral system in which they never won. From 1864 Gladstone supported reform in principle, and after Palmerston's death he and Russell introduced a moderate bill in 1866*. It was defeated by a combination of Conservatives, Whigs and Liberals who thought the bill did too much, and by the hostility of radicals who thought it did too little. The Liberal government resigned. The Derby and Disraeli cabinet which took office introduced a Conservative reform bill; the Conservatives under Disraeli in the Commons accepted a number of Liberal amendments, and the 1867 Reform Act's* household suffrage clauses (enfranchising about fifty-eight per cent of adult males in the boroughs) went much further than the Liberal bill of 1866 would have permitted.

Regrouped on the question of Irish disestablishment, the Liberals won the 1868 election* after a campaign of religious, revivalist intensity. Gladstone's first government (1868-74) carried a number of major reforms, on Ireland*, education, the secret ballot and open careers in army, civil service and universities. This spate of legislation startled contemporaries, and disputes about the role of religion in education estranged many nonconformists; details of measures to legalize trade unions and control the drink trade upset both supporters and opponents. Despite its Irish measures, the government lost support there to Isaac Butt's Home Rule Association, and unsuccessfully attempted resignation after defeat on an Irish University Bill* (1873).

The Conservatives, and especially John Gorst, used the early 1870s to build up constituency organization*, and Disraeli comfortably won the 1874 election. After a Church Discipline Act (1874) and a series of social measures*, the Conservatives became relatively inactive in legislation. Disraeli's strategy of capitalizing on Liberal "mistakes" in foreign policy (such as the arbitration with the USA over the "Alabama"* civil-war damages case) and the alleged lack of Liberal imperial fervour, was crowned by the Royal Titles Act (1876) by which Victoria became Empress of India, which the Liberals foolishly appeared to oppose. Successful symbolically, and in purchasing almost half the shares in the Suez Canal (1875), Disraeli ran into political difficulties over

Budgets of 1860s
Series of free-trade budgets introduced by Gladstone as chancellor of exchequer 1860-66: aimed to simplify fiscal system by concentrating on a few items of general consumption; accordingly 1860 budget reduced items on tariff from 419 to 48. Income tax reduced at same time from 10d 1861 to 4d 1866. Facilitated by 10% drop in government expenditure and 40% increase in value of British exports 1860-66.

Cobden Treaty 1860
Free-trade treaty with France negotiated by Cobden: reduced French duties on coal and most English manufactures; Britain reduced duties on French wines, brandy and several manufactures; reductions effected by Gladstone's 1860 budget. British exports to France doubled in value 1859-69.

Reform League
Formed 1864: predominantly working-class pressure group seeking manhood suffrage and secret ballot; strong support among trade unionists who saw parliamentary reform as precondition for reform of industrial relations law. Supported Liberals in 1868 election and spent £2,000 during campaign, but collaboration caused friction within movement, which was wound up in 1869.

Reform Bill 1866
Proposed £7 rental qualification for borough franchise and reduction of county tenant franchise from £50 to £14. Also proposed enfranchisement of £10 lodgers in boroughs and £50 savings bank depositors in counties. Intended to enfranchise "respectable" urban working class. Would have added 400,000 to register, half of them working class. Tories reached agreement with Liberal right, led by Elcho and Lowe, and secured passage of Dunkellin amendment which would have substituted rateable value for rental qualification and actually restricted franchise in some boroughs. Russell ministry resigned.

Second Reform Act 1867
Bill introduced by minority Tory government proposed household suffrage with minor conditions and additions. Disraeli's determination to pass measure led to almost uncritical acceptance of amendments which greatly radicalized bill. Added 1.12 millions to existing UK electorate of 1.4 millions.

General Election 1868
First election after second Reform Act: returned 382 Liberals and 276 Conservatives. Liberals strongest in Ireland, Scotland and Wales and smaller English boroughs; Conservatives strengthened grip on English counties and made some ground in larger cities.

Irish Church disestablishment
Irish Church Act 1869 ended statutory establishment of "Anglican" Church of Ireland: Irish bishops ceased to sit in House of Lords, Church courts abolished; Commissioners of Church Temporalities sold property of Irish Church with existing tenants given pre-emptive right of purchase. 1869 also saw termination of grants to Presbyterians and Maynooth.

Irish University Bill 1873
Proposal for denominationally neutral Irish university in response to Catholic demands for counterpart to Protestant Trinity College, Dublin. Defeated by three votes, precipitating Gladstone's resignation; Disraeli refused to take office, Gladstone returned for a further ten months as prime minister.

Conservative party organization
1867 franchise extension necessitated changes in constituency organizations of both parties. Conservative organizations federated in National Union of Conservative and Constitutional Associations 1867; its annual conference became main party forum, although selection of candidates and disbursement of central fund remained with party whips and Conservative Central Office founded in 1870. National Union exercised little direct influence over policy.

Disraelian social reform
Social legislation of Disraeli's second ministry supposedly derived from his concern for improvement of condition of people, but measures largely departmental in inspiration, often extending work of previous ministry. Factory Act 1874 limited hours of labour of women and children in textile industry; Employers and Workmen Act and Conspiracy and Protection of Property Act 1875 removed breach of contract from criminal law and protected trade union activities from conspiracy laws; Artisans' Dwellings Act 1875 permitted more local authority slum clearance; Public Health Act 1875 consolidated sanitary legislation; Food and Drugs Act 1875 tightened law on adulteration of food; Education Act 1876 provided for committees to compel school attendance.

massacres in Turkey* (1876) and the Afghan (1878-79) and Zulu (1879) wars. Despite returning from a congress at Berlin* (1878) with "peace with honour" and the island of Cyprus, Lord Beaconsfield, as Disraeli became in 1876, found himself harried by Gladstone's Midlothian* campaigns (1879-80) which skilfully blended moral outrage with denunciation of the government's financial incompetence. The start of the prolonged agricultural depression *c.* 1875 and a sharp trade depression *c.* 1879 added economic distress to political hostility; the Liberals won the 1880 election easily.

Alabama claims
Wooden sloop later named *Alabama* built Birkenhead 1862 to engage in privateering for Confederacy during American Civil War. British government aware of purpose but failed to detain her. Harrassed Union shipping until sunk 1864. US claims for compensation from Britain followed end of Civil War. By Treaty of Washington 1871, GB and USA agreed to arbitration by tribunal of five. Final award 1872 found Britain liable for acts of *Alabama* but limited award to £3¼ millions against £9½ millions demanded by US.

Bulgarian atrocities 1876
Savage Turkish repression of attempted insurrection by Bulgarian nationalists; 15,000 Bulgarians massacred and 70 villages destroyed: wave of anti-Turk feeling in Britain. Gladstone's pamphlet "Bulgarian Horrors and the Question of the East" embarrassed government, whose foreign policy required upholding of Ottoman power.

Mezzotint after the painting by John Phillip of the Palmerston government front bench during the Commons debate on the Cobden Treaty in 1860.

See **Congress of Berlin** (page 267)

Midlothian campaigns 1879-80
Oratorical electoral campaigns in which Gladstone, adopted for Midlothian constituency, spearheaded Liberal victory in 1880. Gladstone exploited his own rhetorical skill, attacking Disraeli's foreign policy, high government spending and agricultural distress; underlined claim to return to Liberal leadership which he had resigned 1875.

Gladstone's second government (1880-85) sprang from the enthusiasm of the campaign against "Beaconsfieldism", an enthusiasm hard to sustain once in power. The ministry was not distinguished by a repeat of the great surge of reforms of the 1868-74 sort, but was beset by imperial and Irish difficulties. Boer hostility to the Conservative's attempts at federation in South Africa was suppressed until the British had eliminated the Zulu threat at Ulundi (1879), but it then erupted in the first Anglo-Boer war* (1880-81) in which British troops were temporarily defeated at Majuba Hill (1881); an uneasy compromise was reached by the Convention of Pretoria (1881), which gave the Transvaal independence under British suzerainty.

In North Africa, also, the Liberal government found itself "in bondage" to the tendencies of long-standing imperial involvement. Disorder and bankruptcy in Egypt led to British bombardment of Alexandria (1882) and the occupation of Egypt (1882-83) to safeguard the Suez Canal; the Liberal government obliged the Egyptian government to withdraw from the Sudan, but when General Charles Gordon* was sent to supervise the evacuation, he and his force were massacred at Khartoum (January 1885) by the Mahdist rebels. Imperial disaster and reluctant expansion thus seemed to characterize Liberal government; the first exposing it to ridicule, the second dismaying many of its supporters, especially the most articulate.

Irish affairs seemed to go no better; a further Land Act (1881, combined with a Coercion Act*) partly dissolved the Land League's campaign, but, despite extraordinary negotiations between Gladstone and the Home Rule leader, Parnell, while the latter was in gaol*, the Irish secretary, Lord Frederick Cavendish, was murdered*, and Fenians resorted to further terrorism both in England and Ireland.

The government's proposal to extend the household suffrage to voters in the counties was delayed by the House of Lords (1884). Salisbury used Conservative control of the Lords to force an important bargain*: household suffrage (enfranchising about sixty-eight per cent of the adult males in the counties) was to be balanced by a redistribution of seats* largely on Tory terms; single-member constituencies (with a few exceptions) became usual, and the increasingly significant phenomenon of suburban Conservatism became a

See **First Boer War 1880-81** (page 268)

See **Gordon and Khartoum** (page 268)

Irish coercion legislation 1881
Measures to restore order to Ireland following campaign of Land League: Protection of Person and Property Bill provided for suspension of Habeas Corpus in parts of Ireland at discretion of lord lieutenant; Peace Preservation Bill restricted holding of arms. Prompted unprecedented display of parliamentary obstruction by Irish Nationalists.

"Kilmainham Treaty" 1882
Agreement on Irish land reform reached between representatives of Liberal government and C.S. Parnell at Kilmainham Gaol, where Parnell had been imprisoned under 1881 Coercion Act. Coercion implicitly abandoned; Parnell agreed to co-operate with Liberal government in Parliament. "Treaty" provoked resignation of chief secretary for Ireland, W.E. Forster.

Phoenix Park murders 1882
Murder of Cavendish, new chief secretary for Ireland, and under-secretary in Phoenix Park, Dublin, by secret society, the Invincibles: led to new measure of coercion, Crime Prevention Act.

Third Reform Act 1884
Extended household and lodger franchise created for boroughs 1867 to counties, and instituted franchise for occupation of land or tenements worth £10 p.a. Under 1884 system seven distinct qualifications existed, though household and occupation franchises accounted for over 80% of electorate.

Redistribution of Seats Act 1885
Comprehensive revision of electoral map, retaining traditional county/borough distinction but creating predominantly single-member constituencies as subdivisions. 36 boroughs of under 50,000 population lost one member, 72 under 15,000 merged in surrounding counties. Seats thus gained redistributed largely in London, Lancashire, Yorkshire and northeast. Increased London representation benefited Conservatives, but Liberals predominant in new seats in industrial areas until rise of Labour party.

Gladstone addressing a crowd at Blackheath 28 October 1871. He recorded in his diary that he spoke for almost two hours, "too long, yet really not long enough for a full development of my points..."

Unauthorized programme

Originated in programme devised by cabinet Radicals Chamberlain and Dilke, after resignation from Gladstone's second ministry 1885, and in anticipation of ensuing general election. Proposed democratic county councils with compulsory purchase power for land transfer, free education and National Councils for local administration in Ireland, Scotland and Wales; later published as Radical Programme, with reform of Lords and disestablishment added. More radical than Gladstone's 1885 manifesto, which rejected free education and compulsory purchase.

First Home Rule Bill 1886

Return of 86 Irish Nationalists, holding balance of power in 1886 Parliament, was followed by Gladstone's espousal of Home Rule. 1886 Bill proposed Irish parliament, with executive responsible to it but denied control of "imperial" functions; Irish MPs to be removed entirely from Westminster. Defeated on second reading by 30 votes, after defection of Liberal Unionists.

Liberal Unionism

93 Liberals opposed second reading of Gladstone's first Home Rule Bill in 1886; 79 returned in 1886 election, usually unopposed by Conservatives; voted with Salisbury in 1886 Parliament. Agreement on fusion of Conservative and Liberal Unionist parties reached by leaders 1890 but not attained at constituency level; final merger 1912.

County councils

Local Government Act 1888 created 62 administrative counties; directly elected county councils inherited administrative functions of justices of the peace; 61 county boroughs also created, with full county powers.

National Liberal Federation

Federation formed 1877: intended as general federation of local associations, though less than half affiliated by 1884. Reflected wish of Chamberlain and Birmingham Liberal Association to encourage participation of party members in direction of policy.

Newcastle programme

Radical manifesto adopted by meeting of National Liberal Federation Council at Newcastle 1891: Irish Home Rule placed first, followed by resolutions reflecting preoccupations of constituency Liberal/Radical associations, including Welsh and Scottish disestablishment, free education,

powerful political force through the Redistribution Act (1885). As a result of the 1884-85 measures, about sixty-three per cent of the adult male population of Britain was enfranchised – the nearest the nation got to universal suffrage before 1918. Beset with threats of ministerial resignation, the unhappy Liberal government resigned in June 1885, succeeded briefly by a Conservative minority government under Salisbury.

The reformed electorate, as in 1868, returned a Liberal government (November 1885), encouraged perhaps by Joseph Chamberlain's "Unauthorized Programme"* for land reform (1885), but whereas in 1868 most Irish MPs had been Liberals they were now Home Rulers. Prompted by the force of the Home Rule case and by the political arithmetic of the election result (the balance of power being held by some eighty Home Rule MPs), Gladstone, in his short third government (1886), declared for Home Rule. However, his first Home Rule Bill* was defeated in the Commons, "Liberal Unionists"* – mainly landed Whigs led by Hartington, but also some urban radicals led by Chamberlain – voting with the Conservatives. Salisbury won the General Election (1886) and his second government lasted, with Liberal Unionist support (though not yet a formal coalition), until 1892.

Salisbury set out to consolidate the gains which the 1885 redistribution made possible. A rigorous anti-Home Rule stance, combined with relative inactivity at home and a "responsible" foreign policy, was intended to soothe the anxieties of the propertied classes; the introduction of county councils* (1888-89) was the only major legislation. Liberal attempts at reunification (1886-87) failed; Gladstone kept control of the National Liberal Federation*, the constituency organization founded by Chamberlain in 1877, and used its annual meetings, especially that at Newcastle* (1891), as the platform on which to consolidate various Liberal causes such as Home Rule for Ireland, Church disestablishment and a reduction in factory work-hours. This and an efficient voting registration campaign allowed the Liberals to win the General Election (1892) with eighty-one Home Rulers' help. Gladstone's fourth government (1892-94) was thus a minority one, primarily committed to Home Rule; his second Irish Home Rule Bill* passed the Commons but was defeated in the Lords, which also rejected or wrecked other Liberal bills. Hostile to his cabinet's support for the annexation of Uganda and for increased naval expenditure, Gladstone resigned; Lord Rosebery succeeded him (1894-95), but lost the 1895 General Election. Salisbury's third government (1895-1902) included the Liberal Unionist leaders in his cabinet, with Chamberlain as colonial secretary. His prescription of domestic inactivity remained the same, though the Workmen's Compensation Act* (1897) reflected the growing importance of trade-union influence.

electoral reform, land reform, reform or abolition of House of Lords and removal of duties on basic foods. Largely disowned by party managers after defeat in 1895.

Second Home Rule Bill 1893

Proposed bicameral Irish legislature, with "imperial" powers withheld from Irish executives as in 1886 Bill, but 80 Irish MPs retained at Westminster (forbidden to vote on purely British questions). Bill passed Commons with Irish Nationalist support but defeated 419 - 41 in Lords.

Workmen's Compensation Act 1897

Chief social reform measure secured by Joseph Chamberlain as Unionist minister: established principle of automatic compensation for industrial accidents as charge upon employer. Offended many Unionist industrialists but supported by Salisbury and Balfour.

Partly because of the success of the Liberals in incorporating a wide spectrum of radical policies and pressure groups, attempts at direct political representation by the working classes came surprisingly late to British politics. As British society became more urban, and industry became more complex, the family firm giving way to more impersonal management, trade unions developed. The Trades Union Congress*, whose origins date from 1868, gradually represented what in the 1880s became known as the "New Unionism"*: unions such as the Miners' Federation (1888), with a base wider than the skilled craftsmen who had made up the unions most characteristic of the mid-century. These unions reflected at an institutional level a growing working-class consciousness. In 1889 a dock strike in London gained much publicity, and in 1893 an Independent Labour party* was founded under Keir Hardie. The Labour Representation Committee*, soon to develop into the Labour party, was formed in 1900 to co-ordinate the parliamentary representation of the trade-union interest, threatened by the Taff Vale judgement.

This striking, if as yet ineffectual, departure from the incorporational tradition of British politics was an aspect of a general dissatisfaction with the performance of the mid-century "minimalist" Liberal state. Anxiety about the relative decline of the British economy began to become general in the 1890s and the growing prevalence of social Darwinism* caused inquiry by men such as Charles Booth and Seebohm Rowntree into the condition of the "imperial race". The Liberal party began to look to the state for "positive liberty" for social reform as well as the "negative liberty" of political emancipation characteristic of the Gladstonian years. The way was already pointed, for, despite the commitment of both parties to retrenchment, Whitehall's *per capita* expenditure on civil government (education, etc.) had nearly doubled between 1868 and 1900 (1868=£0.37; 1900=£0.62), and the expenditure of local authorities at least equalled that of central government.

Salisbury's 1895-1902 government was chiefly concerned with imperial affairs, and especially with consolidating the defence of the route to India. In 1898 the Sudan was finally occupied, and the French warned off the Nile. South African society was transformed by the gold discoveries in the Transvaal in 1886; expansion in Central Africa by Cecil Rhodes's British South Africa Company (1889) meant the Boers were surrounded. An attempt to undermine Boer authority by the Jameson Raid (December 1895) failed, but Alfred Milner, as high commissioner (1897), determined to provoke the Boers to war. In 1899 the Transvaal invaded Cape Colony; the second Anglo-Boer War* (1899-1902) began with disasters for the British, seemed to be won by 1900, but degenerated into a policy of guerrilla warfare, attrition and "concentration camps", as the British attempted to clear the veldt.

Salisbury's government was re-elected in the General Election of 1900, the first time a prime minister had achieved this since Palmerston, but victory turned sour; Queen Victoria died on 22 January 1901, the imperial splendour of her golden and diamond jubilees of 1887 and 1897 diminished in a mood of self-doubt and reappraisal about foreign and domestic policies and even the political structure of the realm, a mood which the Boer War diffused across a wide spectrum of the population.

Trades Union Congress

National federation of trade unions meeting annually from 1868, with smaller Parliamentary Committee between conferences from 1872. Initially acted as pressure group for reform of industrial relations legislation, but from 1890 more political.

"New Unionism"

Attempts from late 1880s to broaden base of trade union movement by organizing semi-skilled and unskilled workers in docks, public utilities, etc. Greatest advances made 1888-90, with victories in London gas-workers' and dockers' strikes of 1888-89. Unions aided by favourable trade conditions of late 1880s, with unemployment down to 2%; fell off after 1892, to revive c.1910.

Independent Labour party

Founded 1893, following formation of local independent labour clubs during 1891-92; concentrated in industrial north and Scotland. Objects included 8-hour day and other workplace reforms, free education and "collective ownership of means of production, distribution and exchange".

See **Labour Representation Committee** (page 294)

Social Darwinism

School of thought applying natural selection principle (especially as outlined in Darwin's *Origin of Species* 1859) to social and political analysis. Most frequently used to develop theories of competitive individualism and *laissez-faire*, but also engendered strain of Liberal collectivism.

Fabian Society

Political society, founded 1884; mainly middle class, intellectual and London-centred. Drew upon radical Liberalism and Marxism; also influenced by Jevonian economics. Leading figures included Sidney and Beatrice Webb, G.B. Shaw, Graham Wallas. Advocated gradual social reform, originally through Liberal party, though inclining towards Independent Labour politics from c. 1893.

Social Democratic Federation

Socialist society founded as Democratic Federation 1881, becoming SDF 1884: hostile to both Liberalism and trade unionism, predominantly middle-class membership. Advocated nationalization of "means of production, distribution and exchange". Organized unemployment demonstrations in 1886 and 1887.

See **Second Boer War** (page 268)

Ireland:
from ascendancy to democracy

D.G. Boyce

The history of Ireland between 1783 and 1901 has been characterized as another chapter in the unceasing struggle by "Ireland" to wrest from "England" the full measure of her lost national rights. In 1782 the Irish patriotic opposition, under the inspiration of Henry Grattan, took advantage of public feeling in Ireland, the international situation, and a change of government in Britain to win certain legislative freedoms for the Irish Parliament. In 1901 there existed a nationalist movement that sought the restoration of that Parliament, which had been merged with the British legislature in the Act of Union of 1800.

This period, however, saw a profound social, political and economic transformation of Ireland of far greater significance than the rise and fall of Irish legislative institutions. Indeed it was the failure of these institutions in the last quarter of the eighteenth century that provided the possibility for this transformation. In 1783 Ireland was controlled, as she had been since the Glorious Revolution of 1688-89, by Irish Protestants of Anglican persuasion; and the "Constitution of 1782" – a series of concessions made by the British government which placed the legislative independence of the Irish Parliament on a more secure footing – was essentially their constitution. It still excluded from power two important groups of Irishmen: Presbyterian dissenters, particularly strong in the north; and Roman Catholics, defeated and degraded after the Revolution, but now taking their first steps towards asking for the removal of political disabilities. Moreover, it failed to clear up the problem of Anglo-Irish relations, for the Irish Parliament was still under the influence of the executive in Dublin Castle; this executive was appointed in Britain, and was only imperfectly answerable to Irish MPs.

It is possible (though hardly likely) that these problems would have resolved themselves peacefully and gradually. But any hope of peaceful change was undermined by the French Revolution, which inspired radicals as much as it frightened the defenders of the present position. The British government hoped to win Roman Catholic support by forcing the Irish Parliament to concede political reforms*; but its failure in 1795 to fulfil the expectations thus raised was followed by the growing conviction among radicals that reform could only be achieved by revolution. The revolutionary cell was the Society of United Irishmen*, founded in 1791 and now under more determined leadership which sought allies among discontented Roman Catholics. This hastened the fragmentation of Irish political life; and when rebellion broke out in 1798* it was less a blow for Ireland than a struggle between Roman Catholics, Anglicans and Presbyterians. Although the rebels included members from all three groups, the '98 soon assumed the character of a sectarian war; and Irish political life was dominated by the mutually suspicious political/religious sections of a divided nation.

The British government resolved upon union* between England and Ire-

Irish Catholic relief in 1790s
Catholic Relief Act 1793, virtually forced on Irish Parliament by Pitt, enabled Catholics to bear arms, become members of corporations, vote as 40-shilling freeholders in counties and open boroughs and hold commissions in army; still barred from Parliament and government office. In 1795, lord lieutenant promised further liberal measures, but his unauthorized approval of full Catholic emancipation led to recall after three months under pressure from Protestant parliamentarians.

Society of United Irishmen
Founded Belfast and Dublin 1791; Irish manifestation of revolutionary enthusiasm. Attempts at suppression in 1794 led to reconstitution 1795 as secret society with complex cellular structure under executive directory in Dublin; became overtly republican under Theobald Wolfe Tone, and predominantly Catholic; developed military organization 1796-97. Claimed membership of 250,000 at time of 1798 rising, but declined rapidly after its failure.

Rebellion of 1798
Wolfe Tone's small invasion force of 1795 was scattered by gales and never landed; nonetheless prompted government to disarm Ulster 1797-98, which neutralized idealistic centre of disaffection when rebellion did break out in 1798. Consequently strong only in south-east, where peasant force of 500 decimated infantry at Oulart Hill, Wexford, but was routed at Vinegar Hill. Small French force which eventually landed in Connacht surrendered to Cornwallis.

Act of Union 1800
Dissolved separate Irish Parliament in return for Irish representation at Westminster; existing Irish Church establishment protected; largely free trade instituted between Britain and Ireland. Ireland to support two-seventeenths of UK expenditure, but debts already incurred to remain separate. Catholic hierarchy accepted Union on understanding that emancipation would follow, but George III resisted.

land in 1800 as the only means of averting further danger. Ireland was to be represented in the United Kingdom Parliament by 100 MPs in the Lower House, and 32 Lords in the Upper; but, until they were organized by the Parnellite Home Rule party in the 1890s, Irish MPs were small, shifting groups, unable (except for the O'Connellite party* of the 1830s and 1840s) to make any sustained mark. Nevertheless, Ireland's serious social and economic problems made her almost a kind of administrative and legislative laboratory, where English officials could apply all sorts of reforms: ecclesiastical, economic, governmental, educational. Some of these were carried out simply because Ireland was an integral part of the United Kingdom; but many were inspired by the conviction that, if the Roman Catholic majority in Ireland could have its material grievances met, then it would forget any aspirations towards restoring the parliamentary independence of Ireland.

For the Union had in British eyes taken on the sanction of fundamental law: in 1843 Sir Robert Peel emphasized his determination to maintain the integrity of the United Kingdom, even at the cost of civil war. But the policy of sound administration and material concessions to the Roman Catholics, followed by the Whigs in the 1830s and by Peel in the 1840s*, failed to reconcile the majority to the Union.

Several reasons help explain this: the initial disappointment over the failure to combine Catholic emancipation with union; its ungracious concession (after strenuous agitation by Daniel O'Connell) in 1829; above all the Great Famine* of 1847-8 which cost Ireland, by death or emigration, over 1,000,000 people, creating a generation of Irish Americans who held Britain responsible for the disaster. Yet the first half century of the Union, whatever its shortcomings, was not followed by any widespread or successful movement for its ending. Young Ireland and then, in the 1860s, Fenians might plot and even attempt rebellion; but there was no political or social opportunity for any kind of sustained pressure on the British government.

Such opportunity was provided by two main developments. British franchise reforms from the 1850s enabled the Irish tenant farmer to play a more active part in politics, and thus form a sound base for a nation-wide political party; and after the famine the tenant farmer saw his material position

O'Connell's party
39 men returned in 1832 General Election pledged to seek repeal of Act of Union; largest single Irish grouping. Allied with English Whigs at Westminster 1837-41, keeping them in power; reduced to 18 MPs in 1841 election, and subsequently overshadowed by extra-parliamentary repeal movement in Ireland. Strength increased after 1847 election, but party disintegrated rapidly after O'Connell's death in same year.

Tory Irish policy 1841-45
Origins of two-pronged policy familiar later in century: firm executive action curbed O'Connell's extra-parliamentary pursuit of repeal, with forced abandonment of "monster meeting" at Clontarf 1843 and severe Arms Act 1843; also attempts to gain support of Catholic hierarchy and moderate nationalists by attention to education, and land questions.

Great Famine
Intensive potato cultivation had accommodated 70% population increase 1791-1841; by mid-1840s potato sole food of third of population and essential to many more. Crop blight first occurred autumn 1845; 1846 and 1848 crops failed entirely, 1847 crop poor. Population fell by 2-2¼ million 1845-51, of whom some 800,000 died through starvation or malnutrition-induced diseases; remainder emigrated, mostly to USA.

Young Ireland
Nationalist movement founded 1842: echoed European romantic nationalism and stressed collective consciousness of Ireland. Split with repeal movement after O'Connell's return to parliamentarianism; divided on adoption of "physical force" policies until arrest of several leaders in 1848 drove it into attempted insurrection, failure of which led to disintegration of movement.

Fenians
Secret revolutionary organization founded 1858, strongly linked with American Irish community: name derived from Old Irish word for Irish warriors. Recruited from Catholic population, Irish soldiers in British army and some parish priests, though Catholic hierarchy hostile. Attempted insurrection in Dublin, Cork

and elsewhere 1867; arrest of leaders led to murder of police guard in Manchester and gunpowder explosion at Clerkenwell prison. Reconstituted as Irish Republican Brotherhood 1873.

Home Government Association/Home Rule League
Association founded 1870: embraced Conservatives, Liberals, moderate nationalists and Fenians, with Protestant majority; pressure group for federalism, with Irish parliament and executive but Westminster control over foreign policy and defence. Replaced by Isaac Butt's Home Rule League 1873; 1874 election (first under secret ballot) returned 59 Home Rulers. Divided over question of federalism versus independence, resulting in attack on Butt by radicals 1879. Parnell's party after 1880 more radical in tone.

Parnell's Irish Nationalist party
61 Home Rulers elected in 1880: resisted Forster's Coercion Bill by parliamentary filibustering, causing one session to last 41 hours – longest on record; moderated obstructionist tactics in return for concessions granted by Gladstone in "Kilmainham Treaty" 1882. 86 Nationalists returned in 1885, 85 in 1886. Pledged to abide by decisions of party majority, making them first fully organized parliamentary third party.

Irish National Land League
Founded 1879 to seek protection of tenants and encouragement of land purchase; leadership included C.S. Parnell and ex-Fenians. Organized popular resistance to eviction (including "boycott") and provided legal support for tenants. Weakened during 1881 as divisions emerged between rural bourgeoisie and poor peasantry and Parnell exchanged land war for parliamentary obstruction. Suppressed 1881 under Coercion Act.

Irish land legislation 1860-81
Landlord & Tenant Law Amendment Act 1860 tightened provisions for ejectment for default on rent. Landlord & Tenant (Ireland) Act 1870 sought to give tenants the right to compensation for eviction and for improvements made with landlord's consent; Treasury loans to tenants to encourage purchase of holdings, but terms (two-thirds price at 5% over 35 years) unenticing. Land Law (Ireland) Act 1881 legalized three f's (fair rent, free sale and fixity of tenure) throughout Ireland and established commission to assess fair rents. Purchase terms relaxed – three-quarters price at 5% over 35 years.

improve, only to be confronted, in the 1870s, by the fear that this process might be halted, or even reversed, by a recurrence of agrarian depression. This is not to underplay the importance of emotions, nor of the widely propagated belief that the British had left the Irish to starve in 1847. But starving people do not make rebellions, as the Young Irelanders* had discovered in 1848; and while Fenians* might gather sympathy, especially among the lower classes, it was becoming increasingly clear to politically alert Roman Catholics that more might be gained by votes than by bullets. Had not Gladstone demonstrated this in 1869, when his disestablishment of the Church of Ireland indicated that the Protestant ascendancy could be undermined by parliamentary means? And such a process could rally also the Roman Catholic Church in Ireland, now increasingly confident and well-organized.

The last quarter of the century saw the emergence of a dominating force in Irish politics: the Roman Catholic voter, sympathetic to the revolutionaries, but able to take care of himself. This democracy's politics, given parliamentary form by Parnell and his party*, were founded upon a deep-rooted conviction: that Roman Catholics were the rightful masters of Ireland, and would make good, by the best means available, their majority status – the Catholic nation would emerge from bondage and enter the promised land. Meanwhile the Parnellite movement, in alliance with Michael Davitt's Land League*, could show successes, as Liberals and Conservatives sought to solve the Irish question by tilting the balance in land tenure* in favour of the tenant as against the Protestant landlord. The Famine had initiated a rapid decline in the population and a rise in holdings of over fifteen acres, thus making possible a system of peasant proprietorship, and the foundation of a predominantly agrarian, conservative but nationalist movement.

It was the Union that enabled this powerful political and social movement to emerge in Ireland; but what response would the Protestant minority make, especially when in 1886 it saw its existence threatened by Gladstone's publicly revealed conversion to the cause of Home Rule for Ireland? Ulster had developed important economic links with Great Britain since the mid-nineteenth century. Irish Protestants were in any event determined not to stand idly by while they were handed over, bound and helpless, to their old enemies. Protestant fears were compounded by the cultural revival* of the 1880s and 1890s, which included among its conflicting aims a Gaelic movement seeking to restore the "true" Irish identity; for while individual Protestants might sympathize with an attempt to recover the Irish past, they could not as a body feel at home in a movement which implied or stated that Protestants were "Saxon interlopers".

But the Gaelic enthusiasm of the period was not the root of the problem. The essential point was that the Union, created for Protestant security (as it was believed), had been used by British politicians, in collusion with Irish nationalists, to undermine that security. After 1886 the Union itself was in danger, as the Home Rule-Liberal alliance was forged: Protestant survival was at stake, and must be defended. Irish Unionists, with their Conservative allies in Britain, defeated the Home Rule bills of 1886 and 1893; but no one doubted that the nationalist party, once recovered from its bitter disputes over the fall of Parnell* in 1891, would try again. And when Home Rulers resolved their differences in 1900, Irishmen of all political persuasions waited to see when – not if – the struggle would be renewed.

Ireland in 1901 was only superficially peaceful. But while the fundamental problems had not been resolved, their form had been changed. In 1783 the whole of Ireland was in the grip of a privileged Protestant minority; by 1901, except in Ulster, that minority had experienced the gradual transfer of power to the Roman Catholic majority. The Church of Ireland had been disestablished; local government* placed in the hands of elective (and therefore mainly Roman Catholic) councils; and peasant proprietorship all but achieved. One essential issue remained unresolved; that of the parliamentary union between Ireland and Great Britain. This final question was to provoke bloodshed and rebellion in the near future. But one thing was clear: whether they supported the Union or rejected it, Protestants and Catholics entered the twentieth century with their relative positions profoundly altered by its existence.

Irish land legislation 1885-1903
Ashbourne's Purchase of Land (Ireland) Act 1885 provided £5m loans for tenants to cover whole purchase price, at 4% over 49 years. Balfour's Act of 1891 provided much larger capital for purchase, but limited by provision for landlords to be paid in land stock rather than cash. Wyndham Act 1903 provided bonuses to encourage landlords to sell if three-quarters of tenants agreed. Total of £83m eventually advanced at 3¼% over 68½ years. Land Acts under Union led to purchase of over 11 million acres for £100 millions.

Irish cultural revival
Fall of Parnell shifted focus of nationalism from Westminster politics to revival of native traditions. Gaelic Athletic Association, founded 1884, comprised 411 clubs by 1900; Irish Literary Society founded by Douglas Hyde and W.B. Yeats 1891; Gaelic League formed by Hyde 1893. League under Hyde avowedly unsectarian and non-political, but GAA more militant and linked to Irish Republican Brotherhood. Acted as school for future nationalist leaders, including several prominent in 1916 rising.

Fall of Parnell 1891
Parnell's affair with Katherine O'Shea, wife of Irish MP, dated from 1880 and had been known of by Liberal leadership since 1882. O'Shea filed divorce petition 1889, citing Parnell as co-respondent. Pressure from within Liberal party, especially nonconformists, led Gladstone to inform Nationalists that parliamentary co-operation towards Home Rule could not continue without Parnell's removal. Nationalist party voted 45-27 against Parnell, who effectively withdrew from politics.

Irish Local Government Act 1898
Extended to Ireland system of elected local councils established in England by legislation of 1888 and 1894; councils dominated by Catholic and nationalist majority, advancing farmers, shopkeepers and publicans at expense of landlord class.

"All that is left: scene at a Mayo eviction". Illustrations such as this, in the Illustrated London News *of 17 April 1886, helped to undermine the Irish landlords' position in the eyes of British public opinion.*

Warfare and International Relations:
Britain, Europe and the "Pax Britannica"

D.W. Sweet

Britain lost her American colonies following an uncharacteristic failure to manipulate the states system of Europe in the interest of her own imperial position. A coalition of maritime powers, led by her traditional rival France and for the time being undistracted by continental preoccupations, was able temporarily to wrest ascendancy in the Atlantic from the British fleet, and to avoid worse disasters the government of Shelburne was forced to concede American independence. This failure served to point up three basic principles, distinct but interrelated, which were to animate British policy from 1783 until the First World War.

The first was control of the sea routes which constituted Britain's essential imperial and commercial communications. Naval ascendancy was secured at the battle of the Nile* (1798) and at Trafalgar* (1805), and was never thereafter seriously threatened (in spite of intermittent naval scares) until the rise of the German navy after 1900. It enabled the British to exercise influence wherever sea power could be brought to bear effectively, around the European littoral and in the islands and coastal provinces of the wider world. A major imperative underlying the expansion of the British Empire was the need for strategically-situated naval bases: thus for instance Malta, the Cape of Good Hope, and Ceylon, which were taken during the French wars in the 1790s, were retained at the general peace settlement of 1814-15. Sea power guaranteed the inviolability of Britain from invasion, the security of her imperial possessions, and the peaceful development of her world-wide trading interests. Britain's island situation, her industrial and technological progress, and her relatively limited population both required and enabled her to remain predominant at sea, which she could not aspire to become on land. Even in prolonged periods of peace, demands for economy in expenditure on armaments were not allowed to compromise naval security. At the end of the nineteenth century, British governments based their naval programmes on the "two-power standard"* – the maintenance of an effective force greater than the combined strength of the two next largest naval powers, which in effect meant France plus Russia.

The second principle was the security of certain strategically sensitive areas which, if they fell under the control of a hostile great power, could threaten Britain's naval communications. In Europe these were the Low Countries, which provided bases from which France might threaten British control of the English Channel; the Baltic Sea, which was of peculiar importance until the 1860s as the source of naval supplies, the very sinews of sea power; the Iberian peninsula, whose harbours lay on the flank of the sea lanes of the eastern Atlantic; and the straits between the Black Sea and the Mediterranean, whose possession by Russia would menace the direct route to India. Much of Britain's diplomatic, naval and, in the last resort, military activity throughout this period was in response to threats to her strategic interests in these vital

Battle of the Nile 1798
Successful lightning attack by Nelson upon French fleet in Aboukir Bay, following Napoleon's occupation of Egypt; ended French hopes of eastern empire, with associated threat to British interests in Levant.

Battle of Trafalgar 1805
Defeat and destruction by British fleet under Nelson of combined French and Spanish fleets under Villeneuve off Cadiz; greatly reduced invasion threat.

India Act 1784
Established Board of Commissioners for the Affairs of India to supervise political activities of East India Company: privy councillors empowered to inspect papers of Company and issue orders; Company retained right of appointment to posts in India, subject to royal veto; British subjects answerable to British courts for crimes in India.

Two-Power Standard
Naval Defence Act 1889 established policy of naval expansion, intended to guarantee margin of superiority over next two largest naval powers combined. Rendered more expensive by expansion of Japanese, German and US naval construction at turn of century, but maintained until 1908.

The Charge of the Light Brigade. *Coloured lithograph after W. Simpson, published in 1855.*

French Revolutionary War 1793-1802
British involvement in continental conflict followed French annexation of Belgium; France declared war on Britain and Holland 1793. First anti-French Coalition, of Britain, Holland, Austria, Prussia and Sardinia, disintegrated by 1795; Second Coalition, with Russia, Austria, Turkey and Naples formed 1799. Peace of Amiens 1802 ended war, but failed to limit French influence.

Napoleonic War 1803-15
Napoleon's expansionism led to renewal of war by Britain 1803: then threatened both with invasion and with strangulation of economy by Napoleon's closure of continental markets. Third Coalition 1805, with Austria, Prussia, Russia, Sweden and Naples, was dismantled 1807 as result of French victories. Tide turned with failure of Napoleon's invasion of Russia 1812, and Wellington's victory over French army in Spain at Vitoria 1813. Fourth Coalition formed with Prussia, Russia, Sweden and eventually Austria 1813. By late 1813 French driven back behind Rhine; Paris fell 1814.

Congress of Vienna 1815
International conference to arrange settlement after defeat of Napoleon: culminated in Final Act 1815. Future French expansion blocked by new kingdom of Netherlands (uniting Belgium and Holland), independent Swiss confederation and strengthened kingdom of Sardinia. Prussian gains built her up as central European obstacle to French or Russian expansion. Britain made colonial gains, including Trinidad, Malta and Cape.

Belgian Revolt 1830
Belgians rebelled 1830 against union with Holland imposed 1814; Dutch called for British support to defend Vienna settlement but Aberdeen, foreign secretary, reluctant to risk war with France. 1830 brought Palmerston to Foreign Office: accepted separation of Belgium and Holland and sought to ensure truly independent Belgium. Dutch attempt to recover Belgium by force resisted by Anglo-French intervention 1831-32; 1831 agreement guaranteed Belgian neutrality; Dutch acknowledged Belgian independence by Guarantee Treaty of 1839.

theatres. Thus, concerning the Low Countries, when the war against revolutionary France* began in 1793, Pitt's immediate aims were limited to expelling the French from the Austrian Netherlands and defending Holland (although the objects and scope of the conflict soon became much more extensive). At the Congress of Vienna* (1814-15) at the end of the Napoleonic wars*, Castlereagh successfully stipulated for a strong and united Netherlands kingdom which would act as a barrier against renewed French expansion. When this stability was endangered by the Belgian revolt* of 1830, Palmerston intervened to assert Britain's interest in a secure and independent Belgium, free from French influences; the guarantee treaty of 1839, which bound all the great powers to maintain the independence and integrity of Belgium, was largely his creation. In 1870 Gladstone, although anxious to keep Britain out of the Franco-Prussian war, successfully stipulated as the condition of British neutrality that the belligerents should respect that of Belgium. And it was Germany's violation of Belgium in August 1914 which was the occasion of Britain's entry into the First World War.

Perhaps the most striking example of Britain's recurrent involvement in these sensitive areas is provided by the long and complicated history of the "eastern question", the problem posed by the decline of the Ottoman Empire and the consequent prospect of Russia becoming preponderant in the Balkans, gaining control of the Straits, and achieving the naval ambitions in the Mediterranean which she had already manifested during the Napoleonic wars. This danger obliged Canning to intervene in the Greek revolt* in the 1820s, and Palmerston to respond to growing Russian influence over Turkey in the 1830s. In 1841 Palmerston secured the assent of all the great powers to a convention* which closed the Straits to their warships, and this was regularly reaffirmed in subsequent treaties dealing with the eastern question. When in 1853 the Russians presented further demands to Turkey and backed them up with warlike measures, even so pacific an administration as that of Aberdeen and Clarendon went to war in alliance with France to preserve Turkey from Russian domination. The Crimean War* (1854-56) was the only occasion between 1815 and 1914 when Britain sent a military expedition to Europe to fight another great power, and the terms of the Treaty of Paris (1856) indicate that the primary war aim was to reduce Russia's power of aggression in the

Greek Revolt 1821-30
Rebellion against Turkish rule broke out in Morea peninsular and Greek islands 1821. Canning negotiated Treaty of London 1827 with Russia and France, offering mediation to Turkey to establish self-governing Greece under Ottoman suzerainty. Turkish rejection led to destruction of Turkish fleet by three powers at Navarino 1827. Protocol of 1830 agreed on Greek independence, with Wellington securing more limited frontiers to reduce potential as Russian satellite.

Straits Convention 1841
1840 four-power agreement with Turkey made protection of Sultan conditional upon Straits being closed to all foreign warships in peacetime; France joined other powers in Straits Convention 1841, substantially reiterating terms of 1840 agreement. Convention neutralized threat of Russian expansion – and thus threat to British Mediterranean route to India – posed by weakness of Turkey.

Crimean War 1854-56
After Turks declared war on Russia 1853, destruction of Turkish fleet revived threat of Russian expansion into Mediterranean: Britain and France declared war on Russia 1854, gained victory at Alma, resisted Russian attacks at Balaclava and

Black Sea area. However, Russia repudiated the relevant clauses as early as 1870, and the question entered a further acute phase with her victory over Turkey in 1878. Disraeli threatened military action, and at the Congress of Berlin* forced the Russians to disgorge their more extreme gains. The Treaty of Berlin (1878) brought an uneasy stability to the Balkans, reinforced by Salisbury's agreements with Italy and Austria* (1887), which envisaged some degree of co-operation to resist further Russian encroachment. But by the late 1890s Salisbury had become pessimistic about the viability of this policy, and later phases of the eastern question, the Bosnian crisis (1908-9) and the Balkan wars (1912-13) saw British diplomacy active in promoting the orderly liquidation of what remained of Turkey in Europe; the Straits, however, remained under Turkish control.

The third principle of British policy was to inhibit the creation of any strong continental coalition, and to prevent a single power from achieving domination over the European Continent and mobilizing its combined resources against the British Empire. Thus Britain emerged as the most implacable opponent of Napoleonic France and was almost continuously at war from 1793 to 1815; she was the one consistent element in successive anti-French coalitions, and made a vital contribution on land as well as at sea to the eventual victory*. The reconstruction of Europe at the Congress of Vienna (1814-15), in which Castlereagh played a decisive role, served British interests well: it provided guarantees against renewed French hegemony, and restored a multi-polar balance of power which rendered a hostile coalition improbable. It was this balance, rather than the specific mechanism of the Congress* or the looser concept of the European Concert*, which was indispensable to British security. When necessary, British governments would associate themselves with

PUNCH, OR THE LONDON CHARIVARI.

"MOSÈ IN EGITTO!!!"

In Tenniel's cartoon in Punch *of 11 December 1875, Disraeli is shown congratulating himself on acquiring the Suez Canal shares. The sphinx evidently approves. The title of Rossini's opera,* Moses in Egypt, *is used as an allusion to Disraeli's Jewish origins.*

Inkerman 1854, captured Sebastopol fortress 1855. Russia forced to accept Treaty of Paris 1856, which guaranteed independence of Ottoman Empire and neutralized Black Sea, preventing formation of Russian fleet there.

Congress of Berlin 1878
Last of the great international congresses, convened to settle affairs of East after Russo-Turkish war 1877-78 and to revise Treaty of San Stefano. By Treaty of Berlin Russia agreed to reduced frontiers for autonomous Bulgaria, Britain occupied Cyprus and Austria occupied Bosnia and Herzegovina, under norminal Turkish sovereignty; relieved immediate danger of Russian domination of Balkans.

Mediterranean agreements 1887
Informal agreements by which Britain, Austria-Hungary and Italy strove to preserve *status quo* in Mediterranean in view of continuing decline of Ottoman empire and threat of Franco-Russian rapprochement. Represented relinquishment of traditional British suspicion of continental alliances.

Battle of Waterloo
Final defeat of Napoleon by British and Prussian forces under Wellington and Blücher at Waterloo, 10 miles south of Brussels, 18 June 1815. Ended Napoleon's "hundred days" – attempt to return to power after escape from Elba in March.

Congress system
Derived from agreement under 1815 Quadruple Alliance (Russia, Austria, Prussia and Britain) upon collective action and regular meetings to maintain Congress of Vienna settlement. France admitted to system after first congress 1818; subsequent congresses held 1820, 1821, 1822, but Britain withdrew 1822 and system largely collapsed.

Concert of Europe
Principle of collective great-power action to maintain peace of Europe, by which limited collaboration was achieved over Greek revolt, Belgian revolt and eastern crisis of 1840-41, and major war averted until Crimean conflict 1854-56.

A still picture, taken from an early film, showing British troops at Spion Kop in January 1900, where the Boers inflicted heavy casualties.

Occupation of Egypt 1882
Growing British trade to India through Suez Canal (opened 1869) and investment in Egypt brought increased British interest in Egyptian affairs. Increasing anti-European nationalist influence in Egypt prompted Anglo-French action to avert any threat to canal, and led to unilateral British occupation; nationalists defeated by Wolseley at Tel-el-Kebir 1882.

Gordon and Khartoum
Mahdist rebellion against Egyptian Khedive began in Sudan 1881: Gladstone's government resolved 1884 to send force under General Gordon to evacuate Egyptian garrisons at Khartoum. Mahdist successes trapped Gordon in Khartoum; cabinet divisions prevented sending of Wolseley's relief expedition in time to forestall fall of Khartoum and Gordon's death 1885. Major blow to public standing of Gladstone's government.

Reconquest of Sudan
Evidence from late 1880s that British could not soon withdraw from Egypt led to policy of warding off any threat to Nile headwaters and thus to Egyptian economy. Resulted in partition of East Africa with Germany 1890, British Protectorate in Uganda 1894 and decision to reconquer Sudan. Kitchener led Egyptian army south 1896, finally defeating dervishes at Omdurman 1898.

First Boer War 1880-81
In 1877 Boers of Transvaal were pushed to accept British annexation, but rebelled 1880 against British rule; defeated British at Majuba Hill 1881. Pretoria Convention 1881 restored Transvaal Republic, with imperial veto over foreign relations and safeguards for natives; London Convention 1884 surrendered powers over native affairs.

Second Boer War 1899-1902
Culmination of seventy years of Anglo-Boer tension. Boers invaded Natal 1899: inflicted defeats on British forces and besieged British garrisons at Kimberley, Ladysmith and Mafeking; all relieved 1900. Orange Free State and Transvaal annexed 1900, but Boers began guerrilla campaign which led British to resort to clearances and concentration camps. Peace of Vereeniging 1902 confirmed annexation of OFS and Transvaal, but promised future self-government.

one power or another to adjust the balance: Palmerston did so in his alignment with France after 1834 (as Grey was to do in the years before 1914), and he evidently regarded the Crimean war as an opportunity to restrain the growing power of Russia in Europe, in the interest of the balance of power. But down to 1900 at least, the antagonisms and alignments of the continental states shifted too frequently to permit the emergence of any stable anti-British coalition. Consequently Britain was able to maintain a position of qualified isolation, which in the 1890s was even characterized as "splendid isolation", and to concentrate her resources upon the development and expansion of her global interests, whether in the shape of formal empire or informal preponderance.

This development went on regardless of the political complexion of the party in office: differences between parties over imperial expansion, as over foreign affairs in general, were more a matter of style and rhetoric than of substance. For instance, it was Disraeli who, by arranging the purchase of shares in the Suez canal in 1875, secured Britain's interest in the canal as the direct route to India and the Far East; but it was Gladstone's government which, by authorizing the occupation of Egypt* in 1882, ensured its physical control. By the close of the century, the British Empire had so expanded as to embrace some eleven million square miles (almost one-fifth of the global land mass) and 372 million people (a quarter of the world's population). The process of imperial consolidation was effectively completed by the Boer War* (1899-1902). Although there was to be one further large increment of empire in altered circumstances after the First World War, Britain in the early twentieth century showed every sign of being a satiated imperial power.

The British Economy:
growth and structural change

P.L. Payne

During the closing decades of the eighteenth century, the British economy was exhibiting many symptoms of economic growth; the population was expanding, the output of agricultural and manufactured goods was rising, and incomes were increasing. Such features are revealed by historians processing inadequate statistics. More visible to contemporaries were, for example, the division of the open fields by rows of quickset hedges, drystone walls, timber fences and rows of trees; the improving state of the roads; the newly constructed tunnels, embankments, aqueducts, inclined planes and locks of the canals, along which travelled barges heavily laden with coal, raw materials for building and manufacture, and foodstuffs; the conversion of long derelict corn mills into factory premises; the blazing light shed by newly-erected blast furnaces and forges; and the thousands of bales of raw cotton which threatened to choke the existing dock facilities of the Mersey and the Clyde. These outward signs of a buoyant economy were obvious to the most casual observer, who was doubtless also conscious that an increasing proportion of the population appeared to be better fed, better clothed, housed and warmed than ever before. What was remarkable was that these trends, interrupted though they may have been by periodic and violent short-term fluctuations, were to continue. For the very first time, the constraints which had inhibited growth in the past no longer possessed the power to arrest, far less reverse, the upward momentum which was boosting the nation's output even faster than the upward surge of population. The majority of the British

Akroyd's loom-shed at Halifax. One of the largest woollen factories in Yorkshire, the careful layout symbolizes the exercise of the new managerial skills required by successful industrialists. In many cases, better organization contributed almost as much to increased production as the use of the machines themselves. Note also the predominantly female labour force and the use of leather belts to transmit power to the looms.

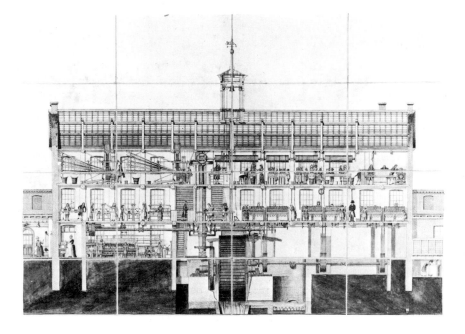

Bedworth worsted mill, drawn c. 1800 by L. Lequesne. In about 1787, Sir Roger Newdegate conceived the idea of using a disused water wheel on his estate as the motive power for a factory. Two large looms can be seen at the top left, with warping mills directly beneath them. On the right are spinning machines.

people, who even in earlier decades of the eighteenth century had enjoyed living standards significantly above those of their continental neighbours, were destined to enjoy even higher standards, although the diversion of resources and the distortion of prices occasioned by the French Wars were important factors in postponing major gains until perhaps the third decade of the nineteenth century.

Economic growth – by which is meant a sustained increase in production per head of population – on this scale was totally new, and since its most obvious outward manifestation was the rise of industry, it is hardly surprising that the period between, say, 1760 and 1830 has been labelled "The Industrial Revolution". The use of this expression is somewhat misleading, however, for it is now clearer than it used to be that the Industrial Revolution was neither cataclysmic nor confined to industry. Even the *rate* of economic growth was surprisingly modest, rarely exceeding two per cent per year. Compared with the experience of several of Britain's continental neighbours and the United States when they too began to industrialize in the nineteenth century, the rate of British economic growth during the years 1783-1901 was hardly exceptional.

Nevertheless, a rate of growth of national product averaging two per cent per annum produces a threefold increase of total output in the space of a lifetime, and an eightfold increase over the span of a century. Had the population not been sweeping upwards too, such a rise in output would have been capable of multiplying living standards by similar factors. As it was, the

Coalbrookdale by Night *by Philip De Loutherbourg, exhibited at the Royal Academy in 1801. It shows the Bedlam furnaces and coke heaps beside the River Severn. Coalbrookdale was a name often given to the entire Severn Gorge, and it was a favourite subject for artists, among them Sandby and Cotman.*

Handloom weavers

Mechanization of cotton spinning from 1770s created demand for handloom weavers; numbers peaked at over 200,000 in late 1820s, concentrated in Bolton, Preston and north-east Lancashire. Spread of powerloom weaving from 1820s brought technological unemployment, only 43,000 handloom weavers by 1850. Many absorbed into factory system where employment was available, though severe poverty in isolated outworking villages.

Coming of the railways

Some 400 miles of railway existed, mostly in collieries, by 1820, before accepted milestones of railway age: Stockton and Darlington Railway 1825, Liverpool and Manchester 1830, London and Birmingham 1838. Bursts of railway investment both reflected and affected swings in capital market, coinciding with "bullish" periods in 1833-36, 1844-47 and mid 1860s. Railways financed by joint-stock companies, locally backed at first but increasingly nationally funded from 1840s. 18,000 route miles built by 1900, owned by over 100 companies, though largest 14 owned 85% of total.

potential rate of increase in income per head was effectively halved by a population increase of slightly over one per cent per annum, and because of the unequal distribution of the national income those at the lower end of the social scale enjoyed even lower rates of increase in their living standards. However, apart from the luckless handloom weavers*, there were few who failed to derive some benefit from the early acceleration of economic activity, though for the majority significant improvement was delayed until the second half of the nineteenth century.

The economic growth that took place involved major changes in the nation's economic structure. There was a relative decline in both the proportion of the national work force engaged in agriculture and the contribution which agriculture made to the national income. From employing roughly a third of the British labour force and generating a similar proportion of the national income in 1801, agriculture's share in the national economy fell to less than ten per cent in 1901, an exceptionally low level by comparison with other advanced and industrializing nations. The obverse of this decline in agriculture was the increasing role of industry (including mining and construction) in the national economy: the relative positions of agriculture and industry were roughly reversed between 1783 and 1901. This reversal of roles is perhaps the strongest justification for the retention of the expression "The Industrial Revolution". Unfortunately, the continued use of the term does obscure the enormous significance of the service sector of the economy. The numbers of those in the service sector were always substantial (rarely more than a percentage point or two below industry) and, by the mid-nineteenth century, their contribution to the national income was quite equal to that of the industrial sector.

This tertiary or service sector comprised not only the tens of thousands of ill-paid female domestic servants (three times as numerous as the total number of men, women and children employed in the cotton mills in 1834), and almost as many workers engaged in transport and distribution, particularly after the coming of the railways*, but members of the professions and a small though increasing number involved in providing mercantile, shipping, banking, insurance and stock broking services. It is the inclusion of these latter occupational categories that helped to boost the disproportionate share of London and the south-east of England in the geographical distribution of the

New Lanark village, c. 1818, built by Robert Owen. The cotton mills are in the foreground, with new housing for the workers behind.

Lithograph of about 1840, showing the North Midland Railway passing beneath the Cromford Canal at Bull Bridge. The line, which ran between Derby and Leeds, was opened for traffic in 1840. The engineer was Robert Stephenson and the architect Francis Thompson, who may have designed the bridge shown here.

national income. The chimneys, mills, forges and steam engines of the north and the midlands may well have captured the imagination of writers, artists and poets, but an overwhelming share of the nation's wealth, and the maximum opportunity for its multiplication, continued to reside in and about the City of London. Few proprietors of textile mills, shipbuilding yards and iron works are to be found in the first rank of the wealth-holders. The very wealthy were invariably landowners, merchants, bankers and, towards the end of the century, those who possessed the bonds of foreign governments, mortgages of overseas real estate, the shares of shipping companies and the debentures of the world's railway network.

But it was the rise of industry that gave a unique character to this century. Perhaps the most important factor in promoting industrial development was the expansion of demand for manufactured products. It was this to which the early entrepreneurs responded. Sensing opportunities to enrich themselves, they took up the new inventions in cotton manufacture; when the cost price squeeze dictated change, the ironmasters adopted smelting with coke*; in the potteries, productivity and quality were improved by systematic specialization, by the energetic adoption of the division of labour; and colliery proprietors laid down cast-iron rails from the pit top to the nearest navigable waterway to supply distant markets. There was a ferment of activity in many branches of industry as individual proprietors, small partnerships and joint stock companies, sought to increase output and cut costs to exploit previously untapped levels of demand.

There was "a wave of gadgets", not only recognizably new inventions, such as Arkwright's waterframe, Cort's puddling and rolling process* and Watt's steam engine, but a myriad of minor improvements to machines, equipment and organizational methods which cumulatively raised productivity and reduced costs. There was, too, a movement towards factory production, though imposing, purpose-designed mills were highly exceptional until well into the nineteenth century. Initially more typical were small workshops, garrets, and converted corn mills. Labour was drawn into such factories, but it was a remarkably slow process. Even the capital sums required by the new entrepreneurs were certainly until 1837 overwhelmingly required more for the purchase of raw materials, the distribution of finished products and the extension of credit, than for investment in fixed, durable plant and machinery.

Coke smelting
Smelting by coke, eliminating sulphur content of raw coal, perfected by Abraham Darby I in 1709. Coke eventually cheaper than charcoal, less likely to clog furnace, allowing greater volume of fuel, thus increasing output. Need for stronger blast inhibited spread of coke smelting until application of Watt's steam engine to blast furnaces from mid-1770s: by 1790, 81 out of 106 furnaces burned coke. Iron industry steadily shifted to sites of coal deposits, S.Wales, Staffordshire and Yorkshire.

Cort's puddling process
Coke-smelted pig iron originally unsuitable for conversion into wrought iron because made brittle by impurities introduced in smelting. Some improvements effected by Abraham Darby II c.1750, but most effective methods those patented by Peter Onions 1783 and Henry Cort 1784. Cort used reverberatory furnace, in which fuel and metal were separated and molten pig iron was stirred and decarburized by circulation of air.

Capital exports

Total British overseas investment rose from £235 million 1854 to £2 billion 1900, yielding annual income then of £100 million p.a. Reflected extent of British capital accumulation and unevenness of its distribution, which depressed domestic interest rates. Average return on foreign securities 1870-1913 24% higher than on British. By 1914 Britain owned 41% of total international investment. Early investment mostly in colonies, but by turn of century chiefly in USA, Argentina and Australia. Generated continuous balance of payments surplus and helped establish City of London as world financial centre.

Retailing revolution

Expansion of consumer market and its concentration in towns encouraged refinement of distribution and retailing in late 19th century. Principles of "vertical integration" – connection of wholesale and retail agencies – and branch system derived from development of co-operative movement from 1840s. Applied to grocery trade by Thomas Lipton from 1872; Liptons had 250 branches by 1900. Nationwide multiple networks spread outside food trade, especially in footwear and clothing, from 1880s. Department stores spread from France during 1870s, transforming existing outlets like Debenham's and creating new ones like Whiteley's. Offered low prices through bulk discount purchases from suppliers.

The Great Eastern, *Brunel's largest iron-clad steamship, in the course of construction 1857. The hull and paddle engines were built on the Thames by Scott Russell & Co and the screw engines in Birmingham by James Watt.*

The capital demands of industry, as such, were remarkably modest in comparison with the investment required for housing the burgeoning population – or even the annual cost of shoeing the horses which, until the coming of the railways, carried or hauled the raw materials, the products of industry, and the foodstuffs needed to feed those clustered in the expanding urban areas.

Furthermore, it is important to recognize the comparatively narrow industrial base being created. During the reign of George III, the great inventions, the new methods, the problems of the recruitment of labour and capital, were pioneered in textiles, particularly cotton textiles. Almost paradoxically, Britain's rise to economic predominance was founded on the manipulation of a foreign raw material and (increasingly) the distribution of cotton goods to every quarter of the globe. Iron-making was initially a far more domestic affair exploiting, as it did, indigenous supplies of coal and ore and depending on home demands for its market. The same is true of pottery, the secondary metal trades, chemicals, glass, and brewing. Yet these were the products which the home population and ultimately the world wanted.

Unfortunately, the world – or at least the developing parts of it – could follow Britain's example and increasingly did so, assisted by both massive capital outflows* from London and by the emigration of skilled labour from all parts of the British Isles. By 1870, the end of British industrial hegemony was becoming apparent. The rate of growth of industrial production was slowing down. Foreign manufacturers, often protected by a wall of tariffs, were supplying their own needs, and British consuls, merchants and manufacturers' agents reported growing competition from indefatigable and ingenious American commercial travellers and persevering, multi-lingual, scientifically trained German salesmen throughout the world.

For some time this competition could be shrugged off, even – in the case of Lancashire – contemptuously ignored. In some cases, it made economic sense to abandon lesser markets and concentrate selling efforts on "softer" areas. Alternatively, improvements in product quality, permitting British manufacturers to move up-market, were implemented, and efforts were made to cater to the whims of buyers to an extent which Americans, with their emphasis on long runs of standardized articles, refused to countenance. New inventions – or cumulatively important improvements to existing technology – in the manufacture of textiles, iron and steel, heavy engineering, shipbuilding, railway locomotives and rolling stock, were taken up when it seemed rational to do so, but the long-term profitability of Britain's staple industries created little incentive to move resources into making entirely new products such as electrical goods, certain machine tools, and several branches of chemicals. The British manufacturing base remained remarkably undiversified, while the market for British coal seemed almost insatiable. In retrospect, it is apparent that many opportunities were missed, but major entrepreneurial errors in existing lines of activity are remarkably difficult to substantiate, despite the British enthusiasm for self-flagellation.

Whatever doubts remain concerning the quality of the entrepreneurial response in the staple industries, few question the vigour of those engaged in the manufacture of consumer goods, the makers of soaps, patent medicines, mass-produced foodstuffs and confectionery; or those pioneering new methods of distribution, the proprietors of departmental and chain stores* in the high streets of the major cities and towns. The best of late-Victorian advertising was sometimes breathtaking in its topicality and ingenuity. Manufacturers and merchants sought to convince and to sell to a public wielding increasing purchasing power, as a flood of cheap imported agricultural products poured in from every corner of the globe and thereby reduced the proportion of household budgets which necessarily had to be diverted to the purchase of basic foodstuffs. There has been little retrospective criticism here, nor much evidence of that shortage of capital which is said to have stifled the rapid development of several new and promising manufactured products.

Was there, in fact, a shortage of capital? And, if so, was it a direct consequence of the truly enormous level of overseas investment? The answer to both these inter-related questions would appear to be "no". The evidence suggests that those seeking to exploit patents, manufacture fresh novelties and establish businesses catering to new or imagined needs experienced little difficulty in getting started. Partnerships continued to be created or expanded; larger needs could be met by an appeal to the public through the instrument of joint-stock limited liability companies registered, since the legislation of 1856*, without fuss and without crippling expense. The London capital market may well have been biased towards large overseas ventures, the flotation of the bonds of foreign governments, the funding of railway companies abroad, but the provincial stock exchanges – growing ever more numerous – did not spurn domestic activities and their existence considerably reduced the illiquidity of risky ventures at home and abroad.

And if the British investor turned to opportunities in the uttermost parts of the globe, was this necessarily detrimental to the British economy and, what was ultimately more important, the well-being of the British people? In an international economy dominated by London and the pound sterling and conducted in acordance with the "rules of the game" for the operation of a gold standard, British foreign investment *did* pay. Overall, the yield from overseas investment was higher than the domestic market could offer; British exports benefited, and the bulk of the population enjoyed a rise in their living standards faster than ever before. These investments were directly responsible, too, for much of the buoyancy of the service sector of the economy in which, as we have seen, a very high proportion of the employed population was engaged. Indeed, many of them were in shipping, and when shipping prospered, so did shipbuilding (in which the British predominance was unquestioned in 1901) and hence a significant part of the iron and steel industry. Not all services owed their genesis and health to industry; in this case perhaps the most progressive and innovative branch of British industry in the closing decade of the 19th century was energized by the service sector.

But what of the individual firm? One factor promoting the rise in the standard of living of the multitude was that for most of their wants the potential purchaser was confronted by a fiercely competitive range of suppliers of goods and services. It is true that product differentiation had enabled a few manufacturers to attain a favourable market position and that the whims of consulting engineers sometimes placed the makers of certain goods, whose products were specified in large contracts by government agencies, railway and shipping companies, in a monopolistic position but, by and large, the necessity to compete kept prices low and the quality of products and services high. Any failures were penalized by loss of sales to rival domestic or foreign suppliers. During the nineteenth century efforts to subvert the sovereignty of the consumer by market-sharing schemes and price-fixing arrangements tended to be brief and ineffective. Yet by the mid-1880s, "there had arisen a

Limited liability legislation

1720 Bubble Act, which had restricted joint-stock enterprises in wake of 1718-19 speculations, repealed 1825; Companies Act 1844 facilitated registration of joint-stock companies; legislation of 1855-56 extended limited liability so that shareholders no longer faced danger of unlimited losses; 1862 Companies Act consolidated previous legislation. Number of companies registered annually rose from average 554 1866-70 to 5017 1896-1900.

Monetary policy after 1844

1844 Bank Charter Act intended to allow Bank of England freedom in commercial operations without jeopardizing monetary stability, but crisis of 1847, following Bank's expansionary role in speculative mania of 1844-46, indicated that two were inseparable. Subsequently Bank retired from commercial role to emphasize that of monetary regulation, keeping Bank Rate above market discount rates and raising it to correct drains of gold on foreign exchanges. From early 1870s open market purchases of government stock used to control money supply: reasonable domestic price stability secured, though sometimes at cost of severe contraction elsewhere in international economy.

Pears' Soap

"For years I have used your soap, and no other."

Lillie Langtry recommending Pears' soap in an advertisement of the early 1880s.

The Devon and Somerset Stores, c.1904, one of the new provincial chain stores which offered lower prices through bulk purchase.

Employers' associations

Price-fixing within trades frequently attempted but not generally effective before *c*.1870. Trade associations emerged from 1860s and especially from 1880s, often as defensive reactions to success of newcomer. From *c*.1890 formal cartels common, especially in textiles and shipping, with price-fixing agreements, production quotas and agreements on profits; most effective in industries where high capital costs dissuaded newcomers.

Industrial mergers in 1890s

Encouraged by growth of joint-stock enterprises under limited liability legislation and by technological advance demanding capital concentration. Major combines in brewing industry formed during 1880s, United Alkali Company 1890, Lever Brothers 1890, Wallpaper Manufacturers 1899, Associated Portland Cement Manufacturers 1900, Imperial Tobacco 1901 – largest firm in Britain – Guest, Keen & Nettlefold 1902. GKN linked firms in vastly different processes, but horizontal organization generally more common than vertical integration.

The Punch *cartoon of 1884 which Pears adopted in a subsequent campaign.*

network of trade associations* buttressed by arrangements and understandings and gentlemen's agreements more numerous", observed the editor of *Engineering*, "than the average man ever dreamed of". And in the dying years of the century more permanent organizations, usually referred to as trusts, were formed by amalgamations in textiles, brewing, iron and steel, cement, wallpaper and tobacco, during which as many as 650 firms valued at a total of £42 million were absorbed in about 200 mergers*. Badly organized and inefficient though they seem to have been, these giant concerns affected only a small part of the entire range of British industry. The largest hundred of them perhaps accounted for barely fifteen per cent of output, but they were the precursors of the corporate economy of the twentieth century by which British industry became dominatd by large, often monopolistic organizations, and the "invisible hand" of the market-place was superseded by the allocation of resources and intermediate products by an administrative rather than a price mechanism.

From being the first industrial nation, Britain, in the course of the nineteenth century became one of several industrial nations. Contemporary observers and later critics have erred in believing that Britain's lead could have been maintained. Their comments betray a belief that British supremacy before the mid-1870s was somehow normal and her accelerating relative decline thereafter, abnormal. But the whole complex of circumstances that produced Britain's early pre-eminence was fortuitous, and as the United States and Germany caught up and eventually surpassed the United Kingdom, and as other countries began to supply their own manufactured goods, British industry tended to assume a relative international position more appropriate to its natural resources, the size of its home market and the share of the export market which it might justifiably expect. For the British economy, then as now, the future lay in services. At the dawn of the twentieth century, Britain continued to lead in shipping, insurance, brokerage and commission services and in international banking and the supply of capital. Britain may have lost her leading position as an industrial power by 1901, but she remained the world's chief financial and trading power. This was no mean achievement.

Society:
the emergence of urban Britain
Michael E. Rose

One of the most dramatic features of Britain's industrial revolution was the rapid growth in her population. In 1700, there were an estimated five and a half million people in England and Wales. At the first official census in 1801, nearly nine million were recorded; by 1851, the population had doubled to almost eighteen million people. Scotland experienced similiar rates of growth, from 1.2 million in 1755 to 1.7 million in 1801 and nearly three million by 1851. By mid-century, the years of most rapid growth were over, and later a distinct slowing down in the rate of growth became visible, a portent of the still more dramatic decline in the rate of growth in early and mid-twentieth century British society.

The "population explosion" of the late eighteenth and early nineteenth centuries supplied labour for the new industries and consumers for their products. Nevertheless contemporaries who had read the gloomy warnings of Malthus in his *Essay on Population* of 1798 as to the tendency of population growth to press upon and outstrip the means of subsistence, viewed the rapid expansion of numbers with concern. In fact their concern proved to be misplaced. As a result of rapid economic growth, Britain was able to support an increasing population without experiencing some severe and distressing check to population growth.

The close links between the industrial revolution and demographic change caught the attention of social and economic historians seeking the causes of growth. Analysis proved difficult, given the absence of official statistics prior to the institution of decennial censuses by the Population Act of 1800, and of a professional machinery of collection and analysis prior to the Registration Act* of 1836. For the crucial period of population growth, therefore, much reliance has had to be placed upon Anglican baptismal, marriage and burial registers for each parish in England and Wales. Earlier interpretation of these and other available statistics placed great emphasis upon a decline in mortality as a major cause of rapid population growth. In recent years, with more sophisticated methods of interpreting the evidence, a rise in fertility rather than a fall in mortality is coming to be seen as the detonator of the "population explosion". Changing patterns of employment in both agriculture and industry brought with them higher earnings and greater freedom from parental or employer control; as a result, marriages were entered into at an earlier age, and fertility rates increased. At the same time, mortality rates remained high and may even have risen as people crowded into insanitary towns. Crude death rates in England and Wales remained obstinately high, at around 22 per 1,000 of population in the early and mid-nineteenth century, whilst of every 1,000 babies born, 150 or more died before they reached the age of one year.

This pattern of high fertility outstripping high mortality began to change around mid-century. Improved public health provision in urban areas brought

Censuses and registration
First census of England and Wales taken 1801; subsequently decennial. Initially used parochial overseers as enumerators, and merely counted population; ages taken from 1821, names, addresses and occupation after adoption of household schedule 1841. Registration of Births, Marriages and Deaths enacted 1836 following recommendation of Select Committee; came into operation 1837.

Population of England and Wales 1781-1901			
Population		Rate of growth	
Date	Millions	% per annum	
1781	7.5	1771-1781	0.5
1791	8.3	1781-1791	1.0
1801	9.2	1791-1801	1.1
1811	10.2	1801-1811	1.1
1821	12.0	1811-1821	1.8
1831	13.9	1821-1831	1.6
1841	15.9	1831-1841	1.4
1851	17.9	1841-1851	1.3
1861	20.1	1851-1861	1.2
1871	22.7	1861-1871	1.3
1881	26.0	1871-1881	1.4
1891	29.0	1881-1891	1.2
1901	32.5	1891-1901	1.2

The urban slum. Bluegate Fields, Shadwell, by Gustave Doré, 1872.

Birth control

Probably conscious family limitation throughout Industrial Revolution period, as 18th-century fertility rate less than half biological maximum of 11 per woman: reflected deferred marriage and practice of coitus interruptus. Rubber sheaths, caps and spermicidal chemicals all appeared in last quarter of 19th century, barrier methods in mass production, but assumed to have had only marginal role in reduction of fertility rate. 1940 sample of women married before 1910 found only 16% of those practising birth control to have used appliance methods.

New Lanark/Saltaire

New Lanark developed by Owen around cotton mills 1800-25 as experiment in social provision for factory workforce: existing houses enlarged and improved, company shops stocked with goods at cost price, new streets laid out and refuse collection and sanitary provisions arranged; Educational Institution founded 1816. New Lanark more utopian in inspiration than Saltaire, community for 4,000 operatives laid out by Liberal worsted manufacturer Titus Salt near Shipley from 1851: 600 new model dwellings provided, with park, club, almshouses and institute. Saltaire inspired subsequent communities at Port Sunlight (Lever Bros 1888) and Bournville (Cadbury's 1890).

cleaner water and more efficient drainage. Living standards for the majority probably rose from the 1850s, boosted by a steep fall in food prices during the last two decades of the century. Mortality fell mainly as a result of a fall in the incidence of infectious diseases such as tuberculosis, scarlet fever, typhoid and smallpox. The fall in mortality was followed from the 1870s by a fall in fertility. In part, this may have been a result of a rise in the average age at marriage for women, but the main cause was undoubtedly the increasing tendency of married couples to limit the size of their families. Increased publicity for, and acceptance of, birth control* techniques from the 1870s provided an enabling factor to those who wished to keep their families small. The later nineteenth century saw a decided shift towards the smaller family, most notably, though not entirely, amongst the wealthier classes. British society was able to contain and stabilize the rate of growth of its population.

An even more dramatic and significant feature of British society in the early nineteenth century was the growth of its towns. Between the censuses of 1821 and 1831, the population of England and Wales increased by 16 per cent, but the population of Manchester grew by 45 per cent, that of Leeds by 47 per cent, Sheffield and Birmingham by 40 per cent and Bradford by 65 per cent. At the beginning of the century there were only fifteen towns in England and Wales with more than 20,000 inhabitants; by 1851, there were sixty-three, and one half of the population could be described as town dwellers compared to about one third in the late eighteenth century. By 1900, almost 80 per cent of the population lived in urban districts with populations of 10,000 or more. In the space of a hundred years, Britain had been transformed into an urban society.

With the development of steam power in the latter part of the eighteenth century, industrialists were better able to site their businesses in urban areas close to markets and transport facilities. Job opportunities increased, drawing in workers from the surrounding countryside. Migrants, often young men and women attracted by the greater freedom of town life, came mainly from communities within a thirty- or forty-mile radius of the town. Some of the newcomers migrated over greater distances, not least the Irish immigrants whose numbers grew to a torrent after the Potato Famine of the mid-1840s. Liverpool, Manchester, Glasgow and the industrial towns of northern England and southern Scotland proved a major attraction for immigrant and migrant alike, although London maintained its magnetic power.

Once established in a town, young men and women married and had families. Thus towns grew not merely by migration but also by the high fertility rates which resulted from these early marriages. Such rapid growth put enormous pressures upon living space. Migrants crammed into the existing housing stock, with multi-occupation of the larger houses left by wealthier townspeople moving to more salubrious outer areas. Such new housing as could be provided was often of poor quality, run up by speculative small builders. These crowded inner urban areas, polluted by smoke and other industrial effluent, often lacked even adequate paving, drainage and water supply, let alone schools, shops or open spaces for recreation.

Whilst large employers in some of the smaller factory towns might provide housing and other facilities for their workers, and a few exceptional ones, such as Robert Owen at New Lanark*, or Titus Salt at Saltaire*, developed complete industrial communities, most larger towns and cities grew in an unplanned muddle. Outbreaks of disease, particularly the horrifying cholera*, in the 1830s and 1840s, alerted contemporaries to the worsening state of their towns. Writers like the young Manchester doctor, James Phillips Kay, pointed to the extreme social dangers of allowing the uncontrolled development of insanitary, impoverished and potentially rebellious communities of young working people in urban areas.

Improvements in municipal government, together with the rapid growth of charitable institutions, helped to focus attention upon the worst areas of neglect. After the Municipal Corporations Act* of 1835 and the Public Health Act* of 1848, town councils and boards of health began to pave streets, build sewers, provide better water supplies and demolish insanitary housing. A host of philanthropic bodies in the shape of domestic missions, visiting societies, voluntary and Sunday schools, sanitary associations and the like, began to take in hand the task of educating and improving the urban poor. By the 1870s, British towns had become healthier places to live in, although slum housing and the extreme poverty of the inner cities remained a major social problem.

Public and philanthropic activity undoubtedly improved urban Britain, but another important factor from the 1860s onwards was the changing geography of many towns. The central districts of cities like London, Manchester or Liverpool began to decline in population, easing the intense overcrowding of the first half of the century. The development of suburban railways and, later, trams* enabled more people to live at a distance from their place of work. The concentrated populations of towns burst outwards, creating rapidly growing suburbs, Tottenham, Willesden or Camberwell in London, Fallowfield, Withington or Levenshulme in Manchester, Handsworth and Smethwick in Birmingham. The better-paid skilled worker and the aspiring clerk were able to follow the merchant, manufacturer and professional man in their flight from the inner city, leaving the low-paid casual labourer in the mean streets of poor housing close to the town centre. British cities expressed the geography of social class.

The industrializing and urbanizing of British society brought with it a change in the way in which the structure of that society was viewed. Pre-industrial society was a hierarchical one of descending ranks and degrees. This pyramid was kept together by the strings of patronage held by those higher in the social scale and by the ropes of dependence which bound tenant farmer to landlord or journeyman to his master. Whilst there remained those in the 19th century who still viewed society in these hierarchical terms, the forces of industrialization and urbanization proved powerful solvents of this structure. The new industrial towns promoted the rise of industrialists, merchants and professional men who increasingly resented the social and political privileges of landed aristocrats, gentlemen and the clergy of the Church of England. By 1815, the term "middle class" had entered the English language; by 1850, the urban, industrial middle class had consolidated its power, and won important concessions from the upper, landed class in the shape of measures like the Parliamentary Reform Act of 1832 or the repeal of the corn laws in 1846. At the same time, factory workers, labourers and handicraft workers found the industrial town provided an environment in which their various political and economic grievances could begin to merge into a common consciousness of being a working class. Robert Dudley Baxter in 1867 showed that upper and middle income earners, whose yearly incomes ranged from less than £500 to well over £5,000, numbered only about 20 per cent of the occupied population, yet obtained more than 60 per cent of the national income. Manual workers,

Cholera
Most startling, though not most persistent, of Victorian morbid diseases. Four epidemics, 1831-32, 1848-49, 1853-54 and 1866, killed around 140,000 in England, Wales and Scotland, over 60,000 of them in second epidemic. Virus generally transmitted by water infected by excreta of previous victim, therefore curbed by sanitary improvements even before identification of virus by Koch in 1883.

Municipal Corporations Act 1835
Legislation to reform and standardize municipal corporations in England and Wales. Covered 178 borough corporations recognized by 1835 Royal Commission (omitting powerful Corporation of London). Burgesses (rated occupiers for last two years) to elect borough council; council to control borough property, police, street lighting, markets, etc; empowered to raise rate to defray cost.

Public Health Act 1848
Fruit of a decade of sanitary agitation, including Chadwick's Sanitary Report 1842 and reports of Royal Commission on Health of Towns 1844-45. Act created General Board of Health empowered to establish elected local boards on petition of ratepayers or by compulsion where death rate high. Borough councils to act as local board in incorporated towns. Local boards empowered, but not obliged, to appoint Medical Officer of Health. Excluded Scotland, not covered until 1867.

Detail from an engraving of 1818 showing the hustings outside St Paul's church, Covent Garden, at the time of an election.

Urban elegance. Thomas Shotter Boys's view of Hyde Park near Grosvenor Gate, 1842.

Suburban transport
Omnibus first and most important form of urban communication; London General Omnibus Company carrying 40 million passengers p.a. by 1860. Railway not significant until urban railway boom of early 1860s, but thereafter some companies legally obliged to run cheap workmen's trains. First English tram in Birkenhead 1860; Tramways Act 1870 provided for local authority approval of construction and right of compulsory purchase. Municipal operation at cheap fares began in Huddersfield 1883; adopted in London and elsewhere in 1890s.

whose weekly wages gave them yearly sums of between £70 and £100, were more than 80 per cent of the occupied population, yet together took less than 40 per cent of national income. The young Friedrich Engels, exploring the slums of Manchester and London in the early 1840s, felt that movements like Chartism were the organization of the working class, the proletariat, for war against the middle and upper classes, the bourgeoisie. The class system, he thought, would destroy class society. Yet, to Engels's chagrin, class society in Britain was not destroyed, for stabilizing forces were at work from mid-century onwards.

The upper class of landed aristocrats and gentlemen proved not to be diametrically opposed to newly rich industrialists and merchants. Landowners like the dukes of Northumberland, Devonshire or Westminster were interested in exploiting the coal and iron deposits on their estates or in developing their land holdings in the cities. Industrialists such as Richard Arkwright or Robert Peel the elder purchased estates with their industrial fortunes and settled for the life of country gentlemen. The second half of the nineteenth century saw the growth of a *rentier* class drawing its income from a wide range of investments at home and overseas. Landowners whose rent rolls fell as a result of agricultural depression from the 1870s sought to recoup their losses in the City, and were welcomed by company promoters for the prestige which a titled name on a prospectus conveyed. By the late nineteenth century, British society was headed by a plutocracy, an aristocracy of wealth rather than of land.

Not all industrialists joined the "super rich", who were a creation of the City of London and inhabitants of the Home Counties rather than of the seedbeds of the industrial revolution in the west midlands, north-western and north-eastern England or southern Scotland. Many successful industrialists remained provincial, living on the fringe of the town where their business interests lay, and playing an active part in urban politics, culture and philanthropy. They were joined by another expanding and prestigious sector of the middle classes, the professional. Industrial urban society required an expansion of older professions like medicine and created new ones such as engineering. More formal standards of entry, often tested by examination, were required for entry and for membership of their associations*. From the 1840s on, schools and universities* responded to a growing demand from those anxious to prepare their children for entry to a gentlemanly profession.

For those unable to afford such expensive training, an increasing range of non-manual, white-collar jobs developed. The expansion of commerce, industry and government required more clerical workers. The growing numbers of elementary schools required teachers, and the new department stores, shop assistants. Such jobs provided a degree of security and respectability which attracted the sons and daughters of aspiring working-class parents. Soberly dressed, suburban-dwelling and often conventional in its religion and politics, the lower middle class gave stability to later nineteenth-century British society.

The manual working class, comprising eighty per cent or more of the occupied population of nineteenth-century Britain, was not a monolithic, uniform creation any more than was the middle class. It was headed by an upper stratum of skilled workers, craftsmen whose skills were essential to expanding industrial production and who protected their privileged position by controlling entry to the craft with stringent apprenticeship regulations. Engineers, printers, instrument makers, boiler makers and others formed a "labour aristocracy" which numbered about ten per cent of the manual working class by mid-century. Their share of expanding industrial production made them more ready to accept the values of the capitalist middle class and less likely to lead fellow workers in some challenge to the dominant social system. Nevertheless, they were prominent in working-class organizations such as trade unions, co-operative societies or political movements.

Below the "labour aristocracy" in earning power and security of employment came a large group of workers employed in manufacturing industry, mining and transport. By 1901, the numbers employed in agriculture had fallen sharply, manufacturing industry employed nearly three million more men than in 1851, and the service sector, trade and

Professional associations
Specialization attendant upon spread of industry and commerce led unions and groups to seek professional status previously accorded only to clergymen, physicians and barristers. Institution of Civil Engineers founded 1818, Law Society 1825, Institute of British Architects 1834, British Medical Association 1855, Institution of Chartered Accountants 1881. Sought to maintain standards by control of entry and codes of practice; some became powerful pressure groups.

London and English civic universities
Ratio of graduates to population fell by two thirds 1700-1850; Oxbridge Anglican, anti-technological and far from expanding population centres. Benthamite University College London (1826) provided vocational courses for dissenters and "middling rich people"; joined with Anglican King's College (1828) in London University, empowered to grant external degrees 1836. Durham, first provincial university 1832, imitated Oxbridge, with 90% of graduates taking holy orders. Later civic universities more science-orientated, many, notably Manchester (from 1851), Birmingham 1874, and Liverpool 1881, depending upon industry for funds. Ten founded in England by 1900, most offering London external degree at first.

	1850-4	1860-4	1870-4	1880-4	1890-4	1900-4
Money wages (1850 = 20s. full work)	21s.	23.4s.	29s.	29.4s.	32.4s.	35.6s.
% unemployed	3.7	5.8	1.9	4.4	5.3	3.7
Cost of commodities (1850 = 16s.)	16.7s.	17.6s.	18.7s.	16.6s.	14.4s.	14.4s.
Cost of housing (1850 = 4s.)	4.1s.	4.3s.	4.6s.	4.8s.	5.1s.	5.3s.
Real wage index (1850 = 100 full work)	101	107	125	137	166	181

**Weekly wages and prices for the average worker
1850-1900**

(1s = 5p)

A sombre view of Oldham in 1870, showing a mix of mills, mines and workers' housing.

Seaside resorts

Railways transformed watering places into day-trip resorts from mid-century, and 1851 Census commented on expansion of seaside towns, but exploitation as places of mass recreation awaited reduction in working hours, introduction of Bank Holidays 1871 and increase in real earnings over last quarter of century. Seaside entertainments developed from 1870s, including minstrel quartets, pierrot troupes (first toured south coast 1892) and piers – 33 of Britain's 54 piers built 1870-1910. Blackpool Tower, completed 1894, epitomized commercialization of seaside.

Professional football

Growth of soccer as working-class pastime followed restriction of working hours and liberation of Saturday afternoon. By 1880s crowds of 10,000 common in industrial north and midlands; gate money charged from 1870s and professionalization followed commercialization, with wages paid to entice and retain players. Changing nature of game symbolized by defeat of Old Etonians by Blackburn Olympic in 1883 Cup Final. In 1885 Football Association accepted professionalism after attempts to suppress it, thus avoiding repeating Rugby Union/Rugby League split. Football League formed 1888 by 12 leading northern and midland clubs.

Booth and Rowntree social surveys

Charles Booth, Liverpool shipowner and philanthropist, began investigations into London poor 1886: unsentimental, empirical survey valuable for analysis of London industry, social geography and religion as well as for findings on poverty; found 30% of Londoners lived below poverty line (pitched at income of 18-21s per week for family of parents and three children). B. Seebohm Rowntree's first survey of York 1899 more sophisticated in analysis of nutrition and relationship of poverty to age: found 10% in "primary" poverty (income inadequate to maintain good health) and further 18% in "secondary" poverty (income inadequate to provide security against unemployment, illness or old age).

transport, had grown even more significantly in relative terms. Factory employment, with its regular hours and routines, became an increasingly common form of work experience in the second half of the nineteenth century.

Throughout the century, however, there existed large numbers of unskilled labourers, competing desperately for work on building sites, warehouses or docks. Others entered sweated trades, producing shoddy goods at low piece rates, often in competition with female and child workers. Even this, however, was often found preferable to the low wages, irregular employment and wretched housing of the agricultural labourer, whose ranks thinned rapidly with the agricultural depression of the late 1870s. Underemployment, insecurity and low earnings characterized this sector of the working classes, in which women workers were more common than in the more fortunate groups.

Because of this diversity of experience within the manual working classes, historians have found great difficulty in coming to any exact conclusions as to their living standards in the nineteenth century. Given the disruption caused by industrialization and urbanization in the early part of the century, it is likely that that period saw little improvement in material standards for the great majority of working people. The 1850s and 1860s brought more stable prices, rising wages, a better urban environment and thus some gains – especially to the labour aristocrat. The last thirty years of the century, however, were undoubtedly the decades of most general improvement. Falling food prices brought an increase of more than one third in real wages. Meat, jam and butter made a more regular appearance on working men's tables. Municipal authorities provided more schools, parks, libraries, baths and washhouses. The rise of seaside resorts* and of professional football clubs* were evidence of a surplus in the working man's pocket to spend on commercial forms of leisure. Despite this, however, social investigation by Charles Booth* in East London in the late 1880s and by Seebohm Rowntree* in York in 1899 revealed that nearly one-third of the population were living at a level below that required for a healthy physical existence.

Britain proved able to absorb and stabilize the massive social changes which it experienced in the nineteenth century, but unable to provide a satisfactory life for a large proportion of its people.

Culture:
revolution, Romanticism and Victorianism
W.E.S. Thomas

The culture of the late eighteenth century had two outstanding features. It was overwhelmingly aristocratic, and it was cosmopolitan. Britain was ruled by an opulent landed aristocracy, whose manner of life was highly enviable. It was epitomized by the large country houses, supported by great estates and filled with collections of antique sculpture, great libraries and fine pictures by old masters. Many of these houses survive, but to capture the magnetism of the culture they once embodied we have to imagine a world in which exhibitions of painting, symphony concerts, opera, chamber music, the best libraries, even scientific experiment, were all heavily dependent on aristocratic patronage and inaccessible to those who had not some connection with the small minority whose property made such things possible. The political dominance of the landed aristocracy was enhanced by this cultural patronage, and all the art and literature of the period has a marked deference to aristocratic values. The careers of writers like Burke and Sheridan were no less dependent on aristocratic patronage than those of painters like Gainsborough and Lawrence, or the architects Wyatt and Nash. But the social ambitions of wealthy upstarts like the East Indian "nabob" Robert Clive, or the iron magnate J.J. Guest, pointed in the same direction, that of making a figure in the landed aristocracy.

The standards of this eighteenth-century culture were as much European as English. The acknowledged measure of taste, at least for the formally educated, was provided by the art and literature of ancient Greece and Rome, whose prestige, spread by the Renaissance, was assured by the adoption of Greek and Latin in the curricula of schools and universities all over Europe. Classicism, as we now call it, is a pattern of taste to be found in all the major European states in the eighteenth century. It meant that a young man seeking to complete his education with foreign travel, went abroad not for the broadening effects of different cultures, but for the elevating effect of the best examples of the same culture.

The French Revolution rudely disrupted this aristocratic internationalism. In overthrowing the most powerful nobility in Europe, it made aristocracies elsewhere more mindful of their security and less inclined to dally with ideas and fashions which had turned out to be so subversive. There was at all levels a general revulsion against change and in favour of established forms and customs. In England the chief gainer from this new caution was religion. Men who before 1789 had mocked the Church as a hollow shell, found themselves caught up in a new mood of serious piety, which often converted their sons and daughters. The Church which had allied with the politicians to keep the dissenting sects out of political power now found itself enjoying the tacit support of many dissenters against democratic and revolutionary ideas. The main manifestation of the new spirit of Christian philanthropy was the evangelical revival*. Its roots antedated the French Revolution by a genera-

Charles Towneley and his friends in his private gallery at Park Street, Westminster, painted by Zoffany between 1781 and 1783. He is seen surrounded by his unique collection of antique marbles.

Evangelicalism
Those Anglicans who remained within established Church after Methodist secession in 1780s but advanced fundamentalist theology, emphasizing personal salvation and primacy of scripture. Devoted to pursuit of humanitarian causes: William Wilberforce and other members of Clapham Sect dominant in successful campaign to end slave trade in British Empire 1807. Earl of Shaftesbury led campaign for reform of factory conditions and limitation of hours of labour in 1840s.

Oxford Movement/Tractarianism
High-Church reaction to perceived threat to Anglican interests from Catholic emancipation, reform and Whig latitudinariansim. Movement generally dated from Keble's Oxford sermon on "National Apostasy" 1833: crystallized around Keble, Newman, Manning and Pusey. Affirmed Catholic doctrine within limits of Anglicanism, stressed Church independence from secular interference.

Views propagated in "Tracts for the Times" from 1833. Accusations of Romanism strengthened by defection of disillusioned leaders to Catholicism – Newman 1845, Manning 1851.

Gibbon's "Decline and Fall of the Roman Empire"

Published in six volumes 1776-88. Survey of decadence of Roman Empire from height in first and second centuries AD to extinction with capture of Constantinople 1453. Marked by measured cynicism towards human ambition, conventional 18th-century scepticism towards Christian religion as agent of destruction of classical civilization, and detached conviction that history amounted to "little more than the crimes, follies, and misfortunes of mankind".

Burke's "Reflections on the Revolution in France" 1790

Forceful polemical assault upon uncritical Whig and Radical espousal of principles of French Revolution: attacked mechanistic application of rationalism to political philosophy at expense of allowance for human nature and emotion; defended monarchy and aristocracy as "Corinthian capital of polished society"; and asserted validity of prescriptive property rights. Burke accurately predicted the Revolution's domestic bloodshed, inflation of currency and eventual military rule.

Lake poets

Term coined by *Edinburgh Review* in 1807 for three English Romantic poets living in and drawing inspiration from Lake District – Coleridge, Southey, Wordsworth. Coleridge defined two cardinal points of poetry as "the power of exciting the sympathy of the reader by a faithful adherence to the truth of nature and the power of giving the interest of novelty by the modifying colours of the imagination"; Wordsworth invoked "impassioned contemplation" of nature in preface to *Lyrical Ballads*, written with Coleridge 1798. Fidelity to nature extended to fidelity to human soul, exemplified by Wordsworth's autobiographical and introspective *Prelude* 1799. All three poets moved from revolutionary enthusiasm to social conservatism.

Fear of the guillotine was still alive in 1819. Cruikshank shows the "mob" pursuing Lords Londonderry, Eldon and Liverpool, with the Prince Regent disappearing from the picture.

tion, but it was during the revolutionary wars that it consolidated its hold upon the upper and middle classes in Britain. Evangelical Christianity threw a long shadow forwards into the Victorian age.

The horrors of the French Revolution discouraged English democrats, who found themselves caught in the contrast between their original hopes and the grim reality of the Terror. Some, like Thomas Paine and Joseph Priestley, despaired of Europe and emigrated to America. Some were cowed by the panicky conservative reaction into silence and conformity. But many, especially the artists and writers, translated their political frustrations into art, and produced a revolution in taste against which the opponents of political change were powerless. For while the French Revolution and the wars that followed did bring about a mood of embattled patriotism, the long-term effects of this were not favourable to the aristocratic way of life. The classical, cosmopolitan culture, at once so rational and so exclusive, was fatally undermined. The cool patrician values which inform a work like Gibbon's *Decline and Fall of the Roman Empire** (completed 1788) came to seem frivolous and facile. The wars of Napoleon encouraged nationalist loyalties and particularist feeling which stimulated a new curiosity about national histories and literatures, and strengthened vernacular standards of taste. An interest in the past for its own sake, because it was irrevocable and therefore nostalgic; a new solicitude about the lives and concerns of simple people remote from Courts and salons; and a new plainness of expression, to free art and literature from the stilted classical conventions which had ruled polite society – all these made up the new mood which historians came to call Romanticism. In England the work which more than any other signalled the new mood was Burke's *Reflections on the Revolution in France** (1790) – short-term comfort to reactionary governments, long-term quarry for romantic literary themes.

Some opponents of the Revolution spoke as if they would have liked to stop popular enlightenment altogether, and some historians have supposed that this is exactly what they tried to do. Actually, harnessing national energies for war meant consulting classes till then disfranchised. And in fact the growth of

a new public consolidated the revolution in taste. The Lake poets* shed their "Jacobinism" but kept their readers. Robert Southey became a Tory historian, Wordsworth an exciseman, and Coleridge wrote the next generation's apology for the historic English constitution. But many writers remained outspoken critics of the evils in English society and still enjoyed great popularity with the growing reading public. William Cobbett, though he was careful to give his radicalism a patriotic twist and insisted that he advocated reform as a restoration of ancient liberties, was the most popular journalist of his day, his *Political Register** a formidable critic of governments.

Not that the aristocratic forces gave up their political and cultural primacy without a struggle. It was in literature that the conflict was most envenomed. Architecture and painting, after all, are arts for the opulent and were comparatively unaffected by the political struggle. The new rich of the industrial revolution were anxious to be assimilated to the old landed aristocracy, and the design and decoration of their houses either followed established conventions, or else revived "Gothic" styles* which suggested a more antique pedigree. But the written word was more contentious, since literacy widens political as well as aesthetic experience, and efforts to teach more people to read were hampered by the fear that they would read the wrong things. So great was the fear of mobs, incited by half-lettered demagogues, that popular unrest was almost invariably followed by constraints on press freedom. It took a long time for the governing classes to realize that a literate population would actually be more governable, and even then educational progress was held up by the disagreement over the place of religious education in schools. This disagreement dogged efforts at popular education until the "March of Mind" movement in the 1820s, which saw the first Mechanics' Institutes*, the Society for the Diffusion of Useful Knowledge*, and the foundation of University College, London. All these ran into opposition from the clergy, whose dominance in the schools and the two ancient universities was threatened. But on two things the reformers and their opponents were agreed. They thought that the government should keep out of the controversy and that education should precede a man's enfranchisement and qualify him for it. The first belief inhibited the state's endowment of education. The second meant that manifestations of political violence usually delayed educational improvement rather than hastened it.

Not surprisingly, the first three decades of the nineteenth century produced a cultural scene shot through with fear, recrimination and reprisal. The insecurity of all classes is particularly clear in popular literature and art. It was the golden age of the political cartoonist, the writer of lampoons, the parodist and the vitriolic literary critic. But just as political agitation became more moderate after 1832, so culture became more decorous. After the failure of Chartism, the fear of revolution receded into a horrid memory. Constitutional change through a Parliament chosen by about a million electors became the rule for all classes. The literate population of about six million ensured that orderly "bourgeois" values permeated the world of art and literature. Industrial growth made reading an essential prerequisite for anyone who wanted do "better his condition", but reading matter was not cheap. A three-volume novel (the most popular literary form) sold for a half-guinea a volume, and between 1836 and 1855, a daily newspaper cost 4½d. To a skilled artisan or a clerk, these were luxuries, and to buy them regularly called for a certain settled prosperity. This is why it is really the tastes and standards of the

"Political Register"
Forerunner of political review, founded 1802 by William Cobbett: moved from Tory to Radical stance. Influence increased from 1816 when published as nominal pamphlet to evade newspaper tax; circulation over 40,000 at 2d price. Act of 1819 applied tax to all frequent periodicals, rise of price to 6d restricted circulation. Published in stamped and unstamped editions from 1821. Ceased publication 1838.

Gothic Revival
Gothic forms never died within English architecture, but revived late 18th century as part of "picturesque" reaction to classicism. Early "Gothick" designs (Walpole's Strawberry Hill, Wyatt's Fonthill Abbey) stylistically frivolous; movement given earnestness by research and propaganda of A.W.N. Pugin and by John Ruskin's work on Venetian forms. Ecclesiological Society advocated decorated style as purest church form; G.E.Street and W. Butterfield applied Ruskinian principles to churches and public buildings; G.G. Scott mass-produced cathedral restorations and commercial buildings.

Mechanics' Institutes
London Mechanics' Institute founded 1823 as part of Radical extension of education: spread through industrial areas, often under patronage of mill-owners. Emphasis on science and technical education, though 1840s saw move towards social and political subjects; political economy sometimes taught as antidote to factory reform agitation. Local examination system inaugurated by Society of Arts 1857: 200,000 members by 1860.

Society for the Diffusion of Useful Knowledge
Founded 1826, in wake of Brougham's call for production of cheap educative publications. Issued 32-page monthly treatises selling at 6d, circulating utilitarian doctrines but avoiding controversy; collectively formed Library of Useful Knowledge. Also produced Penny Magazine, claiming 200,000 circulation. Initially high sales of Library dwindled by mid-1830s, wound up 1845.

"Taxes on Knowledge"
Four duties raised price of newspapers and pamphlets: newspaper tax (4d from 1815), advertisement tax, excise duty on paper, and pamphlet duty; said to have confined newspaper sales per head to quarter of USA level in 1830s. Attacked in early 1830s by middle-class radicals anxious to extend educative power of press, and circumvented

The regal lying-in-state of Matthew Russell, a coal magnate who bought a Northumberland castle.

by illegal unstamped working-class press. Newspaper tax cut to 1d and advertisement duties halved in 1836; pamphlet duty repealed 1833, advertisement tax 1853, newspaper tax 1855, paper duty 1861.

Transformation of public schools

Public-school image to mid-century one of narrow classical curriculum, primitive conditions and licensed brutality: improvement initiated by reforming headmasters, Samuel Butler at Shrewsbury from 1798, Thomas Arnold at Rugby from 1828. Broadened curriculum to include history and geography, systematized internal discipline through prefecture. Inspired foundation of progressive public schools, including Cheltenham 1841, Marlborough 1843 and Wellington 1853.

Education Act 1870

Prompted by franchise extension, collapse of nonconformist voluntary education and foundation of National Education League 1869. Divided all Britain into school districts; elected School Boards to be set up where Education Department found existing provision inadequate, with power to levy rates and build schools; school fees to continue, though Boards empowered to establish free schools.

prosperous middle class that we think of when we use the word "Victorian".

If we try to define Victorianism, what features should we stress? First of all, highmindedness. Education at all levels was dominated by Christian teaching. The Bible and its interpretation formed the central preoccupation of many educated men, not merely of clergymen. Christian ethical teaching shaped the outlook and actions of many more; charity and service to one's fellow men were the standards of public activity. Preaching, secularized as philanthropic oratory, penetrated every corner of Victorian life. It turned the crude commercial agitation for freer trade into a crusade, it made bankers speak of faith when they meant credit, it caused free-booting colonial adventurers to talk like missionaries, and it turned the political platform into a kind of pulpit. It meant that the decline of Christian belief, when it came, was singularly free of anticlerical militancy, and socialism of the doctrines of class hatred and violent revolution.

A second theme was domesticity. Victorian upper and middle class education took place largely in the family; exclusively so in the case of girls, but even boys who were sent to the new public schools* were taught values which were supposed to uphold and reflect those of home. To an extent which our own centralized electronic culture can hardly comprehend, families made their own entertainment, in music, writing and amateur theatricals. Many of the classics of children's literature originated in domestic *jeux d'esprit,* like *Alice in Wonderland,* but family life accounts for more serious work too – such as the novels of the Brontë sisters. In most families the commonest entertainment was reading aloud: the strenuous moral propriety of the fiction of Dickens, George Eliot and Trollope, was largely due to the writers' awareness that they would be read aloud in family circles all over the country. This was what Thackeray meant when he said of his fellow novelists, "our profession seems to me to be as serious as the parson's own". Not only the writer went in awe of the standards of Victorian parents concerned for the morals of their children. Any public figure whose behaviour "violated the domestic tie", as the phrase was, courted disaster, as the careers of Dilke and Parnell show. In this sense the end of Victorianism, in a double blow against marital fidelity as well as sexual normality, came in 1895 with the trial of Oscar Wilde.

A third theme was amateurism, in the sense in which it is opposed to professionalism. One of the attractions of Victorian culture to the modern student is that even its most technical works require little specialist training to understand. This feeling of the accessibility of the Victorian mind accompanies the reader through the period until the 1880s. By then philosophy, economics and the physical sciences were outgrowing their lay readers and becoming too technical. Two factors hastened this specialization, the spread of universal compulsory education after 1870*, which brought about a mass reading public, and the increasing division of labour in the world of higher education which tended to erode the intelligent lay readership for learned works. But it is important to stress how slow this process was. At the mid-century it had hardly begun: at the end we still have only faint portents of that fracturing of idioms which marks the modern mind.

Until their reform* in the 1850s the two ancient universities had been dominated by the Church. Though they taught a traditional curriculum with a heavy emphasis on the classics and mathematics, they gave their degrees only to Anglicans and were run by clergymen. So they were accused, with some justice, of being exclusive, tradition-bound, and indifferent to society's needs. Many distinguished thinkers and writers like J.S. Mill, Dickens and Disraeli did not attend university at all. Many who did, like Byron, Carlyle or Thackeray, proclaimed how little they owed to it. For practical subjects, appropriate to an expanding commercial society, England could draw on the great Scottish universities, which produced a large number of notable economists, doctors of medicine and natural scientists. But in many areas the opportunity for original research was woefully limited. This neglect of research facilities seems scandalous to the modern mind, but it did mean that the Victorian intellectual was obliged to justify his activities before a lay public in plain language. Hence the great confidence, which is so marked a feature of late Victorian culture, in the power of reasoned argument to change society, and the eager interest with which extensions of scientific knowledge were followed and understood, and their implications for other areas of study explored and discussed. This may have led to some clumsy amateurism, but the very fact that most of the experts, however recondite their knowledge, did not disdain to write for the general public in the great non-technical reviews*, like the *Edinburgh* and the *Fortnightly,* meant that charlatanism was soon exposed and shoddy work did not last. In the end, the political benefits of amateurism outweighed the technical shortcomings. The Victorian ruling class was small and its culture was exclusive; but it was an open-minded ruling class, and when faced with universal primary education and a mass electorate, produced original thinkers who were also great popularizers like T.H. Huxley, Bertrand Russell, and J.M. Keynes.

University reform
Reform movement formed part of pressure for educational improvement from 1820s: sought to break clerical monopoly of teaching, end exclusion of non-Anglicans, introduce "modern" subjects and encourage research. Royal Commissions on Oxford and Cambridge reported 1852-53, recommending broader curriculum and professional career structure; legislation of 1854 and 1856 opened BA degree to non-Anglicans; fellowships opened to competition.

Political and literary reviews
Principal source of informed analysis during 19th century. *Edinburgh Review,* founded 1802, at peak in 1820s and 1830s, carried articles by Brougham, Macaulay and leading political economists. Whiggish bias balanced by Tory *Quarterly Review* from 1809 and Radical *Westminster Review* from 1824. Over 100 reviews founded each decade 1830-80; most prominent *Fortnightly Review* (Liberal 1865) and *Contemporary Review* (Tory 1866, later Liberal).

Victorian domestic life depicted by William Frith in Many Happy Returns, *1856.*

7

FROM
IMPERIAL POWER TO
EUROPEAN PARTNER

1901-1975

FROM IMPERIAL POWER TO EUROPEAN PARTNER 1901-1975

Overview

Keith Robbins

In 1901 Queen Victoria died. Subsequent tributes stressed the remarkable changes which had taken place during the many decades of her reign. Some contemporaries feared that the capacity to change, without jettisoning old ways and institutions completely, could not be sustained; something radical would happen. Such fears proved exaggerated as monarch followed monarch and, eventually, another queen reigned securely. Yet the monarchy had its awkward moments, most conspicuously when Edward VIII abdicated. If George VI had not shown singular devotion to duty, republicanism might have made headway. There were moments, too, when it seemed possible that the Crown might be caught up in constitutional issues. The budget crisis of 1909-10 was one such instance. George V, newly on the throne, was worried lest populist attacks on dukes might widen to include the monarchy. He was very relieved when, in the event, he did not have to create a host of new peerages. He continued to believe that he had a role to play in trying to bring the opposing political leaders together, most notably to seek agreement on the Irish question. His successors were also not without political influence in moments of crisis. It was George VI, finally, who chose Winston Churchill as prime minister in 1940, and his daughter later plumped for Macmillan rather than Butler. The more formal processes for the election of their leaders now agreed in all the major political parties may well now have curtailed that ultimate power of choice. It remains true, however, that Elizabeth II has acquired formidable knowledge and experience of public affairs. It is still not inconceivable that the monarch could play a significant role, for example in the event of a hung Parliament.

If the monarchy flourishes, the accompanying Court has faded. The Parliament Act of 1911 removed the power of the House of Lords to veto legislation and substituted a power of delay. Even at the time, that decision did not satisfy all Liberals. While few wanted the abolition of the upper chamber, some urged a reform in its composition and the ending, or at least the dilution, of the hereditary element. Successive non-Conservative governments, and some Conservative, have wrestled with the apparent anomaly of the survival of such a chamber. In 1949 the Labour government further reduced the ability of the Lords to delay legislation. In 1958 life peers were created and they played an increasing part in the proceedings of the chamber. Nevertheless, the dilemma remained: to make the Lords more "representative" challenged the authority of the Commons. Short of total abolition, which only a minority supported, it seemed best to leave the Lords alone. It was thus that Crown, Lords and Commons survived into the final quarter of the twentieth century. It is a record of institutional continuity not matched by any other major European country.

The three major political parties also remain the same, or at least carry the same label: Conservative, Labour and Liberal. Despite their fluctuating support and the splits and divisions that have occurred, all parties see themselves (somewhat fancifully on occasion) as the heirs of organizations that existed in the first decade of the century. There is a radical and a socialist "tradition"; there is a conservatism which advocates change. It has normally been a two-party system, with a third party poised between expansion and oblivion. Coalition government has existed, normally in wartime, though in 1931 it arose out of a peacetime crisis. New parties have come and gone. The Communist party rubbed along ingloriously and the British Union of Fascists proved a frail imitation of continental movements. Governments have not been prepared to dabble with a proportional representation system which might encourage new parties. All that has happened is that Labour has come to occupy the position formerly occupied by the Liberals. Although that breakthrough did come surprisingly quickly, Labour might have found it as difficult to advance as the Liberals have found it to break back. It is again a comment on continuity that these three parties have proved so durable.

The detailed political record naturally shows more movement and ideological change than this concentration upon externals might suggest. Even so, continuity is ubiquitous; disturbingly so for some commentators. On the other hand, if stability be a virtue, then, in general,

Britain has possessed it in a century otherwise marred, or at any rate marked, by revolution, civil war, mass internment and, indeed, extermination. The inter-penetration of Liberal and Conservative values, coupled with the peculiarly British character of the Labour party's socialism, had normally produced more shared assumptions, even in an avowedly "adversarial" system, than frequently exists in other European societies. The notion of a loyal Opposition has been sustained. To emphasize these points is not to overlook times of acute political crisis or moments of industrial confrontation heavy with political significance. For better or worse, however, these moments of tension have passed, despite occasional talk of "ungovernability" and the power of trade unionism as an alternative to the authority of Parliament.

Yet, even amongst those who applauded the course of twentieth-century British politics, there was anxiety by the early seventies. That very continuity and conserva-tism, which could make Britain seem a model, might also be accelerating and accentuating national decline. Where other continental countries had been compelled to make a fresh start by revolution, occupation or libera-tion, Britain had merely patched up and pulled through; perhaps not to her own benefit. The maintenance of established patterns and procedures might be reassuring if the world were static and there was little else to do but admire a British coronation. Unfortunately, the world was constantly changing and resistance to change, whether on the shop floor, in the board-room, or in Whitehall, might prove fatal.

Certainly Britain's international position has drastic-ally changed when we compare the world of 1901 with that of 1975. The British Empire, at the turn of the century, was an extraordinary concoction, embracing under one flag a great diversity of territories and peoples. So far-flung and so heterogeneous was it that it is difficult to discern a single "imperial system". The complexity of India, the aspirations of the self-governing colonies of settlement, and the "undeveloped estate" of Africa were the chief ingredients. Optimists talked of a century of consolidation; pessimists groaned under the burden of imperial administration and defence. Even the Boer War itself could be variously interpreted as salutary shock or ominous precedent. In short, while the Empire could look solid, especially if one's main acquaintance with it was on a map, there was a mass of only half-disclosed uncertainty amongst its guardians.

Territorially, the Empire was not to reach its greatest extent until after the First World War, but the strains of "Recessional" could already be heard. There were still

confident voices. In the Middle East, for example, imper-ial servants assumed that Britain would exercise a more extensive hegemony than she had ever done there in the past. To this confidence add the splendours of the Empire Exhibition at Wembley in the early twenties and its equally glorious counterpart in Glasgow in 1938. The Empire engaged and held the emotions of millions: the British were an imperial race, but they might not be able to remain so. The 1926 Imperial Conference had recog-nized that the British Commonwealth was a voluntary association whose members (the white dominions) were equal in status if not in power. Some of them were more eager than others to secure the formal recognition of their position, but the tendency towards "independence" (though that was not a word used between kith and kin) was obvious. On the left, the Empire was increasingly declared to be morally unacceptable, though in office between the wars Labour did not seriously envisage giving it up. Nevertheless the fundamental incompatibil-ity of a democracy based on participation and consent ruling an empire by command became steadily more evident. Change speeded up with the coming of the Second World War. Independence for India and Pakistan set a pattern for the transfer of power throughout the world, even to colonies long thought not to be "viable". Apart from certain particularly intractable issues, that process was substantially completed by the mid-seventies.

"Decolonization" on this scale was not something which would have been envisaged at the beginning of the century. Victorians would no doubt have interpreted such a change as an indication of decline, indeed of decadence. There was a loss of the "will to govern", though on the other hand there was little zest to shake off the trappings of authority. But it did seem that prot-racted resistance to the transfer of power would be futile. Even so, in Malaya and Kenya, the British were both willing and able to put down insurrectionary movements which might upset their capacity to leave when they chose. British governments, of both parties, remained determined to withstand international pressure and insisted that they should control the timetable. They eagerly drew up new constitutions, only to see most of them disappear within a few years. The process of hand-over was normally amicable, at least in the final stages. Most of the former colonies joined what was now called the Commonwealth of Nations – it was decided in 1949 that a republican constitution was compatible with continued membership and the prefix "British" dropped out of use. Countries with British-descended popula-tions now formed a minority in the association. British pre-eminence also faded, with the establishment of a separate Commonwealth Secretariat and the rotation of meetings around the globe: during the protracted Rhodesia/Zimbabwe crisis, some Commonwealth African states thought that the group would prosper without Britain. By the mid-seventies, it became ever more difficult to say precisely what the Commonwealth was, yet, despite the passage of time and the withering of some contacts, it continued – its curious intimacy being made possible by the English language.

It was, to say the least, an unusual way to dispossess oneself, or be dispossessed, of an empire. The French experienced military defeat in Indo-China and Algeria and the Dutch in their East Indies, but the British beat a dignified retreat – if we are prepared to overlook Aden and Cyprus. During the decades of transition, supporters of this new Commonwealth looked upon the association with enthusiasm and commitment. Here was partnership, not domination, the very symbol of what the modern world needed. It linked developed and developing countries, North and South, East and West. It was these aspects that made the Commonwealth particularly congenial to the left for thirty years. Apparently, it still gave Britain a mission in the world. There was, after all, to be no abrupt descent from British Empire to Little Britain. While this zeal had not disappeared by the mid-seventies, it was becoming clear that the Commonwealth could not quite bear the weight of these expectations.

Whatever the future might hold, however, it had achieved one useful result, whether by accident or design. It had cushioned the psychological impact of loss of empire, and Britain was spared the disruption of domestic politics which happened elsewhere when soured and embittered *colons* returned to the homeland. Luck played a part here. There was no major upheaval in a colony close at hand comparable to Algeria in the case of France, and there was no General de Gaulle for the League of Empire Loyalists to turn to.

What there was, however, was a substantial and growing population either born in or descended from parents who came from the New Commonwealth. It was a development which only became numerically significant after 1945 and at first occurred without serious controversy. By the sixties, however, the issue of immigration, coupled with legislation designed to prevent discrimination, moved steady to the fore, causing divisions which by no means corresponded with party lines. The first substantial Aliens Act had been passed in 1905. It was now followed by further legislation designed to restrict immigration. It was a situation full of irony and, in some cases, tragedy. Britain city-dwellers for the first time formed the acquaintance of Indians and West Indians and this movement of population was occurring at a psychologically sensitive point in British history. A "multi-racial society" to this degree was a new phenomenon. Opinion was divided as to whether immigrants should become assimilated to the British "norm" or whether diversity in language, culture and religion was to be encouraged. It was an odd comment on events that it was easier for an Indian to be elected to the House of Commons in the first decade of the century than it was in the 1970s.

It was partially in the context of immigration that there was increased speculation about what this British "norm" might be. It was a concern which operated at political, educational and cultural levels. Changes in religious belief, sexual behaviour and modes of speech and dress, to mention only a few developments, made it increasingly difficult to say what was acceptable conduct and what was not. A culture bent on permissiveness was not a "norm" to which it was easy to attach oneself, even if it was worth the effort. Politically, however, it was also difficult to be sure what the essence of Britain was – indeed, whether it existed at all. Despite the stress which has been placed on continuity, it is important to note that the United Kingdom of Great Britain and Ireland of 1901 did break up.

In a decade from 1912, after a period when even many Liberals had supposed that Ireland could be dealt with "step by step", without root and branch constitutional change, the Union of 1800 was destroyed and the island of Ireland partitioned – to be followed, over subsequent decades, by intermittent violence and constitutional adjustments, North and South. In the wake of Ireland's departure from the Commonwealth in 1949, on becoming a republic, the British Labour government gave to the people of Northern Ireland their existing constitutional guarantee. In effect, there would be no change in their status as subjects of the Crown and citizens of the United Kingdom unless a majority desired it. They would remain, in their own fashion, "British". The United Kingdom government did not recognize the territorial claims of the republic. How the inhabitants of Northern Ireland are best described admits of no easy answer. We may think of two "communities", if we recognize that they are flawed communities; we may think of them as "Ulstermen", if we recognize that Northern Ireland contains only two-thirds of the province of Ulster – and so on. We may even call at least some of them British, if we recognize that they are not English.

Prolonged exposure of the troubles of Northern Ireland on British television screens and the loss of British

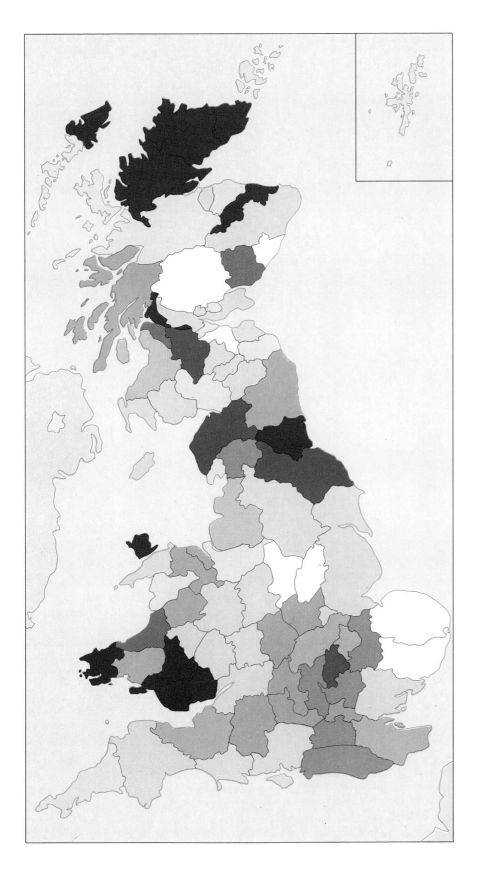

**Relative levels of Unemployment
1931-36**

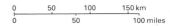

Proportions higher or lower than the national
average (national average 17.7% of insured
population)

Less than average unemployed:

60-70%

50-60%

40-50%

30-40%

20-30%

10-20%

Average

More than average unemployed:

10-20%

20-30%

30-40%

40-50%

50-60%

60-70%

Over 70%

291

soldiers' lives left no doubt that Ireland had not left British political history, as many had supposed likely after 1922. Many in England found it difficult to identify themselves with any faction in Northern Ireland, even if it was accepted that the British army had to remain to keep the uneasy peace. The claim that Ulstermen are (if they say so) authentically British can be greeted with scepticism in England. The truth of the matter is that "British" can mean whatever we want it to mean. The separate treatment of Ireland, Scotland, Wales and England, however difficult, is a recognition in this volume that there can be no facile equation of England with Britain. Such treatment, however, may itself be a product of developments after 1945. At the beginning of the century, at least in England, there was far less sensitivity about these matters. It was not until the sixties that political nationalism showed some signs of sustained activity and success in mainland Britain.

What made such pressures seem ominous was that they occurred in what was commonly referred to as a time of "identity crisis". It was not only the Empire's disappearance which had to be adjusted to, it was also the challenge presented by the consolidation of the European Economic Community. The dimensions of the problem went beyond what is normally thought of as foreign policy. Did Britain "belong" to Europe? What was "Britain"? What was "Europe"? This was a question which, to paraphrase Sir Edward Grey in the more extreme circumstances of 1914, every man had to consider for himself. Was there a continental commitment? Did membership of the EEC mean the end of a thousand years of British history – or some such figure? Did it entail the inevitable erosion of all that was distinctive in British life, not least the inexorable downgrading of Westminster and the intrusion of alien legal codes? Britain had gone to war in 1914, it was supposed, for "gallant little Belgium"; now there was the prospect that gallant little Britain would be dominated by Brussels. The varying answers to these questions, encased as they frequently were with a spurious precision (on both sides of the argument), help to explain the protracted and debilitating delay before Britain entered the Community and the British people ratified the decision. Whatever view was taken of the likely consequences, they would have profound bearings on what one meant by Britain in the latter half of the twentieth century.

Alas, it was also an economic question. It was not merely a matter of weighing up a cultural and political heritage. Entry was feared or advocated as a response to what appeared to be a lengthy and enduring loss of commercial confidence and economic viability. But the record in this respect was not one of such unmitigated disaster that it gave full justification to that sense of failure and decline that was indeed pervasive. As always, in assessing economic performance much depends on the dates chosen for comparison. Even so, it is difficult, on the basis of the figures presented on pages 321 to 322, to paint a picture of absolute decline. Nevertheless, by the close of our period, pessimism was paramount. Things were so serious that not even the recruitment of additional economists to the Treasury might suffice to restore matters. Academics began to write books to explain that Britain's industrial decline stemmed from the failure of suffucent products of public schools and the universities of Oxford and Cambridge to be gripped by the entrepreneurial demon. They received a good deal of acclaim in academic quarters without, apparently, sensing the irony of their own circumstances in relation to their prescriptions.

It was, in short, a crisis. Everybody said so, though perhaps it was just the crisis of capitalism. It was time for a change, though there was no unanimity about the direction, or the extent to which it would be choked by the conservatism which was a feature of twentieth-century British life. It was time to look again at education about which much had already been said, not altogether profitably, in previous decades. Could the cultural clock be turned back in order or preserve the future? Basking in the after-glow of the white heat of technology, it was difficult to explain precisely what had gone wrong, or how it might be put right, but something was amiss. It was all very galling for a country which had played a major part in winning two world wars, at great cost in human lives and financial reserves. Britain, or at any rate England, was an old state and nation, arguably the oldest with an unconquered history in the world. To be swamped by inflation was humiliating for a proud nation which had survived the Battle of Britain. But to stumble at this juncture perhaps gave a chance to leap boldly, even successfully, in the future.

Government and Politics in England:
realignment and readjustment

Peter Clarke

In 1901 the Unionist* government of Lord Salisbury had been in power with no serious challenge for the best part of fifteen years, while the question of Home Rule for Ireland had dominated party controversy. But although the General Election of 1900, at the height of the Boer War, had confirmed them in office, their strong-minded colonial secretary, Joseph Chamberlain, was restive. When Salisbury was replaced by his nephew Balfour in 1902, Chamberlain seized his chance to launch a new initiative. Whereas his Conservative allies represented the cautious defence of the interests of property by an established governing class, Chamberlain's faith in majorities and belief in action reflected his radical origins. His programme of tariff reform*, unveiled in May 1903, sought to commit the Unionist party to a new economic policy as a means to imperialist ends.

After 1903 the Unionist party was acutely divided over tariffs. The Liberal party, which had been in the doldrums since Gladstone's era, pulled itself together to mobilize its traditional support, some of it from nonconformists disaffected as a result of the Balfour Education Act* of 1902. There was also a new section of support, represented by organized labour. The Labour Representation Committee* had been set up to defend the interests of trade unionism*, and it included socialists who likewise wanted independent representation in Parliament. In practice, Liberals and Labour generally worked together in the Edwardian period. An electoral pact between them in 1903 facilitated a "progressive alliance"*, which dominated the next three general elections.

Unionists
Term originally applied to Liberals who left Liberal party 1886 over Irish home rule issue; later extended to Conservative party which also vehemently opposed home rule. Indicated commitment to the political union of Ireland and Great Britain. Conservative party became "Conservative and Unionist Party" 1909; Liberal Unionists merged with Conservatives 1912.

Tariff reform
Campaign for introduction of import duties on some foods and foreign manufactures, launched by Joseph Chamberlain 1903: intended to protect British industry against dumping of foreign goods, and to provide revenue for social reform; hoped to promote imperial economic unification via imperial preference. Campaign won over bulk of Conservative party by 1906; Balfour adhered to compromise position in order to conciliate significant free-trade minority.

See **1902 Education Act** (page 333)

Labour Representation Committee
Formed 1900 in response to resolution at 1899 Trades Union Congress, which called for independent working-class political organization: had no clear aims other than separate parliamentary representation for workers; ideology more "labourist" than socialist; executive had 7 trade union representatives, 2 each from ILP and SDF, 1 from Fabian Society.

Taff Vale judgement 1901
Court decision that trade unions could be sued for company losses during strikes; in consequence unions turned to political activity to change law. LRC membership rose from 350,000 1901 to 700,000 1902; 1906 29 LRC Members of Parliament elected; changed name to Labour party.

The Unionist rally at Blenheim Palace 27 July 1912, attended by some 13,000 people. Bonar Law pledged unmeasured support for resistance to Irish home rule, his fighting words echoed by those of Sir Edward Carson and F.E. Smith.

In the General Election of 1906* the Unionist ascendancy came to an end with a crash. But during its first three sessions, the new Liberal government found many of the bills it passed through the Commons with large majorities checked by the equally large Unionist majorities in the Lords. This was the deteriorating political situation it faced by 1908, together with a budgetary crisis as a result of piling new demands upon a narrow fiscal base. In particular, an expensive programme of naval armaments had been undertaken at the same time as the new scheme for non-contributory old-age pensions, and there were further proposals for state-subsidized health and unemployment insurance.

Lloyd George used his "People's Budget"* of 1909 to solve both problems at once. Politically, it by-passed the House of Lords, whose powers over money bills were limited by convention. Financially, it provided new revenue from a sharp increase in direct taxation, notably death duties and progressive rates on high incomes. This strategy of interventionist social reform and redistributive taxation marked the implementation of a New Liberalism*, in contrast to the Gladstonian tradition, as an ideological buttress for progressive action. The alternative was to seek revenue from tariffs. This gave the Unionist majority in the House of Lords a strong party case for rejecting the Budget – or, as they put it, referring it to the judgment of the people. The conduct of the House of Lords was thus firmly linked with the social and economic interests at stake on both sides in the two general elections of 1910*. The government victories paved the way for a restriction of the Lords' veto through the Parliament Act* of 1911. Armed with this power, the Liberals now had to discharge their longstanding commitment to the Irish Nationalist party, who held the balance in Parliament, so home rule returned to the centre of the stage. The Unionists, true to their name, pledged full support to the Protestants of Ulster in their resistance, and an armed conflict moved into prospect.

When the First World War broke out in 1914, it was envisaged in terms of a British contribution through her navy and a small professional army and it seemed reasonable to speak of "business as usual". With the stalemate on the western front, however, came a shift to the recruitment of Kitchener's "new

Progressive alliance
Political strategy of co-operation between middle-class and working-class radicalism, formalized in 1903 electoral pact: in 1906 24 of 29 Labour victories achieved in absence of Liberal opposition. Based on common ideology of "progressivism", synthesis of liberalism and gradualist socialism finding expression in social reform of 1906-14 Liberal government. After 1910 indications that alliance breaking down at constituency level.

General Election 1906
Landslide victory for Liberals: won 401 seats, Conservatives 157, Labour 29 and Irish Nationalists 83. Fought on issues of 1902 Education Act, Chinese slavery and tariff reform, which Liberals skilfully presented as meaning increases in cost of food.

People's Budget 1909
Introduced by Lloyd George as chancellor of exchequer to make good deficit (incurred by expenditure on pensions and dreadnoughts and by trade depression), by taxing the wealthy: 7 new taxes, including super tax on high incomes, higher rate of tax for unearned income, capital gains tax on land and duty on petrol; higher death duties and duties on liquor and tobacco. Passed by House of Commons but rejected by Lords; finally passed by Lords 1910. Achieved budgetary surplus 1910-14, but effect of redistributive measures limited.

New Liberalism
Reinterpretation of Liberalism from late 1890s, which placed new emphasis on social reform and redistribution of wealth by collective social action; departed from Gladstonian tradition by heightened view of functions of state. New Liberal views expressed by *Progressive Review* and

Manchester Guardian, influenced Liberal social reform 1906-14. Represented last Liberal response to challenge of socialism.

General Elections 1910
January election fought on issue of People's Budget: very high turnout of 86%; results destroyed overall Liberal majority, electorate increasingly polarized along class lines; Liberals won 275 seats and 43.2% of poll, Conservatives 273 seats and 46.9% of poll, Labour 40 seats and Irish Nationalists 82. Second election held December, on issue of reform of House of Lords: result was virtually the same, with Liberals continuing as minority government supported by Labour and Irish Nationalists.

Parliament Act 1911
House of Lords' rejection of People's Budget prompted Asquith to introduce Parliament Bill 1910: passed by House of Lords 1911, after Asquith had threatened to create sufficient Liberal peers to ensure its passage. Removed right of veto from Lords except on bills to extend life of Parliament; Lords permitted delaying powers of one month for money bills and two years for other legislation. Maximum duration of Parliament reduced to five years.

First Coalition 1915
Formation 1915 brought about by resignation of Fisher, First Sea Lord, and a parallel crisis over shell shortage: Bonar Law decided Conservatives must either attack government or join it; Asquith offered coalition. All key posts kept for Liberals except for Admiralty (to Balfour); Bonar Law to Colonial Office. Henderson represented Labour. Lloyd George made minister of Munitions.

Second Coalition 1916
Formed December 1916 after collapse of Asquith's government: Lloyd George, supported by Bonar Law and Carson, challenged Asquith; resulted in fall of government. Lloyd George formed new coalition with support mainly from Conservatives; Asquith refused to serve and Liberals badly split between two leaders. Coalition backed by Labour.

Withdrawal of Labour from Coalition 1917
Arthur Henderson resigned from War Cabinet 1917 as result of "doormat incident" (when he was excluded from cabinet discussion of his behaviour over Russia). Other Labour ministers remained in office, but "incident" marked beginning of Labour's assertion of itself as independent national party.

Fourth Reform Act 1918

Increased electorate from its pre-war level of 8 million to 21 million: gave vote to men over 21 fulfilling 6 months residence qualification, and to women over 30 meeting occupancy requirement; second vote retained for business premises and in university seats. Redistribution Act increased size of House of Commons and adopted principle of equal constituency sizes.

General Election 1918

Known as "coupon election", as coalition candidates received letter of endorsement from Lloyd George and Conservative leader Bonar Law: timing resulted in landslide victory for coalition (526 of 707 seats), benefiting from popular Germanophobia. Labour won 57 seats and 22.7% of poll; Liberals, crippled by schism between Asquith and Lloyd George, won only 28 seats.

Geddes Axe 1922

Popular name for report of Geddes Committee: recommended cuts of £76 million, of which £46.5 million fell on armed services and £24 million on social services; hit education and housing hard, crippling reforms introduced in 1918 Fisher Education Act and in Addison's housing measures.

Carlton Club meeting 1922

Austen Chamberlain called meeting of parliamentary Conservative party at Carlton Club to gain support for continuing participation in coalition under Lloyd George. Bonar Law and Baldwin made effective speeches against coalition. 86 MPs voted in favour of coalition and 187 against; vote brought resignation of Lloyd George and dissolution of Parliament. Bonar Law replaced Chamberlain as Tory leader.

General Election 1922

Resulted in handsome Conservative victory: Conservatives won 345 seats, Labour 142 and Liberals 116. Most significant fact was emergence of Labour as second party with 29.5% of vote against Conservatives' 38.2%, made possible by disunity of Liberals.

General Election 1923

Baldwin succeeded Law as Conservative leader, called election ostensibly to gain mandate for tariff reform. Real motive was desire to unite Conservatives, restore normal party politics and end possibility of coalition by squeezing out Liberals: short-term failure but long-term success. Conservatives won 258 seats, Labour 191 and Liberals 159; followed by formation of first Labour government, with support of Liberals.

armies", with concomitant demands upon the supply of armaments. The formation of the First Coalition* in May 1915 was an attempt by Asquith to retain power in the hands of his own supporters, but the Unionists were now riding high as the champions of sterner military measures, and Lloyd George was impatient with Asquith's dilatory image. Once Asquith had brought in a full scheme of conscription in 1916, despite the deep reservations of many of his Liberal and Labour followers, his usefulness was at an end. After rallying Unionist support for an open challenge, Lloyd George replaced him as prime minister in December 1916. In the Second Coalition*, the Unionists were predominant, with most Liberal frontbenchers now outside the government. Lloyd George brought a new energy to the direction of the war, in presentation as much as substance, and his government was identified, for better or worse, with fighting on to the bitter end.

By the time the Armistice came in November 1918, the pre-war political map had greatly changed. The Liberal party was now separated into Asquithian and Lloyd Georgian factions, the latter working closely with the Conservatives. Alienated from the coalition* in August 1917, Labour prepared itself for an independent bid for power. Moreover, in 1918 the fourth Reform Act* granted manhood suffrage, as a sort of political corollary of the new armies, and along with this came a substantial, though not yet equal, measure of woman suffrage. If this was marginally helpful to Labour, the wartime increase in trade-union membership (from about four million in 1914 to a peak of eight million in 1920) was a more solid benefit. When Lloyd George decided on an immediate general election, a new alignment emerged. He saved the seats of 150 Liberal coalitionists by an electoral pact with the Conservatives who swept the board elsewhere on a tide of triumphant nationalism in this "Coupon Election"*.

The Lloyd George Coalition went on until 1922, settling major external issues through the peace treaties and the Irish Treaty of 1921. Though not devoid of constructive achievements in domestic policy, the shortfall in "homes for heroes" was a living reproach to the Coalition. The spending cuts* which it implemented, once the post-war inflationary bubble burst, indicated the priorities of its Conservative supporters. Ultimately Lloyd George's future depended on fusing with them into a centre party, of which he would be leader, but his own Coalitionist Liberals balked at this step in 1920. The fall of Lloyd George was thereafter only a matter of time. Confident that they could survive without Lloyd George, the Conservative backbenchers who met at the Carlton Club* in October 1922 showed themselves high-minded and high-handed in voting to re-establish their independence.

The party system was thus restored, though it worked on new lines. Bonar Law formed a purely Conservative government, the first since 1886, and was confirmed in power at the General Election of 1922*. Within a year he was succeeded by Stanley Baldwin, who made an unsure start when he called a general election at the end of 1923* on tariff reform, always an electoral handicap for the Conservatives.

The manoeuvre at least united the party under his leadership by dividing the erstwhile Conservative Coalitionists from Lloyd George, who, like other Liberals, reverted gladly to the defence of free trade. But though the Conservatives lost their overall majority, Labour's vote, concentrated in urban industrial constituencies, yielded more seats than the Liberals' broader but thinner support, thus giving it a presumptive right to form the next government. That it did so – with Liberal acquiescence but no working arrangement – was of crucial importance in establishing its credibility. MacDonald looked the part of prime minister, and though his short-lived administration had meagre legislative achievements, this could easily be blamed upon its minority position. The General Election of 1924* revealed a sharp polarization. Though Labour lost seats, it gained votes; but the Liberals lost both, and heavily. This was the moment when the Liberals relinquished major-party status, and thereafter their decline spiralled as the logic of the electoral system tipped sharply against them.

Both Baldwin and MacDonald were adept at squeezing the Liberal vote, and were united too by a strong antipathy to Lloyd George, who finally succeeded Asquith as Liberal leader in 1926. Baldwin's government incorporated Churchill at the Treasury and Neville Chamberlain at the Ministry of Health, who together gave the government a competent and constructive social policy. Despite the industrial confrontation which came to a head in the General Strike* of 1926, therefore, Baldwin developed a reputation as a man of peace whose humane sympathies won the respect of political opponents. The major problem his government faced – or refused to face, as some said – was unemployment, which, under Liberal prompting, emerged as the main subject of political debate. The General Election of 1929*, however, demonstrated the Liberals' failure to reach the necessary threshold of electoral support, and MacDonald was not far short of an outright majority.

The second Labour government lacked any real convictions over unemployment, either for a radical policy such as that urged within the cabinet by Sir Oswald Mosley*, or for Snowden's orthodox policy as chancellor of the exche-

Lloyd George's coalition government became increasingly close-knit as old party differences gave way to cronyism. The pre-war scourge of the aristocracy is seen here with the 17th earl of Derby, Tory magnate and secretary of state for war.

General Election 1924
Held after government defeated on vote of censure. Shortly before polling day "Zinoviev letter" was published, allegedly from president of Communist International to British Communist party inciting it to class war; produced anti-socialist panic. Effect probably marginal, but election gave Conservatives 419 seats and 48.3% of poll, Labour 151 seats and 33.0%, Liberals 40 seats and 17.6%.

General Strike 1926
Called by the TUC in support of miners, who were already on strike against wage cuts and longer hours: brought out workers in key industries such as transport, iron and steel, building, printing and electricity. Government well prepared for strike and helped by middle-class volunteers. Strike collapsed rapidly due to failure of TUC leadership: failure caused disillusionment with strikes; consolidated hold of moderates in trade unions. Government response was Trades Disputes Act 1927, making sympathetic strikes illegal.

General Election 1929
Main issue was unemployment: Labour fought on moderate programme with public works as remedy for unemployment;

Liberal programme influenced by Keynes, in fact more radical. Labour won 288 seats and 37.1% of poll, Conservatives 260 seats and 38.2%, Liberals 59 seats and 23.4%. Labour formed minority government.

Mosley Memorandum 1930
Oswald Mosley, Labour minister, wanted machinery of government overhauled to set up new economic department under prime minister; drastic reduction of unemployment by public works programme along lines advocated by Keynes; long-term economic reconstruction by large-scale mobilization of resources through government planning. Rejected by cabinet, adhering to Snowden's fiscal orthodoxy; Mosley resigned; ideas supported by left of Labour party and rank and file.

Political crisis 1931
Mounting unemployment meant heavy budgetary deficit looming; collapse of German banking system resulted in drain on British money market and run on pound. America only willing to provide loan in return for balanced budget to restore confidence in sterling. Cabinet unable to agree programme of cuts proposed by Snowden (including 10% cut in unemployment benefit): TUC flatly rejected

Snowden's proposal, 9 members of cabinet threatened to resign if cuts implemented. MacDonald formed National Government.

General Election 1931
National Government ostensibly wanted "doctor's mandate" to deal with economic problems: in fact, opportunity to exploit Labour's disarray and for Baldwin to emasculate right-wing of Conservatives. Government won 554 seats and 67.0% of poll: Conservatives predominant in coalition with 473 seats; opposition won 56 seats, of which Labour held 52 (driven back to its heartland areas of high unemployment).

National Government 1931-40
Coalition of Conservatives, Liberals and MacDonald's National Labour supporters, set up to implement programme of economic retrenchment. Liberals withdrew over tariffs 1932. Essentially Conservative administration, though dominated by Baldwin's brand of liberal Conservatism. Its economic policies probably contributed little to economic recovery; some attempt to deal with unemployment in 1934 Depressed Areas Act, but funding inadequate.

See **Tariffs** (page 324)

quer. As the slump mounted, therefore, the inadequacies of the government showed up more sharply, and, in August 1931, faced with a run on the pound, the cabinet fell apart*. MacDonald took a handful of senior ministers with him into the National government, but the rest of the Labour party stood aside. By October, when a general election* was held, public opinion had shown itself unexpectedly ready for sacrifice, albeit mainly at the expense of public servants and the unemployed. Supporters of the National government – predominantly Conservative with some Liberals and a smattering of National Labour – cornered the anti-Labour vote, while Labour's own support slumped badly. The net effect, as magnified by the electoral system, left Labour outnumbered by more than ten-to-one in the Commons.

The National government* remained in power until the Second World War, though time eroded both its National status and its power. Its Liberal support was withdrawn in 1932, when it accepted tariffs*, and the National Liberals who remained in the government, like National Labour, were in due course swallowed by the Conservative party. The government nonetheless remained more centrist than many Conservatives wished. The unlikelihood of Labour supplanting it, confirmed in the General Election of 1935*, was one reason for the persistent advocacy of a "popular front"* during the 1930s, though what was meant by this was so disputable as to vitiate the proposal. Baldwin's achievement was to maintain the moderate right in office despite the slump. Though Mosley launched a fascist movement* after leaving the Labour party, and though Communism* acquired more prominence (and even fashionableness among intellectuals), extreme solutions remained confined to the margins of politics.

After Neville Chamberlain became prime minister in 1937, politics turned increasingly upon issues of foreign policy. Chamberlain's aim of appeasing* Hitler came to a head in the autumn of 1938, with his claim to have brought back peace with honour from Munich. When Hitler violated the Munich settlement in March 1939, the policy of appeasement lay in tatters. Politically, the initiative passed from Chamberlain to his Conservative critics, led by

General Election 1935
Main issue was unemployment with rearmament as minor concern. 9.4% swing to Labour, but National Government retained sizeable majority. Government won 432 seats and 53.7% at poll; Labour won 158 seats and 38% poll. Labour made major gains in areas of high unemployment.

Popular front
From mid-1930s, proposals to mobilize anti-Conservative forces, on model of coalitions of parties in Spain and France: Communist party, ILP and Socialist League called for unity of working-class movement against fascism and National Government; Labour party hostile due to Communist involvement and movement faded. After Munich, alliance of Labour, Liberals and Conservative critics of Chamberlain proposed; united action by Labour and Liberals in 1938 by-elections.

Abdication crisis 1936
Edward VIII became king but intended to marry Mrs Wallis Simpson, American divorcée. Church of England, of which monarch the head, was opposed to divorce, which still carried moral stigma. Baldwin posed stern choice of renouncing Mrs Simpson or abdication: Edward wavered, but announced his abdication; his brother became George VI; he went into exile.

British Union of Fascists
Mosley left Labour party 1930, formed New Party 1931, renamed it British Union of Fascists 1932 after visit to Italy; membership reached 20,000 at highest point; wore uniforms of black shirts; relied on marches and rallies which often degenerated into violence. Stronghold was East End of London, where Mosley exploited working-class anti-semitism; curbed by economic revival and by 1936 Public Order Act, banning political uniforms and controlling marches.

British Communist party
Formed 1920 by amalgamation of British Socialist party and other far-left elements; tried to affiliate to Labour party but repeatedly rebuffed. Parliamentary candidates won at Battersea 1924, West Fife 1935 and 1945; Mile End 1945. Membership rose from 2,500 1930 to 18,000 1939, but reflected middle-class concern about fascism more than working-class allegiance: advocated popular-front strategy against fascism in 1930s.

Sir Oswald Mosley leads a procession of British fascists through the London streets in May 1938.

Churchill, and to the anti-fascist ideologues of the Labour and Liberal left. The outbreak of war in September 1939 brought Churchill into the government but, like Lloyd George in 1915-16, his fortunes were not to be bound up with the misfortunes of the cabinet in which he served. In May 1940, with Germany rampant, enough Conservative MPs withdrew their support from Chamberlain to make a coalition inevitable, and since he was not acceptable as prime minister to Labour (or the Liberals) this meant his downfall.

The coalition government* which Churchill formed had the overriding aim of winning the war, but it also responded to a major shift to the left in public opinion. Labour and Liberal ministers wielded greater influence than their parliamentary numbers warranted. Along with this went a renewed emphasis on welfare measures in the war emergency and an increase in personal taxation which had a levelling effect in society. The Beveridge Report* of 1942 went further in presenting a specific plan for a comprehensive social security system.

Appeasement
Term for much-criticized British foreign policy of 1937-39, aimed at stopping German and Italian expansion by concession rather than force, particularly associated with Neville Chamberlain. Policy culminated in Munich Agreement 1938, but discredited by German invasion of Czecho-Slovakia and ended by British pledge to Poland 1939.

Wartime Coalition
Public opinion disturbed by the fall of Norway 1940; Chamberlain was blamed and attacked in Commons; resigned in order that Churchill might lead coalition government with Labour and Liberal participation. War Cabinet composed of Churchill plus 2 Labour and 2 Conservative representatives; Cabinet offices dominated by Conservatives; War Cabinet dominated by Churchill. Electoral truce declared, but broken by formation of Commonwealth party 1942, which contested by-elections against "reactionary" candidates.

Beveridge Report 1942
Report produced by Sir William Beveridge, after official enquiry, which proposed: introduction of unified scheme of social insurance to abolish "five giants" of want, sickness, squalor, ignorance and idleness; introduction of family allowances, National Health Service; and economic policy directed at avoidance of unemployment. Plan received wide popular support; wartime government accepted report in principle but vacillated on implementation. Labour government adopted its main proposals via 1946 National Insurance Act and establishment of National Health Service 1948.

General Election 1945
Result great surprise, as most commentators anticipated Conservative victory: 12% swing to Labour resulted in Labour 393 seats and 47.8% vote, Conservatives 213 seats and 39.8%, Liberals 12 seats and 9%. Labour benefited from consensus created during war in favour of collectivist policies and state intervention; public interested in social change, welfare and housing. Conservatives, despite Churchill's prestige, blamed for pre-war unemployment and for causing war.

Winston Churchill with Brendan Bracken on the steps of 10 Downing Street in June 1940, soon after becoming premier.

"Socialists!". Vicky's cartoon of July 1951 depicts the Bevanites as street urchins attacking the respectable right wing of the Labour party. The Bevanites, left to right, are Harold Wilson, Aneurin Bevan, Michael Foot and Ian Mikardo. Across the road are Herbert Morrison, Clement Attlee, Hugh Gaitskell and Emanuel Shinwell.

National Health Service

National Health Service Act became law 1946 but not implemented until 1948. Provided public medical service entirely free at point of need, to replace complex and inadequate pre-war provision. Financed out of insurance contributions and taxation. Much obstruction from British Medical Association, who particularly opposed full-time salaried service from doctors, but compromise skilfully achieved by Bevan. 14 regional boards set up to adminster hospitals; 138 executive councils formed to run GP services in England and Wales.

Nationalization

Since 1918 Labour Party pledged to nationalization in Clause IV of its constitution: 1945 manifesto even more committed. Bank of England and civil aviation nationalized 1946; coal mines and electricity 1947; railways, gas and some road transport 1948; iron and steel 1949 with vesting date in 1951. But Labour in fact cautious in its procedures: modelled nationalized industries on public corporations with little industrial democracy. Conservatives denationalized road haulage and iron and steel in 1953; iron and steel renationalized 1967.

General Election 1950

Government went to polls with confidence but overall majority reduced to 4. Sedate campaign but high turnout of 84%. Labour won 315 seats and 46.1% of poll, Conservatives 297 seats and 43.4%, Liberals 9 seats and 9.1%. Electorate dissatisfied with continuance of wartime controls. Labour lost support most heavily in suburbs, especially in Home Counties.

General Election 1951

Labour polled its highest ever total of votes, but Conservatives won small majority of seats; Conservatives won 321 seats and 48% of poll, Labour 295 seats and 48.7%, Liberals 6 seats and 2.6%. Marked feature was collapse of Liberal vote, squeezed out as voting became clearly polarized on class lines; Conservatives benefited from Liberal demise and formed government.

" SOCIALISTS! "

Churchill, with his transparent English nationalism and his image as a man of the right, thus presided over a government which restored the fortunes of the moderate left. His direction of the war effort was widely commended and he drew on the unstinting loyalty of Labour ministers like Attlee and Bevin. But as the tide turned, and the grim defiance of 1940-41 yielded to the prospect of victory in 1942-43, political divisions sharpened, and wartime by-elections showed that, despite the official party truce, the Conservatives were in trouble. In the General Election of 1945*, therefore, Churchill's personal ascendancy could not be translated into votes for his party. Conversely, Labour improved out of all recognition upon its vote in 1935, increasing in round numbers from eight million to twelve million. This was a structural change for which the war was largely responsible, and it put a Labour government into power for the first time with an overall majority.

The Attlee government implemented the new consensus, and the creation of the welfare state was its monument. Able to follow the Beveridge Report as regards national insurance, it had no such blueprint for a national health service. Here the creative talents of Bevan, as minister of health, supplied the need, and his combination of bold administrative decisions with adroit medical diplomacy enabled the new service* to come into operation in 1948. The other aspect of Labour's domestic programme was its socialist policy of bringing certain industries and utilities into public ownership*. Labour's approach to reconstruction involved a continuation of wartime controls and rationing; austerity became a way of life and to some extent the Conservatives were able to capitalize upon this. Weakened by internal dissension, Labour nonetheless polled at record levels in the General Election of 1951*, though the electoral system now exhibited a bias which gave the Conservatives a small majority of seats. This was the peak of the two-party system, with high turnout and sharp polarization which almost squeezed the Liberals out of existence.

299

Churchill returned as prime minister on the cry of setting the people free from socialist controls, but his government embodied substantial continuity in practice. His chancellor of the exchequer, R.A. Butler, sought to manage the economy in much the same way as his Labour predecessor, Gaitskell, as the coinage of the term "Butskellism"* suggested (albeit with exaggeration). Similarly, in industrial relations, the trade unions were handled with kid gloves and the welfare state was maintained in all essentials. Indeed, the Conservatives even scaled down the defence budget and, with the end of the Korean War, this left room for lower taxes and higher personal consumption. Churchill's replacement by Eden in 1955 was smooth and inevitable, but Eden's tenure was to prove rough and unpredictable as the Suez crisis* of 1956 tested him to his limits, both political and physical. He was succeeded in 1957, not by Butler, with his liberal reputation, but by Macmillan, currently the hero of the anti-American right wing of the Tory party.

As prime minister, however, Macmillan set his own course, under cover of artful dissimulation. Not only did he rebuild the alliance with the USA despite right-wing suspicions, but he accelerated the winding-up of Britain's imperial commitments, especially in Africa. At home he reverted to the Keynesian* policies of which he had been an early advocate in the 1930s, and in economic strategy chose to err on the side of inflation rather than unemployment. The consumption-led boom of the late 1950s offered an apparent vindication of his policies, economically and electorally. The Conservatives' easy success* stood in sharp contrast to the factionalism of the Labour party, divided between its Bevanite* left wing proclaiming socialism and its Gaitskellite right wing advocating a revisionist approach. As affluence seemed set to erode its traditional working-class support, political analysts began to ask, Must Labour Lose? Party unity, however, was given a new priority from 1963, under the leadership of Wilson, and in 1964 the long spell of Conservative rule was broken, along with the prosperity which had sustained it.

"Butskellism"
Term first coined by *The Economist* in 1951 to suggest that Butler's handling of balance of payments crisis 1951 took much same form as would have been adopted by Gaitskell, previous Labour chancellor. More widely used to describe economic policy mixing planning and freedom following doctrines of Keynes. Left employed it derisively to indicate similarity in purpose of Labour and Tory leaderships.

See **Suez crisis** (page 318)

See **Keynesianism** (page 326)

General Election 1959
Conservatives increased majority to 100 seats: personal triumph for Macmillan who presented programme based on Britain's new affluence; Labour had no effective answer. Conservatives won 365 seats and 49.4% of poll, Labour 258 seats and 43.8%, Liberals 6 seats and 5.9%.

Bevanites
Group of left-wing Labour MPs, closely associated with Aneurin Bevan, which came into conflict with Labour leadership in 1950s. Gained support in constituency parties and trade union branches; prominent Bevanites elected to National Executive Committee of Labour party at 1952 conference. Clashed with leadership on defence and nationalization. Group lost its leader 1959 when Bevan opposed unilateral nuclear disarmament.

General Elections 1964 and 1966
In 1964: 3.5% swing to Labour gave Wilson working majority of 4. Wilson proved skilful party leader, effectively presenting Labour party as best able to harness science and technology to provide growth. Labour won 317 seats and 44.1% of poll, Tories 304 seats and 43.4%, Liberals won 9 and 11.2%. In 1966, a uniform national swing of 3.1% to Labour resulted in majority of over 90: Labour won 363 seats and 47.9% of poll, Conservatives 253 seats and 41.9%, Liberals 12 seats and 8.5%.

Devaluation 1967
By summer of 1967 government in serious economic trouble with trade deficit and unemployment rising. Chancellor of exchequer Callaghan rejected devaluation July; but dock strike worsened trade figures and confidence in pound declined. In November government announced 14.3%

Harold Macmillan in West Hartlepool in January 1959, on a pre-election tour of the north-east.

devaluation of sterling in attempt to reduce balance of payments deficit. Meant admitting failure of economic policy of deflation and wage restraint.

"In Place of Strife" 1969
White Paper produced by Barbara Castle, secretary for employment, proposing extensive trade union reform. Recommended compulsory 28 day conciliation period and ballot of members backed by legal sanctions when strike threatened. Supported by Wilson but split Labour cabinet; outcry from trade unions; major backbench revolt. Wilson and Castle capitulated: episode major tactical blunder.

General Election 1970
4.7% swing to Conservatives, gave Heath 30-seat majority. Result was deep shock to Labour party: perhaps explained by last-minute change in voting intentions, influenced by poor trade figures published shortly before polling. Conservatives won 330 seats and 46.4% of poll, Labour 287 seats and 43.0%, Liberals 6 seats and 7.5%.

Industrial Relations Act 1971
Introduced fundamental changes into legal framework of industrial relations. Unions had to register if they were to retain special legal status; ballots could be imposed on membership before strikes began; workers and trade unions faced fines for non-compliance. Established new Industrial Relations Court which, together with industrial tribunals, heard complaints of unfair industrial practice. TUC resolved that its members should boycott register; strikes held against Act and unions fined. Repealed by Trade Union and Labour Relations Act 1974.

See **European Economic Community** (page 320)

General Elections 1974
First held February 1974 in circumstances of 3-day working week and state of emergency. Heath stood for firmness against unions and inflation; Labour as party to get country out of crisis. Labour won 301 seats and 37.1% of poll, Conservatives 297 seats and 37.9%, Liberals 14 seats and 19.3%, Nationalists won 9 seats. Labour formed government with Liberals and Nationalists holding balance of power. In October 1974, second election held with government seeking new mandate at earliest opportunity. 2.2% swing to Labour gave Labour small overall majority: Labour won 319 seats and 39.2% of poll, Tories 277 seats and 35.8%, Liberals 13 seats and 18.3%, Nationalists 14 seats.

Labour squeaked home in 1964 and was confirmed in power in 1966*. This was Wilson's heyday, promising better management of the economy to produce faster economic growth to finance higher spending on the social services. In practice, expenditure outran the resources generated by the faltering economy, beset by sterling crises as the exchange rate came under pressure. Wilson and his chancellor, Callaghan, opted to defend sterling, if need be at the expense of growth and the social programme. Only when their efforts failed in 1967 did a devaluation of the pound*, along with allied measures from the new chancellor, Jenkins, pave the way for a recovery in the balance of payments. The central problem of government was increasingly perceived as that of preventing wage rises from pushing up prices too fast. The Wilson government's reliance upon a formal incomes policy here proved double-edged, achieving some success at the price of alienating its trade-union supporters. What the unions finally would not tolerate was an explicit proposal to reform their legal position, envisaged in the white paper *In Place of Strife,** published in 1969, and their influence in the Labour party was accordingly used to abort the Bill which the government brought forward. By 1970 Labour's reputation for economic management was under question and its relations with the trade unions under a searchlight, thus giving the Conservatives a chance to snatch an unexpected victory*.

The new prime minister, Heath, was in an unusually strong position, owing few political debts. He invested much prestige in pushing through an Industrial Relations Act* in 1971 in the face of union hostility, and signalled a break with the interventionist economic consensus of the 1960s. His greatest triumph came when he took Britain into the European Economic Community* in 1972, a step to which exaggerated hopes and fears were attached. But Heath found the economic returns on his policies disappointing, and his abrasive methods had undermined the goodwill necessary to rekindle a consensus between representatives of both sides of industry. When, in 1972, the government moved back towards incomes policy, albeit of an ostensibly egalitarian kind, it found the unions sullen and hostile. The attempt to force a settlement upon the miners in the autumn of 1973, just when the international oil crisis was bidding up energy prices, therefore backfired badly. The General Election of February 1974*, dubbed an unpopularity contest, saw a simultaneous slump in both Conservative and Labour support. For the Conservatives, it was worse than 1945; for Labour worse than 1959. The Liberal party, which had periodically shown dramatic flashes of revival in by-elections, now polled half as well as each of the major parties, though with few seats in reward.

Back in office, Labour abandoned Heath's incomes policy and relied instead upon the concept of a social contract with the trade unions. Anxious now to repudiate Britain's membership of the EEC, it determined to re-negotiate the terms. The government's left-wing stance in these matters, however, was soon tempered. The referendum on the EEC, which the left had relied upon to vindicate their alternative economic strategy, gave a two-to-one vote in favour of continued membership. It followed from this rebuff to the left that the response to the spiralling inflation in the summer of 1975 lay instead in the inception of a new variant of wage restraint – one initiated this time by the union leaders themselves. The policies of consensus were thus reasserted, but from a base of such economic and political weakness that their viability could no longer be presumed.

Twentieth-Century Welsh Politics

D.B. Smith

In 1900 the Scot, Keir Hardie, was elected for Merthyr as the first socialist MP in Wales. By 1966 thirty-two of the thirty-six Welsh MPs elected now represented the Labour party. It would seem that Labour's domination this century, at local and parliamentary level, was an assured success story in a country where what had made Merthyr pioneering in the nineteenth century – industry, urban growth and a proletarian presence – made her merely representative in the next. But on his death in 1915 Hardie remained the only avowed socialist amongst Welsh MPs: the transition from Liberalism to Labourism, let alone socialism, was a slow, turbulent passage.

Down to 1914 the Liberal party's hold was relatively unquestioned in both rural and industrial Wales. Political rhetoric on the question of Land and Religion* may have been by-passed by reality, but the wider social and cultural values which had imbued Liberalism with "Welshness" were potent forces in the southern coalfield, no less than in the countryside or the slate quarrying villages of the north or the metal-working towns of the south-west. In 1906 no Conservative was returned in Wales and even when the Lib-Lab* miners' MPs became officially "Labour" after 1908, their politics remained rooted in the concepts of progressivism and community rather than those of socialism and class.

The First World War, with its collectivist drive and its disregard for Liberal values, notwithstanding the premiership of a Welsh Liberal, David Lloyd

Land and Religion
Welsh Liberalism dominated 1885-1905 by issues of land and disestablishment of Anglican Church in Wales. Welsh land league set up 1886 to protect tenant farmers; Lloyd George and Tom Ellis voiced anti-landlord sentiment at Westminster. Tithes united hostility to landlords and to "alien" Anglican Church. Protest against tithes defused by Tithe Rent Charge Act 1891; Welsh disestablishment fading in importance by early 20th century. Anglican Church in Wales disestablished 1920.

"Lib-Labs"
Working-class MPs elected from 1874 who took Liberal whip and espoused Gladstonian politics: predominantly miners' union officials sitting for mining areas, where able to influence local Liberal associations. Failed to make distinctive political contribution as too easily absorbed into orthodox Liberalism; "Lib-Labbery" ended as separate body when Miners Federation affiliated to Labour party 1908.

National Union of Mineworkers
In pre-war period, the South Wales Miners Federation exerted militant influence; the "Fed" had had strong left-wing leanings due to leaders such as Arthur Horner and S.O. Davies; miners' agents were powerful force in Labour movement. In 1945, national Miners Federation became National Union of Mineworkers, and its political influence was strongest in immediate post-war years. In 1945, 13 South Wales MPs were sponsored by NUM; but NUM lost political power with run-down of coal industry; by 1970 only 2 MPs were direct nominees of NUM; by 1974 none.

The Welsh mining town of Pentre in the Rhondda Valley, photographed in about 1905. The pit was closed in 1959. Apart from the removal of the chimney and the headframe, the town looks very much the same today.

Plaid Cymru

("Party of Wales") Founded 1925 by merger of 2 small nationalist groups, initially little more than small Welsh-language pressure group. Plaid Cymru committed to Welsh self-government on a dominion basis 1932. Rose to prominence in 1936 when leaders imprisoned for involvement in burning RAF bombing school at Pen-y-Berth. Drew in advocates of non-violent direct action late 1930s but insignificant force until 1960s.

Plaid Cymru MPs arriving at Westminster in October 1974. On the left is Gwynfor Evans (Carmarthen), president of the party, with Dafydd Wigley (Caernarfon), right.

Welsh Office

Established 1964 with secretary of state for Wales: Labour's conversion to support for Welsh Office in 1959 was reversal of policy of Attlee government. Owed much to influence of Welsh Labour group. Office's powers covered housing, local government and transport, extended to health, agriculture and education 1969. Seen by some as first step towards devolution.

Welsh language

Welsh Language Society formed 1962: departure from gradualist approach adopted by earlier groups; took militant approach to defence of language, recruited young members especially students. New tactics included demonstrations and sit-ins; from 1963 used sabotage of property and English road signs. Must take partial credit for Welsh Language Act 1967 giving Welsh equal legal validity with English.

George, acted as catalyst on the politics of a society riven with industrial conflict. By 1922 the Labour party held eighteen seats and Liberalism began its long retreat to the more rural west and north. The Labour party's harvest proved as bitter as the protracted strikes that cracked trade union power in Wales until the mid-1930s. The once-dynamic economy, based largely on coal, which had concentrated two thirds of the population into south Wales before 1914, now spiralled into long-term decline. Labour administered a society which had lost almost 450,000 people through emigration by 1939 and was characterized by heavy unemployment throughout the inter-war period. Collectivism, in politics and in industry, was embraced wholeheartedly as the only salvation. The presence of ex-miners' leaders, like Aneurin Bevan and James Griffiths, in the 1945 Labour government signalled the power and appeal of the Labour party in Wales. It had become, like the Liberal party before it, expressive of Welsh needs and identity that went beyond the merely political.

Defiance of a one-party domination has been mostly ineffective. The Liberals were whittled down to one MP by 1979, whilst the Communist party, a strong rival in council elections and in some constituencies until 1945, never won a seat. Communist influence was most felt in the miners' union*, where it often resembled the practice of pre-1914 Welsh syndicalists. Plaid Cymru* (the Welsh Nationalist party, founded in 1925) was an insignificant political force until disillusionment with Labour in government and in local administration combined to send their president, Gwynfor Evans, to Westminster in 1966. Two more nationalist gains, both in the north-west, followed in 1974, and these two were held in 1979. The incoming Labour government of 1964, reversing its long-standing attitude, had appointed a secretary of state for Wales to serve in the cabinet. The Welsh Office* grew in administrative scope. It was a focus for successful lobbying to improve the condition of the embattled Welsh language in schools, in the media, and as an officially recognized language in Wales. Plaid Cymru, buoyed up by a youthful cultural nationalism*, made dramatic progress in the late 1960s even in largely English-speaking areas. However, the politics of culture did not translate smoothly into the language of politics. Though devolution* was official Labour party policy, the referendum held on St David's Day in 1979 saw the Welsh reject an elected Assembly by four to one, exactly the proportion of English to Welsh speakers.

Perhaps 1979 marked the end of Welsh radicalism's long reign. Certainly the return of eleven Conservative MPs – three for constituencies that had not been Tory at all this century – was quite unprecedented. This may be the reflection of a new Wales – white-collar, coastal, suburban, less attached to the old loyalties forged in single-industry communities – or it may only signal the political flux of a Wales that is experiencing a more divisive social and cultural pluralism than has hitherto been its lot this century.

Welsh devolution

Labour lost 3 seats to Plaid Cymru 1974, felt threatened by nationalists, and decided to act on recommendations of 1973 Kilbrandon Report and introduce directly elected assembly for Wales with executive powers. Labour party split on issue: bill introduced 1976 but in trouble from beginning; government forced to concede referendum in which 40% of electorate had to vote in favour for devolution to be implemented. In 1979 referendum 11.8% of electorate voted in favour, 46.5% voted against. Episode was bad miscalculation by Labour party.

Scottish Politics Since 1901

Christopher Harvie

Two themes have dominated twentieth-century Scottish politics: the problems of an over-specialized, socially unequal and depressed industrial economy; and the evolution of a distinctively Scottish administrative system. The result has been political behaviour increasingly at variance with the English norm, and the strength of nationalist ideas, which now extend far beyond the supporters of the Scottish National party.

Nineteenth-century Scotland was overwhelmingly Liberal, and its political class was content to barter the autonomy of its traditional institutions – Kirk, law, education and local government – for a share in the spoils of empire. Mounting difficulties in local administration, however, caused the Westminster parties to sanction the restoration of the Scottish Secretary* in 1885, although he did not seriously begin to accumulate power until after 1926. The secretary was effectively manager of the northern Liberals, although the high tide of imperialism, 1895-1905, saw them at a disadvantage. Conservatives and Liberal Unionists returned thirty-eight out of seventy-two MPs in 1900, with strong support from the Protestant working-class of Clydeside and the established Kirk. But the controversy over Kirk disestablishment was waning, and Clydeside's distaste for tariff reform led to the Liberals' landslide victory of 1906, when they captured fifty-eight seats.

Scottish Office
Established 1885 with Scottish Secretary: powers limited, except over education. 1939 Reorganization of Offices (Scotland) Act introduced major reform: new Scottish Office established with 4 administrative departments (Home, Health, Education and Agriculture); headquarters moved from London to Edinburgh.

The Red Flag in George Square, Glasgow, in 1919, during a strike called to demand a 40-hour working week.

The Scottish Liberal party was cool about social reform and hostile to Labour (which, however, won two seats). Many Liberal MPs were English; most lived in England. As a result the "New Liberalism" took a socialist or nationalist form, expressed in the Young Scots Society or the successful weekly *Forward*, which circulated widely among the members of the Independent Labour party. In comparison with England, however, Scotland remained overwhelmingly Liberal in 1910.

The politics of the skilled workers were important in reshaping the party system after the First World War. In 1915-16 they resisted attempts by the government to enforce the Munitions Act*, and accepted an element of socialist ideology, although post-war working-class disillusionment with Liberalism and the alignment of Catholic voters with Labour over the Irish troubles were as important in causing pronounced swings to Labour in the Glasgow municipal elections of 1920 and the General Election of 1922. The realignment of the centre and right that this provoked penalized the Liberals, already badly divided by the Asquith-Lloyd George split of 1916. After a brief three-party episode, 1922-24, Liberal MPs fell to nine in 1924. The party never recovered.

John Wheatley, the architect of the Labour-Catholic alliance, proved as minister of health the outstanding success of MacDonald's first Labour administration. He secured a housing act* which gave adequate central subsidies to public housing and began the assault on Scotland's wretched living conditions. This, and growing socialist involvement in local government, detracted from the hitherto strong home-rule commitment of Scottish Labour. So too did the experience of British working-class solidarity in the General Strike of 1926. Yet divisions between ILP radicals and the Labour/trade union establishment grew, aggravated by the failures of MacDonald's second government, 1929-31. Wheatley's successor as leader of the Scottish left, James Maxton, proved as inept an organizer as he was a brilliant orator. After Labour's crushing defeat in the "National Government" election of 1931, when their MPs dropped from thirty-six to seven, he led the ILP out of the Labour party, and into the wilderness.

The high unemployment* which gripped the country (over 20 per cent for most of the thirties) compelled intervention by the government, which gave Scotland a commissioner under the 1934 Special Areas Act, and a wide range of state initiatives were taken under the secretaryship of Walter Elliot, 1936-38. Scottish nationalism provided a stronger stimulus to the political class than the poor electoral performance of the National Party of Scotland* (1928) and its successor, the SNP* (1934), would suggest. Elliot backed the strongly-autonomist Scottish Economic Committee* (1936-39) and "popular front" movements in Scotland took on a strongly nationalist tinge. In part this reflected a remarkable cultural renaissance headed by the poet and critic "Hugh MacDiarmid", but a general middle-class concern about the damage inflicted by industrial decline produced many cross-party pressure groups. These got their chance when Churchill made Tom Johnston Scottish secretary in 1941, and Johnston collaborated with Elliot and other leaders to secure a wide range of planning and social welfare initiatives.

Between 1945 and 1957, however, Scotland's politics closely paralleled those of Westminster. Labour's electoral performance in 1945 was relatively disappointing, but by 1950 it had attained its maximum vote and party membership. Arthur Woodburn, Secretary 1947-50, shared the Attlee cabinet's

Munitions Act 1915
Attempt by Lloyd George to tighten controls on munitions workers: made strikes illegal on war work; gave Ministry right to declare workshops "controlled establishments" where it could itself impose discipline; introduced leaving certificate from employer without which worker could not get another job. Act failed to stop strikes, led to formation of Clyde Workers' Committee, of militant shop stewards, to resist compulsion.

The Clydesiders
Group of left-wing ILP MPs first returned to Westminster 1922 when Labour won 10 of 15 seats. Most vocal group on left in Westminster throughout 1920s; best-known figures were split over decision to disaffiliate from Labour party 1932. Secession from Labour led to decline of ILP.

Housing Act 1924
Most successful housing measure of inter-war years, one of few successes of first Labour government. Followed recent policy of encouraging local authority house building by increasing central government subsidies. Produced 508,000 houses by 1933.

See **Unemployment 1921-41** (page 324)

National Party of Scotland
Founded 1928 largely by intellectuals of 1920s Scottish cultural renaissance and former ILP activists. Party was politically radical: vote steadily rose but disastrous by-election result at East Fife 1933 led to purge of fundamentalists.

Scottish National Party
Founded 1934 by amalgamation of National Party of Scotland and Scottish Self-Government party (less radical body formed 1932), aimed to secure Scottish Parliament within framework of United Kingdom. Leadership ousted during war; SNP became explicitly separatist. First electoral success at Motherwell by-election April 1945, but party then in decline until 1966: revival began with victory at Hamilton 1967.

Scottish Economic Committee 1936-39
Sub-Committee of Scottish National Development Council financed by Special Areas Commissioner; worked to promote 1938 Empire Exhibition, Scottish Industrial Estates and Scottish Special Housing Associations. Imbued with Keynesian ideas promoted by Dundee School of Economics; influential exponent of economic and physical planning.

Mrs Winifred Ewing, the former SNP MP for Hamilton, with the veteran nationalist Arthur Donaldson, at the Party's Bannockburn celebrations in 1971.

centralism and staved off the demands of the Scottish Covenant* movement, which gained two million signatures for its home rule petition. His Unionist successors, James Stuart and John Maclay, increased administrative devolution and after 1959, driven by mounting unemployment, revived the idea of economic planning. But by this time Labour, against the English trend, was gaining support (it had taken over most of the local authorities in the densely-populated central belt in the thirties and forties) and in 1964 it captured forty-three out of seventy-one seats, on a programme which promised the integration of Scottish industrial modernization within its National Plan*.

With dwindling public support (50 per cent in 1955, 31 per cent in 1979), and takeovers sapping the autonomy of their Scottish business backers, the Unionists continued to slip. The challenge to Labour, in mounting economic trouble after 1966, came from a revived SNP, which made sweeping gains in the 1968 local elections. Their performance in the 1970 election was disappointing but the Kilbrandon Commission* reported in November 1973 in favour of devolution, just as another SNP revival took off, powered by the six-fold increase in the price of "Scotland's oil" newly discovered off the east coast.

The SNP gained seven seats in February 1974, and a further three in October, when it topped 30 per cent of the vote. The Labour leadership combatted this threat by forcing a policy of legislative devolution* to a Scottish assembly on its Scottish supporters. But the relevant legislation passed through Parliament only with difficulty, the assembly's powers were severely circumscribed, and the Scottish electorate's endorsement of it, in a referendum held on 1 March, 1979, was not sufficient to allow its enactment to proceed.

The SNP provoked the vote of no confidence which toppled the Callaghan government, but its vote fell to 17 per cent in the May General Election and it lost nine seats. Largely because of internal disputes, it found recovery difficult and the initiative passed to Labour, converted to a much stronger assembly with which to combat de-industrialization and the anti-socialist centralization of Mrs Thatcher (who had always been hostile to devolution). Socialism and nationalism were the political indicators of an ever-deeper social and cultural alienation from England.

Scottish Covenant movement
Organized to promote home rule propaganda in post-war years. 1,200 delegates at 1949 convention signed covenant calling for home rule within federal system, which then gained two million signatures. But Labour party hostile and movement lost impetus.

Labour's National Plan 1965
Plan forecast 3.8% annual growth for period 1965-70. Scottish Development Department (set up 1962 with its own regional development division) worked more effectively on its strategy than English counterparts. William Ross, secretary of state, presented "Plan for Scotland" 1966, which placed stress on new industries and social expenditure to create jobs. Ross introduced Highlands and Islands Development Board 1965 financed by block grant.

Kilbrandon Commission
Royal Commission on the Constitution established 1969 by Wilson as response to SNP challenges. Recommendations of 1973 Report were complex and far from unanimous, but all 13 commissioners favoured some form of change. Most popular was creation of elected assemblies for Scotland and Wales, from which would come governments to deal with business of Scottish and Welsh Offices.

Devolution for Scotland
SNP gains in 1974 elections forced Labour to act on Kilbrandon Report and introduce some form of devolution, though issue divided Labour in Scotland. Scotland and Wales Bill introduced 1976; proposed legislative assembly for Scotland; government forced to concede referendum but bill still lost. 1977 new bill produced separately for Scotland: ultimate enactment made dependent on 40% electorate voting for devolution in 1979 referendum. Assembly favoured by 32.85% to 30.78%, but failed to secure 40% target; SNP brought government down on vote of no confidence 28 March 1979.

Ireland and British Government

Patrick Buckland

The history of Anglo-Irish relations between 1901 and 1975 is a story of British failure to understand the nature of political loyalties and conflict in Ireland. This is clear from the fates of the 1914 Home Rule Act*, the 1920 Government of Ireland Act and the 1921 Anglo-Irish Treaty, all of which were designed to end the Act of Union and direct rule over Ireland as well as to secure its adherence to the British Empire.

A combination of political calculation and idealism prompted Asquith's Liberal government to propose in 1912 a limited form of self government which would hand over Ireland to the Irish parliamentary party under the moderate John Redmond. The act of reconciliation proved as abortive as Gladstone's earlier attempts, because it ignored the regionalism of the north-east of Ireland and the fierce opposition of the Protestants of Ulster to home rule. A singular concept of political loyalty, the support of an effective political machine (the Ulster Unionist Council*) and a para-military force (the Ulster Volunteer Force*), and the connivance of the Conservative and Unionist opposition in Britain enabled the Ulster Unionists to bring the United Kingdom to the verge of civil war by 1914. Their opposition rendered the Home Rule Act irrelevant, ensured that Ireland would eventually be partitioned, and stimulated a more uncompromising form of nationalism. The short-lived

Home Rule Act 1914

Home Rule Bill introduced by Asquith 1912: provided for bicameral Irish parliament, but wide powers over revenue and defence reserved for Westminster (where Irish representation retained). Unionist opposition led by Carson (supported by Conservatives under Bonar Law): pledged resistance, by force if necessary, in Solemn League and Covenant 1912. Bill twice passed by House of Commons, twice rejected by Lords. Threat of rebellion in Ulster brought compromise from Asquith 1914: allowed counties to vote to be excluded from arrangement for 6 years. Act passed with proviso not to be implemented until after war and not without amending legislation for Ulster.

Ulster Unionist Council

Formed 1905 with aim of uniting local Unionist associations and Orange Lodges to co-ordinate policy and defend interests of Ulster Unionism. Formation prompted by devolution crisis 1904-5, when Ulster feared UK Unionist government was contemplating Irish devolution. Ruling body was central council composed of 200 representatives of Unionist associations, Orange Lodges, MPs and peers, controlled by landowners and businessmen. Assumed steadily increasing power: co-ordinated opposition to Home Rule Bill 1912, formulated plans for provisional Ulster government in event of home rule.

Ulster Volunteer Force

Paramilitary force formed by Ulster Unionist Council 1913 in attempt to unite local Unionist militia groups into single body. Recruitment limited to 100,000 and succeeded in enrolling 90,000 men: drilled openly, but not fully armed until April 1914 when rifles and ammunition smuggled in from Germany. By summer of 1914, UVF formed significant body prepared to resist home rule by armed force.

O'Connell Bridge, with the ruins of Eden Quay, after the Easter Rising in Dublin, 1916.

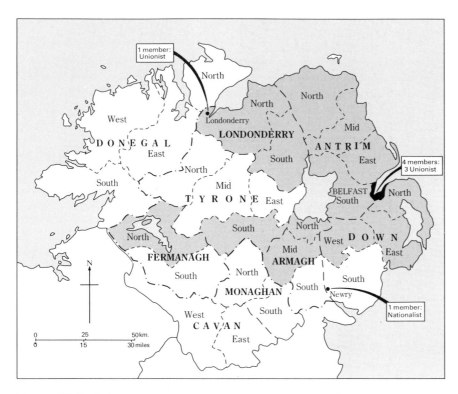

The parliamentary representation of Ulster in 1911

——— Provincial boundary
— — County boundary
- - - - Parlimentary constituency boundary

Unionist constituencies in Ulster

·—·— Present border between Northern Ireland and the Republic of Ireland

Easter Rising* in 1916 was in the tradition of the old Irish Republican Brotherhood*, but the movement which swept aside the old home rulers in 1918 also drew upon the support of a new generation and the new thinking of Arthur Griffith's Sinn Fein*. Through passive resistance and guerrilla warfare, the new nationalists demanded an Irish Republic completely independent of the British Empire, a demand repugnant to Lloyd George's coalition government. The result was the Anglo-Irish war*, 1919-21, in which Michael Collins and the Irish Republican Army faced both the regular and irregular forces of the Crown.

Unable or unwilling to resolve the conflict by force, the British government adopted a number of political measures to end the Anglo-Irish war and to reconcile the aspirations of Irish nationalists with both the needs of the British Empire and the apprehensions of Ulster Unionists. The Government of Ireland Act* of December 1920 partitioned both Ireland and Ulster by establishing two equal Irish parliaments subordinate to Westminster, one for the six counties of Northern Ireland (with a population 66 per cent Protestant), the other for the twenty-six counties of Southern Ireland. The Anglo-Irish Treaty* of December 1921 superseded the 1920 Act in the south, turned Southern Ireland into the Irish Free State with dominion status, and made a half-hearted effort to compel Northern Ireland to accept the sovereignty of Dublin.

These initiatives almost ended in immediate disaster. Northern Ireland was in danger of dissolving amid the anarchy of sectarian conflict in the months following its establishment in May-June 1921, while between June 1922 and May 1923 the twenty-six counties were plunged into a bitter civil war*, as republicans under Eamon De Valera refused to accept the limited status bestowed by the Treaty. However, a degree of stability was achieved in Northern Ireland by August 1922, and the Unionist Party ruled virtually

Easter Rising 1916
Armed nationalist insurrection in Dublin: insurgents numbered less than 2,000- 200 from Citizen Army; rest from "Irish Volunteers" infiltrated by Irish Republican Brotherhood. Insurgents based at General Post Office where Pearse proclaimed Independent Irish Republic and set up Provisional Government. Fighting bitter but rebels heavily outnumbered by British, making ruthless use of artillery. 450 killed during rising, 3,500 arrested, 2,000 deported, 15 leaders executed.

Irish Republican Brotherhood
Fenian Society reorganized 1873 as Irish Republican Brotherhood (IRB): formally linked 1877 with Clan na Gael, American-Irish revolutionary nationalist body; reorganized 1907 by Tom Clarke; from 1910 activity increased, culminating in 1916 Easter Rising.

Sinn Fein
("Ourselves") Formed 1905 by Arthur Griffith to unite competing nationalist bodies. Central tenet was national self-reliance, expressed in policy of electing MPs to abstain from Westminster and to act as de facto parliament. De Valera became leader 1917; won 73 of 105 Irish seats at Westminster 1918; refused to attend; set up first Assembly of Ireland (Dail Eireann) 1919, declaring Free State of Ireland.

Eamonn de Valera with Arthur Griffith in Dawson Street, Dublin, during the Treaty negotiations, 1921.

unchallenged for almost fifty years with only four prime ministers between 1921 and 1968 – two of whom, Viscounts Craigavon and Brookeborough, each held the office for some twenty years. In the south, the traditions of parliamentary and representative government established under the union survived the civil war with the emergence of two main political parties, Fine Gael*, pro-Treaty, and Fianna Fail*. After 1932 the latter, under De Valera, and later Sean Lemass and Jack Lynch, was the predominant party. In power for most of the time, it was occasionally ousted by coalitions of other parties under a Fine Gael taoiseach (prime minister), as with the ministries of John Costello, 1948-51 and 1954-57, and Liam Cosgrave, 1973-77. Thus after 1922 the storm centre of Irish politics moved away from Westminster.

Divided over Anglo-Irish Treaty 1921; moderate elements joined De Valera's Fianna Fail 1926, leaving extremists to act as political wing of republican movement.

Anglo-Irish war 1919-21
Republican forces of IRA led by Michael Collins launched sporadic attacks on British government forces and Royal Irish Constabulary in 1919 which escalated into guerrilla warfare; British responded by violent reprisals through "Black and Tans", reinforcements for RIC who took their name from khaki and black uniforms. Violence culminated in "Bloody Sunday" 21 November 1920 with multiple IRA shootings of Englishmen in Dublin and reprisals from Black and Tans who fired on Gaelic football match. Truce announced

July 1921; negotiations finally led to Anglo-Irish Treaty December 1921.

Government of Ireland Act 1920
Carried into effect partition implicit in political debate since 1914: proposed two parliaments for Ireland, one for six north-eastern counties and one for other 26, with strictly limited powers; Council of Ireland of 20 representatives from each parliament to unite two bodies. Envisaged as temporary solution; single parliament to be introduced with agreement of regional parliaments. Act satisfied neither North nor South.

Anglo-Irish Treaty 1921
Outcome of negotiations between British government and Sinn Fein: Irish Free State became self-governing dominion within

British Empire; MPs to take oath of allegiance to Crown; governor general appointed. Six north-eastern counties opted out of Free State.

Irish civil war 1922-23
Republican die-hards led by De Valera refused to accept Anglo-Irish Treaty 1921 negotiated by Griffith and Collins, since it did not confer full republican status. Summer of 1922 saw open hostilities between De Valera and Irish government: anti-Treaty forces of IRA, known as "Irregulars" used same guerrilla methods as against British and assassinated Collins; Irish government took violent reprisals against rebels, executing 77 and imprisoning 12,000. De Valera called off fight May 1923. Civil war resulted in deep and lasting divisions in Irish society.

Fine Gael
("Tribe of the Gaels") Formed 1933-35 by fusion of Cosgrave's pro-treaty Cumann na nGaedhal, National Centre party led by Dillon and McDermot, and National Guard, Blueshirt movement under General O'Duffy. Stood for united Ireland within Commonwealth, ending of economic war with Britain and establishment of agricultural and industrial corporations.

Fianna Fail
("Warriors of Ireland") Party launched by De Valera 1927, with backing of moderate Sinn Fein supporters who rejected complete opposition to participation in Dail. Second largest Dail party 1927 but refused to take oath of allegiance; in 1928 De Valera agreed to regard oath as mere formality and Fianna Fail entered Dail, still committed to abolition of oath of allegiance: achieved in constitution of 1937. Traditionally more sympathetic to republicanism than Fine Gael.

Nevertheless, three assumptions behind the settlement of 1920-21 proved invalid – the continued place of the south within the British Empire and Commonwealth, the eventual unity of Ireland, and the development of Northern Ireland as a parliamentary democracy on British lines. The Free State proved a very restless dominion, moving inexorably out of the Commonwealth, maintaining its neutrality during the Second World War, refusing to put its ports at the disposal of the Allies, and, finally, declaring itself a republic in 1949.

Partition, regarded by many as only a temporary expedient, became an accepted fact by the 1930s, despite continued nationalist rhetoric about Irish unity. Although they had many problems in common – rural depopulation, inefficient small-scale agriculture, and the need for industrial diversification – the two parts of Ireland went their separate ways. The north remained an integral part of the United Kingdom, determinedly British and Protestant, while the south fostered a particular sense of Irish identity, especially through the promotion of the Gaelic language and the incorporation of Catholic values into the constitution, apparatus and working of the state. The differences became even more marked with the advent after 1945 of the welfare state in the United Kingdom, which for a time gave the north a far higher standard of living than that enjoyed by the south and meant that unity would have imposed an intolerable burden on an already heavily taxed republic.

Finally, although apparently stable, Northern Ireland did not overcome the many obstacles, scarcely recognized by the framers of the 1920 Act, to the development of healthy political life there. These included a narrow and parochial political culture, an ailing economy in the most disadvantaged part of the United Kingdom, and sectarian division, as Protestants and Catholics segregated themselves on this earth and in preparation for the next, not inter-marrying, being educated apart, living in different areas and carrying on separate activities. Unchecked by the sovereign power at Westminster,

Civil Rights movement
Movement seeking "British rights" for Ulster Catholics: demanded political rights (one man, one vote in local government) and welfare rights (such as better housing and fair employment). 1963 Campaign for Social Justice in Northern Ireland; 1967 Northern Ireland Civil Rights Association; followed by local associations in Belfast and Londonderry. Activity peaked 1968 with protest marches, culminating in march in Londonderry and violent exchanges with the police.

Brown Street, off Shankill Road, Belfast, decorated for Orange Day celebrations in 1951.

British intervention 1969
6,000 British troops sent into Northern Ireland in response to escalating sectarian violence. Trouble had broken out in Londonderry on occasion of Apprentice Boys' march, commemorating relief of city from Catholic siege of 1689; spread to Belfast, local authorities unable to contain it. British intervention accompanied by offer of social and economic reform but violence escalated after intervention: 1,391 deaths 1969-75; 20,000 British troops present by 1972.

Social Democratic and Labour party
Founded 1970 by civil rights activists, quickly established itself as voice of moderate Catholic community. Aims included abolition of religious discrimination, public ownership of essential industries, and co-operation between North and South with view to eventual reunification. Participated in 1973-74 power-sharing Executive.

Irish Republican Army
Formed 1919 by reorganization of Irish Volunteers: led by Michael Collins, who waged successful campaign in Anglo-Irish war 1919-21. Split over Treaty 1921: those who rejected it kept title of IRA and pursued civil war; withdrew support from De Valera 1925, set up army council to end partition by force; outlawed 1931. Unsuccessful campaign of violence 1956-62 against "British occupation" of Northern Ireland. Split 1969 into Official and Provisional wings: Provisionals concentrated on driving British out of Northern Ireland, major force since 1972.

Ulster Unionist party
Founded 1886 to organize Ulster opposition to home rule: from 1921-72 it translated Protestant majority in population into unionist majority in Stormont. Only policy was maintenance of union with Britain. Disintegrating by late 1960s over Terence O'Neill's reforms to conciliate Catholics; 1972-73 split over power-sharing; unity regained, but more extreme groupings had emerged.

Democratic Unionist party
Ultra-Loyalist party led by Rev Ian Paisley, pledged to maintain constitution at all costs; advocates closer integration with Westminster. Founded 1971; 1975 formed United Ulster Unionist Council, or Loyalist Coalition, together with official Unionists and Vanguard Unionist party (set up 1973).

Paramilitary groups
46 groups identified 1975, including Ulster Special Constabulary Association and Ulster Defence Association. Semi-legal bodies who use weapons without authority of régime; operations not clear. Some involvement in industrial action: Ulster Workers Council (which organized 1974 general strike) had links with Ulster Defence Association.

Resumption of direct rule 1972
Stormont government suspended 1972, when Unionist administration refused to accept British proposals for transferring responsibility for law and order to Westminster. Britain gave responsibility for government to a secretary of state for Northern Ireland, member of British cabinet. Direct rule failed to stop violence, despite brief truce negotiated by government with IRA 1973.

Sunningdale Agreement 1973
Conference held between representatives of Irish and British governments and new Northern Ireland Executive: agreed to establishment of Council of Ireland to deal with matters concerning both Eire and Ulster; Irish conceded right of Ulster to self-determination; Britain would not oppose unification of Ireland if in North majority consented.

Power-Sharing Assembly and Executive 1973-74
Constitution Act 1973 provided for self-government for Northern Ireland: distinctive feature was "power-sharing", that no Executive could be based on support of only one community. Welcomed by moderates but denounced by traditional Republicans and Unionists. After Assembly elections, government formed by Unionists, SDLP and Alliance party. Executive fell after 4 months due to 14-day general strike organized by ultra-Loyalist Ulster Workers Council. Direct rule resumed.

Northern Ireland developed into a Protestant state for Protestant people, with deliberate discrimination against the Catholic minority in matters of local government, education and law and order. The breakdown of the Catholic ghetto mentality by the early 1960s, as a result of increased education and a measure of economic prosperity and social mobility, posed, through the civil rights movement*, challenges which the Unionist régime was incapable of meeting either by judicious reform or the effective use of force. Increasing violence finally precipitated open British intervention* in August 1969, but the quickened pace of reform polarized opinion still further. The Catholic community found representation and protection in the newly-formed Social Democratic and Labour party* and a revived Irish Republican Army*, while the traditional Unionist party* disintegrated, with the formation of such new parties as Dr Ian Paisley's Democratic Unionist party*, and such para-military forces* as the Ulster Defence Association. Lack of leadership and continued violence, despite the use of internment, led to the suspension of regional government in March 1972.

The resumption of direct rule* from Westminster could have been advantageous. However, some ill-considered security measures and a succession of ill-fated attempts to hand back power to Northern Ireland and recognize "the Irish dimension" (most notably, the Sunningdale Agreement* and the power-sharing Assembly and Executive* in 1974) showed that Britain had learned little from its earlier experiences. At times, too much reliance was placed upon the views of Dublin; there was little appreciation of the complex relationship that existed between para-military groups in Northern Ireland and the communities they claimed to represent and defend; and no clear distinction was made between the separate, though not unrelated, questions of Irish unity and community relations in Northern Ireland. Consequently, "The power to govern did not pass to Westminster with Britain's assumption of responsibility for direct rule of the Province. Instead, it sank almost out of sight" (Richard Rose).

Warfare and International Relations:
Empire, Commonwealth, Community

Peter Lowe

Throughout the twentieth century the conduct of British diplomacy has involved tension between Britain's roles in Europe and in the wider world, the latter being largely determined by the nature of the British Empire-Commonwealth. In 1901 the pride of empire was at its climax in the midst of the South African war, but the war also revealed the resentment of Britain in Europe. The rapid growth of German power and ambitions confronted Britain with a challenge to her vital interests; her colonial territories meant that Britain had to act as a world power, yet she lacked the resources to fulfil her obligations. This was made clear by the 1902 Anglo-Japanese alliance* to resist Russian expansion in East Asia, and became still more obvious with the Anglo-German naval race* and the gradual withdrawal of the Royal Navy from far eastern waters. Irate voices were raised in the British dominions bordering the Pacific – Canada, Australia, and New Zealand – questioning British ability to defend the Empire; finally, in 1942, the question was resoundingly answered by Japan. British leaders were always influenced by emotional ties in contemplating the Empire, which resulted in an inability to face issues and to explain realities to the dominions. British vacillation towards western Europe after 1945 can be similarly explained.

War had immense repercussions upon Britain's role in the twentieth century. The South African war revealed the incompetence of the British army, waging a disappointing campaign against a tenacious foe. The conflict ended in victory, but it dealt a considerable blow to the prestige of British forces, and questioned their conduct towards civilians. Essential continuity existed in

Anglo-Japanese alliance 1902
Defensive treaty concluded between Great Britain and Japan, marking end of British isolationism. Provided for independence of China and Korea, recognition of Japan's special interest in Korea. If either party entered war with third party, its ally was to maintain neutrality but to participate if other powers entered conflict. Treaty renewed 1905 and 1911, alliance finally terminated 1923.

Anglo-German naval race
Naval rivalry dominated Anglo-German relations before 1914: competition began with German Naval Laws of 1898 and 1900, aimed at expanding German navy. British responses were Fisher reforms 1904 and launching of Dreadnought 1905, provoking increased German construction of battleships. Race won by Britain: by 1914 Britain had 20 dreadnoughts to Germany's 13, 9 battlecruisers to Germany's 6.

British battleships passing down the Solent on their way to Spithead for the naval review of 1914.

The British sector of the Western Front 1914-18

Trench Warfare 1914-18

━━━━━ British sector (BEF)

▪ ▪ ▪ ▪ ▪ Belgian and French sectors

─·─·─ Frontiers

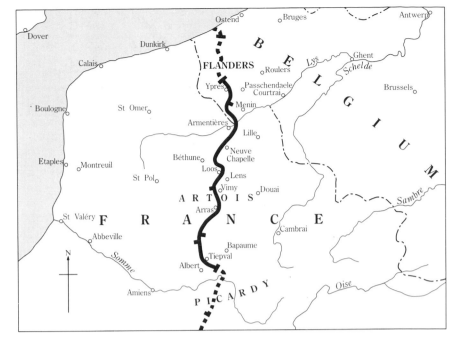

Anglo-French entente 1904
Essentially settlement of colonial differences. France recognized British occupation of Egypt, receiving guarantees over Egyptian debt; Britain recognized French interests in Morocco, pledging diplomatic support; Britain provided free navigation of Suez Canal as agreed 1888.

British soldiers on the Fampoux Road, April 1917, during the Arras offensive on the western front.

British foreign policy from 1901 to 1914; Lansdowne and Grey shared the same objective; to maintain a balance of power in Europe. The Anglo-French entente* of 1904 originally had limited aims; its significance developed when Campbell-Bannerman and Grey authorized military discussions. The British defence chiefs did not anticipate the type of war that occurred in 1914-18: the army believed in a small professional force rather than an enormous expeditionary army, and the navy envisaged a decisive battle between huge capital ships. It was generally held that war would be brief and would not necessitate mass mobilization. Kitchener was one of the few to forecast a lengthy conflict and even he underestimated the duration.

Britain entered war in 1914 for several reasons, especially commitments to France and German aggression against Belgium. There was a large measure of unity in the British Isles, including rather surprisingly Ireland, over participation in the war. A vast army was created, mostly to serve on the battlefields of the western front*, and until 1916 this was recruited without compulsion. The fighting on the western front was grotesque, comprising futile and

Western front 1916-17
Very heavy losses sustained on western front. Assault on Verdun 21 Feb-11 July resulted in loss of 350,000 Frenchmen and as many Germans. In Battle of Somme 1 July-18 November, British advance gained allies 125 square miles of no strategic importance at cost of 400,000 British lives, almost 200,000 French and 400,000-500,000 Germans. In Third Battle of Ypres (Passchendaele) 31 July-10 November 1917, advance of 5 miles made at cost of 400,000 British lives and demoralization of army.

Battle of Jutland 1916
Beatty, commanding British battle cruisers, encountered German counterpart off Norwegian coast; running engagement drew British under guns of German High Seas Fleet, which Beatty managed to draw on to British Grand Fleet under Jellicoe; two brief engagements took place before German fleet withdrew. British losses greater in terms of tonnage, but German fleet had turned tail and remained in port for the rest of war.

bloody attempts at breakthrough; the sickening casualties in the battles of the Somme and Passchendaele starkly underlined the cost of the strategies pursued. At sea there was only one great encounter between the British and German fleets, at Jutland* in 1916. The battle proved indecisive, but the German naval chiefs were frightened by its implications and avoided a confrontation for the rest of the war. But German submarines were successfully deployed and much merchant shipping was lost; Britain was faced with the danger of being compelled to surrender through shortages of food and vital raw materials early in 1917. Convoys were eventually adopted, and these, together with the entry of the United States into the war in 1917, defeated the submarine menace. Ultimately the war was won because of the collapse of Austria-Hungary and the disintegration of German morale in 1918.

The First World War was a tremendous strain on Britain's human, economic, and psychological resources, and her decline was much accentuated. Losses in the fighting resulted in a failure of confidence that characterized British opinion in the interwar years. After the war the British Empire had expanded by mandates over former German and Turkish possessions in Africa, the Pacific, and the Middle East, but the most important effect of the war on the Empire was to accelerate the development of nationalism and autonomy in the dominions. In 1914 the decision to go to war had committed the dominions, but the contribution of dominion forces to the fighting inevitably led to demands for a more effective voice in policy. It was obvious in 1918 that the dominions would follow more independent policies: Canada, South Africa and the Irish Free State led this process; Australia, too, showed a certain truculence at times. New Zealand was largely immune to this trend. India had responded loyally between 1914 and 1918; demands for self-government and ultimately independence were growing, and were to be shrewdly exploited by Gandhi.

In 1919 Britain favoured a punitive peace settlement with Germany, but not one that would go to extremes and provoke German demands for revenge. The Versailles Treaty* was arrived at too hastily and was characterized by malevolence; it did not however necessitate or excuse the subsequent appeasement policies. The League of Nations* was fully supported by Britain; even experienced diplomats felt that, after the horrors of the Great War, nations would appreciate the perils of selfishness and show a greater willingness to compromise. The first major test for the machinery of the League was the Manchurian crisis* of 1931-33. The British attitude was to support use of the conciliatory mechanisms of the League but to oppose sanctions against Japan, but Japan refused to compromise and left the League. The second major crisis arose from Italian aggression against Ethiopia* in 1935. The Baldwin government stated its support for collective adherence to the covenant of the League, but pursued a vacillating policy aimed at buying off Italy if possible: half-hearted economic sanctions were applied against Italy and then withdrawn. The authority of the League had received a savage blow from which it could not recover.

British defences were allowed to decline to wholly inadequate levels in the 1920s, when the "ten year rule" assumed that Britain was unlikely to be involved in a war within the next decade. Imperial defence policy was complicated by the decision to end the Anglo-Japanese alliance in 1921: Britain now had to reckon with the possibility of Japanese antagonism rather than co-operation. It was decided to construct a naval base at Singapore, for a fleet to

Imperial conferences
The conferences were gatherings of self-governing dominions to consider affairs of common interest, especially trade. At 1926 Imperial Conference, Balfour formulated doctrine of British Commonwealth of Nations, codified in Statute of Westminster 1931: defined Britain and dominions as "autonomous communities within the British Empire, equal in status, in no way subordinate one to another in any aspect of their domestic or external affairs, though united by a common allegiance to the Crown and freely associated as members of the British Commonwealth of Nations".

Treaty of Versailles 1919
One of treaties ending First World War drawn up at Paris Conference: 27 victorious powers represented; Germany was excluded. Terms determined by Britain, France, USA and Italy: Wilson for USA and Lloyd George for Britain attempted to moderate French desire for revenge but success only partial. Article 231 declared sole German responsibility for causing war; heavy reparations exacted from Germany for war damage. Chief aim was to ensure Germany could not again become military power: German army limited to 100,000; Germany lost territory; Saar placed under international administration for 15 years; and allies were to occupy Rhineland for 15 years with demilitarized zone on right bank of Rhine. German colonies to become mandates under League of Nations.

League of Nations
Established 1920 as part of post-war attempt to establish collective security by new international bodies: 58 founder members, including self-governing dominions of British Empire, but hampered by refusal of USA to join. Members were to give each other mutual protection; League was to devote itself to disarmament, labour problems and health. Functions transferred to United Nations 1946.

Manchurian crisis 1931-33
Japan invaded Manchuria 1931, and set up puppet state of Manchukuo under Japanese control. League of Nations condemned Japan as aggressor 1933 and refused to recognise Manchukuo, but no attempt to impose sanctions. By 1934 Britain virtually acquiesced in Japanese control of Manchuria.

Italian invasion of Ethiopia 1935
Italy invaded Ethiopia 1935, concluding conflict between Italian and Ethiopian troops in disputed territory between Italian Somaliland and Ethiopia. League of

Nations condemned Italy as aggressor and voted for economic sanctions. Britain and France tried to buy off Mussolini by Hoare-Laval pact, offering Italy territorial concessions if Haile Selassie could retain part of his Ethiopian Empire: public outcry in Britain, and plan withdrawn. League discussed oil sanctions against Italy 1936 but no agreement reached; Italy proclaimed annexation of Ethiopia.

Czechoslovak crisis 1938
First German-Czechoslovak crisis March-May 1938: after annexation of Austria, Hitler turned attention to Sudetenland (included in new state of Czechoslovakia 1919, containing large German population); agitation for autonomy by Sudeten German movement resulted in disorder, crisis averted by firm stand by Britain and France. Second crisis exploded September 1938, with Hitler's Nuremberg speech calling for self-determination for Sudeten Germans, provoking widespread disorder in Czechoslovakia. Chamberlain visited Hitler at Berchtesgaden (where he conceded principle that Sudetenland be transferred to Germany) and at Godesberg (where he rejected Hitler's detailed proposals). Then 24-29 September acute crisis, culminating in Chamberlain's final visit to Hitler in Munich.

Munich Agreement 1938
Culmination of Chamberlain's policy of appeasing Hitler. Czechoslovaks were unrepresented, but pact signed by Britain, France, Germany and Italy transferred 10,000 square miles of Czech territory in Sudetenland and 3,500,000 people to Germany, and other areas to Poland and Hungary. Truncated federal republic of Czecho-Slovakia created. Chamberlain and Hitler signed separate declaration that their countries would not go to war with each other. On return to London, Chamberlain referred to Agreement as "peace with honour ... peace for our time". Six months later, Germany invaded Czecho-Slovakia.

Anglo-Polish Agreement 1939
Ended policy of appeasement. Poland vulnerable after German invasion of Czecho-Slovakia; Chamberlain responded with assurance that Britain would guarantee Polish independence, followed by introduction of measure of conscription. Intensified German pressure on Danzig and Polish Corridor drew Britain into closer alliance, resulting in Pact of Mutual Assistance between Britain and Poland. Made inevitable Britain's declaration of war on Germany 3 September, after German invasion of Poland.

be dispatched from home waters or the Mediterranean in the event of trouble in the Far East, but the base was not opened until 1938. Australia and New Zealand were alarmed at the Japanese threat and British ministers promised that help would be forthcoming; but the undertakings were unrealistic and it was doubtful whether developments in Europe would permit a fleet to be sent. For Hitler's achievement of power in Germany in 1933 increased the danger of conflict. Some sympathy for Germany existed in Britain from reactions against the Versailles treaty and the belief that Hitler had some justified grievances. Neville Chamberlain held that every effort must be made to avoid war: he visited Hitler on three occasions in the autumn of 1938 to defuse the Czechoslovak crisis*; the culmination was the Munich agreement*. After Munich there was a gradual reaction against further acts of appeasement. In March 1939 Chamberlain denounced the German entry into Prague and shortly afterwards the Anglo-Polish agreement* was signed. Chamberlain still hoped war could be averted, but faced pressure from his own backbenchers to take a more resolute line. Following the German attack on Poland, Britain declared war on 3 September supported by the dominions.

After the brief interlude of the "phoney war"*, Hitler implemented a brilliant series of offensives in western Europe leading to the fall of France. Churchill became prime minister and brought a new spirit of defiance to the war leadership. The situation was desperate, with invasion looming, but this

"Phoney war" 1939-40
Derisive term coined by Americans and adopted by British to describe period from September 1939 to April 1940, characterized by Allied and German inactivity on western front. Germans consolidated defeat of Poland while Allies relied on economic blockade and defensive fortification – since pre-war strategy had been disrupted by failure of Italy to declare war. Ended by German invasion of Norway April 1940.

Neville Chamberlain leaving the Dreesen Hotel at Godesberg with Hitler on 26 September 1938. Daladier is just behind them.

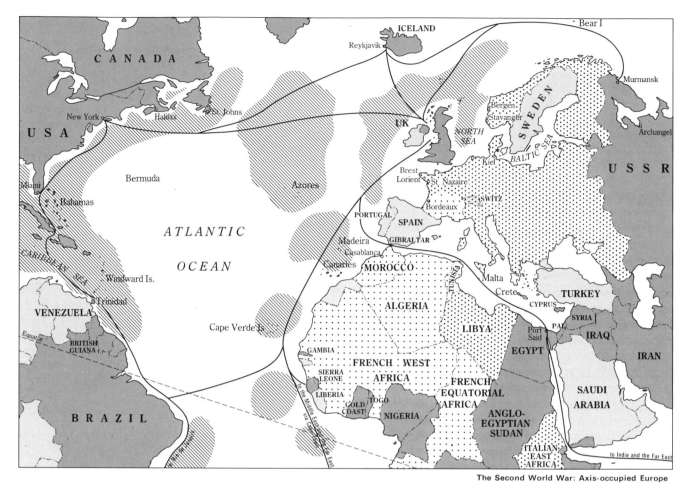

The Second World War: Axis-occupied Europe
and the Battle of the Atlantic 1939-42

▦ Maximum extent of Axis occupation

⋯ Axis-dominated areas

▓ British and allied areas

☐ Neutral zones

— Convoy routes

▨ U-boat operations 1939-42

threat was removed by victory in the "Battle of Britain"*. The United States extended greater support in 1940-1 but there was no likelihood of defeating Germany without direct American participation. This was accomplished following the Japanese attack on Pearl Harbor* in December 1941, for Hitler foolishly declared war on the United States. While Japan had unwittingly brought the Americans into the European war, the price paid in the Far East and Pacific was a heavy one. The Japanese inflicted humiliating defeats on the British in Hong Kong, Malaya, and Burma, and advanced to New Guinea, thus threatening Australia. On 15 February 1942 a large British and dominion army surrendered at Singapore*, the greatest defeat suffered by the Empire since the loss of the American colonies. Australia now looked to the United States for protection; this new relationship was symbolized by General MacArthur establishing his headquarters in Australia. Britain's role in the Far East and Pacific was secondary to that of the United States between 1942 and 1945. The chief British contribution was in Burma, where the final Japanese onslaught was held at the battles of Imphal-Kohima* and Slim's forces subsequently defeated the Japanese in 1945. The fortunes of British forces in North Africa fluctuated in 1941-42, but, after the preparatory work of Auchinleck, Montgomery's victory at Alamein* marked the decisive watershed in the defeat of Rommel's forces. In November 1942 Anglo-American troops landed in French North Africa and this constituted the beginning of the Mediterranean strategy, which produced the swift elimination of Italy from

Battle of Britain 1940

10 July-12 October 1940 air engagement in which RAF Fighter Command under Dowding managed to forestall German invasion of Britain. First stage of invasion plan was to eliminate British air superiority and bombard British cities: Germans began with attacks on merchant shipping; switched to blasting RAF airfields with up to 1,000 planes. Strategy almost succeeded, but on 7 September assault switched to London, to destroy civilian morale ("The Blitz"). Last great German effort 15 September; invasion postponed 17 September and abandoned for winter 12 October. 1,733 German planes lost, 915 British.

Pearl Harbor 1941
Japanese sea and air forces launched surprise attack on United States Pacific Fleet at Pearl Harbor, Hawaii. Inflicted devastating damage, neutralizing fleet for at least a year: 5 battleships and 3 cruisers sunk; 177 aircraft destroyed; 3,000 killed. United States immediately declared war on Japan.

Surrender of Singapore 1942
Surrender of Singapore to Japanese inflicted worst blow of war on British imperial prestige. Singapore was naval base, never really prepared for attack from land; vulnerable when Malayan peninsula captured by Japanese. Held out for week of assault and siege, but had to surrender unconditionally when water supply captured: 70,000-man garrison surrendered.

Battles of Imphal-Kohima 1944
British forces under General Slim managed to beat off Japanese advance into India by relieving towns of Imphal and Kohima in Assam after protracted sieges. There followed collapse of Japanese 15th army, forced back by British with loss of 65,000 men.

Alamein 1942
Decisive battle of North Africa campaign 23 October-4 November 1942: victory for Montgomery and British Eighth Army, initiating decline of Axis forces in North Africa. Eighth Army, reinforced to 200,000 men, attacked Rommel's 96,000 strong forces; 12 days of heavy fighting followed, Eighth Army finally broke through with strong backing from RAF. Rommel retreated for 1,500 miles with Eighth Army in pursuit, to total Axis defeat in Tunisia. Rommel's army lost 20,000 killed and 30,000 prisoners; British lost 10,000 men.

Aerial bombing
In first phase September 1940 ("The Blitz"), Germans directed heavy attack on London: civilian morale not destroyed, but heavy losses; 300-600 a day killed and between 1,000 and 3,000 injured. October 1940-April 1941 attacks spread over country from Plymouth to Glasgow with destructive assault on Coventry 10 November. Culminated in shattering assault on London 10 May. Total losses were 43,000 dead and 51,000 injured. British reprisals under Harris violent and indiscriminate e.g. "Thousand Bomber Raid" on Cologne May 1942; German response was "Baedeker" raids on historic English cities. With American support, British devastated the Ruhr, Hamburg and Berlin 1943.

the war. German submarines in the Atlantic caused heavy losses of merchant shipping in 1941-43; however, the use of convoys and the increasing American naval contribution eventually conquered the U-boat menace. Aerial bombing of Britain* resulted in the loss of many lives and much damage; civilian morale, while not always as high as was claimed, nevertheless proved tenacious. Churchill authorized intensive bombing of Germany, but the air offensives did not achieve the rapid results originally promised. The allied landings in northern France took place in June 1944 and, combined with the Russian successes on the eastern front, inexorably forced back the German armies. Germany surrendered in May 1945; the Second World War terminated with the submission of Japan, after atomic bombs* had been dropped on Hiroshima and Nagasaki in August 1945.

Britain's relationship with the United States was basic to her foreign policy throughout the post-1945 period, but diminishingly so in the later 1960s and 1970s. British leaders had been sceptical of the American commitment to Europe, but these doubts were removed by the Truman doctrine* and Marshall aid*. The principal architect of British postwar policy was Ernest Bevin: he laid down the aims of rebuilding Europe, securing better political and economic understanding in western Europe, achieving a new framework for defence policy, and resisting the further expansion of the Soviet Union.

Atomic bomb
Dropping of atomic bombs on Hiroshima and Nagasaki August 1945 was culmination of research during war years to produce nuclear weapon. President Truman's decision to drop bomb determined by need to secure Japanese surrender at least cost to American lives. Destruction was on massive scale: at Hiroshima 78,000 killed and 70,000 injured; at Nagasaki 40,000 killed. Japanese surrendered a week later.

Truman doctrine 1947
Doctrine outlined by President Truman: United States to support "free peoples who are resisting attempted subjugation by armed minorities and outside pressure"; called for aid to Greece and Turkey, dispatch of military and civil officials as advisers. Prompted by Soviet pressure on Turkey 1946 and end of British assistance to Greece 1947. Doctrine reflected American hostility to Communism and accelerated division of Europe into Eastern and Western blocs through use of language of Cold War.

Marshall aid 1948-51
Informal name for European Recovery Programme 1948-51, financed by United States. Plan proposed 1947 by Secretary of State George Marshall: Paris Conference 1947 attended by 16 European countries (not including Soviet Union), drew up four-year programme. Implemented by Organization for European Economic Recovery set up 1948; involved $12 million

in aid. Encouraged closer integration of European economies, but significant step towards division of Europe into East/West camps.

Commandos of No 1 Special Services Brigade, led by Brigadier Lord Lovat, landing at La Brèche on the Queen Red sector of Sword Beach 6 June 1944.

American commitment to the defence of western Europe was achieved in the formation of the Nato alliance* in 1949, which has proved the most enduring aspect of postwar British foreign policy. Britain was committed to developing her own nuclear deterrent*, which was given priority by Attlee. Relations with the United States were strained at times (as over Communist China* in 1949-50 and the Korean war* in 1950-51), but the only profound problem was created by the Suez crisis* in 1956 when President Eisenhower intervened to compel a change in British policy. Gradually, as British power declined, so Britain became far less important to the United States.

The Second World War accelerated the process whereby the British Empire became the Commonwealth*. The Japanese occupations in the Far East had discredited the colonial empires and made it difficult for the old colonial relationship to be resurrected. A potent impetus had been given to nationalist movements, which forced a change of policy when the colonial powers returned. The most dramatic single change was seen in the Indian sub-continent, where India and Pakistan became independent* in 1947. While the final stages of independence in India came too rapidly, the decision to leave was unavoidable. Burma became independent in 1948 and, after the defeat of communist insurgency, so did Malaya* in 1957. It was widely felt that decolonization in Africa would take appreciably longer, but once again change was swift and African colonies gained their independence between 1957 and 1964, starting with Ghana. The Macmillan government quickened the speed, appreciating both its inevitability and the undesirability of British forces becoming involved in confrontations with nationalist movements, as they had done in Kenya*. Rhodesia presented problems owing the recalcitrance of a white settler régime led by Ian Smith, but this was eventually resolved and Rhodesia* became Zimbabwe. In the older dominions the repercussions of the Second World War and the rapid expansion of the Commonwealth after 1947 diluted the old imperial relationship. Canada moved closer to the United States and became more preoccupied with domestic issues. Australia and New Zealand looked more to the United States for defence, as the Anzus pact* (1951) was to emphasize. South Africa* moved away from Britain after the

United Nations
Founded at San Francisco Conference 1945, attended by 51 nations, implementing 1944 decision by USA, British Commonwealth and Soviet Union to establish international body to replace League of Nations. UN given four organs: general assembly of all members as policy-making body; international court of justice; security council to settle military and political problems; economic and social council. Administration directed by secretary-general.

North Atlantic Treaty Organization
North Atlantic Treaty signed 1949: provided for mutual assistance against aggression in North Atlantic, collaboration in military training, arms production and strategic planning; but emphasized settlement of disputes by co-operation. Establishment encouraged by mounting suspicion of Soviet Union in view of Czech

coup and Berlin blockade. Signatories were Belgium, Britain, Canada, Denmark, France, Iceland, Italy, Luxembourg, Netherlands, Norway, Portugal and USA; Greece and Turkey joined 1952; West Germany 1954.

Independent nuclear deterrent
Decision that Britain should have own atomic bomb taken secretly by Attlee 1946 and hidden from cabinet: motivated by view that atomic bomb was symbol of international status. British atomic bomb first tested 1952; hydrogen bomb 1957. By early 1960s British nuclear technology had become outmoded: in Nassau Agreement 1962 America agreed to sell Britain Polaris missiles as part of NATO multilateral nuclear force, and Britain agreed not to use nuclear weapons without American consent, so weakening independent nature of British deterrent.

British recognition of Communist China 1949-50
Communists defeated nationalist régime and set up Chinese People's Republic 1949. Britain gave de jure recognition to People's Republic, but USA continued to regard nationalists under Chiang Kai-shek as legitimate government. Pressure from USA resulted in Britain taking compromise position; recognized both Communists and nationalist régime in Taiwan.

Korean war 1950-53
Communist North Korea attacked pro-Western Republic of South Korea 1950. On United States initiative, "United Nations" forces under MacArthur were despatched; Britain also provided substantial naval aid. But Britain unhappy about MacArthur's policy of extending operations to frontier with China and war against Chinese: doubts shared by Truman; MacArthur recalled 1951. Britain disturbed by American resolution at United Nations 1951 condemning China for aggression but reluctantly supported it. Armistice ending war signed 1953; Korea de facto divided along 38th parallel into North and South Korea.

Suez crisis 1956
President Nasser of Egypt nationalized Suez Canal Company in order to finance construction of Aswan Dam; Eden denied Nasser's right to nationalize. Together with French government, who thought Nasser was main supporter of Algerian rebels, Eden planned invasion of Egypt and occupation of Canal, to coincide with Israeli attack on Egypt. Israel attacked; Anglo-French intervention followed. America disapproved of British action, which was condemned by United Nations; Labour party objected strenuously. Britain forced to withdraw. Affair was embarrassing blunder for British government, causing loss of diplomatic prestige; resulted in resignation of Eden in 1957.

Commonwealth of Nations
1931 Statute of Westminster established British Commonwealth as association of equal and autonomous partners. In 1949 Commonwealth heads of state decided that republics might remain within Commonwealth provided they acknowledged British sovereign as its head. Since 1957 almost all colonies have become independent and most remained members. Commonwealth Secretariat established 1965 to promote relations between members.

Indian independence 1947
India granted independence after long

campaign by Indian National Congress and Gandhi. India Act 1935 gave large measure of self-government; by end of war British determined to leave India. Mountbatten sent as Viceroy February 1947; government announced intention to leave. Impossible to draw up plan satisfying both Moslem League led by Jinnah and mainly-Hindu Indian Congress Party under Nehru: solution was partition of continent into India and Pakistan. Partition followed by terrible violence, especially in Punjab region: 200,000 deaths; 2 million refugees exchanged. Both countries remained on good terms with Britain.

Malayan independence 1957
Malayan Federation formed 1948, but Communist guerrilla activity began and British, Australian and New Zealand troops sent in; waged successful campaign of counter-insurgency, enlisting Malayan support against Chinese rebels. Independence achieved 1957.

Aden
Colony housing military base of strategic importance to Britain. Britain suspended constitution 1965 because of failure of local authorities to deal with terrorism of National Liberation Front. United Nations called on Britain to give up its military base; all troops withdrawn 1967, Aden independent as People's Republic of South Yemen.

Cyprus
From 1930 Enosis movement for union with Greece gathering strength among Greek Cypriots. Archbishop Makarios became leader 1950 and exerted pressure for union with Greece. Right-wing extremists EOKA launched guerrilla war; Makarios did not denounce it, deported. Britain declared state of emergency 1955. Britain wanted to withdraw, happy to see Cyprus independent 1959: constitution gave Cyprus Greek Cypriot president, Turkish Cypriot vice-president, and set up legislature 70% Greek, 30% Turkish. Britain retained sovereign bases.

Kenya
By 1950s British policy in Kenya running into problems as white settlers refused to concede representation to black majority. Kenyan African Union (founded 1944) gaining support; situation became violent when KAU failed to secure redress of grievances. Mau-Mau revolt 1952-56, perpetrating acts of savage violence, killing 95 Europeans and 13,000 blacks. Led by Jomo Kenyatta, Mau-Mau movement a potent mixture of Kikuyu tribalism and anti-colonialism: put down by British troops. Kenyatta imprisoned 1953-61 but released to become first prime minister of independent Kenya established 1963.

Rhodesia/Zimbabwe
Premier Smith issued Unilateral Declaration of Independence 1965 after Britain refused to grant independence without introduction of black majority rule. Britain responded by ineffective economic sanctions; inconclusive negotiations with Smith. Black guerrilla warfare in Rhodesia forced Smith to negotiate; resulted in setting up of transitional government 1979 under Bishop Muzorewa. Failed to gain support of Nationalist groups who had conducted guerrilla war. All-party talks were held in London 1979-80; elections in Rhodesia 1980; Zimbabwe emerged as independent state.

Anzus pact 1951
Security treaty drawn up between United States, Australia and New Zealand for mutual assistance in Pacific. Pacific Council established 1952 to guard against Communism and maintain peace.

South Africa
Nationalist-Afrikaner bloc won 1948 general election; introduced programme of apartheid (racial segregation) 1949. 1960 referendum approved republican form of government; severed ties with Commonwealth 1961, when it became apparent that, due to apartheid, members unwilling for South Africa to remain.

The first British thermonuclear test, carried out over the South Pacific in June 1957.

Edward Heath signing Britain's agreement to join the EEC. Sir Alec Douglas-Home, foreign secretary, is on his right, with Geoffrey Rippon, chief negotiator for Britain's entry, to his left.

Nationalist electoral victory in 1948 and left the Commonwealth in 1961. The Commonwealth still possessed significance in the 1970s in the sense of certain limited cultural and political attitudes, but it was no longer a homogeneous body with common political and strategic interests. It took time for the consequences to be grasped in London. There was truth in Dean Acheson's remark that Britain had lost an empire and was in search of a role.

It might have seemed obvious in retrospect that this role should have been found in western Europe. The Attlee government was deeply involved in rebuilding Europe, but it opposed a new political community and had more urgent tasks in cementing the Anglo-American relationship and the Commonwealth. British attitudes towards the EEC* after 1957 were hesitant, erratic and timid. It was gradually realized that the Commonwealth had less meaning, that the United States was less close and that Britain's economic problems were intensifying. Membership of the European Community would hopefully resolve some of these problems. The first British initiative failed, but Edward Heath was later successful and Britain formally joined the Community in January 1973. The Conservative party shed most of its old attachment to imperial sentiment and advocated a European policy. The Labour party was deeply divided but accepted the convincing vote to remain in the Community at a referendum* in 1975. The Community was not loved, but accepted for lack of an apparent alternative.

Thus Britain's ambiguous relationship with Europe throughout the twentieth century was resolved on a note of ambiguity. Britain had possessed a vast empire, but from 1901 she struggled to reconcile the defence of such disparate territories with the resources available for the task. Despite reservations about Europe, Britain had no choice but to participate in both world wars, profound as the cost was. The drain on British resources accentuated the disintegration of Empire and the birth of Commonwealth. The arrival of the latter implied, however, the beginning of the end of Britain's old global responsibility. One is surprised, not that this was the eventual outcome, but that Britain attempted for so long to maintain such a role.

European Economic Community.
Established by 1957 Treaty of Rome which set up European Customs Union and Common Agricultural Policy. EEC to be means of promoting harmonious economic development as first step towards political unification. Founder members were France, West Germany, Italy, Netherlands, Belgium and Luxembourg. Britain applied for membership 1961, 1967, but France vetoed it. Heath resumed negotiations 1972 and Britain joined January 1973 together with Denmark and Ireland.

Referendum 1975
Labour manifesto 1974 had committed government to holding a referendum on British membership of EEC on terms it had renegotiated. Labour government recommended "Yes" vote, but cabinet split and Labour party opposed to membership. Contest cut across party lines, with some right-wing Conservatives and socialists both hostile to EEC. In referendum, 67% of votes cast in favour of continued membership.

The Economy:
adjustment, affluence, decline

Barry Supple

Britain's economic experience in the twentieth century has been largely characterized by frequent contrasts and occasional paradoxes – the most striking example of which has been the combination of rapid economic growth and a pervasive sense of failure and decline. The positive achievements have been considerable and are best indicated by the economist's conventional statistical measurements: the rate of growth of the output of goods and services and advances in productivity. Even the interwar period – which is normally considered to have been a time of severe depression and poverty – was at least as buoyant as the late nineteenth century, while the 1950s and 1960s witnessed historically unprecedented advances in levels of productivity and consumption.

Admittedly, the years immediately before 1914 were, in economic terms, inauspicious; and Britain's role as a principal participant in both world wars naturally exacted a toll in terms of normal economic development at the time. But the long-run trends are plain and fairly impressive. Between the beginning of the century and the mid-1970s, the population rose by almost 50 per cent (from 37 to just over 54 million); the annual output of goods by almost 250 per cent; and personal consumption by about 100 per cent. Meanwhile, leisure had also grown: the average working week fell from 56 to barely 41 hours, average annual holidays increased from 1.4 to 4.7 weeks. These were very solid achievements. Even in the two great wars – periods of full employment, the universal harnessing of productive effort, and a more determined effort to ensure equity in living standards – there was some improvement in the lot of many of the poorer groups in society. Between the wars, and especially since the 1940s, poverty has been decisively outweighed (at least in terms of aggregate statistics) by prosperity.

Why, then, should the attitude towards Britain's economic history have been one of disappointment and unease? The answer lies in the fact that aggregate statistics of output and growth in one country, while indispensable for some purposes, conceal two other vital aspects of economic performance: first, the relative achievement of the economy when set against the achievements of other nations or the material ambitions of its members; second, the underlying pressures on economic and social structures and attitudes which are but crudely summarized by figures of total production and average growth.

In comparative terms, Britain's twentieth-century economic performance has been worse than that of other leading industrial countries. In 1901, for example, the average level of output of its labour force was exceeded only by the immensely wealthy United States. But by the mid-1970s, after a generation or more of relatively slower growth, it had fallen behind all the leading industrial nations of western Europe as well as Japan. The psychological effects of what amounted to a dramatic loss of economic pre-eminence were no

	1870	1890	1913	1938	1950	1973	1979
France	60	55	54	64	44	76	86
Germany	61	58	57	56	33	71	84
Italy	63	44	43	49	32	66	70
Japan	24	(23)	22	33	14	46	53
Sweden	44	42	50	59	55	79	81
UK	114	110	81	70	56	64	66
US	100	100	100	100	100	100	100
Average*	61	54	51	55	39	67	73

Comparative Levels of Productivity 1870-1979
US gross domestic product per man-hour = 100
*Arithmetic average (excluding USA)

	GDP	GDP per man-year of labour
Peacetime phases		
1856-1873	2.4%	1.2%
1873-1913	2.0	0.9
1924-1937	2.2	1.0
1951-1973	2.8	2.4
Wartime phases		
1913-1924	−0.1	0.3
1937-1951	1.8	1.0
Long run		
1856-1973	2.0	1.2

Annual Average Growth Rates: gross domestic product (GDP) in Great Britain and Northern Ireland

doubt traumatic; but the material implications were no less serious: in spite of rapid development, the British economy was clearly less capable than many (perhaps most) other leading industrial societies of taking full advantage of modern knowledge, technology and skills. As a result the fall in Britain's share of world manufacturing and trade, although in part inevitable (the supreme dominance of the early nineteenth century could not be retained for ever), was rapid and severe, destroying its earlier pretensions to international economic leadership. Whatever the merits of joining the Common Market, the fact, and the context, reflected an essentially subordinate, dependent and even parochial position compared to 1872 or even 1912. At the same time, of course, this comparative under-achievement was a handicap in the pursuit of military, political and social goals. Impressive increases in national income undoubtedly took place. But they were insufficient to sustain Britain's inherited pretensions in international politics or its burgeoning aspirations to combine enlarged social services and enhanced private affluence. Economic growth was disappointing because it was inconsistent with the nation's perception of its role and needs.

The second set of reasons for a more subtle and variegated reaction to economic development than would be suggested by a simple observation of the statistics of growth, derive from the structural changes which accompanied that growth. The logic of twentieth-century economic development demanded adjustments (of institutions and attitudes) which had their considerable costs as well as their larger benefits.

Although the economy showed some signs of competitive weakness and retardation in the decade before the First World War, nineteenth-century elements were continuing to serve it well. The great industries of the Industrial Revolution – textiles and clothing, iron and steel, coal and engineering – still dominated manufacturing and exports. The service sectors (banking,

UK share in world exports of manufactures		Volume of UK exports
Date	(%)	(1958 = 100)
1899	34.0	33
1913	30.9	91
1929	22.9	74
1937	21.3	59
1950	25.3	91
1970	10.8	170
1975	9.3	221

Levels of UK exports 1899-1975

Gold standard

System of valuing paper currencies at fixed amounts of gold, thus giving fixed exchange rates between currencies. Britain was on gold standard from 1819 to 1914. In 1925 Churchill announced return to gold at pre-war parity of $4.86 to £; but now agreed that £ was over-valued. Effect was to cheapen imports and make British exports more expensive to foreign consumers, which impeded British production, increased unemployment and worsened balance of payments. Economic crisis resulted in Britain abandoning gold standard September 1931; sterling dropped to $3.40 by end of year. Favourable impact on balance of payments; helped to begin recovery from depression.

Above: *coal mining in 1926. An explosive charge is rammed into the coal face as a preliminary to blasting.*

Right: *a modern coal-cutting "shearer" in action at the Daw Mill colliery, Coventry. Water sprays suppress the dust.*

Above: *Sainsbury's supermarket at Coldham's Lane, Cambridge, 1975.*

Left: *opening day at Sainsbury's Guildford shop, 1906.*

Above: *chassis assembly line for the Austin 12 × Six at Longbridge in about 1931.*

Above right: *fourteen robots carrying out welding on the Metro line at Longbridge.*

finance, insurance, trading, transport), whose rapid growth was symptomatic of Britain's maturity as a producing and consuming nation, also generated a huge income from the world economy which still radiated from London; and the vast overseas investments (equivalent to about one-third of the nation's capital and generating some 8 per cent of the annual income in the years before 1914) were a further indication of international pre-eminence. The war of 1914-18, by disrupting the international economic order, hastened the rise of competition, especially in the staple industries, disturbed the bases of Britain's command of the world's financial and trading relationships, and eroded its overseas capital (with sales equivalent to 15 per cent of *all* capital).

These disturbances proved long-lasting, and Britain's generally weaker international position was aggravated by extensive stagnation in those industries and regions (Clydeside, the north-east, Lancashire, south Wales) on which so much of the nineteenth-century industrialization had been based. This, together with the advent of international cyclical fluctuations, resulted in the mass unemployment* and embittering regional distress which continue to dominate popular memories of the 1920s and 1930s. Yet there were other, and more hopeful, developments at work in this period: investment, technical innovation and reorganization which improved productivity; above all the rapid accommodation of skills, capital and labour supplies to the industries and services (chemicals, electrical equipment and supply, motor vehicles, durable consumer goods, food and drink processing, housing, leisure services, distribution) on which the twentieth-century consumer society has been so largely based. These positive aspects of interwar history (together with the low world prices of food and basic commodities) lay behind the beginning of the affluence – in suburbia, the south-east, in the light engineering and vehicle industries of the west midlands – which co-existed with poverty in the paradoxical 1930s.

The war of 1939-45 was both more and less disruptive than that of 1914-18: more, because its sales of investment capital were greater, because its world-wide scale implied a much greater upheaval in the international economy and in Britain's competitive position, and because it was the occasion, within Britain, of more far-reaching social reforms and realignments of internal power (especially that of the trade unions); less, because during the painful adjustments of the 1920s and 1930s the ground had been prepared for the commitment of human and material resources to the modern industries and services which fed the sustained postwar boom. Yet even in the rising prosperity of the 1950s and 1960s, the price of progress often seemed high, involving as it did an initial period of consumer austerity* while the transition to a "normal" peace-time economy was undertaken; severe competition for resources between rival claimants (private consumers, social services, defence); the further running down of surplus capacity in some basic industries (notably coal); the poignant clash between rapidly rising expectations of affluence and an only modestly increasing flow of goods and services; changes in incomes, occupations and geographical location. Although not so stark as in the 1920s and 1930s, the contrast between poverty and affluence, and between the uncomfortable prerequisites and the rewards of the latter, were again in evidence. Despite diffused and unprecedented growth, there were the contrasts of material achievement within Britain, just as there were within the international economy, where, in spite of its effort and dearly-bought attainments, the country still found itself falling increasingly behind the leaders.

The place of social change in Britain's twentieth-century economic history is not always clear. For example, economic growth has facilitated, but is also based upon, increased mobility between social classes and regions. A modern economy is, of necessity, urban in character, with an extended educational system and a diffused pattern of mass communication and popular culture. Economic interests have an irresistible tendency to form themselves into pressure groups and to attempt to monopolize resources. All these developments have taken place in Britain. Moreover, it has been argued that social attitudes in Britain – between classes, towards innovation and material achievement, in relation to the worth of economic effort – have retarded

1931 Crisis

By 1931 Britain was deep in economic depression inaugurated by Wall Street Crash 1929. Unemployment reached 2.5 million, resulting in sizeable budgetary deficit. European financial crisis began 1931 with threatened collapse of Austrian banking system; collapse averted but crisis spread to Germany. Resulted in drain on British gold reserves, sterling began to look vulnerable, causing withdrawal of foreign funds culminating in run on pound. Government sought loan of £80 million in United States: terms of loan were achievement of balanced budget to restore confidence in sterling, by cutting unemployment benefit (although balanced budget irrelevant to real economic problems of depression). Resulted in formation of National Government.

Tariffs

Import Duties Act 1932 marked complete reversal of traditional British adherence to free trade: introduced general tariff of 10% on all goods except foodstuffs and industrial raw materials; British Commonwealth exempt. Import Duties Advisory Committee recommended increasing general tariff to 20% with up to 30% on certain luxury items. Protection was motivated as much by political as economic considerations: Conservative majority in National Government strongly protectionist; desire for dramatic response to 1931 crisis.

Ottawa Imperial Conference 1932

Attended by representatives of Britain and Dominions: hoped to built up "imperial preference" and expand trade within Commonwealth; failed in objectives. Dominions determined to protect own emergent industries; not possible to make Commonwealth economically self-sufficient. Resulted in 12 individual agreements by which tariffs reciprocally lowered: more symbolic gesture than economic strategy.

Unemployment 1921-41

Post-war boom gave way to trade slump 1921-22; unemployment then fluctuated for almost two decades between 8.7% and 22.4% of insured population, and did not fall below 1 million until 1941; trough reached 1931-32 when unemployment hit 2,900,000. Inter-war unemployment caused by structual decline of traditional export industries, e.g. coal, ship-building, cotton, exacerbated by world economic depression. Intensely regional in its impact: "depressed areas" of Scotland, north-east and south Wales hit very hard (e.g. Jarrow had 67.8%

unemployment 1934), while south-east remained relatively prosperous. Government policy had little impact on problem. Special Areas Act 1934 appointed Commissioners to initiate aid measures in depressed areas, assisted by £2 million grant, but largely ineffective.

Treasury view
View held in official circles on how to fight economic depression in inter-war years: cautious and anti-Keynesian. Held that employment could not be created by state borrowing and expenditure, opposed public works. Advocated reductions of government expenditure, debt redemption and balancing budget with aim of encouraging private investment. Approach predominant in government policy.

Lend-Lease aid 1941
Programme of American economic aid to Britain and allies: $27 billion available to Britain; Britain provided $6 billion to USA in reciprocal aid; dominated British economy and relations with USA throughout war. Stringent conditions attached: export of British goods containing raw materials supplied through Lend-Lease prohibited; Britain virtually ceased to be exporting country. Lend-Lease abruptly stopped by Truman 1945: resulted in acute dollar shortage in Britain; forced to negotiate loan from America which came into operation 1946.

Bretton Woods Conference 1944
Conference between Britain and America resulting in creation of international financial institutions 1945: International Monetary Fund (IMF) and Bank for Reconstruction and Development (World Bank). IMF was attempt to safeguard international liquidity: members paid into fund in proportion to economic strength; able to obtain loans when short of currency; bound not to devalue, nor to discriminate against each other. Basis of international financial system for next 25 years.

General Agreement on Tariffs and Trade 1947
Representatives of 23 countries met in Geneva for round of tariff and preference bargaining: Britain made modest concessions on Commonwealth preferences; USA reduced average American tariff to lowest level since 1913. Loosely knit organization built up around Agreement, which was amplified and enlarged 1949, 1951, 1956 and 1961. Aim was to end quantitative restrictions on trade, but proved impossible in climate of 1940s and early 1950s.

growth and impaired competitiveness. Obviously, little of this can be new: nineteenth-century parallels can be found for most modern institutions. But the twentieth century has offered a vastly enlarged scope for (some would say need of) "institutionalizing" attitudes and strengthening social groups. Two different sorts of example can be emphasized.

First, the growing power of organized labour – notably in trade unions – has characterized the period, and come to exercise enormous influence on economic organization, technical innovation, and income determination and distribution. Further (although here the direct influence of trade-union policy is uncertain) the economic position of the wage- and salary-earning groups has been transformed: at the beginning of the century labour income (wages, salaries, employers' contributions) accounted for some 50 per cent of the gross national product; by the early 1970s they accounted for over two-thirds.

The second example of a social change with broad economic implications is the dramatic extension of the role of government in the economy* and society. In part a response to economic vicissitudes, in part a vehicle of welfare policies and institutional reform, the state now dominates economic structures and performance. Here, three sorts of developments took place, each influenced by the necessities of war and the social and economic problems of peace. First, the political demands and manifest social needs of the twentieth century obliged governments to undertake income transfers (raising taxes and insurance levies to pay pensions, unemployment and social security benefits, and allowances of various sorts). Second, certain services – notably education and health – have become major public responsibilities, and have been commensurately extended. Third, a combination of political ideology and the pressure for public subsidy when under market pressure has greatly enlarged the scope of public enterprise, from the negligible range before the First World War (the Post Office was the leading example) to coal, iron and steel, motor vehicles, electricity and gas, railways and airlines, oil, telecommunications, etc. Public

Austerity
Term used to describe economic and social conditions of immediate post-war years, especially associated with economic policies of Stafford Cripps. Rationing of clothing, furniture, petrol and many foods continued after war. Severe winter of 1946-47 resulted in serious fuel crisis; by September 1947 Britain had virtually exhausted dollar reserves and had large balance of payments deficit. Cripps was appointed Minister of Economic Affairs, and inaugurated new tough policy: emphasis on exports and capital investment, attempted to regulate economy by wage restraint. From 1948, with election imminent, controls on food and raw materials gradually lifted, but food was not completely de-rationed until 1954.

Inflation 1945-75
Post-war British economy characterized by rising money prices, in contrast with inter-war years when prices fell by 39% 1920-39: 1945-64 average rate of inflation was 3.7%; 1964-72 was 5.4%; 1972-75 15.8%. By 1975 value of money to consumer not much more

than ⅕ of 30 years before. Causes of inflation controversial: variously explained in terms of expanding money supply, heavy government spending, trade union pressure for higher wages, exchange rates and rising import prices. Two periods of most rapid inflation characterized by rising import prices: 1949-51 prices rose by almost 20% and import prices raised by Korean war; 1972-74 inflation accelerated by oil shortage due to Arab-Israeli war 1973.

Devaluation
Strategy of reducing relative value of currency in order to rectify balance of payments deficit. Pound first devalued 1931. In 1949 Cripps devalued pound by 30.5% as result of weakened trading position of sterling and campaign against pound on international markets, but seen as panic measure and did little to restore confidence in sterling. In 1967 large balance of trade deficit caused Callaghan to devalue by 14.3%. Both 1949 and 1967 devaluations were recognitions of failure of government's economic policy.

expenditure, which accounted for some 15 per cent of national income at the beginning of the century, came to account for over 40 per cent by the early 1970s. And public enterprises were responsible for 11 per cent of the national output and 8 per cent of industrial employment.

The economic effects of this revolution in welfare and the market place are not obvious. On the one hand, it has introduced a greater measure of equity in the distribution and use of resources; provided at least the possibility of an improvement in the health and skills of the population; and opened the way to purposeful planning and investment across large areas of the economy. On the other hand, the political vulnerability of decision-making in the public sector and the potential inefficiencies of large bureaucratic institutions, undermine confidence that the concentration of power and wealth will be used wisely. The welfare state and the public sector absorb resources, and do not necessarily use them in flexible, mobile and productive ways. In protecting the weak against the vicissitudes of economic development, they may also defend vested interests against the need to change, and thereby restrict the further development of the economy. While it is unlikely that Britain's economic decline can be attributed to the growth of state intervention, the reverse may well be the case.

Of course, Britain is not alone in experiencing this sort of transformation. But of all the leading industrial nations it is distinctive in its combination of a relatively poor industrial record, apparently inflexible social institutions and outlooks, and the accessibility of its economic structures to political decision-making and vested interests. That such should be the burdens with which, after the achievement of the first 75 years of the century, it had to confront the potential renewal of international stagnation in the last quarter, is yet another paradox for the pioneer of modern industrialization.

Keynesianism

Economic doctrine formulated by J.M. Keynes, Cambridge economist, which was to revolutionize economic thought: most thorough exposition was *General Theory of Employment, Interest and Money* 1936. Advocated government intervention in economy via monetary and fiscal policy to counteract cyclical depression and unemployment by maintaining aggregate demand. Ideas taken up from late 1920s by Liberal party, advocating ambitious loan-financed programme of public works: ignored by government throughout depression. White Paper on Employment Policy 1944 was decisive turning-point in government acceptance of responsibility for maintaining employment by Keynesian methods.

Incomes policies since 1949

Governments have attempted since 1949 to control inflation by means of imposing wage restraint: policies have in general met with limited success. Wages freeze of 1949

abandoned after year in face of rising import prices. Selwyn Lloyd's call for "pause" in 1961 wages round foundered on wage increase in electrical supply industry. Attempts by Wilson government 1965-69 weakened by deteriorating relationship with trade union movement. Heath's pay freeze 1972-73 ended in industrial unrest and "3-day week".

Beeching Report 1963

By 1960 British Railways had working loss of £68 million; government decided new strategy needed. Beeching, chairman of British Railways, drew up "Reshaping Report" 1963, popularly known as the "Beeching Axe": proposed closure of over one-third of rail system, cuts in stock and manpower, and new emphasis on freight traffic. Report brought government much hostility in rural areas and Scotland. Achieved more efficient freight working and some new traffic, but only limited success: failed to make British Railways break even.

Social Change:
appearance and reality

Michael Bentley

Two types of misapprehension prevail in current conceptions of social development in Britain over the past eighty years. One of them consists in a post-dating of technological advance within this most technological of eras: ask anyone how many cars were on British roads in 1914, after all, and few estimates will climb to the true figure of 140,000; not a few will prove wrong by a factor of ten. A second distortion lies in the widespread assumption that *war* has acted as the most fundamental agent of social change in modern civilizations; thus a mental base-line, redrawn annually in university courses and publishers' catalogues, sharply delineates the origin and termination of social analysis in ways that are not always helpful. Predispositions of this kind colour contemporary history in shades startling enough to alert the critical reader that something is happening, as it were, between the lines of commentary. But perhaps we should recall that conventional judgements and inherited perceptions leave their mark also in less obvious places. Not least, they combine with memory (an instrument of historical treachery on which all modern commentators cut themselves) to build a view of the recent past deeply structured by a determination to find – and often celebrate – radical changes in the character of British society since the end of the Boer War.

Many of these perspectives will not, however, stand scrutiny. If we examine some obvious correlates of social structure (political institutions, distribution of wealth, class and status, sex roles, religion, education) it remains far from clear that the twentieth century exhibits a transformation. Representative democracy achieved its most important consummation, certainly in the creation of universal manhood suffrage in 1918 and the final instalment of female emancipation* in 1928. Nor should one minimize the curtailment of the powers of the second chamber* (1911, 1949) and the partial democratization of its membership through the introduction of life peerages in 1958. But the essential attributes of high politics remain in the forms that Gladstone and Disraeli made their own; and to describe the British political structure as an autocracy operating under constant criticism seems no less relevant to the eighth decade of the century than it did to the first. The structure of wealth in contemporary Britain likewise constrains any optimism over the impact of attempts to redistribute the nation's income in some more equal way. A massive extension of trade unionism between 1912 and 1921 and the legislation of majority Labour governments since 1945 promised some movement in this direction, but little subversion has come to light. The one per cent of the population who owned 65.5 per cent of the country's personal capital in 1911-13 failed, it is true, to keep all of it. But the top one per cent of capital owners in 1951-56 still held 42 per cent of that capital. Initiatives in taxation such as death duties (1894) and the capital gains tax (1962) have brought about some redistribution; and positive discrimination in favour of the lower-paid has prompted definite amelioration in the after-tax economics of working-class family life

Enfranchisement of women
1918 Reform Act gave votes to women over 30 who fulfilled certain occupancy qualifications, largely in recognition of women's contribution to war effort. But reform not gained without long campaign by women's suffrage movement, particularly active after 1903 with formation of Women's Social and Political Union which adopted new militant tactics and gained public attention. Final instalment of reform was 1928 Equal Franchise Act which, despite opposition of Churchill and Birkenhead, reduced voting age for women to 21 (known as "flapper vote") and with same residence qualifications as men.

Reform of House of Lords
1911 Parliament Act began erosion of Lords' powers by ending right of veto, replacing it by right to delay bills; process continued in 1949 Parliament Act, which reduced delaying powers. 1958 Life Peerages Act represented attempt to democratize membership by reducing hereditary element: admitted women for first time; opposition able to make recommendations to provide more political balance. 1963 Peerages Act enabled peers to disclaim peerages and admitted all female hereditary peers.

since 1945. Yet these revisions, not to mention retrogressions after 1979, hardly amount to a remodelling of the economic structure.

Inequalities based on class differences show a similar resilience. The social power of the traditional aristocracy barely survived the Great War and the land sales that followed it, just as the soil continued to lose the battle with urban predominance it had been losing since the 1870s. One ultimate beneficiary was the working class of the towns, with its unions and new parliamentary arm in the Labour party; but an equally significant one emerged in a lower middle class whose experience lay less in the town than in the suburb and its rookeries of semi-detached property-owners* buying for the first time in the 1920s and 1930s. In this context Victorian class privilege acquired a classical status, and developed into a collection of atavistic values depicted in the popular culture dominated by P.G. Wodehouse, Noel Coward, Dorothy Sayers, Agatha Christie and Enid Blyton. A modified class presence nevertheless served to undermine post-war contentions about a general *embourgeoisement*. Private education and health care retained their exclusiveness in the era of the National Health Service, in the late 1940s, and the onset of comprehensive education in the 1950s; the higher civil service continued to recruit through Oxbridge colleges; the clubs of St James's found their waiting lists as long as ever; the golf and rotary clubs of the provinces maintained their depiction of the chambers of commerce at play.

Sex roles, on the other hand, changed more fundamentally: indeed a case could be framed for seeing woman's function in society as a domain of primary importance for the social historian of these years. Yet that case would rest better on shifting attitudes to sexuality, marriage, childbearing and the function of the family than on, for example, female employment-patterns or improvements in legal status, despite significant developments in divorce reform* (1923, 1937, 1949, 1969) and the landmark of the Equal Pay Act of 1970. Plainly the world wars impinged on female participation in economic life, taking women out of the home and into the munitions factory or onto the farm. Many of these encroachments were repulsed, however, when peacetime returned. Those of the Second World War proved permanent in one respect. The employment of married women, in which it had been catalytic, not only continued but accelerated in the consumer boom of the 1950s. By 1966 over five million married women had a job, compared with less than a million in 1931. Congruent with these changing priorities came a more widespread adoption of birth control and a decrease in the size of the average family from three children in 1910 to two by 1940, though later "bulges", peaking in 1947 and 1966, distorted an evident trend. The presence of an aggressive women's rights movement in the 1970s presented double-edged evidence of female self-confidence in a world marked by continuing male dominance.

Examined against any crude structural scaffolding of this kind, a number of important social changes can, of course, easily be obscured. There can be no doubt that the quality of life for a significant proportion of British people altered in the three generations after the turn of the century. The "condition of England" question repeatedly asked in the late-nineteenth century was not forgotten in the twentieth; it found notable continuators in Seebohm Rowntree's surveys of York (1901, 1936, 1951) and a socialist tradition of enquiry embodied in Sidney and Beatrice Webb, for example, or Douglas and Margaret Cole. Some governmental response appeared, moreover, in the wide-ranging recommendations of the Beveridge Report of 1942. The sense of

Owner-occupation
In 1914 only 10% of housing owner-occupied, 90% rented from private landlords – local authority provision had not yet begun; by 1938 proportions were 25%, 65% and 10%; by 1970 50%, 20% and 30%. Inter-war years saw owner-occupation extended to lower middle- and skilled working-class; as prices fell, interest rates were low and building societies flourished.

Divorce reform
1923 Matrimonial Causes Act relieved wife petitioner of necessity of proving cruelty or desertion in addition to adultery as grounds for divorce; desertion and insanity added to adultery as grounds by 1937 Divorce Act. 1949 Legal Aid Act made divorce possible for those previously deterred by expense. Most significant reform was 1969 Divorce Reform Act making irretrievable breakdown of marriage only grounds for divorce. Divorce rate has risen dramatically – 1920 3,747 decrees absolute, 1973 107,471.

Children of evicted miners being given dinner outside the Kinsley Hotel in Yorkshire, 1905, during the Hemsworth colliery strike.

Right: *Edwardian Ascot, 1907.*

Below: *an inspection of the Women's Reserve of the National Motor Volunteers, October 1916.*

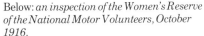

"improvement" can be overstressed. Dietary habits probably remained undisturbed by greater awareness of nutritional needs until at least the 1950s: the loaf, the potato and the margarine kept their place in the pantry.

Health care continued to be rudimentary and expensive, though typhoid had been brought substantially under control by mid-century and the incidence of death from tuberculosis reduced by two-thirds over the same period. Far more apparent to contemporaries, however, was a revolution in leisure and fashion. The exigencies of war had demanded austerities in female dress and hair styles that persisted into the 1920s as *chic* accompaniments to the craze for American dance music. But of course it was to be the cinema that would exert over the next thirty years a remarkable influence over the life-style and values of the British population, and especially of the working class. Between the wars English towns acquired cinemas with the dedication once shown by their Spanish counterparts in sprouting monasteries; and by 1939 four million British cinema seats gave daily access to the romantic escapism of Hollywood. A sporting culture based on football and boxing complemented the cosmology of picture-goers and fed the taste for the virile and outward-bound that underlay the muscular secularism of the period.

Together with traditional practices in the workplace, these activities supplied ritual to a society bereft of religion. One should not post-date the sense of loss: the Christian churches had encountered falling attendance* and membership since before the opening of the century. The pace of secularization appeared to quicken, however, apart from a short-lived revival in the first decade of the century, and became especially marked after the Second World War. Yet if social values before 1950 drew sustenance more from secular than spiritual roots, they nonetheless remained cohesive in their recommendations and effects. Bitter class divisions gave rise, certainly, to waves of strikes and disturbances between 1911 and 1920, during the General Strike of 1926 and at a number of points after 1937. Yet even the chronic deprivation suffered in areas most affected by the depression in primary industry during the 1930s – south Wales, the north-east of England and Clydeside stand out among them – gave rise to very little communist or fascist enthusiasm. Too much stress can be placed on the social significance of a literary coterie which, for all the talent of Auden, Isherwood, Spender and their fellow travellers, left Kipling's large inter-war readership undismayed and unembarrassed by the teaching of Empire given to its children and as impressed by the new naval base at Singapore as by the Peace Pledge Union* (1936). When a backbench Member of Parliament visited a home at Hebburn on the Tyne at the nadir of the depression in 1933, he found it consisted of one room: "The room, which was perfectly clean, was papered with coloured prints from illustrated journals depicting life in the highest circles, the glories of Ascot and Goodwood, of

Cleaning the Morris Eight. Suburban semi-detached housing in the 1930s.

Terraced houses of mill workers in Bradford in the early 1930s.

Church membership

There has been general decrease in participation in organized religion since 1901. Membership of major Protestant denominations fell between 1911 and 1966 by over 5% which, when rise in population is taken into account, meant that proportion of population who were churchgoers fell from 20% to 12%. Between 1901 and 1966 membership of Church of England fell from 1,945,000 to 1,899,000; most Protestant groups have been in severe decline since late 1950s. Only major group to evade this trend has been Roman Catholic Church; Catholic membership has increased from 2,165,900 in 1901 to 4,834,360 in 1966. N.B. Churches calculate "membership" in different ways.

Industrial unrest 1911-20

Decade of almost full employment in which trade union membership rose from 2,565,000 1910 to 8,348,000 1920; characterized by increasing union militancy, despite industrial truce of war. 1911-14 spontaneous strike activity; syndicalist influence at its height in Britain. 1911 railway strike, 1912 national

miners' strike, 1914 Triple Appliance of miners, railwaymen and transport workers. Munitions legislation 1915/16 provoked strikes in engineering by unofficial shop stewards' movements, especially on Clydeside and Sheffield. Triple Alliance formalized 1919. But rising post-war unemployment dampened militancy; Triple Alliance collapsed on "Black Friday" 15 April 1921.

Peace Pledge Union
Britain's largest pacifist movement, founded 1936: basis of membership was Canon Dick Sheppard's letter of October 1934 in appeal for postcard declarations of support for pacifist principles. PPU represented whole range of pacifist opinion and its collective leadership, known as the "sponsors", included Lansbury, Joad, Russell, Vera Brittain and Sassoon. Membership reached peak of 136,000 in April 1940, but then declined as war made position increasingly uncomfortable for pacifists.

Spanish Civil War
Right-wing generals under Franco rebelled 1936 against left-wing Popular Front government: Republican government armed workers and mounted effective resistance until 1939. Rebels received aid from Italy and Germany: British government followed policy of non-intervention, aiding neither party. Spain seen as battleground for confrontation of Fascism and democracy; about 2,000 Britons fought for Republic with International Brigade, including intellectuals like Orwell and large contingent of unemployed Welsh miners.

Foxhunting and Grouse Moors, and the usual obscene follies of a society journal in three colours. There were the familiar oleographs of Victorian England: Queen Victoria reading the Bible, entitled 'The Secret of England's Greatness', an old Crimean print, and portraits of Lord Roberts, Kitchener and Haig. The room measured 14 feet by 12. In it lived, cooked, ate, and slept a man, his wife and six children ..." Such values not only endured but remained hegemonic for a further two decades. With the partial exception of the heroic young men who fought against Franco in the Spanish Civil War* (1936-39), no alternative vision of society arose.

The point may be made in a different way by involving a concept of the American sociologist Edward Shils. In his studies of British society, Shils has identified a "centre" which consists partly of its authority structure, partly "of the order of symbols, of values and beliefs, which govern the society". This "centre" remained intact in 1945 – an observation which generates two thoughts. The first lies in the conclusion that the most significant social shift so far experienced in the twentieth century did not come directly from either of the world wars. The second lies in the residual question: when and why did that change occur? No social transition will appear in retrospect as a momentary threshold, and it would be silly to seek one. There seems little doubt, however, that several currents crossed in the later years of the 1950s; and, of these, three were to manifest considerable social undertow during the next twenty years: the development of rampant consumerism, successive waves of coloured immigration and a heightened self-consciousness among the young.

Advertisements in newspapers and periodicals had, since Edwardian days, drawn attention to luxury consumer products from motor cars to sewing machines and vacuum cleaners. These appealed to an exclusive audience and rarely reached down the class spectrum below the lower reaches of the middle class. What characterized the consumer boom of the 1950s was a proliferation of cheaper goods and, no less important, the provision of widespread credit facilities which brought consumer durables within the reach of most sectors of society without any accompanying social stigma. *Per capita* consumption rose by a quarter on average through the 1950s: the national hire-purchase debt more than doubled. Expenditure on cars, to return to our original criterion, rose by a factor of six, the number of telephones by a half. A boom in house purchases made the domestic mortgage a near-universal reference point among the propertied, the working wife its accompaniment and convenience foods from the new supermarkets (over 800 of them opened in the five years after 1956) an inevitable consequence. Television completed its task of removing working-class audiences from the cinemas, which won back some female sections of it with the bingo which might stand as motif for these years. But consumerism did at least prompt a greater expenditure on food: a notable rise in standards of nutrition took place. Eating habits also became more diversified, especially in the early 1960s, through the dissemination of Indian restaurants, bistros and Chinese take-aways.

The owners of these businesses often came to Britain in a second wave of immigration. An earlier one, beginning in about 1955, consisted centrally of West Indians remedying a desperate labour-shortage in unattractive sectors of employment in the host country. Large-scale immigration had presented a significant problem once before at the very beginning of the century when an influx of Russian and Polish Jews settled, until the flow was staunched by the Aliens Act of 1905, in the East End of London and in some provincial centres of which Leeds was the most conspicuous. Anti-semitism – a fashionable social attitude until the German death camps drove it underground – flourished in such areas and undergirded the initial appeal of Sir Oswald Mosley's British Union of Fascists after 1932. But the coloured immigration of the late 1950s impinged more directly on British social consciousness, despite renewed constraints* imposed by governments (1962, 1968, 1971), through its concentration in decaying inner-city areas and the rhetoric of those, especially Mr Enoch Powell, who campaigned to reverse the trend and repatriate immigrants. Serious race riots in Notting Hill (1958) and later in Brixton, Bristol and Liverpool challenged any organic conception of British society. Economic jealousy among the working class combined with a mood of national insecurity in the aftermath of Russia's invasion of Hungary and the Suez crisis (1956) to add further questions to those insistently put by Britain's youth.

How much importance to grant the mood of teenage rebellion and alienation dating from the "rock" period of the mid-fifties, through the Beatles period of the sixties to the drug culture beyond, will remain problematic until a longer perspective is attainable. In the early 1980s, for example, indications exist that conservative values have reasserted themselves in a generation for whom economic depression and unemployment supply persistent preoccupations. But it seems clear that the youthful depiction of an "alternative" consciousness, later to dovetail into the Campaign for Nuclear Disarmament* and the anti-nuclear lobby of the late 1970s, compounded other changes in post-1950s society and lent some of them an articulateness which they might otherwise have lacked. The universities* and polytechnics of the 1960s gave a voice to radicalism, especially in the heady moments of 1968 when socialist intellectuals looked to events in Paris for their inspiration. Through the satirical reviews whose talents they provided and the revolution in dress and vocabulary in which they played no small part, students continued thereafter to sustain a residual *anomie*.

Beneath the appearance of continuity in British society, broken in 1914 and 1945, lies a more complicated reality. Two "societies" offer themselves for identification and delineation and they point to a socially significant disjunction in the decade after 1955. Structurally, those two societies share many, perhaps most, characteristics and imply a history of transformation in the mechanisms of the social order rather than a fundamental change within the order itself. Yet in its "centre" – in the cluster of assumptions, values and myths that legitimate social practice – important modifications seem traceable. Occasionally a displaced value-structure assumes a former identity: during a royal wedding, perhaps, or a national emergency such as that precipitated by the Argentinian invasion of the Falklands Islands (1982); and indeed the decades from 1950 to 1980 may appear in later years a strange epicycle within the more familiar orbit of twentieth-century social development. But the present understanding of historical material available for scrutiny leads one rather towards a recognition of the distance travelled – too long a road easily to permit of return – since the mythology of national cohesion found its finest hour in the summer of 1940.

Immigration legislation
1962 Commonwealth Immigration Act provided that Commonwealth citizens could apply for entry vouchers if employment obtained in Britain or possessed required skills or qualifications; otherwise entered as part of quota determined by government. Denounced by Labour party as racialist. 1968 Commonwealth Immigration Act passed by Labour government placed controls on UK passport holders with "no substantial connection" with Britain and set aside 1,500 vouchers for them; met by Liberal and back-bench Labour opposition. 1971 Immigration Act ended favourable status of Commonwealth immigrants.

Wolfenden Report 1957
Wolfenden Report was crucial episode in evolution of liberal attitudes towards homosexuality. Wolfenden Committee set up 1954 to consider laws relating to homosexual offences and prostitution in view of rising number of prosecutions and several major scandals. Report recommended that homosexual acts in private could be decriminalized for men over 21, and that maximum penalties should be revised. Homosexual Law Reform Society founded 1958 to press for implementation of Report's recommendations. Sexual Offences Act 1967 permitted homosexual acts in private between consenting adults.

Campaign for Nuclear Disarmament
Established 1958 in response to 1957 British H-Bomb test: called for unilateral British nuclear disarmament. Easter 1958 saw first Aldermaston protest march, which became annual event. Campaign reached peak 1960, when Labour Party Conference supported unilateralism but resolution defeated 1961 and movement lost impetus.

See **Robbins Report** (page 334)

Culture:
élite and mass
Gillian Sutherland

By 1901 the vast majority of the population of the United Kingdom – 99 per cent of those in Scotland, 97 per cent in England and Wales, 88½ per cent in Ireland – were literate, as measured by their ability to sign their names in the register on marriage. But although in this sense Great Britain had caught up with the rest of western Europe and the developed world, the society remained one in which access to more than the very basic educational skills represented by such signatures was limited. Government funds were for the first time made available for secondary education in England and Wales under the Education Act* of 1902, which established county and county borough councils as local education authorities. But the minimum school leaving age had been raised to twelve only in 1899 and grant-aided secondary schools were allowed to charge fees for the majority of their places. In 1920 only 9.2 per cent of children in England and Wales thirteen-year-old were in full-time attendance at a grant-aided secondary school and under half of these had previously attended a public elementary school, i.e. could be described as either working or lower middle class.

The Education Act* of 1918 (known as Fisher's Act) and the associated plans for post-war reconstruction had raised the minimum school leaving age to fourteen, envisaged a further rise to fifteen and promised considerable expansion in educational provision for adolescents. But economic depression led to the shelving of almost all the medium-and long-term plans. The minimum leaving age in England and Wales was eventually raised to fifteen by the Education Act* of 1944 (in Scotland and Northern Ireland by legislation in 1947).

This Act, known as Butler's Act, also abolished fees in state-supported secondary schools and was popularly supposed to provide "secondary education for all". Post-elementary (or post-primary, as it was now coming to be called) educational provision in fact took three forms: the secondary "grammar" school, the secondary "modern" school and the technical school. Children were allocated between them usually by means of an examination at age eleven – the "eleven plus" – and this examination was a ranking process, both intellectual and social. It usually consisted of a group intelligence test and tests in English and arithmetic, in which middle-and upper-class children tended to do disproportionately well. Although the three types of school were supposed to enjoy "parity of esteem", only the secondary grammar school led on to higher education. The children who did best in the examination therefore tended to go to the grammar school, the next best to the technical school and the remainder to the modern school. A first attempt to break down the tripartite division and abolish such ranking was made by central government in 1965, when the Labour secretary of state for Education, Anthony Crosland, issued Circular 10/65, requesting local authorities to reorganize their post-primary provision on a multilateral or comprehensive* basis. Circular 10/70, however, issued by

1902 Education Act
Act designed to streamline educational administration by transferring functions of school boards to county and county borough councils; for the first time, gave them power to provide secondary schools. Most controversial feature was establishment of local authority maintenance of voluntary (largely Anglican) schools, which aroused wrath of Nonconformists (especially in Wales) who objected to subsidizing Anglican education.

1918 Education Act
Promoted by H.A.L. Fisher, president of Board of Education in Coalition government. Gave Board powers to compel local authorities to make adequate educational provision; in return state provided financial aid. Envisaged establishment of nursery education, continuation schools and more senior schools; but nursery provision and continuation schools were first victims of post-war retrenchment. Act ended half-time system and established 14 as minimum leaving age, with some provision for part-time post-school education.

1944 Education Act
Known as Butler's Act after Conservative president of Board of Education. Most significant feature was compulsion on local authorities to provide secondary education. Act raised school leaving age to 15 and scheme for part-time education until 18 revived but not implemented. Local authorities were to provide school meals, free milk and regular medical inspection. Act gave religious instruction a firm basis in schools, requiring a daily act of collective worship.

Comprehensive education
Support for comprehensive education growing in educational circles in post-war years. First purpose-built comprehensive opened by London County Council in 1954, and in 1957 Leicestershire embarked on its two-tier system. Circular 10/65 gave impetus for reorganization; by 1971 there were 1,300 comprehensives in England and Wales, covering 35% of age group.

Drilling at Townmead Road School, Fulham, in 1909.

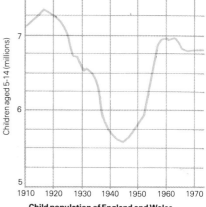

Child population of England and Wales (children aged 5-14 inclusive)

the Conservative secretary of state, Margaret Thatcher, in 1970 cancelled this request.

The 1944 Education Act was followed by a major secondary school building programme. Existing universities were expanded and between 1958 and 1966 nine new universities, seven in England, one each in Scotland and Northern Ireland, were founded. But the expansion overall was not sufficient to keep pace with the rise in the birth rate immediately after the war. The fall in the child population in the inter-war years had improved the chances of access to secondary education, and by extension to higher education, for children from all social classes. The position deteriorated again after the Second World War. Expansion in university places kept pace with the "baby boom" rather better than expansion in selective secondary school places; but this again was insufficient to keep pace with the growing demand represented by the lengthening of school life and the increase in the number of children acquiring the minimum qualifications for entry to university. By 1961 4.6 per cent of the total population of eighteen-year-olds in the UK were entering university; and the chances of doing so were distributed most unequally between social classes. In 1962 it was estimated that 45 per cent of the children of higher professional families were likely to enter some form of higher education, if not university, then an advanced technical college or a college of education, while only 4 per cent of the children of skilled manual workers were likely to do so.

Higher education was expanded* during the 1960s not only by the creation of new universities but also by the expansion and upgrading of work at polytechnics – the development of the "binary system" of higher education. By 1968, twenty-one polytechnics were designated as able to run degree-earning courses and the Council for National Academic Awards (CNAA) had been established as a course-validating and degree-awarding body. Such expansion eased the pressure on places in absolute terms – by 1970 about 15 per cent of the relevant age-group were entering some form of higher education – but brought about no significant redistribution of chances of access between classes.

Robbins Report
Laid down principle that there should be places in higher education for all suitably qualified candidates. Committee on Higher Education appointed 1961 to examine university development. Reported October 1963 and made 178 recommendations: doubling numbers of students in full-time higher education by 1980-81, expanding size of existing universities, creating six new universities and granting full university status to colleges of advanced technology. Report crystallized earlier proposals and was promptly accepted by government: in 1964 total of £56 million given in grant for university expansion.

British Broadcasting Corporation 1926
British Broadcasting Company became public corporation 1926, after government accepted 1925 Crawford Report endorsing principle of monopoly for broadcasting. BBC to be public service body acting in "national interest" and financed by licence fee paid by owners of radios. Royal charter granted BBC licence for 10 years; renewed thereafter. Directed by Board of Governors nominated by government. First public service television opened 1936 from Alexandra Palace; second BBC channel opened 1964.

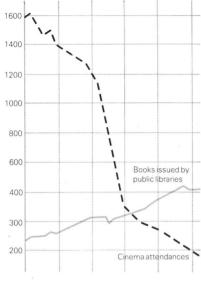

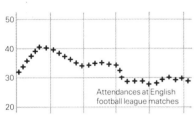

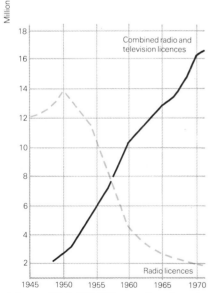

Leisure and Media 1945-1970: comparison of annual UK statistics

The radical, unit-constructed design of Hunstanton Secondary Modern School by Alison and Peter Smithson, 1954.

The educational system thus reflected, embodied and reinforced a continuing divide between high culture in the sense in which Matthew Arnold had defined it, "a study of perfection", and the culture of the society in the anthropologists' sense, the habits of thought, attitudes and expectations of the mass of the population. It was a divide acknowledged by most British intellectuals, whether, like the novelist and essayist George Orwell, they felt a continuing sense of guilt about it; or, like the poets W.B. Yeats and T.S. Eliot, an Englishman by adoption, they contended that true culture could only be the preserve of an élite. In Yeats's case, as to some degree also for Welsh and Scottish writers, the position was complicated by the tensions of nationalism and the problems of a national language. "Finding a voice" presented Irish, Welsh and Scottish writers with problems above and beyond those of class.

Mass literacy contributed little, if anything, to close up this divide. For the achievement of mass literacy also saw the beginning of its devaluation as a skill, through the homogenization dictated by the economics of mass marketing, the development of oral and visual modes of mass communication – radio, film, television – and the increasing importance of pure science and the linked skill of numeracy. At the end of the 1950s daily newspapers were being produced at the rate of two copies for every household in the UK; but the number of *different* newspapers being published was roughly half what it had been in 1901. British publishers succeeded in retaining retail price maintenance for books in 1962, but the protection this was supposed to afford did not obviate the need to develop the "hype", selling – indeed, commissioning – books as if they were new breakfast cereals.

At the same time the written word was being pushed out of its central role in communication. Radio broadcasts began in 1922, the Post Office granting a monopoly to the British Broadcasting Company, a group financed by radio manufacturers. In 1926 the monopoly passed to the British Broadcasting Corporation*, established by royal charter. In 1932 King George V broadcast the first of the royal Christmas messages; and Edward VIII chose radio as the medium by which to make his abdication statement in December 1936. Silent

films had been an occasional curiosity in the years immediately before the First World War. The first "talkie", *The Jazz Singer,* starring Al Jolson, was made in 1927; and in the inter-war years cinemas mushroomed everywhere, bringing the collapse of most music halls and provincial repertory theatres.

After the Second World War the cinema, in its turn, gave way before the advent of television. The BBC's pre-war television station at Alexandra Palace had been closed down for the duration of the war and began to broadcast again in June 1946. In June 1953 56 per cent, over twenty million, of the adult population of Great Britain watched the transmission of the coronation service of Queen Elizabeth II from Westminster Abbey. The (Independent) Television Act* of 1954 brought to an end the BBC's monopoly and the first ITV programmes were shown on 22 September 1955. By then television was in principle available to 92 per cent of the population and there were four and a half million combined sound and television licences. The spread of colour television from the end of the 1950s was but the icing on the cake.

The burgeoning of radio and television was in itself one index of the acceleration of technological and scientific innovation in this period. This served both to distance the scientific élite not only from the mass of the population but also from fellow intellectuals, and to limit the power of the written word still further. For much of the path-breaking work in population genetics, molecular biology, nuclear and astro-physics was numerical and quantitative, sustained and supported by developing computer technology and increasingly difficult of access even to those few members of the population with higher education. At the end of the 1950s it became fashionable to talk not simply of high culture but of two élite cultures*, the literary and the scientific. A first gesture towards solving the problem was made in 1964, when the minister of Education was re-named secretary of state for Education and Science; and the development of the "binary system" in higher education was, in part, an attempt to build upon and develop the work being done in technical colleges. But much of this activity simply reproduced the patterns already prevailing within the universities. The real roots of the problem appeared to lie further back, in early specialization in the secondary school. And devising policies to bridge rather than simply to perpetuate this gap, in a period of increasing financial stringency, was to remain a central issue for the 1970s.

(Independent) Television Act 1954
Conservative government set up Independent Television Authority under postmaster-general for 10 years: to licence contracting companies and regulate their output. Companies established on regional basis from 1955, financed by advertising revenue. 1964 Television Act extended ITA's life for 10 years and increased its membership.

"The Two Cultures"
Concept of gulf between scientists and other intellectuals, first put forward by novelist and scientist C.P. Snow in 1956. Full version delivered as Rede Lecture in Cambridge 1959 and published. Directed much public attention to problem of over-specialization in education producing cultural gap and need to enable laymen to cope with scientific revolution. Labour government set up Ministry of Technology 1964 with Snow as parliamentary under-secretary.

A pop concert in Hyde Park, 7 June 1969.

WHO'S
WHO

WHO'S WHO

Abbot, George 1562-1633 Oxford Calvinist theologian and Vice-Chancellor, Bishop of Lichfield 1609, Archbishop of Canterbury 1610. Favoured hostility to Catholics at home and abroad, alliance with foreign Protestants, and lenience to Puritan nonconformists. Accidentally shot gamekeeper 1621. Lost political influence from 1625 with rise of Laud.

Aberdeen, George Hamilton-Gordon, earl of 1784-1860 Diplomat and scholar, (President of Society of Antiquaries 1812-46); Chancellor of Duchy of Lancaster 1828, Foreign Secretary 1828-30, 1841-46, Secretary for War 1834-35, Prime Minister 1852-55. Supported Peel over corn laws, resigned with him 1846; succeeded to leadership of Peelites 1850; headed Peelite-Whig government 1852-55, resigned over mismanagement of Crimean War.

Acton, John Emerich Dalberg-, Lord 1834-1902 Whig MP 1859-65, associate of Gladstone. A leader of English liberal Catholics, opposed Syllabus of Errors and papal infallibility. Helped found *English Historical Review* 1886; Regius Professor of History at Cambridge 1895-1902; planned *Cambridge Modern History*.

Adam, Robert 1728-92 Most prominent of four architect brothers, studied architecture in Italy. Executed work in the Neo-classical style with attention to detail, care in interior design. Interiors included Harewood House 1758-71, Syon House 1760-69, Kenwood 1767-69; designed Apsley House 1775, and Charlotte Square, Edinburgh 1791.

Addington, Henry, Viscount Sidmouth 1757-1844 Lawyer; MP from 1784, Speaker of Commons 1789-1801, Prime Minister 1801-4, Lord President 1805, 1806, 1812, Home Secretary 1812-22; viscount 1805. Protégé of Pitt, who broke with him over 1802 Treaty of Amiens. As Home Secretary, responsible for repression of radical movements, especially by Six Acts 1819.

Addison, Joseph 1672-1719 Whig MP 1708-19, minor offices, Chief Secretary for Ireland 1708-10, 1714-17. Influential essayist, a leading contributor to *The Tatler*, co-founder of *The Spectator* 1711, to which he contributed as "Clio".

Adrian IV, *c.*1100-59 Born Nicholas Breakspear; a monk and abbot in France. Cardinal 1146, papal legate to Norway. Pope 1154-59, the only Englishman ever to be elected. Reputed to have granted authority over Ireland to Henry II in 1158.

Aelfric ("the Grammarian") *c.*955-*c.*1020 Monk at Winchester, Abbot of Cerne 987, Eynsham 1005. Wrote homilies and lives of saints in English, for use by parish clergy, expressing ideals of Dunstan's reforms.

Aethelbald, d. 757 King of Mercia 716-57; built up powerful military and political base for a greater Mercian kingdom. Murdered by his bodyguard.

Aethelbert, *c.*552-616 King of Kent. *c.*560-616, bretwalda of southern English from 591. Married Bertha, daughter of a Frankish king, before 588, permitted her to practise Christianity; admitted Augustine's mission 597, converted as first English Christian king. Promulgated earliest surviving Anglo-Saxon legal code.

Aethelfleda, d. 918 Daughter of Alfred the Great, married Aethelred, ealdorman of Mercia, *c.*887. With her husband, and from 911, as "Lady of the Mercians", organized Mercian resistance to Danes and fortified sites such as Bridgnorth, Tamworth, Stafford and Runcorn.

Aethelfrith, d. 616 King of Bernicia 593-616, annexed Deira *c.*604 to rule all Northumbria. Defeated British and Scots Dál Riáta forces, but killed in battle with Edwin.

Aethelred I, d. 871 As King of Wessex 866-71, organized resistance to Danish attacks: forced withdrawal of Danes from Nottingham 868, defeated by them at Reading 870, overcame them at Ashdown 871, suffered two reverses before death.

Aethelred II, *c.*968-1016 King of England from 978, nicknamed "unready" (i.e. redeless, or lacking in counsel) by later writers, though improvements made in government, law and finance. Bought off Danish invaders with Danegeld, deposed by Svein I Estrithson 1013, but restored on Svein's death 1014.

Aethelwulf, d. 858 Sub-king of Kent, Essex, Sussex and Surrey 825, King of Wessex 839-56. Defeated by Danes at sea 842, but routed them at Aclea 851. Made a pilgrimage to Rome 855, and shared kingdom with eldest son on return to avert civil war. Four sons by his first wife became successive kings of Wessex.

Agricola, Gnaeus Julius AD 39-93 Served twice in Britain before appointed Governor, 78: completed subjugation of north Wales, occupied the lowlands of Scotland and defeated combined Caledonian tribes at Mons Graupius 84. Then recalled to Rome.

Aidan, d.651 Monk at Iona, then settled at Lindisfarne at request of Oswald of Northumbria and was consecrated bishop 635. His humility and asceticism aided evangelization of Northumbria for Celtic Christianity. Canonized.

Ailred of Rievaulx 1109-67 Son of a Saxon priest, lived at Scots Court before entering monastery of Rievaulx *c.*1133; Abbot of Revesby 1143, of Rievaulx 1147. Wrote works of mysticism, theology and life of Edward the Confessor. Canonized 1191.

Albany, Alexander Stewart, duke of *c.*1454-85 Son of James II of Scots; fled to France to escape brother James III. Acknowledged English supremacy over Scotland in return for Edward IV's recognition of him as king and help to make good his claim. Attempted to seize power in Scotland 1482, 1484, then withdrew to France; accidentally killed.

Albany, John Stewart, duke of 1484-1536 Son of above: brought up in France. Sent to Scotland by Francis I to secure alliance: governor of child James V, had himself declared heir to throne. Recalled to France 1517, when Anglo-French relations improved, returned to Scotland 1522, invaded England unsuccessfully 1522, 1523, then retired to France. Employed by Francis I in military and diplomatic missions.

Albany, Robert Stewart, duke of c.1340-1420 Son of Robert II, took part in a number of military actions against English 1385-1402; virtual ruler of Scotland because of incapacity of brother Robert III, regent on Robert III's death 1406, when young James I was captured by English.

Albert, Prince 1819-61 Son of Ernest, duke of Saxe-Coburg-Gotha, married cousin Queen Victoria 1840. As a foreign Prince Consort, his position was a delicate one, but he was respected for his political advice and his dedication to arts, sciences and living conditions of working class. Organized Great Exhibition 1851.

Alcock, John 1430-1500 Master of Rolls 1462-72; Bishop of Rochester 1472-76, of Worcester 1476-86, of Ely 1486-1500; Lord Chancellor 1475, 1485-87. Founder of Jesus College, Cambridge.

Alcuin c.735-804 English name Ealhwine. Master of great cathedral school at York 766; adviser to Charlemagne from 781 and tutor to royal household; abbot of Tours 796. Influential poet, religious writer and teacher, and one of the inspirations of Carolingian renaissance.

Alexander I c.1077-1124 Son of Malcolm III; King of Scots 1107-24. Never effectively ruled southern Scotland, controlled by brother David I. Defeat of rebellious northern clans earned epithet "the fierce"; reputation for piety, and sought to maintain independence of Scottish Church against English archbishops.

Alexander II 1198-1249 Son of William I the Lion; King of Scots 1214-49. Intervened in England, exploiting troubles of John and Henry III, but made peace 1219; extended royal control in Argyll and Caithness, repelled Norse invasion 1230. Died while attempting to wrest Hebrides from Norway.

Alexander III 1241-86 Son of Alexander II; King of Scots 1249-86: annexed the Western Isles by Treaty of Perth 1266.

Alexander, Sir William, earl of Stirling 1576-1640 Tutor to James VI's sons Henry and Charles, promoted unsuccessful colony in Nova Scotia; poet and courtier, Scottish Secretary 1626-40.

Alexander of Tunis, Harold Rupert Leofric George, Earl 1891-1967 Served in First World War; commanded evacuation of Dunkirk 1940; stemmed Japanese advance in Burma 1942; successful Commander-in-Chief in Middle East 1943; Supreme Allied Commander in Mediterranean 1945. Governor-General of Canada 1946-52; Conservative Minister of Defence 1952-54.

Alfred ("the Great") 849-99 Son of Aethelwulf; fought against Danes with brother Aethelred I; King of Wessex 871-99. Secured peace with Danes until 875, then faced new attacks: after setbacks, victory at Edington 878 forced Danes to leave Wessex. Strengthened defences by constructing fortresses, improving fyrd and building fleet: resisted further invasion 892-96. Attracted scholars to Court, translated Latin texts and promulgated influential code of law.

Allen, William 1532-94 Oxford Catholic scholar, went into exile 1561; founded seminary for training English Catholic priests at Douai 1568; helped found English College at Rome 1579; supervised mission to England. Cardinal 1587. Political propagandist, called on English Catholics to support Philip II's Armada 1588.

Allenby, Edmund, Viscount 1861-1936 Served in Boer War 1899-1902. Cavalry commander on Western Front in First World War, highly successful Commander-in-Chief of Egyptian Expeditionary Force 1917: drove Turks from Jerusalem and Damascus. Field Marshal 1919, High Commissioner in Egypt 1919-25.

Amherst, Jeffrey, Lord 1717-97 Served in Germany and Netherlands; successfully commanded expeditionary force against French in North America 1758-60; Commander-in-Chief and Governor-General of British North America 1761-70; Commander-in-Chief 1777-82, 1793-97. Field Marshal 1796.

Anderson, Elizabeth Garrett 1836-1917 First woman to qualify as a doctor in England 1865, founded St Mary's Dispensary for Women (Elizabeth Garrett Anderson Hospital). First woman mayor elected in England 1908.

Andrewes, Lancelot 1555-1626 Cambridge academic and London preacher; Bishop of Chichester 1605, of Ely 1609, of Winchester 1618. Court preacher, influential theologian and controversialist, responsible for large parts of Old Testament in Authorized Version.

Aneurin fl.600 Welsh poet, whose *Y Goddoddin* describes defeat of British by Saxons at Catterick, c. 590.

Anne 1665-1714 Daughter of James II, married Prince George of Denmark 1683. A Protestant, supported her father's deposition and accession of Mary II and William III 1689. Queen of Great Britain and Ireland 1702-14. Despite 18 pregnancies, produced no surviving direct heir and reluctantly accepted Hanoverian succession. Her Anglican-Tory views and susceptibility to influence of friends were important factors in political conflicts.

Anne Boleyn 1507-36 Queen consort of Henry VIII 1533-36. Upon her return from residence at French Court, Henry VIII became infatuated with Anne Boleyn and in 1527 began attempts to secure divorce from Catherine of Aragon. She married Henry VIII 1533, gave birth to Elizabeth I. With failure to produce male heir, victim of faction at Court; convicted of alleged adultery and incest, and beheaded.

Anne of Cleves 1515-57 Queen consort of Henry VIII 1540. Daughter of duke of Cleves: marriage to Henry VIII 1540 promoted by Thomas Cromwell for political reasons, but Henry found her unattractive and diplomatic needs changed; marriage annulled. Anne remained in England with pension.

Anselm c. 1033-1109 Born in Piedmont, Abbot of Bec 1078, Archbishop of Canterbury 1093. Forced into exile by William II 1097, returned on accession of Henry I 1100, exiled again 1103 over lay investiture; compromise allowed return 1107. Influential theologian, devised ontological proof of God. Canonized.

Anson, George, Lord 1697-1762 Naval officer protecting English commerce in Atlantic; made a successful circumnavigation of world 1740-44. As admiral, defeated French off Cape Finisterre 1747. First Lord of Admiralty 1751-62, carried out important reforms in naval administration and dockyards.

Argyll, Archibald Campbell, earl of 1530-73 Promoted Reformation in Scotland, but then supported Mary Queen of Scots: privy to plot to murder Darnley, fought for Mary at Langside 1568. Chancellor of Scotland 1573.

Argyll, Archibald Campbell, marquis and earl of *c.*1606-1661 Leading Covenanter, opposing Charles I's religious policy in Scotland in 1630s; fought against Montrose and royalists in Civil War. Opposed Scots Engagement with Charles I 1647, but proclaimed and crowned Charles II as King of Scotland 1650-51. After defeat, submitted to Cromwellian rule, MP in 1659; executed at Restoration.

Argyll, Archibald Campbell, earl of **1629-85** Son of above, though vigorous royalist in 1650s; Scottish Councillor 1664, active against Covenanters 1667. After opposition to Scottish Test Act 1681, sentenced to death and fled to exile; invaded Scotland on behalf of Monmouth 1685, but captured and executed.

Argyll, Archibald Campbell, duke of **1682-1761** Prominent in Scottish politics, helped to promote Union with England 1707, fought at Sheriffmuir 1715; Walpole's chief adviser on Scotland.

Argyll, John Campbell, duke of 1678-1743 Elder brother of above: an able soldier, served in Flanders 1702, 1706-9, Commander-in-Chief in Spain 1710, in Scotland 1712. Supported 1707 Union and Hanoverian succession, terminated Jacobite rebellion at Sheriffmuir 1715; duke of Greenwich 1719. Dominated Scottish politics, allied with Walpole.

Arlington, Henry Bennet, earl of 1618-85 Supported Charles I in Civil War and Charles II in exile; Secretary of State 1662-74; expert on foreign policy and parliamentary management. Member of Cabal ministry 1667-74; Parliament attempted to impeach him 1674, but he resigned political offices.

Arnold, Matthew 1822-88 Son of Thomas: prolific, influential poet and literary critic; saw culture as means of moral reform. Inspector of Schools 1851-83, opposing mechanical learning; Oxford Professor of Poetry 1857-67.

Arnold, Thomas 1795-1842 Headmaster of Rugby School 1828-42, pre-eminent in creating English public school ideal: widened curriculum, stressed value of organized games, encouraged responsibility among pupils, and made chapel focus of school life. Regius Professor of Modern History, Oxford, 1841.

Arran, James Hamilton, earl of *c.***1516-75** Governor of Scotland 1542-54, in minority of Mary Stuart: initially pursued English alliance, but then joined pro-French party; defeated by English at Pinkie 1547. Replaced by Mary of Guise 1554; defected to Lords of Congregation 1559; opposed Queen Mary's marriage to Darnley, but then supported her against reformers 1569-73.

Arran, James Stewart, earl of *c.***1545-96** Served in Netherlands against Spain, returned to Scotland 1578; became close adviser to James VI, especially after 1583; lost power 1585, went into exile: returned and was murdered.

Arthur *fl.c.***500** Probably Roman-British leader of resistance to Saxon invasions. Real importance is uncertain, but by 9th century he was credited with British victory at Mount Badon *c.*518. Later, became inspiration of medieval legendary tales of chivalry and search for Holy Grail.

Arthur of Brittany 1187-1203 Named heir by uncle Richard I 1190, but Richard later adopted brother John as heir. When John succeeded to throne 1199, Philip Augustus of France pressed Arthur's rival claims; John had Arthur captured and murdered.

Arundel, Thomas 1353-1414 Bishop of Ely 1347, Archbishop of York 1388, of Canterbury 1396; Lord Chancellor 1386-89, 1391-96, 1407-10, 1412-13. Supported Appellants, impeached and banished 1397; returned 1399 to crown Henry IV. Vigorously suppressed Lollards, banned English Bible 1408.

Ascham, Roger 1515-68 Greek scholar, tutor to Princess Elizabeth, Latin Secretary to Edward VI, Mary and Elizabeth. Influential writer on education, advocating milder discipline of children and teaching of languages, music and games.

Asquith, Herbert Henry, earl of Oxford and Asquith 1852-1928 Barrister, Liberal MP from 1886; Home Secretary 1892-95. Chancellor of Exchequer 1905-8; Prime Minister 1908-16; Liberal leader 1908-26. Led reforming Liberal government 1908-14 and war coalition 1914-16, but overthrown by Lloyd George over conduct of war; continuing split with Lloyd George divided Liberal party and contributed to its decline.

Asser d.*c.***909** Welsh monk, tutor and adviser to Alfred; Bishop of Sherborne, wrote chronicle of England and life of Alfred.

Astor, Nancy, Viscountess 1879-1964 Born in the USA, first woman MP (Conservative) 1919-45: campaigned for women's causes, temperance and education.

Athelstan 895-940 Son of Edward the Elder: King of Wessex and Mercia 924-39, of England 927-39. By crushing Danish rule at York 927, became ruler of all English; supremacy also recognized by kings of Scotland and Strathclyde, and later by Welsh princes; defeated invasion by minor kings of Ireland and Scotland at Brunanburh 937. Summoned royal councils, issued many laws, made alliances with continental princes.

Atholl, John Murray, earl and marquis of 1631-1703 Active Royalist, at Restoration was sworn to Privy Council; Justice-General of Scotland 1661-75. Quarrelled with Lauderdale over treatment of Covenanters 1679: lost offices, but restored to favour 1684; irresolute in 1688 revolution, equivocal in his loyalties thereafter.

Atholl, John Stewart, earl of d. 1579 Leading Catholic, councillor to Mary Queen of Scots; member of regency council 1567, but secretly worked for Mary's restoration; joined in overthrow of Morton 1578; Chancellor 1578-79.

Attlee, Clement Richard, Earl 1883-1967 Lawyer, Labour MP from 1922; junior minister 1924, 1929-31 but refused to join National Government; Labour party leader 1935-55. Opposed rearmament, but condemned Munich Agreement 1938; Lord Privy Seal 1940-42 and Deputy Prime Minister 1942-45 in coalition war cabinet; Labour Prime Minister 1945-51. His governments laid foundations of welfare state, undertook major schemes of nationalization and decolonization.

Attwood, Thomas 1783-1856 Banker, advocate of paper money and flexible credit, founded Birmingham Political Union 1829. Radical MP 1832-39; a Chartist leader, presented petition to Parliament 1839.

Auchinleck, Sir Claude 1884-1981 Served in Near East in First World War; Commander in Middle East 1941-43, halted German advance on Egypt, but replaced by Montgomery. Commander-in-Chief in India 1943-47.

Augustine of Canterbury d. 604 Monk at Rome, sent by Pope Gregory to establish Church in England: landed in Kent 597, received by King Aethelbert, organized missionary work. First Archbishop of

Canterbury 597-604, nominated suffragan bishops; failed to reach agreement over differences with Celtic Church. Canonized.

Austin, Herbert, Lord 1866-1941 Began motor car production 1895; founded Austin company 1905; produced "Baby" Austin Seven 1922, helping to bring motoring within price range of wider public. Benefactor of hospitals.

Bacon, Francis, Lord Verulam, Viscount St Albans 1561-1626 Lawyer, MP from 1584; served Elizabeth as counsel; Solicitor General 1607, Attorney General 1613, Privy Councillor 1616, Lord Keeper 1617, Lord Chancellor 1618-21; impeached by Commons for corruption, dismissed 1621. Influential scientific writings developed inductive theories of knowledge, maintained that science could be of practical benefit, and advocated organized scientific associations.

Bacon, Roger 1210/14-94 Franciscan friar and Oxford philosopher of much originality, in recurrent conflict with Church authorities. Studied alchemy, experimented in optics.

Baden-Powell, Robert, Lord 1857-1941 Commanded beseiged garrison at Mafeking 1899-1900, holding out against Boers for 7 months before being relieved. Founded Boy Scouts 1907 and Girl Guides 1909.

Bagehot, Walter 1826-1877 Lawyer, political theorist, editor of *The Economist* 1860-77: believed truth was discovered by trial and error, requiring individual freedom; emphasized importance of mature institutions in *The English Constitution* 1867.

Baldwin, Stanley, Earl 1867-1947 Conservative MP from 1908: President of the Board of Trade 1921-22; influenced Conservative MPs against the Lloyd George coalition and helped bring it down 1922. Chancellor of Exchequer 1922-23, Prime Minister 1923-24, 1924-29, 1935-37; a leader of National Government 1931-35. Faced General Strike 1926, disavowed Hoare-Laval Pact 1935, managed abdication crisis 1936, retired 1937.

Balfour, Arthur James, Earl 1848-1930 Conservative MP from 1874: Secretary for Scotland 1886-87; Secretary for Ireland 1887-91, opposing Home Rule, but supporting land reform. Prime Minister 1902-5; Leader of Opposition 1906-11. First Lord of Admiralty 1915-16 and Foreign Secretary 1916-19, in war coalition: issued Balfour Declaration 1917, favouring a Palestinian homeland for Jews. Lord

President of Council 1919-22, 1925-29: Balfour Definition 1926 was foundation for 1931 Statute of Westminster.

Ball, John d. 1381 Imprisoned for preaching Wycliffite doctrines 1376, freed by rebels in Peasants' Revolt 1381, accompanied the insurgents to London. Preached social equality and used couplet "When Adam delved and Eve span, Who was then a gentleman?" Executed.

Bancroft, Richard 1544-1610 Opponent of nonconformists and presbyterians, as preacher, writer and prosecutor: Bishop of London 1597, Archbishop of Canterbury 1604; responsible for Canons of 1604; defended independence of Church jurisdiction.

Baring, Evelyn, earl of Cromer 1841-1917 After early career as soldier and administrator in India and Egypt, British agent and Consul General in Egypt 1883-1907: as virtual ruler, he promoted agricultural, social, legal, and industrial improvements, and supported Kitchener's reconquest of Sudan.

Barnardo, Thomas John 1845-1905 Worked as evangelist, trained as medical missionary; founded mission for destitute children 1867, Boys' Home 1870 and Girls' Home 1876. These became nuclei of national organization.

Beaton, David 1494-1546 Employed on Scottish diplomatic missions; Keeper of Privy Seal 1520; Cardinal 1538, Archbishop of St Andrews 1539. As Chancellor 1543-46, furthered Catholic and pro-French policies; murdered by Protestant opponents.

Beatty, David, Earl 1871-1936 Admiral, commanded British fleets at Heligoland 1914, Dogger Bank 1915 and Jutland 1916; commanded Grand Fleet 1916-19; First Sea Lord 1919-27.

Beauchamp, Guy de, earl of Warwick 1272-1315 Fought in Edward I's Scottish wars; one of Lords Ordainers 1310-11; assisted in 1312 capture of Piers Gaveston, who had nicknamed him "the Black Dog of Arden".

Beauchamp, Richard de, earl of Warwick 1382-1439 Fought against Percies at Shrewsbury 1403, against Glyndŵr and in France 1415-21. Member of regency council 1422, entrusted with education of Henry VI; lieutenant of France and Normandy 1437-39.

Beaufort, Henry c.1377-1447 Son of John of Gaunt: Bishop of Lincoln 1398, of Winchester 1404; Lord Chancellor 1403-5, 1413-17, 1424-26; a leading member of regency council for Henry VI, rival of Humphrey of Gloucester. Cardinal 1426; attempted to organize crusades against Bohemian Hussites and to negotiate peace with France. Famed for wealth.

Beaufort, Margaret 1443-1509 Wife of Edmund Tudor and mother of Henry VII: a wealthy and influential woman, who promoted piety, learning and new colleges and professorships at Oxford and Cambridge.

Beaverbrook, William Maxwell Aitken, Lord 1879-1964 Canadian-born politician and newspaperman: Conservative MP from 1910, helped Lloyd George to premiership, but disappointed of high office. Developed newspaper empire based on *Daily Express,* founding *Sunday Express* 1921 and buying *Evening Standard* 1923; campaigned for Empire Free Trade; Minister of Aircraft Production 1940-41; post-war champion of Commonwealth trade.

Becket, Thomas 1118-70 Agent of Archbishop Theobald, then Chancellor 1155-62; Archbishop of Canterbury 1162. Resisted Henry II's attempts to bring clergy under jurisdiction of secular courts; in exile 1164-70; after return to England, was murdered in cathedral. Canonized 1173: shrine at Canterbury became centre of pilgrimage.

Bede c.673-735 Monk of Jarrow, influential scholar and writer of biblical commentaries, history, verse, and natural science: modern fame rests on *Ecclesiastical History of the English People* 731, which showed unprecedented grasp of historical method.

Bedford, John of Lancaster, duke of 1389-1435 Son of Henry IV, Regent of France and Protector of England 1422-35. Chiefly occupied in France whilst Humphrey of Gloucester ran England in Henry VI's minority; had Joan of Arc burned at the stake, 1431.

Bentham, Jeremy 1748-1832 Influential political theorist, legal reformer and exponent of utilitarianism: "It is the greatest happiness of the greatest number that is the measure of right and wrong". Distrusted French revolutionaries; advocated parliamentary reform.

Bentinck, Lord George 1802-48 Tory MP from 1828: political ally of Disraeli and leader of protectionists, opposed repeal of corn laws and helped topple Peel 1846.

Bessemer, Sir Henry 1813-98 Developed original processes in metallurgy: invented process (known by his name) for cheap conversion of pig iron into steel; established steel works at Sheffield 1859.

Bevan, Aneurin 1897-1960 Miner, Labour MP from 1929: Minister of Health 1945-51; established National Health Service 1948; Minister of Labour 1951, resigned in protest against financial cuts in social services; led discontented left wing of party; defeated in 1955 leadership election.

Beveridge, William Henry, Lord 1879-1963 Economist, administrator and expert on the problems of poverty and unemployment: his 1942 report formed basis for post-war social reconstruction and national insurance scheme.

Bevin, Ernest 1881-1951 Dockers union leader 1910-21; a founder of Transport and General Workers 1921, General Secretary 1921-40. Labour MP from 1940, Minister of Labour 1940-45; Foreign Secretary 1945-51, involved in post-war European reconstruction and foundation of NATO.

Blackstone, Sir William 1723-80 Jurist, Professor of Law at Oxford from 1758: his *Commentaries on the Laws of England* 1765-69, which gave comprehensive account of laws and constitution of England, was attacked as idealized and partial. MP 1761-70; judge of Common Pleas 1770.

Blake, Robert 1599-1657 MP and Parliamentary military commander in Civil War; naval commander from 1649, member of Council of State 1651-52, and of Barebones Parliament 1653. Led English fleet against Dutch 1652-54, and, more successfully, against Spanish 1656-57; helped create professional navy and develop naval tactics.

Bolingbroke, Henry St John, Viscount 1678-1751 Tory MP from 1701, Secretary for War 1706-8, Secretary of State 1710-14; opposed Hanoverian succession, fled to France 1715 and was impeached. Returned and was pardoned 1723, wrote and intrigued against Walpole.

Bonner, Edmund c.1500-69 Lawyer and diplomat, Bishop of Hereford 1538-39, of London 1539-49, 1553-59; active persecutor of Protestants under Henry VIII and Mary, known (somewhat unfairly) as "Bloody Bonner"; deprived of bishopric and imprisoned 1549 and 1559 for opposing official religious policy.

Booth, William 1829-1912 Revivalist preacher; founded East London Revival Society 1865, reorganized as Salvation Army 1878, offering fundamentalist religion and social welfare: Army spread rapidly in Britain and abroad. *In Darkest England and the Way Out* 1890 propounded his solutions to evils of his time.

Bothwell, Francis Stewart, earl of c.1563-1611 Favourite of James VI, who made him earl 1587, but from 1590 involved in plots against and attempts to seize the king; fled 1595.

Bothwell, James Hepburn, earl of c.1535-78 Unruly Scottish commander and Privy Councillor 1561; won favour of Mary Queen of Scots; implicated in murder of Darnley 1567; divorced his wife and married Mary. On Mary's surrender to opposition 1567, fled to Denmark and was imprisoned until death.

Boudicca d. AD61 On death of husband, King of Iceni, kingdom was plundered by Romans, Boudicca assaulted and her daughters raped; she led revolt that destroyed Colchester, St Albans and London; defeated by Roman governor Paullinus and committed suicide.

Boyle, Richard, earl of Cork 1566-1643 Powerful and unscrupulous Anglo-Irish landowner and official: Privy Councillor for Ireland 1612, Lord Boyle 1616, earl 1620, and Irish Lord Treasurer 1631. Intrigued against Wentworth, and gave evidence at his impeachment.

Bradlaugh, Charles 1833-91 Journalist, political and social reformer, an able and vigorous propagandist: ejected from House of Commons four times 1880-86 for refusing to swear on Bible, being re-elected MP each time, but eventually allowed to retain his seat. Advocated birth control.

Bradwardine, Thomas c.1290-1349 Academic and diplomat, confessor to Edward III, Archbishop of Canterbury 1349; major international scholastic philosopher, known as "Doctor Profundus".

Brian Boru c.926-1014 Son of minor Irish king, defeated Danes of Limerick c.968; became a chief 976, and asserted authority over all Munster and beyond; took Dublin 1000, recognized as High King of Ireland 1002. Continued operations against chiefs who resisted him and the Danes.

Bright, John 1811-89 Lancashire mill-owner, powerful orator, advocate of free trade in campaign to repeal corn laws 1839-46. Radical MP from 1843, supported financial reform and franchise extension; President of Board of Trade 1868-70, Chancellor of Duchy of Lancaster 1873-74, 1880-82.

Brindley, James 1716-72 Engineer on Duke of Bridgewater's canal 1761, constructed Barton aqueduct and miles of underground canals in Worsley coal mines: Bridgewater Canal inspired many others, and Brindley built over 360 miles of canal.

Brougham, Henry Peter, Lord 1778-1868 Energetic and eccentric lawyer, writer: Whig MP 1810-12, 1816-30, Lord Chancellor 1830-34, advocated abolition of slavery, law reform and popular education. Became popular when he defended Queen Caroline at her trial 1820. Helped found Society for the Diffusion of Useful Knowledge 1825, and University College, London 1828.

Brown, Lancelot ("Capability") 1716-83 Developed style of landscape gardening in which expanses of grass, clumps of trees, and stretches of water combined to give balanced naturalism; parks include Warwick Castle c.1750, Blenheim 1765, and Nuneham Courtenay 1778.

Bruce, Edward c.1276-1318 Brother of Robert I the Bruce, campaigned with him and fought at Bannockburn. Led resistance to English in Ireland 1315; crowned High King of Ireland 1316; defeated and killed at Battle of Dundalk.

Bruce, Robert ("the Competitor") 1210-95 Descendant of David I, claimed Scottish throne on death of Margaret 1290 but agreed to accept arbitration of Edward I: prepared to resist unfavourable decision, but old age prevented him and he passed claim to son 1292.

Brunel, Isambard Kingdom 1806-59 Engineer of determination and genius, built some of earliest iron steamships, Clifton suspension bridge 1864, and was chief engineer to Great Western Railway 1833-46.

Buchanan, George 1506-82 In trouble in Scotland and on Continent as Protestant heretic, returned to Scotland 1561 as tutor to Queen Mary: Moderator of General Assembly 1567; involved in Mary's overthrow; tutor to James VI. Historian and political theorist, author of *De Jure Regni* 1579, a defence of limited monarchy.

Buckingham, George Villiers, duke of 1592-1628 Introduced to James I by anti-Spanish faction 1614; viscount 1616, earl 1617, marquis 1618, duke 1623. King's favourite: virtually monopolized patronage, but furthered some administrative reform and influenced foreign policy; organized failed expeditions to Cadiz 1625, La Rochelle 1626, 1627: protected from impeachment by friend Charles I; assassinated.

Buckingham, George Villiers, duke of 1628-87 Son of above, exiled 1648-57 and imprisoned 1658-59 for royalism; Privy Councillor 1662, member of ruling Cabal 1667-74; parliamentary criticism secured dismissal. Profligate and dilettante, interested in arts and sciences.

Buller, Sir Redvers 1839-1908 Soldier in India, China, Canada, Africa and Middle East: won VC in Zulu War 1879; General 1896. As Adjutant General 1890-97, responsible for army reorganization; commanded South African Field Force in 1899-1902 Boer War, but criticized.

Bunyan, John 1628-88 Parliamentarian in Civil War, Baptist preacher from 1657; imprisoned at Bedford 1660-72 for illegal preaching; published *Grace Abounding* 1666, *Pilgrim's Progress* 1678, 1684, and other spiritual works of great force.

Burdett, Sir Francis 1770-1844 Radical MP from 1796, campaigned for parliamentary reform, and against corporal punishment in army; imprisoned 1810 for breach of privilege and 1820 for condemnation of Peterloo massacre. Supported Catholic emancipation and Reform Bill, but defected to Tories 1837.

Burgh, Hubert de, earl of Kent. d. 1243 Served Richard I and John; justiciar 1215; held Dover against French 1216, defeated French fleet off North Foreland 1217; under Henry III, headed opposition to foreign officials in England; justiciar 1228-32, but overthrown by rivals.

Burgoyne, John 1722-92 Served in Portugal, then commanded British troops against American colonists 1777, but was forced to surrender at Saratoga: controversy over whether he or government was responsible for failure, dismissed 1779. Commander in Ireland 1782; playwright.

Burke, Edmund 1727-97 Rockingham Whig MP from 1765: defended constitutional rights of Parliament, opposed war in American colonies; campaigned for administrative reform, abolition of slavery, and Ireland. Political theorist and pamphleteer: broke with Whigs on publishing *Reflections on the French Revolution* 1790, advocating freedom under aristocratic constitution.

Burnet, Gilbert 1643-1715 Glasgow Professor of Divinity 1668, London preacher from 1675; Whig historian and propagandist, exiled 1685-88, returned with William III as chaplain; Bishop of Salisbury 1689; opponent of Catholics but supported concessions to Dissenters.

Burns, Robert 1759-96 First published poetry 1786 with a view to raising money to emigrate from Scotland, but success led him to stay; following the popularity of dialect poetry, wrote mostly songs.

Bute, John Stuart, earl of 1713-92 Close friend of Princess of Wales, influential tutor to her son (future George III); after George's accession, Secretary of State 1761-62, Prime Minister 1762-63. Negotiated Treaty of Paris 1763, but resigned after criticism; retained power in Closet until 1765.

Butler, Josephine Elizabeth 1828-1906 Energetic campaigner for women's education, abolition of state regulation (and thus legalization) of prostitution (achieved 1886), and against "white slave trade"; intensely religious.

Butler, Richard Austen, Lord 1902-1982 Conservative MP 1929-65: minor offices 1932-41, minister of Education 1941-45, framed important 1944 Education Act; Minister of Labour 1945; Chancellor of Exchequer 1951-55; Leader of Commons 1955-61; Home Secretary 1957-62; Foreign Secretary 1963-64. Despite vast ministerial experience, failed to achieve premiership 1957, 1963. Life peer and Master of Trinity College, Cambridge 1965.

Butt, Isaac 1813-79 Irish Protestant lawyer and academic; MP from 1852. Defended Fenian prisoners 1865-69, converted to Irish nationalism. First person to use "Home Rule" as effective slogan; leader of Home Rule party 1871-78.

Byng, George, Viscount Torrington 1664-1733 Naval officer: support for William of Orange 1688 brought important commands in wars against France. Rear-Admiral 1703, Admiral 1708. Thwarted invasion by Pretender 1708; his control of seas vital in defeat of Jacobites 1715.

Defeated Spanish off Cape Passaro 1718. First Lord of Admiralty from 1727.

Byng, John 1704-57 Son of above: unspectacular naval career, until Admiral 1756. Sent to relieve Minorca 1756 he retired without doing so, considering forces insufficient; after public outcry, court marshalled for negligence and shot.

Byrd, William *c.* 1543-1623 Organist of Lincoln Cathedral and Chapel Royal, wrote Anglican church music despite his Catholicism; composed three masses, much other religious music, and was a pioneer of verse anthem and English madrigal.

Byron, George Gordon, Lord 1788-1824 Travelled abroad 1809-11, began to publish poetry 1812 with first part of "Childe Harold's Pilgrimage". Left England 1816 and did not return; contributed money and leadership to Greek struggle for independence.

Cadwaladr ap Gruffudd d. 1172 Welsh prince, son of Gruffudd ap Cynan. Conquered Meirionydd 1121 and Ceredigion 1135-36, but quarrelled with brother Owain, fled to Ireland, and returned with fleet of Danes. Then reconciled with Owain and seized, blinded and ransomed by Danes. Restored by Henry II 1157, but resisted 1165 expedition into Wales.

Cadwallon d. 633 King of Gwynedd: after defeats by Edwin of Northumbria, allied with Penda of Mercia and devastated Northumbria 632. Overthrown and killed by Oswald.

Cadwgan d.1111 Welsh prince, successfully resisted Normans in Wales in 1090s, but failed to save Anglesey 1099; came to terms with the Normans 1100. Murdered in family feud.

Caedmon 7th century According to Bede, was oxherd at Whitby Abbey when he miraculously acquired poetic skills. Versified many passages of Scripture, one of which has survived as oldest English poem.

Caedwalla *c.*659-89 A landless adventurer, who secured the throne of Wessex 685 and quickly subjugated Isle of Wight, Sussex and Kent (although the Kentishmen promptly rebelled). Went to Rome 688, baptized and died there.

Caesar, Julius 102-44 BC Roman general: whilst campaigning in Gaul, crossed to Britain 55 BC, but bad weather forced him to withdraw. He undertook more prolonged campaign 54 BC, defeated Cassivellaunus, forced him to pay tribute and then again withdrew.

Cambridge, George William Frederick Charles, duke of 1819-1904 Cousin of Queen Victoria, Lieutenant-General in Crimean War, General Commanding-in-Chief 1856, and Commander-in-Chief 1887; played important part in army reforms which followed the Crimea, but from 1868 opposed nearly all Cardwell's proposals.

Campbell, Colin, Lord Clyde 1792-1863 Served in Peninsular War, in China 1842-46, in Crimea, and was Commander-in-Chief in India during the Mutiny. A talented commander, respected his men.

Campbell-Bannerman, Sir Henry 1846-1908 Liberal MP from 1868, held junior posts before serving as Secretary for Ireland 1884-85 and for War 1886, 1892-95. Liberal leader 1899, Prime Minister 1905-8. After a landslide victory in 1906 election, passed Trades Disputes Act 1906, Merchant Shipping Act 1907 and granted self-government to colonies in South Africa. Resigned through ill health.

Campion, Edmund 1540-81 Oxford scholar, attended English Catholic college at Douai, became a Jesuit in Rome, and sent to Prague and Brno. With Parsons, conducted first Jesuit mission to England 1580, but was arrested and executed on false charges.

Canning, George 1770-1827 Tory MP from 1794, held junior posts 1796-1801, 1804-6, Foreign Secretary 1807. Fought duel with Castlereagh after arguments over prosecution of Peninsular War 1809, left office and travelled abroad. Secretary of India Board 1816, but resigned in sympathy with Queen Caroline 1821. Foreign Secretary 1822-27; Prime Minister 1827, but ministry dogged by dissention and his failing health.

Canning, Stratford, Viscount Stratford de Redcliffe 1786-1880 Served as diplomat in Turkey, Switzerland, Russia and USA; grasp of Near Eastern affairs gave him important roles in Napoleonic and Crimean Wars. MP 1828-41.

Cantelupe, Thomas d. 1282 Chancellor 1264-65, Bishop of Hereford 1275. Pious and learned, the last Englishman canonized before Reformation.

Caratacus 1st century AD As chief of Catuvellauni, led resistance to Romans in Kent, AD 43; defeated at Medway, fled west and continued resistance among Silures and Ordovices. His fortress was stormed and family captured AD 51. Fled to Brigantes, but Queen Cartimandua surrendered him and he was sent captive to Rome.

Cardigan, James Thomas Brudenell, earl of 1797-1868 MP and army officer: long history of friction with fellow officers compounded the errors which resulted in his leading charge of Light Brigade at Balaclava, 1854. He survived to be acclaimed a popular hero.

Cardwell, Edward, Viscount 1813-86 MP from 1842, in government almost continuously 1852-74. As Secretary for Colonies 1864-66, encouraged colonial self-reliance and ended transportation. As Secretary for War 1868-74, responsible for reforms in army recruitment, organization, and discipline.

Carlyle, Thomas 1795-1881 Influential Scots writer who propounded criticisms of contemporary society and of schemes of reform, making wide use of historical examples. His epic *French Revolution* published 1837.

Carnarvon, Henry Howard Molyneux Herbert, earl of 1831-90 As Conservative Colonial Secretary 1866-67, 1874-78, created Federal Dominion of Canada, but failed with a similar scheme for South Africa. Lord Lieutenant of Ireland 1885-86, negotiated unsuccessfully with Parnell for limited self-government. Scholar and President of Society of Antiquaries 1878-85.

Caroline of Ansbach 1683-1737 Daughter of margrave of Brandenburg-Ansbach, she married future George II 1705, Queen 1727. Relations with both father-in-law George I and eldest son Frederick were strained, but she maintained her influence over her husband and supported Walpole in office.

Caroline of Brunswick 1786-1821 Daughter of duke of Brunswick, married the future George IV 1795, but they separated 1796 after birth of Charlotte, their only child. Excluded from Court and denied access to Charlotte, Caroline embarked on continental tour in which indiscretions gave rise to scandal. Returned 1820 on husband's accession; an attempt to deny her title as Queen and dissolve marriage was abandoned in face of her popular support. Barred from entering Westminster Abbey for husband's coronation, died 19 days later.

Carr (or Kerr), Robert, earl of Somerset c.1586-1645 Accompanied James I to England 1603 as page, went to France, but reappeared at English Court 1607 and rapidly became favourite of James I. Viscount Rochester 1611, earl of Somerset 1613. Replaced in king's favour by George Villiers 1614-15, implicated in the murder of Sir Thomas Overbury. Imprisoned 1616-22.

Carson, Edward, Lord 1854-1935 Dublin lawyer, MP 1892-1921, Leader of Ulster Unionists from 1910. Organized Ulster Volunteer Force 1911, opposed Liberal plans for Home Rule. First Lord of Admiralty in War Cabinet. Resigned 1918 in protest at Lloyd George's Irish policy, Lord of Appeal 1921-29.

Carteret, John, Lord Carteret and Earl Granville 1690-1763 Diplomat 1719-20, Secretary of State 1721-24 and favourite of George I, Lord Lieutenant of Ireland 1724-30. Secretary of State 1742-44. Accused of favouring Hanoverian against British interests. Prime Minister 1746, but unable to form a ministry.

Cartwright, Thomas 1535-1603 Cambridge Puritan Professor of Divinity 1569-70, forced by religious disputes to withdraw from university. Probably wrote presbyterian *Second Admonition to Parliament* 1572, which led him into long controversy with Whitgift. Protected by Leicester, but spent time in exile and in prison, especially after 1590 Star Chamber trial.

Casement, Sir Roger 1864-1916 Member of consular service, reported on conditions of native workers in Congo and Peru. Retired 1912 to devote himself to Irish nationalism: went to Germany 1914 to seek aid and returned by German submarine on eve of Easter Rising. Captured, and hanged as a traitor.

Cassivellaunus 1st century BC Ruler of Catuvellauni; attacked Trinovantes, whose appeal to Rome for assistance was occasion of Caesar's 54 BC invasion. His stronghold, probably in Hertfordshire, was taken, and he came to terms with Romans.

Castlereagh, Robert Stewart, Viscount 1769-1822 Secretary for Ireland 1798-1801, and promoted union with Great Britain, but resigned when George III blocked Catholic emancipation. War Secretary 1805-6, 1807-9, but conduct of war made him unpopular and brought a duel with Canning. Foreign Secretary

1812-22. Favoured peace through a congress system and an alliance of conservative states. Committed suicide.

Catherine of Aragon 1485-1536 Daughter of Ferdinand and Isabella of Spain, married Prince Arthur 1501, but Arthur died 1502; married Henry VIII 1509. Failure to produce male heir, political machinations and attractions of Anne Boleyn led Henry to seek divorce 1527; withheld by pope, it was granted by an English court 1533. One surviving child, future Mary I.

Catherine of Braganza 1638-1705 Portuguese princess, married Charles II 1662: no children. Her Roman Catholicism led to an unsuccessful attempt to implicate her in Popish Plot. Left England 1692.

Catherine of Valois 1401-37 Daughter of Charles VI of France, married Henry V in 1420 at conclusion of Henry's French war: mother of Henry VI. After Henry's death in 1422, secretly married Owen Tudor, from which match descended House of Tudor.

Catherine Howard *c.*1521-42 Grand-daughter of duke of Norfolk, who promoted her at Court and in affections of Henry VIII: married Henry 1540. Her indiscretions before and after marriage were used by factions at Court to destroy her, and she was executed.

Catherine Parr 1512-48 Widowed twice before she became Henry VIII's sixth wife 1543. She was a beneficial influence on Henry's children, and her tolerant Protestantism was followed by Elizabeth. Married Thomas Seymour 1547.

Caxton, William *c.*1422-91 Merchant at Bruges, then learnt printing and issued first books at Cologne from 1474. Returned to England 1476, and published first book printed in England 1477. Established his press at Westminster, and published nearly eighty volumes.

Cecil, Robert, earl of Salisbury 1563-1612 Son of William Cecil, groomed by him as successor. Elizabeth's Secretary of State 1596; smoothness of the accession of House of Stuart owed much to him. Lord Treasurer 1608-12, responsible for 1608 Book of Rates and abortive 1610 Great Contract, but his influence on James waned in face of more prepossessing younger men.

Cecil, William, Lord Burghley 1520-98 Held political office under Edward VI and Mary; Elizabeth's Secretary of State 1558-

72, Lord Treasurer 1572-98: worked in close harmony with her. Supported a comprehensive Church while favouring stern measures against recusants; and Church reform while resisting presbyterianism. In foreign policy, was conscious of threat of Catholic powers, but sensitive to complexities of international politics. Urged execution of Mary Queen of Scots, and that Elizabeth should marry.

Cenwulf d.821 Succeeded Offa's son and ruled Mercia from 796: pre-eminent among kings of southern England. Attempted to remove the southern archbishopric from Canterbury to London; raided Wales.

Cerdic d.534 Regarded as founder of West Saxon dynasty in England. According to *Anglo-Saxon Chronicle,* King of Wessex: probably led Saxon invasion up Southampton Water to establish kingdom to south and west of middle Thames.

Chadwick, Sir Edwin 1800-90 Friend of Jeremy Bentham, whose utilitarian ideas he applied to social reform: was,inspiration behind Poor Law Amendment Act 1834, which created the Poor Law Commission (of which he was secretary). Report *The Sanitary Condition of the Labouring Population* 1842 prepared way for the Public Health Act 1848, which created Board of Health: he was one of commissioners. The board was abolished 1854; Chadwick did not hold important public office again.

Chamberlain, Sir J. Austen 1863-1937 Son of Joseph and half-brother of Neville: MP from 1892, held minor offices. Chancellor of Exchequer 1903-5, contender for Conservative leadership 1911, Secretary of State for India 1915-17, member of War Cabinet 1918. Chancellor of Exchequer 1919-21, Conservative leader 1921-22; ousted when Conservative support withdrawn from Lloyd George's coalition. Foreign Secretary 1924-29, negotiated Locarno pact 1925. Declined office after 1931, but continued to exercise influence.

Chamberlain, Joseph 1836-1914 Mayor of Birmingham 1873-75: furthered municipal reform and transformed local politics. Radical Liberal MP from 1876, President of Board of Trade 1880-85, of Local Government Board 1886. Resigned on Gladstone's conversion to Home Rule, and led Liberal Unionists into alliance with Conservatives. Secretary of State for Colonies from 1895, but resigned 1903 to campaign against free trade and for imperial preference, which split the party.

Chamberlain, A. Neville 1869-1940 Son of Joseph and half-brother of Austen: Conservative MP from 1918, Postmaster General 1922; Minister of Health 1923, 1924-29, Chancellor of Exchequer 1923-24, 1931-37; Prime Minister 1937-40. Attempted to halt deteriorating relations with Germany and Italy and negotiated Munich agreement 1938. Gave guarantee to Poland 1939, declared war on Germany when Poland was invaded 1939. Resigned when he lost support on fall of Norway 1940. Briefly member of Churchill's War Cabinet.

Chancellor, Richard d. 1556 Pilot on Sir Hugh Willoughby's 1553 expedition to find north-east passage to India, became separated from companions, reached White Sea and went overland to Moscow. Negotiated important trade agreement with Ivan IV; wrote an account of Russia,

Charles I 1600-49 Second son of James I: heir on death of brother 1612, succeeded to throne 1625. Married Henrietta Maria of France 1625. Encountered reluctance of Parliament to grant money for his expensive foreign policy in time of economic depression. Ruled without Parliament 1629-40 but used unpopular financial expedients. Forced to call "Short" and "Long" Parliaments by expense of Bishops' Wars 1640; policy and ministers attacked by Parliament, and with mistrust on both sides the breach became irreparable: Civil War began 1642. Taken by Scots at Newark 1646, but handed over to Parliamentarians. Negotiated Engagement with Scots, promising to establish presbyterianism in return for Scottish support. But after Scots defeat 1648, Charles was tried for treason, and executed.

Charles II 1630-85 Son of Charles I: after father's execution attempted to recover Crown with support from Scotland; fled abroad after defeat at Worcester 1651. His return as king in 1660 was organized by Monck; married Catherine of Braganza 1662; no legitimate children, but at least 14 illegitimate. Attempted to secure toleration for religious dissidents, and followed pro-French foreign policy; provoked distrust, hence Popish Plot and Exclusion crisis. Died a Roman Catholic.

Chaucer, Geoffrey *c.*1340-1400 Held a number of official posts, travelled on Continent: his earlier poems show French and Italian influence. His most famous poem, *The Canterbury Tales* was conceived *c.*1387 and is a collection of stories as if retold by pilgrims on their way to Canterbury.

Chesterfield, Philip Dormer Stanhope, earl of 1694-1773 Critic of Walpole and Hanoverian interest, Lord Lieutenant of Ireland 1745-46 Secretary of State 1746-48. Responsible for 1751 calendar reform. Wrote famous *Letters to his Son* on life in fashionable society.

Chichele, Henry c.1362-1443 Used as diplomat by Henry IV, Bishop of St David's 1408, Archbishop of Canterbury 1414; helped administer country in absence of Henry V. Careful Church administrator and persecutor of Lollards, but some conflict with Rome over limits to papal authority. Founded All Souls' College, Oxford.

Churchill, Lord Randolph 1849-95 Son of Duke of Marlborough: Conservative MP from 1874, but independent and leader of "Fourth Party". Built up Conservative clubs. Secretary for India 1885-86, Chancellor of Exchequer 1886: resigned in face of opposition to defence cuts in budget. Subsequently travelled in South Africa.

Churchill, Sir Winston 1874-1965 Son of Randolph. Entered army and served in India 1897 and Sudan 1898. Worked as correspondent in South Africa in Second Boer War 1899-1902. Conservative MP 1902 but joined Liberals 1904 through support for free trade. President of Board of Trade 1908-10, Home Secretary 1910-11, First Lord of Admiralty 1911-15: left government after failure of Dardanelles landing 1915. Minister of Munitions 1917, Secretary for War 1918, Colonial Secretary 1921-22. Returned to Conservatives 1924, unsuccessful Chancellor of Exchequer 1924-29. Advocated measures to combat German menace in 1930s. First Lord of Admiralty 1939, Prime Minister 1940-45, 1951-55. An outstanding war leader, forged alliance with USA and USSR which defeated Axis.

Clare, Gilbert de, earl of Hertford and Gloucester 1243-95 Member of baronial party at Oxford Parliament 1258, refused allegiance to Prince Edward 1263, took arms with Simon de Montfort. Reconciled with Henry III, acted as mediator between king and rebels; proclaimed Edward I king 1272. Married Edward's daughter 1290.

Clare, Richard de, earl of Pembroke and Striguil ("Strongbow") d. 1176 Invaded Ireland at behest of dethroned Dermot MacMurrough, 1170: stormed Waterford and Dublin. Created his own Irish fief in Leinster.

Clarence, George, duke of 1449-78 Son of Richard, duke of York, brother of Edward IV and Richard III. Taken to Flanders for safety after the Battle of Wakefield 1460, returned on accession of Edward IV 1461. Lord Lieutenant of Ireland 1462-69. Married daughter of Warwick the Kingmaker 1469, and with Warwick deposed Edward 1470. But helped to reinstate Edward 1471, though continued friction between brothers resulted in his arrest and murder.

Clarendon, Edward Hyde, earl of 1609-74 MP in Short and Long Parliaments and critic of Charles I's personal rule, but reacted against radicals and became one of King's closest advisers and leader of constitutional royalists. Went into exile 1646. As Charles II's chief adviser, helped to negotiate Restoration. Lord Chancellor and Charles II's chief minister 1660-67, earl of Clarendon 1661. Fell with mishandling of Second Dutch War, and went again into exile. Author of *History of the Rebellion*, written during exiles.

Clifford, Thomas, Lord 1630-73 MP from 1660, Roman Catholic member of Charles II's Cabal; privy to secret clauses in Treaty of Dover 1670. Lord Treasurer 1672, but forced to resign under Test Act 1673; died shortly afterwards.

Clinton, Sir Henry 1730-95 Fought with distinction at Bunker Hill 1775. Commander-in-Chief in North America 1778, but resigned 1781 after errors of judgement and quarrel with Cornwallis. MP 1772-84, 1790-94, and Governor of Limerick and Gibraltar.

Clive, Robert, Lord 1725-74 Worked as clerk for East India Company in Madras. Served in Company's army and won renown with victories at Arcot 1751 and Plassey 1757. Governor of Madras 1756, and of Company's Bengal possessions 1757-60. Returned to England 1760, hoping for political career; as Governor of Bengal 1765-66 carried out administrative reforms. Forced back to England by ill health. His financial probity the subject of parliamentary inquiry 1772-73. Cleared, but committed suicide under influence of drugs and depression.

Cnut c.994-1035 Accompanied Svein Estrithson to England 1013, divided English kingdom with Edward II Ironside 1016. King of England 1016-35; King of Denmark 1019-35; effective ruler of Norway from 1028: rule of England marked by domestic peace, a concern for law and patronage of Church.

Cobbett, William 1762-1835 From 1802 published number of political newspapers and journals, advocating radical democratic Tory viewpoint. His activities earned official denunciation and imprisonment. His *Rural Rides* describes the England of his day with a medieval nostalgia.

Cobden, Richard 1804-65 Textile manufacturer in Manchester; leader with John Bright of Anti-Corn Law League 1839-46. MP from 1841. Advocacy of repeal helped to convert Peel. Campaigned for peace and free trade. Declined political office.

Coke, Sir Edward 1552-1634 Lawyer, MP from 1589, Solicitor General 1592, Speaker of House of Commons 1593, Attorney General 1594. Prosecuted Essex 1601, Raleigh 1603, and Gunpowder Plotters 1606; Chief Justice of Common Pleas 1606, Chief Justice of King's Bench and Privy Councillor 1613. Championed common law against prerogative courts; antagonized James, who dismissed him 1616. MP from 1621, and continued to oppose royal prerogative over monopolies, extra-parliamentary taxation, and illegal imprisonment. Author of important law books, *Reports* and *Institutes*.

Colet, John c.1466-1519 Studied at Oxford, Paris and in Italy, taught theology at Oxford, where he developed critical humanist approach to the Bible. Close friend of More and Erasmus, preached against Church abuses. Dean of St Paul's 1505-19, founder of St Paul's School.

Collingwood, Cuthbert, Lord 1750-1810 His career followed closely that of friend Nelson: fought at Cape St Vincent 1797, took command at Trafalgar 1805 after Nelson's death. Subsequently employed safeguarding British interests in Mediterranean.

Collins, Michael 1890-1922 Member of Irish Republican Brotherhood, active in Easter Rising 1916. Minister of Finance in Sinn Fein government 1919-21. Helped to negotiate Anglo-Irish Treaty 1921. Chairman of transitional government, but assassinated by republicans opposed to the Free State.

Columba c.521-97 Established churches in Ireland, then c.563 founded monastery on Iona and began conversion of Scottish mainland. Canonized.

Compton, Henry 1632-1713 Ordained 1662 after brief army service. Bishop of

Oxford 1674, London 1675. Suspended by James II for opposition to religious policy, and was a signatory of invitation to William of Orange 1688; crowned William and Mary. Disappointed at not being offered archbishopric of Canterbury, he increasingly withdrew from public affairs.

Comyn, John the Black, Lord of Badenoch d.c.1303 Scottish magnate of great wealth and influence, one of six Guardians of Scotland named for minority of Maid of Norway 1286. Claimed throne 1290, but then supported John Balliol, whose sister he had married.

Comyn, John the Red, Lord of Badenoch d.1306 Son of John the Black: supporter of John Balliol, his uncle. One of three Guardians of Scotland after Battle of Falkirk 1298. Rival claimant of throne to Robert Bruce, who murdered him.

Constable, John 1776-1837 The most notable English landscape painter of his day. Chose unexceptional subjects and aimed for a naturalism shorn of affectation.

Constantine d.820 Became King of the Picts by dethroning Conall in c.789, and probably extended his authority over Dál Riáta after 811.

Constantine I d. c.877 Son of Kenneth MacAlpin and nephew of Donald I, King of Scotia c.862-c.877. His reign was marked by Viking incursions and he was killed in battle against them.

Constantine II d. 952 King of Scotia from 900, and was first king to exercise authority south of the Forth. Early in reign, preoccupied repelling Viking attacks. Joined alliance of kings against Athelstan of England 937, but decisively beaten at Brunanburh. Constantine abdicated and retired to a monastery 943.

Constantine III d. 997 Became King of Scotia 995, possibly through procuring murder of Kenneth II. He was then murdered, perhaps at instigation of successor Kenneth III.

Cook, Captain James 1728-79 Made name as seaman in Canada, commander of three voyages to Pacific which greatly extended geographical knowledge, particularly of Australia and New Zealand. Devised a diet to combat scurvy. Killed by Hawaiian natives.

Coote, Sir Eyre 1726-83 Served against Jacobites 1745, and then with great effect under Clive in India. After period in England, returned to India, and was Commander-in-Chief from 1777.

Cornwallis, Charles, Marquis 1738-1805 General in American War of Independence, achieved some success prior to surrender at Yorktown 1781. Governor General in India 1786-93, where he undertook judicial and financial reforms. Diplomat in Brussels 1794. Lord Lieutenant of Ireland 1798-1801, where he suppressed 1798 rebellion. Helped to negotiate Peace of Amiens 1801-2. Reappointed Governor of India, but died on arrival.

Cosgrave, William Thomas 1880-1965 Co-founder of Sinn Fein 1905, active in Easter Rising 1916. Sinn Fein MP 1918 and Minister for Local Government 1919-21. Accepted Anglo-Irish Treaty 1921. Chairman of Provisional Government, first President of Executive Council of Irish Free State 1922-32. Led opposition Fine Gael party 1933-44. His son Liam was Prime Minister 1973-77.

Courtenay, William c.1342-96 Chancellor of Oxford 1367, Bishop of Hereford 1370, of London 1375, Archbishop of Canterbury 1381. Opponent of Wycliff and John of Gaunt, called Blackfriars Council 1382, at which Wycliff's doctrines were condemned.

Coverdale, Miles 1488-1568 Augustinian friar, fled abroad to avoid prosecution for heresy, and there completed work of Tyndale and published first complete English Bible 1535. Bishop of Exeter 1551-53, in exile under Mary, declined reinstatement as bishop under Elizabeth.

Cranfield, Lionel, earl of Middlesex 1575-1645 Merchant and financier, tax official from 1613; Privy Councillor 1620, Lord Treasurer 1621. Attempted to restrict royal expenditure: impeached in 1624.

Cranmer, Thomas 1489-1556 Early Cambridge Protestant, employed by Henry VIII in efforts to obtain divorce; secretly married 1532. Archbishop of Canterbury 1533, annulled Henry's marriage. With Cromwell, promoted measures of Church reform in 1530s. In Edward VI's reign advanced Protestant Reformation and issued English prayer books 1549, 1552. Burnt for heresy under Mary.

Cripps, Sir Richard Stafford 1889-1952 Lawyer, Solicitor General 1930, Labour MP from 1931; declined to join National Government 1931. Expelled from Labour party 1939 for advocacy of popular front including communists. Diplomat and cabinet minister under Churchill. Re-admitted to Labour party 1945, President of Board of Trade 1945-47. Chancellor of Exchequer, with policy of austerity, 1947-50. Resigned through ill health.

Cromwell, Oliver 1599-1658 Huntingdonshire squire, MP from 1628. A skilled cavalry commander, his Civil War victories and creation of New Model Army gave him leadership of Parliamentarian cause. Defeated Scots fighting for Charles I at Preston, 1648, subjugated Ireland 1649, defeated Scots at Dunbar 1650 and Prince Charles at Worcester 1651. Forcibly dissolved Rump Parliament 1653, and became Lord Protector, but attempts to secure a stable constitutional settlement failed.

Cromwell, Richard 1626-1712 Eldest son of Oliver, with little experience of public life when nominated father's successor as Protector 1658. Unenthusiastic for office and abdicated 1659. Went into exile 1660; returned c.1680 to live in retirement.

Cromwell, Thomas, earl of Essex c.1485-1540 After varied career as merchant and soldier, entered service of Wolsey. MP from 1523, survived Wolsey's fall, Privy Councillor 1531 and later Henry VIII's chief minister. Responsible for legislation which separated English Church from Rome and provided Henry VIII with his divorce 1532-34. Promoted ecclesiastical, social, financial and administrative reforms. Fell from favour and executed 1540.

Cumberland, William Augustus, duke of 1721-65 Son of George II. Served as unsuccessful commander in War of Austrian Succession and Seven Years War. Defeated Jacobites at Culloden 1746, and became known as "the Butcher" because of atrocities which followed.

Cunedda fl. early 5th century Migrated with his kin from south-east Scotland to north Wales to defend area against invaders from Ireland. Welsh princely dynasties claimed descent from him: the preservation and development of his legend probably owed much to later political alliances between British kingdoms.

Cunobelinus d.c. AD 40-43 King of Catuvellauni from c.AD 10, extended his control to other tribes in south-east, including Trinovantes, into whose territory at Colchester he moved his capital. Avoided conflict with Romans: death probably helped to precipitate Roman invasion.

Curzon, George Nathaniel, Marquis 1859-1925 Conservative MP from 1886: served as junior minister and developed interest in Indian affairs. Viceroy of India 1898-1905: period of office marked by administrative reforms and ceremonial splendour. Lord Privy Seal 1915-16, Foreign Secretary 1919-24.

Cuthbert d.687 Celtic monk at Melrose, then settled in Lindisfarne 644, where he adopted some Roman usages; lived as hermit on Farne Island 676-84; reluctantly Bishop of Lindisfarne 685-87. Renowned as preacher and for simplicity of his life. Canonized.

Dafydd ap Gruffudd d. 1283 Son of Gruffudd ap Llywelyn. After quarrel with his brother Llywelyn, withdrew to England where he was maintained by Edward I, precipitating war between Edward and Llywelyn 1276. After Llywelyn's surrender, Dafydd deserted Edward and reopened hostilities 1282. Captured by English and executed.

Dafydd ap Llywelyn c.1208-46 Son of Llywelyn ap Iowerth and Joan, illegitimate daughter of King John. Defeated his illegitimate half-brother Gruffudd for Gwynedd succession 1240; recognized as prince by, but subsequently at war with, Henry III.

Dalhousie, James Ramsay, marquis of 1812-60 MP and minister before being appointed Governor-General of India 1847: promoted industry and commerce with construction of railway and telegraph network, and social reforms including abolition of *sati*. Annexed former protectorates. His westernization was a cause of Indian Mutiny.

Dalrymple, James, Viscount Stair 1619-95 Taught philosophy at Glasgow University 1641-47, lawyer. Negotiated with Charles II terms of return to Scotland 1649-50. Advised Monck prior to Restoration. Uneasy under Charles II, went into exile after Test Act 1681. Returned with William of Orange and became William III's leading agent in Scotland. His *Institutions of the Law of Scotland* (1681) was an important codification of Scottish law.

Dalrymple, John, earl of Stair 1648-1707 Son of above: imprisoned after father fled to Netherlands, subsequently served James II

and William III as Lord Advocate. Hostile to MacDonalds and implicated in Glencoe massacre. A commissioner in negotiations for Union of 1707.

Dalton, Hugh, Lord 1887-1962 Academic and Labour MP from 1924. Refused to serve in National Government 1931, held offices in Churchill's wartime coalition. Chancellor of Exchequer 1945-47, but forced to resign for leaking budget secrets. Subsequently held other ministerial offices.

Danby, Thomas Osborne, earl of; duke of Leeds 1632-1712 MP from 1665: joined attack on Clarendon. Lord Treasurer and Charles II's chief minister, 1673-79. Attempted to manage House of Commons to own political and financial advantage. During Exclusion and Popish Plot crises, impeached for duplicity of his foreign policy and imprisoned 1679-84. Opposed James and welcomed William of Orange: William's chief minister 1690-95, when he was once more accused of corruption and resigned.

Darnley, Henry Stuart, Lord 1545-67 An attractive but weak courtier: married Mary Queen of Scots 1565. His unreliability resulted in estrangement; jealous of Mary's secretary Riccio, and took part in his murder 1566. Was himself murdered 1567.

Darwin, Charles Robert 1809-82 Sailed as naturalist on *Beagle* 1831-36. Observations led to his formulation of theory of evolution published in 1859 as *The Origin of Species*. The book gave rise to major intellectual debate and had consequences in areas beyond biology.

David (or **Dewi**) **6th century** Son of British chief, founded a number of monasteries. His chief residence as abbot-bishop became St David's. Patron saint of Wales.

David I c.1084-1153 Son of Malcolm III, King of Scots 1124-53. Reign marked by increasing Norman influences at Court, in government, and in country. Defeated at Battle of Standard 1138, when intervening in England on behalf of Matilda. Generous to Church.

David II 1324-71 King of Scots 1329-71, taken to France to evade Edward Balliol 1334, returned 1341. Invaded England but defeated at Battle of Neville's Cross 1346. Imprisoned in England until 1357.

Davies, Richard c.1501-81 Welsh Protestant scholar, in exile at Geneva in

Mary's reign. Bishop of St Asaph 1560, of St David's 1561. Helped in preparation of Salesbury's Welsh Bible 1567 and revised Bishop's Bible 1568.

Davison, William d.1608 Elizabethan diplomat, especially responsible for negotiations with Dutch. Secretary of State 1586, but Elizabeth's scapegoat for execution of Mary Queen of Scots, and disgraced.

Davitt, Michael 1846-1906 Member of Irish Fenian brotherhood, imprisoned for nationalist activities 1870-77, 1881-82, 1883. Organizer of Irish Land League 1879. MP 1882 (while in gaol), 1892 and 1895.

Davy, Sir Humphrey 1778-1829 Experimented with effects of electricity and developed the process of electrolysis by which he was able to isolate several new elements. Devised a miners' safety lamp. President of Royal Society 1820-29.

Dee, John 1527-1608 Welsh astrologer, alchemist and mathematician of European reputation. Imprisoned under Mary but held in some regard by Elizabeth I.

Defoe, Daniel 1660-1731 In political writings, supported Revolution of 1688 and War of the Spanish Succession, but satirical pamphlets were condemned and brought imprisonment. Wrote novels, including *Robinson Crusoe* 1719, and the topographical *Tour through the whole Island of Britain* 1724-27.

Derby, Edward George Stanley, earl of 1799-1869 MP from 1822, held office in both Whig and Tory administrations: Under-Secretary for War 1827-28, Secretary for Ireland 1830-33, Secretary for Colonies 1833-34 (promoted abolition of slavery) and 1841-45. Opposed Peel on free trade, Tory leader from 1846. Prime Minister 1852, 1858-59, and 1866-68; carried the Reform Bill of 1867. Orator and Greek scholar.

Derby, Edward Henry Stanley, earl of 1826-93 Son of above: Conservative MP from 1848, Secretary for India 1858-59, Foreign Secretary 1866-68, 1874-78. Resigned 1870 over Eastern Question, joined Liberals 1880. Colonial Secretary 1882-85. Opposed Gladstone on Home Rule 1886, and became leader of Liberal Unionists in Lords 1886-91.

Derby, Thomas Stanley, earl of c.1435-1504 Married Margaret Beaufort c.1482. At Bosworth 1485 betrayed Richard III to ensure victory and accession of stepson Henry VII; rewarded with earldom.

Dermot MacMurrough *c*.1110-71 King of Leinster 1126-71, but driven out by Rory O'Connor 1166. Secured aid of Richard de Clare, who restored him to his throne 1170. Succeeded following year by de Clare.

Despenser, Henry le *c*.1341-1406 Bishop of Norwich 1370, but active militarily: helped to suppress Peasants' Revolt 1381, and led "crusade" in Flanders against antipope Clement VII 1383. Remained loyal to Richard II and was imprisoned.

Despenser, Hugh le, the Elder, earl of Winchester 1262-1326 Served Edward I, favourite of Edward II: virtually controlled government 1320, but banished with son 1321. Returned and made earl of Winchester 1322. Captured and executed by Queen Isabella and Roger de Mortimer 1326.

Despenser, Hugh le, the Younger *d*.1326 Son of Hugh le Despenser the Elder, and favourite of Edward II. With father, banished and recalled 1321-22: defeat of opposition left him without rival in kingdom. Fled on the return of Isabella and Mortimer, but taken and executed.

De Valera, Eamon 1882-1975 Participated in Easter Rising 1916; condemned to death but reprieved 1917. Leader of Sinn Fein and MP 1917-26. President of Provisional Government 1919-22. Rejected Anglo-Irish treaty 1921. Founded Fianna Fail party 1926, won 1932 election, president of Executive Council 1932-37. Prime Minister 1937-48, 1951-54, 1957-59; President 1959-73.

Devonshire, Spencer Compton Cavendish, marquis of Hartington, duke of 1833-1908 Liberal MP 1857-68, 1869-91. Secretary for War 1866, 1882-85, Postmaster General 1868-71, Secretary for Ireland 1871-74, Liberal leader 1875-80. Secretary for India 1880-82. Opposed Irish Home Rule and left Liberals 1886; President of Council in Conservative and Unionist cabinets 1895-1903.

Devonshire, William Cavendish, duke of 1641-1707 Committed Protestant and opponent of Court under Charles II and James II; welcomed William of Orange 1688, by whom he was entrusted with various offices and created duke 1694. Also served Anne.

Dickens, Charles 1812-70 Journalist, but turned to novels with *Pickwick Papers*, begun 1836. Followed by *Oliver Twist* 1837-38 and many others. Attempted to alert readers to degradation of contemporary living and working conditions and to iniquities in poor law and education.

Digges, Sir Dudley 1583-1639 Prominent in East India Company, MP from 1621. Prosecuted Buckingham 1626, helped to frame Petition of Right 1628, but reconciled to Court and became Master of Rolls 1636.

Dilke, Sir Charles Wentworth 1843-1911 Vigorous advocate of imperial expansion and radical domestic reform. Liberal MP 1868-86, 1892-1911. Under-secretary at Foreign Office 1880-82, President of Local Government Board 1882-85. Scandal in private life terminated ministerial career.

Dillon, John 1851-1927 Irish nationalist, MP 1880-83, 1885-1918. Turned against Parnell 1890, and led United Nationalist Party until superseded by Redmond 1900.

Disraeli, Benjamin, earl of Beaconsfield 1804-81 Jewish, but was baptized 1817. Flamboyant and opportunistic Conservative MP from 1837. Leader of Young England group, whose principles found expression in his political novels. Opposed Peel on corn law repeal 1846. Chancellor of Exchequer 1852, 1858, 1866-68. Responsible for 1867 Reform Act. Prime Minister 1868, led opposition 1868-74, Prime Minister 1874-80. His ministry espoused moderate social reform and an activist foreign policy.

Donald III Bane *c*.1031-1100 Seized Scottish throne on death of brother Malcolm III Canmore 1093, but deposed by Malcolm's son Duncan II after six months; king again six months later, on Duncan's murder. Deposed 1097 by another of Malcolm's sons, Edgar, assisted by Edgar's English uncle Edgar the Aetheling. Blinded and died in prison.

Donne, John 1572-1631 Held official posts before entering Church 1615. Dean of St Paul's 1621, and notable preacher. The first of the Metaphysical poets, his verse combines harshness and wit, passion and urbanity.

Douglas, Sir Archibald *c*.1296-1333 Defeated Edward Balliol 1332 to become Regent of Scotland 1333, in minority of David II, but killed at Halidon Hill.

Douglas, Archibald, earl of Angus, *c*.1449-1513/14 Led noble attack on favourites of James III, and briefly took James prisoner 1482. Intrigued with Albany and Edward IV 1483, and with Henry VII 1491. Chancellor of Scotland 1493-98.

Douglas, Archibald, earl of Angus *c*.1489-1557 Married Margaret Tudor, mother of James V of Scotland 1514; appointed to Council of Regency 1517, exiled to France 1520. Returned 1524 and contested custody of James V with Margaret and others. Margaret divorced him and he fled to England 1528. Returned 1542 on James's death, and held military commands against England.

Douglas, Sir James ("the Good") *c*.1286-1330 Vigorous supporter of Robert I the Bruce: a commander at Bannockburn, 1314, and leader of raids into England. Killed fighting Moors in Spain.

Dowding, Hugh, Lord 1882-1970 Artillery officer then air squadron commander in First World War. Subsequently responsible for 1930s build-up of Fighter Command and development of Spitfire and Hurricane. Organized fighter defences in Battle of Britain 1940.

Drake, Sir Francis *c*.1543-96 Undertook privateering voyages to Spanish Main 1566-68 and West Indies 1570-73. First Englishman to circumnavigate the globe 1577-80. Renewed raids on West Indies 1585-86, and attacked Spanish fleet in Cadiz 1587. Helped defeat Armada 1588. Led unsuccessful Lisbon expedition 1589.

Dryden, John 1631-1700 Came to prominence 1659-60 with poems lamenting Cromwell's death and then celebrating Restoration. Poet Laureate 1667. Published political satires on Whigs and in defence of Anglicanism, especially 1681 "Absalom and Achitophel". Roman Catholic after accession of James II, and lost offices under William III.

Dudley, Lord Guildford *d*.1554 Son of duke of Northumberland, married by father to Lady Jane Grey 1553: on failure of attempt to make Jane queen, he was tried and sentenced to death, but sentence not carried out until after Wyatt's rebellion.

Duncan I *c*.1010-40 King of Strathclyde from *c*.1016, and when in 1034 he succeeded his grandfather, Malcolm II, as King of Scots the kingdom of Scotland was created. Fought Earl Thorfinn of Orkney. Defeated besieging Durham 1035. Murdered by Macbeth who then succeeded him.

Duncan II *c*.1060-94 Eldest son of Malcolm III, probably in England 1072-94.

With Norman help he defeated uncle Donald III Bane to gain throne 1094, but murdered by Donald six months later.

Duncan of Camperdown, Adam, Viscount 1731-1804 Admiral 1795, Commander-in-Chief North Sea 1795-1801. Defeated Dutch off Camperdown 1797.

Dundas, Henry, Viscount Melville 1742-1811 Scottish lawyer, Lord Advocate 1775. MP from 1774, held ministerial office from 1782 and was a leading ally of Pitt, but career terminated 1805 by accusations of misappropriating Admiralty funds.

Dunstan c.925-88 A monk, councillor to Edmund I, Abbot of Glastonbury c.940. Treasurer and adviser to Edred, but banished by Edwy 956. Recalled by Edgar, Bishop of Worcester 957, of London 959, Archbishop of Canterbury 960. Responsible with Oswald and Aethelwold for rejuvenation of English Church and monastic life. Canonized.

Durham, John George Lambton, earl of 1792-1840 Whig MP 1813-28, Lord Privy Seal 1830-33. Ambassador to Russia 1832, 1835-37, Governor General of Canada 1838. Provoked opposition in Canada and was recalled, but his *Report on the Affairs of British North America* 1839 later formed the basis of much British colonial administration.

Eden, Sir Anthony, earl of Avon 1897-1977 Conservative MP 1923-57. Foreign Secretary 1935-38, but resigned over Appeasement. Dominions Secretary 1939-40, Foreign Secretary again 1940-45, 1951-55. Natural successor to Churchill as Prime Minister 1955; resigned after Suez crisis 1957.

Edgar 943-75 Younger son of Edmund I, succeeded Edwy as King of Mercians and Northumbrians 957, King of England 959: crowned as first king of all England at Bath 973. Established relations with Kenneth of Scotland and with the Emperor Otto the Great. Patronized reforms of Dunstan and carried out administrative reforms.

Edgar the Aetheling 1053-c.1125 Grandson of Edmund II Ironside, chosen king 1066 by Witenagemot on death of Harold II at Hastings. Unable to make good his claim, submitted to William. Underwent periods of exile. Helped to dethrone Donald III Bane 1097 and fought for Duke Robert against Henry I in 1106.

Edmund I 921-46 Son of Edward the Elder, half brother and successor of Athelstan. King of England 939-46, faced Viking invasion 940 and only regained north 944. Conquered Strathclyde 945. Murdered by robber. Patron of Dunstan.

Edmund II Ironside c.993-1016 Son of Aethelred II, on whose death he was declared king in London 1016. His title was disputed by Cnut, who defeated him at Ashingdon. Died in uncertain circumstances.

Edred d. 955 Son of Edward the Elder, succeeded brother Edmund as King of England 946. Fought for control of Northumbria, which he achieved with expulsion of Eric Bloodaxe 954.

Edward I 1239-1307 Son of Henry III: helped formulate Provisions of Westminster 1259; defeated de Montfort at Evesham 1265, King of England 1272-1307. Reign marked by expansionist wars in Wales 1277, 1282-83, 1294-95, and Scotland from 1296; and by significant legal and administrative reforms.

Edward II 1284-1327 Son of Edward I: first English Prince of Wales 1301, King of England 1307-27. Reign disrupted by his reliance on favourites Piers Gaveston and Hugh le Despenser the Younger; prestige further undermined by his defeat at Bannockburn 1314. Baronial opposition, led by wife Isabella of France and Roger de Mortimer, secured his deposition and murder.

Edward III 1312-77 Son of Edward II, King 1327-77, personal rule began 1330. Restored respect for Crown, especially by military achievements. Re-opened Scottish wars 1332. Initiated war with France 1337, claimed French throne 1340: met with initial spectacular success (Sluys 1340, Crécy 1346, Poitiers 1356) but after campaign of 1359-60 renounced claim in return for concessions. Senile in later years.

Edward IV 1442-83 Son of Richard, duke of York. Defeated Lancastrian forces at Mortimer's Cross and Towton 1461; deposed Henry VI. King of England 1461-70, 1471-83. Marriage 1464 to Elizabeth Wydeville and favour to her relations drove Warwick to depose him 1470, but regained his throne 1471. Invaded France 1475, but withdrew in return for French subsidies.

Edward V 1470-83 Son of Edward IV, succeeded as King April 1483. Declared illegitimate by uncle Richard duke of Gloucester and deposed June 1483. Imprisoned with younger brother in Tower. Not seen alive after 1483; probably murdered.

Edward VI 1537-53 Son of Henry VIII and Jane Seymour: King of England and Ireland 1547-53. Was precocious and held articulate Protestant views, but was manipulated by Somerset and Northumberland. Often in poor health, he died of consumption, leaving a "Devise" to change succession from Catholic Mary to Protestant Jane Grey.

Edward VII 1841-1910 Son of Victoria, who largely denied him political responsibilities as Prince of Wales. Had little political influence as King 1901-10, but his Paris visit of 1903 helped cement the Entente Cordiale.

Edward VIII 1894-1972 Son of George V, served in the army in First World War. King 1936, but Baldwin and the Church opposed his marriage to an American divorcée, Mrs Wallis Simpson. Abdicated, became duke of Windsor, married Mrs Simpson and retired to France.

Edward, Prince of Wales 1453-71 Son of Henry VI: brought up in Scotland and France during the Wars of the Roses. Joined Warwick's invasion 1470, but killed at Tewkesbury 1471.

Edward, the Black Prince 1330-76 Son of Edward III and Philippa of Hainault: duke of Cornwall 1337. A distinguished participant in campaigns in France, fighting at Crécy 1346 and Poitiers 1356, and in Spain. As Prince of Aquitaine 1362-72, an unpopular heavy-handed ruler: nobles rebelled and Edward retaliated with the massacre at Limoges 1370.

Edward Balliol c.1283-1364 Son of John Balliol King of Scots. Seized the throne in David II's minority in 1332, but was forced to abdicate. Restored by Edward III of England in 1333, but unable to enforce authority, retired to England 1338 and in 1356 he resigned his title to Edward.

Edward of Norwich, duke of York 1373-1415 Grandson of Edward III. Earl of Rutland 1390, duke of Albemarle 1397. Deserted Richard II for Henry IV, but loyalty suspect. Killed at Agincourt fighting alongside Henry V.

Edward the Aetheling d.1057 Son of Edmund II Ironside. On King Cnut's accession fled to Hungary marrying into the imperial line. In 1057 he returned home as Edward the Confessor's closest heir but died soon after arriving.

Edward the Confessor c.1003-66 Son of Aethelred II and Emma of Normandy. Exiled in Normandy 1016-41, King of England 1042-66; unpopular in some circles because of Norman advisers. Withdrew from government in later years. Noted for his piety: founded Westminster Abbey. Canonized 1161.

Edward the Elder c.870-924 Son of Alfred: King of Wessex 899-924. Reconquered southern Danelaw 910-18 and extended West Saxon influence into Wales and Scotland.

Edward the Martyr c.962-78 Son of Edgar: King of England from 975, but claim challenged by supporters of half-brother Aethelred (the Unready). Murdered. Canonized.

Edwin c.584-632 Succeeded father, Aelle, as King of Deira, 616; annexed Bernicia to rule united Northumbria. Recognized as overlord (bretwalda) of all England except Kent 626. Advanced Christianity in Northumbria after his conversion by Paulinus 627.

Edwy or **Eadwig d.959** King of England from 955, when only fifteen; came into conflict with Dunstan, Archbishop of Canterbury, and had him exiled. The Mercians and Northumbrians renounced their allegiance to him 957 for Edgar, his brother.

Egbert d.839 In exile 789-802 at Charlemagne's Court, until elected King of Wessex. After military successes against Mercia and Northumbria, recognised as bretwalda 829, but Mercia regained independence.

Eldon, John Scott, earl of 1751-1838 Lawyer, Tory MP 1783-99; Solicitor General 1788-93, Attorney General 1793-99, Lord Chief Justice in 1801, Lord Chancellor 1801-6, 1807-27. An extreme Tory, resisted legal reform and Catholic emancipation.

Eleanor of Aquitaine c.1120-1204 Heiress to Aquitaine and Queen of France by marriage to Louis VIII 1137, divorced Louis 1152 and became Queen of England as Henry II's wife, 1154-89. Imprisoned for helping her sons rebel against Henry from Aquitaine in 1173. Active supporter of her sons, Richard and John, as kings.

Eleanor of Castile 1246-90 Queen consort of Edward I 1272-90. Edward built twelve Eleanor crosses at resting places on her funeral route from Hadby, Notts, to Westminster Abbey.

Eleanor of Provence 1223-91 Queen consort of Henry III 1236-72. Hated for advancing Savoyards at Court. Exiled in France during Second Barons' War 1264-67, she raised money and troops to support Henry.

Elgar, Sir Edward 1857-1934 Composed the *Pomp and Circumstance* marches, the *Enigma Variations* and set Newman's *Dream of Gerontius* to music. Master of the King's Musick from 1924; baronet 1931.

Elizabeth I 1533-1603 Daughter of Henry VIII and Anne Boleyn: on Anne's death was declared illegitimate, but restored to succession 1544. Queen 1558-1603. Well educated; cautiously reformist in religion, she restored Protestantism in 1559 and supported, sometimes reluctantly, Protestants in Scotland, France and Netherlands. Remained unmarried, despite pressure to ensure Protestant succession: used marriage offers in diplomacy. Through portraits and pageantry, made herself a unifying cult figure.

Elizabeth II b.1926 Daughter of George VI; married Philip, duke of Edinburgh, 1947. Queen from 1952.

Elizabeth Wydeville (Woodville) 1437-92 Married Edward IV secretly in 1464: husband promoted her relations to counterbalance Neville interest. Fled to sanctuary 1470 and 1483, retired to abbey 1485. Mother of Edward V.

Emma of Normandy d. 1052 Daughter of Richard I of Normandy, wife of (1) Aethelred II 1002-16, (2) Cnut 1017-35. Attempted to gain the throne for her son Harthacnut in 1035, later opposed Edward the Confessor, her son by Aethelred.

Essex, Robert Devereux, earl of 1567-1601 Succeeded his stepfather, Robert Dudley, earl of Leicester, as Elizabeth I's favourite. Captured Cadiz in 1596 but his 1597 Azores expedition failed. Lost favour in 1599 when he failed to suppress the O'Neill revolt in Ireland. Opposed the Cecil faction at Court, attempted a rebellion in London; executed for treason.

Essex, Robert Devereux, earl of 1591-1646 Son of above. Soldier in Europe in 1620s, a commander of English army

against Scots 1639. Opposed king in Lords 1640, led Parliamentary forces in the Civil War, resigned 1645.

Fairfax, Ferdinando, Lord 1584-1648 Commanded Parliamentary troops in Yorkshire during the Civil War. Governor of Hull 1643-44, and York 1644-45.

Fairfax, Thomas, Lord 1612-71 Son of Ferdinando. Fought in Netherlands and in 1639 Bishops' War. Commanded the northern forces in the Civil War; won battle of Marston Moor 1644. Commander of the New Model Army 1645, defeated Royalists at Naseby. Resigned his command, 1650. Later supported the return of Charles II and a constitutional monarchy.

Falkland, Lucius Cary, Viscount 1610-43 Member of "Great Tew Circle"; served in First Bishops' War; MP from 1640, and opponent of Laud. Later, leader of constitutional royalists, Secretary of State 1642. Killed at the battle of Newbury.

Fawcett, Dame Millicent Garrett 1847-1929 President of the National Union of Women's Suffrage Societies 1897-1919, advocating peaceful means to win the vote. Sister of Elizabeth Garrett Anderson.

Fawkes, Guy 1570-1606 Fought for Spain in Netherlands; Catholic conspirator in the Gunpowder Plot; remembered on 5th November.

Finch, Sir John, Lord 1584-1660 MP from 1625; aided Charles I as Speaker 1628-29; Chief Justice of Common Pleas 1635-40. Unpopular for 1637 ship money judgement. Impeached 1640, sought exile in Holland.

Fisher, Herbert Albert Laurens 1865-1940 As President of the Board of Education 1916-26, introduced compulsory education up to 14, in 1918 Education Act. Widely-read author of *History of Europe,* 1935.

Fisher, John, Lord 1841-1920 Energetic naval commander and administrator, First Sea Lord 1904-10, 1914-15. Rebuilt British navy before 1914. Resigned 1910 because Asquith failed to support re-armament; again in 1915 in opposition to Gallipoli campaign.

Fisher, John 1469-1535 An influential theologian, Bishop of Rochester from 1504. Opposed Protestantism, and Henry VIII's divorce from Catherine of Aragon. Executed for alleged denial of royal supremacy. Canonized 1936.

Fitzgerald, Gerald, earl of Kildare d. 1513 Irish magnate, Lord Deputy of Ireland 1481-94, 1496-1513. Supported the Yorkist cause until 1494, when temporarily deprived of office after Warbeck landed in Ireland; thereafter loyal to the king.

Fitzgerald, Gerald, earl of Kildare 1487-1534 Lord Deputy of Ireland 1513-20, 1524-26, 1532-33 between imprisonments for feuding with rival family. Died in the Tower of London.

Fitzgerald, Thomas, Lord Offaly and earl of Kildare 1513-37 Son of above: rebelled on his father's arrest 1533, but was defeated and executed.

Fitzosbern, William d. 1071 Norman lord, earl of Hereford 1067; co-regent during king's absence 1067; prolific builder of castles in Welsh Marches.

Flambard, Ranulf d. 1128 Bishop of Durham 1099-1128 and counsellor to William II. Fled from Henry I in 1100, but later reconciled.

Fleming, Sir Alexander 1881-1955 Professor of bacteriology at London University 1928-48; discovered penicillin, shared the 1945 Nobel Prize for medicine.

Foliot, Gilbert d. 1187 Bishop of Hereford 1147-63, and London 1163-87. Conflicts with Becket led to his excommunication by the archbishop on three occasions. Counsellor to Henry II after Becket's death.

Forster, William Edward 1818-86 Liberal MP 1861-86. His Elementary Education Act 1870 made education available to all children in England and Wales of between 5 and 13 years. Chief Secretary for Ireland 1880-82: pursued an aggressive policy against agrarian revolt.

Fortescue, Sir John d. c.1477 Lawyer, Chief Justice of King's Bench 1442. Lancastrian supporter, attainted and exiled 1461-73. Author of *De Laudibus Legum Angliae* and *The Governance of England*.

Fox, Charles James 1749-1806 Son of Henry, MP from 1768, leader of the Whigs. Foreign Secretary 1782, 1783, 1806, but otherwise in opposition. Opposed North's policy towards North American colonies. In 1806, initiated banning of the slave trade. Supporter of the French Revolution, but eventually took anti-Napoleonic line.

Fox, George 1624-91 Missionary preacher throughout Britain from 1647, and in North America and Holland. Founder of the Quakers.

Fox, Henry, Lord Holland 1705-74 MP from 1735. Secretary at War 1746-55, Secretary of State 1755-56, Paymaster General 1757-65, in which office he enriched himself. Expert parliamentary tactician and controller of patronage.

Foxe, John 1516-87 Protestant preacher and author, he compiled his *Acts and Monuments* 1563 in exile during Mary's reign, tracing the triumph of Protestantism through the sufferings of English Protestants.

Foxe, Richard 1448-1528 Bishop of Exeter 1487, Bath and Wells 1492, Durham 1494, and Winchester 1501. Diplomat and councillor to Henry VII and Henry VIII; Lord Privy Seal 1487-1516, when Wolsey superseded him and he turned to pastoral work.

French, John, earl of Ypres 1852-1925 Field Marshal, much criticized for his management of British Expeditionary Force in 1914; replaced by Haig in 1915. Lord Lieutenant of Ireland 1918-21.

Frobisher, Sir Martin, 1535-94 Sailed to Labrador 1576-78 searching for gold and a passage to China. Distinguished commander of the English fleet fighting the Armada 1588.

Frontinus, Sextus Julius 1st century AD Governor of Roman Britain AD 74-78; defeated the Silures; established a legionary fortress at Caerleon. A writer on military subjects and on aqueducts.

Gage, Thomas 1721-87 Soldier, served in America from 1751. Commander-in-Chief, North America 1763-72; Governor of Massachusetts 1774-75. Resolute stand after Boston Tea Party led to fighting at Lexington and Bunker Hill, first engagements of the War of Independence.

Gaitskell, Hugh 1906-63 Labour MP 1945-63. Chancellor of Exchequer 1950-51 and leader of the opposition 1955-63. Countered influence of Campaign for Nuclear Disarmament on Labour party.

Gardiner, Stephen 1490-1555 Secretary to Wolsey and Henry VIII, keen supporter of the king's divorce. Bishop of Winchester 1531-51, 1553-55. Accepted royal supremacy 1534, but doctrinally conservative and opposed Cromwell. Deprived of office and imprisoned under Edward VI, but under Mary became Lord Chancellor and supported Catholic restoration.

Gaveston, Piers d.1312 The Gascon favourite of Edward II. Earl of Cornwall 1307, Keeper of the Realm 1307-8; aroused the distrust and opposition of the barons; banned from England 1308 and 1311, killed by earl of Lancaster.

Geoffrey of Brittany 1158-86 Son of Henry II: unsuccessfully rebelled against Henry with mother and brothers 1173. In 1182 fought his brother Richard. Died in France, still plotting against Henry.

Geoffrey Plantagenet d. 1212 Illegitimate son of Henry II: Bishop of Lincoln 1173-82, Chancellor 1182-89, Archbishop of York 1189-1207. Rebelled against Henry in 1173, but remained loyal in 1189.

George I 1660-1727 Great grandson of James I, via marriage of James's daughter to Elector Palatine; Elector of Hanover 1698-1727; King of Great Britain 1714-27, succeeding under Act of Settlement 1701. Favoured Whigs and Hanover.

George II 1683-1760 Son of George I: when Prince of Wales, he quarrelled with his father and from 1716 became focus of opposition. King of Great Britain and Elector of Hanover 1727-60. Relied heavily on advice of Queen Caroline and Robert Walpole for policy. After 1746 retreated from politics. Keen patron of music and the arts; as a soldier, fought at Oudenarde 1708 and was the last British king to lead his own troops into battle – at Dettingen 1743.

George III 1738-1820 Son of Frederick Louis, Prince of Wales (died 1751), grandson of George II: King of Great Britain 1760-1820. Urged by Bute, first minister 1762-63 to exert personal control over patronage and policy: from 1770-82 supported Lord North, against strong opposition, in resisting the American revolt; overthrew unsympathetic 1783 Fox-North coalition and appointed Pitt the Younger. Afflicted by porphyria, intermittently from 1788, permanently after 1811, when his son became Regent. Opposed Catholic emancipation 1801-7.

George IV 1762-1830 Son of George III: Prince Regent from 1811, King 1820-30. Idle, extravagant and unpopular. In 1785 illegally married Mrs Fitzherbert, a Catholic, but denied the marriage to conciliate Parliament; in 1795 he married

Caroline of Brunswick, deserting her in 1796. He lived a great deal in Brighton, at the pavilion he had built. Strongly opposed Catholic emancipation and in later years had aspirations to command the army, which position Parliament denied him.

George V 1865-1936 Son of Edward VII: naval officer, heir to throne 1892, Prince of Wales 1901, King 1910-36. Toured the Empire as prince and as king. Married Mary of Teck 1893, and the two earned popularity in First World War as symbols of unity. Had some political influence, choosing Baldwin as Prime Minister in 1923 and forming the National Government of 1931.

George VI 1894-1952 Son of George V: naval officer, became King 1936 after Edward VIII's abdication. Like his father, popular, and a symbol of national resolve in Second World War.

Gibbons, Grinling 1648-1720 Born in Rotterdam, but worked in England as woodcarver; carved the stalls in St Paul's cathedral and the woodwork in Trinity College Library, Cambridge.

Gibbons, Orlando 1583-1625 Organist of Chapel Royal 1604, and of Westminster Abbey 1623. Fashionable composer of church music, madrigals and viol music.

Giffard, Walter d. 1279 Bishop of Bath and Wells 1265, Chancellor 1265-66, Archbishop of York 1266. One of three regents to Edward I in 1272-74 and 1275.

Gilbert, Sir Humphrey 1539-83 A navigator, from 1566 he wished to seek a north-west passage to India, but Elizabeth I sent him to fight in Ireland, then Netherlands. Finally made two voyages, 1578, 1583; claimed Newfoundland for England, first British colony in North America. Lost at sea on return.

Gladstone, William Ewart 1809-98 MP from 1832. Tory Junior Lord of Treasury 1834-35, President of Board of Trade 1843-45, Secretary for Colonies 1845-46. Peelite Chancellor of Exchequer 1852-55, 1859-66. Leader of the Liberal party from 1867. Reforming Prime Minister 1868-74, 1880-85, 1886, 1892-94. Resigned over Lords' rejection of Home Rule bill.

Glanvill, Ranulf de d.1190 Fought the Scots and captured William the Lion in 1174. Chief Justiciar 1180-89. Went on crusade with Richard I, although he had supported Henry II against him, and died at

Acre. Reputed author of *De Legibus et Consuetudinibus Angliae*.

Glyndŵr (Glendower) Owain c.1359-c.1416 Served Richard II and Bolingbroke, but after local feud led a revolt against Henry IV 1400, assuming title "Prince of Wales". Gained control of much of Wales, with French and some English support, and called a Welsh Parliament 1404, but support declined from 1407. Disappeared 1415. Symbolic hero of Welsh nationalism.

Goderich, Frederick John Robinson, Viscount 1782-1859 President Board of Trade 1818-23, Chancellor of Exchequer 1823-28. Prime Minister 1827-28 but failed to heal the division in Tory party and resigned. Earl of Ripon 1833, President of Board of Trade 1841.

Godolphin, Sidney, earl of 1645-1712 Served Charles II, James II and Anne. MP 1668-81, Secretary of State 1684; First Lord of Treasury 1690-97, 1700, 1702-10; an able financier, helped sustain Marlborough's campaigns; promoted union with Scotland 1707.

Godwin d.1053 Earl of Wessex 1019. Supported Edward the Confessor's accession 1042 and married his daughter to the king. Headed Saxon opposition to Edward's Norman advisers; exiled 1051, but forced Edward to reinstate him to favour in 1052. His son became Harold II of England.

Gordon, Charles George 1833-85 Distinguished soldier of the Crimean War and Chinese Wars of 1859-60 and 1863-64. Governor in Sudan 1874-76, 1877-80 where he tried, unsuccessfully, to abolish slave trade. Attempted to evacuate Egyptian troops from Khartoum 1884, but killed by Mahdi's troops after siege of 317 days.

Grafton, Augustus Henry Fitzroy, duke of 1735-1811 First Lord of Treasury 1766-70, Prime Minister on Pitt's resignation 1768. Conciliatory towards the American colonists but king's opposition and the distraction of the Wilkes affair prevented him implementing such a policy. Served under North 1771-75, and Rockingham 1782-83.

Granville, George Leveson Gower, Earl 1815-91 Liberal MP 1836-46, Foreign Secretary 1851-52, 1870-74, 1880-85; a close associate of Gladstone.

Grattan, Henry 1746-1820 Patriot MP in Irish Parliament from 1775, he obtained

its legislative independence in 1782. Unsuccessfully opposed union with England. As Westminster MP for Dublin 1806-20, supported Catholic emancipation.

Grenville, George 1712-70 MP 1741-70. Treasurer of the Navy 1757-62. Secretary of State 1762, First Lord of Admiralty 1762-63, Prime Minister and Chancellor of Exchequer 1763-65. Proceeded against Wilkes 1763, enacted Stamp Act 1764.

Grenville, Sir Richard 1541-91 MP 1571 and 1584, advocate of colonies. Second in command of Azores fleet 1591; fought in the *Revenge* for 15 hours against 15 Spanish ships before being mortally wounded.

Grenville, William Wyndham, Lord 1759-1834 Son of George Grenville: MP 1782-90, Speaker 1789; Home Secretary 1789-91, Foreign Secretary 1791-1801. Broke with cousin Pitt in 1804 to ally with Fox. Premier of "Ministry of all the Talents" 1806-7.

Gresham, Sir Thomas 1519-79 Merchant and financier, founder of Royal Exchange in 1566. Government financial agent at Antwerp.

Grey, Charles, Earl 1764-1845 Whig MP 1786-1807, campaigned for parliamentary reform. First Lord of Admiralty 1806, Foreign Secretary 1806-7; resigned when George III refused Catholic emancipation. Prime Minister 1830-34, his 1831 reform bill was defeated in Commons and, after a general election, in Lords. Succeeded with the 1832 Reform Act, the first stage of franchise extension. Resigned in 1834 over Irish affairs.

Grey, Edward, Viscount 1862-1933 Liberal MP 1885-1916. Foreign Secretary 1905-16, worked hard to avert a European war; strengthened relations with Italy, France and Russia.

Grey, Lady Jane 1537-54 Grand-daughter of Mary Brandon, Henry VIII's sister; married Northumberland's son, Lord Guildford Dudley 1553. Edward VI named her his successor; she was proclaimed queen on 9th July 1553, but after 9 days her régime collapsed and she was replaced by Queen Mary. Executed 1554.

Griffith, Arthur 1872-1922 Irish nationalist campaigner and founder of Sinn Fein 1905. Vice-president of Republic under De Valera 1919. President of the Irish Free State 1922.

Grindal, Edmund *c.*1519-83 Protestant chaplain to Edward VI, exile in Strasbourg under Mary where he became sympathetic to Calvinism. Bishop of London 1559, Archbishop of York 1570, Archbishop of Canterbury 1575. Refusal to suppress "prophesyings", or sermon-meetings, in his province led to his suspension in 1577.

Grosseteste, Robert *c.*1175-1253 A noted scholar at Oxford and Paris, became Bishop of Lincoln 1235. Preached against clerical and papal abuses, defended Church against secular power and opposed granting of English benefices to foreigners.

Gruffudd ap Cynan *c.*1055-1137 After childhood in Ireland, finally secured his inheritance by allying with Rhys ap Tewdwr in 1081. King of Gwynedd 1081-1137. Compelled by Normans to retire to Ireland in 1098, eventually paid tribute to Henry I. Patron of literature and music.

Gruffudd ap Llywelyn *d.*1063 King of Gwynedd 1039, and of Deheubarth 1044. Attacked Herefordshire, ruled virtually all Wales by 1055; allied with Aelfgar of Mercia 1058. Defeated by forces led by Earl Harold at Rhuddlan; killed by own followers.

Guthrum, d.890 Danish chief who conquered Mercia 871. Attacked Wessex; forced to treat with Alfred: became a Christian, moved his army from Wessex to East Anglia 878-79.

Haig, Douglas, Earl 1861-1928 Commander-in-Chief of the British Expeditionary Force in France 1915-18, his policy of attrition led to great loss of life.

Hailsham, Quintin Hogg, Lord b.1907 Conservative cabinet minister 1956-64. Renounced viscountcy in 1963 in attempt to succeed Macmillan as Prime Minister, but failed. Life peer 1970, Lord Chancellor, 1970-74, 1979.

Haldane, Richard Burdon, Viscount 1856-1928 Liberal MP 1885-1911, viscount 1911. Secretary for War 1905-12, responsible for readiness of British army in 1914; founded Territorial Force and General Staff. Lord Chancellor 1912-1915, dismissed on suspicion of pro-German sympathies. Joined Labour party; again Lord Chancellor 1924.

Halifax, Charles Montagu, earl of 1661-1715 Whig MP 1689-1700. Treasury Commissioner 1692-99, originated the National Debt by proposal to raise a government loan of £1 million. Established Bank of England 1694; Chancellor of Exchequer 1694-99. First Lord of Treasury 1697-99, baron 1700, earl 1714. Impeached 1701 and 1703 for supposed neglect. Acquitted, returned as First Lord 1714.

Halifax, George Montagu Dunk, earl of 1716-71 First Lord of Board of Trade 1748-61; promoted North American trade. Lord Lieutenant of Ireland 1761-63; Secretary of State 1762-65; led assault on Wilkes.

Halifax, George Savile, marquis of 1633-95 Moderate in opinions, he opposed Charles II's pro-French policies, Test Act against Catholics 1673, and second Exclusion Bill 1680. Lord Privy Seal 1682-85 and again 1689-90 as supporter of William of Orange; chief minister to William and Mary 1689-90. Nicknamed "The Trimmer".

Hamilton, James, marquis and duke of 1606-49 Charles I's adviser on Scottish affairs; negotiated with the Covenanters 1638. Charles suspected his loyalty and imprisoned him 1644-46; in 1648 he led a Scottish army into England. Defeated at Preston and executed.

Hamon, Robert Fitz d.1107 Norman lord who established lordship of Glamorgan. Supported Crown against rebellion 1088; rewarded with lands in Gloucestershire, Buckinghamshire and Cornwall. Built Cardiff castle; second founder of Tewkesbury abbey.

Hampden, John 1594-1643 MP from 1621; consistently opposed Charles I's arbitrary taxation and government. Imprisoned for refusing to pay a forced loan 1627; his resistance to ship money in 1635 encouraged opposition. Initiator of Strafford's impeachment. Parliamentarian commander in Civil War; killed at Chalgrove Field.

Handel, George Frederick 1685-1759 Born in Saxony, Kapellmeister to Elector of Hanover 1710. Settled in England 1712; prolific composer of operas, oratorios and music for royal occasions; royal pension granted 1713, doubled on accession of former patron, now George I, 1714.

Hankey, Maurice, Lord 1877-1963 Secretary to Imperial Defence Committee 1912-38. Created cabinet secretariat 1916; secretary to cabinet committee until 1938, cabinet minister 1939-42.

Harcourt, Sir William Vernon 1827-1904 Lawyer, Liberal MP 1868-98, Home Secretary 1880-85; Chancellor of Exchequer 1886, 1892-95; introduced death duties 1894. Liberal leader 1896-98.

Hardie, James Keir 1856-1915 A coalminer, union leader from 1879; secretary of Scottish Miners' Federation 1886. Founded Scottish Labour party 1888. Independent Labour MP 1892-95; chairman of Independent Labour party 1893-1900; Labour MP 1900-15; chairman of parliamentary Labour party 1906-7.

Harley, Robert, earl of Oxford 1661-1724 MP 1689-1711, first Whig, then Tory, always moderate. Secretary of State 1704-8, Chancellor of Exchequer 1710, Lord Treasurer 1711-14. Removed Marlborough and created 12 new peers to carry through Peace of Utrecht. Dismissed 1714 having alienated Bolingbroke and the queen.

Harold I Harefoot *c.*1016-40 Son of Cnut and Aelfgifu. Chosen regent for half-brother Harthacnut 1035; King of England 1037.

Harold II *c.*1020-66 Son of Earl Godwin, whom he succeeded in Wessex 1053. Strongest of the Saxon earls. Helped Duke William of Normandy against Bretons in 1064, and, according to Norman sources, pledged to aid William's succession in England. Elected king on Edward the Confessor's death 1066. Defeated and killed at Hastings by William.

Harthacnut *c.*1018-42 Son of Cnut, ruled Denmark from 1028, remaining there on Cnut's death because of Norwegian threat. Allowed his half-brother Harold I to take English throne. Succeeded on Harold's death: King of England 1040-42.

Harvey, William 1578-1657 Discovered the circulation of blood, publishing the discovery 1628. Royal Physician 1628, 1642. Warden of Merton College from 1645.

Hasilrig, Sir Arthur, baronet d. 1661 Opposed Laud's religious policy, active in Strafford's impeachment 1641. Charles I tried to arrest him in Commons 1642; fought against king throughout Civil War, but as republican opposed Cromwell from 1653. Opposed Restoration; imprisoned 1660, died in Tower.

Hastings, Francis Rawdon, marquis of 1754-1826 Governor General of India, Commander in Chief 1813-22; pacified Nepal 1814-16, and central India, by defeating the Mahrattas 1817-18.

Hastings, Warren 1732-1818 Clerk in East India Company 1750, member of Bengal Council 1761 and Madras Council 1768. Governor of Bengal 1771; first Governor General of India 1774, pacified much of India, showing respect of Indian customs and culture. Criticized for arrogance, returned to England 1785 and was impeached for corruption 1788. Seven-year trial resulted in acquittal.

Hatton, Sir Christopher 1540-91 Politician and courtier, favourite of Elizabeth I. Privy councillor 1577, strongly anti-Spanish; took part in trials of Catholic plotters and Mary Queen of Scots. Lord Chancellor 1587-91, supported Whitgift against Puritans.

Hawke, Edward, Lord 1710-81 Naval officer: commanded *Berwick* in Battle of Toulon 1744. MP for Portsmouth 1747. Commanded home fleet 1748-52, western fleet 1755-56, Mediterranean fleet 1756. Defeated the French at Quiberon Bay 1759, frustrating French plans to invade Britain. First Lord of Admiralty 1766-71, Admiral of the Fleet 1768.

Hawkins, Sir John 1532-95 Re-designed Elizabethan navy and harassed Spanish shipping in years before Armada. Slave-trader on West African coast 1561-69. MP for Plymouth in 1572, Treasurer of Navy 1577, later Comptroller. Able commander against Armada; sailed with Drake to raid Spanish West Indies 1595.

Hawksmoor, Nicholas 1661-1736 Worked as architect with Wren at St Pauls, with Vanbrugh at Blenheim. Surveyor General of Westminster Abbey 1723, designing west towers. Worked on Queen's College, Oxford and many London churches.

Heath, Edward b. 1916 MP from 1950, leader of Conservative party 1965, Prime Minister 1970-74: his main achievement was to take Britain into EEC. Lost party leadership election 1975.

Henderson, Arthur 1863-1935 Labour MP from 1903; as party secretary 1911-34 played important role in drafting party constitution 1918. Served in War Cabinet, Home Secretary 1924, Foreign Secretary 1929-31; briefly party leader. Disarmer, he won 1934 Nobel Peace Prize.

"Hengist" 5th century A Jute, invited to England with brother Horsa to aid Briton, Vortigern, in 449. Perhaps mythical, by tradition the brothers revolted and seized Kent, founding the Kentish kingdom.

Henrietta Maria 1609-69 Daughter of Henry IV of France, unpopular Catholic Queen consort of Charles I 1625-49. Mother of Charles II and James II, she supported Charles I in Civil War by raising troops and funds; forced into exile in France 1644.

Henry I 1068-1135 Son of William I: King of England 1100-35. Married Matilda, niece of Edgar the Aetheling, uniting English and Norman dynasties in 1100. Seized throne on death of brother William II, defeated resistance and took Normandy from brother Robert 1106. Reign saw improvements of the judicial system and royal administration, successful wars in France, and a healing of split between Crown and Church over lay investiture. His only son died in 1120. Henry extracted an oath from barons to accept daughter Matilda as heir, but Stephen seized the Crown.

Henry II 1133-89 Grandson of Henry I, son of Matilda: 1152 married Eleanor of Aquitaine, and 1153 recognized as heir. King of England 1154-89, and ruler of Normandy, Brittany, Anjou, Aquitaine, etc. He subdued rebellious barons, established jury system and exacted homage from Malcolm III of Scotland, restoring border counties to England. Quarrelled with Becket after Constitutions of Clarendon 1164: this led to Becket's murder 1170, for which Henry did penance. Enforced authority on Welsh and Irish, but sons Geoffrey and Richard rebelled and, with French support, defeated Henry in 1189.

Henry, the Young King 1155-83 Son of Henry II: crowned 1170, he joined the 1173 rebellion against Henry. Rebelled with brother Geoffrey against brother Richard I in Aquitaine, 1183.

Henry III 1207-72 Son of King John: King of England 1216-72. As king, Henry provoked the barons by promoting foreigners at Court: his government was ineffectual, and, when he asked the country to fund wars in Sicily, the Baronial Reform Movement ensued 1258. In the Barons' War, Simon de Montfort captured Henry at Lewes 1264, and ruled England until 1265.

Henry IV 1367-1413 Son of John of Gaunt: styled "Bolingbroke" after his birthplace. "Appellant" opponent of Richard II from 1386; exiled in 1398; estates seized in 1399. Henry invaded England, forcing Richard's abdication: King 1399-1413. Subdued Glyndŵr rebellions in Wales, 1400-9, and by Percies and others.

Henry V 1387-1422 Son of Henry IV: Prince of Wales 1399; campaigned against Owain Glyndŵr. King of England 1413-22. Resumed war with France, capturing Harfleur and defeating the French at Agincourt 1415: by the Treaty of Troyes, 1420, Charles VI recognized Henry as heir to throne of France. He suppressed Lollardy at home and reformed the Benedictine monasteries, but died in France whilst fighting against the dauphin.

Henry VI 1421-71 Son of Henry V: King of England 1422-61, 1470-71. Crowned in 1429 as King of England and in 1430 as King of France. An incompetent monarch, who suffered from occasional insanity, his reign was marred by baronial conflicts. Henry was deposed by Edward of York in 1461; in 1470 Warwick, the Kingmaker, secured his restoration, but Edward returned and, after the Battle of Tewkesbury, Henry was murdered. He was a patron of learning and genuinely pious: Henry VII proposed his canonization.

Henry VII 1457-1509 Son of Edmund Tudor, earl of Richmond: a Lancastrian supporter, went into exile 1471. In 1485 he invaded England, defeating Richard III at Bosworth Field: King of England 1485-1509. He was crowned in 1486 and, by marrying Elizabeth of York, united the two warring factions, although Perkin Warbeck and Lambert Simnel plots threatened his throne. Protected himself by intimidation of nobility, and his strong rule restored financial and political stability.

Henry VIII 1491-1547 Son of Henry VII: King of England 1509-47, Ireland 1540-47. Early reign characterized by aggressive foreign policy: defeated French at Battle of Spurs 1513, while Scots were defeated at Flodden. Henry's reign was dominated by search for secure succession and a male heir. By Catherine of Aragon he had only a daughter, Mary; from 1527, Henry actively sought divorce, and in 1533 he broke from allegiance to pope, divorced Catherine and married Anne Boleyn, by whom he had Elizabeth. Henry next married Jane Seymour, who died after giving birth to Edward, 1537; in 1540, to secure support of German princes, married Anne of Cleves, whom he immediately divorced to marry Catherine Howard (executed 1542). Married Catherine Parr 1543. In the 1540s returned to war with France and Scotland, imposing great financial strain on England.

Henry of Grosmont, duke of Lancaster c.1300-61 Fought alongside Edward III in France from 1338. Trusted counsellor, headed embassy to Navarre 1354 and helped to negotiate Treaty of Brétigny 1360. His daughter Blanche brought her Lancastrian claims to her husband, John of Gaunt.

Herbert, Arthur, earl of Torrington 1646-1716 Rear-Admiral 1678; Admiralty Commissioner 1684; MP from 1685; Vice-Admiral 1685, but dismissed by James II. Commanded the fleet which brought William of Orange to England 1688; First Lord of Admiralty 1689-90; resigned 1690 and court martialled for hesitating to engage the French at Beachy Head. Acquitted.

Herbert, William, earl of Pembroke *c*.1423-69 From 1461, Edward IV's chief counsellor. Earl 1468, on capture of Harlech and attainder of Jasper Tudor. Executed.

Herbert, William, earl of Pembroke 1580-1630 Courtier and politician; Lord Chamberlain 1615-25. Patron of Ben Jonson and Inigo Jones. Chancellor of Oxford 1617, Pembroke College named after him.

Hereward the Wake *fl*.1070 Led a revolt against William I 1070-71: sacked Peterborough Abbey and escaped, though beseiged by William on the Isle of Ely. Symbol of resistance to Normans.

Hill, Sir Rowland 1795-1879 Pamphleteer, inventor of penny post and postage stamps 1839-40, but dismissed from office 1842. Chairman of Brighton Railway Company, introducing express and excursion trains. Secretary of the Post Office 1854-64.

Hilliard, Nicholas 1537-1619 English miniature painter, goldsmith and carver. Painted Elizabeth I, James I, and many at Court. Made Elizabeth I's second Great Seal in 1586.

Hoadly, Benjamin 1676-1761 Controversial and influential Whig bishop, of Bangor 1715, Hereford 1721, Salisbury 1723, Winchester 1734. Wrote against nonconformists, and nonjurors, and for toleration, and provoked crisis which led to suspension of Convocation 1717.

Hoare, Sir Samuel, Viscount Templewood 1880-1959 Conservative MP 1910-44; Secretary for India 1931-35; Foreign Secretary 1935. Resigned after Hoare-Laval pact was repudiated 1935. Home Secretary 1937-40, ambassador to Spain 1940-44.

Hobbes, Thomas 1588-1679 Influential philosopher of science, and political theorist; author of *Leviathan* 1651 in which he argued the necessity of an absolute ruler to overcome human selfishness.

Hobhouse, John Cam, Lord Broughton de Gyffard 1786-1869 Radical MP 1820-51; President of India Board 1835-41, 1846-52. Writer and friend of Byron.

Hogarth, William 1697-1764 Painter and engraver, excelled in pictorial satire, e.g. *A Rake's Progress* 1735. In *Gin Lane* he exposed the social evils of gin-drinking.

Holinshed, Raphael, *c*.1520-80 Author of *Chronicles of England, Scotland and Ireland,* 1577, used by Shakespeare for his historical plays.

Holland, Henry Richard Vassall, Lord 1773-1840 Whig politician; Lord Privy Seal in Ministry of All the Talents 1806-7; Chancellor of Duchy of Lancaster 1830-40. Holland House, London, was political centre of Whig society.

Holles, Denzil, Lord 1599-1680 MP from 1624; Charles I attempted to arrest him in Commons in 1642. Opposed the king in Civil War, but broke with Cromwell and went into exile. Supported Restoration; baron 1661; used as diplomat by Charles II.

Home Alexander Frederick Douglas-Home, Lord b.1903 Conservative MP from 1931; Commonwealth Secretary 1960-63. Renounced earldom to become Prime Minister in 1963, but lost General Election 1964 and Conservative leadership 1965. Foreign Secretary 1970-74. Life peer 1974.

Hood, Samuel, Viscount 1724-1816 Naval commander in North American waters. Rear-Admiral 1780. Admiralty commissioner 1788-95; successful Commander-in-Chief Mediterranean 1793-94.

Hooker, Richard *c*.1554-1600 Preacher and theologian: defender of episcopacy against presbyterians and apologist for established Church of English in *Of the Laws of Ecclesiastical Polity,* published from 1597.

Hooper, John d.1555 Protestant minister, he fled England in 1539, chaplain to Somerset in 1549. Bishop of Gloucester and Worcester 1550-54: a diligent diocesan, especially as judge. Deprived by Mary, sentenced for heresy and burned.

Hopton, Ralph, Lord 1596-1652 Royalist general in Civil War, although originally Puritan. Led Royalist armies to victories at Stratton and Lansdowne in 1643; surrendered to Fairfax at Truro in 1646; went into exile.

Horsa *see* **Hengist**

Howard, Charles, earl of Carlisle 1629-85 Member of Cromwell's Council of State 1653; led English troops against Scots 1654. Earl, 1661; ambassador of Charles II to Russia, Sweden and Denmark.

Howard, Charles, earl of Nottingham, Lord Howard of Effingham 1536-1624 Lord Chamberlain 1574-85, Lord High Admiral 1585-1618. Led English fleet against Spanish Armada 1588; fought with Essex at Cadiz 1596. Earl 1597. Ambassador to Spain 1605.

Howard, Henry, earl of Northampton 1540-1614 A Catholic, associated with Mary Queen of Scots, and imprisoned 1583. Assisted accession of James I 1603, earl 1604, Lord Privy Seal 1608; James I's leading adviser 1610-14.

Howard, Thomas, earl of Suffolk, Lord Howard de Walden 1561-1626 Fought against Armada, served on 1596 Cadiz expedition. Lord Chamberlain 1603-14, Lord High Treasurer 1614-18: fined for corruption.

Howard, William, Lord Howard of Effingham *c*.1510-73 Lord High Admiral 1554-73; defended London against Wyatt's rebellion 1554. Lord Chamberlain to Elizabeth I; Lord Privy Seal 1572.

Howe, Richard, Viscount and Earl 1726-99 Naval commander in the Seven Years War, fought at Quiberon Bay in 1759 and at the blockade of Brest. A Lord of the Admiralty 1762-65, Treasurer of Navy 1765-70. Relieved Gibraltar 1782. First Lord of the Admiralty 1783-88. Commanded victorious English fleet against French on "Glorious First of June" 1794.

Hume, David 1711-76 Scots philosopher and historian: his sceptical empiricism was a turning-point in metaphysics. Author of *Treatise of Human Nature* 1738-40, and a *History of England* 1754-62.

Hume, Joseph 1777-1855 MP from 1812-1855, a Tory until 1818 then radical. Secured repeal of the Combination Acts 1824; helped draft 1838 Charter.

Humphrey, duke of Gloucester 1391-1447 Son of Henry IV: a patron of learning. Member of Council of Regency for Henry VI and protector in Bedford's absence. Quarrelled with colleagues mainly over French policy. Died in custody whilst awaiting trial for designs on the king's life.

Hunt, Henry ("Orator Hunt") 1773-1835 Radical politician, agitated for parliamentary reform, contested several seats unsuccessfully; present at Spa Fields and Peterloo 1819, after which he was imprisoned. MP for Preston 1830-33.

Huntingdon, Selina Hastings, countess of 1707-91 Founder of Lady Huntingdon's Connexion, a Methodist sect; established chapels in Brighton, London and Bath from 1761. Hoped to evangelize other aristocrats, but faced much opposition.

Huntly, George Gordon, earl and marquis of 1562-1636 Led the Catholic earls against James VI. Imprisoned 1588-89, he defeated royal forces at Glenlivet in 1594, was pardoned by James and in 1599 made marquis. Once James inherited the English throne, Gordon's power declined.

Huskisson, William 1770-1830 Liberal Tory MP, President of Board of Trade 1823-27, modified Navigation Acts. Attacked for supporting Catholic emancipation and for free-trade views. The first person killed by a train – at the opening of the Manchester-Liverpool railway.

Huxley, Thomas Henry 1825-95 Darwinian biologist with scientific interests stretching from fossils to public health. Influenced London's education scheme 1870. President of the Royal Society 1883-85.

Hywel, Dda ("the Good") d.950 King of Gwynedd, Powys and Deheubarth. Co-operated closely with English kings and codified a system of laws which survived until Edward I.

Ine d.c.726 King of West Saxons from 688; extended territory over Somerset and made war on South Saxons. His laws, promulgated from 690, were the most significant until Alfred's time.

Ireton, Henry 1611-51 Parliamentary commander in Civil War, Cromwell's son-in-law. Fought at Naseby, signed Charles I's death warrant; Lord Deputy of Ireland 1650.

Isaacs, Rufus Daniel, marquis of Reading 1860-1935 Lawyer, Attorney General 1910-13; criticized in Marconi affair. Lord Chief Justice from 1913; ambassador to USA 1918-19. Viceroy of India 1921-26, Foreign Secretary 1931.

Isabella of France 1292-1358 Queen consort of Edward II, daughter of Philip the Fair: neglected by homosexual husband. Angry at loss of her estates she returned to France in 1325, where she became mistress of Roger de Mortimer, with whom she deposed Edward II in 1326. The two ruled as Edward III's regents from 1327, until Edward had Mortimer executed in 1330, retiring his mother on a generous pension.

Isabella of France, 1389-1409 Queen consort of Richard II 1396-99. Daughter of Charles VI of France, the marriage brought peace between the two countries.

James I 1394-1437 Son of Robert III: King of Scots 1406-37, but in English captivity 1406-24. Married Joan, cousin of Henry V, in 1424. Curbed the power of the duke of Albany and attempted social reform, but unpopular because of authoritarian rule over the nobility. Murdered in attempted *coup*, but his son succeeded him.

James II 1430-60 Son of James I: King of Scots 1437-60. Assumed royal powers in 1449 with the help of the Douglases, although he killed Earl William himself in 1452, attainted the family and annexed its estates 1455. Killed at the siege of Roxburgh Castle.

James III 1452-88 Son of James II: King of Scots 1460-88. Gained Orkneys and Shetlands for Scotland by 1469 marriage to Margaret of Denmark. Reign troubled by factionalism: overcame Albany's rebellion in 1484, but was killed in a revolt led by son.

James IV 1473-1513 Son of James III: as King of Scots 1488-1513, established strong government and promoted education and culture. Invaded England in support of Warbeck 1496, but married Margaret, Henry VII's daughter, 1503. When England attacked his ally France in 1513, invaded England and was killed at Flodden.

James V 1512-42 Son of James IV: King of Scots 1513-42. Attained full royal power 1524, but reign troubled by factionalism worsened by his aggression. Cemented the French alliance by marrying Madeleine of France 1537, and on her death married Mary of Guise-Lorraine 1538.

James VI and I 1566-1625 Son of Mary Queen of Scots: King of Scots 1567-1625; married Anne of Denmark 1589, accepted presbyterianism in Scotland by law in 1592. He was promised throne of England by childless Elizabeth: as King of England 1603-25, maintained religious settlement, but some dispute with Parliament over the extent of authority and financial expedients. In 1604 he made peace with Spain and followed peaceful foreign policy.

James II 1633-1701 Son of Charles I: duke of York 1634. Exiled 1648-60, Lord High Admiral 1660-73, fought in Dutch Wars. Became a Catholic and resigned offices after 1673 Test Act: parliamentary attempts to exclude him from succession 1678-81. As King 1685-88, sought to promote Catholicism and granted toleration to Catholics and dissenters 1687. The birth of a son in 1688 and prospect of a Catholic succession prompted opposition's invitation to William of Orange and deposition of James. Defeated at the Boyne 1690, went into exile in France.

Jane Seymour 1509-37 Pawn in Court politics, becoming third Queen consort of Henry VIII, 1536-37. Died after birth of Edward VI.

Jeffreys, George, Lord 1648-89 A cruel judge, Lord Chief Justice 1682-85. Presided over "bloody assizes" after Monmouth rebellion 1685. Lord Chancellor 1685. Died in Tower after James II fled.

Jellicoe, John Rushworth, Earl 1859-1935 Commanded Grand Fleet 1914, fleet at Jutland 1916, organized convoy system in 1917, Admiral of the Fleet 1919. Governor-General of New Zealand 1920-23.

Jervis, John, Earl St Vincent 1735-1823 Served in North America 1759-60, helped relieve Gibraltar 1780-82; MP 1783-94. Involved in capture of Guadeloupe and Martinique in 1794, and in suppression of 1797 naval mutinies. Defeated the Spanish off Cape St Vincent 1797. First Lord of the Admiralty 1801-4. Commander of Channel fleet 1800-1, 1806-7.

Jewel, John 1522-71 Protestant exile in Mary's reign, returned on Elizabeth's accession and made Bishop of Salisbury, 1560. Famous as apologist of the Church of England: *Apologia Ecclesiae Anglicanae* 1562 led to a long controversy with Catholic Thomas Harding.

John 1166-1216 Youngest son of Henry II: King of England 1199-1216. Conflict with France resulted in loss of most of Angevin Empire. Excommunicated 1209-13 for refusing to let pope's nominee as archbishop of Canterbury into England. The barons thought his rule despotic, and forced him to accept Magna Carta 1215, but civil war broke out 1216.

John Balliol c.1250-1313 Created King of Scotland by Edward I in 1292, unpopular with Scottish nobility as a result. To appease them,he resisted Edward, was defeated in 1296 at Dunbar, and resigned throne to Edward, dying in France.

John of Gaunt, duke of Lancaster 1340-99 Son of Edward III, father of Henry IV. Increasingly in control of affairs as his father grew senile, he retained power under Richard II. He attempted, 1386-89, to claim and take Castile, but in his absence England was on the brink of civil war. He restored peace, but on his death his son Henry seized the throne.

John of Salisbury c.1115-80 Close friend of Becket, he upheld his cause and went into exile 1164-70. Bishop of Chartres 1176. Author of *Policraticus*, a life of St Anselm, and other works: regarded as the most learned classical writer of medieval times.

Johnson, Samuel 1709-84 Lexicographer, essayist, poet and critic: author of *Dictionary of the English Language* 1755 and *Lives of the Most Eminent English Poets* 1779-81.

Johnston, Archibald, Lord Warriston 1611-63 Scots presbyterian opponent of Charles I and leader of Covenanters; supported Cromwell, fled 1660, captured and hanged.

Jones, Inigo 1573-1652 Designer of masques for Ben Jonson; Surveyor General of King's Works 1615, designed Queen's House at Greenwich, Banqueting House, Whitehall; revamped Old St Paul's.

Jonson, Ben c.1573-1637 Actor and playwright, whose satirical plays include *Epicoene, The Alchemist* and *Bartholomew Fayre*. Also wrote a number of masques, staged by Inigo Jones, for James I and Charles I.

Jowett, Benjamin 1817-93 Oxford classical scholar: Professor of Greek 1855, Master of Balliol. University reformer and promoter of careers open to talents in politics and civil service.

Juxon, William 1582-1663 Laudian churchman: Bishop of London 1633, Lord Treasurer 1636-41, attended Charles I at execution. Archbishop of Canterbury 1660.

Kemp, John c.1380-1454 Bishop of Rochester 1419, of London 1421, Archbishop of York 1426, of Canterbury 1452. Chancellor of Normandy 1419-22, Lord Chancellor 1426-32: supported Beaufort against Gloucester, and had to resign as Chancellor. Cardinal 1439, Lord Chancellor again 1450-54.

Kenneth I MacAlpin d. 858 King of Dál Riáta from 841; conquered the Picts and united them with the Scots; King of Scotia c.843-58.

Kenneth II d.995 King of Scotia 971-95, who recognized Edgar of England as his overlord in 973 and was granted Lothian. Killed in a feud by Constantine III after securing Edinburgh.

Kenneth III d.1005 King of Scotia 997-1005, grandson of Malcolm I: murdered Constantine III and was in turn killed by Malcolm II.

Keppel, Augustus, Viscount 1725-86 Entered the navy in 1735 and voyaged round the world with Anson 1740. Commander of North American station 1754, Commissioner of Admiralty 1766, Commander in Chief of grand fleet 1778. Acquitted at court martial 1779 for conduct at Brest blockade. First Lord 1782-83.

Keynes, John Maynard, Lord 1883-1946 In *The Economic Consequences of the Peace* 1919, warned against severe reparations from Germany. His proposal that governments should use budgets to regulate demand and thus employment was published 1936 in *The General Theory of Employment, Interest and Money*. Influential Treasury adviser from 1940, and a founder of International Monetary Fund.

Kingsley, Charles 1819-75 Anglican churchman, writer and social reformer: Christian socialist from 1848, Professor of Modern History at Cambridge 1860-69. Popular author of *Westward Ho!* 1855, and *The Water Babies* 1863.

Kipling, Rudyard 1865-1936 Born in India, which formed setting for many of his books, such as the *Jungle Books* 1894-95, *Just So Stories* and *Kim*. Vigorous imperialist and anti-liberal propagandist.

Kirkby, John d.1290 Treasurer from 1284, Bishop of Ely 1286-90. Travelling fund-raiser for Edward I's Welsh wars.

Kitchener, Horatio Herbert, Earl 1850-1916 Defeated Dervishes at Omdurman 1898, re-establishing British power in the Sudan. Commander in Chief in South Africa 1900-2 and in India 1902-9. Field Marshal 1909. Secretary for War 1914-1916, responsible for the mobilization of 70 new divisions. Drowned in the *Hampshire* en route to Russia.

Knox, John c.1505-72 By 1547 he was a convinced Protestant reformer. Captured by French after siege of St Andrews and sent to the galleys 1547-49. Preached in England 1549-53, then went to Geneva and adopted Calvinist views. Leader of Scots Reformation, as minister at Edinburgh from 1560. Wrote against women rulers so both Mary Queen of Scots and Elizabeth I distrusted him.

Lambert, John 1619-83 Commissary General to Fairfax, led the cavalry at Marston Moor 1644. Commander of army in the north 1647, defeating the Scots at Preston. Broke with Cromwell in 1657 and unsuccessfully tried to stop Monck's invasion in 1659. Imprisoned in Guernsey after Restoration.

Lanfranc c.1005-89 Lawyer and scholar. As Archbishop of Canterbury from 1070, asserted the primacy of his province over York, defended William I's rights to ecclesiastical patronage and supported king in his refusal to swear fealty to Pope. Crowned William II in 1087 and supported him in the revolt of 1088.

Langham, Simon d. 1376 Abbot of Westminster, Bishop of Ely 1362, Archbishop of Canterbury 1366-68, Cardinal 1368; ecclesiastical reformer. Treasurer 1360-63, Lord Chancellor 1363-67.

Langland, William c.1330-c.1400 Probably educated at Great Malvern monastery. His great poem *The Vision of Piers the Plowman* was written, in three versions, 1362-92: criticized the clergy for their moral laxity and worldliness, but remained theologically orthodox.

Langley, Edmund de, duke of York 1341-1402 Son of Edward III: accompanied his father on the French wars from 1359. Earl of Cambridge 1362, duke of York 1385. He acted as regent in Richard II's absences 1394-99, but yielded to superior force of Henry IV in 1399.

Langton, Stephen d. 1228 Studied theology and arts in Paris, went to Rome and made Cardinal 1206. Appointed Archbishop of Canterbury by Pope 1207, excluded by John until 1213; played part in drawing up Magna Carta. Mediator in Church and state affairs.

Langton, Walter d. 1321 Bishop of Lichfield 1297, Treasurer 1295. Councillor to Edward I, arrested by Edward II for irregularities as Treasurer 1308, but restored to office 1312. Member of King's Council 1315-18.

Lansbury, George 1859-1940 MP 1910-12 and 1922-40, leader of the Labour party 1931-35, supporter of women's suffrage; pacifist; lost leadership to Attlee 1935.

Lansdowne, Henry Petty-Fitzmaurice, marquis of 1780-1863 Chancellor of Exchequer in Ministry of All the Talents 1806-7. Supported anti-slave movement and other liberal causes. President of Council in 1830, he sat in every Whig or Liberal cabinet until 1863.

Lansdowne, Henry Petty-Fitzmaurice, marquis of 1845-1927 Governor-General of Canada 1883-88, Viceroy of India 1888-94, Secretary for War 1895-1900. Foreign Secretary 1900-05, negotiating Entente Cordiale 1904. Led Conservatives in Lords 1903-16.

Lansdowne, William Petty, marquis of 1737-1805 As earl of Shelburne, President of Board of Trade 1763, Secretary of State 1766-68, resigned over criticism of his conciliatory policy towards North American colonies. Prime Minister 1782-83. Marquis 1784. Patron of Bentham and Priestley.

Latimer, Hugh c.1485-1555 Protestant reformer: Bishop of Worcester 1535-39, but resigned over Six Articles. Noted preacher on moral issues under Edward VI, and under Mary remained firm in his views; burned for heresy.

Laud, William 1573-1645 Bishop of St David's 1621, of Bath and Wells 1626, London 1628; Archbishop of Canterbury 1633. Privy Councillor 1627, Treasury Commissioner 1635. Attempted to impose liturgical uniformity which, in Scotland, led to Bishops' Wars. Impeached by Commons 1640, for alleged treason; attainted 1644 and executed.

Lauderdale, John Maitland, earl and duke of 1616-82 Commissioner for Solemn League and Covenant 1643-46, and for Engagement with Charles I 1647. Followed Charles II at Worcester in 1651 and was prisoner until 1660, when he became Secretary for Scottish affairs. Member of the Cabal. Tried to enforce absolute power of Church and Crown in Scotland and became unpopular as a result.

Law, Andrew Bonar 1858-1923 Conservative MP 1900-23, party leader 1911, Colonial Secretary 1915, Chancellor of Exchequer 1916-19: introduced war bonds. Lord Privy Seal 1919-21, Prime Minister 1922-23.

Lawrence, Thomas Edward 1888-1935 Led Arab revolt against Turks 1917-18, known as "Lawrence of Arabia". At the Paris Peace Conference of 1919 condemned decision on Arab affairs. Adviser to Colonial Office 1921-22. Arabian experience described in *Seven Pillars of Wisdom* 1926.

Leicester, Robert Dudley, earl of c.1532-88 Elizabeth I's favourite: rumoured to have killed his wife, Amy Robsart, in 1560, to obtain Elizabeth's hand. Courtier and councillor, earl 1564; favoured an aggressive foreign policy and further "reform" of Church of England. Led an ineffective campaign in support of Dutch rebels 1585-87.

Lennox, Esme Stuart, duke of 1542-83 Came to Scotland from France 1579, and, despite hostility from rivals, dominated young James VI; after James was seized in Ruthven Raid, he fled to France.

Lennox, Matthew Stuart, earl of 1516-71 Opponent of Arran, Scottish supporter of Henry VIII. His son, Darnley, married Mary Queen of Scots, and Lennox acted as regent for grandson James VI in 1570.

Leslie, Alexander, earl of Leven c.1580-1661 Served in army of Gustavus Adolphus; led Scots in Bishops' Wars, defeating English at Newburn 1640. Supported the Parliamentarians in Civil War, and took Charles I's surrender at Newark 1646, but reverted to Royalists and fought for them at Dunbar 1650.

Leslie, David, Lord Newark d.1682 Commanded the pro-Parliamentarian Scottish cavalry at Marston Moor, but was later defeated by Cromwell at Dunbar 1650 and Worcester 1651.

Lilburne, John c.1614-57 Imprisoned 1638 for pamphleteering, fought for Parliament in Civil War but criticized Army and Parliament and became a Leveller leader. Exiled 1652, imprisoned 1653-55, became a Quaker in last years.

Liverpool, Charles Jenkinson, earl of 1729-1808 Secretary to Treasury 1763-65, Secretary at War 1778-82, President of Board of Trade 1786-1804.

Liverpool, Robert Banks Jenkinson, earl of 1770-1828 Tory MP from 1790-1803, then peer. Foreign Secretary 1801-3, Home Secretary 1804-6, 1807-9 and Secretary for War and the Colonies 1809-12. As Prime Minister, 1812-27, his régime repressed disorders in post-war depression, but became more reformist later.

Lloyd George, David, Earl 1863-1945 Liberal MP 1890-1945, then earl. As President of Board of Trade 1905-8, set up Port of London Authority; as Chancellor of Exchequer 1908-15 presented his 1909 "People's" Budget advocating social reform. Successful Minister of Munitions 1915-16. In 1916, replaced Asquith as Prime Minister of coalition government; despite disagreements with generals, led country to victory. His post-war Irish policy forced many Conservatives to withdraw support from coalition and he resigned 1922. Led Liberals again 1926-31.

Llywelyn ab Gruffudd d.1282 Son of Gruffudd ap Llywelyn: established authority over Gwynedd 1246. Assumed title "Prince of Wales" 1258, acknowledged by Henry III at Treaty of Montgomery 1267; but lost land in war 1277 and died in second war against the English.

Llywelyn ap Iorwerth ("Llywelyn the Great") 1173-1240 Consolidated Gwynedd to 1202, and extended his authority at expense of lesser Welsh rulers and English Marches: gains recognized by Treaty of Worcester 1218. Laid foundation of united Welsh feudal principality.

Locke, John 1632-1704 Adviser to Shaftesbury and Whig political theorist. In *An Essay Concerning Human Understanding* 1690, argued human ideas were not innate but came from experience. In *Two Treatises of Government* 1690, attacked divine right of kings and expounded social contract as defence of 1688 Revolution.

Longchamp, William d. 1197 Bishop of Ely and Chancellor 1189-97; administered the country 1189-91 in Richard I's absence, until overthrown.

Loudoun, John Campbell, earl of 1598-1662 Opposed Charles I's Church policy in Scotland and promoted Covenant; Scottish Chancellor 1641-50. Supported Charles II at Dunbar 1650, but penalized at Restoration.

Lovell, Francis, Viscount 1454-?87 Lord Chamberlain 1483-85 and adviser of Richard III. Fought at Bosworth 1485, led an unsuccessful rebellion against Henry VII, and supported Simnel. Probably killed at battle of Stoke.

Lovett, William 1800-77 Moderate Chartist leader, chief author of the People's Charter of 1838.

Lowe, Robert, Viscount Sherbrooke 1811-92 Liberal MP from 1852, educational reformer 1859-64, Adullamite leader 1866, Chancellor of Exchequer 1868-73, Home Secretary 1873-74.

Lucan, George Charles Bingham, earl of 1800-88 Led the Charge of the Light Brigade at the Battle of Balaclava 1854, having misunderstood Lord Raglan's orders.

Lucy, Richard de d.1179 Justiciar 1154-79, helped draw up the Constitutions of Clarendon 1164, and consequently excommunicated by Becket. Suppressed rebellion against Henry II in 1173.

Ludlow, Edmund 1617-92 Lawyer, MP from 1646, a judge at Charles I's trial and signed death warrant 1649. Military commander in Ireland from 1651, but opposed the Protectorate. Exiled from 1660.

Lugard, Frederick, Lord 1858-1945 Colonial administrator, whose notable contribution was policy of "indirect" rule through tribal chiefs. High Commissioner Northern Nigeria 1900-6, Governor General of all Nigeria 1914-19.

Macadam, John Loudon 1756-1836 As surveyor general of Bristol roads from 1815, employed a wear-resistant road surface of layers of broken stone. His method was adopted throughout the world.

Macaulay, Thomas Babington, Lord 1800-59 Whig MP from 1830, member of Supreme Council of India 1834-38, helped compose criminal code for India 1835. Secretary for War 1839-41, Paymaster of Forces 1846-47. Baron 1857. Wrote an unfinished five-volume *History of England* in which archetypal "Whig interpretation" of English history is found.

Macbeth c.1005-57 Earl of Moray, perhaps grandson of Malcolm II: King of Scots 1040-57. Killed Duncan I at Elgin in 1040, but defeated at Dunsinane 1054 by Siward. Killed in 1057 by Duncan's son Malcolm Canmore.

MacDonald, James Ramsay 1866-1937 Joined Social Democratic Federation 1885, Fabian Society 1886, Independent Labour party 1894. First secretary of Labour Representation Committee (from 1906 the Labour party) 1900-12. Labour MP from 1906, leader of the Parliamentary Labour party 1911-14, opposed the war, but then agreed it must be won. Labour Prime Minister and Foreign Secretary 1924 and 1929-31. In 1931 formed National Government and divided Labour party; Prime Minister until 1935.

Macdonald, John, last Lord of the Isles, earl of Ross d. 1498 Rebelled against James II 1453, but pardoned. Attempted to establish himself as King of Hebrides, with English support: attainted for treason 1475, was pardoned but retired to Paisley Abbey.

Macmillan, Maurice Harold, earl of Stockton b.1894 Conservative MP 1924-64. Critic of appeasement, first achieved office during war; Minister of Housing 1951-54, of Defence 1954-55, Foreign Secretary 1955, Chancellor of the Exechequer 1955-57. As Prime Minister 1957-63, saw colonies to independence. Retired on health grounds 1963 after Profumo scandal.

Madog ap Maredudd d.1160 Prince of Powys from 1132, defeated by Owain of Gwynedd 1150 but recovered some lands with English support 1157.

Maitland of Thirlestane, John, Lord 1543-95 Keeper of Privy Seal 1567-70, Secretary of State 1584 and the most important of James VI's advisers. Chancellor 1587. Careful administrator, responsible for creating presbyterian form of Kirk.

Malcolm I (Macdonald) d.954 King of Scotia 943-54, harried Northumbria but preoccupied with internal rebellion.

Malcolm II (MacKenneth) c.950-1034 Son of Kenneth II, King of Scotia 1005-34: succeeded by killing Kenneth III. Captured Lothian from the English 1018, but submitted to Cnut after English invasion 1031.

Malcolm III Canmore c.1031-93 Son of Duncan I, defeated Macbeth 1054 with English help, and succeeded to throne after killing Macbeth 1057. Married Margaret, sister of Edgar the Aetheling, but submitted to William I in 1072.

Malcolm IV ("the Maiden") 1141-65 Grandson of David I: King of Scots 1153-65. Surrendered Northumberland and Cumberland to Henry II 1157, becoming his vassal 1163. Engaged in suppressing rebellions 1160-64.

Malthus, Thomas Robert 1766-1834 Influential demographic theorist, whose *Essay on the Principle of Population* 1798 stated that rising population cannot be fed by expanding food production, so growth will be checked by famine.

Manchester, Edward Montagu, earl of 1602-71 Parliamentary leader 1640-41, Parliamentarian commander at Marston Moor 1644. Resigned after Cromwell charged him with incompetence at Newbury 1645. Opposed Charles I's trial and welcomed the return of Charles II.

Manning, Henry Edward 1808-92 Anglican Archdeacon of Chichester 1841, but became Roman Catholic 1851 after Gorham Judgement. As priest, involved in mission work in Bayswater from 1857. Archbishop of Westminster 1865, campaigned for papal infallibility, Cardinal 1875. Member of royal commissions on housing 1884-85, and education 1886-87.

Mansfield, William Murray, earl of 1705-93 MP 1742 and Solicitor General, Lord Chief Justice 1756-88. Reversed Wilkes's outlawry on a technicality, improved mercantile law, judgement declared slavery illegal in England 1772. But strict interpretation of law earned unpopularity, especially in "Letters of Junius" 1770-72. His house was sacked in Gordon riots 1780.

Mar, John Erskine, earl of d.1572 Supported Mary Queen of Scots, suppressing Moray's rebellion 1566, but her marriage to Bothwell alienated him. From 1566, guardian of Prince James (King James VI from 1567), regent 1571-72.

Margaret c.1046-93 Queen consort of Malcolm III Canmore, sister of Edgar the Aetheling. She introduced Roman uses and Benedictine monks into Scottish Church. Canonized 1250.

Margaret of Anjou 1430-82 Daughter of duke of Anjou: Queen consort of Henry VI 1445. Defeated Warwick at St Albans 1460, but after Yorkist victory at Towton 1461 fled to Scotland with Henry. Appealed to Louis XI for aid, and unsuccessfully invaded Northumberland with French troops 1462. Landed in England again 1471 but she and Warwick were defeated at Tewkesbury: her son Edward was killed and husband later murdered. She was imprisoned, but ransomed by Louis XI and died in France.

Margaret, duchess of Burgundy 1446-1503 Sister of Edward IV: married Charles, duke of Burgundy 1468. Reconciled Edward and Clarence in 1470; supported Warbeck and Simnel against Henry VII but was pardoned 1498. Patroness of Caxton.

Margaret of Denmark 1457-86 Daughter of Christian I of Denmark and Norway: Queen consort of James III of Scotland 1469. Part of her marriage dowry 1469 was Orkney and Shetland Islands.

Margaret of France 1282-1318 Daughter of Philip III of France: Queen consort of Edward I from 1299; marriage was part of a treaty between the two kings.

Margaret Tudor 1489-1541 Daughter of Henry VII: Queen consort of James IV 1503. After husband's death at Flodden 1513, Margaret was regent and guardian of her son James V. Married earl of Angus 1514, but in 1515 was compelled to give up the regency and left for England. Returned to Scotland 1517. Quarrelled with Angus, and in 1527 divorced him, marrying duke of Albany, temporarily ending disputes between pro-French and pro-English parties.

Marlborough, John Churchill, duke of 1650-1722 Entered army 1667, Colonel of Foot 1678. Served as agent between the duke of York and Charles II, envoy to Louis XIV in 1685, crushed Monmouth's rebellion, and was created a peer, 1685. Shifted support to William of Orange, rewarded with earldom 1689. Privy Councillor 1690 but imprisoned for two months for correspondence with James II. In 1702, at accession of wife's friend Queen Anne, made duke, Captain-General of forces and Commander of the allied troops in War of Spanish Succession. Victories at Blenheim 1704, Ramillies 1706, Oudenarde 1708 and Malplaquet 1709. Lost favour after 1710 Tory election victory: dismissed 1711, but active in arranging Hanoverian succession and restored to favour.

Marlowe, Christopher 1564-93 His plays include *Tamburlaine the Great, Dr Faustus*

and *Edward II,* as well as *Henry VI* – completed by Shakespeare: notable for psychological insight and portrayal of human ambition.

Marshal, William, earl of Pembroke d.1219 Fought alongside Henry II in France 1168, guardian of Prince Henry from 1170. Crusader in Syria 1183-87. Remained loyal to Henry II against the rebel princes, but served under Richard I and was John's chief counsellor. Regent to Henry III from 1216, drove out Louis of France 1217, confirmed Magna Carta and reimposed order.

Martineau, Harriet 1802-76 Unitarian popularizer on a wide range of topics: authoress of *Illustrations of Political Economy* 1832-34, *Poor Law and Paupers Illustrated* 1833 and books about American society and her experiences in Middle East; cabinet ministers sought her advice.

Marvell, Andrew 1621-78 Puritan poet, tutor to Cromwells and Fairfaxes, and assistant to Milton as Latin secretary 1657. Under Charles II, advocated a republic and published pamphlets and satires of the king and ministers.

Mary 1542-87 Daughter of James V and Mary of Guise: Queen of Scots 1542-67. Sent to France 1548; married dauphin Francis 1558; widowed 1560 and returned, Catholic and pro-French, to a Protestant Scotland 1561. Married cousin Lord Darnley 1565, son James born 1566. After Darnley's murder 1567 her marriage to earl of Bothwell turned opinion against her, and she was forced to surrender to Protestant lords at Carberry Hill. Escaped from imprisonment but was defeated at Langside 1568 and fled. In prison in England, she became focus of Catholic opposition to Elizabeth; after suspected complicity in Catholic plots, was executed.

Mary I 1516-58 Daughter of Henry VIII and Catherine of Aragon: Queen of England and Ireland 1553-58. She was a devout Catholic and set about restoring the faith to England. Her marriage to Philip of Spain in 1554 was unpopular and caused rebellion and plotting: the marriage also led to expensive unpopular war with France in which Calais was lost 1558. Mary re-enacted the heresy laws and about 280 Protestants were burned. She died childless, succeeded by sister Elizabeth.

Mary II 1662-94 Daughter of James II: married William of Orange 1677; Queen of England, Scotland and Ireland from 1689.

Accepting the Crown jointly with William, played little part in politics, although carefully exercised ecclesiastical patronage.

Mary of France 1496-1533 Daughter of Henry VII by Elizabeth of York, Queen of Louis XII of France. On Louis' death, 1515, married Charles Brandon, duke of Suffolk. Her daughter by him, Frances, was mother of Lady Jane Grey.

Mary of Guise 1515-60 Daughter of duke of Guise: Queen consort of James V of Scotland 1538-42, mother of Mary Queen of Scots. After 1542, advanced French interests against pro-English regent earl of Arran; as regent 1554-60, sought to crush Protestantism and maintain French alliance.

Mary of Modena 1658-1718 Queen consort, second wife of James II, married 1673. Unpopular in England as a Catholic, fled to France 1688, corresponded actively with Jacobites.

Masham, Lady Abigail d. 1734 Replaced her cousin and patroness, Sarah Churchill, as Queen Anne's favourite 1710. Ally of Harley, but involved in his dismissal 1714; associated with Jacobites 1715.

Matilda (Maud) 1102-67 Daughter of Henry I: married Emperor Henry V 1114 and after his death, Geoffrey of Anjou 1128. Recognized as Henry I's successor from 1126 (confirmed 1131 and 1133), but Stephen seized the throne in 1135. Matilda invaded England 1139 and had some success, but forced to flee to Normandy 1147. Her son became Henry II.

Matthew, Tobias 1546-1628 Oxford Calvinist theologian, Dean of Christ Church 1576, Vice-Chancellor 1579, Dean of Durham 1584 and Bishop 1595, Archbishop of York 1606. Sympathetic to Puritans, active pastor and preacher, persecutor of Catholics.

Melbourne, William Lamb, Viscount 1779-1848 Whig MP from 1806, supporter of Catholic emancipation, Irish Secretary 1827-28, Home Secretary 1830-34, Prime Minister 1834, 1835-41. Repressed working-class disorders and influenced the young Queen Victoria.

Melville, Andrew 1545-1622 Studied in France and Geneva, returned to Scotland 1573 and assisted in reforming Glasgow, Aberdeen and St Andrews universities. Drafted 1578 presbyterian *Second Book of Discipline,* moderator of Kirk assemblies, but resisted by James VI who sought royal control of Church. Imprisoned in London 1607-11, then professor in France.

Methuen, John 1650-1706 MP 1690, envoy to Portugal 1691. Lord Chancellor of Ireland 1697. Ambassador to Portugal 1703, concluded Methuen Treaty permitting English textiles into Portugal in return for lower duties on port wine.

Mill, James 1773-1836 Leading philosophic radical and disciple of Bentham: founded school to teach utilitarian principles 1814, which became London University. He wrote a *History of British India* 1818 *Elements of Political Economy* 1821 and *Analysis of the Phenomena of the Human Mind* 1829.

Mill, John Stuart 1806-73 Son of James, who educated him. Founder of Utilitarian Society 1823, and leading contributor to radical *London Review*. Author of *A System of Logic* 1843, *Utilitarianism* 1863 and *On Liberty* 1859. Liberal MP 1865-68.

Milner, Alfred, Viscount 1854-1925 Under-Secretary for Finance in Egypt 1889-92, Chairman of Board of Inland Revenue 1892-97. High Commissioner of South Africa 1897-1905, advocate of "enlightened" imperial rule; served in Lloyd George's War Cabinet 1916-18; as Colonial Secretary 1919-21, worked for Egyptian independence.

Milton, John 1608-74 Wrote lyric poems in 1630s, political pamphlets in 1640s (against episcopacy and in defence of divorce and free press) and epic poems in last years (*Paradise Lost* 1667, *Paradise Regained* 1671). Latin secretary to Council of State 1649, defended execution of Charles I.

Monck, George, duke of Albemarle 1608-70 Professional soldier, fought against Scots 1640 and Irish rebels 1642-43, and Parliament in Civil War: taken prisoner at Nantwich 1644. Commanded Parliament's forces in Ireland 1647, and in Scotland 1650-51, 1654-60. Marched to London 1660, secured dissolution of Long Parliament and restoration of monarchy. Duke and Captain General 1660, Governor of London in 1665 Plague, Admiral in Dutch War 1665-67.

Monmouth, James Scott, duke of 1649-85 Illegitimate son of Charles II, acknowledged 1663 and created duke. Privy councillor 1670, military commander against Dutch 1672-73, French 1678, Covenanters 1679. Exclusionist candidate for throne, banished 1679-80, 1684:

returned 1685, claimed throne and raised support in West, but defeated at Sedgemoor, captured and executed.

Montfort, Simon de, earl of Leicester c.1208-65 Married Eleanor, sister of Henry III, 1238, fought in Palestine 1240-41, and Poitou 1242, Governor of Gascony 1248-52. As leader of baronial opposition to king, helped draw up Provisions of Oxford 1258. Withdrew to France 1261; after failure of mediation, defeated royal forces at Lewes 1264, capturing king and Prince Edward. Summoned a parliament 1265, the first to include borough representatives. After escape of Edward, Montfort was defeated and killed at Evesham.

Montgomery, Bernard Law, Viscount 1887-1979 Soldier from 1908, Commander of Eighth Army, defeated Rommel at El Alamein 1942. Commanded land forces in invasion of Normandy 1944, and occupation forces in Germany after war. Chief of General Staff, Deputy Supreme Commander of NATO forces 1951-58.

Montrose, James Graham, earl and marquis of 1612-50 Joined Covenanters 1638 but switched to Charles I 1641; won several victories for king in Scotland 1644-45, but was defeated at Philiphaugh 1645. In exile 1645-50, then raised new army and was defeated at Invercarron; executed.

Moore, Sir John 1761-1809 Soldier from 1776, served in North America, Mediterranean, West Indies and Ireland. Commander in Mediterranean 1806, Sweden and Peninsula 1808. Led the 250-mile retreat in winter to Corunna, where he was killed in successful battle against French. Pioneer of modern light-infantry tactics.

Moray, James Stuart, earl of c.1531-70 Illegitimate son of James V, played leading role in Scottish Reformation 1559-60. Held power under Mary Queen of Scots, promoting a Protestant pro-English policy. Opposed Darnley marriage and rebelled 1565, but was defeated: regent of Scotland on Mary's abdication 1567. Assassinated.

More, Sir Thomas 1478-1535 London lawyer, MP from 1504. Humanist scholar, friend of Erasmus, Lily and Colet, highly favoured by Henry VIII. Knighted 1521, Speaker of House of Commons 1523. Served on diplomatic missions 1514-15, 1527 and 1528; Chancellor of Duchy of Lancaster 1525-29, Lord Chancellor 1529-32: vigorous policy against heresy, but resigned in opposition to Henry's divorce and its

implications. Imprisoned 1534, convicted of treason on perjured evidence, and executed. His best known work is *Utopia* 1516, which describes an ideal society. Canonized 1935.

Morgan, Sir Henry c.1635-88 Commanded a privateer 1663, and sailed against Spanish in Caribbean. Plundered Panama 1670-71 but arrested for piracy 1672: acquitted, knighted 1675, and appointed Lieutenant Governor of Jamaica.

Morley, John, Viscount 1838-1923 Liberal MP from 1883; Chief Secretary for Ireland 1886, 1892-95. Secretary for India 1905-10; Lord President of Council 1910-14. Journalist and author, biographer of Cobden and Gladstone.

Morris, William 1834-96 Poet, artist and socialist, disliked industrialization and sought return to individual craftsmanship. Founded Society for Protection of Ancient Buildings 1877, pioneered return to medieval styles in his fabric and wallpaper designs. Joined Social Democratic Federation 1883, seceded and formed Socialist League 1884.

Morrison, Herbert, Lord 1888-1965 London Labour councillor 1922-45, Labour MP from 1923, life peer 1959. Minister of Transport 1929-31, creator of London Passenger Transport Board 1933, Home Secretary 1940-45, Lord Privy Seal 1945-51, Foreign Secretary 1951.

Mortimer, Edmund, earl of March 1352-81 Married a grand-daughter of Edward III, thus giving the House of York its claim to the throne. Led Court opposition to John of Gaunt; Earl Marshal of England 1369-77, Lieutenant of Ireland 1379-81.

Mortimer, Roger, earl of March c.1287-1330 Lieutenant of Ireland, from 1316, fought there and in Wales against Despensers. Imprisoned by Edward II 1322, but escaped to France 1324 and became lover and adviser of Isabella, Edward's estranged wife. They invaded England 1326, deposed Edward II 1327 and installed his son as king. Mortimer ruled until Edward III had him executed.

Morton, James Douglas, earl of 1516-81 Privy Councillor to Mary Queen of Scots, Lord Chancellor 1563-66. Involved in murder of Riccio, Mary's favourite 1566, defeated Bothwell at Carberry Hill 1567 and Mary at Langside 1568. Regent 1572-78, overthrown by Lennox and executed. Promoted alliance with England and tried to continue episcopal system in Scotland.

Morton, John c.1420-1500 Master of Rolls 1473, Bishop of Ely 1479, arrested 1483 but escaped to Flanders until returned with Henry VII. Privy Councillor 1485, Archbishop of Canterbury 1486, Lord Chancellor 1487, Cardinal 1493. Chief adviser to Henry VII.

Morton, Thomas 1564-1659 Chaplain to James I, Dean of Gloucester 1606, Bishop of Chester 1616, Lichfield 1618, Durham 1632. A Calvinist, he made vigorous efforts to convert Catholics to established Church, and to justify conformity to its rituals against Puritan criticism. Deprived of his see by Parliament in 1645.

Mosley, Sir Oswald 1896-1981 MP from 1918, first Conservative, then Independent, then Labour, until 1931. Founded British Union of Fascists 1932; imprisoned 1940-43. Founded right-wing Union Movement 1948.

Mountbatten, Louis, Earl 1900-79 Great-grandson of Queen Victoria: naval officer, Chief of Combined Operations 1942-43, Supreme Allied Commander South East Asia 1943-45. In 1947, as Viceroy of India, supervised transition to independence in India and Pakistan. Commander-in-Chief Mediterranean Fleet 1952-54. First Sea Lord 1955-59. Murdered by IRA.

Mountjoy, Charles Blount, Lord 1563-1603 Elizabethan MP, courtier and soldier. Fought in Netherlands, served on Azores expedition 1597. As Lord Deputy of Ireland 1601-3, defeated Spanish force at Kinsale and suppressed O'Neill's revolt. Earl of Devonshire 1603.

Mowbray, Thomas, duke of Norfolk c.1366-99 Fought against Scots 1384, Lord Appellant 1387, reconciled to Richard II and made warden of Scottish Marches 1389 and governor of Calais 1391. Probably involved in murder of Thomas of Woodstock 1397. Banished after Bolingbroke accused him of treason.

Murray, Lord George c.1700-60 Jacobite leader, defeated government troops at Prestonpans 1745, captured Carlisle and routed official forces at Falkirk 1746. A commander at Culloden, and on defeat retired to France.

Napier, Robert Conelis, Lord 1810-90 Soldier and engineer, served with Bengal Engineers in India on irrigation schemes 1828-42, in Sikh Wars 1845, 1848, against Indian Mutiny 1857-58, and in China. Successful commander of Abyssinian expedition 1867-68. Baron 1868, Commander-in-Chief in India 1870, Governor of Gibraltar 1876.

Nash, John 1752-1835 Architect, patronized by Prince Regent: laid out Regent's Park 1811 and Regent Street, London. Enlarged Buckingham Palace, designed Brighton Pavilion.

Nelson, Horatio, Viscount 1758-1805 Joined navy 1770, served in West Indies, North America and French Revolutionary Wars. Lost right eye at Calvi, Corsica 1794 and right arm at Santa Cruz 1797. Helped defeat French and Spanish at Cape St Vincent 1797; destroyed French fleet at Aboukir Bay 1798; crushed a rebellion in Naples 1799; defeated Danish fleet at Copenhagen 1801. Blockaded French at Toulon 1803-5: they escaped, but after six-month chase across Atlantic and back he defeated French and Spanish fleet at Trafalgar, where he was killed. Rear Admiral 1797, baron 1798, viscount 1801.

Neville, George c.1432-76 Brother of Warwick the Kingmaker, Bishop of Exeter 1455, Archbishop of York 1465. Lord Chancellor 1460-67, 1470-71, but removed on Edward IV's return and imprisoned 1471-74.

Neville, Richard, earl of Warwick and Salisbury ("The King Maker") 1428-71 Enormously wealthy landowner, supported Richard of York in 1455, but after defeat in 1459 retired to Calais. Returned 1460, gained victories against Henry VI at Northampton, St Albans, Towton, and established Edward of York as King Edward IV. As Lord Chamberlain had great influence until Edward married Elizabeth Wydeville 1464. Intrigued with duke of Clarence, Edward's brother, and in 1470 captured Edward briefly; joined Lancastrians, but defeated and killed by Edward IV at Barnet 1471.

Newcastle, Thomas Pelham-Holles, duke of 1693-1768 Rich landowner, Secretary of State 1724-54, First Lord of Treasury 1754-56, 1757-62, Lord Privy Seal 1765-66. Skilled manipulator of patronage to main governments of Walpole and brother Pelham.

Newcastle, William Cavendish, duke of 1592-1676 Courtier, earl of Newcastle 1628; Royalist commander in north of England in Civil War, but, after 1643 successes, fled to Continent following defeat at Marston Moor 1644. Duke 1664, in compensation for expenditure in Royalist cause.

Newman, John Henry 1801-90 Vicar of St Mary's Oxford 1828-43, a leader of Oxford Movement from 1833 and author of many *Tracts for the Times*. Became Roman Catholic 1845, priest 1847, Cardinal 1879. Founded Dublin University from 1851, published *Apologia pro vita sua* 1864, *Grammar of Assent* 1870.

Newton, Sir Isaac 1642-1727 Natural philosopher, discovered differential and integrated calculus; formulated idea of universal gravitation; published laws of motion in *Philosophiae Naturalis Principia Mathematica* 1687; experimented with optics, building several reflecting telescopes and showing that white light is composed of rays of different colours. Fellow of Royal Society from 1672, President from 1703; Warden of Royal Mint from 1696.

Nightingale, Florence 1820-1910 Superintendent of nurses in British hospitals in Crimean War from 1854, she improved conditions and organization and laid the foundations of modern nursing.

Norfolk, John Howard, duke of c.1430-85 Fought in Gascony 1453, household officer and ambassador for Edward IV, created baron by Henry VI 1470. Supporter of Richard III, who made him duke, Earl Marshal and Admiral of England 1483. Killed at Bosworth Field.

Norfolk, Thomas Howard, earl of Surrey and duke of 1443-1524 Fought for Edward IV at Barnet, earl 1483, fought for Richard III at Bosworth but pardoned by Henry VII, subdued 1489 Yorkshire rebellion. Lord Treasurer 1501-22, Earl Marshal 1510, duke 1514. Defeated Scots at Flodden 1513, campaigned against French 1522 and Scots 1523.

Norfolk, Thomas Howard, duke of 1473-1554 Lord Admiral 1513, led the van at Flodden, earl of Surrey 1514. Lord Lieutenant of Ireland 1520-21, Lord Treasurer 1522-46, duke 1524. Opponent of Wolsey and then Cromwell at Court; worked through nieces Anne Boleyn and Catherine Howard to influence Henry VIII. Fought Scots and French in 1540s; imprisoned 1546-53, but released by Mary.

Norfolk, Thomas Howard, duke of 1536-72 Lieutenant in the North 1559-60, a leader of conservatives in 1560s and plotted to marry Mary Queen of Scots; arrested 1569 after northern rebellion, but released; arrested and executed after Ridolfi plot.

North, Frederick, Lord 1732-92 MP from 1754, Junior Lord of Treasury 1759-66, Paymaster of Forces 1766, Chancellor of Exchequer 1767-82, Prime Minister 1770-82. Policy failures in North America caused mounting unpopularity, and he submitted resignation several times from 1777, until George III accepted after Yorktown. Home Secretary in 1783 Fox-North coalition.

Northumberland, John Dudley, duke of *c.*1502-53 Courtier, Warden of Scottish Marches 1542, Admiral 1543-47, 1549-50, successful against French. Earl of Warwick and member of regency council 1547, Lord President of Council and virtual ruler 1550-53, duke 1551. Furthered administrative reform and Protestant cause under Edward VI; attempted to place daughter-in-law, Jane Grey, on throne at Edward's death. Executed for treason.

Nottingham, Daniel Finch, earl of 1647-1730 Son of Heneage: First Lord of the Admiralty 1681-84, negotiated with William of Orange 1687, Secretary of State 1688-93, 1702-4, Lord President of Council 1714-16.

Nottingham, Heneage Finch, earl of 1621-82 Solicitor General 1660, prosecuted regicides, Attorney General 1670, Lord Keeper 1673-75, Lord Chancellor 1675-82. Earl 1681.

Nuffield, William Morris, Viscount 1877-1963 Motor car manufacturer, producing his first car 1913; first to mass-produce automobiles in Britain. Endowed Nuffield College, Oxford and Nuffield Foundation.

Oates, Titus 1649-1705 After discreditable career as Anglican chaplain, infiltrated Catholic circles. Invented Popish Plot 1678, and informed against Catholics; convicted of perjury and imprisoned 1685, although released and pensioned 1689.

O'Brien, James Bronterre 1805-64 Chartist journalist, editor of *Poor Man's Guardian* 1831-35; advocated force in *Northern Star,* founded 1837, and was imprisoned for sedition in 1840.

O'Brien, William 1852-1928 MP 1885-86, 1887-92, 1910-18; keen supporter of Irish Land League, voicing its views as editor of the *United Ireland* from 1881.

O'Connell, Daniel ("The Liberator") 1775-1847 Irish barrister, campaigned against 1800 Union and for Catholic emancipation; formed Catholic Association 1823, MP from 1828, founded anti-Union Repeal Association 1840, tried for conspiracy 1843. Used mass meetings to achieve political change, although advocated peaceful means: responsible for re-creation of national feeling in Ireland.

O'Connor, Feargus 1794-1855 Irish radical MP 1832-35, joined Chartists, founded *Northern Star* 1837, advocating peasant proprietorship of land. Imprisoned for seditious libel in 1840, MP 1847, died insane after Chartist petition of 1848 failed.

Odo *c.*1030-97 Bishop of Bayeux, earl of Kent, half-brother to William I. Regent of England in William's absence 1067, 1080; acquired vast wealth and attempted to succeed to papacy. Imprisoned 1082-87, led baronial opposition to William II and was exiled to Normandy 1088. Died on crusade.

Offa d.796 King of Mercia 757-96: extended his power across southern England, probably building Offa's Dyke as boundary with Welsh tribes; claimed to be king of all England by 774. His daughters married into houses of Wessex and Northumbria and he traded and corresponded with Charlemagne.

Oglethorpe, James Edward 1696-1785 Soldier, founder of colony of Georgia 1732, as a refuge for paupers and debtors and a barrier against Spanish expansion. He banned slavery there, despite opposition. Returned home 1743, fought against Jacobites. MP for 32 years.

O'Higgins, Kevin Christopher 1892-1927 Sinn Fein MP from 1918, in 1921 he supported the treaty establishing the Irish Free State. Minister of Justice 1923; murdered 1927.

O'Kelly, Sean Thomas 1883-1966 Founder member of Sinn Fein with De Valera; repudiated the 1921 treaty establishing the Irish Free State. President of Ireland 1945-59.

Olaf Sihtricson d.981 King at York 940-44, 949-52. Driven out of York by Edmund 944, returned to Ireland to establish kingdom there; King of Dublin 945-80; failed to retain York at second attempt 949-52. Defeated at Tara by Irish 980.

Oldcastle, Sir John d. 1417 Soldier, friend of Henry V, convicted of heresy 1413, but escaped and tried to organize Lollard rebellion 1414. After three years in hiding, captured and executed.

O'Neill, Con Bacach, earl of Tyrone *c.*1484-1559 Irish chieftain, invaded Pale 1520, 1539, 1541, but submitted to the English 1542: earl 1543, councillor of Ireland, but authority declined as he co-operated with English.

O'Neill, Hugh ("The Great O'Neill"), earl of Tyrone *c.*1540-1616 Set up as pro-English counterpoise to rival chieftain, gave nominal allegiance to Elizabeth, but rebelled from 1594, demanding restoration of confiscated land and freedom of religion. Submitted and pardoned 1603, but distrusted by James I and when summoned to England 1607 fled to Rome.

O'Neill, Owen Roe *c.*1590-1649 Irish soldier, nephew of Hugh: served Spanish for many years; from 1642 led Catholic cause in Ulster, winning the battle of Benburb 1646.

O'Neill, Sir Phelim *c.*1604-53 A leader of Ulster rebellion 1641, commanded Catholic forces until Owen Roe succeeded him 1642; tried and executed by English 1653.

O'Neill, Shane, earl of Tyrone *c.*1530-67 Expelled father Con Bacach from chieftainship 1556, recognized by Elizabeth 1560. His wilful independence and harrying of Pale provoked punitive expedition by Sir Henry Sidney 1567; murdered.

Ormonde, James Butler, earl and duke of 1610-88 Irish nobleman, educated in England as a Protestant. Commanded Royalist forces in Ireland from 1641, but went into exile after defeat 1649. Lord Lieutenant of Ireland 1661-69, 1677-84; restored Protestant episcopate. Opposed James II's Catholic policies.

Ormonde, James Butler, duke of 1665-1745 Soldier, fought for William III in Ireland; Lord Lieutenant of Ireland 1703-5, 1710-11, Commander in Chief in Flanders 1711, opposed George I's accession, attempted Jacobite invasions, lived in exile.

Oswald *c.*604-642 Defeated Caedwalla near Hexham in 634, uniting Bernicia and Deira; King of Northumbria. Helped Aidan, Bishop of Lindisfarne, to bring Christianity to kingdom. Acknowledged bretwalda by West Saxons and Kent, but died in battle with Mercians. Canonized.

Oswald d.992 Bishop of Worcester 961-92, Archbishop of York 972-92; founded monasteries at Worcester, Winchcombe, Ramsey and Westbury; followed Dunstan's policy of removing married clergy from cathedrals. Patron of learning. Canonized.

Oswy 612-70 Succeeded brother Oswald as King of Bernicia 642, re-united Northumbria 654 after killing Oswin of Deira; King of Northumbria 654-70; defeated overlord Penda 655, becoming bretwalda. Presided over synod at Whitby 664, accepted Roman rite.

Owain Gwynedd (Owain ap Gruffudd) c.1110-70 King of Gwynedd 1137-69, expanded his territory in north Wales, paid homage to Henry II in 1157, but allied with Rhys ap Gruffudd to repel Henry's invasion of south Wales in 1165.

Owen, Sir Hugh 1804-81 Chief Clerk of Poor Law Commission 1853-72. As Secretary to Cambrian Educational Society from 1846, organized deaf and dumb education, state-aided education and founding of University College, Aberystwyth, teacher-training colleges and charities.

Owen, Robert 1771-1858 Philanthropist and socialist, introduced improved conditions at mills in New Lanark. Promoted Factory Act 1819 and experimental co-operative communities; tried to organize Grand National Consolidated Trades Union 1834 but opposed by employers.

Oxford, Robert de Vere, earl of 1362-92 One of Richard II's favourites: created marquis of Dublin 1385, duke 1386. Angered by his influence, Lords Appellant charged him with treason 1387; he raised army at Chester, marched on London, but defeated by Bolingbroke at Radcot Bridge.

Paget, William, Lord 1505-63 Diplomat and politician: Secretary of State from 1543, and one of closest advisers to Henry VIII and Protector Somerset. Distrusted by Northumberland, in 1552 was degraded from Garter and fined. Mary restored him; Lord Privy Seal 1555-58.

Paine, Thomas 1737-1809 Inspired by revolutions in North America and France, his *Rights of Man* 1791-92 attacked Burke's *Reflections on the Revolution*. An important influence on English radical thought.

Palmerston, Henry John Temple, Viscount 1784-1865 MP from 1807, Secretary at War 1809-28. Foreign Secretary 1830-41, 1846-51, supporting nationalist and constitutionalist movements abroad. Reforming Home Secretary 1852-55; Prime Minister 1855-58, 1859-65.

Pandulf d. 1226 Sent by pope to England 1211 to determine succession to Canterbury; excommunicated King John. Bishop of Norwich 1215-26, papal legate 1218-21. From 1219-21, in virtual control of the country after regent's death.

Pankhurst, Emmeline 1858-1928 Campaigner for female suffrage: formed Women's Franchise League 1889, and more militant Women's Social and Political Union 1903; frequently imprisoned for militant methods.

Parker, Matthew 1504-75 Chaplain to Anne Boleyn 1535, Master of Corpus Christi, Cambridge 1544, Dean of Lincoln 1552; deprived by Mary; Archbishop of Canterbury 1559. Attempted to impose liturgical uniformity, and 1565 "Advertisements" provoked Vestments Controversy with Puritans. A noted scholar and historian of the English Church.

Parnell, Charles Stewart 1846-91 Irish MP from 1875, leader of MPs supporting Home Rule 1878. First President of National Land League 1879; imprisoned in 1881 for inflammatory speeches. Supported Gladstone's Irish policy, hoping for success by parliamentary means. Resigned party leadership in 1890 when cited in a divorce case.

Parsons, Robert 1546-1610 Oxford scholar, went to Italy 1575 and became a Jesuit. In 1580 he and Campion returned on Catholic mission to England, working amongst the gentry. Returned to Continent 1581, directed the mission and intrigued against Elizabeth. Author of anti-Protestant propaganda and *The Christian Directory* 1585.

Patrick c.373-c.463 Captured in northern Britain by Irish raiders and sold as a slave, escaped to Gaul and studied under Martin of Tours. Became a priest and bishop, and at an uncertain date returned to Ireland as a missionary. Canonized.

Paulinus d.644 Roman missionary to England 601, consecrated bishop 625, converted Edwin of Northumbria 627 and evangelized Northumbria. In 633 he fled south, becoming Bishop of Rochester. Canonized.

Pearse, Patrick Henry 1879-1916 A leader of Gaelic League; commander of Irish forces in 1916 Easter Rising; proclaimed the Irish Republic, surrendered to British and was tried and executed.

Peckham, John c.1225-92 International scholar, Provincial of English Franciscans, Archbishop of Canterbury 1279. Defended papal authority and the interest of his order, summoned councils to remedy abuses in Church. Came into conflict with Edward I for advancing ecclesiastical claims.

Peel, Sir Robert 1788-1850 Tory MP from 1809, Under Secretary for War 1810-12, Chief Secretary for Ireland 1812-18, Home Secretary 1822-27, 1828-30. Established Metropolitan Police 1829. Reversed opposition to Catholic emancipation and introduced 1829 bill. Reforming Prime Minister 1834-35, 1841-46. In 1846, after poor harvests and Irish potato famine, he repealed corn laws, divided his party and had to resign.

Pelham, Henry 1696-1754 Whig MP from 1717, Secretary for War 1724, Paymaster of Forces 1730, Prime Minister and Chancellor of the Exchequer 1743-54. Followed policy of economy, and with brother Newcastle managed Parliament through patronage.

Penda c.580-654 Powerful pagan prince of Mercians, who was certainly King from 632 after his defeat of Edwin of Northumbria; sought power over West and East Saxons, slew Oswald of Northumbria in 642; killed in great battle near Leeds.

Penn, William 1644-1718 Became a Quaker 1667 and, to avoid persecution obtained from Charles II a grant of land in America. Established colony of Pennsylvania 1681, which tolerated all monotheistic religions and espoused peace.

Pepys, Samuel 1633-1703 Diarist of period 1660-69, presenting revealing picture of Restoration London. As Secretary of Admiralty 1673-79, responsible for reforms in supply and provisions. President of Royal Society 1684.

Perceval, Spencer 1762-1812 Lawyer, Tory MP from 1796, Solicitor General 1801, Attorney General 1802. Chancellor of the Exchequer 1807-9, Prime Minister 1809-12. Assassinated in House of Commons.

Percy, Henry, earl of Northumberland 1342-1408 Marshal of England 1377, Warden of Scottish Marches, captured Berwick 1378 and made earl. Supported Richard II, but turned to Henry Bolingbroke in 1399. Rebelled 1403 but pardoned; joined Mortimer and Glyndŵr against Henry IV 1405; fled to Scotland, invaded England 1408, and was killed.

Percy, Sir Henry ("Hotspur") 1364-1403 Son of above: fought on the Scottish marches with distinction but joined father's 1403 rebellion and was killed.

Percy, Henry, earl of Northumberland 1421-61 Warden of East Marches 1439, defeated duke of York at Wakefield 1460, and Warwick at St Albans 1461, but was killed at Towton.

Percy, Henry, earl of Northumberland 1446-89 Confined to Tower by Edward IV but restored to title 1469. Great Chamberlain 1482, shifted allegiance to Henry VII at Bosworth. Killed near Thirsk, Yorkshire whilst trying to collect a subsidy.

Perkins, William 1558-1602 Seminal Cambridge Calvinist preacher and theologian; wrote against Catholics and extended doctrines of predestination and assurance.

Perrers, Alice d.1400 Influential mistress of Edward III. Accused of corrupting judges 1376 and banished by Good Parliament, but sentence was reversed 1379.

Peterborough, Charles Mordaunt, earl of 1658-1735 Intrigued against James II and as supporter of William III became First Lord of Treasury 1689. Commanded forces in Spain 1705-7, capturing Barcelona 1705; recalled 1707 to explain financing of his campaigns.

Philip of Spain 1527-98 King consort of England 1554-58 by marriage to Mary I. Left England in 1555, returned briefly in 1557 to draw Mary into Spain's war with France, in which England lost Calais. King of Spain 1556-98: supported English Catholics, dispatched Armada 1588.

Pitt the Elder, William, earl of Chatham 1708-78 MP from 1735, opposed continental involvement, especially in War of Austrian Succession. Paymaster General 1746, but dismissed in 1755. Secretary of State 1756-61: implemented policy of fighting France outside Europe. Earl 1766, Lord Privy Seal 1766-68 but resigned in ill health. Opponent of American War.

Pitt the Younger, William 1759-1806 MP from 1781, Prime Minister 1783-1801, 1804-6 (Britain's youngest ever). Reduced customs duties, brought East India Company under government control 1784, introduced Sinking Fund 1786. Formed three international coalitions, 1793, 1798, 1805 against France, but cost of wars led to introduction of income tax 1799. Resigned

when George III opposed Catholic emancipation 1801.

Place, Francis 1771-1854 Radical tailor, agitator and political organizer: opposed Sinking Fund 1816-23, helped achieve repeal of Combination Acts 1824, campaigned for 1832 Reform Act.

Plunket, Oliver 1629-1681 Catholic Archbishop of Armagh, titular primate of Ireland. Tried for treason as part of Titus Oates's fictitious Popish Plot and executed. Canonized 1976.

Plunket, William Conyngham, Lord 1764-1854 Irish MP from 1798, opposed Union. Solicitor General in 1803, Attorney General 1805. Westminster MP from 1807, campaigned for Catholic emancipation. Baron 1827, Lord Chancellor of Ireland 1830-41.

Pole, John de la, earl of Lincoln c.1462-87 Earl 1467, President of Council of North 1483, Lord Lieutenant of Ireland 1484. Nominated successor by Richard III, was killed at battle of Stoke, supporting Simnel.

Pole, Michael de la, earl of Suffolk d.1389 Baron 1366, Chancellor 1383-86, earl 1385, adviser to Richard II. Impeached for corruption 1386, fled to avoid Lords Appellant 1387, died in exile.

Pole, Reginald 1500-58 Student in Italy and humanist scholar, refused to return to England after 1534 Royal Supremacy of Henry VIII. Cardinal 1536, papal legate at Council of Trent; legate to England 1554-57 after Mary's restoration of Catholicism. Archbishop of Canterbury 1556, active in reform of Church and persecution of Protestants.

Pole, William de la, earl and duke of Suffolk 1396-1450 Fought against France 1415-31; but opposed war policy of Humphrey duke of Gloucester and promoted marriage of Henry VI to Margaret of Anjou 1445. Secured Gloucester's overthrow 1447; duke 1448, but when he ceded Anjou and Maine to France hostility to his policy peaked 1450 and he was impeached. Banished by Henry VI, but killed on leaving the country.

Portland, William Bentinck, earl of 1649-1709 Dutch noble and friend of William of Orange, negotiated with opponents of James II 1687 and came to England with William. Diplomat, involved in Treaty of Ryswick 1697 and Partition Treaties 1698, 1700.

Portland, William Henry Cavendish Bentinck, duke of 1738-1809 MP 1760-61, succeeded to dukedom 1762, Privy Councillor 1765, Lord Lieutenant of Ireland 1782. Prime Minister 1783 and 1807-9. As Home Secretary under Pitt, 1794-1801, important in passing Act of Union.

Pride, Thomas d. 1658 Parliamentary soldier who, on orders of Army Council, prevented 130 MPs from entering the Commons ("Pride's Purge" 1648), the remainder, "the Rump", voting for Charles I's trial. Pride was a commissioner at Charles's trial and signed his death warrant.

Priestley, Joseph 1733-1804 Scientist, theologian and philosopher: discoverer of oxygen 1774; experimented with electricity; anticipated many utilitarian views. Forced to emigrate to Pennsylvania 1794, after support for French Revolution.

Prynne, William 1600-69 Lawyer and Puritan pamphleteer, wrote against Arminianism 1627, stage-plays 1632, bishops 1637. Twice tried in Star Chamber, had ears removed and was imprisoned. Released by Parliament 1640, MP 1648 but attacked Parliament over taxation and was imprisoned 1650-53. Later supported Restoration.

Purcell, Henry 1658-95 King's Composer for the Violins 1677, Organist of Chapel Royal 1682; probably organist of Westminster Abbey 1680. Especially famous for choral work, also wrote music for theatre and royal occasions.

Pym, John c.1584-1643 MP from 1614, managed Buckingham's impeachment 1626, critic of Arminianism and Crown financial expedients. In Long Parliament participated in impeachments of king's ministers and helped draft Grand Remonstrance 1641. In Civil War, managed finances of Parliamentary war effort and maintained Scottish alliance.

Raedwald. d.c.627 King of East Angles: accepted Christianity probably alongside old gods. Became fourth bretwalda, defeated Aethelfrith of Northumbria 617. Probably commemorated at Sutton Hoo.

Raffles, Sir Thomas Stamford 1781-1826 Employed by East India Company, Lieutenant Governor of Java 1811-15, persuaded company to buy Singapore 1819 and started its development as commercial centre. Founded Zoological Society 1825.

Raglan, Fitzroy James Henry Somerset, Lord 1788-1855 ADC to Wellington, wounded at Waterloo, Military Administrator 1827-52, Field Marshal 1854. Commanded British troops in Crimea 1854: won battle of Alma 1854, issued ambiguous order that caused charge of Light Brigade at Balaclava.

Raleigh, Sir Walter c.1522-1618 Courtier from 1581, knighted 1584; explorer of eastern seaboard of America; attempted to colonize Virginia. Undertook an unsuccessful expedition to find El Dorado 1595; served in expeditions to Cadiz 1596 and Azores 1597. After 1603 Main Plot, imprisoned in Tower, until released 1616 to search for El Dorado again; he destroyed a Spanish settlement; executed on return. Wrote poetry and *History of the World* 1614.

Redmond, John Edward 1856-1918 Irish lawyer, MP from 1880, supported Parnell. United Irish parties in 1900, joining with Liberals 1910 to fight for Home Rule.

Reith, John Charles Walsham, Lord 1889-1971 BBC's first General Manager 1922 and Director General 1927-38: formative influence in development of broadcasting. Minister in war government.

Remigius d.1092 Monk, accompanied William the Conqueror to England. Bishop of Dorchester 1067, in 1072 moved to Lincoln and founded the cathedral.

Reynolds, Sir Joshua 1723-92 Portrait painter and founder of Literary Club 1764; first President of Royal Academy 1768.

Rhodri, Mawr ("The Great") d.877 Ruler of north Wales from 844 and expanded his territory; defeated Viking leader Gorm 856, but was killed fighting Saxons.

Rhys ap Gruffudd c.1132-97 Prince of Deheubarth by 1155, submitted to Henry II 1158 and supported him against 1173 rebellion. Justice of south Wales 1172, but resumed independence on Richard's accession.

Rhys ap Tewdwr d.1093 Prince of Deheubarth from 1078, defeated northern princes at Mynydd Carn 1081. Killed in battle against Norman invaders at Brecon.

Ricardo, David 1772-1823 In *Principles of Political Economy and Taxation* 1817, asserted that value of goods arises from labour incorporated in them. As MP 1819-23 he supported free trade.

Riccio, David c.1533-66 Secretary and favourite of Mary Queen of Scots: Darnley and other Scottish nobles resented Riccio's influence, so they murdered him.

Rich, Edmund 1175-1240 Studied at Paris and taught at Oxford. Archbishop of Canterbury from 1234: his archiepiscopate was marked by friction with the Crown, the papacy and his own monks at Canterbury. Canonized 1248.

Rich, Richard, Lord c.1496-1567 Lawyer, Solicitor General 1533; obtained evidence by deceit against Fisher, gave perjured evidence against More; Speaker 1536, Lord Chancellor 1548-51.

Richard I, Coeur de Lion 1157-99 Son of Henry II and Eleanor of Aquitaine: duke of Aquitaine 1170, in 1173-74 he and brothers rebelled against father but submitted. King of England 1189-99. In 1190 he went on crusade; defeated Saladin at Arsuf and made a truce. Kidnapped by Leopold of Austria, handed over to Emperor Henry VI and forced to pay homage and ransom. Returned to England 1194, fought against Philip Augustus in France 1194-98.

Richard II 1367-1400 Son of Edward the Black Prince: Prince of Wales 1376, King of England 1377-99. Met rebels led by Wat Tyler and personally conciliated them 1381. Country under control of John of Gaunt for much of reign. Accused of extravagance, Richard forced to accept commission to regulate household 1386; Lords Appellant persuaded Parliament to outlaw his favourites 1388. Richard took revenge on Appellants 1397; confiscated lands of Henry Bolingbroke who then invaded England. Richard abdicated 1399, died prisoner in Pontefract Castle.

Richard III 1452-85 Son of Richard, duke of York: duke of Gloucester 1461. Commanded vanguard at Barnet and Tewkesbury for brother Edward IV 1471, fought against Scots. Protector for young nephew Edward V 1483, but imprisoned him and his brother in Tower (where they were probably murdered), destroyed Wydeville faction, and took throne: King 1483-85. Put down Buckingham's revolt 1483 and ruled through northern allies, but overthrown and killed at Bosworth by Henry (VII) Tudor.

Richard, earl of Cornwall 1209-72 Son of King John: fought in France 1225-27; a leader of baronial opposition to Henry III's foreign counsellors; reconciled to Henry 1239; crusader 1240; regent 1253-54.

Elected King of Romans 1257, but never crowned Emperor. Fought for Henry in second Barons' War, captured at Lewes 1264, released 1265.

Ridley, Nicholas c.1500-55 Cambridge Protestant theologian, chaplain to Cranmer from 1537; Bishop of Rochester 1547, London 1550: energetic reformer. Supported Lady Jane Grey 1553, deprived by Mary, burned for heresy.

Ripon, George Frederick Samuel Robinson, marquis of 1827-1909 Liberal MP from 1853, earl 1859. Lord President of the Council 1868-73, Viceroy of India 1880-84, sympathetic to Indian cause. Lord Privy Seal and leader of Liberals in Lords 1905-8.

Riveaux, Peter des d.1258 Favourite of Henry III, Treasurer from 1232, but deprived 1234 because of baronial opposition to Poitevin favourites.

Rivers, Anthony Wydeville, Lord and Earl 1440-83 Transferred allegiance to Edward IV after Towton, brother of Queen Elizabeth, accompanied Edward into exile, 1470-71, guardian to Edward V 1483, executed by Richard of Gloucester. Poet and patron of Caxton.

Robert I ("the Bruce") 1274-1329 Acknowledged Edward I as King of Scotland 1295, rebelled with Wallace 1297, a Guardian of realm 1298-1300, submitted to Edward 1302-4, but had himself crowned King of Scots 1306. After 1306 defeats, gradually won back Scottish lands and in 1314 defeated Edward II at Bannockburn. Recognized as king by pope 1323, and by Edward II 1328 after invading England.

Robert II 1316-90 Grandson of Robert I: helped rule in David II's absences 1334-38, 1346-57. King of Scots 1371-90.

Robert III c.1340-1406 Eldest son of Robert II: King of Scots 1390-1406, but incapacitated and left government to Robert Stuart, duke of Albany.

Robert II Curthose, duke of Normandy c.1054-1134 Eldest son of William I. Rebelled against father 1077, 1082, but succeeded to duchy 1087. Claimed English throne from brothers William II and Henry I, but Henry defeated him at Tinchebrai 1106 and kept him in prison.

Robert, earl of Gloucester d.1147 Illegitimate son of Henry I: submitted to Stephen 1135, but quarrelled 1137 and invaded England with Matilda 1139, capturing Stephen at Lincoln 1141. Defeated Stephen again at Wilton 1143, but death led to Matilda's withdrawal.

Robert of Jumièges *fl.*1050 Norman abbot, Bishop of London 1044-51, Archbishop of Canterbury 1051-52. Leader of Norman influence at Court of William the Conqueror; expelled by Godwin.

Roberts, Frederick, Earl 1832-1914 Served in India during Mutiny and awarded Victoria Cross 1858; fought in Afghan War 1878-79; Commander in Chief in India 1885-93; Field Marshal and Commander in Ireland 1895; Commander in Chief in South Africa in Second Boer War 1899-1900, capturing Pretoria.

Roches, Peter des d.1238 Born in Poitou, Bishop of Winchester 1205, Justiciar 1214, guardian and leading adviser of Henry III; unpopular for appointing his countrymen to high office; fell from power 1234.

Rockingham, Charles Watson Wentworth, marquis of 1730-82 Leading Whig politician, Prime Minister 1765-66, 1782; mainly in opposition. Opposed war with American colonies, advocated economical reform and Catholic emancipation.

Roderic O'Connor *c.*1116-98 King of Connacht 1156, acknowledged as High King of Ireland 1166. Seized lands of Dermot MacMurrough who called in Norman assistance; defeated by Strongbow 1171, acknowledged Henry II's overlordship 1175.

Rodney, George Brydges, Lord 1719-92 Naval officer; Governor of Newfoundland 1749-50; took Grenada and St Lucia 1762. Admiral 1778, defeated Spanish off Cape St Vincent 1780, defeated French at Battle of Saints 1782.

Roger of Salisbury d. 1139 Chancellor 1101-2 and leading adviser to Henry I; Bishop of Salisbury 1102; regent in King's absences. Supported Stephen 1135 but disgraced and forced from office 1139.

Rosebery, Archibald Philip Primrose, earl of 1847-1929 Under Secretary for Scottish affairs 1881-83, Lord Privy Seal 1885, Foreign Secretary 1885-86, 1892-94, Prime Minister 1894-95. A Liberal imperialist with little enthusiasm for social reform.

Rotherham, Thomas 1423-1500 Keeper of Privy Seal 1467-74, Bishop of Rochester

1468, of Lincoln 1471. Chancellor 1474-83, Archbishop of York from 1480. Diplomat and administrator under Edward IV; kept to Church affairs under Henry VII.

Rothschild, Lionel Nathan de 1808-79 German by birth, he inherited position of Chief Manager of family's banking business in England. The first Jewish MP elected 1847; only allowed to sit 1858 when parliamentary oath was changed.

Rupert, Prince 1619-82 Son of Frederick V Elector Palatine and nephew of Charles I. Joined Charles I's forces 1642; flamboyant cavalry commander, successful at Edgehill 1642 but defeated at Marston Moor 1644, Naseby 1645. Forced to surrender Bristol 1645, exiled 1646; privateer 1649-52. Naval commander after Restoration: Lord Admiral 1673-79.

Ruskin, John 1819-1900 Influential art critic and social theorist, who advocated naturalism in art and social welfare in politics. Oxford Professor of Art 1870-79, 1883-84.

Russell, Bertrand, Earl 1872-1970 Philosopher, author of *Principles of Mathematics* 1903 and, with Whitehead, *Principia Mathematica* 1910. Social theorist and political activist: a founder member of Campaign for Nuclear Disarmament 1958.

Russell, John, Earl 1792-1878 Whig MP from 1813, moved repeal of Test and Corporation Acts 1828, managed Reform Bill 1831-32. Paymaster General 1830-34, Home Secretary 1835-39, Secretary for War 1839-41, Prime Minister 1846-52, 1865-66, Foreign Secretary 1852-53, 1859-65. Defeated over franchise reform 1866.

Rutherford, Ernest, Lord 1871-1937 New Zealand physicist, discovered nucleus of atom. Director of Cavendish Laboratory, Cambridge 1918-37. Nobel prize 1908.

Sacheverell, Henry *c.*1674-1724 High Church Tory preacher, whose 1709 sermon condemning occasional conformity and toleration led to state trial 1710 with major political consequencies.

Sackville, George Sackville Germain, Viscount 1716-85 Distinguished but erratic soldier, court martialled for neglecting to pursue enemy at Minden 1759. MP 1741-82. George III restored him to favour; Secretary of State for Colonies 1775-82.

Sackville, Thomas, earl of Dorset 1536-1608 Elizabethan diplomat and Privy Councillor: Lord Buckhurst 1567; Lord Treasurer 1599-1608, mocked as "Lord Fill-Sack"; earl 1604.

Salesbury, William *c.*1520-*c.*1600 Welsh lexicographer and Protestant scholar, wrote *Dictionary in Englyshe and Welshe* 1547; from 1563 translated the Bible into Welsh (printed 1567) with Richard Davies.

Salisbury, Robert Arthur Talbot Gascoyne-Cecil, marquis of 1830-1903 Conservative MP from 1853, marquis 1868. Secretary for India 1866-67, 1874-78, Foreign Secretary 1878-80. Prime Minister 1885-86, 1886-92, 1895-1902. Somewhat reactionary in domestic matters, imperialist in foreign affairs.

Samuel, Herbert, Viscount 1870-1963 Liberal MP from 1902. Home Secretary 1916, 1931-32. Leader of Liberals in opposition 1932-35, and in Lords 1944-1955.

Sancroft, William 1617-93 Charles II's chaplain from 1661, Dean of York, St Paul's, Archbishop of Canterbury 1678. Opposed James II's Declaration of Indulgence 1688 and was tried for resistance. Opposed William III's coronation, deprived as a non-juror 1690.

Sandwich, John Montagu, earl of 1718-92 First Lord of Admiralty 1748-51, 1763, 1771-82; Secretary of State 1763-65, 1770-71. Blamed for navy's unpreparedness in American War of Independence.

Savery, Thomas *c.*1650-1715 Invented steam engines for raising water from mines 1698, and patented paddles as means of propelling ships.

Saye and Sele, William Fiennes, Viscount 1582-1662 Viscount 1624, opposed 1626 forced loan; involved from 1630 in establishing colonies in New England. Leading parliamentary critic of Charles I 1640-42.

Scott, Sir Walter 1771-1832 Romantic poet and author of "Waverley" novels between 1814-32. Historian and collector of ballads, aided revival of interest in past.

Scrope, Richard le *c.*1350-1405 Bishop of Lichfield 1386, Archbishop of York 1398. Resisted lay spoliation of Church, rebelled with Northumberland 1405, captured and executed. His tomb at York became focus of pilgrimage.

Selden, John 1584-1654 Lawyer and historian, MP from 1624, constitutionalist critic of arbitrary government, especially in Long Parliament.

Septimus Severus, Lucius d. AD 211 Roman Senator, governor of Pannonia AD 192 when Emperor Commodus murdered. Emerged as victor in subsequent civil wars: ruthless and efficient Roman emperor 193-211. Defeated Parthians in East AD 197-99, reorganized Egypt, returned to Rome AD 203. Went to Britain AD 208 with two sons to campaign in north.

Seymour, Thomas, Lord c.1508-49 Ambassador to France 1538, Hungary 1540-42 and the Netherlands 1543. Member of regency council and Lord Admiral 1547. Married Queen Catherine Parr 1547, and on her death (1548) tried to marry Princess Elizabeth. Conspired against his brother Somerset.

Shaftesbury, Anthony Ashley Cooper, earl of 1621-83 Parliamentarian supporter from 1644 but reconciled to Charles II; Chancellor of Exchequer 1661, First Lord of Treasury in Cabal ministry 1667-72, Lord Chancellor 1672-73 but dismissed. Led Whig critics of Court from 1673, exploited Popish Plot, attempted to exclude James from succession; arrested for treason 1681, acquitted and fled to Holland.

Shaftesbury, Anthony Ashley Cooper, earl of 1801-85 Evangelical reformer, MP 1826-51. Advocated reform of lunacy laws 1829, factory reform 1833-34, improvement for colliery workers and chimney sweeps 1842, and better housing for poor.

Shakespeare, William 1564-1616 Acted with Lord Chamberlain's players from 1592, helped establish Globe Theatre London 1598. Major playwright and poet: works include tragedies, comedies, histories and sonnets.

Shaw, George Bernard 1856-1950 Irish playwright, author of *Pygmalion* 1912, and *St Joan* 1923. Leading member of Fabians.

Shelley, Percy Bysshe 1792-1822 Friend of Byron, poet and writer, atheist and democrat. Poems include *Prometheus Unbound*, *Ode to the West Wind*.

Sheridan, Richard Brinsley 1751-1816 Playwright, author of *The Rivals* 1775, *School for Scandal* 1777. Friend of Prince Regent, MP from 1780, leading parliamentary orator; Treasurer of Navy 1806-7.

Shrewsbury, Charles Talbot, earl and duke of 1660-1718 Catholic by birth, Anglican 1679, invited William III to England 1688. Secretary of State 1689-90, 1694-98, duke 1694. Lord Chamberlain 1710, ambassador to France 1713, Lieutenant of Ireland 1713, Lord Treasurer 1714: helped assure Hanoverian succession.

Shrewsbury, John Talbot, earl of c.1388-1453 Lieutenant of Ireland 1414, campaigned in France 1420-44, 1452-53. His death in battle ensured loss of Gascony.

Sidney, Algernon 1622-83 Fought against Charles I in Civil War, MP from 1646, member of Council of State in 1653, 1659. At Restoration he went abroad, but returned 1677. Convicted of complicity in Rye House Plot 1683, executed.

Sidney, Sir Philip 1554-86 Elizabethan courtier and poet, ambassador to Elector Palatine and Low Countries from 1577, MP 1581, Governor of Flushing 1584, killed fighting Spanish at Zutphen. Influential writings published posthumously, *Arcadia* 1590, *Astrophel and Stella* 1591, *Apologie for Poetrie* 1595.

Simnel, Lambert, c.1475-1525 Impersonator of Edward, earl of Warwick; crowned at Dublin as "Edward VI" 1487. His attempted invasion and rebellion was defeated at Stoke. Simnel pardoned.

Simon, John Allsebrook, Viscount 1873-1954 Liberal MP 1906-18, 1922-40; Home Secretary 1915-16. Led Liberals in National Government: Foreign Secretary 1931-35, Home Secretary 1935-37, Chancellor of Exchequer 1937-40, Lord Chancellor 1940-45.

Siward, earl of Northumberland d.1055 Dane, came to England with Cnut, receiving earldom 1041. Supported Edward the Confessor against Godwin 1051, resisted Scottish invasions, defeating Macbeth and protecting Malcolm, son of Duncan, who later became King of Scots.

Smith, Adam 1723-90 Philosophy professor at Glasgow University 1751-64. Political economist, whose *Wealth of Nations* 1776 advocated division of labour, *laissez-faire* trade and minimal government interference.

Smith, Frederick Edwin, earl of Birkenhead 1872-1930 Lawyer, Conservative MP 1906-18, Attorney General 1915-18, Lord Chancellor 1919-22, Secretary for India 1924-28.

Snowden, Philip, Viscount 1864-1937 Independent Labour party activist from 1893, Labour MP from 1906, Chancellor of Exchequer 1924, 1929-31. Briefly member of National Government, critic from 1932.

Somers, John, Lord 1651-1716 Lawyer, defended Seven Bishops 1688, Attorney General 1689, Lord Keeper 1693-97, Lord Chancellor 1697-1700. Leading minister of William III and member of Whig Junto. Lord President of Council 1708-10.

Somerset, Edward Seymour, earl of Hertford and duke of c.1506-52 Brother of Queen Jane Seymour, uncle to Edward VI. Privy Councillor from 1537, Lieutenant General in North from 1544, invaded Scotland, ravaged Lowlands and sacked Edinburgh; fought in France 1544-46. After skilful *coup* 1546-47, Protector for Edward VI 1547-49. Pursued aggressive policy in Scotland and religious and social reform in England. Overthrown as Protector 1549, remained on Council until executed by Northumberland.

Southcott, Joanna 1750-1814 Religious fanatic, from 1792 she wrote and published prophecies; attracted many followers and in 1814 announced that she was to give birth to a "Prince of Peace".

Spencer, Herbert 1820-93 Originally an engineer, he published *A System of Synthetic Philosophy* 1862-96 in nine volumes, in which he extrapolated from Darwin's theory of evolution a comprehensive social philosophy.

Stanhope, Charles, Earl 1753-1816 Eccentric radical politician, supported American independence and ideas of French Revolution. Invented various steam engines, methods of printing, calculators and experimented with electricity.

Stanhope, James, Earl 1673-1721 MP from 1701, fought in Spain 1704-5, Commander in Chief there 1708-10. Secretary of State 1714-17, checked Jacobite revolt and secured the Hanoverian succession; Lord Treasurer 1717-18, Secretary of State 1718-21. Negotiated Quadruple Alliance 1718.

Stanley, Sir Henry Morton 1841-1904 Explorer and journalist, sent by *New York Herald* to find Livingstone in Central Africa 1871. Helped organize Congo for King of Belgians 1879-84, and to establish British East African Protectorate, from 1899. Liberal Unionist MP 1895-1900.

Stephen c.1097-54 As grandson of William the Conqueror, claimed throne 1135 and was recognized by nobles, pope and David I. But rival claimant, Matilda, and Robert, earl of Gloucester, rebelled and anarchic civil war followed 1138-48. Stephen was defeated and captured at Lincoln 1141, but released after supporters' victory at Winchester. Stephen defeated Matilda at Faringdon 1145, and she withdrew 1148. After death of his only son, Stephen acknowledged Matilda's son Henry as heir by Treaty of Winchester 1153.

Stephenson, George 1781-1848 Railway inventor: his mineral line from Stockton to Darlington opened in 1825, and his Liverpool to Manchester passenger line in 1830, using "Rocket" engine.

Stigand d.1072 Chaplain to Cnut and Harold Harefoot, Bishop of Elmham 1038, Winchester 1047-70, Archbishop of Canterbury 1052-70, but deprived for uncanonical pluralism.

Strafford, Thomas Wentworth, earl of 1593-1641 MP from 1621, critic of royal financial expedients, but accepted office after death of Buckingham: President of Council in North 1628, Lord Deputy of Ireland 1632. Implemented policy of "thorough" government, and provoked fear as "Black Tom Tyrant". Recalled from Ireland 1639 to defeat rebellious Scots and manage Parliament, but impeached 1640 and executed.

Stratford, John d.1348 Diplomat, Bishop of Winchester 1323. Archbishop of Canterbury 1332; Lord Chancellor 1330-34, 1335-37, 1340. Accused of treason by Edward III 1341, but insisted on trial in Parliament; returned to royal service.

Stuart, Arabella 1575-1615 Daughter of Charles Stuart, earl of Lennox, Darnley's younger brother, second in line to throne after James I and centre of Main Plot of 1603. Married William Seymour (later duke of Somerset) 1610, another claimant to throne, so James imprisoned them.

Stuart, Charles Edward ("the Young Pretender") 1720-88 Known as "Bonnie Prince Charlie". Son of James Edward Stuart, "the Old Pretender". Raised an army in Scotland 1745, took Edinburgh and marched south to Derby before retreating. Army crushed at Culloden 1746. Fled to France and took to drink.

Stuart, James Edward ("The Old Pretender") 1688-1766 Son of James II,

taken to France in 1688. His followers proclaimed him King James III and VIII in 1701. Attempted to invade Scotland in 1708 but failed; landed in 1715 after supporters' victory at Sheriffmuir, but forced to flee in 1716; settled in Italy.

Sunderland, Charles Spencer, earl of 1674-1722 Whig MP from 1695, advanced by father-in-law Marlborough. Envoy to Vienna 1705, Secretary of State 1706-10, 1717-18, Lord Privy Seal 1715, First Lord of the Treasury 1718-21, forced to resign over South Sea Bubble crisis.

Sunderland, Robert Spencer, earl of 1641-1702 Secretary of State 1679-81, 1683-88. Opportunist in religion and politics: became Catholic 1687 but on William's accession reverted to Protestantism and helped Whig Junto to power 1696-97. Lord Chamberlain 1697, but unpopular and forced to resign.

Svein Estrithson (Forkbeard) d.1014 Driven from Denmark, attacked England 994 and 1003, and mounted full invasion 1013 with son Cnut. Took London, accepted as King of England 1013-14.

Swift, Jonathan 1667-1745 Political pamphleteer and satirist, wrote against Whigs from 1710, for which Tories made him Dean of Dublin 1713. *Drapier Letters* 1724 opposed introduction of Wood's Halfpence into Ireland; best known for satirical novel *Gulliver's Travels* 1726.

Tallis, Thomas c.1505-85 Organist at Waltham Abbey until 1540; later one of organists of Chapel Royal. In 1575 he and William Byrd received a 21-year monopoly to print music, and they published *Cantiones Sacrae* 1575. Compositions included motets, liturgical settings and instrumental pieces.

Taverner, John c.1495-1545 Master of Choristers and organist at Cardinal College, Oxford, but became involved in heretical groups and was probably dismissed 1530. Composed many motets and masses, notably *Western Wynde* mass.

Telford, Thomas 1757-1834 Builder of roads, bridges and canals from 1787: especially Ellesmere Canal 1793-1805, Caledonian Canal 1803-23, and Menai suspension bridge 1819-25. First president of Institute of Civil Engineers 1818.

Temple, Richard Temple Grenville, Earl 1711-79 MP from 1734, earl 1752; First Lord of Admiralty 1756-57, Lord

Privy Seal 1757-61. Patron of John Wilkes, whose legal expenses he paid in *North Briton* affair 1763; forced to resign as Lord Lieutenant of Buckinghamshire.

Temple, William 1881-1944 Bishop of Manchester 1921, Archbishop of York 1929, of Canterbury 1942. Influential advocate of ecumenism and social welfare programmes.

Theobald d.1161 Abbot of Bec, Archbishop of Canterbury 1138. Supported Matilda against Stephen, but crowned Stephen as King 1141; exiled 1148 and 1152 in disputes with Stephen, but reconciled him to Henry of Anjou 1153. Forwarded Thomas Becket as his successor; defended episcopal rights.

Theodore of Tarsus c.602-690 Sent to England from Rome as Archbishop of Canterbury 668: held first national English synod at Hertford 673, at which he reorganized diocesan boundaries and established parish system. Conflict with Wilfrid of York over diocesan reorganization, but reconciled 686.

Thomas, earl of Lancaster c.1277-1322 Nephew of Edward I: one of Lords Ordainers 1310, responsible for execution of Piers Gaveston 1312. Virtually governed England 1314-18, until Edward recovered power with Despensers; he struck back 1321, but defeated by Edward at Boroughbridge and executed.

Thomas of Woodstock, duke of Gloucester 1355-97 Son of Edward III: fought against French in 1380s, led opposition against Richard II 1386, one of Lords Appellant in Merciless Parliament of 1388. Richard took revenge 1397, Gloucester being arrested and, probably, murdered.

Tiptoft, John, earl of Worcester 1427-70 Lord Treasurer 1452, 1462-63, 1470, Constable of England 1462-67, 1470. As supporter of Edward IV, became known as "Butcher of England". Executed by Henry VI. Cultivated and learned, patron of Caxton.

Tone, Theobald Wolfe 1763-98 Irish lawyer, involved in anti-government activity, partly inspired by French Revolution. Founded Society of United Irishmen 1791; organized a French expedition to invade Ireland 1796, though it never landed; brought another fleet to assist 1798 revolt, was captured and committed suicide.

Tooke, John Horne 1736-1812 Briefly

supported Wilkes, and founded "Society for Supporting the Bill of Rights"; formed Constitutional Society 1771; imprisoned for trying to raise a subscription for American colonists 1778; tried for treason in Corresponding Society 1794, but acquitted.

Tostig, earl of Northumbria d.1066 Son of Earl Godwin, with whom was banished 1051. Earl 1055, fought in Scotland and Wales, but provoked Northumbria to revolt 1065 and fled abroad. In 1066 raided southern England, allied with Harold Hardrada of Norway, was killed at Stamford Bridge.

Townshend, Charles, Viscount 1675-1738 Diplomat until 1714, Secretary of State 1714-16, 1721-30. President of the Council 1720-21. Active in foreign affairs under brother-in-law Walpole, but resigned after policy disputes and turned to farming; became known as "Turnip" Townshend, for development of crop rotation.

Townshend, Charles 1725-67 MP from 1747, Secretary at War 1761-62, President of Board of Trade 1763, Paymaster General 1765. As Chancellor of Exchequer from 1766-67, implemented unpopular American Import Duties Act 1767.

Tudor, Jasper, duke of Bedford c.1431-95 Fought for Henry VI at St Albans 1455, Mortimer's Cross 1461; landed with Warwick 1470, fled after Tewkesbury 1471, returned with nephew Henry (VII) 1485, fought at Bosworth; duke 1485; helped suppress rebellions.

Tull, Jethro 1674-1741 Invented wheeled seed drill c.1701, and published *Horse Hoeing Husbandry* 1733 and other treatises which helped revolutionize agriculture.

Turner, Joseph Mallord William 1775-1851 Romantic painter, best known for such works as *The Fighting Temeraire* 1839, paintings of Venice, and experiments with colour and light such as *Rain, Steam and Speed* 1844.

Tyler, Walter or **Wat d.1381** Led 1381 Peasants' Revolt from Kent to London, where negotiated with Richard II; killed while negotiations in progress.

Tyndale, William c.1494-1536 Began to translate New Testament into English, but forced to leave for Hamburg 1524 to complete work, published 1526. Protestant, wrote against Catholic Church, including *Obedience of a Christian Man* 1528, and *Practice of Prelates* 1530.

Tyrconnell, Richard Talbot, earl of 1630-91 At Restoration, leader of Irish Catholics incriminated in fake Popish Plot 1678. Army commander in Ireland 1683, earl 1685, Lord Deputy of Ireland 1687. Implemented James II's Catholic policies, raised Ireland for him 1689, fought at Boyne 1690.

Ussher, James 1581-1656 Dublin Calvinist theologian, Bishop of Meath 1621, Archbishop of Armagh 1625. Drafted Calvinist articles of 1615 for Irish Church, proposed compromise "reduced episcopacy" for English Church 1641.

Valence, Aymer de, earl of Pembroke d. 1324 Fought for Edward I in Flanders and Scotland, Warden of Scotland 1306-7. Defeated Robert Bruce 1306, critic of Edward II; but King's Lieutenant in Scotland from 1312 and helped reconcile king and opponents 1318.

Vanbrugh, Sir John 1664-1726 Had great success as playwright to c. 1705, then architectural interests took priority: inspired by French style, visible in Castle Howard 1701, Blenheim Palace 1705.

Van Dyck, Sir Anthony 1599-1641 Portrait painter in Antwerp until invited to England 1620, when worked for James I. From 1632-40, worked for Charles I and members of Court, producing idealized and propagandist pictures.

Vane the Elder, Sir Henry 1589-1655 Diplomat and household official, Privy Councillor 1630, Secretary of State 1640-41. Opponent of Strafford in Long Parliament, dismissed by Charles I and supported Parliament.

Vane the Younger, Sir Henry 1613-62 Son of above: Puritan Governor of Massachusetts 1636-37, returned 1637, Treasurer of Navy 1639-41. MP from 1640: pressed Strafford's impeachment and abolition of episcopacy. Negotiated Solemn League and Covenant 1643; republican critic of Protectorate; opposed Restoration and was executed.

Victoria 1819-1901 Grand-daughter of George III: Queen of United Kingdom 1837-1901. Was instructed in state duties by Melbourne; married cousin Albert 1840, by whom she had nine children. Demanded to be informed on all government matters, especially foreign affairs: took close interest in Crimean War 1854-56. A decade of seclusion followed Albert's death 1861, but her popularity recovered thereafter as she

appeared in public more frequently. Her long reign was enthusiastically celebrated in Golden Jubilee 1887, and Diamond Jubilee 1897.

"Vortigern" fl.450 The word means "supreme lord"; Gildas and Bede named him as the king who invited Saxons to Britain to repel Picts and Scots. His terrritorial powers are uncertain, but probably covered the south-east.

Wade, George 1673-1748 Soldier from 1690, MP from 1715; Commander in Chief, Scotland 1724-38, built extensive road network. Field Marshal 1743; Commander in England 1745, dismissed for failing to stop Prince Charles Edward's march southwards 1745.

Wallace, William c. 1272-1305 Organized support for John Balliol against English 1297, and drove them out of southern Scotland; defeated at Falkirk by Edward I 1298. Sought help from pope and France, continued to fight Edward until captured and executed.

Waller, Sir William 1597-1668 Soldier in Germany, MP from 1640, unsuccessful Parliamentary commander in Civil War. Leading presbyterian, alienated from Army, supported Restoration.

Walpole, Sir Robert, earl of Orford 1676-1745 Whig MP from 1701, Secretary for War, 1708-10, Treasurer of Navy 1710-11. Imprisoned for corruption 1712. First Lord of the Treasury 1715-17, 1721-42. Restored public credit after South Sea Bubble, retained office by skilled use of patronage, support of Crown, and policy of peace and economy.

Walsingham, Sir Francis c. 1530-90 Diplomat, Secretary of State 1573-90, supervised collection of intelligence on foreign governments and English Catholics; probably manipulated Catholic plots to government advantage. Zealous Protestant, advocate of war with Spain.

Walter, Hubert d.1205 Archbishop of Canterbury 1193, Justiciar 1193-98, Chancellor 1199-1205 and virtual ruler of England 1194-98 when Richard I was in France. Papal legate 1195.

Walter of Coutances d. 1207 One of Henry II's clerks, Vice-Chancellor of England 1173, Bishop of Lincoln 1183, Archbishop of Rouen 1184; ambassador to France until 1191; Justiciar of England 1191-94, ruled in Richard I's absence.

Warbeck, Perkin 1474-99 Impersonator of Richard, duke of York, son of Edward IV, from 1491; received support of James IV of Scotland, Margaret of Burgundy and Emperor Maximilian I. Invasion of England from Ireland 1497 was quickly defeated; imprisoned and hanged.

Warenne, John de, earl of Surrey and Sussex c.1231-1304 Supported Henry III against barons 1258-59, de Montfort 1260-63, and Henry again 1263. Fought in Edward I's Welsh and Scottish campaigns; Warden of Scotland 1296; defeated by Wallace 1297, fought at Falkirk 1298.

Warenne, John de, earl of Surrey and Sussex 1286-1347 Accompanied Edward II to Scotland 1310; joined baronial opposition 1312; opposed Gaveston's execution and returned to Edward 1313. Feud with Thomas of Lancaster 1317-19. Took Edward II's side against Isabella, but supported abdication and Edward III's coronation 1327. Member of regency councils 1327, 1338, 1340, 1345.

Warham, William c.1450-1532 A lawyer, Master of Rolls 1494-1502, Lord Keeper 1502-4, Lord Chancellor 1504-15; Bishop of London 1502, Archbishop of Canterbury 1504. Critic of Wolsey, opposed Henry VIII's divorce from Catherine, defended clergy against lay encroachment 1529-32.

Wavell, Archibald Percival, Earl 1883-1950 Soldier, Commander in Chief in Middle East 1939-41, successful against Italians in North Africa; Commander in India and in South-East Asia, combatting Japan; Viceroy of India 1943-47.

Webb, Beatrice 1858-1943 Fabian reformer, married Sidney Webb 1892. Together they wrote on social history and welfare, sat on Royal Commission on Poor Laws 1905-9 and advocated reforms.

Webb, Sidney, Lord Passfield 1859-1947 Fabian reformer, founder of *New Statesman* and London School of Economics with wife Beatrice. Labour MP from 1922, President of Board of Trade 1924, peer 1929.

Wedgwood, Josiah 1730-95 Started pottery works at Burslem, Staffordshire, 1759, eventually in partnership with Thomas Wedgwood and Thomas Bentley. Used new materials and designs, responsible for extending roads and canals in area; highly successful industrialist.

Wellesley, Richard Colley, Marquis 1760-1842 MP from 1784, Governor-General of India 1797-1805: expanded British power by conquest and negotiation. Foreign Secretary 1809-12, tried to form a ministry himself 1812 but unsuccessful. Advocate of Catholic emancipation; Lord Lieutenant of Ireland 1821-28, 1833-34.

Wellington, Arthur Wellesley, duke of 1769-1852 Brother of above: soldier from 1787, MP from 1790; soldier and administrator in India 1797-1804; Chief Secretary of Ireland 1807-9. Commander in Portugal 1809, major victories 1813-14, duke 1814; Commander in Chief against Napoleon 1815, victory at Waterloo. Tory Cabinet minister 1818-27, active in foreign affairs; Prime Minister 1828-30, 1834; Foreign Secretary 1834-35; Cabinet minister 1841-46.

Wentworth, Peter c.1530-96 Aggressive Protestant MP from 1571, clashed with Elizabeth over limits to free speech in Parliament, but other members gave little support and he was imprisoned three times.

Wesley, John 1703-91 Anglican leader of Oxford "Holy Club" with brother Charles from 1729; was "converted" 1738 after contact with German Moravian brethren, began evangelical campaign of field-preaching 1739 and preached widely thereafter, laying foundations of Methodism.

Weston, Richard, earl of Portland 1577-1635 Customs official, Chancellor of Exchequer 1621-28, Lord Treasurer 1628-35. Leading adviser of Charles I, advocating non-parliamentary financing and Spanish alliance.

Wharton, Thomas, marquis of 1648-1715 Whig MP from 1679, supported Exclusion, mocked James II's policies with his song "Lillibullero"; joined William of Orange, Comptroller of Household 1689-1702, leader of Whig Junto; Lord Lieutenant of Ireland 1708-10, led anti-Tory opposition 1710-14; Lord Privy Seal 1714-15, marquis 1715.

Whitgift, John c. 1530-1604 Cambridge Professor of Divinity and Vice-Chancellor 1563-77, opposed nonconformity and wrote against presbyterianism; Bishop of Worcester 1577, Archbishop of Canterbury 1583. Sought to maintain liturgical conformity with 1583 Three Articles, and theological unity with moderate Calvinist Lambeth Articles 1595.

Whittington, Richard d. 1423 Mercer, Alderman 1393, Sheriff 1394 and Mayor of London 1397-98, 1406-7, 1419-20. Gave generously to almshouses and churches; lent money to Richard II, Henry IV and Henry V.

Wiglaf d.838 King of Mercia 825. Deposed *c.*828 by house of Wessex, recovered kingdom 830.

Wihtred d.725 King of Kent from 690; drew up one of earliest British law codes.

Wilberforce, William 1759-1833 Tory MP from 1780, campaigned from 1787 to success in 1807 for abolition of slave trade. Eventually succeeded in abolishing slavery in British Empire altogether 1833. Founder member of the Church Missionary Society 1798, and philanthropist.

Wilfrid 634-709 Monk, studied at Rome, Abbot of Ripon 661, where he introduced customs based on those of Italy and Gaul. Opposed Celtic party at Synod of Whitby 664. Influential in Northumbrian Church, with chief church at York. Quarrelled over jurisdiction with Theodore of Canterbury 677, Aldrid of Northumbria 692, Brihtwald of Canterbury 703. Canonized.

Wilkes, John 1727-97 MP from 1757, attacked Bute in pamphlets; published *North Briton* 1762, arrested 1763 for libel on George III but discharged; obtained verdict against general warrants 1769. Outlawed 1764, elected to Parliament three times from 1768 but election quashed despite riots. Society of Supporters of Bill of Rights helped him to take his seat in 1774.

William I ("the Conqueror") 1027-87 Duke of Normandy 1035; visited England 1051 and was probably promised throne of England; exacted promise from Harold of Wessex to uphold his claim 1064. When Harold became king 1066, William invaded England and defeated him at Hastings: King 1066-87. Quelled insurrections 1067-71, repelled Danish invasion 1069-70, invaded Scotland 1072. Set about Normanization of Church and state in practice and personnel, but had also to attend to problems in Normandy.

William II Rufus c.1060-1100 Son of William I, he fought with him against rebellious brother Robert 1079. King of England 1087-1100. Bishops Odo of Bayeux and William of Durham rebelled on behalf of Robert 1088, desiring one ruler for both England and Normandy, but William suppressed the revolt; gained Cumbria from Scots 1092; quarrelled with Archbishop Anselm. Killed while hunting.

William III 1650-1702 Grandson of Charles I, Stadtholder of the Netherlands 1672-1702, married Mary, daughter of James, duke of York 1677. Invited by critics of James II to assist in overthrow 1688, landed at Torbay. James abdicated, and William and Mary accepted throne of Great Britain from Convention Parliament; defeated James's army at Boyne 1690. Devoted himself to breaking French dominance in Europe.

William IV 1765-1837 Son of George III, served at sea 1779-90, Rear-Admiral 1790, Admiral of the Fleet 1811, heir presumptive 1827, King of United Kingdom 1830-37.

William I, the Lion *c.*1143-1214 Grandson of David I: King of Scots 1165-1214. Accompanied Henry II of England to France 1168, but joined Henry's sons in 1173 revolt; invaded England but captured at Alnwick. Forced to do homage to Henry as overlord 1175, but Richard I relinquished this hold for 10,000 marks 1189. William faced intermittent revolt, especially from Galloway.

Williams, John 1582-1650 Welsh pluralist churchman, Lord Keeper 1621-25, Bishop of Lincoln 1621; accused several times of betraying Council secrets, imprisoned 1637-40. Critic of Laudian innovations, nominated Archbishop of York 1641 as concession to opposition. Retired to Wales.

Wilmington, Spencer Compton, earl of *c.*1673-1743 MP from 1698, Speaker of Commons 1715-27, Paymaster General 1727-30, Lord Privy Seal 1730-31; First Lord of the Treasury 1742-43. Friend of George II, but overshadowed by Walpole and Carteret.

Wilson, James Harold, Lord b.1916 Labour MP from 1945; President of Board of Trade 1947-51; Leader of Labour party 1963-76; Prime Minister 1964-70, 1974-76. Life peer 1983. Pragmatic rather than socialist, sought to make Labour "the natural party of government."

Winchelsey, William d. 1313 Scholar in Paris and Oxford, Archbishop Canterbury 1294; involved in conflicts with Edward I over clerical taxation; supported Lords Ordainers against Edward II.

Wingate, Orde Charles 1903-44 Soldier in Sudan 1928-33, Palestine 1936-38. Commander of Chindits, jungle fighters who fought behind enemy lines, in Burma in Second World War.

Winstanley, Gerrard *fl.*1650 Leader of "Diggers"; with William Everard established community to assert people's right to cultivate common land. Wrote *The Law of Freedom in a Platform* 1652, defending his ideals and attacking all landowners.

Wiseman, Nicholas Patric Stephen, 1802-65 Noted Hebrew scholar, rector of English College at Rome 1828-40. Vicar Apostolic of London district 1847, Cardinal-Archbishop of Westminster 1850, when English Catholic hierarchy restored.

Wishart, George *c.*1513-46 Scottish Protestant reformer, forced to flee to Continent 1538; returned home 1543; joined Knox in denouncing ecclesiastical abuses; arrested 1545, for heresy, burned.

Wolfe, James 1725-59 Served in Flanders 1744, at Culloden 1745 and at the siege of Louisbourg 1758. Commander of successful assault on Quebec 1759, which guaranteed British control of Canada.

Wollstonecraft, Mary 1759-97 Teacher and governess; published *Thoughts on the Education of Daughters* 1787, and a pioneer feminist work *Vindication of the Rights of Women* 1792. Died in childbirth.

Wolseley, Garnet, Viscount 1833-1913 Fought in Crimean, Ashanti and Zulu Wars, in Egypt 1882, and led relief force for Gordon to Khartoum 1884-85. Colonial governor, Field Marshal 1894, a reforming Commander in Chief of forces 1895-99.

Wolsey, Thomas *c.*1475-1530 Chaplain to Henry VIII 1507, Dean of Lincoln and almoner to Henry VIII 1509. Privy Councillor 1511, involved in planning the French campaign. Bishop of Tournai 1513, of Lincoln 1514, Archbishop of York 1514; also Bishop of Bath and Wells 1518, of Durham 1523, of Winchester 1523. Cardinal 1515, Legate 1518; Lord Chancellor 1515-29. Dominated both Church and state, active in cautious ecclesiastical and judicial reform and in international negotiation. Founder of Ipswich School and Christ Church, Oxford. Fell from power 1529 as result of aristocratic plotting and failure to secure king's divorce.

Wordsworth, William 1770-1850 Romantic democrat inspired by French Revolution, published innovatory *Lyrical Ballads* with Coleridge 1798. Much of his poetry was inspired by the simplicity of rural life; major works include *The Prelude* 1799 and *Intimations of Immortality* 1807. Later opponent of liberalism; Poet Laureate 1843.

Wren, Sir Christopher 1632-1723 Professor of Astronomy in London and Oxford 1653-73; founder member of Royal Society, President 1680-82. First architectural ventures were Pembroke College Chapel, Cambridge, and Sheldonian Theatre, Oxford 1663-69. Great Fire of London 1666 gave him, as Surveyor General, opportunity to re-build St Paul's and design 52 new churches 1670-1720.

Wulfstan *c.*1010-95 Bishop of Worcester 1062, supported William I and was allowed to retain bishopric; rebuilt his cathedral and ended Bristol-based slave trade. Canonized 1203.

Wycliff, John d.1384 Oxford theologian who denied transubstantiation and papal authority, and advocated lay reading of Bible; protected by John of Gaunt from heresy charges because of his attacks on Church property and power. His pupils spread his ideas and inspired Lollards.

Wykeham, William of 1324-1404 Bishop of Winchester 1367, Lord Privy Seal 1363-66, Lord Chancellor 1368-71, 1389-91. Leading opponent of John of Gaunt, founded Winchester School and New College, Oxford.

York, Richard, duke of 1411-60 Descendant of Edward III, Lieutenant in France 1436-37, 1440-45. Sent to Ireland as Lieutenant 1447, but marched on London 1452 and displaced rivals. Protector during Henry VI's incapacity 1454-55, but driven to rebellion with Neville allies and defeated Henry at St Albans 1455; Protector 1455-56. Rebelled again 1459, claim to succession accepted, but defeated and killed at Wakefield by Lancastrian forces.

Young, Arthur 1741-1820 Agricultural writer who travelled widely in Britain and France, publishing *Travels in France* 1792 and *Annals of Agriculture* 1784-1809. Co-founder and secretary to Board of Agriculture 1793.

FURTHER READING

The following lists provide a short guide to further reading rather than a full scholarly bibliography, and they are confined to books. Wasteful repetition of key titles has been avoided, so the allocation of works to specific sections is sometimes arbitrary. The place of publication is London unless otherwise stated.

BRITONS AND ROMANS
c. 100 BC-AD 409

Overview
BIRLEY, A.R. *The People of Roman Britain* (1979)
CUNLIFFE, B.W. *Iron Age Communities in Britain* (1974)
FRERE, S. *Britannia: a History of Roman Britain* (2nd ed. 1974)
SALWAY, P. *Roman Britain* (Oxford, 1981)
TODD, M. *Roman Britain* (1981)

Government and Politics
BIRLEY, A.R. *The Fasti of Roman Britain* (Oxford, 1981)
BROWN, P. *The World of Late Antiquity* (1971)
STEVENSON, G.H. *Roman Provincial Administration* (Oxford, 1949)
WACHER, J. *Roman Britain* (1978)

Warfare and International Relations
BREEZE, D.J. *The Northern Frontiers of Roman Britain* (1982)
CONNOLLY, P. *Greece and Rome at War* (1981)
JOHNSON, J.S. *Roman Forts of the Saxon Shore* (revised ed. 1979)
NASH-WILLIAMS, V.E. *The Roman Frontier in Wales* (2nd ed., revised by M.G. Jarrett, Cardiff, 1969)
WEBSTER, G. *The Roman Imperial Army of the First and Second Centuries AD* (revised ed. 1979)

Economy
CUNLIFFE, B.W. (ed.) *Coinage and Society in Britain and Gaul* (1981)
MCWHIRR, A.D. *Roman Crafts and Industries* (Aylesbury, 1982)
STRONG, D.E. and BROWN D. *Roman Crafts* (1976)
TAYLOR, J. DU PLAT and CLEERE, H. (eds.) *Roman Shipping and Trade: Britain and the Rhine Provinces* (1978)

Society
JONES, M. and DIMBLEBY, G. (eds.) *The Environment of Man: Iron Age to the Anglo-Saxon Periods* (Oxford, 1981)
MILES D. (ed.) *The Romano-British Countryside: Studies in Rural Settlement and Economy* (Oxford, 1982)
REYNOLDS, P.J. *Iron Age Farm* (1979)
TODD, M. (ed.) *Studies in the Romano-British Villa* (Leicester, 1978)

Culture
MUNBY, J. and HENIG, M. (eds.) *Roman Life and Art in Britain* (1977)

RIVET, A.L.F. and SMITH, C. *The Placenames of Roman Britain* (1979)
RODWELL, W. (ed.) *Temples, Churches and Religion: Recent Research in Roman Britain* (1980)
THOMAS, C. *Christianity in Roman Britain to AD 500* (1981)

SAXONS, DANES AND NORMANS
409-1154

Overview
HUNTER BLAIR, P. *An Introduction to Anglo-Saxon England* (2nd ed., Cambridge, 1977)
LOYN, H.R. *The Norman Conquest* (3rd ed. 1982)
MAYR-HARTING, H. *The Coming of Christianity to Anglo-Saxon England* (1972)
STENTON, F.M. *Anglo-Saxon England* (Oxford, 1943)

Government and Politics 409-1042
BYRNE, F.J. *Irish Kings and High Kings* (1973)
CAMPBELL, J. (ed.) *The Anglo-Saxons* (1982)
DAVIES, WENDY *Wales in the Early Middle Ages* (Leicester, 1982)
DUNCAN, A.A.M. *Scotland. The Making of the Kingdom* (revised ed., Edinburgh, 1978)

Government and Politics 1042-1154
BARLOW, F. *Edward the Confessor* (1970)
BATES, D. *Normandy before 1066* (1982)
DAVIS, R.H.C. *King Stephen* (1967)
DOUGLAS, D.C. *William the Conqueror* (1964)
LE PATOUREL, J. *The Norman Empire* (Oxford, 1976)

Warfare and International Relations
ALCOCK, L. *Arthur's Britain* (1971)
BROWN, R.A. *English Castles* (3rd ed., 1976)
HOLLISTER, C.W. *Anglo-Saxon Military Institutions* (Oxford, 1962)
LEVISON, W. *England and the Continent in the Eighth Century* (Oxford, 1946)

Economy
BIDDLE, M. *Winchester: the development of an early capital* (Gottingen, 1972)
DOLLEY, R.H.M. (ed.) *Anglo-Saxon Coins* (1961)
LOYN, H.R. *Anglo-Saxon England and the Norman Conquest* (1962)
WILSON, D.M. (ed.) *The Archaeology of Anglo-Saxon England* (Cambridge, 1976)

Society
O'CORRAIN, D. *Ireland before the Normans* (Dublin, 1972)
SAWYER, P.H. *From Roman Britain to Norman England* (1978)

Culture
DODWELL, C.R. *Anglo-Saxon Art* (Manchester, 1982)
GRABAR, A. and NORDENFALK, C. *Early Medieval Painting* (Geneva, 1957)
NORDENFALK, C. *Celtic and Anglo-Saxon Painting* (1977)

WORMALD, F. *English Drawings of the 10th and 11th Centuries* (1952)

MEDIEVAL EMPIRE: ENGLAND AND HER NEIGHBOURS 1154-1450

Overview
FORTESCUE, J. *The Governance of England*, ed. C. Plummer (Oxford, 1885)
KEEN, M.H. *England in the Later Middle Ages* (1973)
MACFARLANE, ALAN *Origins of English Individualism* (Oxford, 1978)
STRAYER, J.R. *On the Medieval Origins of the Modern State* (Princeton, 1970)

Government and Politics 1154-1272
CLANCY, M.T. *England and its Rulers, 1066-1272* (1983)
HOLT, J.C. *Magna Carta* (Cambridge, 1965)
POWICKE, F.M. *Henry III and the Lord Edward* (2nd ed., Oxford, 1966)

Government and Politics 1272-1450
MCFARLANE, K.B. *The Nobility of Later Medieval England* (Oxford, 1973)
MCKISACK, M. *The Fourteenth Century 1307-1399* (Oxford, 1959)
PRESTWICH, M. *The Three Edwards, War and State in England 1272-1377* (1980)

Wales
EDWARDS, J.G. (ed.) *Littere Wallie* (Cardiff, 1940)
LLOYD, J.E. *A History of Wales from the Earliest Times to the Edwardian Conquest* (3rd ed., 1939)
Owen Glendower (Oxford, 1931)

Scotland
BARROW, G.W.S. *Kingship and Unity* (1981)
Robert Bruce and the Community of the Realm of Scotland (2nd ed., Edinburgh, 1976)
BROWN, J.M. (ed.) *Scottish Society in the Fifteenth Century* (Edinburgh, 1976)
DICKINSON, W.C. *Scotland from the Earliest Times to 1603* (3rd ed., revised by A.A.M. Duncan, Oxford, 1977)
DUNCAN, A.A.M. *Scotland, the Making of the Kingdom* (Edinburgh, 1975)

Ireland
CURTIS, EDMUND *A History of Medieval Ireland* (2nd ed., 1938)
FRAME, ROBIN *English Lordship in Ireland 1318-1361* (Oxford, 1982)
LYDON, J.F. *The Lordship of Ireland in the Middle Ages* (Dublin, 1972)
OTWAY-RUTHVEN, A.J. *A History of Medieval Ireland* (1968)
WATT, J.A. *The Church and the Two Nations in Medieval Ireland* (Cambridge, 1970)

Warfare and International Relations 1154-1327
CUTTINO, G.P. *English Diplomatic Administration 1259-1339* (2nd ed., Oxford 1971)
GILLINGHAM, J.B. *Richard the Lionheart* (1978)

LABARGE, M.W. *Gascony: England's First Colony 1204-1453* (1980)
POWICKE, F.M. *The Loss of Normandy (1189-1204)* (Manchester, 1913)
POWICKE, M.R. *Military Obligation in Medieval England* (Oxford, 1962)

Warfare and International Relations 1327-1450
ALLMAND, C.T. (ed.) *Society at War. The Experience of England and France during the Hundred Years War* (Edinburgh, 1973)
FOWLER, K. *The Age of Plantagenet and Valois* (1967)
FOWLER, K. (ed.) *The Hundred Years War* (1971)
PERROY, E. *The Hundred Years War*

Economy
BOLTON, J.L. *The Medieval English Economy, 1150-1500* (1980)
DARBY, H.C. (ed.) *A New Historical Geography of England* (Cambridge, 1973)
HATCHER, J. and MILLER, E. *Medieval England: Rural Society and Economic Change, 1083-1348* (1978)
KING, E. *England 1175-1425* (1979)
REYNOLDS, S. *An Introduction to the History of English Medieval Towns* (Oxford, 1977)

Society
HYAMS, P.R. *King, Lords and Peasants in Medieval England: the Common Law of Villeinage in the Twelfth and Thirteenth Centuries* (Oxford, 1980)
KING, E. *Peterborough Abbey 1086-1310* (Cambridge, 1973)
RAZI, Z. *Life, Marriage and Death in a Medieval Parish: Economy, Society and Demography in Halesowen, 1270-1400* (Cambridge, 1980)
SAUL, N. *Knights and Esquires: the Gloucestershire Gentry in the Fourteenth Century* (Oxford, 1981)

Culture
ANDERSON, W. *Castles of Europe* (1970)
EVANS, J. (ed.) *The Flowering of the Middle Ages* (1966)
MARTINDALE, A. *Gothic Art* (1967)
PLATT, C. *Medieval England. A Social History and Archaeology from the Conquest to AD 1600* (1978)

REFORMATION AND INFLATION 1450-1625

Overview
ELTON, G.R. *England under the Tudors* (2nd ed., 1974)
LOADES, D.M. *Politics and the Nation, 1450-1660* (1974)
RUSSELL, C. *The Crisis of Parliaments, 1509-1660* (1974)
STONE, L. *The Crisis of the Aristocracy, 1558-1641* (Oxford, 1971)
WILLIAMS, P. *The Tudor Regime* (Oxford, 1979)

Government and Politics: England 1450-1553
DAVIES, C.S.L. *Peace, Print and Protestantism: 1450-1558* (1977)
ELTON, G.R. *Reform and Reformation: England 1509-1558* (1977)
LANDER, J.R. *Government and Community: England 1450-1509* (1977)
SCARISBRICK, J.J. *Henry VIII* (1968)

Government and Politics: England 1553-1625
COLLINSON, P. *The Elizabethan Puritan Movement* (2nd ed., 1982)
HAIGH, C. (ed.) *The Reign of Elizabeth I* (1984)

LOADES, D.M. *The Reign of Mary Tudor: Politics, Government and Religion in England 1553-1558* (1979)
MACCAFFREY, W.T. *The Shaping of the Elizabethan Regime* (1968)
TOMLINSON, H. (ed.) *Before the English Civil War* (1983)

Wales
DODD, A.H. *Studies in Stuart Wales* (Cardiff, 1952)
JONES, G. *The Gentry and the Elizabethan State* (1977)
THOMAS, H. *A History of Wales, 1485-1660* (1972)
WILLIAMS, G. *Welsh Reformation Essays* (Cardiff, 1967)
WILLIAMS, P. *The Council in the Marches of Wales under Elizabeth I* (Cardiff, 1958)

Scotland
COWAN, I.B. *The Scottish Reformation* (1982)
DONALDSON, G. *Scotland: James V-VII* (Edinburgh, 1965)
LARNER, C. *Enemies of God: the Witch-hunt in Scotland* (1981)
LYTHE, S.G.E. *The Economy of Scotland, 1550-1625* (Edinburgh, 1960)
WORMALD, J. *Court, Kirk and Community: Scotland, 1470-1625* (1981)

Ireland
BRADSHAW, B. *The Irish Constitutional Revolution of the Sixteenth Century* (Cambridge, 1979)
CANNY, N.P. *The Elizabethan Conquest of Ireland: a pattern established 1565-76* (Hassocks, 1976)
ELLIS, S.G. *Reform and Revival: English government in Ireland, 1470-1534* (1985)
MOODY, T.W., MARTIN, F.X. and BURNE, F.J. (eds.) *A New History of Ireland. III. Early modern Ireland 1534-1691* (Oxford, 1976)

Warfare and International Relations
LEE, M. *James I and Henry IV* (Urbana, 1970)
LOCKYER, R. *Buckingham* (1981)
WERNHAM, R.B. *Before the Armada* (1966)
The Making of Elizabethan Foreign Policy, 1558-1603 (Berkeley, Cal., 1980)
WILSON, C.H. *Queen Elizabeth and the Revolt of the Netherlands* (1970)

Economy
COLEMAN, D.C. *The Economy of England 1450-1570* (Oxford, 1977)
HOSKINS, W.G. *The Age of Plunder: The England of Henry VIII 1500-1547* (1976)
PALLISER, D.M. *The Age of Elizabeth: England under the Later Tudors 1547-1603* (1983)
THIRSK, J. (ed.) *The Agrarian History of England and Wales: IV. 1500-1640* (Cambridge, 1967)

Society
CLARK, P. and SLACK, P. *English Towns in Transition 1500-1700* (Oxford, 1976)
HOSKINS, W.G. *Provincial England* (1964)
THOMAS, K. *Religion and the Decline of Magic* (1971)
YOUINGS, J. *Sixteenth-Century England* (1984)

Culture
GIROUARD, M. *Life in the English Country House* (1978)
MASON, H.A. *Humanism and Poetry in Early Tudor England* (1959)
STEVENS, J. *Music and Poetry in the Early Tudor Court* (1961)
STRONG, R. *Portraits of Queen Elizabeth I* (Oxford, 1963)

DISORDER TO STABILITY: BRITAIN AND IRELAND 1625-1783

Overview
CARSWELL, J.P. *From Revolution to Revolution: England 1688-1776* (1973)
POCOCK, J.G.A. (ed.) *Three British Revolutions, 1641, 1688, 1776* (Princeton, 1980)
ROGERS, P. (ed.) *The Context of English Literature: the Eighteenth Century* (1978)

Government and Politics: England and Wales 1625-1701
ASHTON, R. *The English Civil War 1603-1649* (1978)
COWARD, B. *The Stuart Age* (1980)
JONES, J.R. *County and Court 1660-1714* (1978)
OLLARD, R. *The Image of the King: Charles I and Charles II* (1979)
ROOTS, I. *The Great Rebellion* (1966)

Government and Politics: England and Wales 1701-1783
CANNON, J. (ed.) *The Whig Ascendancy* (1981)
DICKINSON, H.T. *Liberty and Property: Political Ideology in Eighteenth-Century Britain* (1977)
OWEN, J.B. *The Eighteenth Century 1714-1815* (1974)
PLUMB, J.H. *The Growth of Political Stability 1675-1725* (Oxford, 1967)
SPECK, W.A. *Stability and Strife: England 1714-1760* (1977)

Scotland
FERGUSON, W. *Scotland: 1689 to the Present* (Edinburgh, 1968)
LENMAN, B.P. *The Jacobite Risings in Britain 1689-1746* (1980) *Integration, Enlightenment and Industrialisation: Scotland 1746-1832* (1981)
SMOUT, T.C. *A History of the Scottish People 1560-1830* (1969)

Ireland
BARTLETT, T. and HAYTON, D.W. (eds.) *Penal Era and Golden Age: Essays in Irish History 1690-1800* (Belfast, 1979)
CULLEN, L.M. *The Emergence of Modern Ireland 1600-1900* (1981)
LECKY, W.E.H. *History of Ireland in the Eighteenth Century* (5 vols., 2nd ed., 1892)
MCDOWELL, R.B. *Ireland in the Age of Imperialism and Revolution 1760-1801* (Oxford, 1979)
MOODY, T.W., MARTIN, F.X. and BYRNE, F.J. (eds.) *A New History of Ireland: Volume III, Early Modern Ireland 1534-1691* (Oxford, 1976)

Warfare and International Relations 1625-1689
CHILDS, J. *The Army, James II, and the Glorious Revolution* (Manchester, 1980)
HUTTON, R. *The Royalist War Effort* (1981)
JONES, J.R. *Britain and Europe in the Seventeenth Century* (1966)
OLLARD, R. *Man of War* (1969)
This War Without an Enemy (1976)

Warfare and International Relations 1689-1783
HORN, D.B. *Great Britain and Europe in the Eighteenth Century* (Oxford, 1967)
HOULDING, J.A. *Fit for Service: the Training of the British Army 1715-1795* (Oxford, 1981)
LANGFORD, P. *Modern British Foreign Policy: The Eighteenth Century* (1976)
MACKESY, P. *The War for America, 1775-83* (1964)
RICHMOND, H. *Statesmen and Sea Power* (Oxford, 1946)

Economy

COLEMAN. D.C. *The Economy of England 1450-1750* (Oxford, 1977)
CULLEN, L.M. and SMOUT, T.C. (eds.) *Comparative Aspects of Scottish and Irish Economic and Social History 1600-1900* (Edinburgh, 1977)
DEANE, P. and COLE, W.A. *British Economic Growth 1688-1959* (2nd ed., Cambridge, 1967)
HOLDERNESS, B.A. *Pre-Industrial England* (1977)
WILSON, C. *England's Apprenticeship 1603-1763* (1965)

Society

CANNON, J. *Aristocratic Century: The Peerage of Eighteenth-Century England* (Cambridge, 1984)
LASLETT, P. *The World We Have Lost* (2nd ed., 1972)
MALCOLMSON, R.W. *Life and Labour in England 1700-1780* (1981)
MINGAY, G.E. *The Gentry: the Rise and Fall of a Ruling Class* (1976)
PORTER, R. *English Society in the Eighteenth Century* (1982)
WRIGHTSON, K. *English Society 1580-1680* (1982)

Culture

HARRIS, J., ORGEL, S. and STRONG, R. *The King's Arcadia: Inigo Jones and the Stuart Court* (1973)
GOWING, L. *Hogarth* (1971)
LITTLE, B. *Sir Christopher Wren: a Historical Biography* (1975)
WAIN, J. *Samuel Johnson* (1974)
WHINNEY, M. and MILLAR, O. *A History of English Art* vol. 6, (Oxford, 1957)

POLITICAL REFORM AND ECONOMIC REVOLUTION 1783-1901

Overview

BRIGGS, A. *The Age of Improvement* (1979 ed.)
BURN, W.L. *The Age of Equipoise* (1964)
WIENER, M.J. *English Culture and the Decline of the Industrial Spirit* (Cambridge, 1981)
WILLIAMS, R, *Culture and Society* (1958)
YOUNG, G.M. *Victorian England, Portrait of an Age* (1936)

Government and Politics 1783-1846

BEALES, D. *From Castlereagh to Gladstone, 1815-1885* (1969)
BROCK, M. *The Great Reform Act* (1973)
CHRISTIE, I.R. *Wars and Revolutions: Britain 1760-1815* (1982)
GASH, N. *Aristocracy and People. Britain 1815-1865* (1979)
THOMPSON, E.P. *The Making of the English Working Class* (1963)

Government and Politics 1846-1901

BEST, G. *Mid-Victorian Britain 1851-1870* (1971)
BLAKE, R. *The Conservative Party from Peel to Churchill* (1970)
HAMER, D.A. *Liberal Politics in the Age of Gladstone and Rosebery* (Oxford, 1972)
HANHAM, H.J. *The Reformed Electoral System in Great Britain 1832-1914* (1968)
VINCENT, J. *The Formation of the Liberal Party 1857-1868* (1966)

Ireland

CURTIS, L.P. *Coercion and Conciliation in Ireland, 1886-1892* (Princeton, 1963)
LEE, J. *The Modernisation of Irish Society, 1848-1918* (Dublin, 1973)
LYONS, F.S.L. *Ireland Since the Famine* (1971)

LYONS, F.S.L. and HAWKINS, R.A.J. (eds.) *Ireland under the Union: Varieties of Tension* (Oxford, 1980)
TUATHAIGH, G.O. *Ireland before the Famine, 1798-1848* (Dublin, 1972)

Warfare and International Relations

BARTLETT, C.J. *Great Britain and Sea Power 1815-1853* (Oxford, 1963)
BOURNE, K. *The Foreign Policy of Victorian England 1830-1902* (Oxford, 1970)
HOWARD, C. *Britain and the Casus Belli 1822-1902* (1974)
HYAM R. *Britain's Imperial Century 1815-1914* (1976)
SETON-WATSON, R.W. *Britain in Europe 1789-1914* (Cambridge, 1937)

Economy

FLOUD, R. and MCCLOSKEY, D. (eds.) *The Economic History of Britain since 1700*, 2 vols. (Cambridge, 1981)
CROUZET, F. *The Victorian Economy* (1982)
LANDES, D.S. *The Unbound Prometheus: Technological Change and Industrial Development in Western Europe from 1750 to the Present* (Cambridge, 1969)
MATHIAS, P. *The First Industrial Nation: An Economic History of Britain, 1700-1914* (Cambridge, 1969)
MITCHELL, B.R. and DEANE, P. *Abstract of British Historical Statistics* (Cambridge, 1962)

Society

BEDARIDA, F. *A Social History of England Since 1850* (1976)
BRIGGS, A. *Victorian Cities* (1968)
HOBSBAWM, E.J. *Industry and Empire* (1968)
MORRIS, R.J. *Class and Class Consciousness in the Industrial Revolution* (1979)
PERKIN, H.J. *Origins of Modern English Society 1780-1880* (1969)

Culture

BUTLER, M. *Romantics, Rebels and Reactionaries: English Literature and its Background, 1760-1830* (Oxford, 1981)
GEORGE, M.D. *Hogarth to Cruikshank: Social Change in Graphic Satire* (1967)
GIROUARD, M. *The Victorian Country House* (Oxford, 1971)
GROSS, J. *The Rise and Fall of the English Man of Letters* (1969)
HEYCK, T.W. *The Transformation of Intellectual Life in Victorian England* (1982)

FROM IMPERIAL POWER TO EUROPEAN PARTNER 1901-1975

Overview

LLOYD, T.O. *Empire to Welfare State: English History 1906-1976* (Oxford, 1979)
PORTER, B. *Britain, Europe and the World 1850-1982* (1983)
ROBBINS, K.G. *The Eclipse of a Great Power: Modern Britain 1870-1975* (1983)

Government and Politics in England

MACKINTOSH, J.P. *The British Cabinet* (2nd ed., 1968)
MIDDLEMAS, K. *Politics in Industrial Society. The experience of the British System since 1911* (1979)
PELLING, H. *A Short History of the Labour Party* (7th ed., 1982)
PUGH, M. *The Making of Modern British Politics, 1867-1939* (Oxford, 1982)
TAYLOR, A.J.P. *English History, 1914-1945* (Oxford, 1965)

Wales

FRANCIS, H. and SMITH, D. *The Fed: A History of the South Wales Miners in the 20th Century* (1980)
JAMES, A.J. and THOMAS, J.E. *Wales at Westminster: A History of the Parliamentary Representation of Wales 1800-1979* (Llandysul, 1981)
MORGAN, K.O. *Rebirth of a Nation: Wales 1880-1980* (Oxford, 1981) *Wales in British Politics 1868-1922* (3rd ed., Cardiff, 1980)
SMITH, D. (ed.) *A People and A Proletariat: Essays in the History of Wales 1780-1980* (1980)

Scotland

BUDGE, I. *Labour Records in Scotland* (Edinburgh, 1980)
HANHAM, H.J. *Scottish Nationalism* (1969)
HARVIE, C. *No Gods and Precious Few Heroes: Scotland, 1914-1980* (1981)
MACDOUGALL, I. *Labour Records in Scotland* (Edinburgh, 1980)
MIDDLEMASS, R.K. *The Clydesiders, a Left-wing Struggle for Parliamentary Power* (1965)

Ireland

BOWMAN, J. *De Valera and the Ulster Question, 1917-1973* (Oxford, 1982)
BUCKLAND, P. *Factory of Grievances: Devolved Government in Northern Ireland, 1921-1939* (Dublin, 1979) *A History of Northern Ireland* (Dublin, 1981)
FANNING, R. *The Irish Department of Finance, 1922-1958* (Dublin, 1978)
TOWNSHEND, C. *The British Campaign in Ireland, 1919-1921. The Development of Political and Military Policies* (Oxford, 1975)

Warfare and International Relations

BARNETT, C. *The Collapse of British Power* (1972)
LOWE, P. *Britain in the Far East: a Survey. 1819 to the Present* (1981)
MANSERGH, N. *The Commonwealth Experience* (1969)
NORTHEDGE, F.S. *Descent from Power: British Foreign Policy, 1945-1973* (1974)
STEINER, Z. *Britain and the Origins of the First World War* (1977)

Economy

ALDCROFT, D.H. *The Inter-War Economy: Britain, 1919-1939* (1970)
FLOUD, R. and MCCLOSKEY, D. (eds.) *The Economic History of Britain since 1700*, vol. 2, (1981)
GLYNN, S. and OXBORROW, J. *Interwar Britain: A Social and Economic History* (1976)
KIRBY, M.W. *The Decline of British Economic Power since 1870* (1981)
MATTHEW, R.C.P., FEINSTEIN, C.H. and ODLING-SMEE, J.C. *British Economic Growth, 1855-1973* (Oxford, 1982)

Society

HALSEY, A.H. *Trends in British Society since 1900* (1972)
MARWICK, A. *British Society since 1945* (1982)
ROEBUCK, J. *The Making of Modern English Society from 1850* (1973)
SILVER, H and RYDER, J. *Modern English Society* (1970)
STEVENSON, J. *British Society 1914-1945* (1983)

Culture

BRIGGS, A. *The History of Broadcasting in the United Kingdom*, 4 vols., (Oxford, 1961-79)
HALSEY, A.H., HEATH, A.F. and RIDGE, J.M. *Origins and Destinations: family, class and education in modern Britain* (Oxford, 1980)
HOGGART, R. *The Uses of Literacy* (1957)
LYONS, F.S.L. *Culture and Anarchy in Ireland, 1890-1939* (Oxford, 1979)
WERSKEY, G. *The Visible College* (1978)

INDEX

Italic numbers refer to illustrations;
bold type to Who's Who

Abbot, George, Archbishop of
 Canterbury **338**
Aberdeen 112; university 165
Aberdeen, George Hamilton-
 Gordon, earl of 255, 266, **338**
Aberlemno 82, *87*
Abernethy, Peace of (1072) 66
Aberystwyth 111–12
Abhorrers 205
Abingdon 72, 90
Abjuration, Oath of, Ireland (1703)
 217
Accord, Act of (1460) 147
Acheson, Dean 320
Aclea, Battle of (851) 61
Acre 118, 120
Acton, John Emerich Dalberg, Lord
 338
Acton Burnell, Statute of (1283)
 106
Adam, (architect brothers) 240,
 241, **338**
Adam, William 241–2
Addedomaros, King of Trinovantes
 15, 39
Addington, Henry, Viscount
 Sidmouth 253, **338**
Addison, Christopher, Viscount
 295
Addison, Joseph 242, **338**
Addled Parliament (1614) 160
Aden 290, 319
Admonitions to Parliament (1572)
 157
Adrian IV, Pope 115, **338**
Adventurers Act (1641) 215
advertising 273–4, *274*, *275*, 331
Advocates Library, Edinburgh 214
Aelfric ("the Grammarian"), Abbot
 of Eynsham 92, **338**
Aelle, King of Sussex 60
Aethelbald, King of Mercia 60, 72,
 78, **338**
Aethelbert, King of Kent 60,
 62, **338**
Aethelfleda ("lady of the Mercians")
 338
Aethelfrith, King of Northumbria
 59, 60, 71–2, **338**
Aethelred I, King of Wessex **338**
Aethelred II ("the Unready"), King
 of England 57–8, 60, 66, *71*,
 74–6, 78–9, 79, 85, **338**
Aethelwold, Bishop of Winchester
 57, 69, 90, 92
Aethelwulf, King of Wessex 61–2,
 64, 76–7, **338**
Afghan war (1878–79) 256
African Company 229
Agincourt, Battle of (1415) 121
"Agreement of the People" (1647)
 232
Agricola, Gnaeus Julius 10, 12–13,
 17, 25–8, 30–1, 45, 48, **338**
agriculture and farming:
 pre-Roman 10, 37; under Romans
 13, 32–3, 41; Anglo-Saxon 79–80;
 in Scotland 112, 213–14, 227; in
 13th–14th centuries 124–6;
 output 124, 196–7, 225–6, 269;

and disasters 127–8; under
 Lancastrians and Tudors 175–8,
 177; wage labour in 184, 271, 276;
 improvements 226–7; protection
 withdrawn 253; late 19th-century
 depression 257; decline of labour
 271, 276
Aidan, St **338**
Aidan Mac Gabran, King of Dál
 Riáta 59, 72
Ailred, Abbot of Rievaulx **338**
Aix-la-Chapelle, Peace of (1748)
 222
Akroyd's loom-shed, Halifax *269*
Alabama case 256–7
Alamein, Battle of (1942) 316–17
Alban, St 48
Albany, Alexander Stewart, duke
 of **338**
Albany, John Stewart, duke of **338**
Albany, Robert Stewart, duke
 of **339**
Albert, Prince Consort 248, 255,
 339
Albinus, Clodius, Roman emperor
 12, 20–1, 36
Alciston manor, Sussex 124
Alcock, John, Bishop of Ely **339**
Alcuin 76, 78, 88, 90, **339**
Aldborough (Isurium) 17
Alehouses 232
Alexander I, King of Scots **339**
Alexander II, King of Scots **339**
Alexander III, King of Scots
 114, **339**
Alexander IV, Pope 104, 120
Alexander, Sir William, earl of
 Stirling **339**
Alexander of Tunis, Harold Rupert
 Leofric George, Earl **339**
Alfred ("the Great"), King of
 Wessex: court aristocracy 57;
 Jewel 57, *89*; and Danes 58, 61,
 73–4; laws 62, 82; and overseas
 contacts 76, 92; and learning 90,
 92; **339**
Aliens Act (1905) 290, 331
Allectus 10, 12, 20
Allen, William, Cardinal 157, **339**
Allenby, Edmund Henry Hynman,
 Viscount **339**
Alliance Party (N. Ireland) 311
Alma, Battle of (1854) 267
Almanza, Battle of (1707) 222
Amboina 218, 221
America 209, 223–4, 229, 245,
 249; Civil War 257; War of
 Independence 197, 214, *223*, 224,
 252; *see also* United States of
 America
Amherst, Jeffrey, Lord **339**
Amicable Grant (1525) 150
Amiens, Judgment of (1264) 104;
 Peace of (1802) 266
Ammianus Marcellinus 10
Amminus 16
Anderson, Elizabeth Garrett **339**
Andrewes, Lancelot, Bishop of
 Winchester **339**
Aneirin 82–3, **339**; see also
 Gododdin

Angevins *see* Anjou
Anglesey (Mona) 25
Anglo-Irish Treaty (1921)
 307–9, 311
Anglo-Irish War (1919–21) 308–9
Anglo-Japanese alliance 312, 314
Anglo-Polish Agreement (1939)
 315
Anglo-Saxon Chronicle 60–1,
 69, 72
Anglo-Saxons: settlement 54, 71,
 79–81; law-codes 56, 81–2, 84;
 administration and rule 59–64;
 royal succession 63–4, 76, 77;
 Normans defeat 66; warfare 71–2,
 75; Church 74, 76, 77; trade and
 economy 78–80; society 81–7; art
 and learning 82, 88–92, *90*, *91*;
 arms *83*
Anjou, Angevins: and English
 succession 66–7, 76, 105; power
 and administration 96–8, 100–1;
 and Wales 110; Empire 118–19;
 and Hundred Years War 121–2;
 and feudal society 131
Anjou, Henry, duke of (*later* Henry
 III of France) *174*
Anne, Queen of Great Britain 204,
 206, 212–13, 222, 224, **339**
Anne Boleyn, Queen of Henry VIII
 142, 144, 150–1, 168, 190, **339**
Anne of Cleves, Queen of Henry
 VIII 150, 172–3, **339**
Anne of Denmark, Queen of
 James I 159, 238
Annual Register 244
Anselm, St 69, 77, 84, **339**
Anson, George, Lord **339**
Anthony, St 89
anticlericalism 133
Anti-Corn Law League 253
anti-semitism 332
Antonine Wall 10, 28–9, *29*
Antoninus Pius 10, 29
Anzus Pact (1951) 318–19
Apprentices Act (1802) 252
Aquitaine 121
Argyll, Archibald Campbell, earl of
 (1530–73) **339**
Argyll, Archibald Campbell, earl of
 (*c.* 1606–61) 210–11, **340**
Argyll, Archibald Campbell, earl of
 (1629–85) 212, 221, **340**
Argyll, Archibald Campbell, duke
 of (1682–1761) 214, **340**
Argyll, John Campbell, duke of
 212, **340**
aristocracy: Anglo-Saxon 57–8,
 82; Norman 66–7, 69, 74, 87;
 warrior 71–2, 75, 82–3, 87; conflict
 with Angevin kings 98; taxed 98;
 feudal development of 132;
 post-industrial values 246; and
 political power 250–1; and
 industrialists 279, 284; culture
 282; 20th-century decline 328
Arkwright, Sir Richard 225, 272,
 279
Arles, 22–3; Council of (314) 48
Arlington, Henry Bennet, earl of
 203, 221, **340**

Armada, Spanish 145, 174, *174*
Arminianism 194, 197, 200–1, 210
Armorica 15, 39
Arms Act (1843) 262
arms and armour (weapons) 24,
 71, 74, *75*, 82, *83*, 87, *122*
army: Roman 12–13, 18–19, 22,
 24–31, 36, 47, 52; Anglo-Saxon
 71–5; and feudal service 120;
 tactics 120; in Hundred Years War
 123; professional standing 196;
 and Cromwell's parliament 202,
 219; New Model 219; disbanded
 (1660) 220; self-supporting 220;
 18th-century decline 224; in Boer
 War 312; in World War I 313
Arne, Thomas 240–1
Arnold, Matthew 335, **340**
Arnold, Thomas 285, **340**
Arran, James Hamilton, earl
 of **340**
Arran, James Stewart, earl of
 165–6, **340**
Arras, Congress of (1435) 123
Arsuf, Battle of (1191) 118
Arthur, King 54, 106, 138, **340**
Arthur, Prince (brother of Henry
 VIII) 150, 172
Arthur, duke or count of Brittany
 340
Artificers, Statute of (1563) 185
artillery *122*, 123, 140, 173
Artisans' Dwellings Act (1875) 257
Arundel, Thomas, Archbishop of
 Canterbury 133, **340**
Arundel, Thomas Howard, earl of
 192, 240
Ascanius, Nipius 33
Ascham, Roger **340**
Asclepiodotus 20
Ascot 329
Ashbourne, Edward Gibson,
 Lord 264
Ashley, Lord *see* Shaftesbury,
 earl of
Aske, Robert 154
Asquith, Herbert Henry, earl of
 Oxford and Asquith 294–6, 305,
 307, **340**
Asser, Bishop of Sherborne 90, **340**
"assessment" (tax) 219
Associated Portland Cement
 Manufacturers 275
Astor, Nancy, Viscountess **340**
Athelney (monastery) 90
Athelstan, King of Wessex and
 Mercia 74, 78, 82, 90, **340**
Atholl, John Murray, marquis
 of **340**
Atholl, John Stewart, earl of **340**
atomic bombs 317; *see also* nuclear
 weapons
Atrebates 14–15, 19, 39
Attacotti 10, 22
Attainder, Acts of 152
Attlee, Clement Richard, Earl
 299, *299*, 305, 318, 320, **340**
Attwood, Thomas **340**
Auchinleck, Gen. Sir Claude
 316, **340**
Auden, W.H. 330

Aughrim, Battle of (1691) 216
Augsburg League, War of (1689–97) 222
Augustine, St, Archbishop of Canterbury 76, 92, **340**
Augustus, Roman emperor 17, 21, 24, 46
Aurelianus, Ambrosius 71
Aurelius, Marcus, Roman emperor 28
Austen, Jane 242, 247
austerity 325
Austin factory, Longbridge *323*
Austin, Herbert, Lord **341**
Australia 314–16, 319
Austria and Austria-Hungary 222–3, 314–15
Austrian Succession, War of (1740–48) 207, 222–4
auxilia (Roman) 24–5
Ayscough (Ayscue), Admiral Sir George 221

Babington plot (1586) 157
Bach, J.C. 241
Bacon, Francis 160, 178, 237, 240, **341**
Bacon, Roger **341**
Badbury Rings, Dorset 81
Baden-Powell, Robert, Lord **341**
Bagehot, Walter 246, **341**
Bakewell, Robert 226
Baldwin, count of Flanders 77
Baldwin, Stanley, Earl 295–6, 314, **341**
Balfour, Arthur James, Earl 248, 259, 264, 293, 294, **341**
Ball, John 134, **341**
Balliol family 112; *see also* Edward Balliol; John Balliol
Bamburgh 60, 74
Bancroft, Richard, Archbishop of Canterbury **341**
Bank Charter Act (1844) 253, 274
Bank Holidays 281
Bank for Reconstruction and Development (World Bank) 325
Bank of England 221–2, 225, 253, 274, 299
Bannockburn, Battle of (1314) 107, 114, 116, 120
Banqueting House, Whitehall 239
Baptists 234
"barbarian conspiracy" (367) 10, 22, 30
barbarian invasions (Roman empire) 10, 20, 22
Barbour, John: *The Bruce* 114
"Barebones Parliament" (1653) 202
Baring, Evelyn, earl of Cromer **341**
Barnardo, Thomas John **341**
Barnet, Battle of (1471) 148, *149*
baronetcies 159, 183
barons 94, 97, 100, 102–4, 106–7; War, 104, 107
Basset, Sir Ralph 120
Bastwick, John 200
Bateman, Stephen: *Crystal Glass of Christian Reformation* 181
Bath 13, 42, 45, 46, *49*, 232
Bath, William Pulteney, earl of 207
baths (Roman) 45
Battle of Britain (1940) 316
Baxter, Robert Dudley 278
Bayeux Tapestry *67*, 74, *75*, 87–8
Bayonne 122
Beachy Head, Battle of (1692) 222
Beaton, David, Cardinal **341**
Beatty, Admiral David, Earl 313, **341**
Beauchamp, Guy de, earl of Warwick **341**

Beauchamp, Richard de, earl of Warwick **341**
Beauchamp Pageant MS (1485–90) *123*
Beaufort, Henry, Cardinal **341**
Beaufort, Margaret 148, **341**
Beaumaris castle 111
Beaverbrook, William Maxwell Aitken, Lord **341**
Becket, St Thomas, Archbishop of Canterbury 100, *103*, 106, **341**
Bede, Venerable 56, 59–61, 75, 77–8, 88–9, 92, **341**
Bedford, John of Lancaster, duke of 122, **341**
Bedford, John Russell, duke of 223
Bedworth worsted mill *269*
Beeching Report (1963) 326
Belfast *310*, 311
Belgic people 10, 14, 15
Belgium 266–7, 292, 313
Benedictine order 57, 90
Bentham, Jeremy 252, **341**
Bentinck, Lord George **341**
Bentley, Richard 240
Beowulf (poem) 54, 56, 82, 88, *89*
Berlin, Congress of (1878) 257, 267
Bermingham family 117
Bermondsey fête *186*
Berners, Sir James *107*
Bernicia 60
Berwick 112, 211; Treaty of (1639) 210
Bessemer, Sir Henry **342**
Bevan, Aneurin 299, *299*, 300, 303, **342**
Beveridge Report (1942) 298–9, 328
Beveridge, William Henry, Lord **342**
Beverley 180; Minster 136
Bevin, Ernest 299, 317, **342**
Bible, Holy 96, 140, 150, 153, *153*, 159, 162, 190
Bigod, Hugh 104
Bill of Rights (1689) 204–5
Birkenhead, F.E. Smith *see* Smith, F.E.
Birmingham 180, 250, 277, 280
birth control 277, 328
Biscop, Benedict 56, 88
bishops: lay investiture 76–7; and royal authority 102; royal appointments 152; in Scotland 166, 210, 212–13, 234; abolished (1646–60) 201
Bishops' Wars (1639–40) 201, 210, 218
"Black Acts" (Scotland, 1584) 166
"Black and Tans" 309
Black Death 98, 117, 126, 128–9, 132, 175
Blackpool Tower 281
Blackstone, Sir William **342**
Blake, Admiral Robert 221, **342**
Blanche, Queen of Louis VIII of France 118
Blenheim, Battle of (1704) 222
Blenheim Palace 239
"Blitz, The" 316–17
Blois, Treaty of (1572) 174
"Bloody Assizes" (1685) 221
Bloody Sunday (21 Nov., 1920) 309
Blount, Charles 234
Blücher, Marshal Gebhardt Lebrecht von 267
Bluegate Fields, Shadwell *277*
bluestockings 242
Blyton, Enid 328
Boarstall, Buckinghamshire 128–9
Boccaccio, Giovanni 140
Boer Wars: First (1880–1) 258, 268; Second (South African War, 1899–1902) 260, 268, *268*, 289, 293, 312
Bolingbroke, Henry *see* Henry IV, King

Bolingbroke, Henry St John, Viscount 208–9, 223, 234, **342**
Bolton, Edmund 241
bonds (for royal duty) 148–9
Boniface (Wynfrith) 76–7
Bonner, Edmund, Bishop of London **342**
bookland 85
Book of Discipline (Scotland) 166
Booth, Charles 260, 281
Booth, William **342**
Boroughbridge, Battle of (1322) 107
Boston, Lincolnshire 125
Boston Tea Party (1773) 224
Boswell, James 238
Bosworth, Battle of (1485) 142, 148–9
Botero, Giovanni 180
Bothwell, Francis Stewart Hepburn, earl of *165*, **342**
Bothwell, James Hepburn, earl of 166, **342**
Boudicca, Queen of the Iceni 12–13, 16–17, 21, 26, 28, 39, 46, **342**
Boulogne 173
Boulton, Matthew 228
Bournville 277
Bouvines, Battle of (1214) 102, 118
"Boy Patriots" (1737–8) 223
Boyce, William 241
Boyle, Henry 217
Boyle, Richard, earl of Cork **342**
Boyle, Robert 237
Boyne, Battle of the (1690) 216
Boys, Thomas Shotter *279*
Bracken, Brendan *298*
"Bracton" (legal treatise) 96
Bradford 277, *330*
Bradford-on-Avon *89*, 90
Bradlaugh, Charles **342**
Bradwardine, Thomas, Archbishop of Canterbury **342**
Bradwell 30
Bramham Moor, Battle of (1408) 112
Breda: Declaration of (1660) 202; Treaty of (1667) 221
Brétigny, Treaty of (1360) 121
Bretton Woods Conference (1944) 325
bretwaldas 60
Brian Boru, High King of Ireland 64, 73, 115, **342**
Bridgewater, Francis Egerton, duke of 229
Bright, John **342**
Brighton: French assault (1514) *171*
Brihtnoth, *ealdorman* of Essex 75
Brigantes 16–18, 26
Brindley, James 229, **342**
Bristol 229, 233
British Broadcasting Corporation 334–6
British Medical Association 280, 299
British Museum: library 240
British Railways 326
British Socialist Party 297
British South Africa Company 260
British Union of Fascists 288, 297, *297*, 332
Briton, The (journal) 208
Brittain, Vera 331
Broad Bottom Ministry (1744–46) 207
Brontë sisters 285
Brookeborough, Basil S. Brooke, Viscount 309
Brough-on-Humber (Petuaria) 34
Brougham, Henry Peter, Lord 284, 286, **342**
Brown, Lancelot ("Capability") *240*, 242, **342**
Bruccius 35

Bruce family 112
Bruce, Edward 116, **342**
Bruce, Robert ("The Competitor") 114, **342**
Bruce, Robert *see* Robert I, King of Scots
Bruges, Truce of (1375) 121
Brunanburh, Battle of (937) 74
Brunel, Isambard Kingdom *273*, **342**
Bubble Act (1720) 274
Buchanan, George **342**
Buckingham, Edward Stafford, duke of 142, 161
Buckingham, George Villiers, duke of (1592–1628) 146, 160, 174, 192, 200, 218, **343**
Buckingham, George Villiers, duke of (1628–87) 203, **343**
Buckingham, Henry Stafford, duke of 148
budgets: (1860s) 256; (1909 "People's") 288, 294; (1910) 288
Bulgarian atrocities (1876) 257
Buller, Sir Redvers **343**
bullion outflow 128
Bunker Hill, Battle of (1775) 224
Bunyan, John **343**
Burdett, Sir Francis 253, **343**
burgesses 97, 106–7
Burgh Castle 30
Burgh, Hubert de, earl of Kent **343**
Burghley, William Cecil, Lord *see* Cecil, Sir William
Burgoyne, Gen. John 224, **343**
Burgred, King of Mercia 77
Burgundy 121, 123, 137, 172
Burgundy, Charles, duke of 172
Burgundy, John, duke of 121
Burgundy, Philip III (the Good), duke of 121–3
burhs 73, 78
Burke, Edmund 209, 238–9, 242, 282–3, **343**
Burlington, Richard Boyle, earl of 239
Burma 316–18
Burnet, Gilbert, Bishop of Salisbury **343**
Burns, Robert 214, 242, **343**
Burton, Henry 200
Bury St Edmunds *125*, 129; Psalter 92
Bute mazer *114*
Bute, John Stuart, earl of 208, *209*, 223, **343**
Butler family 117, 167
Butler, Josephine Elizabeth **343**
Butler, R.A., Lord 300, 333, **343**
Butler, Samuel 285
Butser Hill farm, Hampshire 37
"Butskellism" 300
Butt, Isaac 256, **343**
Butterfield, William 284
Byng, George, Viscount Torrington **343**
Byng, Admiral John 223, 236, **343**
Byrd, William 189, **343**
Byron, George Gordon, Lord 286, **343**

Cabal, The 203, 221
Cadbury's (company) 277
Cade, Jack 109, 147
Cadiz 218
Cadwaldr ap Gruffud **343**
Cadwallon, King of Gwynedd 60, **343**
Cadwgan, Prince **343**
Caedmon, St **343**
Caedwalla, King of Wessex 77, **343**
Caerleon 12, 20, 28
Caernarfon: castle 111
Caerwent 46

Caesar, Julius, Roman emperor   10, 14–15, 24–5, 38, 82, **343**
Caister-by-Yarmouth   30
Caistor-by-Norwich   17, 34
Calais   121, 122, 155, 173
Caledones (Caledonians)   12, 25, 27–9
Calgacus   25–7
Caligula, Roman emperor   24
Callaghan, James   300–1, 306, 325
Calvinism   156, 236–7
Cambridge   42; university 135, 191, *227*, 286, 292; Plot (1415) 109
Cambridge, George William Francis Charles, duke of   **344**
Cambridge, Richard, earl of   109
Cameron, Richard   212
Campaign for Nuclear Disarmament (CND)   332
Campbell clan   210, 212; *see also* Argyll
Campbell, Colen   240
Campbell, Colin, Lord Clyde   **344**
Campbell, Captain Robert   212
Campbell-Bannerman, Sir Henry   313, **344**
Campion, Edmund   **344**
Camulodunum *see* Colchester
Canada   223, 314, 318
canals (inland)   229, 245, *272*
Canmore dynasty (Scotland)   112, 114
Canning, George   253, 266–7, **344**
Canning, Stratford, Viscount Stratford de Redcliffe   **344**
Canons of 1640 (Church of England)   201
Canons, Book of (Scotland, 1636)   210
Cantelupe, Thomas, Bishop of Hereford   **344**
Canterbury: under Romans 42, 44; archbishopric 58, 69, 75–6; and Kentish kingdom 59; Vikings raid 60; Anglo-Saxon settlement 80; art and culture 88, 92; cathedral 92, 135–6; Tudor decline 180; Hexateuch 92; Psalter 88, 92; *see also* individual archbishops
Cantiaci   14
cantref (administrative unit)   64
Caracalla, Roman emperor   19, 21, 29
Caratacus   15–18, 25–6, **344**
Caratius   35
Carausius, M. Mausaeus   12, 20, 22
Cardigan, James Thomas Brudenell, earl of   **344**
Cardwell, Edward, Viscount   **344**
Carlos, Don   155
Carlton Club meeting (1922)   295
Carlyle, Thomas   286, **344**
Carmarthen   111
Carnarvon, Henry Howard Molyneux Herbert, earl of **344**
Caroline of Ansbach, Queen of George II   207, **344**
Caroline of Brunswick, Queen of George IV   **344**
Carr, Robert, earl of Somerset   **344**
Carrawburgh   48
Carson, Sir Edward, Lord   *293*, 294, 307, **344**
Carter, Elizabeth   242
Carteret, John, Earl Granville   207, **344**
Cartimandua, Queen of Brigantes   16–17, 26
Cartwright, Thomas   157, **344**
carucage   68
Casement, Sir Roger   **344**
Cassius, Dio   10
Cassivellaunus   15, 24, **344**
Castell Dwyran   *61*
Castillon, Battle of (1453)   123
Castle Combe   130

Castle Hedingham   135
Castle Howard   239
Castle, Barbara   301
Castlereagh, Robert Stewart, Viscount   266, **344**
castles   69, 74, *77*, 92, *101*, 111, *116*, *119*, 135–6
Cateau-Cambrésis, Peace of (1559)   173
Catesby, Robert   159
Catherine of Aragon, Queen of Henry VIII   144, 150–1, 172, 188, **345**
Catherine of Braganza, Queen of Charles II   **345**
Catherine of Valois, Queen of Henry V   **345**
Catherine Howard, Queen of Henry VIII   **345**
Catherine Parr, Queen of Henry VIII   **345**
Catholic Relief Act (1790)   261
Catholics *see* Roman Catholics
Cato's Letters (1720–22)   196
Catraeth, Battle of (600)   71
Catuvellauni   14–16, 24, 26, 36, 39, 44
Catus Decianus (procurator)   18
"Cavalier Parliament" (1661–79)   203
Cavendish, Lord Frederick   258
Caxton, William   **345**
Ceawlin, King of Wessex   60, 72
Cecil family   146
Cecil, Sir Robert, earl of Salisbury   158–60, **345**
Cecil, Sir William, Lord Burghley   145, **345**
Celatus   *35*
"Celtic" fields   32, 41, 80
Celts: immigration and language 10, 14; society 14, 81–2, 84; army and warfare 24, *26*, *87*; fields 32, 41, 80; art 40, *43*, *47*, 88; culture 44, 46, 48; dress 45; place-names 48; and Picts 59; rulers 64; Church 76; law 81
Cenimagni (tribe)   17
Cenred, King of Mercia   77
censorship   233
censuses   248, 276; *see also* population
Cenwulf   **345**
Ceolfrith, Abbot of Wearmouth   88–92
ceorl   84
Cerdic   60, **345**
cereals and grain   10, 33, 36, 80, 124, 178
Chadwick, Sir Edwin: Sanitary Report (1842)   278, **345**
Chalton Down, Hampshire   *38*, 79, 80, 81
Chamberlain, Sir J. Austen   295, **345**
Chamberlain, Joseph   246, 259, 293, **345**
Chamberlain, Neville   296–8, 315, *315*, **345**
Chambers, Sir William   239, 241
Chancellor, Richard   **345**
Chancery   101, 105, 132, 154
Chantries Acts (1545, 1547)   150, 153, 155
Charlemagne, Emperor   56, 80, 90
Charles I, King of England: proposed Spanish marriage 160, 174; and Scotland 167, 210–12, 219; sells baronetcies 183; constitutional changes and Civil War 194, 196, 198–201, 210–11, 219; and arts 198, 238–40; portraits *199*, 238; "personal rule" 200; defeat and execution 201–2, *202*, 211; and Ireland 214; foreign relations 218; **345**

Charles II, King of England: and *quo warranto* 196; Restoration and reign 202–5, 212; receives French pension 204–5; proclaimed in Scotland 211–12; alliance with France 220; and Dutch wars 220–1; Catholicism 221; will and succession 222; supports dissenters 234; **345**
Charles V, Holy Roman Emperor   144, 155, 171–3
Charles VI, Holy Roman Emperor   223
Charles III (the Simple), King of France   66
Charles IV, King of France   120
Charles VI, King of France   121, 123
Charles VII, King of France   98, 121–3
Charles II, King of Spain   222
Charles Edward Stuart (Young Pretender; Bonnie Prince Charlie) *see* Stuart, Charles Edward
Chartists, Chartism   251–2, *254*, 279, 284
Chaucer, Geoffrey   96, *138*, 140, **345**
Cheltenham school   285
Chertsey Abbey, Surrey   *135*
Chester   12, 20, 28; mystery plays 140
Chesterfield, Philip Dormer Stanhope, earl of   207, **346**
Chesterholm (Vindolanda)   35
Chesterton   42
chi-rho monogram   48, *51*
Chiang Kai-shek   318
Chichele, Henry, Archbishop of Canterbury   **346**
Chichester (Noviomagnus)   15, 45, 73
child labour   252, 257, 281
Chillingworth, William   234
Chiswick House   239–40
chivalry   96, 137–8
cholera   278
Christianity and Christian Church: under Romans 13, 48; Anglo-Saxons and 54, 56–8, 74, 76; Picts accept 59; under Normans 69, 76; internationalism of 74, 94; early missionaries in Britain 74–6; taxation 80, 150; books and learning 88–92, *138*; and anti-papalism 96; relations with feudal state 100, 102; in Ireland 116–17; 13th-century reforms 135; and medieval art 135–9; mysticism and heresies in 138, 140; foundations and endowments 138; Reformation 144, 150; subjection under Tudors 150, 152–4; and dress 156; 20th-century attendance 330; *see also* Church of England
Christie, Agatha   328
Church Discipline Act (1874)   256
Church of England: beginnings 156–7, 159; in Wales 162, 302; in Civil War 200; Laudian reforms 201; abolished (1646) 202; re-established 203; Tories support 204, 206; and social order *230*; and dissent 234, 236, 252, 282; disestablishment question 259; opposes revolutionary ideas 282; High-Church reaction in 282; and universities 285; membership decline 330
Church of Ireland   256–7, 264
Church of Scotland *see* Kirk
Church-scot   80
Churchill, Lord Randolph   **346**
Churchill, Sarah, duchess of Marlborough   206, 222
Churchill, Sir Winston S.   288,

298–300, *298* 305, 317, 322, 327, **346**
cinema   329–30, 336
Cirencester (Corinium)   21, 34, *47*
Cistercian order   94
Civil Service Commission   255
Civil War: Tudor origins 145; and constitutional change 194, 196, 200; outcome 201; and Scots 210–11; in Ireland 214–15; Second 219; and social order 232
civitas capital (Roman)   13, 16
Clan na Gael   308
Clapham Sect   282
Clare, Gilbert de, earl of Hertford and Gloucester   **346**
Clare, Richard de, earl of Pembroke and Striguil ("Strongbow")   **346**
Clarence, George, duke of   148
Clarence, Lionel, duke of   117
Clarence, Thomas, duke of   **346**
Clarendon: Assizes of (1166) 100; Constitutions of (1164) 101
Clarendon Code   203
Clarendon, Edward Hyde, earl of   203, 240, **346**
Clarendon, George William Frederick Villiers, earl of   266
Clarke, Tom   308
class (social):   stratification 98, 131–3; Tudor rural 182; 18th century 230; and urban life 278–9; Engels on 279; and economic effort 324–5; and inequalities 328; and 20th-century values 330–1; and university entrance 334
classes (evangelical)   156–7
Classicianus, Julius (procurator)   12, 17–18
Classis Britannica (Roman British fleet)   30, 33
Claudia Rufina   13
Claudius, Roman emperor: and conquest of Britain 10, 12, 14–16, 18, 24–6; and Amminus 16; Colchester temple 39
Claverhouse, John Graham of *see* Dundee, Viscount
clergy: secular 133; in social order 133; submission of (1532) 153; and Reformation 156; numbers 198; resignations under Act of Uniformity 203; status 278; opposes popular education 284; *see also* Church of England; Roman Catholics
Cleveley, Robert   *223*
client-kingdoms (Roman)   16–19
Clifford family   146
Clifford of Chudleigh, Thomas, Lord   203, 221, **346**
Clinton, Sir Henry   **346**
Clive, Robert, Lord   223–4, 229, 282, **346**
Clontarf, Battle of (1014)   73, 115
cloth: exports 130, 137, 172, 179–80; production 127; as Devon industry 227; *see also* textile industry; woollen industry
Clouet, François   *166*
"Club, The"   238
clubs   198, 233, 238
Cluny   90, 92
Clyde Workers' Committee   305
Cnut, King of England   57, 59–60, 62, *63*, 64, 66, 74, 76–7; law code 68, 81; **346**
Cnut IV, King of Denmark   76
coal and coalmining   179, 227, 227–8, *272*, *322*, *329*
Coalbrookdale   *270*
Coalition governments: (1915–16) 294–5; (1940) 298–9
Cobbett, William   284, **346**
Cobden, Richard   256, *257*, **346**
Cobham, William Brooke, Lord   *185*
"Cocoa Tree" coffee house   238

Coercion Act (1881) 258, 263
coffee houses 233, 238
Cogidubnus, Tiberius Claudius 15–16, 19, 41, 42, 44, 45
coins, coinage: pre-Roman 10, 14–15, 32, 32; Roman 23, 36, 44, 45; Offa's 56; Anglo-Saxon 63, 78, 79; Norman 58; Tudor debasement 176; see also silver
coke smelting 228, 272
Coke, Sir Edward 160, **346**
Coke, Thomas 226
Colchester (Camulodunum; Colonia Victricensis): under Romans 10, 13, 15–16, 18, 21, 24, 35, 38–9, 41–2, 44–5; Claudius temple 39, 45–6
Cold War 317
Cole, Douglas (G.D.H.) and Margaret 328
Coleridge, Samuel Taylor 283–4
Colet, John **346**
College of Arms 183
Collingwood, Cuthbert, Lord **346**
Collins, Michael 308–9, 311, **346**
Coloniae 13, 16
colonies 223–4, 245, 266, 289; see also Empire, British
Columba, St 76, 89, **346**
Combination Acts 250
Commission for Ecclesiastical Causes 205
commissions of array (1642) 218–19
Committee of the Articles 210
Commius 10, 12, 15
Commodus, Roman emperor 20
Common Pleas, Court of 100–1, 105
Commons, House of: and supply 98; hostility to papal use of Church 105; relations with Crown 106–9; and taxation 107–8, 207; in constitution 108; Puritans in 156; and James I 160; illustrated 160, 251; and impeachment 160; changes in 17th century 194, 196; "place men" 205; 18th-century position 208; see also Parliament
Commonwealth (1649–53) 202
Commonwealth of Nations, British 289–90, 312, 314, 318–20; Secretariat 290, 318; see also Empire, British
Commonwealth Immigration Act (1962) 332
Commonwealth Party 298
commotes (Wales) 64
Communist Party of Great Britain 288, 296–7, 303
Companies Acts (1844, 1862) 274
Compton, Henry, Bishop of London **346**
Comyn, John the Black, Lord of Badenoch **347**
Comyn, John the Red, Lord of Badenoch **347**
Concert of Europe 267
Concord, Battle of (1775) 224
"Confession of Faith", Scotland (1560) 165
Congreve, William 238
Connacht, Council of 169
Conservative party: organization 246, 256–7; J. Chamberlain splits 246; governments 255, 259; Irish policy 262; 20th-century survival 288; and Unionists 293; and denationalization 299; in Wales 302–3; and EEC 320; protectionism 324; see also General Elections; Tories
Consolidation Act (1787) 252
Conspiracy and Protection of Property Act (1875) 257
Constable, John **347**
constable (royal office) 101

Constans, Roman emperor 22
Constantine II, Roman emperor 22
Constantine III, Roman emperor 13, 22–3
Constantine the Great, Roman emperor 21–2, 30
Constantine Mac Fergus, King of Picts **347**
Constantine I, King of Scotia **347**
Constantine II, King of Scotia **347**
Constantine III, King of Scotia **347**
Constantius I (Chlorus), Roman emperor 10, 20, 22, 30
Constantius II, Roman emperor 22
constitution (British) 99, 102, 194, 206–8, 222, 246, 303, 306
consumerism 274–5, 323 324, 331
Contemporary Review 286
Conventicle Acts (1664, 1670) 203
Convention Parliament (1660) 202–3
Convocation (Church) 135
Conwy castle 111; Treaty of (1277) 110
Cook, James **347**
Cooley, Thomas 239
Cooper, Samuel 237
Coote, Sir Eyre **347**
Cope, Anthony 157
copper 13, 33, 39
corn see cereals
corn laws 253; repealed 246, 253–4, 255
Cornwall 33, 60, 81
Cornwallis, Charles, Earl 224, 261, **347**
coroners 106
Corporation Act (1661) 197, 203; repealed (1828) 252–3
Corresponding Societies 197, 250; Act (1799) 250
Cort, Henry 272
Cosgrave, William Thomas 309, **347**
Costello, John 309
cottage industries 176–8
cotton industry 227, 271–3; see also textiles
Council for National Academic Awards (CNAA) 334
Council in the Marches of Wales 153, 161, 200
Council of the North 153, 200
Counter-Reformation 172, 191
County and Borough Police Act (1856) 252
county committees 219
"Country" party 205
Courtenay, William, Archbishop of Canterbury **347**
courts of law 97–8, 100–2, 132–3, 200; see also individual courts
Covenanters (Scotland) 210–12, 219; see also National Covenant
Coventry 140, 180
Coverdale, Miles, Bishop of Exeter 150, 347
Coward, Noel 328
Craftsman, The (journal) 207
Craggs, James 207
Craig, James 239
Craigavon, James Craig, Viscount 309
Cranfield, Lionel, earl of Middlesex 160, **347**
Cranmer, Thomas, Archbishop of Canterbury 144, 152, 153, 156, 188, **347**
Crawford Report (1925) 334
Crécy, Battle of (1346) 121, 173
Crichton castle, Midlothian 165
Cricieth castle 111
Cricklade 73
Crimean War (1854–5) 244, 255, 266–8
Cripps, Sir R. Stafford 325, **347**
Crompton, Samuel 225

Cromwell, Oliver 196, 201–3, 211, 214–16, 219, 232–3, **347**
Cromwell, Richard 202, **347**
Cromwell, Thomas, earl of Essex: and Reformation 144, 150, 153, 165; and royal succession 151; and Great Bible 153; and Wales 161; and Ireland 168; downfall 173; and arts 190; **347**
crops (agricultural) 33, 41, 80, 124, 177; see also agriculture; individual crops
Crosland, Anthony 333
Crown (monarchy; kings): Anglo-Saxon 63–4, 79; and feudalism 94, 97; authority, status and conventions 94, 97–8, 100–9; and barons 97, 102; and war 97–8, 106; household 105, 191; and taxation 98–9, 106, 108, 146; and Parliament 107–9, 154, 222; and Tudor rule 142, 144, 160; and Church supremacy 153; prerogative 160; culture and pastimes 188–92, 198; 17th-century changes 194, 196; and divine right 205, 208; 18th-century position 208–9; marriages regulated 236; arts patronage 238–9; 19th-century decline 249–50; in 20th century 288
Cruikshank, George 249, 283
Crusades 118, 120
Culloden, Battle of (1746) 213, 213
"Cum Universi" (Bull, 1192) 113
Cumann na nGaedhal 309
Cumberland, William Augustus, duke of 213, 213, 223, 236, **347**
Cunedda **347**
Cunobelinus (Cymbeline) 10, 15–16, 39, **347**
Curia Regis 100–1
Curzon, George Nathaniel, Marquis **348**
Cuthbert, St 88–9, **348**
Cyprus 257, 290, 319
Czechoslovakia 315, 318

D-Day (1944) 317
Dacre family 146
Dafydd ap Gruffud **348**
Dafydd ap Llewelyn **348**
Dagworth, Thomas 121
Dál Riáta 59, 64, 72
Daladier, Edouard 315
Dalhousie, James Ramsay, marquis of **348**
Dalrymple, Sir James, Viscount Stair 212, **348**
Dalrymple, John, earl of Stair **348**
Dalton, Hugh, Lord **348**
Danby, Thomas Osborne, earl of 204, **348**
Danebury, Hampshire 37
Danegeld 68, 74–5, 78
Danelaw 73, 74
Danes 57–8, 61, 73–4; see also Vikings
Danzig 315
Darby, Abraham 225, 272
Darien scheme (1695–99) 212–13
Darnley, Henry Stuart, Lord 166, **348**
Darwin, Charles: *The Origin of Species* 245, 260, **348**
Davenant, William 240
David, or Dewi, St **348**
David I, King of Scots 70, **348**
David II, King of Scots 114, **348**
David, Prince of Gwynedd 110
Davies, John 174
Davies, Richard, Bishop of St David's 162, **348**
Davies, S.O. 302

Davison, William D. **348**
Davitt, Michael 263, **348**
Davy, Sir Humphrey **348**
Daw Mill colliery, Coventry 322
de Burgh family 117
de Clare, Richard ("Strongbow") 115
De Donis (1285) 106
De Excidio Britonum (Gildas) 71
De Heretico Comburendo (1401) 140
de la Mare, Peter 108
de Vesci, Eustace 102
Debenham's (store) 273
Declaratory Acts, Ireland (1720, 1782) 217
Decorated style (architecture) 136
Dee, John **348**
Defoe, Daniel 198, 207, 241, **348**
Deheubarth 110
Deira 60
Deism 234–5
Delany, Mary 242
demesnes 124, 126–7, 129
Democratic Unionist Party (N. Ireland) 311
Denain, Battle of (1710) 222
Depressed Areas Act (1934) 296
Derby, Edward George G.S. Stanley, earl of 255–6, **348**
Derby, Edward Henry Stanley, earl of **348**
Derby, Thomas Stanley, earl of **348**
Dere Street 29, 40
Dermot MacMurrough **349**
Descartes, René 237
Despenser family 107
Despenser, Henry Le, Bishop of Norwich 134, **349**
Despenser, Hugh Le, the Elder, earl of Winchester **349**
Despenser, Hugh Le, the Younger **349**
Dettingen, Battle of (1743) 223
De Valera, Eamon 308–9, 309, 311, **349**
devaluation (sterling) 300, 325
Devis, Arthur 239
Devon and Somerset Stores 275
Devonshire, Spencer Compton Cavendish, marquis of Hartington, duke of 239, **349**
Devonshire, William Cavendish, duke of 279, **349**
Devotio moderna 165
Dickens, Charles 248, 285–6, **349**
diet 98, 186–7, 226, 269, 329, 331; see also food supply
Diggers 232
Digges, Sir Dudley **349**
Dilke, Sir Charles Wentworth 259, 285, **349**
Dillon, John 309, **349**
Dinas Powis 54
Diocese (Roman) 21
Diocletian, Roman emperor 12, 20–1, 30, 34, 36, 45
Disarming Act, Scotland (1715) 213
disease 277–8, 329; see also epidemics; plague
Disraeli, Benjamin, earl of Beaconsfield 246–8, 255–8, 267, 268, 286, **349**
dissenters see nonconformists
divorce 328; Divorce Acts (1937, 1969) 328; see also marriage
Dobunni 15, 39
Dolocauthi, Carmarthenshire 33, 34
Domesday Survey and Book (1086) 59, 68–9, 69, 80–1, 84–6
Dominican order 132
Donald III Bane **349**
Donaldson, Arthur 306
Donnchad macDomnall, King of the

380

Uí Néill   72
Donne, John   **349**
Dorchester-on-Thames   48, 75,
   134, 136
Doré, Gustave   *277*
Dorset, Thomas Sackville, earl of
   see Sackville, Thomas
Douai   157
Douglas family   113–15; Black
   Douglases 164
Douglas, Sir Archibald   **349**
Douglas, Archibald, earl of Angus
   (*c.* 1449–1513/14)   **349**
Douglas, Archibald, earl of Angus
   (*c.* 1489–1557)   **349**
Douglas, Sir James ("the Good")
   349
Douglas-Home, Sir Alec *see* Home,
   Lord
Dover   30, 78; castle *101*; Treaty
   of (1670) 221
Dowding, Air Marshal Hugh, Lord
   316, **349**
Drake, Sir Francis   174, **349**
"draperies, new"   179–80, 227
Dream of the Rood (poem)   88–9
dress   45, 87, 132, 184, 186, *187*,
   329
Drogheda: 1649 massacre   215
Drogheda Parliament (1494–5)
   167
druids   14, 44
Dryden, John   241–2, **349**
Dublin: Vikings in 73–4; charters
   115; as capital 116–17; and Pale
   117; population growth 180, 225;
   1771 riots 217; Trinity College
   238; cultural life 238–9; 1916
   Easter Rising *307*
Dublovellaunos   15
Dudley, Lord Guildford   **349**
duelling   233
Dugdale, William   240
Dumnonia, kingdom of (Devon)
   60, 81
Duncan I, King of Scots   **349**
Duncan II, King of Scots   **349**
Duncan of Camperdown, Adam,
   Viscount   **350**
Dunbar, Battles of: (1296) 114;
   (1650) 211
Dundas, Henry, Viscount Melville
   350
Dundee, John Graham of
   Claverhouse, Viscount   212–13
Dunkellin amendment (1866 Reform
   Bill)   256
Dunkirk   220–2
Dunning, John, Lord Ashburton
   209
Dunstan, St, Archbishop of
   Canterbury   57, 69, 90, **350**
Durham (city)   *68*, 69, 92, 105, 280
Durham (county)   81
Durham, John George Lambton,
   earl of   **350**
Durotriges   36
Dutch Wars   203, 218, 220–1, *221*

ealdormen   60–2, 75
Ealhswith, Queen of Alfred   78
earls (Anglo-Saxon)   61–2, 82
East Anglia   56, 60, 73–4, 81,
   134, 136
East India Bill (1783)   209
East India Company   180, 224,
   229, 265
East India Regulating Act (1773)
   224
Easter: date of   76
Easter Rising, Ireland (1916)
   307–8
"eastern question"   266
Ecclesiological Society   284
Ecgfrith, King of Mercia   64

Eddius   89
Eden, Sir Anthony, earl of Avon
   300, 318, **350**
Edgar, King of the English   57, 60,
   63, 79, 90, **350**
Edgar the Aetheling   76, **350**
Edgecote, Battle of (1469)   148
Edinburgh   114, 175, 210, *212*,
   232, 239
Edinburgh Review   253, 286
Edington, Battle of (878)   74
Edith, Queen of Edward the
   Confessor   67
Edmund I, King of the English   **350**
Edmund II Ironside, King   **350**
Edmund, Prince (son of Henry III)
   · 120
Edred, King of the English   **350**
education: Roman 13; and 19th-
   century reform 246, 284–5;
   religion and 256; professional 280;
   secondary 333–4, 336; higher 334,
   336; *see also* polytechnics; public
   schools; universities
Education Acts: (1870) 285; (1876)
   257; (1902) 293–4, 333; (1918)
   295, 333; (1944) 333–4
Edward I, King of England: and
   foreign wars 94; and church taxes
   96; and Scots 97, 106, 114; and
   Parliament 98, 107; and franchise
   103; power 105–7; and conquest of
   Wales 106, 110–11, 120, 125, 161;
   and French 118–19; on Crusade
   120; and new towns 125; expels
   Jews 126; castles 135; **350**
Edward II, King of England   98–8,
   105–7, 114, 116, 118, 120,
   137, **350**
Edward III, King of England: and
   French 94, 106, 121, 123; and
   Church 96; success of reign 97,
   105; and Commons 98; finances
   107–8; seizes power 107; grants
   and rewards 107; conquests 109;
   and Ireland 117; wool taxes 127;
   and bullion loss 128; and Windsor
   Castle 137–8; and Garter 138;
   captures Calais 173; **350**
Edward IV, King of England   142,
   146–9, *149*, 161, 171, 184,
   191, **350**
Edward V, King of England
   148, **350**
Edward VI, King of England   144,
   150–1, *152*, 154–5, *154*, 165, **350**
Edward VII, King of Great Britain
   350
Edward VIII, King of Great Britain
   288, 297, 335, **350**
Edward, Prince of Wales (1453–71)
   147–8, **350**
Edward, the Black Prince   121, **350**
Edward Balliol, King of Scots   **350**
Edward of Norwich, duke of York
   350
Edward the Aetheling   **350**
Edward the Confessor, King of the
   English   57–60, 66, *67*, 74, 76–7,
   103, 105, **351**
Edward the Elder, King of the
   Angles and Saxons   60, 73,
   78, **351**
Edward the Martyr, King of the
   English   **351**
Edwin, King of Northumbria   60,
   72, 75, **351**
Edwin, Earl   66
Edwy, or Eadwig, King of the
   English   **351**
Egbert, King of Wessex   60, 64,
   351
Egypt   258, *267*, 268, 313
Eisenhower, Dwight D.   318
Elcho, Francis, Lord (*later* earl of
   Wemyss)   256
Eldon, John Scott, earl of   *283*, **351**

Eleanor of Aquitaine, Queen of
   Henry II   100, 105, **351**
Eleanor of Castile, Queen of
   Edward I   **351**
Eleanor of Provence, Queen of
   Henry III   **351**
electoral registration   253
"Eleven Years' Tyranny" ("personal
   rule" 1629–40)   200
Elgar, Sir Edward   **351**
Eliot, George   245, 248, 285
Eliot, T.S.   335
Elizabeth I, Queen of England: and
   Reformation 145, 155–7; death
   146; finances and economy 146,
   156, 160, 192; birth 150–2;
   succession 156–7; rule and
   character 157–8, 160; portraits
   158, *187*, *190*, 192; and
   international politics 173–4; and
   power of London 180; and social
   order 184; and Knole 188; court
   pastimes 188; and constitution
   194; **351**
Elizabeth II, Queen of Great Britain
   288, 336, **351**
Elizabeth Wydeville (Woodville),
   Queen of Edward IV   148, **351**
Elizabeth, Queen of Bohemia   160,
   174
Elizabeth of York, Queen of Henry
   VII   *154*
Ellenborough, Edward Law, Lord
   253
Elliot, Walter   305
Ellis, Tom   302
Elmet   54, 81
Elphinstone, William, Bishop of
   Aberdeen   165
Ely   57, 69, 72, 90; cathedral
   92, 136
Emma of Normandy, Queen of
   Aethelred II   66, 76, **351**
Empire, British   265, 268, 289–90,
   292, 312, 314, 318; *see also*
   Commonwealth of Nations;
   imperialism
Empire Exhibitions: Wembley (1924)
   289; Glasgow (1938) 289, 305
employers' associations   275
Employers and Workmen Act (1875)
   257
enclosure (land)   177, 186, 226–7
"Engagement" (Scots Treaty, 1647)
   211–12, 219
Engels, Friedrich   279
England, unification of   59–60,
   63–4, 94, 96, 105–6
Enniskellin Castle, siege of (1594)
   170
entertainment (popular)   329–30;
   see also sport
epidemics   181, 277–8, 329; *see also*
   plague
Eppillus   15, *45*
Equal Franchise Act (1928)   327
Equal Pay Act (1970)   328
Erasmus, Desiderius   165, 190
escheators   106
esquires   183
Essex, Robert Devereux, earl of
   (1567–1601)   158–9, 169, **351**
Essex, Robert Devereux, earl of
   (1591–1646)   219, **351**
Ethiopia   314–15
eucharist   152
European Economic Community
   (Common Market)   292, 301,
   320, *320*, 322
European Recovery Programme
   (Marshall Aid)   317
evangelical movement   236, 283–4
Evans, Gwynfor   *303*
Evesham, Battle of (1265)   104, 120
Ewing, Winifred   *306*
Eworth, Hans   *185*
Exchequer   69–70, 79, 101,

105–6, 191
Exchequer, Stop of (1672)   221
Excise crisis (1733)   207, 236
Exclusion crisis (1678–81)   194,
   197, 204–5, 233, 241
Exclusion Parliament (1681)   205
Exeter   73, 136
Explanation, Act of (1660)   216
eyre, court of   97, 100

Fabian Society   260, 293
Factory Acts (1833, 1844)   252
Fairfax, Ferdinando, Lord   **351**
Fairfax, Gen. Thomas, Lord
   219, **351**
Falkirk, Battle of (1298)   114, 120
Falkland Islands   332
Falkland, Lucius Cary, Viscount
   351
family   182, 185, *185*, 231, *231*,
   239, 248, 277, *286*, 328
famine   128, 178, 234; Irish
   (1847–8) 262, 277
Farquhar, George   238
Fawcett, Dame Millicent   **351**
Fawkes, Guy   159, **351**
fealty   131
Fenianism   258, 262–3, 308
feoffees   131–2
feorm (food rent)   79, 84
Fergusson, Robert   242
fertility (human)   276–7
feudalism: Anglo-Saxons and 63;
   Normans and 68, 74, 86–7; and
   military service 69, 87, 120, 131;
   rule 94, 97, 100; and monarchy
   106–8; and social order 131–2;
   and land tenure 131–2; "bastard"
   142, 148, 184; fiscal 158, 160
Fianna Fail   309
fiefs   69, 87, 131
Field of Cloth of Gold (1520)   172
field systems   32, 41, 80
Field, John   157
Fielding, Henry   234, 242
Fielding, Sir John   234
"Fifteen", The (Jacobite rebellion,
   1715)   197, 206, 207, 212–13
Fifth Monarchists   202, 233
Finch, Sir John, Lord Finch of
   Fordwich   **351**
Fine Gael   309
Fishbourne   41, *42*
Fisher, H.A.L.   295, 333, **351**
Fisher, John, Bishop of Rochester
   151, **351**
Fisher, Admiral John Arbuthnot,
   Lord   294, 312, **351**
Fitton, Sir Edward   169
Fitzgerald earls (of Desmond and
   Kildare)   167
Fitzgerald, Gerald, earl of Kildare
   (d. 1513)   **352**
Fitzgerald, Gerald, earl of Kildare
   (1487–1534)   **352**
Fitzgerald, Thomas, Lord Offaly and
   earl of Kildare   **352**
Fitzosbern, William, earl of
   Hereford   **352**
Fitz Walter, Robert   102
Five Articles (Scotland, 1621)   166
Five Knights Case (1626)   200
Five Mile Act (1665)   203
Flambard, Ranulf, Bishop of
   Durham   70, **352**
Flanders   80, 119, 125, 127,
   130, 179
Fleetwood, Charles   216
Fleming, Sir Alexander   **352**
Fleury, André Hercule de, Cardinal
   222
Flint, Wales   111
Flitcroft, Henry   *240*
Flodden, Battle of (1513)   164, 172
Flood, Henry   217

Foliot, Gilbert, Bishop of London **352**
Folkestone 41
Fonthill Abbey 284
Food and Drugs Act (1875) 257
food supply 80, 124–5, 176, 177, 196–7, 226
Foot, Michael *299*
football 281, 330
fora (Roman) 40–1, 45
Fordwich 78
Forest Charter 107
Formigny, Battle of (1450) 123
Forster, William Edward 258, **352**
Fortescue, Sir John 99, 109, **352**
Fortnightly Review (journal) 286
forts 22, 26–30, 41, 73; *see also* castles; hill-forts
Forty-Five", "The (Jacobite rebellion, 1745) 197–8, 206, 213
Forward (journal) 305
Fotheringhay, Northamptonshire 137
Fountains Abbey 94
Fox, Charles James 194, 209, 233, 246, 253–4, **352**
Fox, George 233, **352**
Fox, Henry, Lord Holland (1705–74) **352**
Foxe, John: *Acts and Monuments (Book of Martyrs)* 157, **352**
Foxe, Richard, Bishop of Winchester **352**
France: English rule in 94, 97, 100; cultural dominance 96; monarchical rule 98; barons seek unity with 102; Angevin wars with 106, 118; invades England (1216–17) 118; and Hundred Years War 121–3; and Scots Reformation 164–5; supports Scotland 171; in international power struggle 171–4; famines 178; Charles I's war with 200, 218; 18th-century wars with 205–6, 222–3; and war in Netherlands 220; and Hanover 223; naval rivalry 224, 265; in American War of Independence 224; commercial rivalry 229; revolutionary wars 244, 265–6; and 1860 Cobden Treaty 256, *257*; in Africa 260; in Ireland 261; and Russia 267; Palmerston aligns with 268; 1904 entente with Britain 313; falls to Germany (1940) 315
franchise (parliamentary): late medieval 103; pre-1832 system 249; 1832 Reform Act 250–1, 253; and Reform League 256; and household suffrage 258–9; and Ireland 262; and 1918 Reform Act 295, 327
Francis I, King of France 172, *173*
Francis, Dauphin of France 165
Francis, Philip 208
Franciscan order 132
Franco-Prussian war (1870) 266
Franco, Gen. Francisco 331
Franks 54, 59, 76–7, 92
Frederick Louis, Prince of Wales 207, 223, 236
free trade 248, 254, 256, *257*
freedmen 35
freemen 84–6
French Revolution 194, 245, 250, 282–3, *283*
French, John, earl of Ypres **352**
friars 132–3; *see also* Dominican order; Franciscan order
Frith, William *286*
Frobisher, Sir Martin 174, **352**
Frontinus, Sextus Julius 25, **352**
Fullofaudes, Duke 22
Fursey, St 89
fyrd 97

Gaelic Athletic Association 264
Gaelic League 264
Gaelic revivals 167, 264, 310
Gage, Thomas 239
Gaillard, Château 118–20, *119*
Gainsborough, Thomas 240–1, *282*
Gaitskell, Hugh *299*, 300, **352**
Galba, Sulpicius, Roman emperor 19
Gallienus, Roman emperor 30
Gandhi, Mohandas Karamchand 314, 319
Gandon, James 239
Gardiner, Stephen, Bishop of Winchester 155, **352**
Garrick, David 233, 238, 241
Garter, Order of the 138
Gascony 118–23
Gaul 10, 14–15, 22, 24, 35–6, 82
Gaulle, Charles de 290
Gaunt, John of *see* John of Gaunt
Gaveston, Piers 107, **352**
Gawain and the Green Knight (poem) 140
Gay, John 209, 240
Geddes Committee ("Axe") (1922) 295
geld 96
General Agreement on Tariffs and Trade (1947) 325
General Elections: (1841) 254; (1868) 256–7; (1880) 257; (1885) 259; (1900) 260, 293; (1906) 294; (1910, Jan. & Dec.) 294; (1918, "Coupon election") 295; (1922) 295, 305; (1923) 295; (1924) 296; (1929) 296; (1931) 296, 305; (1935) 297; (1945) 298–9, 305; (1950) 299; (1951) 299; (1959) 300; (1964) 300–1; (1966) 300; (1970) 301; (1974) 301; (1979) 306
General Strike (1926) 296, 305, 330
genius and *numen* 46
gentry: social hierarchy 98, 132, 183, 239; as local officials 106; and Crown 108; anticlericalism 133; under Tudors 145, 181; and integration of Wales 161; housing 186; and Cromwell's military rule 219; social life 232, *239*
Geoffrey, Count of Anjou 66–7, 76–7, 100
Geoffrey, Count of Brittany **352**
Geoffrey Plantagenet, Archbishop of York **352**
George I, King of Great Britain: accession 197, 205–6, 223; quarrel with son 207; foreign relations 222; supports Latitudinarians 234; mistresses 236; **352**
George II, King of Great Britain 207, 223, 234, **352**
George III, King of Great Britain: and constitution 194, 208; and political consensus 198; and arts 198; reign 209, 249; foreign policy 223; and farming 226; morality 236; and Ireland 261; **352**
George IV, King of Great Britain 249–50, *283*, **352**
George V, King of Great Britain 288, 335, **353**
George VI, King of Great Britain 288, 297, **353**
Geraldine family 117; *see also* Fitzgerald
Germain, George Sackville *see* Sackville, Viscount
Germanic peoples 54, 59–60, 71, 81
Germanus, St 30, 48
Germany: Romans in 15; and English cloth trade 80, 130; economic dominance 130; naval

rivalry 265, 312; in East Africa 268; economic competition from 275, 312; banking collapse 296, 324; and World Wars 298; 313–17; and Czechoslovakia 315
Gerontius 13
gesith 84
Ghana 318
Gibbon, Edward 238, 240; *Decline and Fall of the Roman Empire* 283
Gibbons, Grinling 237, **353**
Gibbons, Orlando **353**
Gibraltar 223
Giffard, Walter **353**
Gilbert, Sir Humphrey **353**
Gilbert, John 229
Gildas (monk) 71, 81, 85
gin 234, *235*; Gin Act (1751) 241
Ginkel, Godert, Baron von, earl of Athlone 216
Giraldus Cambrensis *117*
Gladstone, William Ewart: liberalism 246–7; and income tax 254; in office 255–6; supports reform 256; administration and legislation 256–60; Midlothian campaigns 257; and Bulgarian atrocities 257; conflicts with Disraeli 257–8; illustrated *258*; and Ireland 259, 263–4; foreign policy 266, 268; **353**
Glanvill, Ranulf de 96, **353**
Glasgow 165, 213, 225, 229, *304*
Glasgow General Assembly (1638) 210
Glastonbury 90
Glencairn, William Cunningham, earl of 212
Glencoe massacre (1692) 212–13
Globe theatre, London 192
Glorious Revolution (1688) 194, 196, 213, 221–2
Gloucester, Richard, duke of *see* Richard III, King
Gloucester (Glevum) 13, 16, 34, 136–7
Gloucester, Statute of (1278) 103
Gloucester, Thomas Despenser, duke of 105, 108–9, *115*
Glyndŵr, Owain 109, 112, 129, **353**
Goderich, Frederick John Robinson, Viscount **353**
Godfrey, Sir Edmund Berry 204
Godmanchester 42
Gododdin (poem) 54, 71, 83, 88
Gododdin, kingdom of the 54, 71
Godolphin, Sidney, earl of 206, **353**
Godwine, Earl 66, 68, 77, **353**
Goes, Hugo van der *165*
Gokstad ship *73*
gold 13, 33, *34*, 78; *see also* bullion
gold standard 253, 274, 322
"Golden Act" (Scotland, 1592) 166
Goldsmith, Oliver 238, 241
"Good Parliament" (1376) 107–9
Gordon riots (1780) 236
Gordon, Gen. Charles George 258, 268, **353**
Gordon, Thomas 196
Gorst, John 256
Gosbecks, Essex 46
Gothic art 135–6; revival 284
Gough, Richard *230*
Government of Ireland Act (1920) 307–8, 309–10
governors (Roman) 17
Gower, John 140
Graces, The (Ireland, 1626, 1628) 214
Grafton, Augustus Henry Fitzroy, duke of 208, **353**
Graham, Sir James Robert George 255
Grand Assize 100
Grand Remonstrance (1641) 201
Grand Tour 240

Granville, George Leveson Gower Earl **353**
Granville, John Carteret, Earl *see* Carteret
Gratian, Roman emperor 23
Grattan, Henry 217, 261, **353**
Gravelines, Battle of (1588) 174
Great Chesterford 34
Great Contract (1610) 160
Great Council (1376) 108
Great Eastern (ship) *273*
Great Exhibition (1851) 246, 255
Great Revolt (1381) 109
Great Seal of England (1651) *203*
Great Sessions 161
Great Wardrobe, Keeper of the 105
Greece 266–7
Greenwich: pageant (1527) 190–1; Treaty (1543) 165; Queen's House 192, *199*, *238*, 239; Park *199*
Gregory I (the Great), Pope 54, 74–6, 88–9, 92; *Pastoral Care* 90
Grenville family 223
Grenville, George **353**
Grenville, Richard Temple, Earl Temple *see* Temple, Richard
Grenville, Sir Richard **353**
Grenville, William Wyndham, Lord 253, **353**
Gresham, Sir Thomas *180*, **353**
Grey family *152*
Grey, Charles, Earl 254, **353**
Grey, Sir Edward, Viscount 268, 292, 313, **353**
Grey, Lady Jane 152, 155, **353**
Grey of Ruthin, Reginald de, Lord 112
Griffith, Arthur 308, *309*, **353**
Griffiths, James 303
Grindal, Edmund, Archbishop of Canterbury 165
Grosseteste, Robert, Bishop of Lincoln **354**
Gruffud ap Cynan 70, **354**
Gruffud ap Llywelyn, ruler of Gwynedd 64, 70, **354**
Guarantee Treaty (1839) 266
Guest, Keen and Nettlefold (company) 275
Guest, J.J. 282
Guines 121
Gunpowder Plot (1605) 159, 200
Gussage All Saints 32, 37
Guthlac, St, Mercian prince 56, 89
Guthrum, King of East Anglia **354**
Gwynedd (Welsh principality) 54, 64, 110

Habsburg dynasty 171–3
Hadrian, Roman emperor *17*; Wall 10, 12, 28–31, *28*, *31*, 42, 46
Haig, Douglas, Earl **354**
Haile Selassie, Emperor of Ethiopia 315
Hailsham, Quintin Hogg, Lord **354**
Hakon IV, King of Norway 114
Haldane, Richard Burdon, Viscount **354**
Hales, Robert 134
Halévy, Elie 245
Halifax, Charles Montagu, earl of 205, **354**
Halifax, George Montagu Dunk, earl of **354**
Halifax, George Savile, marquis of **354**
Halley, Edmund 237
Hallstatt culture 40
Hamilton, John, Archbishop of St Andrews 165
Hamilton, James, duke of 211, **354**
Hamilton, James Douglas, duke of 213

Hamon, Robert Fitz **354**
Hampden, John 200, **354**
Hampton Court: conference (1604) 159; Palace *190*
Hanbury 136
Handel, George Frederick 240, **354**; *Messiah* 238, 240–1
Hankey, Maurice, Lord **354**
Hanoverians 194, 197, 205–6, 222, 236
Hanseatic League 80, 130, 172
Harcourt, Sir William Vernon **354**
Hardie, James Keir 260, 302, **354**
Hardwicke, Philip Yorke, Earl 231
Hargreaves, James 225
Harlech: castle 111–12
Harley, Robert, earl of Oxford 206, 222, **354**
Harold I (Harefoot), King of England **354**
Harold II (Godwinson), King of England 64, 66, *67*, 68, 87, **354**
Harrington, Sir Henry *170*
Harrington, James: *Oceana* 196
Harris, Air Marshal Sir Arthur 317
Harthacnut, King **354**
Hartington, Spencer Compton Cavendish, marquis of, *see* Devonshire, duke of
Hartshill 35
Harvey, William 240, **354**
Hasilrig, Sir Arthur **354**
Hastings, Battle of (1066) 66, 74, *75*, 87
Hastings, Francis Rawdon, marquis of **354**
Hastings, Warren **355**
Hattin, Battle of (1187) 118
Hatton, Sir Christopher **355**
Hawke, Edward, Lord **355**
Hawkings, Sir John 174, **355**
Hawksmoor, Nicholas 242, **355**
Hayling Island 46
Hayman, Francis 241
Hayter, Sir George *251*
Heads of Proposals (1647) 219
Health of Towns, Royal Commission on (1844–5) 278
Heath, Edward 301, 320, *320*, 326, **355**
Hell-fire Club 238
Henderson, Alexander 210
Henderson, Arthur 294, **355**
Hengist 54, 59, **355**
Hengistbury Head, Dorset 36, 38–9
Henley, Walter of 124
Henrietta Maria, Queen of Charles I 174, 200, **355**
Henry I, King of England 62, 66–70, 76–7, **355**
Henry II, King of England: succeeds to throne 66–8, 76, 96–8; and Exchequer 69, 70; rule and administration 70, 98, 100–1; and control of Church 96, 100, 102–3; and royal justice 97; and France 97, 118; in Anjou 100; burial 105; and Becket *103*, 106; and Welsh 110; invades Ireland 115; foreign interests and alliances 120; and social order 133; **355**
Henry III, King of England: foreign expeditions and interests 94, 97, 120; and papacy 96; and Magna Carta 97–8, 102; and taxation 98; government and authority 102–4; death 105; and Wales 110; surrenders French territories 118–19; and French invasion 118; and Sicily 120; and Westminster Abbey 135–6; encourages art 135–6; encourages Cambridge University 135; **355**
Henry IV (Bolingbroke), King of England 105–6, 108–9, 112,

117, **355**
Henry V, King of England: reign 97; popularity 105; in France 106, 109, 121, 123; and Lancastrian legitimacy 109; marriage 123; endows monasteries 138; and Oldcastle 140; **355**
Henry VI, King of England: political conflicts 97; and taxation 98; authority 105; and French wars and claims 122–3; and succession 142, 147–8; insanity 147; readeption 148, 172; **355**
Henry VII (Tudor), King of England: rule 142; and Wars of Roses 147; succeeds 148–9; and retaining 152; and Council of North 153; portraits 154; and Ireland 167; and international affairs 171–2; household administration 191; **355**
Henry VIII, King of England: rule 142, 154; marriages 142, 144, 150–1, 172–3; and Reformation 144, 150, 165, 172; accession 150; finances 150; succession and will 150–2; portraits *151*, *154*; and Council of North 153; and Wales 161; claims to Scotland 164, 173; and Ireland 168; wars and international affairs 171–3; and debasement of coinage 176; appropriates Knole 188; culture and pastimes 188, 191; **355**
Henry the Young King (1155–83) **355**
Henry Frederick, Prince of Wales 192
Henry Grace à Dieu ("Great Harry": ship) *171*
Henry of Grosmont, duke of Lancaster **355**
Herbert family (earls of Pembroke) 146, *163*
Herbert, Arthur, earl of Torrington **356**
Herbert, William, earl of Pembroke (*c.* 1423–69) **356**
Herbert, William, earl of Pembroke (1580–1630) **356**
Herbert of Cherbury, Henry, Lord 237
Herbert, Sidney 255
Herefordshire School (stone carving) 135
heresy 140, 155
Hereward the Wake 66, **356**
heriot 84
heritability (property) 57–8, 84, 131–2, 161
Hermitage castle, Roxburgh *113*
Hertford, Edward Seymour, earl of *see* Somerset, duke of
Hexham 88, 90
hides and hidage (land measure) 59–61, 68–9, 73, 75, 84
High Commission Court 200–1, 233
Highlands and Islands Development Board 306
Hill, Sir Rowland **356**
hill-forts 10, 37, 39, 71
Hilliard, Nicholas *190*, **356**
Hingston Down, Battle of (838) 60
Hinton St Mary, Dorset 13, 34, 48, *51*
Hiroshima 317
Hitler, Adolf 297, 315–16, *315*
Hoadly, Benjamin, Bishop of Winchester **356**
Hoare-Laval Pact (1935) 315
Hoare, Sir Samuel, Viscount Templewood **356**
Hobbes, Thomas **356**
Hobhouse, John Cam, Lord Broughton de Gyfford **356**

Hoccleve, Thomas 140
Hod Hill, Dorset 37
Hogarth, William 198, 237, **356**; *Gin Lane* 235, 241
Hohenstauffen family 120
Holbein, Hans *151*, *154*, 190, 192
holidays 232, 281, 321
Holkham Bible *119*
Holland, Henry Richard Vassall Fox, Lord **356**
Hollar, Wenceslas *211*, *221*, *223*
Holles, Denzil **356**
Holt, Denbighshire 34
Holy (Catholic) League 172
Holy Roman Empire 171–2
homage 131
Home Rule: Act (1914) 307; Association 256; Bills (1886 & 1893) 259, 264; League 263
Home, Sir Alec Douglas-Home, Lord **356**
Homosexual Law Reform Society 332
Honorius, Emperor in the East 23
Hood, Admiral Samuel, Viscount **356**
Hooke, Robert 237
Hooker, Richard **356**; *Ecclesiastical Polity* 156–7
Hooper, John, Bishop of Worcester **356**
Hopton, Ralph, Lord **356**
Horner, Arthur 302
Horsa 59, **356**
Hotspur *see* Percy, Sir Henry
household (royal) 105, 188
households (family) 185, 188–9, 191
housing: Roman 13, 20, *21*, 22–3, 32–3, 37, 41, *42*, 45; Tudor upper class 186; 18th-century improvements 269; slum 278; 20th-century legislation 295, 305; owner-occupation 328, 331; and class *330*
Housing Act (1924) 305
Howard family 142, 146
Howard, Charles, earl of Carlisle **356**
Howard, Charles, Lord Howard of Effingham, earl of Nottingham **356**
Howard, Henry, earl of Northampton **356**
Howard, Thomas, earl of Suffolk and Lord Howard de Walden **356**
Howard, Lord William Howard of Effingham **356**
Howe, Admiral Richard, Earl **356**
Huddersfield 279
Hudson, Jeffrey 233
Hugh, St, Bishop of Lincoln 135
Huguenots 218, 227
Hull 125, 229
Humble Petition and Advice (1657–59) 202
Hume, David 214, 237, 240, **356**
Hume, Joseph **356**
Humphrey, duke of Gloucester **357**
hundred (administrative division) 59–61
Hundred Years War (1337–1453) 94, 120–3, 128, 130, 136
Hunstanton Secondary Modern School *335*
Hunt, Henry ("Orator") **357**
Huntingdon, Selina Hastings, countess of **357**
Huntly, George Gordon, marquis of **357**
husbandmen 184
Huskisson, William **357**
Huxley, Thomas Henry 286, **357**
Hyde Park, London *279*, *336*
Hyde, Douglas 264

Hywel Dda, ruler of Gwynedd 64, 82, **357**

Iceni 15–17
Ida, Bernician king 54
immigration 290, 331–2
Imperial Conferences 289, 314, 324
Imperial Tobacco company 275
imperialism 245, 256, 289; *see also* Empire, British
Imphal-Kohima, Battles of (1944) 316–17
Import Duties Act (1932) 324
In Place of Strife (white paper) 301
income tax 254, 256
incomes and earnings: gentry 126, 132, 181, 183; growth of 269–71, 325; distribution 271–2, 278–9; government policies on 326; *see also* prices; wages
Incorporated Society of Artists 241
Indemnity and Oblivion, Act of (1660) 202
Independence, War of (Scotland, 1296–1357) 114
Independent Labour Party 260, 293, 297, 305
Independent Television Authority 336
Independents (17th-century group) 201, 219, 234
India 223, 224, 256, 289–90, 314, 318–19
India Acts: (1784) 265; (1858) 256; (1935) 319
Indian National Congress 319
indulgences (religious) 190
Indulgence, Declarations of (1662–63, 1672, 1688) 205, 234
Industrial Relations Act (1971) 301
Industrial Revolution 245, 250, 270–6
industry: Roman 33–4; in Weald 175, 179; Tudor 179–80; early 18th-century development 225, 227–8; 19th-century expansion 245–6, 249, 270–5; company and trade organization 275; and aristocracy/plutocracy 279–80; 20th-century fortunes 323–6
Ine, King of Wessex 62, 71, 77, 84, 86, **357**
inflation 36, 124, 325; *see also* prices
Ingham 136
Injunctions (royal: 1536 & 1538) 153; (1559) 155
Innocent III, Pope 102
Innocent IV, Pope 96
Inns of Court 183, 191
Inquisition, Holy 104
Institute of British Architects (Royal) 280
Institution of Chartered Accountants 280
Institution of Civil Engineers 280
Instrument of Government (1653–57) 202
insurance (state) 294
Interdict (1208–13) 102
International Monetary Fund 325
"Intolerable Acts" (1774) 224
Iona: monastery 60, 76, 88
Ipswich 78
Ireland: Celts in 14; invasions of Britain 23; Roman objects in 30; early art 54, 56; Christianity in 59, 74, 88; hierarchy of kings 64, 72; Vikings in 73, 78, 115; missionaries from 74, 76; laws 82, 86, 116–17; social order 84, 86; culture and learning 88, 238–9, 264; relations with

Scotland 114; linked by King John's succession 100, 102; Henry II's invasion and administration 115; church in 116–17; Pale *116*, 117, 167, 169; Scots invade (1315) 116, 129; Parliament 116, 216–17, 261; and English domination 116–17, 215–17; population 124, 225; urban growth 125; economic decline 129; plague 129; Tudor wars in 146; plantation of 159, 169–70, 214–15; Catholicism in 162, 170, 214, 238, 253, 261–4; as kingdom 167–70; Reformation in 168; agriculture 175, 178; debasement of coinage 176; industry in 180; 1641 rebellion 201, 214–15; in Civil War 214–15; agrarian risings 217; Protestant ascendancy 217, 261; legislative independence (1782–83) 217; exports 225; food supply 226, 254; parliamentary franchise 249, 251, 253; church disestablishment 256–7, 264; Home Rule 256, 259, 262–4, 294; land reform 258, 263–4, *264*; coercion, terrorism and political proposals 258; nationalist activities 261–4; Union with Great Britain 261–4, 290; Great Famine (1847–48) 262, 277; population fall 262; emigration 262, 277; evictions *264*; independence 290, 292; 20th-century politics 307–11; war with England (1919–21) 308–9; 1920 partition 308, 310; 1922–23 civil war 309; declares republic 310; literacy 333; language and literature 238–9, 335
Ireton, Henry **357**
Irish Arms Bill (1846) 254
Irish Church Act (1869) 257
Irish Declaration of Rights (1782) 217
Irish Free State 308–10, 314
Irish Land Acts (1881–1903) 258, 264
Irish Literary Society 264
Irish Local Government Act (1898) 264
Irish Nationalist Party 263–4, 294
Irish Republican Army 308–9, 311
Irish Republican Brotherhood 263–4, 308
Irish Treaty (1921) 295
Irish University Bill (1873) 256–7
iron and steel 13, 30, 33, 272, 274
Isaacs, Rufus Daniel, marquis of Reading **357**
Isabella, Queen of Edward II 107, 118, 121, **357**
Isabella, Queen of Richard II **357**
Isherwood, Christopher 330
Italy 98, 125, 127, 130, 314–15

Jacobitism, Jacobites 197, 206–7, 212–13, 217, 222
Jaffa 118
Jamaica 220–1
James I, King of Scots 114, **357**
James II, King of Scots 114–15, **357**
James III, King of Scots *164*, **357**
James IV, King of Scots 164, 172, **357**
James V, King of Scots 164–5, **357**
James VI, King of Scots; I of England: and Mary, Queen of Scots' loss of throne 145; and Church 145, 156, 166; accession and rule on English throne 146, 158; extravagance 146, 160; sells peerages and honours 146, 158–9;

administration 158–60; and Gunpowder Plot 159; portrait *159*; and witch-hunts 167; and Ireland 170; and international affairs 172, 174, 218; and Spanish war 174, 218; and power of London 180; culture and pastimes 192; and arts 239; **357**
James II, King of England: succession question and Exclusion crisis 194, 196, 204–5; interference in local government 196; excluded by Test Acts 203; reign 204–5; and Scotland 212–13; and Ireland 216–17; crushes Monmouth rebellion 220; flight and exile 221–2; supports dissenters 234; **357**
James Edward Francis Stuart (Old Pretender) *see* Stuart, James Edward
Jameson Raid (1895) 260
Jane Seymour, Queen of Henry VIII 151, *154*, **357**
Japan 265, 312, 314, 316–18, 321
Jarrow 56, 59–60, 88–90, 324–5
Jeffreys, George, Lord (Judge) 221, **357**
Jellicoe, Admiral John Rushworth, Earl 313, **357**
Jenkins' Ear, War of (1739) 222–3
Jenkins, Roy 301
Jerome, St 92
Jervis, John, earl of St Vincent **357**
Jesuits 156–7, 253
Jewel, John, Bishop of Salisbury **357**
Jews, expulsion of (1290) 126
Jinnah, Mohammed Ali 319
Joad, C.E.M. 331
John, King of England 100, 102, 105, 110, 118, **357**
John II, King of France 121
John Balliol, King of Scots 114, **358**
John of Gaunt, duke of Lancaster 108, 138, **358**
John of Salisbury **358**
Johnson, Samuel 198, 237–8, **358**; *Dictionary* 240, 242
Johnston, Archibald, Lord Warriston **358**
Johnston, Tom 305
joint-stock companies 274–5
Jones, Inigo 192, *199*, 238–40, *238*, **358**
Jonson, Ben 188, 238, **358**
Josephus 24
journalism 206–8, 242; *see also* newspapers
jousting 188
Jovinus 22
Jowett, Benjamin **358**
Julian (the Apostate), Roman emperor 22, 45
"Junius" letters 208
Junius of Leyden 237
juries 69, 100
justice, administration of *see* courts of law; law
Justices of Labourers 129
Justices of the Peace 100–1, 106, 161, 185, 204
justiciar 70, 104
Jutes 59
Jutland, Battle of (1916) 313–14
Juxon, William, Archbishop of Canterbury **358**

Kay, James Phillips 278
Keble, John 282
Kedleston, Derbyshire *241*
keepers of the peace 106
Kells, Book of 90, *91*

Kemp, John, Cardinal **358**
Kempley frescoes 135, *136*
Kenilworth, Dictum of (1265) 104
Kenneth I MacAlpine, King of Scots 30, 59, 64, **358**
Kenneth II, King of Scots **358**
Kenneth III, King of Scots **358**
Kent: 54, 59–60, *61*, 62, *62*; 1450 rebellion 147
Kent, William 240
Kenya 289, 319
Kenyatta, Jomo 319
Kepler, Johann 237
Keppel, Augustus, Viscount **358**
Ket, Robert 186
Keynes, John Maynard, Lord 286, 296, 300, 326, **358**
Khartoum 258, 268
Kilbrandon Commission Report (on the Constitution, 1973) 303, 306
Kildare, Butler earls of 167
Kildare, earls of *see* Fitzgerald
Kildare Rebellion (1534) 168
Kilkenny: Statutes of (1366) 117; Grammar School 238
Killiecrankie, Battle of (1689) 212–13
"Kilmainham Treaty" (1882) 258, 263
Kilpeck, Herefordshire 135, *136*
King's Bench, court of 101, 105
King's Chamber 191
King's College, London 280
Kingsley, Charles **358**
Kingston, Treaty of (1217) 118
Kinloss Abbey 165
kinship 84–7
Kipling, Rudyard 330, **358**
Kirk (Scots): and Reformation 166; and Charles I 210–11; and Restoration 212; secessions and divisions 234; and arts 241; and 20th-century politics 304
Kirkby, John, Bishop of Ely **358**
Kit Kat Club 238
Kitchener, Horatio Herbert, Earl 268, 294, 313, **358**
Klosterzeven, Convention of (1757) 223
Kneller, Sir Godfrey 238, 240
knights 69, 97, 107, 126, 131–2, 183, 200; *see also* gentry
knitting machine *229*
Knole, near Sevenoaks (house) 188
Knox, John 164, **358**
Korea 312
Korean War (1950–51) 300, 318

La Hogue, Battle of (1690) 222
La Rochelle 121, 218
La Tène art 40
labour: late medieval 124, 129; after Black Death 134; and social order 230; redistribution in Industrial Revolution 245, 271, 276–7; division of 272, 285; emigration 273; and class 280; factory 280; organized 325; *see also* child labour; women
Labour party: origins 260, 293; and Lords reform 288; and party system 288, 294; and Empire 289; alliance with Liberals 293–4; as second party in 1922 295; early administrations 296; and National government 296–7; post-World War II governments 298–9, 301, 327; and nationalization 299; factionalism 300; in Wales 302–3; in Scotland 305–6; and 1975 EEC referendum 320; and social improvements 328; and immigration 332; supports unilateral nuclear disarmament 332; *see also* General Elections

Labour Representation Committee 260, 293
Labourers, Ordinance of (1349) 129; Statute of (1351) 129
Laissez-faire policy 252
"Lake poets" 283–4
Lambert, George 241
Lambert, John **358**
Lancaster 46
Lancaster, Thomas, earl of *see* Thomas, earl of Lancaster
Lancastrian dynasty 109, 121–2, 147
land: cultivation area 124–5; and natural disasters 127–8; and feudalism 131; *see also* agriculture
land tenure: Roman 32; Anglo-Saxon 56–7, 81, 84–5; Norman redistribution 69; and feudalism 87, 131–2; inheritance and alienation 98, 131; and Exchequer leases 106; and social order 132–4; leasehold 134; *see also* Ireland
land and religion (Wales) 302
Land League (Ireland) 258, 263
Landlord and Tenant Acts, Ireland (1860, 1870, 1881) 263
Lanfranc, Archbishop of Canterbury 69, **358**
Langham, Simon, Cardinal **358**
Langland, William 96, 140, **358**
Langley, Edmund de, duke of York **358**
Langton, Stephen, Archbishop of Canterbury 102, **359**
Langton, Walter, Bishop of Lichfield **359**
Langtry, Lillie *274*
Lansbury, George 331, **359**
Lansdowne, Henry Petty-Fitzmaurice, marquis of (1780-1863) **359**
Lansdowne, Henry Petty-Fitzmaurice, marquis of (1845-1927) 313, **359**
Lansdowne, William Petty, marquis of **359**; *see also* Shelburne, William Petty, earl of
Largs, Battle of (1263) 114
Lateran Councils: 2nd (1123) 77; 4th (1215) 126, 135
Latimer, Hugh, Bishop of Worcester **359**
Latin language 48, 52, 68, 90
Latitudinarianism 234–5
Laud, William, Archbishop of Canterbury 200–1, **359**
Laudabiliter (Bull, 1155) 115
Lauderdale, John Maitland, earl and duke of 203, 212, **359**
Lavenham 130, 180
law: Anglo-Saxon 56, 62–3, 69, 81; Norman 68–70; early codes 81–6; Irish 82, 86, 116; development of common law 96–7, 100–1, 104, 106–7, 132–3; and Crown 97; accessibility 133, 144; Tudor reforms 144, 154; in Wales 161; criminal 236
Law Society 280
Law, Andrew Bonar 293, 294–5, 307, **359**
Lawes, Henry 241
Lawrence, Sir Thomas 282
Lawrence, Thomas Edward ("of Arabia") **359**
Laxton, Nottinghamshire *226*
lead (metal) 13, 33, *35*, 39, 56, 127, 180
League of Empire Loyalists 290
League of Nations 314–15
Leake, Treaty of (1318) 107
leasehold 134
leather industry 34
Lee, Rowland, Bishop of Coventry & Lichfield 161
Lee, William *229*

Leeds 277
Leemput, Remigius van *154*
Legal Aid Act (1949) 328
legions (Roman) 12–13, 24, *25*
Leicester 34, 129
Leicester, Robert Dudley, earl of 145, 156–7, 186, *187*, **359**
Leinster 115, 117
leisure 329–30; *see also* holidays; sport
Leix-Offaly plantation 169
Lely, Sir Peter 238, 240
Lemass, Sean 309
Lend-Lease aid 325
Lennox, Esmé Stuart, duke of **359**
Lennox, Matthew, earl of **359**
Leslie, Alexander, earl of Leven **359**
Leslie, David, Lord Newark **359**
Levant Company 180
Levellers 194, 197, 232
Lever Brothers 275, 277
levies (military) 69, 106
Lewes, Battle of (1264) 104, 120
Lewes, Song of 94
Lexden Tumulus 36, 39
Lexington, Battle of (1775) 224
Liberal party: organization 246; split by J. Chamberlain 248; administrations 255–7, 259–60, 294; suppression 256; and imperialism 258; Irish policy 263–4; and tariff reform 293; alliance with Labour 293–4; and New Liberalism 294, 305; Lloyd George and 295; decline 296, 299; in World War II government 298; in Wales 302–3; in Scotland 304–5; adopts Keynesianism 326; and immigration 332; *see also* General Elections; Whigs
Liberal Unionists 259, 293, 304
libraries 240–1
Library of Useful Knowledge 284
Licensing Act (1662) 233
Lichfield: cathedral 136
life expectancy 181–2
Life Peerages Act (1958) 327
Light Brigade, Charge of (1884) *266*
Lilburne, John 232, **359**
Limerick 115; Treaty of (1691) 216–17
limited liability companies 274–5
Lincoln (Lindum): and Roman rule 13, 16, 21, 46; overseas trade 79; mint 79; decline 129, 180; cathedral 135; Battle of (1217) 118
Lincolnshire revolt (1536) 154
Lindisfarne 60, 72; Gospels 88, *91*
Lipton, Sir Thomas 273
literacy 187, 284, 333, 335
Little Hadham 239
Little Woodbury 37
Liverpool 229, 280
Liverpool, Charles Jenkinson, earl of **359**
Liverpool, Robert Banks Jenkinson, earl of 253, *283*, **359**
"livery" 147
livestock 33, 80, 124
living standard 98–9, 270–1, 274, 277, 281
Lloyd, Edward 233
Lloyd, J. Selwyn B. 326
Lloyd George, David Earl 294–6, 298, 302–3, 305, 314, **359**
Llywelyn ap Gruffud "the Last", Prince of Wales 110, **359**
Llywelyn ap Iorwerth (the Great), Prince of Gwynedd 110, **359**
local government 196, 246, 264
Local Government Act (1888) 259
Locke, John 237, **359**
Locke, Matthew 241
Loggan, D.: *Cantabrigdia Illustrata* *227*

Lollardy, Lollards 96, 140, 144
London: under Romans 13, 20–1, 39, 41, 48; early trade 36; Latin in 48; Mithraism *50*; Vikings raid 60, 74; White Tower 69; under Anglo-Saxons 73, 78–9; episcopal see 75; Bede on 78; and Domesday survey, 81; population 124, 175, 180, 184, 225; dominance 130, social structure 183; views *182–183*, *186*, *235*; poor-rates 185; as financial centre 229, 272, 274; social life 232; Great Fire (1666) and rebuilding 234, 237; architecture 239; incomes 271–2; suburbs 278–9; university 280; social surveys 281; Convention of (1884) 268; Council of (1107) 77; Treaties of: (1518) 172; (1604) 174; (1827) 267
London Corresponding Society 250
London Gazette 233
Londonderry 238, 310, 311
Londonderry, Robert Stewart, marquis of *283*
Long Melford 180
Long Parliament (1640–60) 200–2, 210, 241
Longchamp, William **359**
Lords, House of: development of 107; prosecutions before 109, 160; relations with Crown 109; and social status of peerage 132, 182; power under Tudors and Stuarts 146; and 17th-century revolutions 194, 196; abolished (1649) 202; reforms 259, 288, 327; obstructs Liberal legislation 294
Lords of the Articles (Scotland) 210, 213
Lords of the Isles (Scotland) 105
lordship 86, 131, 134; *see also* feudalism
Lothian, kingdom of 112
Loudoun, John Campbell, Earl **360**
Louis VII, King of France 118
Louis VIII, King of France 118
Louis IX, St, King of France 104, 119
Louis XII, King of France 172
Louis XIII, King of France 174
Louis XIV, King of France 196, 205, 221–2
Loutherbourg, Philip de 241, *270*
Lovat, Simon Fraser, Lord 317
Lovell, Francis, Viscount **360**
Lovett, William **360**
Lowe, Robert, Viscount Sherbrooke 256, **360**
Lucan, Charles Bingham, earl of **360**
Lucy, Richard de **360**
Ludlow, Edmund **360**
Lugard, Frederick **360**
Lull (monk) 76
Lullingstone 48, *51*, 52, *52*
Lusignans 102
Lutheranism 144, 152
Luttrell Psalter *126*, *127*
Lutudarum 35
Lydgate, John 140, 189
Lydney, Gloucestershire *47*, 48
Lympne 30
Lynch, Jack 309
Lynn, Norfolk 125

Mabel of Bury St Edmunds 135
Macadam, John Loudon 229, **360**
MacArthur, Gen. Douglas 316, 318
Macaulay, Thomas Babington, Lord 286, **360**
Macbeth, King of Scots **360**
McDermot, Frank 309
MacDiarmid", "Hugh 305

MacDonald clan 211, 212–13
MacDonald, James Ramsay 296–7, 305, **360**
MacDonald, John, Lord of the Isles and earl of Ross **360**
Mackay, Gen. Hugh 212
Macklin, Charles 238
Maclay, John 306
Macmillan, Harold, earl of Stockton 288, 300, *300*, 318, **360**
MacMurrough, Art, King of Leinster *115*
Macpherson, James ("Ossian") 214
MacSwinney, Owen 238
Madog ap Maredudd, Prince of Powys **360**
Madox, Thomas 240
madrigals 189
Maeatae 25
Mael Secnail 64
Mafeking, Relief of (1900) 245, 268
Magna Carta (1215) 97–8, 102, 104, *104*, 106–7; resumed (1216) 118, 131
Magnentius, Roman emperor 22
Magnus Intercursus (1496) 172
Magnus, son of Hakon IV 114
Mahdist rebellion 258, 268
Maine (France) 118–19, 121
"maintenance" (retaining) 147
Maitland of Thirlestane, John, Lord **360**
Majuba Hill, Battle of (1881) 258
Makarios III, Archbishop of Cyprus 319
Malachy, High King of Ireland 115
Malaya 289, 316, 318–19
Malcolm I (Macdonald), King of Scots **360**
Malcolm II (MacKenneth), King of Scots **360**
Malcolm III, King of Scots 67, **360**
Malcolm IV, King of Scots 114, **360**
Maldon, Battle of (991) 75
Malmesbury 88
Malory, Thomas 140
Malplaquet, Battle of (1710) 222, *223*
Malthus, Thomas Robert **360**; *Essay on Population* 276
Man, Isle of 114
manbot 86
Mancetter 35, *36*
Manchester 180, 250, 277, 280
Manchester Guardian (newspaper) 294
Manchester, Edward Montagu, earl of **360**
Manchuria 314
Mandeville, Geoffrey de 67
Manning, Henry Edward, Cardinal 282, **360**
manorial villages 175
manors 80–1, 85, 124, 126–7, 129; courts 133
Mansfield, William Murray, earl of **360**
Mantuan (Gonzaga) art collection 238–9
manuscripts: early Christian 88–92
Mar, John Erskine, earl of 197, 212–13, **360**
"March of Mind" movement (1820s) 284
March, Edmund Mortimer, earl of 109, 112
Margaret, St, Queen of Scotland **361**
Margaret of Anjou, Queen of Henry VI 123, 147–8, 172, 191, **360**
Margaret, Duchess of Burgundy 149, 172, **360**
Margaret of Denmark, Queen of James III of Scots **361**
Margaret of France, Queen of

Edward I **361**
Margaret, Maid of Norway, Queen of Scots 114
Margaret Tudor, Queen of James IV of Scots 151, 172, **361**
markets (fairs) 125
Marlborough: College 285; Statute of (1267) 104
Marlborough, John Churchill, duke of 205, 221–2, *223*, **361**; *see also* Churchill, Sarah
Marlowe, Christopher **361**
Marprelate Tracts 156–7
marriage 182, 231, 277
Marriage Act (1753) 231
marshal (royal office) 101
Marshal, William, earl of Pembroke 118, **361**
Marshall, Gen. George 317
Marston Moor, Battle of (1644) 211, 219
Martin, St 89
Martineau, Harriet **361**
Martinus, Vicar of Britain 22
Marvell, Andrew **361**
Marxism 260
Mary I (Tudor), Queen of England: raises rebellion 144; and religion 145, 152–5, 200; legitimacy and succession 150–2, *154*, 173; accession and rule 155; marriage to Philip 155, 173; and Welsh Marches 161; and militia 219; **361**
Mary II, Queen of England, Scotland and Ireland 196, 204–5, 241, **361**
Mary of France, Queen of Louis XII 151, 155, 172, **361**
Mary of Guise, Regent of Scotland 165, **361**
Mary of Modena, Queen of James II **361**
Mary, Queen of Scots 145, 156–7, 164–6, *166*, **361**
Masham, Lady Abigail 206, **361**
masques *191*, 238–9
Matilda (Maud) 66–7, 76, 100, **361**
Matrimonial Causes Act (1923) 328
Matthew, Tobias, Archbishop of York **361**
Maximian, Roman emperor 20
Maximus, Magnus 22–3, 30
Maxton, James 305
Mau-Mau revolt (Kenya, 1952–56) 319
Mayerne, Sir Theodore Turquet de 240
Maynooth seminary 254, 257
Mechanics' Institutes 284
Medina del Campo, Treaty of (1489) 172
Mediterranean agreements (1887) 267
Meikle, Andrew 213
Melbourne, William Lamb, Viscount 254, **361**
Melcombe Regis, Dorset 128
Melville, Viscount *see* Dundas, Henry
Melville, Andrew 166, **361**
mercantilism 228–9
Merchant Adventurers 172
Mercia: kingdom 56–8; dominance 60, 72; Egbert defeats 60; administrative boundaries 61; law codes 62; Vikings in 73–4; scholarship in 90; monasteries 92
Merciless Parliament (1388) 109
Meredith, George 248
metals, mining of 13, 33
Metcalf, William 229
Methodism 197, 236; *see also* nonconformists
Methuen, John **362**
Metropolitan Police Act (1829) 252
middle class 230, 232, 278, 280, 285, 328

Middlesex elections (1768 & 1769) 209
Middlewich 35
Mikardo, Ian *299*
Milan, Edict of (313) 48
militia, 158; *see also* army
Militia Ordinance (1642) 218
Mill, James **362**
Mill, John Stuart 256, 286, **362**
Millenary Petition (1603) 159
Millenarianism 233
Milner, Alfred, Viscount 260, **362**
Milton, John 237, **362**; *Paradise Lost* 241–2
Minden, Battle of (1759) 223–4
Miners Federation 260, 302
mining and minerals 13, 33; *see also* coal
Ministry of all the Talents (1806–7) 253
Minorca 223–4
mints *see* coins
missionaries (Christian) 76–7
Mithras, Mithraism 48, *50*
mob, the 236, *283*, 284
Moderates (Kirk) 234
Molasses Act (1764) 224
monasteries, monasticism: Anglo-Saxon 57, 90; Norman 69; Vikings raid 72; Celtic 76; and learning 88, 90; revival and reforms 90–92, 94; and social order 133; and endowments 138; and education 138; Henry VIII dissolves 150, 153, 155, 168; taxed 150
Monck, George, duke of Albemarle **362**
Money Bill, Ireland (1753) 217
Monmouth, James Scott, duke of 204–5, 212, 220, **362**
monopolies 158, 200
Mons Badonicus (?Badbury Rings, Dorset) 71, 81
Mons Graupius, Battle of (AD83 or 84) 26–8
Montfort, Simon de, earl of Lancaster 94, 104, 108, **362**
Montgomery, Treaty of (1267) 110
Montgomery, Field-Marshal Bernard Law, Viscount 316–17, **362**
Montrose, James Graham, earl of 210–11, **362**
Moore, Gen. Sir John **362**
morality plays 140
Moray, James Stuart, earl of **362**
Morcar, Earl 66
More, Hannah 242
More, Sir Thomas 151, 153–4, 189–90, **362**; *Utopia* 190; *Richard III* 191
Morgan, Sir Henry **362**
Morgan, William 162
Morier, David *213*
Morley, John, Viscount **362**
Morley, Thomas 189
Morris, William **362**
Morrison, Herbert, Lord *299*, **362**
Mortimer, Blanche 137, *140*
Mortimer, Edmund, earl of March 112, **362**
Mortimer, Roger, earl of March 107, 116, **362**
Mortmain, Statute of (1279) 106
Morton, James Douglas, earl of **362**
Morton, John, Cardinal **363**
Morton, Thomas, Bishop of Durham **363**
mosaics 34, *50*, *51*, *52*
Mosley, Sir Oswald 296–7, *297*, 332, **363**
motor cars: industry *323*; ownership *330*, 331
Mountbatten of Burma, Admiral of the Fleet Louis, Earl 319, **363**

Mountjoy, Charles Blount, Lord 169, **363**
Mousehold Heath, near Norwich 186
Mowbray, Thomas, duke of Norfolk **363**
Much Marcle, Herefordshire 137, *140*
Mucking, Essex 80
Muggletonians 233
Munich Agreement (1938) 297–8, 315
Municipal Corporations Act (1835) 252, 278
Municipium 16
Munitions Act (1915) 305
Munster 169–70
Murray, Lord George 213, **363**
Muscovy Company 180
music 92, 188–9, *191*, 240–1
Mussolini, Benito 315
Muzorewa, Abel, Bishop 319
Myddle, Shropshire *230*
Mynyddog the Wealthy 71
mystery and the miracle plays 140
Mytens, Daniel *159*, 238

Nagasaki 317
Napier of Magdala, Field-Marshal Robert Cornelis, Lord **363**
Napoleon Bonaparte, Emperor of France 266–7
Napoleonic wars 266, 283
Naseby, Battle of (1647) *220*
Nash, John 282, **363**
Nassau Agreement (1962) 318
Nasser, Gamal Abdel 318
National Covenant (Scotland, 1638) 210
National Debt 205–6, 225, 252
National Education League 285
National Government (1931–40) 296–7, 305, 324
National Guard (Ireland) 309
National Health Service 298–9, 328
National Insurance Act (1946) 298
National Liberal Federation 259
National Plan (1965) 306
National Union of Conservative and Constitutional Associations 257
National Union of Mineworkers 302
nationalist parties 301, 303–6
Nationalist Party of Scotland 304–5
nationalization 299
Naval Defence Act (1889) 265
Navigation Acts: (1651–96) 228–9; (Ireland, 1662, 1663, 1667) 216; repealed (1849) 255
navy (Royal Navy): financing 218; development and strength *220*, 224; ascendancy 265, *312*; and German rivalry 265, 312; 20th-century armaments 294; withdrawal from East 312; in World War I 313
Nayler, James 233, *233*
Nechtansmere, Battle of (685) 59
Nectaridus, Count 22
Nehru, Jawaharlal 319
Nelson, Admiral Horatio, Viscount 265, **363**
Nero, Roman emperor 12, 18–19, 33
Netherlands (Low Countries): economic dominance 98, 130; 1338–40 campaign in 107; and King John coalition 118; resistance to Spain 171, 174; and 1496 trade treaty 172; commercial rivalry with 218, 228–9; 17th-century wars in 203, 218, 220–1; Spanish wars in 220; alliance with

221–4; arts and sciences 237; French in 266
Nettleton Shrub, Wiltshire *47*
Neville family 109, 121, 146–7
Neville, George, Archbishop of York 148, **363**
Neville, John, marquis of Montagu and earl of Northumberland 148
Neville, Richard, earl of Warwick and Salisbury ("the kingmaker") 148, *149*, **363**
Neville's Cross, Battle of (1346) 121
New England 200
New Lanark *271*, 277
New Liberalism 294, 305
New Party (*later* British Union of Fascists) 297
New York 220–1
New Zealand 314–15, 319
Newburn, Battle of (1640) 210
Newcastle upon Tyne 180, 210–11, 229
Newcastle programme (National Liberal Federation) 259
Newcastle, Henry Pelham Fiennes Pelham Clinton, duke of 259
Newcastle, Thomas Holles-Pelham, duke of 198, 207–8, 223, **363**
Newcastle, William Cavendish, duke of **363**
Newcomen, Thomas 225, 228, *228*
Newdegate, Sir Roger *269*
Newman, John Henry, Cardinal 282, **363**
newspapers 284, 335; *see also* journalism
Newton, Sir Isaac 237, 242, **363**
Niger, Pescennius 20
Nightingale, Florence **363**
Nile, Battle of the (1798) 265
Nine Years War, Ireland (1594–1603) 169
Nine Years War (1688–97) 205, 225
Nineteen Propositions (1642) 194, 201–2
IXth (Hispanic) Legion 28
"No Quarter" Ordinance (1644, Ireland) 215
nobility: and peers of Parliament 132; status under Tudors 146, 152, 183; in Wars of Roses 148; pastimes 190; Scots 210–12; 18th-century status 232; *see also* aristocracy
Nominated Assembly 202
nonconformists (dissenters): banned from official positions 197; increase 198, 234–6; restrictions on 203, 206, 234; 19th-century rights 252–3; oppose revolutionary ideas 282; and school education 333
Nonsuch, Treaty of (1585) 174
Norfolk, John Howard, duke of **363**
Norfolk, Thomas Howard, earl of Surrey and duke of (1443–1524) **363**
Norfolk, Thomas Howard, duke of (1473–1554) 164, 165, **363**
Norfolk, Thomas Howard, duke of (1536–72) 145, 157, **363**
Normandy: Duchy of 66–8; lost to French 94, 102–3, 118–20, 122, 172; Angevin rights to 100; in Hundred Years War 121, 123
Normans: and English succession 66, 76, 94; Conquest of England 66–8, 74, 76, 86; in Wales 66, 70, 86, 110; administration 68–9; and Church 69, 77; warfare 74, 87; society and culture 81, 86–7, 92; and Scotland 112
North, Frederick, earl of Guildford (Lord North) 194, 208–9, 217,

224, 246, **364**
North Atlantic Treaty Organization (NATO) 318
North Briton (journal) 209
Northampton: Assizes of (1176) 100; Battle of (1460) 147; Statute of (1328) 106
Northcote, Sir Stafford 255
Northern Rebellion (1569) 156–7
Northern Star (newspaper) 251
Northumberland, Henry Percy, earl of (1342–1408) 112, **365**
Northumberland, Henry Percy, earl of (1394–1455) 147
Northumberland, Henry Percy, earl of (1421–61) **366**
Northumberland, Henry Percy, earl of (1446–89) **366**
Northumberland, John Dudley, duke of 144, 152, 155, 173, **364**
Northumberland, Thomas Percy, earl of 157
Northumberland, Percy dukes of 279
Northumbria: kingdom 54, 56, 60, 72; and Aethelred 57–8; Vikings in 73; converted to Christianity 75; coins and minting in 78; cultural continuity 81; omitted from Domesday Survey 81; monasticism and learning in 88
North-West Passage 174
Norway 72–3, 114, 315
Norwich 69, 185
Notitia Dignitatum (Roman directory) *19*
Nottingham 137
Nottingham, Daniel Finch, earl of **364**
Nottingham, Heneage Finch, earl of **364**
novel (fiction) 242, 284
nuclear weapons 318, *319*, 332; *see also* atomic bombs
Nuffield, William Morris, Viscount **364**

Oakboys (of Ulster) 217
Oakham Castle 135
Oates, Titus 204, *204*, **364**
O'Brien, James Bronterre **364**
O'Brien, William **364**
Occasional Conformity 206
O'Connell, Daniel ("the liberator") 253, 262, *262*, **364**
O'Connor, Feargus 251, **364**
O'Connor, Rory, High King of Ireland *see* Roderick O'Connor
Octennial Act, Ireland (1768) 217
Odo, Bishop of Bayeux 68–70, 87, **364**
O'Duffy, Gen. Eoin 309
Oengus mac Fergus, King of Picts 72
Offa, King of Mercia 56–7, 60, 64, 71–2, 76, 78, 80, 90, **364**; Dyke *65*
Offa, King of East Saxons 77
Oglethorpe, James Edward **364**
O'Higgins, Kevin Christopher **364**
oil (North Sea) 306
Oisc, King of Kent 59
O'Keefe, John 238
O'Kelly, Sean Thomas **364**
Olaf Sihtricson, King of Dublin 73–4, **364**
Olaf Tryggvasson, King of Norway 75
"Old English" (Ireland) 214–17
Oldcastle, Sir John 140, **364**
Oldham *281*
Omdurman, Battle of (1898) 268
omnibuses 279
O'Neill, Con Bacach, earl of Tyrone **364**

O'Neill, Hugh ("the Great O'Neill"), earl of Tyrone **364**
O'Neill, Owen Roe **364**
O'Neill, Sir Phelim **364**
O'Neill, Shane ("the Proud"), earl of Tyrone **364**
O'Neill, Terence 311
Onions, Peter 272
open field system 175
oppida 39
opus anglicanum (embroidery) 135, *139*
Orange Free State 268
Orange Lodges 307; Parades *263, 310*
Ordinances of 1311 97, 107
ordo (Roman council) 16–17
Ordovices 24–6, 28
Organization for European Economic Recovery 317
Orkney 165
Ormonde, James Butler, earl and duke of (1610–88) **364**
Ormonde, James Butler, duke of (1665–1745) **364**
Orwell, George 331, 335
O'Shea, Katherine 264
Oswald, St, King of Northumbria 60, 72, **364**
Oswald, Archbishop of York 57, 69, 90, **364**
Oswy, King of Northumbria 60, 76, **365**
Ottawa Conference (1932) 324
Otto IV, Emperor 118
Ottoman Empire see Turkey
Oudenarde, Battle of (1708) 222
Oulart Hill, Battle of (1798) 261
overassignment 122
Overton, Richard 232
Ovid 52
Owain Gwynned (Owain ap Gruffud) **365**
Owen, Sir Hugh **365**
Owen, Robert *271, 277*, **365**
Oxford 35, 138; university 96, 135, 191, 286, 292; Provisions of (1258) 97, 104
Oxford Movement 282–3
Oxford, Robert de Vere, earl of **365**

Paget, William, Lord 151, 155, **365**
Paine, Thomas 241, 283, **365**
Paisley, Ian 311
Pakistan 289, 318–19
Pale, The (Ireland) *116*, 117, 167, 169
Palladio, Andrea 239
pallium 76
Palmerston, Henry John Temple, Viscount 255, *257*, 260, 266–7, 365
Pandulf, Bishop of Norwich **365**
Pankhurst, Emmeline **365**
papacy, popes 96, 102, 104–5, 113, 144; *see also* Roman Catholics
Paris: Peace of (1763) 209, 223; (1783) 224; Treaties of (1259) 118–19; (1856) 266–7
Paris, Matthew *103*, 136, 140
parish: evolution of 86–7
Park Street 41
Parker, Matthew, Archbishop of Canterbury 156, **365**
Parliament: rise to power 97–8, 106–9; rejects papal overlordship 105; summoning of 106–7; and taxation 107–8, 150, 205–6, 219; and Tudors 144–6, 154, 157, 160; and Reformation 156–7, 168; and military finance 160; and James I 160; and impeachment 160; and patriarchalism 184; and Charles I 194, 200–1, 219; 18th-century character 198, 208–9; under

Cromwell 201–2, *203*; supremacy established (1689) 205; duration of 205, 208, 294; reform and extension of franchise 249–51, 253–4, 256, 258–9, 295, 327; *see also* Commons, House of; Lords, House of; *and* individual parliaments
Parliament (Scots) 165, 210–13
Parliament Act (1911) 288, 294
Parnell, Charles Stewart 258, 263–4, 285, **365**
Parsons, Robert **365**
Partition Treaty (1698) 222
patriarchalism 184, *231*
Patrick, St 48, **365**
Paulinus, St 75, **365**
Paullinus, Suetonius 12, 17–18, 25
Paulus Catena (Paul "the Chain") 22
Pax Romana 44–5
Peace Pledge Union 330–1
Peake, Robert *187*
Pearce, Edward Lovett 239
Pearl (poem) 140
Pearl Harbor (1941) 316–17
Pear's soap *274, 275*
Pearse, Patrick Henry 308, **365**
peasants: and church dues 79; in Anglo-Saxon society 85–7; unfree 126; economic hardship 127; and Black Death 128–9; reject villeinage 129; and social structure 133–4; and leasehold 134; decline of 184; revolts 129, 133–4, 140, 186
Peckham, John, Archbishop of Canterbury **365**
Peel, Robert (the elder) 279
Peel, Sir Robert 246, 252–5, *255*, 262, **365**
peerage (parliamentary) 98, 132, 182, 288; life 327
Peerage Act (1963) 327
Pelagius 13, 48, 52
Pelham, Henry 206–7, **365**; *see also* Newcastle, duke of
Pelham, Thomas 206–7
Pembroke, John Hastings, earl of 121
Pembroke, earl of *see* Marshal, William
Pembroke, earls of *see* Herbert
Penda, King of Mercia 60, 72, **365**
Penn, Sir William 221, **365**
Penny Magazine 284
Penruddock, John 219
Penry, John 157
pensions 294
Pentre, Rhondda Valley *302*
Pen-y-Berth 303
Pepys, Samuel **365**
Perceval, Spencer 253, **365**
Percy family 108–9, 112, 121, 146; *see also* Northumberland, earls and duke of
Percy, Sir Henry (Hotspur) 109, **366**
Perennis 20
Perkins, William 185, **366**
Perpendicular style (architecture) 96, 136
Perrers, Alice **366**
Perrot, Sir John 169
Perth 112: Synod of (1618) 116; Treaty of (1266) 114
Peterborough 57, 66, 69, 72, 90, 92
Peterborough Chronicle 61
Peterborough, Charles Mordaunt, earl of **366**
Peterloo (St Peter's Fields, Manchester, 1819) *249*, 250–1
Petillius Cerialis 17
Petition of Right (1628) 200
Petty Assizes 100
Pevensey 30
pewter 33

philanthropy 278, 282
Philip I, King of France 77
Philip II, King of France 118
Philip IV (the Fair), King of France 118–19, 121
Philip VI, King of France 94, 121
Philip II, King of Spain 155, 157, 173–4, **366**
Phoenix Park murders (1882) 258
Picts: invasions 10; Romans and 22–3, 30–1, 59; Scots and 72; kings 64; converted to Christianity 76; society 82; art *87*, 90; inter-Scottish rivalries 112
pigs 33, 80
pilgrimage, pilgrims 77
Pilgrimage of Grace (1536) 154
Pinkie Cleugh, Battle of (1547) 173
Pitt, William (the Elder, earl of Chatham 198, 207–8, 223–4, **366**
Pitt, William, the Younger 209, 229, 246, 252–4, 261, 266, **366**
Pius V, Pope 174
Place, Francis **366**
Plaid Cymru 303
plantation (Ireland) 159, 169–70, 215–16
Plassey, Battle of (1757) 223
Playhouse Licensing Act (1737) 241
Pleshey, Essex 77
Plumpton Plain 32
Plunket, Oliver, Archbishop of Armagh **366**
Plunket, William Conyngham, Lord **366**
Plutarch 48
Poitiers, Battle of (1356) 121
Poitou, Poitevins 102, 118–19, 121
Poland 315
Pole, John de la, earl of Lincoln **366**
Pole, Michael de la, earl of Suffolk **366**
Pole, Reginald, Cardinal **366**
Pole, William de la, earl and duke of Suffolk 123, 147, **366**
police 252
Police Act (1839) 252
Political Register (Cobbett) 284
polytechnics 332, 334
poor, poverty: and population increase 126–7, 187; Tudor relief measures 153, 158, 175, 185; in Scotland 166; and social order 230; 18th-century relief for 231, 234, 252; 19th-century values questioned 245; 1834 "New" Law 252; urban 278; revealed by social surveys 281; in 20th century 321, 327
Pope, Alexander 209, 242
Popery, Act to prevent the further growth of (1704) 217
Popish Plot (1678) 204, 216
popular front 297
population: under Romans 12, 32; in Anglo-Saxon times 79; and Black Death 98, 129, 134, 175; and living standard 99; expansion (1100–1300) 124–6; in Scotland 124, 126, 166, 225, 276; growth under Tudors 176, 181–2; 17th-century trends 196, 225; 18th-century movements 225–6, 234, 269, 276; in 19th century 248, 276–8; Irish 262; 20th century 321
Population Act (1800) 276
Port Sunlight 277
Portchester 30, *31*
Portland 60
Portland, William Bentinck, earl of **366**

Portland, William Henry Cavendish Bentinck, duke of **366**
Portugal 224
pottery 34, 35–6, 44
Powell, Enoch 332
Power family 117
Powys (Welsh principality) 110
Poynings, Sir Edward 167, 216–17
Praemunire, Statute of (1393) 105
Praetorian Prefects (Roman) 21
Pragmatic Sanction (1713) 223
Prasutagus, King of Iceni 17–18
Prayer Books: (1549 and 1552) 152, 154–5; opposition to 157, 186; amended 159; Welsh 162; (1662) 203; in Scotland 210, *211*
presbyterianism 156–7, 166, 201, 210–13, 217, 219, 261
Preston, Battle of (1648) 211, 219
Pretoria, Convention of (1881) 258, 268
prices and living costs: fluctuations (1180–1220) 124–5; fall (1330s) 128; under Tudors 153, 176–8, 181; in Scotland 166; in 18th century 226; and "Speenhamland" system 252; and cash payments 253; in competitive market 274–5; 19th-century fall in food 277, 281
Pride, Col. Thomas **366**; "purge" (1648) 201–2
Priestley, Joseph 283, **366**
Princes in the Tower 148–9
Privy Chamber 188
Privy Council 146, 152, 203
Privy Seal 105
procurators, provincial (Roman) 17
productivity 270, 273, 321–2
"Progressive alliance" (Liberal-Labour) 293–4
Progressive Review 294
property tax 254
Protectorate (1653–59) 202
Protestant Society 253
Protestantism: and peaceful Reformation 144–5, 156; and eucharist 152; and patriotism 155, 174; in Scotland 164–7; ascendancy in Ireland 170, 215–17; and Civil War 200–1; and royal succession 204–5; in France 218; decline in Ireland 264; *see also* Church of England; Reformation
Protestation (1621) 160
provinces (Roman) 17
provincial councils (Roman) 17
Provisors, Statute of (1390) 105
Prussia 223, 266–7
Prynne, William 200–1, **366**
Public Health Acts: (1848) 278; (1875) 257
Public Order Act (1936) 297
public schools 246, 285, 292
Pugin, A.W.N. 284
Pula Run, Jamaica 220
Pulteney, Sir William *see* Bath, earl of
Pumpsaint fort 33
Purcell, Henry 240–1, **366**
Puritanism 145, 156, 197, 232, 241
Pusey, Edward Bouverie 282
Putney debates (1647) 232
Pym, John 194, 201, **366**

Quadruple Alliance (1815) 267
Quakers (Society of Friends) 233
Quarterly Review 253, 286
Quebec Act (1774) 236
Quebec, Battle of (1759) 223
Quia Emptores (1290) 106
Quo Warranto 103, 106, 196, 216

Radical Programme (1885) 259
radicalism 197, 232, 250–1, 332
Radicals 255–6
radio 334–6
Raedwald, King of East Anglia 56, 60, 75, 83, **366**
Raffles, Sir Thomas Stamford **366**
Raglan, Fitzroy James Henry Somerset, Lord **367**
Raglan Castle, Gwent *163*
railways: and Industrial Revolution 245, 271, *272*; urban 278; and holidays 281; Beeching Report on 326
Raleigh, Sir Walter 158, **367**
Ramillies, Battle of (1706) 222
Ramsay, Allan (poet and editor) 241
Ramsay, Allan (painter) 241
Ramsay, James 236
Ramsey monastery 90, 92
Ramsey, William of 136
Ranters 233
Ready Money (print) *207*
recreations and sports 232, 281
Rectitudines Singularum Personarum 84–5
Reculver 30
Recusancy 157; *see also* Roman Catholics
Redistribution of Seats Acts: (1885) 258–9; (1918) 295
Redmond, John Edward 307, **367**
Reform Bills and Acts: (1785) 249; Great, or First (1832) 250, *250*, 251, 253, 278; proposed 256; Second (1867) 256; Third (1884) 258; Fourth (1918) 295, 327
Reform League 256
Reformation: and early anti-papal movement 96; and Tudor rule 144–5, 152–3, 155; and Wales 162; in Scotland 164–5; ends religious plays 180; effect on status of women 184
Reformation Parliament, Ireland (1536–7) 168
Regini (tribe) 15, 19
Registration Act (1836) 276
Regnans in Excelsis (Bull, 1570) 157
Reith, John, Lord **367**
religion and cults: under Romans. 13, 21–2, 44–52, *47, 49, 50, 51*; Celtic 44, 46, *47*, 52; and Christian conversions 76; anti-papal 96; questioned in 19th century 245; 20th-century decline 330; *see also* Christianity
Remigius, Bishop of Lincoln **367**
Renaissance (Italian) 96, 140, *165*, 188–92, 239, 282
Renunciation Act (1783) 217
Reorganization of Offices (Scotland) Act (1939) 304
Repton, Humphrey 242
Restoration (1660; Charles II) 202–3, 212, 241
retailing 273–4
retaining 131–2, 147, 152, 184
Revocation, Act of (1625) 210
Reynolds, Sir Joshua 238, 241, **367**
Rhode Island *223*
Rhodes, Cecil 260
Rhodesia *see* Zimbabwe
Rhodri Mawr, King of Gwynedd 64, **367**
Rhondda Valley *302*
Rhuddlan, Wales 111; Statute of (or "of Wales", 1284) 106, 111
Rhys ap Gruffud **367**
Rhys ap Tewdr 70, **367**
Ricardo, David **367**
Riccio, David 166, **367**
Rich, Edmund, St, Archbishop of Canterbury **367**
Rich, John 241

Rich, Richard, Lord **367**
Richard I, Duke of Normandy 66
Richard I (Lionheart), King of England 100, 118, 120, *135*, **367**
Richard II, King of England: and English art 96; political conflicts 97; reign 105–6, 108; rebellion against 106; and Parliament 108–9; foreign policy 108; favours 109; tyranny 109; deposed 109; in Ireland 116–17; and patents for peerage 132; and Peasants' Revolt 134; and White Hart 138; and Lollardy 140; **367**
Richard III, King of England 142, 148, 153, **367**
Richard, duke of York *see* York, Richard, duke of
Richard, earl of Cornwall 120, **367**
Richardson, Samuel 242
Richborough 22, 30, 48
Ridley, Nicholas **367**
Rievaulx Abbey 94
Rimini, Council of (359) 48
Riot Act (1715) 197
riots and disorder 236. 250–2, 332
Ripon, Treaty of (1640) 210–11
Ripon, George Frederick Samuel Robinson, marquis of **367**
Rippon, Geoffrey *320*
Rising in the North (1569) 186
Riveaux, Peter des 102, **367**
Rivenhall 41
Rivers, Anthony Wydeville, Earl **367**
roads *23*, 28, 40, 44, 79, *128–9*, 229, 269
Robbins Report (on Higher Education, 1963) 334
Robert I (the Bruce), King of Scots 114–5, *128–9*, **367**
Robert II Curthose, duke of Normandy 66–8, **367**
Robert II, King of Scots **367**
Robert III, King of Scots **367**
Robert, earl of Gloucester **367**
Robert of Jumièges, Archbishop of Canterbury **368**
Roberts, Frederick Sleigh, Earl **368**
Robertson, William 214
Roche Derrien, la, Battle of (1347) 121
Roches, Peter des 102, **368**
Rochester 60, 75
Rockingham, Charles Watson-Wentworth, marquis of 208–9, 224, 253, **368**
Roderick O'Connor, High King of Ireland 115, **368**
Rodney, Admiral George Brydges, Lord 224, **368**
Roger, Bishop of Salisbury 70, **368**
Rolle, Richard 138
Roman Catholics, Roman Catholicism: and Celtic Church 76, 88; restored under Mary Tudor 145, 155; and eucharist 152; and Reformation 156–7; missionaries 157; suppressed 157; plots by 159; and Scots Reformation 165–6; post-Tridentine 170; and indulgences 190; under Stuarts 200, 204; excluded from office 203, 253; and Scots Restoration settlement 212; and Jacobitism 213; in Ireland 214, 216–17, 238, 253, 261–4; and Declarations of Indulgence 234; rioting against 236; emancipation (1829) 252–4; 19th-century hostility to 254; Oxford defections to 283; in Scottish 20th-century politics 305; in Northern Ireland 310–11; rise in membership 330
Romanesque art 92
Romanticism 283

Rome, Romans: in Britain 10–13; army 12, 18, 24–32, *25*, 36; administration and control 12–23; religion and culture 13, 44–52, *47, 49, 50, 51*; citizenship 18–19; British deputation to (AD 185) 20; barbarian invasions 20; end of rule 22–3; frontiers, conquest and occupation 28, 31, 45, 47; and economy 32–6; settlement and social organization 37–42
Rommel, Field-Marshal Erwin 316–17
"Root and Branch" petition (1640) 201
Rosebery, Archibald Philip Primrose, earl of 259, **368**
Roses", "Wars of the 142, *143*, 147–8, *144*, 167, 172
Ross, William 306
Rossini, Gioacchino Antonio: *Moses in Egypt* 267
Rotherham plough 226
Rotherham, Thomas, Archbishop of York **368**
Rothes, John Leslie, Earl 210
Rothschild, Lionel Nathan de **368**
"Rough Wooing" (Scotland) 165
Rowntree, B. Seebohm 260, 281, 328
Royal Academy, London 241
Royal Exchange, London *180*
Royal Marriages Act (1772) 236
Royal Society 237
Royal Titles Act (1876) 256
Rubens, Sir Peter Paul 238, 240
Rump Parliament 201–2
Runnymede 102
Rupert of the Rhine, Prince 211, **368**
Ruskin, John 284, **368**
Russell family 146
Russell, Bertrand, Earl 286, 331, **368**
Russell, John, earl of Bedford 188
Russell, John, Earl 253–6, **368**
Russell, Matthew *285*
Russia (and USSR) 266–8, 312, 317–18
Russo-Turkish War (1877–78) 267
Rutherford, Ernest, Lord **368**
Ruthwell Cross, Dumfriesshire 89
Ryswick, Treaty of (1697) 222

Sabbath and Sundays 185, 232
Sacheverell, Henry 205–7, **368**
Sackville, Lord George Sackville Germain, Viscount 233, **368**
Sackville, Thomas, earl of Dorset **368**
Sainsbury's stores *323*
St Albans (Verulamium): under Romans 13, 15, 18, 34, 38–9, *39*, 41–2, 44; early Christianity 48; Abbey 136; scholarship at 140; Battle of (1455) 147
St Andrews: university *113*, 212
St James's Day Fight (1666) *221*
St James's Park, London *235*
St Leger, Sir Anthony 168
St Ninian's Isle, Shetland *87*
St Paul's Cathedral 234, 237, 239
St Paul's church, Covent Garden *278*
Saint-Sardos, War of (1324) 120
saints' lives 89
Saints, The, Battle of (1782) 224
Salesbury, William 162, **368***
Salisbury 124, 129, 135, *137*, 180
Salisbury, Robert Arthur Talbot Gascoyne-Cecil, marquis of 258–60, 293, **368**
Salisbury, William Longespée de, earl of 118
salt 34–5, 56

Salt, Titus 277
Saltaire 277
Saltonstall family *231*
Samuel, Herbert Louis, Viscount **368**
San Francisco Conference (1945) 318
San Juan de Ulua 174
San Stefano, Treaty of (1878) 267
Sancroft, William, Archbishop of Canterbury 205, **368**
Sandby, Paul 241
Sandwich, Kent 78
Sandwich, John Montagu, earl of **368**
Saratoga, Battle of (1777) 224
Sarre, Kent 78
Savery, Thomas **368**
Saxon Shore, Count of 12, 22, 30; forts 30
Saxons 10, 21–3, 59; *see also* Anglo-Saxons
Saye, James Fiennes, Lord 147
Saye and Sele, William Fiennes, Viscount **368**
Sayers, Dorothy L. 328
Schism Act (1714) 206
schools *334, 335*; *see also* education; public schools
science and scientists 335–6
Scotland: and Romans 10, 12, 26–30; Celts in 14; unification 59, 64, 70, 112–14; and Normans 66–7, 70, 86; monarchy 70; warfare in 72; early laws 82, 86; English wars with 94, 107, 114, 120–1, 127, 172–3; and Angevin kings 106; farming 112, 124, 126, 175, 213, 227; Church in 113; Wars of Independence (1296–1357) 114–15; invades Ireland 116; population 124, 126, 166, 225, 276; Black Death in 128–9; Reformation in 145, 164–5; stability and culture 164, 166; Parliament 165; inflation in 166; Charles I and 167, 210–12; French alliance 171–2, 174; garrisoned 173; and debasement of coinage 176; famines 178; Tudor industry in 180; 1707 Act of Union 197, 212–13; and Jacobites 197–8, 212–13; in Civil Wars 200, 210–11, 218–19; Privy Council 210; religion in 210, 213; incorporated in Commonwealth 212; and 1660 Restoration 212; industrialization 213, 225; "Enlightenment" 214; English domination 214; clans decline 214; emigration to Ulster 217; exports 225; food supply 226, 234; Highland society and culture 236; arts 241–2; Parliamentary franchise 249, 250; university education 286; position in Britain 292; politics in 20th century 304–6; unemployment 324; literacy 333; language and literature 335
Scotland and Wales Bill (1976) 306
Scots, Scotti (people) 10, 22–3, 59, 112
Scott, Sir George Gilbert 284
Scott, Sir Walter 147, 248, **368**
Scottish Covenant movement (1949) 306
Scottish Economic Committee 305
Scottish National Development Council 305
Scottish National party 305–6, *306*
Scottish Secretary (and Office) 304
Scottish Self-Government party 305
Scrope, Richard Le, Archbishop of York 106, 112, **368**
seaside resorts 281

sects 232–3
Sedgemoor, Battle of (1685) 221
Selden, John 240, **369**
Self-denying Ordinance (1645) 219
Senchas Mar 82
Senchus fer nAlban 64, 72
Sens, William of 135
Septennial Act (1716) 197, 205, 208
Septimius Severus, Roman emperor 10, 12, 20–2, 26, 28–9, 31, **369**
servants (domestic) 185, 271
Settlement, Acts of: (1662) 231; (1701) 205–6
"Seven Bishops' Case" (1688) 204–5
Seven Years War (1756–63) 214, 223–4
Sevenoaks, Battle of (1450) 147
seviri augustales 46
Sexual Offences Act (1967) 332
Seymour, Thomas, Lord **369**
Shaftesbury, Anthony Ashley Cooper, Lord Ashley and earl of (1621–83) 203–5, **369**
Shaftesbury, Anthony Ashley Cooper, earl of (1801–85) 252, 282, **369**
Shakespeare, William 192, 241, **369**
Sharp, Granville 236
Shaw, George Bernard 245, 260, **369**
sheep 33, 80, 177
Sheffield 180, 277
Sheffield, John Baker Holroyd, earl of 229
Shelburne, William Petty, earl of and marquis of Lansdowne 209, 229, 265, **359**
Shelley, Percy Bysshe **369**
Sheppard, Canon Dick 331
Sherborne Abbey 136
Sheridan, Richard Brinsley 233, 282, **369**
sheriffs 62, 70, 79, 100, 106
Shinwell, Emanuel, Lord *299*
ship burials 82–3, *91*
ship money 196, 200, 218
shipbuilding *273, 274*
shires 60–2, 70
shops and shopping 273, *275, 323*
Short Parliament (1640) 201, 210
Shrewsbury, Battle of (1403) 109
Shrewsbury, Charles Talbot, earl and duke of 206, **369**
Shrewsbury, John Talbot, earl of 123, **369**
Sicily 104, 120
Sidmouth, Henry Addington, Viscount *see* Addington, Henry
Sidney, Algernon **369**
Sidney, Sir Henry 169
Sidney, Sir Philip **369**
Signet Seal, Keeper of the 105
Silchester (Calleva) 15, 34, 36, 42, 44, 48
silk 35, 227
Silures (people) 25
silver 13, 22, 33, 39, 78, 80; *see also* coins
Simnel, Lambert ("Edward VI") 149, 172, **369**
Simon, John Allsebrook, Viscount **369**
Simpson, Mrs Wallis (duchess of Windsor) 297
Singapore 314, 316–17
Sinking Fund (1786) 252
Sinn Fein 308–9
Siward, earl of Northumberland **369**
Six Articles, Act of (1539) 150
slaves: Roman 35–6; Anglo-Saxon 84–5, 87, 133; Danes and 58; Africa trade 180; in New World 229; abolition movement 236,

253, 282
Slezer, Thomas: *Theatrum Scotiae* 212
Slim, Gen. William 316–17
Smiles, Samuel 244
Smith, Adam 214, 238, **369**; *The Wealth of Nations*, 229
Smith, Frederick Edwin, earl of Birkenhead *293*, 327, **369**
Smith, Ian 318–19
Smithson, Alison and Peter *335*
Smythson, Robert *192*
Snape 83
Snow, C.P., Lord 336
Snowden, Philip, Viscount 296, **369**
social Darwinism 260
Social Democratic and Labour party (N. Ireland) 311
Social Democratic Federation 260, 293
social welfare 252, 295, 298, 325–6
socialism 289, 294
Socialist League 297
Societies for the Reformation of Manners 236
Society for the Diffusion of Useful Knowledge 284
Society of Arts 284
Society of United Irishmen 261
Solemn League and Covenant (1643) 203, 211; (Ireland 1912) 307
Solway Moss, Battle of (1542) 164, 173
Somers, John, Lord 205, **369**
Somerset Case (1772) 236
Somerset, Edmund Beaufort, duke of 147
Somerset, Edward Seymour, duke of 151–3, 165, 173, 176, 190, **369**
Somme, Battle of the (1916) 313–14
Sophie, Electress of Hanover 205
soul-scot 79
South Africa 258, 260, 314, 318–19; *see also* Boer Wars
South Africa Company 260
South Cadbury, Somerset *71*
South Sea Bubble (1720) 207
South Wales Miners Federation 302
Southampton 78, 80
Southbroom, Wiltshire *47*
Southcott, Joanna **369**
Southey, Robert 283–4
Spa Fields meeting (1816) 250
Spain: Tudor wars with 146, 156; and James I 160; and Irish rebellion 169; European struggle against 171, 174; 1489 alliance with 172; in New World 174; Charles I's war with 200, 218; Commonwealth war with 220–1; 18th-century wars 222; Stanhope allies with 223; naval rivalry 224; and slave trade 229
Spanish Civil War (1936–39) 331
Spanish Succession, War of (1702–13) 205, 222
Special Areas Act (1934) 305, 325
Spectator (journal) 242
"Speenhamland" system 252
Spencer, Herbert **369**
Spender, Sir Stephen 330
Spion Kop *268*
Spithead naval review (1914) *312*
sport 281, 330
Sprigge, Joshua: *Anglia Rediviva 220*
Stamp Act (1765) 224
Stanegate 28–9, 40
Stanhope, Charles, Earl **369**
Stanhope, James, Earl 207, 223, **369**
Stanley family 146, 149; *see also* Derby, earls of

Stanley, Sir Henry Morton **369**
Star Chamber, Court of 154, 200–1
steam power 213, 225, 228, 272, 277
Steelboys (Ireland) 217
Steele, Richard 242
Stephen, King of England 66–8, 70, 76, 110, **370**
Stephenson, George **370**
sterling: exchange rates 322–3, 325
Stewart family *see* Stuart *and* Albany, dukes of
Stigand, Archbishop of Canterbury 67, 69, **370**
Stilicho, Count 23, 30
Stirling Castle 114
Stoke, Battle of (1487) 149
Strafford, Thomas Wentworth, earl of 194, 201, 214–15, **370**
Straits Convention (1841) 267
Stratford, John de, Archbishop of Canterbury **370**
Strathclyde 81, 112
Strawberry Hill 239, 284
Street, G.E. 284
strikes (industrial) 260, *304, 329*, 330–1
Stuart family 164, 167, 197–8
Stuart, Arabella **370**
Stuart, Charles Edward ("the Young Pretender") 197, 213, **370**
Stuart, James (Scottish nationalist) 306
Stuart, James Edward ("the Old Pretender") 197, 213, 222, **370**
Stubbs, George 240, *242*
subsidy (Parliamentary tax) 150
Succession Act (1534) 151
Sudan 256, 260, 268
Sudbury, Simon of, Archbishop of Canterbury 134
Sudetenland 315
Suez Canal 256, 258, *267*, 268; 1956 crisis 300, 318, 332; free navigation 313
Suffolk, William de la Pole, duke of *see* Pole, William de la
Sulcoit, Battle of (968) 115
sumptuary laws 132, 184
Sunderland, Charles Spencer, earl of 205–6, **370**
Sunderland, Robert Spencer, earl of **370**
Sunningdale Agreement (1973) 311
Supremacy Act (1534) 153
Surrey, Henry Howard, earl of 191
Surrey, Thomas Howard, earl of *see* Norfolk, Thomas Howard, duke of
Susa, Peace of (1629) 218
Sussex, Thomas Radcliffe, earl of 169
Sutton Hoo ship treasure 54, 56, 82, *83*, 88, *91*
Svein Estrithson (Forkbeard) 76, **370**
Swan theatre, London *192*
Sweden 221, 223
Sweyn *see* Svein
Swift, Jonathan 196, 207, 209, 217, 237–8, 242, **370**
Syon cope *139*

Tacitus 10, 13, 45, 48, 62, 82
Taff Vale judgment (1901) 260, 293
Talbot family 146
Talbot, John, earl of Shrewsbury *see* Shrewsbury, earl of
Taliesin 82–3
Tallis, Thomas **370**
Tamworth 73
Taplow 83

Tara *65*; Battle of (980) 115; brooch 54, *85*; meeting (1843) *262*
tariffs 229; reform 293, 295, 304; and revenues 294; and 1930s crisis 324; and GATT 325
Tasciovanus, King of Catuvellauni 15
Tatler (journal) 242
Taverner, John **370**
taxation: Roman 16, 22, 36; Anglo-Saxon 57, 59–61, 79, 94; Norman 68–9; for Church 79, 84; on Church 96; and Angevin wars 97–8; and social class 98–9; Parliament and 107–8, 150, 205–6, 219; on wool exports 127; as a cause of Peasants' Revolt 133; Tudor 146, 150, *178*; in Scotland 166; and 17th-century standing army 196; under Hanoverians 205; county 219; property (repeal of) 254; newspapers 284–5; and 1909 budget 294; and distribution of wealth 327
Technology, Ministry of 336
Tel-el-Kebir, Battle of (1882) 268
television 336
Television Acts (1954, 1964) 336
Telford, Thomas 229, **370**
Temple, Richard, Earl Grenville 208, **370**
Temple, William, Archbishop of Canterbury **370**
Tenniel, Sir John *267*
Tennyson, Alfred, Lord 248
Test Acts (1673, 1678) 197, 203; repealed (1828) 252–3
Tewkesbury, Battle of (1471) 148
textile industry 13, *35*, 227–9, 271, 273; *see also* cloth; woollen industry
Textus Roffensis 62
Thackeray, William Makepeace 285–6
Thatcher, Margaret 306, 334
theatres 192, 198, 241
thegns 74–5, 84–5
Theobald, Count of Blois-Champagne 76, **370**
Theodore of Tarsus, Archbishop of Canterbury 86, 88, **370**
Theodosius, Count 10, 22–3
Theodosius the Great, Roman emperor 23
Thirty-Nine articles (1563) 156, 203, 214
Thirty Years War (1618–48) 160, 218
Thomas, earl of Lancaster 106–8, **370**
Thomas of Woodstock, duke of Gloucester **370**
Thorney monastery 57, 90
"Thorough" (1633–40) 214
Three Choirs Festival 241
Throckmorton, Job 157
tiles 34, 48, *135*
Tillotson, John, Archbishop of Canterbury 234
tin 13, 33, *127*, 130
Tinchebrai, Battle of (1100) 66, 68
Tincommius 15
Tiptoft, John, earl of Worcester **370**
Tithe Rent Charge Act (1891) 302
tithes 79
Togodumnus 15–16, 26
Toland, John 234
Toleration Acts: (1689) 234; (1719) 217
Tone, Theobald Wolfe 261, **370**
tonnage and poundage 200
Tooke, John Horne **370**
Tories: taxes on 196; and popular support 197, 254; support Hanoverians 197, 206; principles

204, 206; name 205; rivalry with Whigs 206–7, 217, 253–4; and Treaty of Utrecht 222; and journals 242, 286; and dear money 253; early 19th-century domination 253–4; 1846 split 255; and Ireland 262; *see also* Conservative party
Torksey, Lincolnshire *35*
Tostig, earl of Northumbria **371**
Toulouse 118
Tournai 172
tournaments 96, 188, *189*
Tours, Truce of (1444) 123
Towneley, Charles *282*
towns and cities: pre-Roman 10; Roman 13, 16–17, 20, 23, 38–42, 44; Anglo-Saxon 73, 78–80; development (12th–15th centuries) 124–5; labour conditions in 130; decline (15th-century) 130; under Tudors and Stuarts 146, 180; population 175, 278; slums 187, *277*; provincial 231; 19th-century growth 277–8; suburbs 278; *see also* individual places
Townshend, Charles, Viscount ("Turnip") 226, **371**
Townshend, Charles 224, **371**
Townshend, George, Viscount and Marquis 217
Towton, Battle of (1461) 147–8
Tractarianism 254, 282
trade associations 275
trade unions, trade unionism: pragmatism 246; and Combination Acts 250; growth and influence 259–60, 325, 327–8; "New Unionism" 260; and craftsmen 280; power opposed to Parliament 289; Labour represents 293; membership numbers 295; and social contract 301
Trades Disputes Act (1927) 296
Trades Union Congress 260, 293, 296, 301
Trafalgar, Battle of (1805) 265
Tramways Act (1870) 279
Transvaal 258, 260, 268
Treason Act (1534) 153
Treasons, Statute of (1352) 108
Treasury (in Angevin administration) 101
Trenchard, John 196
Trent, Council of (1545–63) 170
Trevelyan, Sir Charles 255
Triennial Act (1694) 205
Trier 20, 22–3
Trim Castle, County Meath *116*
Trinity College, Dublin 257
Trinovantes 14–15, 18, 24, 36, 39
Tripartite Indenture (1405) 112
Triple Alliance (1668: Anglo-Dutch-Swedish) 221
Triple Alliance (trade unions) 331
Trollope, Anthony 248, 285
Tromp, Admiral Maarten Harpentszoon 221
Troyes, Treaty of (1420) 123
Truman, Harry S. 317–18, 325
tuatha (Ireland) 64, 72
Tudor, Jasper, duke of Bedford **371**
Tudors 142, 144–9, 152, 167–8
Tull, Jethro 226, **371**
Tumultuous Risings Act (1766) 217
Turgeis, King of N. Ireland 73
Turkey (Ottoman Empire) 171, 180, 257, 266–7
Turkish Cypriots 319
Turner, Joseph Mallord William **371**
turnpikes 229
"two cultures" 336
Two-Power Standard (naval) 265
Twyn, John 233

Tyler, Wat 134, **371**
Tyndale, William **371**
Tyrconnel *117*
Tyrconnel, Richard Talbot, earl of **371**
Tyrone, Hugh O'Neill, earl of *see* O'Neill, Hugh

Uffington White Horse *43*
Uganda 259, 268
Uhtred of Bamburgh, earl of Northumberland 58
Uí Néill dynasty 64, *65*
Ulster (Northern Ireland): plantation 159, 170, 215, 217; 1798 rebellion 261; relations with Great Britain 263; Protestant majority 264, 307–8, 311; constitutional position 290; opposition to Irish Home Rule 294, 307; 1920 partition 308–11; civil rights movement 310–11; British intervention (1969) 311
Ulster Defence Association 311
Ulster Special Constabulary Association 311
Ulster Unionist Council 307
Ulster Volunteer Force 307
Ulster Workers Council 311
"undertakers" (Ireland) 217
unemployment *291*, 296, 305, 324–5
Uniformity Acts: (1549) 152; (1552) 152, 155; (1662) 203
Union, Acts of: (1707, Scotland) 197, 212–13; (1800, Ireland) 261–4
Unionists 293–5, *293*, 308, 311
United Alkali Company 275
United Committee of Congregationalist, Baptist and Unitarian Ministers 253
United Nations 318
United States of America: independence 244; and *Alabama* case 257; Irish in 262; naval power 265; industrialization 270; economic and trade competition from 273, 275; Macmillan alliance with 300; in World Wars 314, 316–17; post-war relations with 318, 320; and Anzus pact 319; economic output 321; UK borrowings from 324–5
United Ulster Unionist Council (Loyalist Coalition) 311
universities: Dominicans and 132; founding 135; in Scotland 165, 191, 214, 286; and gentry 183; Tudor expansion 191; 19th-century values 246; in Ireland 256; and professions 280; London and provincial 280; Church and 285; Victorian 285–6; reforms 286; radicalism in 332; 20th-century expansion 334
University College, London 280, 284
Unton, Sir Henry *191*
Urien, King of Rheged 83
Ussher, James, Archbishop of Armagh **371**
Utrecht: Peace of (1713) 222, 223; Treaty of (1474) 130
Utrecht Psalter 92

vagrants 166, 182, 184–6
Valence, Aymer de, earl of Pembroke **371**
Valentia (Roman province) 23
Valentinian, Roman emperor 22
Valentinian II, Roman emperor 23
Valor Ecclesiasticus (1535) 150

Van de Velde, Willem (father and son) 237
Van Dyck, Sir Anthony 238, 240, **371**
Vanbrugh, Sir John 239, **371**
Vane, Sir Henry, the Elder **371**
Vane, Sir Henry, the Younger **371**
Vanguard Unionist Party 311
vassalage 131
Veneti (tribe) 15
Venutius 17
Verdun, Battle of (1916) 313
Vere of Tilbury, Lord 218
Vereeniging, Peace of (1902) 268
Vergil 52
Verica, King of Atrebates 10, 15, 26
Verneuil, Battle of (1424) 123
Versailles Treaty (1919) 314–15
Verzelini, Giacomo *179*
Vesey, Agmondisham 239
Vespasian, Roman emperor 19, 28
Vestiarian controversy (ecclesiastical) 156
Vicar of Britain (Roman) *19*, 21
Vicky (cartoonist) *299*
Victoria, Queen of Great Britain 244, 248, 249, 256, 260, 288, **371**
Vienna, Congress of (1814–15) 266–7
Vikings: invasions and conquests 60–1, 64, 72–6, 85; and Normans 66; and Danegeld 68, 78; and warfare 72–4; ships *73*; destruction by 90; in Ireland 115
villas *see* housing, Roman
villeins, villeinage 81, 86, 98, 129, 133–4
Villeneuve, Admiral Pierre C.J.B. Sylvestre de 265
Vindex, C. Iulius 19
Vindolanda *35*
Visscher, Nikolaas, the Elder *183*
Vitellius, A. 19
Vitoria, Battle of (1813) 266
Volunteer movement (Ireland) *215*, 217
Vondel, Joost van den 237
Vortepor, ruler of Deisi *61*
Vortigern **371**

Wade, Field-Marshal George **371**
wages: late medieval 125; Tudor 176, 181; 18th century 225; Victorian 279; restraint policy 301; 20th-century growth in 325; government freeze on 321; *see also* incomes
Wakefield: mystery plays 140; Battle of (1460) 147
Waleran, Count of Meulan 68
Wales: under Roman rule 12, 26, 28; early mining 33, *34*; Latin words in 48; and Offa's Dyke 56, *65*; disunity 64, 70; royal dues in 64; and Norman Conquest 66, 70, 86, 110; warfare in 72; early Christianity in 76; laws 82, 86; female heritability 84; bondmen 86; English conquest of 94, 110–12; and Angevin kings 102, 106, 110; Marches 110; 1282 rebellion 110; population 124; economic decline 129; Acts of Union (1536, 1543) 153, 161–2; Council in Marches of 153, 161, 200; integration and administration 161–2; culture 162; agriculture 178; Parliamentary franchise 249; position in Britain 292; 20th-century politics 302–3, 306; nationalism 303, 335; Church disestablishment 302;

unemployment 324, 330; literacy 333; language and literature 335
Wales, Statute of *see* Rhuddlan, Statute of
Wall Street crash (1929) 324
Wallace, Alfred Russel 244
Wallace, William 114–15, **371**
Wallas, Graham 246, 260
Waller, Sir William **371**
Wallingford, Oxfordshire *72*, 73
Wallpaper Manufacturers (company) 275
Walpole, Horace 239, 284
Walpole, Sir Robert, earl of Orford 197, 206–7, *208*, 209, 217, 222–3, 241, **371**
Walsingham, Sir Francis 156, **371**
Walsingham, Thomas 140
Walter, Hubert, Archbishop of Canterbury **371**
Walter of Coutances **371**
Waltham Black Act (1724) 197, 236
Waltheof, Earl 66
Walton Castle 30
Walworth, William 134
Wansdyke 81
wapentakes 59
Warbeck, Perkin ("Richard IV") 149, 167, 172, **372**
wardships 158
Wareham 73
Warenne, John de, earl of Surrey and Sussex (c. 1231–1304) **372**
Warenne, John de, earl of Surrey and Sussex (1286–1347) **372**
Warham, William, Archbishop of Canterbury **372**
Warwick Castle 137, *139*
Warwick, John Dudley, earl of *see* Northumberland, duke of
Warwick, Richard Neville, earl of *see* Neville, Richard
Water Newton (Durobrivae), Cambridgeshire 13, 34, 42, 48, *51*
Waterford 115
Waterloo, Battle of (1815) 244, 267
Watling Street 40
Wat's Dyke *65*
Watt, James 213, 225, 228, 272
Wavell, Archibald Percival, Earl **372**
Wavrin, Jean: *Chronique d'Angleterre 122*
Weald 175, 179, 227
weapons *see* arms and armour
Wearmouth 56, 59, 88–9
weaving, weavers 271; *see also* cloth
Webb, Sidney and Beatrice 260, 328, **372**
Weddell, William 240
Wedgwood, Josiah 229, 240, **372**
Wellesley, Richard Colley, Marquis **372**
Wellington school 285
Wellington, Arthur Wellesley, duke of 253, *255*, 267, **372**
Welsh language and literature 162, 303, 335
Welsh Language Act (1967) 303
Welsh Language Society 303
Welsh Office 303
Wells, H.G. 244, 248
Wendover, Roger of 140
Wentworth, Peter 157, **372**
Wentworth, Thomas *see* Strafford, earl of
wergeld 82, 84
Wesley, John 236, **372**
Wessex: kingdom 54, 57, 60, 64, 72; laws 62; and Danes 58, 73–4; land boundaries 80; monasteries 92
West Horsley, Surrey *107*
West Indies 223–4, 229, 331

West Stow, Suffolk 80
Westbury-on-Trym 90
Western Isles 114
Westminster 105, *105, 108*, 135–6; Provisions of (1259) 104; Statutes of: (1275) 106; (1931) 314, 318; Treaties of (1654, 1674) 221
Westminster Assembly of Divines (1643) 211
Westminster Review 286
Westminster, Hugh Lupus Grosvenor, duke of 279
Westmorland, Charles Neville, earl of 157
Westmorland, Ralph Neville, earl of 112
Weston, Richard, earl of Portland **372**
Wexford 115, 215
Wharton, Thomas Wharton, marquis of 205, **372**
Wheatley, Francis *215*
Wheatley, John 305
Whethamstede, John 140
Whigs: favoured by taxation 196; and popular support 197; principles 204, 206; name 205; Junto 205; rivalry with Tories 206–7, 217, 253–4; 18th-century fortunes 206–8; foreign policy 222; and journals 242, 286; early 19th-century decline 253; in office 255; and Ireland 262; *see also* Liberal party
Whitby, Synod of (664) 76
White Hart (livery) 138, *139*
Whiteboys (of Munster) 217
Whiteley's (store) 273
Whitgift, John, Archbishop of Canterbury 157, **372**
Whittington, Richard **372**
Wiglaf, King of Mercia **372**
Wigley, Dafydd *303*
Wihtred, King of Kent 62, **372**
Wilberforce, William 253, 282, **372**
Wilcox, Thomas 157
Wilde, Oscar 245, 248, 285
Wilder, Philip Van 188
Wilfrid, St 56, 75–6, 88–9, **372**
Wilkes, John 198, 208–9, 233, **372**
Wilkins, John 234
William I (the Conqueror), King of England 62, 66–70, 74, 76–7, 81, 87, **372**
William II (Rufus), King of England 66–7, 69–70, **372**
William III (of Orange) King of England, Scotland and Ireland:

accession 196, 202, 204–5, *205*, 221; and Scotland 212–13; in Ireland 216; and French war 222, 224; **373**
William IV, King of Great Britain 249, **373**
William I (the Lion), King of Scots 113–14, **373**
William Longsword 66
Williams, John, Archbishop of York **373**
Willibrord, St, Archbishop of Utrecht 76
Wilmington, Spencer Compton, earl of **373**
Wilson, Harold, Lord *299*, 300–1, 326, **373**
Wilson, Woodrow 314
Wilson, Richard 242
Wilton Diptych 96, 138, *139*
Wilton House 239
Wimpole Hall, Cambridgeshire *240*
Winchelsey, William, Archbishop of Canterbury **373**
Winchester (Venta): under Romans 15; woollen industry 34; and early Exchequer 69–70; under Anglo-Saxons 73, 78–80; and Domesday survey 81; monastery 90; art and learning in 92, 135; cathedral *63*, 92, 136; decline 180; Council of (1070) 69; Statute of (1285) 106; Treaty of (1153) 67–8
Windsor castle 138
Windsor, William 117
wine 35–6, 44
Wingate, Gen. Orde Charles **373**
Winstanley, Gerrard 232, **373**
Winterton, Lincolnshire 32
Wiseman, Nicholas Patrick Stephen, Cardinal **373**
Wishart, George **373**
Witan (Anglo-Saxon counsellors) 62
witchcraft *165*, 167, 185
Witte, Johannes de *192*
Wodehouse, P.G. 328
Woffington, Peg 241
Wolfe, Gen. James 223, **373**
Wolfenden Committee Report (1957) 332
Wollaton Hall, Northamptonshire 192, *192*
Wollstonecraft, Mary **373**
Wolseley, Gen. Garnet, Viscount 268, **373**

Wolsey, Thomas, Cardinal: intrigue 142; administration 150, 152; and Star Chamber 154; and Welsh Marches 161; international relations 172, 191; and coinage 176; and Oxford university 191; **373**
women: in Anglo-Saxon society 84–5; social status 184; on stage 241; authors 242; emancipation 248; factory work 252, 257, 281; domestic servants 271; fertility 277; win vote 295, 327; peers 327; 20th-century role 328
Women's Social and Political Union 327
Wonderful Parliament (1386) 108
Wood, William 217
Woodburn, Arthur 305
woollen industry: in Roman period 34, *35*; in Anglo-Saxon period 56, 80; in Scotland 112; exports 125, 127, 130; taxed 127, 130; flourishes 129–30; trade 171, 179, 180, 227–8; mills *269*; *see also* cloth; textile industry
Worcester, Battle of (1651) 211–12
"Word of God" 190
Wordsworth, William 283–4, **373**
working class: movement 245, 249, 251, 279–80; values 245–6, 330–1; political representation 260; size and composition 280; employment 281; 20th-century improvements 328; *see also* trade unions
Workmen's Compensation Act (1897) 259
World Wars: First (1914–18) 244, 292, 294–5, 302, *312*, 313–14, 323, *329*; Second (1939–45) 298–9, 315–16, 323
Worlington, Cambridgeshire 34
Worms, Concordat of (1122) 77
Worth, Kent 46
Wren, Sir Christopher 234, 237, 239, 242, **373**
Wright, John Michael 238
Wright, Joseph, of Derby 242
writ (royal) 68, *70*, 100
Wroughton, Battle of (825) 60
Wroxeter (Viroconium Cornoviorum) 17
Wulfhere, King of Mercia 56
Wulfstan II, Archbishop of York 58, 84–5
Wulfstan, St, Bishop of Worcester **373**

Wyatt, James 282, 284
Wyatt, Sir Thomas (the elder) 191
Wyatt, Sir Thomas (the younger; conspirator) 155
Wycliff, John 96, 133, 138, 140, **373**
Wykeham, William of, Bishop of Winchester **373**
Wyndham, George 264
Wynegaerde, Antonius van den *190*
Wyvill, Christopher 209

Ximenes de Cisnero, Francisco, Cardinal 165

Year of the Four Emperors (AD 68–9) 19
Yeats, William Butler 264, 335
Yellow Ford, Battle of (1598) 169
yeomen 183–4, 186–7
Yevele, Henry 136
York: Roman base in 12–13, 20–22, 28, 46; archbishopric 58, 69, 76; Viking kingdom of 73–4; Alcuin on trade in 78; mint 79; as intellectual centre 88, 90; Parliament (1322) 107; Statute of (1322) 106; population 124; minster 136; mystery plays 140; and Council of North 153; 1536 rebellion 154; Tudor decline 180; social life 232; social surveys 281, 328
York, Richard, duke of 117, 147–8, **373**
Yorkshire Movement (1779–80) 209
Yorktown: surrender (1781) 224
Young Ireland (movement) 262–3
Young Scots Society 305
Young, Arthur 226, **373**
Ypres, 3rd Battle of (Passchendaele, 1917) 313–14

Zimbabwe (Rhodesia) 290, 318–19
Zinoviev letter (1924) 296
Zoffany, Johann 198, *285*
Zong case (1783) 236
Zosimus 10
Zouche, William de la, Archbishop of York 121
Zulu War (1879) 257, 258

ACKNOWLEDGEMENTS

Illustrations are reproduced by permission of, or have been provided by, the following:

Reproduced by Gracious Permission of H.M. The Queen: 164, 166, 173, 199, 213, 235*t*, 254, 278.

11 modified from P. Salway, *Roman Britain*, OUP, 1981, maps I, V, VI; 15 based on P. Salway, *op. cit.*, map II; 16 BM; 17 V&A; 18 based on P. Salway *op. cit.*, map VII; 19 Bodleian (MS. Canon. Misc. 378, f.150v); 21*l* Sorrell; 21*r* Museum of London; 23 E. Smith; 25 artist Peter Connolly, © Römisch-Germanisches Zentralmuseum, Mainz; 26 National Museum of Wales, Cardiff; 27/9 data from D.J. Breeze; 29 Antiquities,

Edin.; 31*tl* Turner's Ltd., Newcastle upon Tyne; 31*tr*, *bl* CUC; 31*cr* Hazel Harrison; 32 Institute of Archaeology, Oxford; 34 adapted from *The Carmarthenshire Antiquary*, VI, 1970, fig. 2, © Prof. G.D.B. Jones; 35*t* Audio Visual Centre, University of Newcastle upon Tyne; 35*c*, *r* BM; 36 based on *CBA Research Report*, 10, 1973, p. 49. fig. 6; 38*tr* modified from *British Archaeological Reports*, suppl. series No. 11, OUP, 1976, B. Cunliffe, "Oppida in Barbarian Europe", in *The Antiquaries Journal*, 53, 1973, B. Cunliffe, p. 183, fig. 5; 39 adapted from J.S. Wacher, *The Towns of Roman Britain*, Batsford, 1975 (after S.S. Frere); 40 data from M. Millett; 42 Sussex Archaeological Society;

43*tl* Aerofilms Ltd.; 43*r*, *b* BM; 45 Institute of Archaeology, Oxford; 47*tl*, *bl* Warburg; 47*tr*, *c* Society of Antiquaries of London Research Reports IX, 1932, fig. 7, and XL, 1982, plate XIb; 47*br* Corinium Museum, Cirencester; 49*t* Sorrell; 49*l* Bath Museums Service; 49*r* Warburg; 49*b* Clarendon Press, Oxford; 50*l* Warburg; 50*tr* His Grace the Duke of Northumberland (photo BM); 50*b*, 51 BM; 52 Warburg; 55 compilation; 61*t* adapted from K.P. Witney, *The Kingdom of Kent*, Philimore, 1982, p. 59; 61*b* Dept. of Archaeology, University College, Cardiff; 62 Dean & Chapter, Rochester Cathedral/Kent County Archives, Maidstone; 63 BL (Cotton Vesp. A. viii, f. 2v; Stowe 944, f. 6r)/ Bridgeman; 65*l* adapted from

J. Campbell (ed.), *The Anglo-Saxons*, Phaidon, 1982, p. 121, pl. 2; 65*tr*, *br* CUC; 67*t* Michael Holford; 67*b* compilation; 68 E. Smith; 69 PRO; 70 London Records; 71 Camelot Research Committee; 72 CUC; 73 University Museum of National Antiquities, Oslo; 74/5 Michael Holford; 77*t* CUC; 77*b* Sorrell; 79 Ashmolean; 83*tl*, *bl*, *br* BM; 83*tr* York Archaeological Trust (photo Mike S. Duffy); 85 National Museum of Ireland, Dublin; 87*tr* Scottish Development Dept. (Ancient Monuments), Edinburgh; 87 others Antiquities, Edin.; 89*tl* BL (Cotton. Vitell. A, XV); 89*tc*, *tr* NMR; 89*br* Ashmolean; 90 BL (Add. 24199, f. 18); 91*tl* BL (Cotton. Nero D. iv., f. 94b)/Bridgeman; 91*tr* the Board of Trinity College, Dublin/

Bridgeman; 91 others BM; 95 compilation; 101*t* PRO; 101*b* DoE; 103*tl* BL (Cotton. Claudius D. ii, f. 76); 103*tr* Corpus Christi College, Cambridge (MS. 16, f. 215)/ Courtauld; 103*b* Cambridge University Library (MS. Ee.III.59)/ Courtauld; 104 BL (Cotton. Aug. ii. 106)/Mansell; 105 DoE; 107 NMR (Corpus Vitrearum Medii Aevii), © Sarah Brown; 108 NMR; 111*l, r* compiled by R.R. Davies; 112 data by B. Webster and J. Wormald; 113*r* E. Smith; 113*l* University Library, St Andrews; 114 Antiquities, Edin.; 115*tl* Archives de France, Paris; 115*br* BL (MS. Harley 1319)/ facsimile Mary Evans; 116 Office of Public Works, National Parks & Monuments Branch, Dublin; 117 Bodleian (MS. Laud Misc. 720, f. 226*r*, v); 119*t* BL (Add. 47680, f. 40); 119*b* Michael Holford; 122 BL (Royal E.14, f. 59v); 123 BL (Cotton. Jul. E. IV. Art. 6 f. 18v); 125*l* adapted from *The Economic History Review*, A. Oosthoek, Utrecht, Dec. 1965, p. 506, R.S. Schofield, "The Geographical Distribution of Wealth in England, 1334–1649"; 125*br* A.F. Kersting; 126 BL (Add. 42130, ff. 172b, 173b, 158); 127*tl, tr* BL (Cotton. Tib. B.v., f. 7r; Add. 42130, f. 181); 127*bl* The Board of Trinity College, Dublin (MS. 177, f. 60r); 128*l* Bodleian (MS. Gough Gen Top. 16); 128*r* Buckinghamshire Record Office; 129 BL (Royal 15.E.III, f. 269); 130 London Records; 134*l* A.F. Kersting; 134*r* BL (Cotton. Dom. A. xvii, f. 150v); 135 BM; 136/7 NMR; 138 Corpus Christi College, Cambridge (MS. 61, frontisp.); 139*tl, tr* Trustees of the National Gallery, London/Bridgeman; 139*bl* V&A; 139*br* A.F. Kersting; 140 NMR; 143 adapted from M. Falkus & J. Gillingham (eds) *Historical Atlas of Britain*, Granada, 1981, p. 82; 149*l*, 151*b* compiled by C.S.L. Davies; 149*r* Ghent University Library (MS. 236, f. 2r); 151 The Worshipful Company of Barbers, London (photo Brian Harris); 152 The Masters of the Bench of the Inner Temple, London (Petyt MS. – photo Freeman); 153 Mansell; 154 Lord Egremont, Petworth House, Sussex (photo Martin Trelawney)/ Courtauld; 157 Trewin Copplestone

Collection; 158 Tyrwhitt-Drake Collection, East Meon, Hants./ Bridgeman; 159 NPG; 160 BL (MS. Harley 159, f. 2); 162, 163*t, bl* adapted by R.R. Davies from W. Rees, *Historical Atlas of Wales*, Faber, 1959, maps 53, 55, 56; 163*br* PSA. (artist Alan Sorrell); 164 Royal, Holyrood House, Edinburgh (photo Tom Scott); 165*l* Scottish Development Dept. (Ancient Monuments), Edinburgh; 165*r* Glasgow University Library, Ferguson Collection (A1-a. 36); 166 National Galleries of Scotland, Portrait Gallery, Edinburgh; 168/9 data by S.G. Ellis, incl. Margaret MacCurtain, *Tudor and Stuart Ireland*, Dublin, 1972, p. 18, and maps by K.W. Nicholls, Aidan Clarke; 170*tl* BL, Dept. of Maps; 170*br* BL./Bridgeman; 171*tl* BL; Dept. of Maps (Cotton. Aug. I. i. 18 (1545)); 171*r* the Master and Fellows, Magdalene College, Cambridge; 173 Royal; 174 BL, Dept. of Maps (C.7.c.l.(2)); 176 adapted from Joan Thirsk (ed.) *The Agrarian History of England and Wales*, Vol. IV, CUP, 1967, p. 4, and D.M. Palliser, *The Age of Elizabeth*, Longman, 1983, p. 163; 176*r* BM; 177 adapted from Joan Thirsk, *op. cit.*, p. 609, fig. 13; 178 adapted from original map by Dr. John Sheail; 179*l* Birmingham Museums & Art Gallery; 179*r*, 180 Museum of London; 181*t* Mansell; 181*b* based on E.M. Carus-Wilson (ed.), *Essays in Economic History*, Vol. II, Edward Arnold, 1962, p. 186, fig. 3; 182 based on E.A. Wrigley & R.S. Schofield, *The Population History of England*, Edward Arnold, 1981, p. 207, fig 7.1; 182/3 Mansell; 185 the Marquess of Bath, Longleat House, Warminster, Wilts.; 186 the Marquess of Salisbury, Hatfield House, Hatfield, Herts.; 187*tl* NPG; 187*tr* Simon Wingfield Digby, Sherborne Castle, Dorset; 187*bl* based on D. Cressy, *Literacy and the Social Order*, CUP, 1980; 189*t* The College of Arms (Westminster Tournament Roll); 189*b* Courtauld, Photographic Survey (Loseley Park, from ?Nonsuch Palace, by Toto di Annunziata); 190*l* Ashmolean, Dept. of Western Art (DB.13); 190*r*, 191 NPG; 192*b* NMR; 192*t* Mansell; 195

based on G. Barraclough (ed.) *Times Concise Atlas of World History*, Times Publishing, 1982, p. 76; 199 Royal; 202 the Earl of Rosebery/ National Portrait Gallery of Scotland, Edinburgh; 203 BL (Seal XXXIV, 17); 204, 205 Mansell; 207, 208, 209 BM, Prints & Drawings (Satires Nos. 1798, 2447, 3983); 211 Mansell; 212 BL; 213 Royal; 215*t* L.G. Stopford Sackville; 215*b* National Gallery of Ireland, Dublin; 216 adapted from J.G. Simms, *The Williamite Confiscation in Ireland 1690–1703*, Faber, 1956; 219 BL (669. f. 6. (12)); 220 Mansell; 220/1 NMM; 223*t* Mansell; 223*b* NMM.; 226 Bodleian (Maps Notts. A.2); 227 the Syndics of Cambridge University Library; 228 Topham; 229 Freeman; 230 Shropshire County Council (SRO.1525/1); 231 the Trustees of the Tate Gallery, London; 233, 235*b* Mansell; 235*t* Royal; 238 A.F. Kersting; 239 private collection on loan to the Bowes Museum, Barnard Castle, Durham (photo NPG); 240 Aerofilms; 241 IPC; 242 Merseyside County Council, Walker Art Gallery, Liverpool; 247*t, b* modified from P. Mackesy, *The War for America 1775–1783*, Longman, 1964, facing p. 536, and A. J. Marder, *The Anatomy of British Sea Power*, Archon Books, Hamden, Conn., 1964, endpapers; 249 Freeman; 250 based on J. Holladay Philbin, *Parliamentary Representation, 1832, England and Wales*, Yale University Press, New Haven, Conn., 1965, map 1; 251 NPG; 254 Royal (The Queen's Archives, Windsor); 255 Mansell; 257 PSA, Crown Copyright; 258 Gladstone Family Album, by permission of Sir William Gladstone; 262, 263, 264 Mansell; 266 National Army Museum, London; 267 Mansell; 268 Schultze Collection, National Film Archive; 269*bl* F.H.M. FitzRoy Newdegate, c/o Warwickshire County Archivist; 269*tr* Freeman; 270 Science Museum, London; 271, 272 Mansell; 273 V&A; 274/5 Mansell; 275*tr* Topham; 276 adapted from N. Tranter, *Population since the Industrial Revolution*, Croom Helm, 1973, p. 44, graph I, and official statistics; 277 Mansell; 278 Royal Library, Windsor; 279 Bridgeman;

280 based on G.H. Wood in *Journal of the Royal Statistical Society*, 1909; 281 Oldham Metropolitan Borough, Central Library; 282 Towneley Hall, Burnley Borough Council Art Gallery & Museums; 283 Freeman; 285 Lord Boyne; 286 Harrogate Museums & Art Gallery Service; 291 modified from M.P. Fogarty, *Prospects of the Industrial Areas of Great Britain*, Granada, 1945, map III, and M. Falkus & J. Gillingham (eds), *Historical Atlas of Britain*, London, 1981; 293 BBC Data; 296 The Derby Papers, Knowsley, Prescot, Merseyside; 297 BBC Data; 298 The Photo Source; 299 News Chronicle; 300 Associated Press, 302 John Cornwell, Bristol; 303 PA.; 304, 306 George Outram, Glasgow; 307 PA.; 308 based on P.J. Buckland, *Parliamentary Representation of Ulster 1911*, London (Historical Assoc.), 1973, p. 27; 309 Cashman Archive, Radio Telefis Eireann, Dublin; 310 The Photo Source; 312 Topham; 313*t* compilation; 313*bl* IWM; 315 BBC Data; 316 compiled and adapted from B.H. Liddell Hart, *History of the Second World War*, Cassell, 1970, and other sources; 317 IWM; 319 Central Office of Information, Crown Copyright; 320 The Photo Source; 321*t* based on B.R. Mitchell, *European Historical Statistics 1750–1970*, London, 1981, pp. 820–36; 321*b* based on Matthews, Feinstein & Odling-Smee, *British Economic Growth 1856–1973*, London, 1982, p. 22; 322*tr* based on Floud & McCloskey (eds.), *Economic History of Britain since 1700*, Vol. 2, CUP, 1981, Sir Alex Cairncross, "The Postwar Years". p. 388; 322*bl* Topham; 322*br* National Coal Board; 323*tl, tr* J. Sainsbury PLC (Archives); 323*bl* BBC Data; 323*br* Austin Rover Group Ltd., External Affairs; 328–9 BBC Data; 329*t* Dr. Robert G. Neville (Keith Neild), Abingdon; 329*b*, 330*t, b*, 334*r* BBC Data; 334*r* based on Halsey, Heath & Ridge, *Origins and Destinations*, OUP, 1980, p. 196, fig. 11.1; 335*l* adapted and updated from Asa Briggs, *History of Broadcasting*, Vol. IV, OUP, 1979, p. 15, fig. 1; 335*r* British Architectural Library, RIBA, London; 335 The Photo Source.